SAGE was founded in 1965 by Sara Miller McCune to support the dissemination of usable knowledge by publishing innovative and high-quality research and teaching content. Today, we publish over 900 journals, including those of more than 400 learned societies, more than 800 new books per year, and a growing range of library products including archives, data, case studies, reports, and video. SAGE remains majority-owned by our founder, and after Sara's lifetime will become owned by a charitable trust that secures our continued independence.

Los Angeles | London | New Delhi | Singapore | Washington DC | Melbourne

मत्कर्मकृन्मत्परमो मद्भक्त: सङ्गवर्जित:
निर्वैर: सर्वभूतेषु य: स मामेति पाण्डव || ५५

श्रीमद्भगवद्गीता: अध्याय ११

55 *maṭkarmakṛnmatparamo*
madbhaktaḥ saṇgavarjitaḥ
nirvairaḥ sarvabhūteṣhu
yaḥ sa māmeti pāṇḍava

He who does work for Me, he who looks upon Me as his goal,
he who worships Me, free from attachment,
he who is free from enmity to all creatures,
he goes to Me, O Pandava (Arjuna).

The Bhagavadgīta: Chapter 11

Indian Administration

Indian Administration

A Foundation of Governance

Radhakrishan Sapru

Professor (Retired), Department of Public Administration,
Panjab University, Chandigarh

SAGE | TEXTS

Los Angeles | London | New Delhi
Singapore | Washington DC | Melbourne

First published in 2018 by

SAGE | TEXTS

SAGE Publications India Pvt Ltd
B1/I-1 Mohan Cooperative Industrial Area
Mathura Road, New Delhi 110 044, India
www.sagepub.in

SAGE Publications Inc
2455 Teller Road
Thousand Oaks, California 91320, USA

SAGE Publications Ltd
1 Oliver's Yard, 55 City Road
London EC1Y 1SP, United Kingdom

SAGE Publications Asia-Pacific Pte Ltd
3 Church Street
#10-04 Samsung Hub
Singapore 049483

Published by Vivek Mehra for SAGE Publications India Pvt Ltd, typeset in 10/12 pts Cambria by Zaza Eunice, Hosur, Tamil Nadu, India and printed at Sai Print-o-Pack, New Delhi.

Library of Congress Cataloging-in-Publication Data

Name: Sapru, Radhakrishan, author.
Title: Indian administration: a foundation of governance/Radhakrishan Sapru.
Description: New Delhi, India; Thousand Oaks, California: SAGE Publications Inc, 2018. | Includes bibliographical references and index.
Identifiers: LCCN 2018012492 | ISBN 9789352807239 (pbk.)
Subjects: LCSH: Public administration—India. | Decentralization in government—India. | India—Politics and government.
Classification: LCC JQ231 .S328 2018 | DDC 351.54—dc23 LC record available at https://lccn.loc.gov/2018012492

ISBN: 978-93-528-0723-9 (PB)

SAGE Team: Amit Kumar, Indrani Dutta, Vandana Gupta, Kumar Indra Mishra and Rajinder Kaur

This piece of work is dedicated to the sweet memory of my father, Lala Diwan Chand (1919–81), who asked me to shun the sense of egoistic mind and have faith in the All Pervading Supreme Self, the source of all phenomena.

Prayer

Thou who art Radiance, fill me with radiance
Thou who art Valour, fill me with valour
Thou who art Strength, give me strength
Thou who art Vitality, endow me with vitality
Thou who art Wrath (against wrong), instil that wrath into me
Thou who art Fortitude, fill me with fortitude

(*Śukla Yajur Veda*, XIX, 9)

Contents

Detailed Contents

Preface

There are many editions of books on Indian administration—several of these are in Indian languages—and there would be no justification for another one. However, changes and adjustments, not necessarily rational and conducive to administrative efficiency, necessitate analysis and discussion on the subject. Important developments bearing upon it, such as abolition of the Planning Commission, scrapping the practice of a separate Railway budget, parliamentary clearance of the Finance and Appropriation Bills before the end of the fiscal year on 31 March, supplanting plan and non-plan division of expenditure in the Union Budget, setting up of NITI Aayog, demonetization of currency notes of the values of ₹500 and ₹1000 (in November 2016), repealing of the dysfunctional laws, the resumption of the Supreme Court Collegium system, setting up of the Goods and Services Tax Council at the federal level, are standing out. In addition, there are changes of international significance, for example, Britain's full exit from the European Union by December 2020, US President Donald Trump's immigration policy and US Court's refusal to reinstate president's travel ban on certain Muslim nationals, North Korea's intercontinental ballistic missile test, India's entry into the Missile Technology Control Regime, China's insistence on blocking India's NSG membership bid, and so on. All these developments, at both national and international levels, have not only altered the federal character of the Indian Constitution but also affected the theory and practice of Indian administration.

This attempt of mine is coloured by the reflections of the recent period marked by 'less government' but with a maximum of 'good governance and development'. Common good is the cry of nation's judiciary, media and intelligentsia. The political masters and senior civil servants, on whose exercise of authority depends the country's governance and development, have a constitutional role and duty in this task. Authors' writings and social media reflect what is welled-up in the common man's eyes. This book on Indian administration is an attempt to deal with various changes and developments bearing upon the subject.

In writing this book, my gratitude goes to my wife Sushma, son Yudhishthira, and daughters Sugeeta (Mutreja) and Ujjawal (Khurana), whose encouragement and inspiration have always been the source of my will power. For lapse, if any, in this book, I am solely responsible.

About the Author

Radhakrishan Sapru studied at Panjab University, Chandigarh, which awarded him Master's degrees in Political Science (1970), Public Administration (1972), English (1976) and subsequently doctorate in Public Administration in 1983 and an LLB degree in 1992.

Initially appointed as a Teaching-cum-Research Assistant at the Department Chandigarh, in February 1976, Dr Sapru rose to the position of Professor. He headed the Department of Public Administration, Panjab University, from 1 April 1990 to 31 March 1993 and again from 1 April 2002 to 31 March 2005. He retired as a Professor in August 2005 after serving nearly three decades at the Panjab University. During his academic career and after superannuation, Dr Sapru published more than 50 articles in national and international journals and 10 books in the field of public administration.

1 Evolutionary History of Indian Administration

LEARNING OBJECTIVES

1. **To understand the significant relevance to the contemporary Indian administration**
2. **To comment on the Mughal administrative system as a form of centralized despotism**
3. **To evaluate the impact of British rule on the present administrative system**

Introduction

'Indian administration' has a chequered and colourful historical past. Although administration (to use the term as a force for administering public affairs) is marred by political, economic, social and geographical upheavals of the periods, it has successfully survived and is being carried out on a continuous basis ever since the formation of a political state. The present-day administration reflects an amalgam of features of the ancient Indian administration, Moghul (Mughal) rule administration and British India administration.

For expository convenience, the ensuing discussion on the historical growth of the Indian administration is divided into the following:

1. Introduction
2. Ancient Indian Administration
3. Kautilya's *Arthashastra* and Administrative State
4. Mughal Administration in India
5. British India Administration
6. Development of the Civil Services
7. Evolutionary Measures Towards Unity of Constituent Units
8. Evolution of Parliamentary Democracy

1.1 Ancient Indian Administration

Enough literature is not available touching upon administration in the ancient India. However, passages relating to statecraft were inserted in the epic Mahabharata, especially in the form of the twelfth book, 'in the early centuries of the Christian era'. About this time, similar subject matter was found in the Section 7 of the law book attributed to Manu.[1] Kautilya's *Arthashastra* probably is the most important work containing diverse ideas which included many prevailing customs and rules. It also reflected Brahminical ethics and earlier *Smriti*, 'ideas about the authority and sources of law of the social order'.[2] For, as Aiyangar remarks, 'In India, more than in many parts of the world the past persists in the present'.[3] The beauty of this country is that some of the values and principles described in *Arthashastra* still exist.

In ancient times, the whole of India was known as Bharatavarsha—the country of the Bharatas. In the ancient India, Hindus were acquainted with the ideal of sovereignty. Early Hindu political institutions were not imperial; there were several democratic republics on one side and several monarchies with some ethical and institutional controls on power on the other. Most republics were conquered and absorbed by neighbouring kingdoms, but the Indian republican tradition is preserved for us not only in the writings of Greek scholars but also in the republican councillor constitutions of the Buddhist Sangha. For a quite long while, the monarchs fought each other following well-known rules, without absorbing and integrating rival kingdoms into a larger empire, being satisfied with proclaiming a vague suzerainty.

A brief description of the ancient Indian administration is discussed in this section.

1.1.1 King's Position and Functions

In the ancient India, the government was monarchical, with the royal power upheld by the sacerdotal power. The king enjoyed ownership of much of the soil and subsoil, although not quite so absolutely as in the contemporary Hellenistic world, and he also had the right of eminent domain.[4]

Manu called a king foolish who would attempt to carry on administration by himself.[5] The king was the head of the state. According to Havell,

> He was bound to consult his ministers, who as the elders of the village were representatives of all the five classes of freemen and were selected for their knowledge of Aryan tradition to advise the king in all important affairs of the state and to assist him in the administration of Aryan law.[6]

The main duties of the king, according to Manu, were to restrain violence and to punish evil-doers. The state was a trust and the king's key role was to protect the state. The Emperor Asoka proclaimed, 'All men are my children and just as on behalf of my own children, I desire that they may be provided with complete welfare and happiness both in this world and next, the same I desire also for all men'.[7]

Since the king was getting one-fourth of the farm produce, he is duty-bound to protect his subjects. To quote *Manusmriti*, 'Brahma has created the king to be protector of the Varna and public order (common good) so that they discharge their several duties according to their Dharma and rank'.[8]

---

[1] A. L. Basham, *The Wonder That Was India* (London: Oxford, 1954), 80.
[2] U. N. Ghoshal, *A History of Indian Political Ideas* (London: Oxford, 1959), 113.
[3] K. V. Rangaswami Aiyangar, *Aspects of Ancient Indian Economic Thought* (Benares: Digital Library of India, 1934), 6.
[4] Ghoshal, *A History*.
[5] G. Buhler, tr., *The Laws of Manu* (1500 BC), Chapter VII.
[6] E. B. Havell, *The History of Aryan Rule in India* (London, 1918), 36.
[7] The Kalinga Rock Edict II.
[8] Buhler, *The Laws*, Verse 35.

1.1.2 Structure of Central Administration

The structure of central administration is discussed both in Kautilya's *Arthashastra* and in the Asokan inscriptions.[9] They agree about two or three top levels in central administration—a minister or ministers called *mantrin* (Kautilya) or *mahamatra* (Asoka), a council of ministers at the next level (*mantrin parishad*) and many top officers and public servants variously called *amatyas* or *sachivas*, in a clear hierarchy. These three levels were retained with modified names in the later Gupta regime in the 5th century AD and under Harsha in the 7th century. The army general was also a *mantri* of equal status as were the viceroys of *kumaras* of the four large regions or provinces of the Maurya Empire.

The army administration was given a great deal of importance in the central administration. It was separately organized, as was accounting and financial administration through district hierarchies. The office of collector general (*samahartri*) and the accountant general (*akshapataladhyaksha*) were separate and each had its own hierarchy.

1.1.3 Provincial Administration

Accounts of the provincial administration are also described. The state in ancient India was divided into provinces or regions governed by viceroys.[10] These were subdivided into divisions and districts. In Maurya and Gupta Empires, the provincial viceroys (governors) were appointed directly by the king and were usually members of the royal family.

The district was headed by then called *pradeshtri* or *sthanika*. He combined revenue collecting and magisterial duties and supervised the work of other technical or clerical officials (*yuktas*) as well as village government under the *gopa*.

1.1.4 Village and Local Administration

In the ancient India, a village was described as a self-governing community. Hugh Tinker, who has had practical experience of local government institutions in India, wrote, 'Indian village throughout the ages has been a corporate, guided and guarded by a council, the panchayat'.[11]

The village (*gram*) was the political unit of the state. The leader of the village (*graman*) was the key figure of village. The village council (Panchayat) was endowed with executive as well as judicial powers. There was, however, no clear dividing line between a town and village.

Cities also had their local councils. Megasthenes gives a vivid account of municipal administration of Chandragupta's capital, Pataliputra. The city council was composed of 30 members divided into 6 committees. It was an elective body, although certain matters were reserved for the central and imperial officials. The committees were functional bodies and the councils in their cooperative capacity administered general local affairs such as finance, sanitation, water supply and so on.

In sum, traditionally, Indian state had not interfered with the activities of the people except to prevent 'hindrances to their lawful pursuits'. This administrative system founded by Kautilya,

---

[9] B. N. Puri, *History of Indian Administration*, vol. I (Bombay: Bharatiya Vidya Bhavan, 1968), Chapter 3.

[10] Puri, *History of Indian*, Chapter 3.

[11] Hugh Tinker, 'The Village in the Framework of Development', in *Administration and Economic Development in India*, ed. Ralph Braibanti and Joseph Spengler (Durham: Duke University Press, 1963), 95.

Chandragupta and Asoka was adopted by the successive empires of the Guptas and of Harsha with minor changes in name and substance. Thus, we find an officer for war and peace, *sandhivigraha*; another officer *uparika* associated with provincial administration; *kumaramatyas* or experienced officials; and *dandanayaka* standing for a police or an army officer. The Guptas in the north and the Cholas in south made a sophisticated system of village self-government as an integral part of the administrative system. But the overall structures of central and provincial administration were essentially modifications of the *Arthashastra*—Asoka model.[12]

During the post-Mauryan period (say from 184 BC to 200 AD), administrative conditions remained much as in the Mauryan period, although fluctuating with political circumstances and with the extent of external factors.

1.2 Kautilya's *Arthashastra* and Administrative State

In a historical context, it would be worthwhile to refer to Kautilya's *Arthashastra* which throws light on the manual of statecraft designed to guide the ruler of a state and perhaps others engaged in the governance of the people.

Kautilya, also known as Chanakya or Vishnugupta, was a great scholar who played a dominant role in founding and growth of the Indian Empire during the 4th century BC. He was also an adviser, a minister and a kingmaker, who helped overthrow the Nanda Dynasty (an empire in the Gangetic valley) and placed Chandragupta Maurya on the throne of Magadha in 321 BC. Through his statesmanship and diplomacy, Kautilya established Maurayan suzerainty over the whole of northern India.

Kautilya's *Arthashastra*, a scholarly treatise, is claimed to have been written in the period 321–296 BC. Some historians assert the work was written between 1st and 3rd centuries AD. The work, consisting of 15 *adhikaranas* or books, containing 413 maxims or *sloka*s, attempts to set forth general principles and detailed rules for the administration of a despotic State. The work was long lost but was retrieved in 1904 and published in 1909 by R. Shamasastry.[13] The scheme of the work is as follows:

Book I is concerned with education and duties and qualities of a king, the appointment of ministers and other executive officials. Book II exhibits a picture of State activities in different fields. Book III sets forth a code of law. Book IV is concerned with suppression of crime. Book V is devoted to the methods of recruitment, training and grades of salaries of State employees. Book VI gives an introduction of the State's relations with its neighbour. Book VII is devoted to the tactics of foreign policy. Book VIII deals with calamities and certain other matters. Book IX deals with matters related to the preparation for war. Book X deals with fighting. Books XI, XII and XIII are concerned with problems related to conquest. Book XIV presents occult practices. And Book XV describes methods of dealing with a study subject. Out of 15, Books I, II, V and VI deal with the pattern of public administration.

---

[12] V. Subramaniam, 'Administrative Legacy of Ancient India in Relation to Modern Public Administration', *Indian Journal of Public Administration* (1991): 2–3.

[13] R. Shamasastry, tr. *Kautilya's Arthashastra*, 4th ed. (Mysore: Mysore Printing and Publishing House, 1951). An English translation of this book was done in 1915. Satyaketu Vidyalankar, a famous historian, opines that it was written during the Mauryan period between 320 BC and 185 BC.

In brief, the *Arthashastra* concerns with political, social and economic management of the State. It is a work on the organization and management of human affairs. Specifically, Kautilya wanted to devise a statecraft that would keep this large empire unified, guard its integrity against the intrigues of power-seeking nobles and attack from abroad, and prevent a dissolution of the sort that took place less than 150 years later.

1.2.1 *Arthashastra's* Term Signified

The term *artha* signifies 'wealth', 'the subsistence of mankind', 'the earth which contains mankind'; the term *sastra* (science), when affixed to *artha*, designates the 'science of polity' which 'treats of the means of acquiring and maintaining the earth'. At times, Kautilya defines 'wealth' broadly and loosely as 'wealth, virtue, and enjoyment form the aggregate of the three kinds of wealth'.[14]

'Arthashastra' is the combination of the science of wealth and the science of government. The first constituent—the science of wealth—is of great value. Kautilya says, 'It is by means of the treasury and the army obtained solely through *Varta* that the king can hold under his control both his and his enemy's party'. Referring to the importance of the second constituent, Kautilya says, 'It is on the science of Government that the course of the progress of the world depends'. *Artha* is usually 'understood to stand for material well-being as well as the means of securing such well-being, particularly wealth'.[15]

1.2.2 Principles Governing Machinery of Government

Kautilya's *Arthashastra* reflects some principles governing the machinery of the administration and State. These principles can be grouped into two sets—one dealing with the State and the second with the machinery of the administration. The first set of principles encompassing authority, responsibility, duty and discipline reflects the sovereignty of the State. The second set of principles encompassing division of labour, coordination, speciality, hierarchy and enquiry governs the actual method of work of the administration.

The principle of authority is the essence of the State. 'Thus people consisting of four castes and four orders of religious life, when governed by the king with his scepter, will keep to their respective paths, ever devotedly adhering to their respective duties and occupations'.[16] Authority is obeyed by the people on account of sanctions backed by a series of punishments. Kautilya avers,

> For punishment, (*danda*), when awarded with due consideration, makes the people devoted to righteousness and to works productive of wealth and enjoyment; while punishments, when ill-awarded under the influence of greed and anger owing to ignorance, excites fury even among hermits and ascetics dwelling in forests, not to speak of householders.[17]

Any disobedience to authority should be dealt with severe fines and punishments.

[14] Book IX, Chapter 7.

[15] R. P. Kangle, *The Kautilya Arthashastra*, Part 3 (Delhi: Motilal Banarasidas, 1986), 1.

[16] Book I, Chapter 4.

[17] Book I, Chapter 4.

Unity of command is another principle which should govern the machinery of administration. Unity of command principle is maintained because of king's authority. The king must take care to secure his person from external dangers so that he is able to exercise authority vested with him.[18] Not merely for the purpose of security of the King's person but also for the purpose of maintaining security, integrity and stability of administration against the dangers of internal dissension and external aggression, Kautilya outlines an elaborate system of spying and allurements. On the death of the king, Kautilya does not favour usurpation of royal power of the minister. He says, 'But it is unrighteous to do an act which excites popular fury; nor is it an accepted rule'.

According to *Arthashastra*, fear, duty and interest are the three main motivators behind the act of obedience of the orders of administration. He emphasizes the need on securing cooperation of the people as well as of the bureaucracy in carrying out orders of administration. People's cooperation could be secured by giving positive financial help to the needy and distressed, so also by ensuring just treatment to the people in administrative and economic matters. Government employees are to be enthused by granting them promotion in salary, pension, financial and other kinds of help.

Kautilya also lays down a series of qualities, differing in number and order, for officers holding different positions of responsibility. His job specification for a State officer covers many of today's demands.

'The world, when maintained in accordance with injunctions of the triple Vedas, will surely progress, but never perish. Hence, the king shall never allow people to swerve from their duties'.[19]

Kautilya also prescribes the principle of responsibility not only for the king but also for the government officers. To quote famous dictum in *Arthashastra*, 'In the happiness of his subjects lies his happiness; in their welfare, his welfare... The king is, as it were, the aggregate of the people'.[20] This idealism, Kautilya says, is the object and purpose of the exercise of sovereign power by the king.

The second set of principles—division of labour, coordination, speciality, hierarchy—governs the machinery of administration. The principle of division of labour is fundamental for the smooth and efficient working of the machinery of government. Kautilya says that 'sovereignty is possible only with assistance'. Hence, the king 'shall employ ministers, and hear their opinion'.[21] The principle of coordination evolves out of the principle of division of labour. The principle of hierarchy is followed to make coordination and division of labour possible.

1.2.3 King's Attributes, Duties and Position

Kautilya's king is the head of the State and embodiment of the power. Further Kautilya says, 'A King has no personal likes; it is the likes of the subjects'.[22] In Kautilya's world, the king should surrender his individuality in the interest of his duties, and was virtually a 'constitutional slave'.[23] Kautilya lists numerous personal attributes to a king in Book VI, Chapter I, and Book III, Chapter 2. Yet, given that the king possesses many of these attributes, he must understand science if he has to

[18] Book I, Chapter 21.
[19] Book I, Chapter 3.
[20] Book I, Chapter 19.
[21] Book I, Chapter 7.
[22] Shamasastry, *Kautilya's Arthashastra*, Book I, Chapter 19, p. 39.
[23] K. P. Jayaswal, *Hindu Polity* (Bangalore: Bangalore Publishing, 1968), 40.

administer well and strengthen his sovereignty.[24] As it is also essential that the king's councillors and ministers be proficient in the sciences, Kautilya implied that persons chosen for these posts must have not only suitable personal attributes but also some knowledge of the relevant sciences (Book I, Chapters 8–10; Book V, Chapters 5–6; Book VIII, Chapters 1–2).

Kautilya identifies four sciences crucial for the King's role. The first *Anvikshaki*, dealing with philosophical matter, 'is most beneficial to the world, keeps the mind steady and firm in weal and woe alike, and bestows excellence of foresight, speech and action' (Book I, Chapter 2). The second, 'triple Vedas', 'are the most useful' in that they 'determine the respective duties of the four castes (Brahman, Kshatriya, Vaisya and Sudra)[25] and of the four orders of religious life' (Book I, Chapter 3)[26] for the observance of these duties assures happiness 'here and hereafter' to him who also follows the 'customs of the Aryas' and 'the rules of caste division of religious life' (Book I, Chapter 3). The third science, 'economics', or *Varta*, comprises 'agriculture, cattle-breeding and trade'. 'It is by means of the treasury and the army obtained solely through *Varta* that the king can hold under his control both his and his enemy's party' (Book I, Chapter 4). *Varta* is thus represented as the science dealing the occupations that supply the king with the sinews of war and power. The fourth science is that which treats of *danda* (punishment) on which 'the well-being and progress' of the first three sciences depend. This, the 'science of government (*dandaniti*)', has to do with coercion and the appropriate use of 'punishment' as a means of keeping people in 'their respective duties and occupations' (Book I, Chapter 4).[27]

His conception of law, although not wholly free of metaphysical content, was essentially empirical, and his conception of justice consisted in compliance with what the law sanctioned, on the ground that it promoted the common good. Punishment of various types of crime is dealt with particularly in Book IV, although touched upon in other books as well. Some three hundred offences, together with the fines to be imposed, are indicated, principally in Books II–IV.[28]

---

[24] A king who hates 'the science of polity' cannot 'maintain his sovereignty' (Book V, Chapter 4; also Book VI, Chapter 1). 'A wise king, trained in politics, will, though he possesses a small territory, conquer the whole earth with the help of the best fitted elements of his sovereignty, and will never be defected' (Book VI, Chapter 1). 'The King who is well educated and disciplined in science, devoted to good government of his subjects, and bent on doing good to all people will enjoy the earth unopposed' (Book I, Chapter 5).

[25] Concerning the duties of the castes the author writes, 'The duty of the Brahman is study, teaching, performance of sacrifice, officiating in other's sacrificial performance and the giving and receiving of gifts'.

'That of a Kshatriya is study, performance of sacrifice, giving gifts, military occupation, and protection of life'.

'That of a Vaisya is study, performance of sacrifice, giving gifts, agriculture, cattle-breeding, and trade'.

'That of a Sudra is the serving of the twice-born (dvijati), agriculture, cattle-breeding, and trade (varta), the profession of artisans and court-bards (*karukusi-lavakarma*)' (Book I, Chapter 3). The term 'twice-born' refers to those who have undergone initiation into one of the three foregoing classes.

[26] The orders include besides three ascetic orders (student, forest-recluse, and ascetic), the householder whose duties are defined: 'The duty of a householder is earning livelihood by his own profession, marriage among his equals of different ancestral Rishis, intercourse with his wedded wife after her monthly ablution, gifts to gods, ancestors, guests, and servants, and the eating of the remainder' (Book I, Chapter 3).

[27] Kautilya observes of 'punishment': 'For punishment (danda), when awarded with due consideration, makes the people devoted to righteousness and to works productive of wealth and enjoyment; while punishment, when ill-awarded under the influence of greed and anger owing to ignorance, excites fury even among hermits and ascetics dwelling in forests, not to speak of householders'.

'But when the law of punishment is kept in abeyance, it gives rise to such disorder as is implied in the proverb of fishes (matsyanyayamudbhavayati); for in the absence of a magistrate (dandadharabhavre), the strong will swallow the weak; but under his protection the weak resist the strong'.

[28] Quoted in Sapru, R. K. *Administrative Theories and Management Thought*, 2nd edition (New Delhi: PHI Learning, 2009), 70.

It was essential, therefore, that the king be active; after all, activity give rise to wealth, and presumably wealth made for the welfare and happiness of his people and for the progress of virtue. In virtue of his power to guard against the violation of the *dharmas*, the king is the fountain of justice (*dharmapravartaka*). As the duty of the king consists in protecting his subjects with justice, its observance leads him to heaven. 'The king who administers justice in accordance with sacred law (dharma), evidence (*vyavahara*), history (or usage) (*samstha*), and edicts of kings (*nyaya*), which is the fourth, will be able to conquer the whole world bounded by the four quarters (*chaturantam mahim*)'.[29]

1.2.4 Administrative Machinery of Government

To Kautilya, State is of critical importance of ensuring order in the affairs of the society. Kautilya, gliding lightly over contractual theories of kinship, assumes that a high concentration of power is necessary for civilized society to carry on and advises the king against all sorts of stratagems to be strong and diligent. Kautilya identified following as the constituent elements of the State:

1. King
2. Officials
3. Territory
4. Forts
5. Army
6. Treasury
7. *Mitras* or allies

Kautilya also indicated the qualities whereon depended the strength of these elements, among which are the qualities of a good king (Book VI, Chapter 1; Book VIII, Chapter 2) and of a 'good country' or territorial division. According to Pran Nath, a territorial division was 'sufficiently large and varied to constitute a self-supporting independent state, though much smaller than a country of which there were eighty four in India in the 7th century AD'.[30] The structure of administration comprised the following:

1. Central executive machinery (headed by the king)
2. *Mantriparishad* (council of ministers)
3. Civil service (government officials)
4. Provincial and local governments

The chief officials of the State were as follows:

1. *Mantrin*—Minister/Counsellor
2. *Purohita*—Priest

---

[29] Book III, Chapter I. The term *dharma* signifies the Sacred Canon; *vyavahara*, current law; *samstha*, usage; and *nyaya*, reasoning. Kautilya was the first to emphasize the importance of secular law and to make reasoning a source of state law, along with the Sacred Canon, current law and usage.

[30] Pran Nath, *A Study in the Economic Condition of Ancient India* (London: Oxford, 1929), 14, 45–50.

3. *Senpati*—Commander of the Army
4. *Yuvraj*—Prince
5. *Duvarika*—Chief of Palace Attendants
6. *Antaravamsika*—Chief of the King's Guards
7. *Prasastri*—Magistrate
8. *Samaharta*—Collector-General
9. *Sannidhata*—Chief Treasurer
10. *Pradesta*—Commissioner
11. *Nayaka*—Town Guard
12. *Paura*—Chief of the Town
13. *Durgapal*—Guardian of the Forts
14. *Karmantika*—Superintendent of Mines
15. *Mantriparishad Adhyaksha*—Chief of Council of Ministers
16. *Adhyaskas* —Chief of the Records-Audit Office
17. *Dandapalas*—Officer of the Army Department
18. *Antapalas*—Officer in-charge, boundaries
19. *Ativahikas*—Officer-in-charge, forests

The description on the machinery of government is the most important part of *Arthashastra*. At the top of the structure of the machinery of government is the king who is the supreme executive of the land. In the discharge of his duties, the king 'shall employ ministers, and hear their opinion'. 'These ministers shall have to consider all that concerns the parties of both the king and his enemy',[31] and shall be individually and collectively responsible to the king. The prime minister, the high priest and with one or two additions, they might form an inner cabinet. It is this inner cabinet which assists the king to examine the character of ministers appointed in government departments. In times of emergency, Kautilya asks the king to consult the council of ministers—a body larger than the inner cabinet (*antarmatyas*).

The chief functions of the *mantriparishad* were as follows:

1. Commencement of the work
2. Completion of the work
3. Improvement of the accomplished work
4. Proper execution of the order passed
5. General supervision over public administration of the country

The administrative machinery comprising the *mantris* (topmost part of the administrative pyramid), *amatyas* and *mahamatras* (departmental heads) formed the core of the central executive. The administrative structure of the departmental head was as follows:

[31] Book I, Chapter 15.

Departmental Head (*Mahamatra*)
|
Collector-General (*Samaharta*)
|
Commissioners
|
Chief Superintendent (*Sarvadhikarana*)
|
Superintendent (*Adhyaksha*)
|
Chief Officer (*Yukta*)
|
Karnika
|
Clerks

In the management of domestic affairs, Kautilya points out the difficulty of finding men of high character to serve as ministers and other officials. Men 'are naturally fickle minded and exhibit constant change in their temper'. They are apt to be disloyal to plot rebellion.

In his discussion of the structure of the machinery of the government, he counts the high priest, the prime minister, the commander of the army, treasurer general, the collector general, the teacher and the sacrificial priest as the important ministers. In the hierarchy of officers, Kautilya attaches importance to superintendent, lower in position than the ministerial officer and belonging to the sixth order according to remuneration. He is not the head of the department; he is the chief of the section dealing with varied economic and administrative activities of the government. An excerpt from his job description for superintendent of commerce is as follows:

> The superintendent of commerce shall ascertain demand or absence of demand for, and rise or fall in the price of various kinds of merchandise which may be the products either of land or of water, and which may have been brought in either by land of by waterpath. He shall also ascertain the time suitable for their distribution, centralization, purchase, and sale.[32]

He is under a dual control. He is under the collector general for the services of the personnel and collection of revenue. But in the matter of supply of produced and collected commodities and articles, he is accountable to the treasurer general. In addition, he is directly under the control of the king to which all officers are finally subject.

The functions of the government have been arranged according to services required by people. They seem to have been arranged horizontally. Under the collector general are the commissioner, the district officer, and the circle officer in charge of a division, a district and a circle of villages, respectively.

[32] Book II, Chapter 16.

1.2.5 Principal Government Departments

The functioning of the State was not subjected to explicit administrative or economic analysis, although theoretical inferences are implied. For the management, affairs of the State were divided into several departments. The principal departments and functions which they performed are briefly discussed here.

Finance Department: The finance department in *Arthashastra* includes three officers: (a) the collector general of ministerial level in charge of revenue collection, (b) the treasurer general of ministerial level in charge of treasury and (c) the superintendent of accounts much below the ministerial level according to remuneration. Both, the collector general and the treasurer general, are independent, the former controlling revenue collection and the latter controlling supplies of expenditure. Both exercise control over superintendents of several actions. Both the accounts and audit are looked after by the superintendent of accounts, who is under the collector general.

The king is required to attend to the accounts of receipts and expenditure personally.[33] He is also expected to listen to the narrative of the whole of actual accounts pertaining to each department from the minister concerned.

Home Department: The home department consists of a minister (duty not mentioned), the doorkeeper and the superintendent (takes care of personal safety of the king), the superintendent of country parts and boundaries (partakes defence duties), the superintendent of passports (issues passes to those who want to leave or enter the country) and the superintendent of pasturelands (protects forests, arrests thieves to secure safety of traffic, protects lands and also keeps roads in repair). The collector general, like the deputy commissioner of today, also performs magisterial function.

Defence Department: The defence department is headed by the *senapati*, but he is not the commander. Under his supervision, there are two branches. To the defence forces branch, belong the commander, the chief constable in charge of infantry, the chiefs of elephants, cavalry and chariots, physicians of the army and trainers of horses. The defence supplies branch consists of superintendents of infantry, cavalry, chariots and elephants and guards of elephant forests.

Foreign Affairs Department: References are also made in *Arthashastra* to envoy, *chargé d'affaire* and conveyor of royal and their duties. The duties of an envoy (such as, transmission, maintenance of treaties, issue of ultimatum, gaining of friends) are looked at in *Arthashastra* more from the point of view of advancing the war-and-peace policy of the country rather than of advancing the cause of country in economic, social and cultural aspects. Foreign policy consists of adjustments in the various concentric rings.

Social Welfare Department: Social welfare activities are given a great deal of importance in *Arthashastra*. Chapter 1 of Book I details many activities of social welfare in which the government ought to take interest. Kautilya writes that the king should provide the orphans, the aged, the helpless women, the infirm, the afflicted and the helpless with maintenance. The king is under an obligation to carry out injunctions about social and economic justice in

[33] Book V, Chapter 2.

dharmashastras and customs among the people. The departments in the charge of the superintendent of a slaughterhouse, of prostitutes, of liquor and of weaving are social welfare departments.

Public Works and Stores Department: Housing in villages, cities and forts and town planning has been a special care of government in Kautilya's work. An important officer for public works is the *sannidhata* (the chamberlain). He is to build and maintain important state buildings. 'The sannidhata shall build the treasury, the house of saleable commodities, the house of the produce of the land, the house of forest producer, the armoury and the jail'. He also has overall responsibility for the safekeeping and storage of all State wealth, cash and kind. The work also attaches significance of administrative architecture in the context of the construction of harem and of buildings in forts.

The number of departments mentioned in *Arthashastra* is exhaustive. Each department is again subdivided into sections. For example, under the treasurer general, there are officers (coordinating the work of clerks), clerks (drafting and noting) and servants (performing merely physical work). Functions in sections seem to have been arranged horizontally, that is, according to subjects.

He attaches importance to statistics as well. The district and circle officers are asked to collect variety of statistics regarding lands and other property, families and persons. He decries retrenchment of expenditure on profitable works.[34] He advocates frequent meetings between the king and members of public, as he is alive to the evils of bureaucratization.[35] In his description of business departments, Kautilya makes reference to the laws of supply and demand and to other business methods.

1.2.6 Administration of Law

Administrative courts consisting of three persons proficient in *dharmashastras* and three ministerial officers in the administration of law are referred to in *Arthashastra*. A hierarchy of courts from the court of a group of ten villages rising up to the king's court is presented in Kautilya's work. It is not clear whether the king personally or the court of justice presides over the Supreme Court.

Sacred laws (dharma), evidence (*vyavahara*), history (*samstha*) and edicts of kings (*nyaya*) are said to be the four bases of law. In case of conflict, edicts of kings are to override the other bases. Under the law, slavery is legitimate.

Arthashastra also contains references to code of law. The code is set forth under 17 heads including marriage, property, slaves and labourers, forcible seizure of an object, physical injury, theft, defamation, assault and so on.

1.2.7 Personnel Administration

In the administration of domestic affairs, Kautilya emphasizes the difficulty of men of high calibre to serve as officials. He gives more attention to the higher officials for the fact that they are invested with more authority and responsibility than the lower officials. The officials in the higher

---

[34] Book II, Chapter 7.

[35] Book I, Chapter 19.

rung are expected to possess intellectual, moral and physical qualities. There is little about the education, training and qualities to be possessed by the lower officials except that they should be incorruptible and good at work.

Nothing is said in detail about the grades of each category of personnel, training after recruitment, methods of promotion, leave, pension and superannuation. Recruitment of those getting 1,000 panas per annum seems to be made by the king assisted by the higher priest and the prime minister.

Superintendents are vested with the power to regulate the salaries, transfer and appointments of the servants under him getting 100–1,000 panas per annum. Transfer of personnel is suggested as a precaution and a remedy against misappropriation of government money.[36] He does not favour the transfer of employees employed in guarding royal buildings, forts and country parts.

Each government employee is subject to punishment if he is found corrupt, disloyal or harassing the people. A code of conduct to be observed by government servants, of course, figures in *Arthashastra*. Although *Arthashastra* does not prescribe rules of pension for retired employees, pensions to sons and wives of those servants who die in harness are allowed. 'The fundamental principle which Kautilya wants the king to observe is that he should look to the bodily comforts of his servants by providing such emoluments as could infuse in them the spirit of enthusiasm to work'. Government servants do not seem to come within the purview of the courts of law if they violate rules in administration. But for the breach of law in their private conduct, they can, of course, be tried by courts of law.

Kautilya gives great attention to the education and training of the king and the princes. Kautilya's approach is more practical. One of his principles in the training of princes is the selection of mature and learned men. In the morning, he should receive training in military science. The second half can be divided between the 'sacred canon', philosophy, economics and politics. The prince shall also learn self-discipline and self-control 'at first from the teachers' and afterwards, he shall constantly associate with those of mature learning.

Qualities of State Officials: In his discussion of administration, Kautilya lays down a series of qualities, differing in number and order, for officers holding different positions of responsibility. His job specification for a State officer covers many of today's demands:

> Native born of high family, influential, well trained in arts, possessed of foresight, wise, of strong memory, bold, eloquent, skilful, intelligent, possessed of enthusiasm, dignity, and endurance, pure in character, affable, firm in loyal devotion, endowed with excellent conduct, strength, health and braver, free from procrastination and fickle mindedness, affectionate, and free from such qualities as excite hatred and enmity—these are the qualifications of a ministerial officer.[37]

Building Competencies: *Arthashastra* prescribes certain tests before assigning the critical responsibilities to the administrators. These include the following:[38]

1. Test person's training in possession of the eye of science through those learned in the same science. Thus, technical competence must be tested.
2. Test intelligence, perseverance and dexterity.

[36] Book V, Chapter 3.
[37] Shamasastry, *Kautilya's Arthashastra*, 14.
[38] Kangle, *The Kautilya Arthashastra*, Book I, Chapter 9, Sutra 3, p. 17.

3. Test eloquence, boldness and presence of mind.
4. Test ability to bear troubles during the emergencies.
5. Test uprightness, friendliness and firmness of devotion in dealing with others, and amiability and absence of disposition of animosity.
6. Test strength of character.

Thus, the important competencies can be broadly classified as (a) technical/professional competence, (b) decision-making competence, particularly in emergency situations, (c) communication competence, (d) behavioural competence as reflected in dealings with others and (e) character competence.

Arthashastra places great stress on building competencies. In fact, the very first chapter is titled as 'Concerning the Topic of Training'. It emphasizes the twin qualities of the 'skill-in-action' and 'quest for perfection'. *Arthashastra* identifies basic characteristics of the trainable persons:

> For training disciplines suitable stuff, not one unsuited. A science imparts discipline to one, whose intellect has (the qualities of) the desire to learn, listening (to the teacher), learning, retention, through understanding, reflection, rejection (of false views) and intentness on truth, (and) not to any other person.[39]

Further *Arthashastra* recommends, 'And constant association with elder in learning for the sake of improving his training, since training has its root in that'.[40]

1.2.8 Financial Administration

Kautilya's principal concern was to strengthen the State, and this depended upon the adequacy of revenue. He devoted more attention, in fact, to administrative aspects of public finance than to any other economic subject.

It was the revenue yielded by wealth that was of major concern, in Kautilya's opinion. Revenue was of general importance:

> All undertakings depend upon finance. Hence foremost attention shall be paid to the treasury.... Public prosperity (*pracarasamrddhih*), rewards for good conduct (*charitranugrahah*), capture of thieves, dispensing with (the service of too many) government servants, abundance of harvest, prosperity of commerce, absence of troubles and calamities (*upasargapramokshah*), diminution or remission of taxes, and income in gold (*hiranyopayanam*) are all conducive to financial prosperity.[41]

He listed 66 or 67 sources of the king's revenue, based predominantly on land, and grouped them under 7 heads, resting essentially upon the geographical location of the activities and individuals subject to taxation, tolls and so on.[42]

For purposes of administration, Kautilya divided the kingdom into four districts, distinguished the urban centres from the villages, and classified the villages according to size and nature of tax

---

[39] Kangle, *The Kautilya Arthashastra*, Book I, Chapter 5, Sutra 4-5, p. 10.

[40] Ibid., Sutra 11, p. 11.

[41] Book II, Chapter 8.

[42] Those found in fortified and urban areas and those found in rural situations; those found at sites of mineral exploitation, or in pastoral, forest, or intensely cultivated (e.g., horticultural) areas; and those situated along traffic-carrying roads and waterways (Book II, Chapter 6). He also distinguished seven forms of revenue by type (Book II, Chapter 6).

liability.[43] An accountant was made responsible for each five or ten villages and charged with registering the population, estimating income and expenditure by family, collecting taxes and so on, although under the surveillance of inspectors and spies.[44]

Book II (Chapters 6–9, 15–16, 35) deals with the collection of revenue, the keeping of governmental accounts, the detection of embezzlement and the prevention of undesirable fiscal conduct. Other chapters (Book II, Chapters 15, 24) deal with the production and use of agricultural products, taxes thereon and the administration of crown lands. Another chapter (Book II, Chapter 17) deals with forest produce. The duties of a city superintendent, seemingly confined to the police of the city, included ascertaining the income and expenditure of households, as did the duties of parallel officials responsible for districts and villages (Book II, Chapters 35–36). The prevention of false weighing is treated in Book II, Chapters 14 and 19.

Various chapters are devoted to tolls and their collection (Book II, Chapters 21–22), mining and manufacture (Book II, Chapter 12), the production and sale of liquor (Book II, Chapter 25), commerce and forest produce (Book II, Chapters 16–17), navigation and fishing (Book II, Chapter 28), dairy husbandry (Book II, Chapter 29) and the duties of prostitutes (Book II, Chapter 27). The role of the State goldsmith is treated in Book II, Chapters 13–14.

Public expenditure, of which there were many forms, prompted a number of Kautilya's observations. First, it was essential that expenditure on staff be limited. Second, it was essential that wasteful and unnecessary expenditure be avoided by the king and his servants.[45] Third, while Kautilya was opposed to indiscriminate mendicancy and idleness (Book II, Chapters 1, 23), he stated it was essential to keep in hand a reserve of food, clothing, munitions of war, and so on, sufficient to support the population in times of calamity, for years if necessary, and to be able at all times to sustain the currently needy, the helpless, the orphans and so on.[46] Fourth, the king had to undertake various kinds of overhead capital and other improvement expenditures on irrigation, roads, highways, buildings, fire protection and so on. Fifth, it was desirable that the king undertake profitable forms of expenditure such as those upon objects that yielded income periodically (Book II, Chapters 6, 9). Sixth, it was important that the king's stewards manage his properties, together with expenditure upon them, so as to render them profitable (Book II, Chapters 12, 17, 23–24).

Narayan Chandra Bandyopadhyaya identifies 11 objects of public expenditure in Kautilya's work—royal household; religious establishments; magistracy, judiciary, spies and menial staff; military personnel and establishment, together with pensions; government factories; hired labour; loans to cultivators, colonization costs, irrigation expense; widows, orphans, indigents; teachers and teaching establishments; pensions to widows and children of those killed in the king's services; and public works, roads, canals, embankments.[47]

Respecting revenue, Kautilya also observed that the king would suffer if either too little or too much revenue were collected. He who 'lessens the revenue eats the king's wealth' while he who 'doubles the revenue eats into the capital of the country' (Book II, Chapter 9).

---

43 Some villages were exempted from cash taxation.

44 Book II, Chapter 35.

45 Kautilya urged the king to avoid 'expensive sports' and advocated that villagers should not be diverted by sports, plays and so on (Book II, Chapter 1).

46 Book II, Chapters 1, 4, 15.

47 N. C. Bandyopadhyaya, *Kautilya* (Calcutta: Hare Press, 1927), 167–68.

Kautilya thus implied that the king should adjust his demands to the 'capacity' of various parts of the country to supply revenue, taking into account the effect of current taxation upon this capacity in the future (Book V, Chapter 2). In this context, Kautilya remarks,

> Just as fruits are gathered from a garden as often as they become ripe, so revenue shall be collected as often as it becomes ripe. Collection of revenue or of fruits, when unripe, shall never be carried on, lest their sources may be injured, causing immense trouble.[48]

1.2.9 Information Collecting and Decision-making

For decision-making, information is a precondition. *Arthashastra* recommends collection of comprehensive information on various aspects. An illustration of village/rural information system is as follows:

> He should record the number of villages by fixing their boundaries, the number of fields by an enumeration of ploughed and unploughed (fields), dry and wet fields, parks, vegetable gardens, (flower and fruit) enclosures, forests, structures, sanctuaries, temples, water-works, cremation grounds, rest houses, sheds for drinking water, holy places, pasture lands and roads, (and) in conformity with that he should keep records of size of boundaries, forests and roads, and of grants, sales, favours and exemptions, concerning village-boundaries and fields, and (keep records) of houses by an enumeration of tax payers and non-tax payers.[49]

In addition to these classifications and details, emphasis is also laid on the amounts of income and expenditures of families: 'And of males and females in the family, he should know the number of children and old persons, their work, customs and the amount of their income and expenditure'.[50]

Arthashastra recommends group decision-making. 'One wheel alone does not turn'. In order to turn the wheel, others are also needed. 'All undertakings should be preceded by consultation'. Kautilya also advised against relying only on a few advisors. 'Holding a consultation with one (only), he may not (be able to) reach a decision in difficult matters'. 'With more (councillors), it is with difficulty that decisions on matters are reached'.[51] In addition to the soundness of the decision, an important advice is not to put off decisions as 'an (affair/decision) postponed becomes difficult to settle or even impossible to settle'.[52]

1.2.10 State Intervention

Arthashastra recommends State intervention to protect the interest of customers. The superintendent of markets 'is to fix the prices, raising or lowering them according to the availability of the goods, always keeping in mind the customers' interests'. However, producers' interests are also taken care of.

Further, a penalty is recommended in case of unfair trade practices. Cornering of a particular commodity and forcing its price above that fixed by the state involves heavy fine.[53] *Arthashastra*

---

[48] Book V, Chapter 2.

[49] Ibid., Chapter 35, Sutra 3, pp. 182–83.

[50] Ibid., Sutra 5, p. 183.

[51] Kangle, *The Kautilya Arthashastra*, Sutra 40, p. 34.

[52] Ibid., Book I, Chapter 19, Sutra 30, p. 47.

[53] Ibid., Book IV, Chapter 2, Sutra 19, p. 260.

further recommends, 'He is to fix prices of various commodities after taking into consideration such factors as investment of capital, interest charges, duties paid, rent and so on'.[54]

Arthashastra suggests that the idea of managing by contracting out should be practiced particularly in those cases where the State finds it costly to run the activity itself. For example, it is stated that a mine costly in its working should be leased out for a fixed share of the output or for a fixed rent, and only a light mine should be undertaken by the State directly.[54] The most common feature of contracting out was the system of labour contract through the institution of *sanghas*. The *sanghas* or the associations/unions of labourers were allowed to negotiate with the employers. In case of disputes, the matter was referred to the State.

1.2.11 Conclusion

Kautilya's *Arthashastra* is a comprehensive treatise that attempts to set forth general principles and detailed rules to be applied to specific problems of government. Dealing with a large variety of subjects, it covers almost every aspect of the public administration—duties of the king, his ministers and his councillors, diplomats, organization and management of agriculture, trade, commerce, law and law courts, municipal governments, factories, markets, social customs, marriage and divorce, rights of women, census operations and so on. Kautilya was satisfied to lay down administrative rules based on past or current experience and apparently deemed adequate.

Because of his contempt for morality and human compassion, as is evident from *Arthashastra*, Kautilya's name has become synonymous with sinister and unscrupulous administration.[55] His approach is no different from that of Machiavelli which laid stress on unscrupulous practices that ought to be followed for political success in the future.

But, Kautilya's *Arthashastra* is a sincere attempt at scientific enquiry which deals with the organization and management of human affairs of the state. *Arthashastra* is a classical work on ancient Indian administration. In the 12th century, a minister of the King of Banaras classed the *Arthashastra* as a sixth Veda, the Mahabharata having been declared the fifth.[56] Written nearly 2,325 years ago, the work gives a picture of ancient past respecting social, economic, political and administrative aspects of India.

1.3 Mughal Administration in India

The Mughal rule at its height embraced much of India and her population. Its dimensions, much greater than those of previous Hindu rulers, reflected the unifying influence generated by foreign invasions of India that vast territories could be administered.

The Mauryan Empire gradually declined under Asoka's rule (273–232 BC), and India was divided into a number of independent kingdoms with the border areas being occupied by Greeks and Persian satraps. The Indianized Kushan Empire, after occupying a good part of North India, lasted for a century after Christ. This was followed by another period of border incursions and independent states until the Guptas in the 4th century welded a good part of India into an empire after subduing the Saka Invaders. The empire declined due to Hun invasions and other

[54] Ibid., Sutra 36, p. 262.

[55] Ibid., Book 2, Chapter 12, Sutra 22, p. 198.

[56] K. V. R. Aiyangar, *Indian Cameralism* (Madras: The Adyar Library, 1949), 30.

disintegrative factors giving way to several independent states. The empire of Harsha in the 7th century, covering North India up to the Narmada River, was the swansong of the Hindu imperial tradition.[57]

After four centuries of smaller and some independent kingdoms, the Muslim invaders established a Sultanate in Delhi from 1206 to 1526. The Sultanate period had some important rulers such as Iltutmish, Balban, Alauddin Khalji and Muhammad Bin Tughluq. It included the Slave Dynasty (1206–90), the Khaljis (1290–1320), the Tughluqs (1320–1414), the Saiyyads (1414–51) and the Lodis (1451–1526). While their rule covered a good part of North India, it was chequered by change of dynasties, rebellions and intrigues, and was not characterized by steady patterns of administration. During the Mughal period, some six years of Sher Shah Suri's rule (1540–45 AD) were significant from the point of view of government and administration of the country. His revenue administration formed the basis for Mughals. He was the first Muslim ruler of India who displayed a real aptitude for civil government.

After Babur's victory in the First Battle of Panipat in 1526, the Mughal rule was firmly grounded. With this advent, many significant dimensions were added in the administrative system, especially during Akbar's emperorship (1556–1605). The first two rulers, Babur (died in 1530) and Humayun (1530–56) continued the administrative arrangement of the Sultanate and did not introduce any fundamental change either in the political divisions of the kingdom or the administrative machinery. Jahangir (1605–27), and the last of great Mughal emperors, Aurangzeb, who died in 1707, also made some changes in the administrative system during their regimes.

But it was during Akbar's time that the Mughal Empire was best organized. In this context, Sri Ram Sharma writes, 'Nevertheless, the main framework of the administrative organization, though in a considerably attenuated form, endured till the English East India Company (EIC) stepped into the shoes of the Mughal Emperors'.[58]

1.3.1 Emperor's Position

During the Mughal rule, the emperor was all-powerful. The emperor was a 'perfect autocrat' and 'the embodiment of all power'.[59] In 1507, Babur had proclaimed himself as *Padshah*, and the subsequent Muslim rulers followed the suit. The word 'pad' denotes stability and overlordship, and word 'shah' means ruler. As such, the emperor was invested with all political, administrative and religious powers. He was the supreme authority in the State, the head of the government, the supreme commander of the State forces, the lawmaker and law enforcer. The Mughal rulers had faith in the doctrine of divine rights and regarded themselves as the representatives of divinity.

1.3.2 The Council of Ministers and Departments

It may be mentioned here that the Mughal administration centred round the sovereign whose power was unlimited. But for administrative convenience, he had a number of ministers, of whom four were certainly more important: (a) *diwan* in charge of revenue and finance; (b) the *mir-i-baksi*

[57] P. Saran, *The Provincial Government of the Mughals: 1526–1658* (Bombay: Asia Publishing House, 1973), 47–49.
[58] S. R. Sharma, *Mughal Government and Administration* (Bombay: Asia, 1951).
[59] A. L. Srivastava, *The Mughal Empire: 1526–1803 A.D.* (Agra: Shiva Lal Agarwala, 1969), 479.

at the head of the military department; (c) the *mir saman* in charge of factories and stores; and (d) the *sadr-us-sudur*, the head of the ecclesiastical and judicial department.

Besides, there were other chief officers of the state who virtually enjoyed the rank of ministers (e.g., chief quazi, in charge of civil and criminal law; *darogah-i-topkhana*, in charge of the artillery; *darogha-i-dak-chauki*, in charge of information and intelligence).

Besides these, the other important officials included the *mir bahri* (revenue secretary), *mir barr* (superintendent of forests), *quir begi* (lord standard bearer), *hakt-begi* (superintendent of the royal stud), *mushrif* (chief admiral and officer of harbours), *nazir-i-buyutad* (superintendent of imperial workshops), *mustaufi* (auditor general), *awarjah nawis* (superintendent of daily expenditure at the court), *khuwan salar* (superintendent of royal kitchen) and *mir arz* (the officer who used to present petitions before the king).

According to J. N. Sarkar, these officials were equivalent to 'secretaries rather than ministers'.[60] Even on non-acceptance of their advice by the emperor, they never resigned.[61]

1.3.3 Mansabdari System

The Mughal system of administration had a hierarchy of officials called *mansabdars. Mansabdars* held both civil and military powers and functions. Every public officer held a *mansab* or official appointment of rank and profit and every *mansabdar* was expected to supply a given number of troops for the military service. During Akbar's time, there were 33 grades of *mansab*, ranging from 'commanders of 10' to 'commanders of 10,000'. The highest rank an ordinary officer could hold was that of a commander of 5,000; the exalted upper grades were reserved for members of the royal family. These *mansabbar*s were directly recruited, promoted, suspended or removed by the emperor himself. It is noteworthy that the system never worked as it was expected to maintain a quota, and the *mansabdar*s rarely fulfilled the condition of maintaining their due quota.

The Mughals had an efficient civil service. There were no fixed rules for recruitment or service conditions. However, the Mughals were great believers in merit. The Mughal bureaucracy, despite its efficiency, had certain weaknesses. It was 'land-based' and 'highly urbanized institution'.[62]

1.3.4 Revenue Administration

Emperors of the Mughal rule attached a great deal of importance to revenue collection. Early Muslim conquerors followed the Hindu revenue system because it was seen to be more convenient.[63]

Land revenue was the main source of the income of the empire, and the system of land revenue administration was taken from the system introduced by Sher Shah Suri. The architect of the new system was Raja Todar Mal who was later (in 1582) appointed *Diwan-i-Ashraf*. Land revenue was fixed at one-third of the gross produce. This revenue system was based on the *rayatwari* system under which the actual cultivator was the assessee. Lands were carefully surveyed with the use of a new measurement called 'ilahi gaz' or yard, which was equal to 33 inches *tanab* or tent-rope, and

[60] J. N. Sarkar, *Mughal Administration* (Calcutta: M. C. Sarkar, 1935), 17.

[61] Ibid., 18.

[62] B. B. Mira, *The Administrative History of India 1834–1947* (London: Oxford University Press, 1970), 639–40.

[63] Sarkar, *Mughal Administration*, 9.

jarib or bamboos joined by iron rings which assured a constant measure. Land was divided into four classes on the basis of production. These were *polaj* or land capable of being annually cultivated; *parti*, that is, land kept fallow for some time to recover productive capacity; *chachar* or land that had remained fallow for three or four years; and *banjar*, that is, land which had remained uncultivated for five or more years. Only the area under actual cultivation was assessed. There was an officer called *malguzar* in charge of the revenue collection in each district, who was assisted in his task by a number of officials.

In the revenue department, there used to be at the headquarters of a province, a *diwan*, with an administrative head of the *khalsa*, the chief revenue officer; a superintendent called the *serishtadar*; a chief accounts officer called *karkun*, in addition to *naik diwan* who headed the revenue administration of the districts, with village *patwaris* at the bottom of the departmental hierarchy.

1.3.5 Law and Order and Judicial System

Law and order machinery of the Mughal rule became the precursor for the modern-day police system, although substantial changes were made by the British during their two hundred years of rule. Since the emperor himself was in charge of external and internal security, there was no official specifically assigned with the task of looking after law and order problems for the empire. At the provincial level, the subject of law and order was vested with the *fauzdar* (equivalent to the collector-cum-superintendent of police) at the sub-divisional level (district). An important lacuna with regard to the law and administration of the Mughal rulers was the omission of vast rural areas in a *sarkar* (an administrative unit at the district level). Rather, taking urbanized areas as the unit of administration, a *kotwal*, assisted by a number of *darogahs*, was appointed for the maintenance of the law and order in the *sarkar*.

Kotwal was the in-charge of the city. His main duty was to maintain law and order in his area. *Ain-i-Akbari* delineated his duties clearly; these are as follows:

1. To detect thieves
2. To regulate prices and check weights and measures
3. To keep watch at night and patrol the city
4. To keep the registers of houses, frequented roads and of citizens, and watch the movements of strangers
5. To employ spies
6. To gather information about the affairs of the neighbouring villages, and the income and expenditure of the various classes of people
7. To prepare an inventory of and take charge of the property of deceased or missing persons who left no heirs
8. To prevent the slaughter of oxen, buffaloes, horses and camels
9. To prevent the burning of women against their will

The list of duties so outlined is too comprehensive to be followed in actual practice.

Policing of rural areas was the job of the local *chowkidars* who were maintained by villages themselves.

The Mughal judicial system was well organized. The *qazi* and the *sadr* helped the kings in the dispensation of justice. Every *sarkar* (district) had its *faujdar* who was in charge of criminal justice, police and the local military forces. His task was to maintain law and order within his area.

Aurangzeb was an orthodox Sunni Muslim who wanted to set up the rule of the 'shariat' throughout his empire and yet he was keen to be known as an impartial and just emperor. The king, as already mentioned, was the fountain of justice and the final court of appeal. Except for Aurangzeb, the Mughal kings had organized a judicial system open to their subjects.

1.3.6 Provincial and Local Administration

For purposes of administration, the empire was divided in *subas* (provinces) and *sarkars* (districts), and each *sarkar* into *paraganas* or union of several villages. (Akbar divided his empire into 15 *subas*; the number of *subas* rose to 18, to 21 and to 23 during the rules of Jahangir, Shah Jahan and Aurangzeb, respectively.) The provincial government reflected the system of central administration, with one important difference: the headship in the provincial administration was virtually divided between the governor—variously called *nazim*, *sipah salar* or *subedar*—who was the executive head of the administration, and *diwan* who was in charge of the revenue administration. The emperor directly appointed them and they were accountable to him alone.

The entire burden of provincial administration rested on the shoulders of *subedar*. His multifarious duties had three main aspects—civil, military and judicial. He was the head of civil administration and his main duty was to maintain law and order. He was also the head of the provincial army and was responsible for the upkeep of armed forces. He was also the supreme judge in the province and as such was the final court of appeal from the lower courts. However, the *subedar* was dependent on *diwan* in financial matters, and *diwan* had to depend on the *subedar* in military and law and order matters. Both were interdependent, and, for good administration of the province, their cooperation was called for.

As already mentioned, a *suba* or *prant* was further divided into a number of *sarkars*. The district administration had thus two wings, executive and revenue. The head of the executive wing was the *fauzdar*. He was the highest officer in the *sarkar* and can be compared with the present collector and district magistrate (DM). He was the executive head of the district administration. He held a *mansab* and was appointed by the king. He worked under the control of the provincial *subedar*. Similarly, the *amal-guzar* was the revenue official in charge of financial and revenue matters. He was the highest revenue officer at the district level and worked under the control of the provincial *diwan*, and had a number of subordinates assisting him in his duties.

For further administrative convenience, the *sarkar* was divided into a number of *parganas* (equivalent to present tehsil or *taluq*) and each *pargana* was headed by a *shiqqadar*. Decentralization was necessary for a big empire like that of the Mughals that had not disturbed the local set-ups under *muqaddams* and *chaudharies*. The supervision of the *faujdar* hardly reached the village. While the village local institutions (panchayats) continued to manage local affairs; in the towns and cities, the local state government was vested in the *kotwal*, who played the role of the prefect of the municipal administration.

In laying the foundation of a well-organized and strong provincial administration. Akbar took care to devise an elaborate system of checks and balances. But the Mughal emperors 'wisely respected provincial feelings and interfered little in the day-to-day life of the provinces'.[64]

[64] S. A. Khan, *The Indian Federation* (London: Oxford, 1937), 24.

1.3.7 Conclusion

Akbar's successors, Jahangir and Shah Jahan, functioned within the given administrational framework. But Aurangzeb's reactionary policy undermined the administrative work. His highly centralized despotism and the attempt to order and supervise all civil and military administration in every minute detail brought about a complete disintegration of the administrative machinery. The Mughal Empire decayed because of administrative inefficiency, religious intolerance and bigotry of Aurangzeb. Vincent Smith remarked:

> The Mughal Empire, like all Asian despotisms had shallow roots. Its existence depended mainly on the personal character of reigning autocrat and on the degree of his military power. It lacked popular support, the strength based on patriotic feeling, and on the stability founded upon ancient traditions.[65]

The Mughal rule in the 16th and 17th centuries provided a steady pattern of administration, but its decline in the 18th century (the last of the great Mughal emperors, Aurangzeb died in 1707) was followed by total anarchy in the larger of India, when the British EIC began its rule. The disintegration of Mughal power in the 18th century, especially after Aurangzeb's demise, had weakened its authority over the outlying provinces.

1.4 British India Administration

Here, the expression 'British India' means all territories and places within Her/His Majesty's dominions governed through the governor general in India. The British Raj was established in India by Government of India (GoI) Act, 1858, that ended in August 1947.

The present system of Indian administration, judicial system, federal structure of the polity and various laws governing parliamentary institutions are largely a legacy of the British imperial rule. The credit of establishing that rule went to a private trading shareholders' corporation known as the East India Company (EIC) which was itself formed in England by a special royal charter issued by Queen Elizabeth on 31 December 1600 under the name of 'the Governor and Company of Merchants of London trading into the East Indies', conferring on it the monopoly of trade in eastern waters. The charter empowered EIC to assemble in any convenient place and there hold court and 'make, ordain and constitute reasonable laws and constitutions, orders or ordinances for the good government of the Company, of all factors and officers and for the advancement of traffic and trade'. The direction of the affairs of the company was vested in a governor to be elected annually by the members and in 24 committees, each consisting of an individual, also annually elected.[66] The total number of original members incorporated in the company was 217 with a total capital subscription of £68,373.

The management of the company's business was vested in a governor (first being Mr Thomas Smythe) and 24 committees (not bodies but individuals who later on became the Court of Directors) who were to be annually elected by the Regulating Act, 1773. Director's tenure was increased to four years, a quarter of them being annually re-elected from the Court of Proprietors (shareholders who jointly owned the company) until 1854 when it was reduced to 18 of whom 6 were to be nominated by the Crown.

---

[65] V. Smith, *The Oxford History of India* (London: Oxford, 1923), 465.

[66] J. E. Woolacott, *British Rule in India* (Delhi: Anmol, 1986), 4–8.

The period between 1600 and 1757 was marked by the issuance of charters for advancement of trade and good governance of the company, after which the company became a predominantly political body. Important charters issued and events held before 1757 were as under:

1600: Grant of the first charter to EIC by Queen Elizabeth

1609: Renewal of the charter by James I

1615: Empowering the company to proclaim martial law

1657: Uniting the rival association started by Sir W. Courten with EIC

1661: Granting the right to company of coining money and jurisdiction over English subjects

1669: Granting Bombay to EIC for an annual rent for £10

1677–83: Extension of company's privileges

1687: Empowering EIC for establishing municipal corporations

1693–94: Making changes in the constitution of company (governor to be a holder of £4,000 stock and his tenure to be not more than two years)

1698: First parliamentary measure for regulating Indian trade and commerce

1708: Godolphin's Award and formation of 'the Untied Company of Merchants of England Trading in the East Indies'

1726: Establishment of mayor's courts in municipal towns of Madras, Bombay and Calcutta

1730–44: Extension of privileges to the United Company

1754: Laying down regulations for strengthening the Indian forces of the company

1757–58: Retention of booty or territory which the company might have acquired in its struggles with native powers

Thus the British Crown and Parliament literally patronized the company during 1600–1757 and strengthened its position by the grant of various charters.

The history of the transformation of EIC formed for the purpose of trading activities is colourful. Within a span of 150 years, it emerged as a big political power administering vast territories in its own rights and laid the foundation of the Empire of the British Crown.

The Mughal Empire became a hopeless failure in the 18th century.[67] The disappearance of capable and powerful emperors from the Indian stage during the 18th century created a dangerous void in the political and social life of India. In this state of political confusion, EIC, which had been in existence for over a century, began to be drawn into the vortex of Indian politics. It began to enlist armies, fight wars and conquer territory. The winning of Battle of Plassey (between the Nawab of Bengal, Siraj-ud-daula, and Lord Clive) in which EIC was recognized as zamindar of 24 *paraganas* with an area of 882 square miles in 1757, and subsequent win in the Battle of Buxar (in which *nizamat* responsibilities and powers of Nawab of Bengal were taken over by EIC) in 1764 and conferment of *diwani* rights (legalizing EIC of wielding political power invested with the

[67] Sarkar, *Mughal Administration*, 254–55.

task of revenue collection in the three extensive provinces of Bengal, Bihar and Orissa and administration of civil justice in them) in 1765 changed the status of the company from mere traders to rulers. As *diwan*, the company directly collected its revenues, while through the right to nominate the deputy *subedar*, it controlled the *nizamat* or the police and judicial powers. This arrangement is known in history as the 'dual' or 'double government'.

Parliament's focus meantime came to be directed towards India after the momentous events which changed the company's status. The question began to agitate minds of the English people as to whether a trading corporation should be allowed to have territorial sovereignty at all. Further, there were reports that while the servants of the company were amassing colossal fortunes, the company itself was advancing rapidly towards bankruptcy (the company's debt amounted to £6,000,000). The directors of the company approached Lord North begging for a loan from government. The company's request for pecuniary assistance came before the Parliament in 1773, and Lord North's government proposed extensive alterations in the system of the government of the company's Indian possessions. Two Acts were passed by the Parliament. By one, a loan of £1,400,000 at 4% was granted to the company, and the second Act was the famous Regulating Act, 1773.

1.4.1 Parliamentary Enactments (1773–1858) and Impacts

1.4.1.1 The Regulating Act, 1773

In response to financial resources drain and territorial expansion, the Parliament tried to modify the company's administration for the whole of British India. For the Government of Bengal, a governor general (first being Warren Hastings) with an executive council of four councillors for a five years' term was appointed to 'superintend, direct and control' the governments of three presidencies of Bengal, Bombay and Madras (each governed by a governor in council responsible directly to the court of directors in England). The system by which the three presidencies had been independent of one another was abolished. The Act restricted the powers of the presidencies from making war or treaty without the approval of the governor general in council. The latter were to obey the orders of the court of directors who in turn was required to keep the treasury informed of the civil, military and revenue affairs of the government of the company. A supreme court of judicature was also established at Fort William (Calcutta) which consisted of a chief judge and three other judges. Thus, the control of British Parliament and its right to be acquainted with the affairs of a private corporation were clearly demonstrated.

This Act may, therefore, be treated as a landmark step in the evolution of parliamentary institutions in India.

1.4.1.2 The Pitt's India Act, 1784

The Pitt's India Act of 1784 placed EIC in direct and permanent subordination to a body representing the British Government. It created a board of six commissioners for the affairs of India, popularly known as the board of control.

The board was to consist of the chancellor and one of the secretaries of state and four privy councillors nominated by the Crown to hold office during its pleasure. The commissioners were empowered to superintend, direct and control all Acts regarding the civil and military administration of the company's possessions in India. The directors had to give obedience to the board, which might disapprove of or modify the dispatches of the directors. The court of proprietors lost its chief governing power.

The importance of Pitt's Act lies in its creation of a separate Department of State in England under the official style of 'the commissioner for the affairs of India', whose special function was to control the court of directors. One of the commissioners was appointed president, having a casting vote in matters of difference. The Act thus inaugurated what is described as double government in the Indian administration. The company's officers continued to be in actual charge of the management, while the representatives of Parliament, sitting in a separate body, controlled all important matters of policy and detail from day to day.

As the president had cabinet status, the Parliament was able to exercise complete and direct control over Indian administration because of the complete responsibility of the British Cabinet to the British Parliament.

1.4.1.3 The Charter Act, 1793

By the Regulating Act of 1793, the governor general and the governors were empowered to override the majority in their councils. Further, the members of the board of control and its staff were to be paid out of Indian revenues.

Lord Cornwallis (1786–93) who came to India as governor general in 1786 was responsible for improving substantially the terms of employment of the employees of the company, who, in the course of time, began to be called covenanted civil servants. The other step which he undertook was the exclusion of Indians from the higher administration.

Cornwallis believed that 'every native of Hindustan is corrupt'. It was laid down officially in 1793 that all higher posts in administration worth more than £500 a year in salary were to be held by Englishmen.[68] The exclusion of Indians from higher grades of services had been 'to make the whole Indian nation subservient', wrote John Shore who succeeded Cornwallis. It was felt that tempo to consolidate British rule could not be left to Indians who did not possess the same understanding of British interests as Englishmen. Further, the British were convinced that an administration based on British ideas, institutions, and practices could be grounded only by English personnel. Moreover, the directors of the company and members of the British Cabinet were keen to preserve the monopoly of lucrative appointments in the higher civil services for their sons. Cornwallis also laid down that promotion in the civil service would be based on seniority so that its members would remain independent of outside influence. A little later, Lord Wellesley (1798–1805), another governor general initiated the idea of careful training of recruits to the higher administrative (covenanted) posts. In 1800, he set up College of Fort William at Calcutta which was replaced in 1806 by East India College at Haileybury, England.

1.4.1.4 The Charter Act, 1813

The Parliamentary Act of 1813 was preceded by an inquiry of parliamentary committee into Indian affairs from 1808 to 1812. In 1812, it issued the famous Fifth Report, which is stated by Ilbert to be still a standard authority on the question of Indian land tenures and on the judicial and

[68] G. Chesney, *Indian Polity* (London: Longmans, 1870), 48.

police arrangements of the time. Enquiry led to the passage of 13 resolutions by the government on which was based the Charter Act, 1813. Parliament's interference now covered not only the internal administration of Indian affairs, but it reduced the company's trade monopoly itself, confining it to article of tea in their trade with India.

1.4.1.5 The Charter Act, 1833

The Charter Act of 1833 introduced a highly centralized system of administration and deprived the governors in council of provinces of their lawmaking powers. It abolished trading monopoly of the company and completely stopped its commercial activities. By this Act, the governor general in council of Bengal was named governor general in council of India which was empowered to make laws and regulations (subject to disallowance by the board of control) for the whole of India (for all persons, for all places and things, for all servants of the company, for Indian officers and soldiers in the military service and for the administration of courts martial over them).

The Indian Law Commission, of which T. B. Macaulay was the most prominent member, was appointed to inquire into the jurisdiction, powers and rules of the existing courts of justice and the nature and operation of all laws prevailing in the country. Its labour resulted in the preparation of the Indian Penal Code.

By this Act, slavery was also abolished and no subject because of his birth, descent or colour was precluded from holding office and land.

In 1833, the central government had eight departments: military, secret, general, foreign, finance, political, revenue and judicial. But in 1843 when the secretariats were completely separated, GoI had four departments: home department (general, judicial, legislative and ecclesiastical branches); foreign department; finance department; and military department.

1.4.1.6 The Charter Act of 1853

The Charter Act of 1853 created for the first time a separate legislative council for India which eventually developed into the Indian Parliament. In the words of the authors of the Montford Report, 'legislation, for the first time, was treated as a special function of the government, requiring special machinery and special processes'.

Further, by Charter Act of 1853, directors were deprived of their right of patronage of Indian appointments, for the Civil Service of India was thrown open to competition. Their number was also reduced from 24 to 18, of whom six were to be the nominees of the Crown.

Lord Macaulay in his *Report on the Indian Civil Service* (November 1854) advocated the introduction of the principle of entry by open competition in order to bring into the higher civil service the best qualified university graduates in place of the school boys who had been previously nominated by the directors of the company. His plea for recruitment on the basis of merit was accepted by the British Government, and the first such examination took place in 1855 in London conducted by the Civil Service Commission (set up in 1854).

1.4.1.7 Act for Better Government of India, 1858

The mutiny and revolt of 1857 gave the deathblow to the existence of EIC. The Act for the Better Government of India (Mr Stanley introduced the bill) with 75 sections was passed in August 1858 but the assumption of the GoI by the Crown declared on 1 November 1858 by the Queen's proclamation (read out by Lord Canning to the assembled princes and people at a *darbar* held at Allahabad and in all the district towns in India).

The Act transferred the power to govern from EIC to the British Crown to be exercised by a secretary of state for India (a member of the British Cabinet) aided by a council of 15 members (the board of control and the court of directors were abolished). Thus, the ultimate power over India remained with the Parliament. Under the Act, government was to be carried on as before by the governor general who was given the additional title of 'viceroy' as personal representative of the Crown. Although the governor general had an executive council whose members were to act as head of different departments, he had the power to override any important decision of the council.

Impact of the Mutiny

The Indian rebellion commonly called the mutiny (the revolt of 1857) had a two-fold impact on the administration. As India passed constitutionally from the hands of EIC to the British Government itself, the composition and purposes of bureaucracy were liberalized. The government demonstrated a greater sensibility to the demands that Indians be given the opportunity to enter the higher administrative rungs and that the administration's concern for the welfare of the people be extended. Second, the rebellion began to bring home to the British administrators in India the fact that sections of the people were no longer as willing as before to put up with the paternalism of an imperially oriented bureaucracy.

This period also witnessed the passage of the Code of Civil Procedure (1859), Macaulay's (Indian) Penal Code (1860) and the Code of Criminal Procedure (1861) and also the constitution of the high courts (1861).

1.4.1.8 The Indian Councils Acts, 1861, 1892 and 1909

The Indian Councils Act of 1861 strengthened the governor general's Council to work in the capacity of the imperial legislative council for the purpose of making laws. The Act of 1861 also restored to the presidency government the power of legislation which had been withdrawn by the Act of 1833. The legislative councils, analogous to central legislative council (Calcutta), were established in Bombay and Madras. Under the Act, the north-western provinces, Bengal and the Punjab, had their legislative councils in course of time. But the councils both at the Centre and provinces possessed no real powers and were merely advisory bodies. Legislative councils had no control over the executive. Moreover, no bill passed by them could become an Act until it was approved by the governor general. The secretary of state could also disallow any of its Acts. However, the Act of 1861 marked the birth of the provincial legislatures in India and also laid the foundation of cabinet government in India.

The Indian Councils Act, 1892, increased the scope of the legislature's activities and strengthened the non-official element by inaugurating in an indirect manner, the principle of election.

However, it is in the Act of 1909 which may be considered a well-developed product of the policy of association. The Morley-Minto Reforms[69] (1909), which were embodied in the measure,

---

[69] Lord Curzon was recalled in November 1905 who appointed Mr Minto as his successor. John Morley was appointed as the secretary of state for India in the cabinet.

are a landmark in the administrative history of India before the First World War. The Act, 1909, empowered the governor general to create executive councils for the governors in the large provinces. By this Act, the legislative councils were empowered to move resolutions on the budget, with the exception of specified subjects such as the armed forces, foreign affairs and Indian states on any matter of public interest. This gave the councils increased opportunities of influencing policy, but the argument of members remained with the central government. The Act legitimized the election of Indians to the various legislative councils in India for the first time.

1.4.1.9 The Montford Reforms and the GOI Act, 1919

The Montague–Chelmsford (the Montford Report, 1918) Reforms made a real beginning of representative government.[70]

The August or Montague Declaration

Before the passage of the GoI Act, 1919, in August 1917, the new Secretary of State for India Edwin Motague made the historic declaration on behalf of the British Government in the House of Commons which ran as follows:

> The policy of His Majesty's Government, with which the Government of India are in complete accord, is that of the increasing association of Indians in every branch of administration and the gradual development of self-governing institutions with a view to the progressive realization of Responsible Government in India as an integral part of the British Empire.

The authors of the *Report of the Indian Constitutional Reforms* (known as the Montford Reforms) regarded it as 'the most momentous utterance ever made in India's chequered history'. According to Lord Curzon, 'more time and energy were devoted to the drafting of the announcement than perhaps to any other document, including the Queen's Proclamation of 1858'.

The Montford Report, 1918, accepting the principle of Montagu's declaration became the bases of the GoI Act, 1919. The new scheme actually began working in the beginning of 1921. Until this Act, the Indian administration had been 'a benevolent and beneficent autocracy'. This Act may be regarded as a milestone along the road to mark self-government in India. There were three main concepts on which the new scheme was based.

1. *Division of subjects*: The GoI Act, 1919, assigned 51 subjects to the provinces and 47 subjects (defence, foreign political relations, customs, posts and telegraphs, currency, etc.) to the Centre for administration. Further, provincial subjects were split up into (a) reserved subjects (land revenue, famine relief, law and order, irrigation, industrial matters, etc.) that were to be administered by the governor and his councillors and (b) transferred subjects (local self-government, public health, sanitation, education, primarily the subjects concerned with nation-building activities) that were to be controlled by the governor acting with the ministers.[71] Thus, a larger measure of independence was granted to the provinces. Provincial ministers were selected from among the elected members of the provincial

[70] E. S. Montague was the secretary of state for India and Lord Chelmsford was the governor general of India.

[71] M. V. Pylee, *Constitutional Government in India* (Bombay: Asia, 1968), 82.

legislative council and were made fully responsible to that chamber for their actions and policy. The legislative councils themselves were greatly enlarged in size and were provided with a majority of elected members. The franchise for their election was also largely reduced.

2. *Central legislature*: The central legislature was to consist of two chambers: (a) the council of state for a 5-year term (consisting of 60 members, one of whom was to be appointed as the president, 34 of whom were to be elected and 25 nominated); and (b) the legislative assembly for a 3-year term (consisting of 143 members, 103 of whom were to be elected and 40 nominated, comprising 25 officials and 15 non-officials). The upper house was indeed oligarchical in character while the lower house was expected to be more representative of Indian political talent. A wider franchise was prescribed for its election. A part of the central budget was made subject to its vote.
3. *Relaxation of the control of secretary of state*: Many powers of the secretary of state for India were delegated to the governor general in council. The Act provided for transfer of some of the secretary's functions to a new official to be designated as the high commissioner of India.

Comments

As a first step towards realization of responsible government in the domain of provinces, it turned out to be an utter failure. The key factors responsible for its failure was (a) the absence of stable political parties, (b) communal electorates, (c) the joint purse, (d) the presence of large blocs of officials and nominated non-officials, (e) the powers of the governors to over-rule the advice of popular ministers and (f) the rights of the services. It had merely a façade of responsible government. It provided no effective training in parliamentary government. There was no real transfer of powers to the people and no genuine responsible government even in the limited field of transferred subjects.

The Muddiman Committee set up in 1925 to examine the working of dyarchy condemned it, and, in 1930, the Simon Commission concurred in that condemnation. Since then the dyarchy has had no defender. In the words of Sir Edward Blunt, 'in a dyarchical system government was not a matter of policies but a matter of opportunism'.[72]

1.4.1.10 The Lee Commission Report, 1924

In 1923 the Royal Commission on the Superior Civil Services in India was set up under the chairmanship of Lord Lee of Farham which recommended the establishment of a public service commission. Accordingly, the Federal Public Service Commission, consisting of a chairman and four other members, was constituted and it started functioning with effect from 1 October 1926.

1.4.1.11 The Simon Commission Report, 1930

As per provision of the GoI Act, 1919, a statutory commission under the presidency of Sir John Simon was appointed to make inquiries into the system of government and to recommend an

[72] E. A. H. Blunt, *The I.C.S., The Indian Civil Service* (London: Faber and Faber, 1937).

extension, modification or restriction of responsible government. The report of the Simon Commission published in 1930 recommended that (a) provincial autonomy should be strengthened by further devolution from the Centre and by the extension of responsible government over the whole field of administration, including law and order and (b) no change should be made for the present in the central structure, but that the central legislature should be re-oriented on a federal instead of an unitary basis, its members being indirectly elected by the provincial legislatures and not directly by British Indian constituencies.

1.4.1.12 The Government of India Act, 1935

The introduction of Montford reforms under the GoI Act, 1919; the obnoxious Rowlatt Bills (Criminal Law Amendment Bills conferring comprehensive powers of preventive detention on the Executive) of February 1918; the Muddiman Enquiry Committee Report, 1924; the Simon Commission Report, 1930; the Nehru Report, 1928; the First Round Table Conference (opened on 12 November 1930 in London); the Gandhi–Irwin Pact, March 1931; Second Round Table Conference, September 1931; the Communal Award, 1932; the Poona Pact, 1932; and Third Round Table Conference, 1932, were some events which took place before the passage of the GOI Act, 1935.

The White Paper

On the basis of discussions at the Round Table Conferences and reports of the various committees, the British Government published a White Paper in March 1933 which was submitted to the Joint Parliamentary Committee (the Indian assessors like Sir Tej Bahadur Sapru and M. R. Jayakar participated in the JPC, and Lord Linlithgow was the Chairman) of the British Parliament for examination. After the publication of the JPC's report, a Bill was introduced in the Parliament in December 1934 which got the royal assent on 4 August 1935. It was 'the last and most important of the great landmarks along the road to self-government and eventually independence for India'. The Act ran into 451 clauses with 15 schedules. Main features of the Act were as follows:

1. *All India federation*: The Act envisaged an all India federation (could not come into being) which was to consist of 11 governors' provinces and 6 chief commissioners' provinces (compulsory joining) and Indian states (to sign an instrument of accession for joining). The federal executive powers of the federation were to be exercised by the governor general on behalf of His Majesty (the executive head), and the federal legislature consisting of governor general (representative), the council of state (156 representatives in which princes to nominate two-fifths of the seats) and federal assembly (princes to nominate one-third of the seats) was to have the power to legislate on subjects included in the Federal List.
2. *Provincial autonomy*: The chief prize awarded to the Indians by the Act of 1935 was the provincial autonomy (introduced from April 1937) which gave an independent and autonomous status to the British Indian provinces. Dyarchy was abolished and all the provincial departments were transferred to the Indian ministers who were responsible to the provincial legislatures. The governor, who was to select the ministers in consultation with the person having stable majority in the legislature, was to carry on the government in accordance with the advice of the popular ministers. However, the Act gave special

responsibilities to the governors in respect of subjects, such as (a) prevention of any grave menace to the peace and tranquillity of the province; (b) safeguarding the legitimate interests of the minorities, public services; and (c) securing the execution of orders and directions issued by the governor general in his discretion. The provincial governors were also vested with adequate legislative and administrative powers for the proper discharge of their special responsibilities.

3. *Dyarchy at the centre*: The Act envisaged a kind of dyarchy at the Centre with (a) reserved subjects (defence, ecclesiastical affairs, external affairs, etc.) to be administered by the governor general in his discretion and (b) transferred subjects to be administered by the governor general on the advice of the council of ministers (consisting of not more than 10 persons who were to be appointed by the governor general from amongst the members of the federal legislature to which they were collectively responsible. Although the governor general was expected to act as the constitutional head, yet he had a number of special responsibilities and discretionary powers that made him very powerful in relation to the ministers.
4. *Distribution of powers*: The distribution of powers between the federal and provincial governments was spelled out in (a) Federal List containing 59 subjects (of all India concern), (b) Provincial List containing 54 subjects (of local interest) and (c) Concurrent List containing 36 subjects (on which both the federal and provincial legislatures could make laws), and, in case of a conflict between the two authorities, the law of the federal government was to prevail. The governor general in his discretion could allocate subjects not mentioned in the Lists.
5. *Federal court*: In anticipation of the completion of the federal structure, a federal court (to consist of one chief justice and two judges to be appointed by the Crown and to hold office until the age of 65) was set up at Delhi which had original appellate and advisory jurisdictions.
6. *Abolition of India Council*: The 1935 Act abolished the India Council—an advisory body to the secretary of state for India.
7. *Supremacy of the British Parliament*: The 1935 Act expressly provided that no legislature, provincial or federal, could make any law affecting the British sovereignty.

Some other important events were as follows:

1. The August Offer, 1940
2. The Cripps Mission, March 1942
3. The Wavell Plan, 1945
4. The Cabinet Mission, March 1946
5. Prime Minister Attlee's statement on 20 February 1947 for effecting the transfer of power

1.4.1.13 The Mountbatten Plan, June 1947

Recognizing the intolerable situation, Lord Mountbatten, then viceroy and governor general of India, announced on 3 June 1947, with the approval of the British Government, a plan, which was the partition of the country and transfer of power to two dominions.

1.4.1.14 The Indian Independence Act, 1947

On 4 July 1947, the Indian Independence Bill was introduced in the House of Commons which received the royal assent on 18 July 1947 under which as from 15 August 1947 two independent dominions—India and Pakistan—were created. Under this Act, the British Government would cease to have any responsibility of the Government of British India from 15 August 1947.

1.4.2 Conclusion

The modern system of Indian administration is, by and large, a legacy of the British Raj in India which was paramount for almost a century. During the British rule, a framework of administration emerged that has stood the test of time and may well be regarded as one of the most precious legacies bequeathed by the British to India. Lloyd George described the British Civil Service in India as 'the steelframe of the whole structure'. Such a system of administration suited the British. It was more in the nature of preserving the societal structure in India, as it then existed. It was not oriented to socioeconomic development in the country. Thus, at the time of India's Independence (August 1947), the administrative system was not appropriately prepared to handle the massive developmental, democratic and post-independence tasks.[73] The solemnity of the transfer of power was, unfortunately, marred by communal violence in Punjab in the west and by the mass migration of people across the boundary lines of two dominions—India and Pakistan.

1.5 Development of the Civil Services

A brief description of the development of the civil services in India is given in the section of the chapter.

1.5.1 1601–1772 Period

EIC (founded on 31 December 1600) had to appoint a large staff of merchants, factors and writers to carry on its commercial business. These servants of the company who conducted its trade overseas were known as civil servants so as to distinguish them from those, whose duties were of a naval or military character. When the trading character of the company was replaced by the responsibilities of government, its civil servants were transformed from traders into administrators.

In 1675, the company established a regular gradation of posts consisting in the ascending order of (a) apprentices, required to serve for seven years with pay ranging from £5 to £10, (b) writers, required to serve a covenanted term of five years (c) factors, (d) merchants and (e) senior merchants.

Salaries paid to the mercantile services were extremely poor and they conducted trade on their own account. On this issue, O'Malley writes, 'The root cause of abuses prevalent at this time was

[73] E. N. M. Rai, *Patterns of Administrative Development in Independent India* (London: University of London, 1976), 30.

the obstinate and foolish refusal of the Directors (of the East India Company) to pay their employees decent salaries'.[74]

1.5.2 1773–93 Period

With a view of reducing corrupt practices, the Regulating Act of 1773 forbade collectors and persons engaged in collection of the revenue or the administration of justice from participating in private trade and forbade persons holding military or civil offices to accept presents from 'the natives of Asia'. During his regime (1772–86), Warren Hastings laid the foundation of a civil service in the modern sense of an administrative corps, toned up morale, although corruption had not been eradicated.

Later Lord Cornwallis introduced far-reaching changes in administration reserving exclusively all the superior jobs for men of overseas origin and raising their salaries.

After 1786, a single officer combined the office of collector, judge and magistrate; however, in 1793, judicial powers were withdrawn from the collector and transferred to civil courts.

The Charter Act of 1793 required that all positions in the company's civil service with a salary of more than £500 per annum 'shall' be filled by covenanted servants, that is, regular officials who entered into a covenant with the EIC, or after 1858, with the secretary of state. Appointments to these posts were to be made in England by the court of directors.

1.5.3 1794–1858 Period

For training of covenanted servants, Lord Wellesley founded a college called College of Fort William in Calcutta in 1800, but six years later Haileybury College was established in England as a training college for the company's covenanted servants, who were nominated either by the directors or the board of control.

The Charter Act of 1833 laid down that 'no subject of Her Majesty should, by reason only of his religion, place of birth, descent, colour or any of them be disabled from holding any place, office or employment under the Company'. This clause in 1833 Act remained a dead letter until the enactment of the Charter Act, 1853, which made appointment to the covenanted civil service open to competition among natural subjects of Her Majesty. In 1855, Haileybury College was closed down. The higher civil service was open exclusively to British and nothing had been done to admit Indians to it although they were employed in lower offices.

1.5.4 1858–1947 Period

By Section 32 of the GoI Act, 1858, the power of regulating appointments to the Indian Civil Service (ICS) was made over to the secretary of state in council who would act with the aid and advice of His Majesty's civil service commissioners.

[74] L. S. S. O'Malley. *Bengal District Gazetteers: Darjeeling.* (New Delhi: Logos Press, 1999 Reprint), 20.

1.5.5 The Indian Civil Service Act, 1861

The Act was intended to (a) legalize certain appointments which had been made in the past in contravention of the Act of 1793 and (b) reserve all higher civil appointments for members of covenanted civil service, for recruitment to which open competitive examinations were to be held in London every year under the supervision of the civil service commissioners. The first competitive examination was held in 1855 in London on the basis of the Report of the Macaulay Committee (1854).

In 1859, the maximum age for admission was lowered to 22 years; in 1866, it was lowered to 21 years; and in 1878, it was reduced to 19 years.

1.5.6 The Aitchison Commission, 1886

With a view to doing 'full justice to the claim of natives of India to higher employment in the public service', a commission under the presidency of Sir Charles Aitchison was appointed. On commission's recommendations, the system of filling appointments by means of statutory civil service (created in 1878–79) was dropped and the terms 'covenanted' and 'uncovenanted' services were abolished and resultantly, three services were created—the Imperial, Provincial and Subordinate Civil Services. The members of the Provincial Civil Service were made eligible for promotion to the listed posts in the Imperial Civil Services. It suggested that the age limit be raised to 23 years. The secretary of state directed that the covenanted civil service should be known in future as 'the Civil Service of India' and that each branch of the provincial service should be called by the name of the particular province to which it belonged. The provincial governments were ordered to fill one-sixth of the offices hitherto reserved for the ICS with provincial servants when the claims of existing statutory civil servants had been satisfied.

1.5.7 The Islington Commission, 1915, and the Montford Reform, 1918

The Royal Commission on Public Services, which assembled in 1912, submitted its report in 1915. Its recommendations became obsolete because of the First World War and the August Declaration of 1917.

The Montford Report stated that recruitment of a larger proportion of Indians should be started at once, although there was to be no swamping of the European element. This report also recommended the holding of simultaneous examinations in India and England. Total 33% of the superior posts in ICS, to begin with, were to be recruited in India and the percentage was to increase annually by 1.5%. Similar percentage was to be fixed for other services as well.

1.5.8 The Government of India Act, 1919

The GoI Act of 1919 dealt in a separate part with the services in India. According to it, every person in the civil service of the Crown in India held office during His Majesty's pleasure and could not be dismissed by any authority subordinate to that which appointed him.

By rules made under section 96(B)(2) of the GoI Act, 1919, public services under the administrative control of the provincial government were classified in the following divisions:

1. All India Services
2. Provincial Services
3. Subordinate Services
4. Officers holding special posts

The All India Services were to consist of the following:

1. All officers serving under provincial governments who were members of any of the following services:
   a. Indian Civil Service
   b. Indian Police Service (IPS)
   c. Indian Forest Service (IFS)
   d. Indian Educational Service
   e. Indian Agricultural Service
   f. Indian Service of Engineers
   g. Indian Veterinary Service
   h. officers of the Indian Medical Service in civil employment
   i. the Indian Forest Engineering Service, and any other Service declared by the secretary of state in council to be an All India Service
2. Military officers holding posts borne on the provincial cadres of the aforementioned services

1.5.9 Secretariat Procedure Committee, 1919

Before 1920, each individual department recruited its own staff independently. But in 1920, on the basis of recommendations of the Secretariat Procedure Committee (1919), the GoI made upper division clerks of the secretariat part of an Imperial Secretariat Service and appointed a Central Staff Selection Board to supervise the recruitment process. For recruitment to the lower division of the secretariat, the Staff Selection Board alone could determine the necessary qualifications.

1.5.10 The Lee Commission, 1924

In 1923, a commission under the presidency of Lord Lee was appointed and made recommendations, several of which were accepted by GoI.

1. The all India services serving in the reserved part of the provincial administrations were to continue to be appointed and controlled by the secretary of state and their position was to be safeguarded by legal covenants enforceable in civil courts and by the public service commission, to whom appeal was to lie against provincial or central

governments. Civilians serving in transferred departments could either retain all India status, enter into new contracts with the provincial governments or retire on proportionate pensions.

2. The commission recommended the constitution of the public service commission without further delay.
3. In regard to Indianization of services which were still to be recruited by the secretary of state, the Lee Commission recommended as follows:
   a. For ICS, it recommended that 20% of the superior posts should be filled by the appointment of provincial service officers to 'listed posts' and that direct recruitment in the future should be Indian and European in equal members.
   b. For IPS, direct recruitment was to be in proportion of five Europeans to three Indians, allowing for promotion from provincial service to fill 20% of all vacancies.
   c. For IFS, recruitment should be in the ratio of 75% Indians and 25% Europeans in those provinces in which forest administration was reserved.
   d. For the irrigation branch of the Indian Service of Engineers, recruitment should be in the ratio of 40% Europeans, 40% directly recruited Indians and 20% Indians promoted from the provincial service.

1.5.11 The Simon Commission Report, 1930

The Simon Commission referred to 'the very important role which the Indian Services fill in the government of the country'. About the work of ICS, the Commission said, 'Its primacy is justified not only by the range and importance of its activities but by the distinguished and devoted public service rendered by both its Indian and its British members, who, now as formerly sustain its great reputation'.[75]

1.5.12 The Government of India Act, 1935

The GoI Act, 1935, made a special responsibility of the governor general and the governors to secure 'to members of the public services any right provided for them by the Constitution Act and the safeguarding of their legitimate interests'. In case of premature abolition of any office, the persons affected were to receive compensation; in case of wrongful dismissal, they could bring an action against the Crown; and no member of such services could be dismissed or reduced in rank without being given reasonable opportunity of showing cause against the action proposed to be taken in regard to him unless he was convicted of a criminal offence. Officers could address complaints to the governor general or the governor, and could also refer appeals to the secretary of state against any order of punishment, censure or termination or the alteration in the conditions of service. Their salaries, pensions and emoluments were not votable by the legislatures, and their pensions, if they resided permanently outside India, could not be taxed in India. They were indemnified against civil and criminal proceedings in respect of all actions done in good faith in the course of the discharge of their duty (and on the question of good faith, the certificate of the governor general was to be conclusive); and no such proceedings could be initiated without the discretionary permission of the governor general or the governor.

[75] *Report of the Simon Commission*, vol. I (1930), 372.

The 1935 Act also provided for the establishment of the Federal Public Service Commission besides similar provincial commissions, in some cases common to two or more provinces. These commissions were to conduct examinations for recruitment to various services within their respective spheres. They were to be consulted on all matters relating to methods of recruitment, principles to be followed in making appointments, promotions and inter-service transfers, all disciplinary matters.

With the grant of provincial autonomy under the Act of 1935, recruitment to all India services with the exception of ICS and IPS was discontinued. When India became a dominion under the Indian Independence Act, 1947, there were only two residuary all India services, namely, ICS and IPS, with the vanishing remnant of other All India services since discontinued.

1.5.13 The Maxwell Committee, 1937, and the Tottenham Committee, 1946

In 1937, the Maxwell Committee gave the recommendations that the ministerial staff should be divided into two main grades, namely, assistants and clerks; the former being able to note on files and to deal with paper work, while the latter could deal with work of routine nature.

On the Tottenham Committee's recommendations (1945–46), the staffing pattern of the imperial secretariat was changed. Later in 1950, the old Imperial Secretariat Service was replaced by the Central Secretariat Service.

Thus, the structure of the civil services which emerged after India's Independence can be classified into (a) all India services, (b) central services, (c) state services (previously provincial) and (d) subordinate services.

1.5.14 Conclusion

It may be pertinent to mention that the ICS enjoyed a mixed image in the pre-Independence period. As L. S. Rathore observed in an article:

> To the masses of the people, it symbolized terror; to the educated middle class, it was object of awe; to the rich, it was the embodiment of government to whom the submission was naturally due. Its paternalistic outlook and 'fatherly imaged' created an attitude of 'dependence-obedience among the people'.[76]

1.6 Evolutionary Measures Towards Unity of Constituent Units

The transition of the 550 or so princely states, which have been in existence in different stages of social, economic and political development, into union of states after India's independence presented a complex problem of their future constitutional relationship with the union government. It was also a problem of introducing democratic principles and practices and uniformity in their

[76] L. S. Rathore, 'The Legacy of Indian Administration', in *The Indian Administrative System*, ed. Ramesh K. Arora et al. (New Delhi: Associates, 1978), 12.

administrations. The political situation at the time of transfer of sovereign power presented a picture of disruption of territorial integrity of India. This was a major problem. This section deals with measures of uniformity in the administration of princely states before India's independence.

The disintegration of Mughal power in the mid-18th century had weakened its authority over the provinces. EIC, which obtained trading concession and a foothold in Surat, Bombay, Madras and Calcutta, found that the deterioration in the political situation was not only interfering with its normal trading activities but also endangering its security. It sought and obtained permission to fortify its factories and arrange for their defence. But this was not so simple. Moreover, the maintenance of the garrisons constituted a heavy drain on the resources of the company. The company adopted, therefore, the expedient of obtaining the grants or lease of areas of land, contiguous to its concessions, sufficient for maintaining the garrisons. Thus, self-supporting settlements sprung up as adjuncts of the fortresses.

It is argued that the primary objective of EIC was profitable trade, but gradually it acquired political power and hold the foundation of British raj in India. Josiah Child, its governor, had come to canvass the idea of 'the foundation of a large, well-grounded, sure British dominion in India for all times to come', as early as 1681. The victory at the Battle of Plassey (between the Nawab of Murshidabad and the troops of the company) in 1757 had laid the foundation of British domination in India. With this, EIC acquired the appointment as the *diwan*s (revenue authority) for Bengal by the Mughal emperor.

In 1798, Lord Wellesley who became governor general of the company, inspired by the imperial dreams, embarked on a policy of territorial expansion, allowing the survival of the princes only on the surrender of their political independence. In pursuance of this policy, Lord Wellesley introduced the 'subsidiary system'. On the one hand, this guaranteed to the rulers their positions and possessions against both external aggression and internal revolt, rebellion and opposition; on the other, it ensured the fidelity of the princes by the presence of subsidiary forces maintained by the Company at the cost of the states, which also enabled 'the British to throw forward the military, considerably in advance of their political frontiers'. This policy of annexation and subjugation was pursued vigorously in the period between 1813 and 1857.

After the disintegration of Mahratta power and the conquest of the Punjab, the company had established and stabilized itself as the unquestioned dominant power. The company entered into a series of treaties of cooperation, allegiance and loyalty, with the Indian states which had survived annexation. By 1820, all the princes had been enmeshed in the web of British paramountcy. The policy of non-involvement, beyond its ring fence had, now, given way to the policy of 'subordinate isolation', initiated by Lord Hastings who became governor general in 1813. Under the principle of this arrangement, the princes had no international status and the British company was in the position of being 'the managing representative of the Empire as a whole'. Moreover, the princes were forbidden from forming any confederation or taking any concerted action hazardous to the security of the British power. The assumption of responsibility for defence was, also, given a wider connotation, which meant the establishment of a common system of road, rail, postal and telegraphs communication.

The doctrine of paramountcy shaped by Lord Wellesley for regulating relations between the States and the British power did not deter the Company from intervening in 1804, and once again in 1820, as it could 'not obviously remain indifferent spectators of the disorder and misrule'.

The deliberate process of gradual absorption of the States with or without provocation led to the revolt of 1857. During this upheaval, which shook the very foundation of British authority in

India, the princes stood, in the words of Lord Canning, as a 'break-water in the storm which would have swept over us in one great wave'. The Queen's proclamation of 1858 gave recognition to the loyal role the princes had played, by pledging. 'We shall respect the rights, dignity and honour of native Princes as our own'. This conception of paramountcy was restated, in 1860, by Lord Canning, who became the first Viceroy of India in 1858, in the following words: 'The Crown of England stands forth as the unquestioned Ruler and Paramount Power in India'. This led to a reversal of the policy of annexation. In his dispatch of 1860, Lord Canning laid down the two great principles which the British Government had, subsequently, observed in dealing with the states: first, 'the integrity of the states' should be preserved by perpetuating the rule of the princes whose power to adopt heirs was recognized by *Sanads*; and second, 'flagrant misgovernment' must be prevented or arrested by timely exercise of intervention.

Subsequently, Indian States Committee, reporting in 1929, observed that 'the relationship of the Paramount Power with the States was not merely a contractual relationship'. It concluded, 'Paramountcy must remain paramount; it must fulfil its obligations, defining or adapting itself according to the shifting necessities of the time and the progressive development of the State'.[77]

As India passed constitutionally from the hands of EIC to the British Government itself, the Indian states, in different stages of economic and political development, came thus to be interwoven in the fabric of India's geographical, cultural, political and economic entity. With the exception of a few Rajputana States which had survived the waves of invasion, retaining their sovereignty more or less unimpaired, nearly all the others were subordinates or tributaries of the Mughal emperor, the Mahratta Supremacy or the Sikh Kingdom and dependent on them. Some were rescued, others were created by the British Empire.

From the administration point of view, there was little to distinguish between British India and Indian states. Both were autocratic in character, except that one was an impersonal, benevolent autocracy and, the other, a personal autocracy. The political forces which came to be generated in British India in the later half of the 19th century by the emergence of an informed intelligentsia, influenced the gradual evolution of a democratic form of government. These forces were held in check in the states. The princes of states were becoming restive and apprehensive that their absolutism might get submerged in the waves of nationalism encircling them. The Indian states were, therefore, kept outside the scope of parliamentary legislation introduced from time to time to expand democratic institutions in the British Indian provinces. But it became difficult to maintain the policy of isolating the Indian states from the impact of constitutional developments in the Indian provinces, when in 1919 it was decided to transfer partial responsibility to the provincial legislatures and to introduce the rudiments of a cabinet form of government in their administration.

The Montford (Montague–Chelmsford) Report which formed the basis of the GoI Act, 1919, visualized the picture of future India as 'representing the external semblance of some form of federation' with units of a comparable pattern, but the last thing its authors desired was to force the pace in the Indian States.[78]

---

[77] Indian States Committee was appointed in December 1927, with Sir Harcourt Butler as the chairman, to report upon the relationship between the paramount power and the Indian states with reference to the rights and obligations arising from treaties and usage, sufferance and other causes.

[78] The Rt. Honourable E. S. Montague, secretary of state for India (1917–23); Lord Chelmsford, viceroy and governor general of India (1916–21).

The authors of the report said, 'In extenuation, it would be a strange reward for loyalty and devotion to force new ideas upon those who had not desired them'. It contented itself merely with suggesting the constitution of a 'Chamber of Princes' as a deliberative and consultative body. This Chamber was set up in 1921, but if failed to establish itself as an effective or representative organ to make its contribution towards a solution of India's constitutional problems. In the 1930s, the princes did not agree to join the proposed federal constitution for India. They claimed that they should have individually the right to determine the extent of abrogation of sovereignty.

The GoI Act, 1935, gave full recognition to the claim of the princes. This Act instituted a new office of Crown Representative to place the Indian princes in direct relationship with the British Crown. The Act also conceded the right of the princes to join the federation on individual instruments defining the scope and extent of accession. The federal part of the 1935 Act could not be brought into operation as the negotiation with the princes initiated in 1937 had not made sufficient progress when, at the outbreak of the Second World War in 1939, the federal provisions of the Constitution were formally suspended.

The GoI Act, 1935, gave full autonomy to the British Indian provinces. The provincial part of the Act was introduced in 1937 and responsible governments were formed in the provinces. But this Act did not make any provision regarding the internal administration of the Indian states. As a result, these states continued with their archaic autocratic forms of government.

In March 1946, the three cabinet ministers from UK visited India with a mission to settle the political future of India's administration. It realized that the problem was also one of reconciling the sovereignty of the proposed Union. The cabinet mission issued a memorandum in regard to the states' treaties and paramountcy in May 1946, giving categorical assurance to the princes that the British Government would not, in any circumstances, transfers paramountcy to an Indian Government. But, once such a government was formed, the British Government would not be in a position to carry out the obligations of paramountcy by retaining British troops for this purpose.

In July 1947, the Indian Independence Bill was introduced in the House of Commons which received the royal assent on 18 July 1947 under as from 15 August 1947 two independent Dominions—India and Pakistan—were created. Under this Act, the British Government would cease to have any responsibility of the Government of British India from 15 August 1947.

After India's independence, the new GoI has also invited the states to continue relations to mutual friendship and cooperation with the rest of India, especially because of their geographical contiguity. The GI stressed that it would be in the interests of the princely order itself to accept gracefully the ultimate paramountcy of popular interests and welfare.

The transfer of sovereignty to the people at the Centre and in the provinces had rekindled the hopes and aspirations of the subjects of the princely states of receiving a comparable measure of freedom and responsibility. Congress in power had also the obligation to honour its earlier pledge to secure the establishment of responsible governments in the states.

Most of the rulers were conscious of this inherent weakness of their position, and negotiations initiated to secure their consent to the merger of their states did not generally present any great difficulty. The rulers signed covenants ceding to the dominion government 'exclusive authority, jurisdiction and powers for and in relation to the governance of the states'.

As a result of persuasion, cooperation and pressure, 552 Indian states were integrated with either states or Union of India with a complete transfer of power and authority from the rulers to the elected legislature or brought under direct central control. The disruption of the integrity of India was undoubtedly a major problem, but it is also not correct that the British administration had seriously sought to bring about an absolute unity of territorial administration in India. The continued existence of 552 Indian states with sovereignty of their own had stood in the way of introducing a measure of uniformity in the administration of her constituent units.

Later Sardar Vallabhbhai Patel had successfully secured merger of all the states through 'Instruments of Accession' which provided for regular payment of certain amounts, called 'Privy Purse' to the princes. He pointed out to the constituent assembly that the annual liability of the Union would not succeed four crore of rupees, which was 'too small a price for bloodless revolution which has affected the destinies of millions of our people'. Jawaharlal Nehru agreed and a constitutional guarantee was given to princes by incorporating Article 291 made non-justiciable by Article 362.

1.7 Evolution of Parliamentary Democracy

The chief prize which the Britishers gave to the Indians was the 'parliamentary democracy'. But this has a long history and is linked with the growth and dissolution of EIC which was set up under a charter in December 1600 for the 'advancement of lawful traffic'. The company had emerged within a period of 150 years as a significant political force in India.

Although profitable eastern trade was the primary objective of EIC, it slowly adopted the policy of territorial expansion and consolidation which constituted a heavy drain on the financial resources of the company. The company sought financial assistance from the British Government. This attracted the intervention of the Parliament which enacted the well-known Regulating Act in 1773. To strengthen the political responsibilities of the company, the Act provided for the consolidation of authority in the person of a governor general, assisted by an executive council, with powers to make 'rules, ordinances and regulations, for the good order and civil government' of the company. This Act may, therefore, be treated as a convenient landmark in this historical retrospection of the evolution of parliamentary democracy in India.

By the Charter Act of 1833 a law member assisted by a law commission, was added to the governor general's council. By the Charter Act of 1853, a number of additional members were appointed to the legislative council, which was vested with comprehensive powers to make laws for the whole of India.

After the outbreak (mutiny) in the armed forces of the company in 1857, which seemed at one time to threaten the very survival of British authority in India,[79] the British Crown assumed sovereignty over India and EIC vanished from the stage of history.

It was clear that the mutiny was the outcome of the imposition of British laws in complete disregard of the religious beliefs and practices of the Indian people. In the words of Bartle Frere, then governor of Bombay, 'to continue to legislate for millions of people with few means of knowing, except by a rebellion, whether the laws suit them or not'. An attempt was made, therefore, in the Indian Councils Act of 1861, to establish closer contact between the government and the governed. By this Act, governor general's executive council was enlarged by the nomination of 50% of additional members from outside the ranks of the civil service. The admission of a non-official element in the legislature was a step of historic significance as it conceded the right of

[79] This threat was averted by the loyal support of the Indian princes, who stood as a breakwater to stem the tide of armed opposition.

Indians to have a voice in the making of laws for the governance of their country. The council was not, however, a deliberative body. In the words of Lord MacDonnel, a law member,

> The character of the Legislative Councils established by the Act of 1861 is simply this, that they are committees for the purpose of making laws—committees by means of which the executive government obtain advice and assistance in their legislation, and the public derive the advantage of full publicity being ensured at every stage of the law-making process.[80]

The enactment of the Indian Councils Act, promulgated in 1892, 'widened the opportunities for the non-official members of the legislatures for criticism, suggestions, remonstrance and inquiry'. It also conceded the right of members to discuss the annual financial statement.

By the Indian Councils Act of 1909, not only elective principles were introduced but also the provincial legislatures were given a non-official majority. But these enlarged legislatures were not armed with any real power or authority. On the other hand, the executive councils continued to be accountable to the British Parliament.

Significant changes were introduced with the enactment of the GoI Act of 1919. This Act gave the legislatures—both central and provincial—an elected non-official majority. The most striking feature of the Act was, however, the demarcation of the field of administration into two spheres—the central and the provincial. Certain subjects such as education, medical, public health and public works were declared to be wholly provincial subject, while defence, communication, foreign relations, customs, income tax and criminal law were amongst the principal subjects retained by the Centre. The provincial subjects were divided into two groups, 'transferred' and 'reserved'. The transferred subjects were entrusted to the ministers, but the reserved subjects remained the responsibility of the executive council. A second legislative chamber—the Council of State—was created to neutralize, when necessary, any adverse vote by the legislative assembly which had now an elected majority. The constitution of the council was such that the government could, in certain situations, rally support for its policies and action. The Act of 1919 also introduced the rudiments of a cabinet form of government in each province by the provision of ministers answerable to the legislature and dependent on its confidence for continuing in office. Ministerial responsibility was, however, restricted by a clumsy device known as 'dyarchy'.

The GoI Act of 1935 effected a more significant transfer of responsibility to Indian hands. This Act embodied two main principles: the creation of autonomous provinces with governments responsible to elected legislative assemblies and the introduction of a dyarchic form of government at the Centre, based on the federation of the autonomous provinces and the princely states. The provincial section of the new constitution was inaugurated in 1937 and the responsible governments were installed in all the provinces. But the federal provisions could not be bought into operation, as planned, since the specified minimum number of princes had not joined the federation on the basis of individual 'instrument of accession' before the declaration of the Second World War in 1939.

In the wake of the unilateral declaration of war by the viceroy on behalf of India in 1939, the responsible governments in the majority of provinces resigned, leading to a suspension of the Constitution and to the assumption of administrative responsibilities by their governors. The resulting political unrest placed the war effort in serious jeopardy and deterrent measures were taken to suppress opposition. As there was a serious threat to the

[80] Quoted in Report of the India Statutory Commission, Vol. I, p. 116 (New Delhi: Logos Press, 1930, 1988 reprint).

security of India, with Japan's spectacular victories over the allied forces in Southeast Asia, the British Government sent Stafford Cripps, a member of the British War Cabinet, to India in 1942 to conciliate Indian political opinion and to enlist cooperation in the war effort. Cripps' offer defined the object of His Majesty's Government as being the creation of a new Indian Union which would constitute a dominion associated with the UK and other dominions by a common allegiance to the Crown. As a result of discussions with the two major political parties and other minority interests, a settlement appeared at one time imminent, but there was an inexplicable change in the attitude of Stafford Cripps, and the negotiations were terminated. Meanwhile, the tide of the war had turned and the threat to India's security receded.

The failure of the mission deepened the feeling of frustration which found its expression in 'Quit India' resolution of Congress in August 1942, which demanded the immediate withdrawal of the British from India, leaving it to the Indians to work out their own salvation and destiny.

A concerted effort was made, however, after the Second World War, in 1946, when a cabinet mission, consisting of the secretary of state for India, the president of the board of trade and the first lord of the Admiralty visited India to explore the possibilities of finding a common measure of agreement in the implementation of the plan earlier announced. Even after prolonged consultation with various interests, the mission failed to evolve an accepted basis of political settlement, but undeterred by this setback, it put forward its own plan on 16 May 1946. The cabinet mission suggested a three-tier constitution, consisting of a Union, provinces and an intermediate authority formed by grouping contiguous provinces in the northwest and in the east according to a certain pattern. The mission contemplated the setting up of a constituent assembly formed by representatives drawn from the provincial assemblies in proportion to the numerical strength of the communities in the respective provinces. It also suggested the formation of an Interim government consisting of the leaders of the major political parties.

The cabinet mission plan was formally accepted by two major political parties, although not without both expressed and unexpressed reservations. These reservations manifested themselves after the formation of an interim government in October 1946, and the League representatives refused to participate in the deliberations of the constituent assembly. Ultimately, this impasse was ended by the announcement on 20 February 1947 of the definite intention of the British Government 'to take necessary steps to effect the transference of power to responsible Indian hands by a date not later than June 1948'. However, the position was left vague and the question of the authority to whom power would be transferred was left for future determination. There appeared to be a mad struggle between the Congress and the Muslim League to establish itself as the successor authority in the provinces with a Muslim majority. The internal situation was explosive and required immediate solution to arrest the communal mass movements which were being organized.

To end the bitterness which might otherwise spill over into any new administrative arrangements, Lord Mountbatten, who was appointed in March 1947 as the new viceroy and governor general, was convinced that the idea of forming an all India union had to be discarded and replaced by the partition of the country into two dominions. As a result of his representations to the British Government and the latter's initiative, the British Parliament enacted the Indian Independence Act in July 1947. The pivotal provisions of the Act established the sovereign character of the legislatures of the two dominions and gave them the fullest measure of independence. But the administrative system had to face massive developmental tasks following India's independence.

Summary

Since country's independence in August 1947, Indian administration appears to have manifested impressive adaptability and resilience. Without departing from the essential concept underlying the civil service, it has emerged as an essential organ of the government. It has not engendered hostility on the part of the public or other services. It has retained its prominent position despite many upheavals. It has been able to eliminate many of the objectionable qualities of an extreme exclusiveness incompatible with democratic values. The major problems of administration have been overcome through administrative reforms and judicial action. The gradual transition of the colonial rule to independence was made possible by the nationalist forces. A strong administrative system was inherited as is from the British rule. It was further invigorated by political and administrative reforms.

2 Constitutional Ideals as Directives for State Action

LEARNING OBJECTIVES

1. **To understand the basic values of the Indian Constitution**
2. **To examine the importance of the Preamble and Directive Principles of State Policy**
3. **To discuss the socio-economic philosophy underlying the Indian Constitution**

Introduction

The Constitution of India has been drafted after 'ransacking all the known constitutions of the world'. It embodied what suited to the genius of the people. Although the Constitution is criticized for it 'carries the slavish imitation of the West', yet it has survived against all odds since its adoption on 26 January 1950.

The Constitution of India is remarkable for many ideals and objectives underlying its edifice. Pandit Jawaharlal Nehru, one of the architects of the Constitution, pronounced the historic *Objectives Resolution* which was adopted by the Constituent Assembly on 22 January 1947. This Resolution, which inspired the shaping of the Constitution through all its subsequent stages, reads thus, 'This Constitution Assembly declares its firm and solemn resolve to proclaim India as an Independent Sovereign Republic and to draw up for her future governance a Constitution'.[1]

2.1 The Preamble

The Preamble enshrines values or basic concepts as well as objectives intended by the Fathers of the Constitution to serve as authoritative guidelines for the edifice and functioning of the new state. Although the Preamble is not enforceable in a court of law,[2] it has provided inspiration for inclusion of various constitutional provisions which reflect these concepts, for example, Part III relating to Fundamental Rights, Part IV relating to Directive Principles, Article 326 concerning adult suffrage, Articles 75 and 164 regarding ministerial (executive) responsibility to legislature.

[1] Constituent Assembly Debate 304 (moved by Pandit Jawaharlal Nehru on 13 December 1946). In the words of Pandit Nehru, the aforesaid Resolution was 'something more than a resolution. It is a declaration, a firm resolve, a pledge, an undertaking and for all of us a dedication'.

[2] *A. K. Gopalan v. State of Madras* (1950), SCR 88 (198); *Union of India v. Madan Gopal* (1954), SCR 541 (555).

As amended in 1976,[3] the Preamble summarizes the aims and objectives of the Constitution as follows:

> WE, THE PEOPLE OF INDIA, having solemnly resolved to constitute India into a *SOVEREIGN SOCIALIST SECULAR DEMOCRATIC REPUBLIC* and to secure to all its citizens:
>
> JUSTICE, social, economic and political;
>
> LIBERTY of thought, expression, belief, faith and worship;
>
> EQUALITY of status and of opportunity; and to promote among them all;
>
> FRATERNITY assuring the dignity of the individual and the unity and integrity of the Nation:
>
> IN OUR CONSTITUENT ASSEMBLY this twenty-six day of November, 1949, do HEREBY ADOPT, ENACT AND GIVE TO OURSELVES THIS CONSTITUTION.

The concepts of 'socialism' and 'secularism' were added to the Preamble by 42nd Constitutional Amendment in 1976 so as to make them prominently explicit in the Indian polity. Also, same Amendment carried the sub-concept of 'integrity' so as to reinforce the concept of 'unity of nation' already included in the Preamble.

Parliament and state legislatures have enacted several laws to give effect to these concepts. The union and state governments have taken many policy decisions and practical steps under the inspiration of these values or concepts. The Supreme Court and high courts have been tending to take into consideration these concepts while exercising judicial review of laws or executive action brought formally to their attention.

During the last seven decades, the country has been striving to bring about social, political and economic changes in consonance with the letter and spirit of the Preamble. The Preamble reflects the objectives which the Indian Constitution seeks to establish and promote. It also helps the legal interpretation of the Constitution where the language is found to be ambiguous.[4] Further, the Preamble indicates the source from which the Constitution derives its authority.

2.2 Sovereign Independent State

With the enactment of the Constitution since 26 January 1950, the newly born State, that is, India, has been declared as an Independent Sovereign Republic. The Constitution is ordained by the people of India through their representatives assembled in a sovereign Constituent Assembly which was competent to determine the political future of the country in any manner it liked. The words, 'We, the people of India ... adopt, enact and give to ourselves this Constitution', signify that the people are sovereign. 'Sovereignty' means the independent authority of a State. Legally, it means that the State has the power to legislate on any subject and that it is not subject to the control of any other State or external authority or even the UNO.

It may be pointed out that while Pakistan remained a British Dominion until 1956, India ceased to be a Dominion and declared itself a 'Republic' since the making of the Constitution in 1949. Further, as against the British Crown, we have an elected president as the head of our State.

[3] The words in italics were inserted by the Constitution (42nd Amendment) Act, 1976.

[4] Berubari Union, AIR 1960 SC 845.

Although India declared itself a Republic, it did not sever all ties with the British Commonwealth. India's decision to adhere to the Commonwealth, 'without acknowledging allegiance to the Crown', took place at the Prime Ministers' Conference at London on 27 April 1949, where Prime Minister (PM) Pandit Nehru declared that notwithstanding its becoming a Sovereign Independent Republic, India will continue to maintain 'her full membership of the Commonwealth of Nations and her acceptance of the King as the symbol of the free association of the independent nations and as such the Head of the Commonwealth'. It is to be noted that this declaration does not mean that the country has sacrificed its sovereignty. It accepts the Crown of England only as a symbolic head of the Commonwealth. And it would be open to India to cut off that association at any time the country finds it not to be honourable or useful. As Pandit Nehru explained in the Constituent Assembly, 'It is an agreement by free will, to be terminated by free will'.[5] Hence, the voluntary association of India with any country does not affect its sovereignty in any manner.

2.3 Democratic Republic

The Preamble to the Indian Constitution envisages not only a democratic form of government but also a democratic society, infused with the spirit of 'justice, liberty, equality and fraternity'. The Indian system of government purports to be democratic. This requires it to ensure that the wishes of the people are reflected in the policy decisions of the government. There are two essential requirements, according to Dorothy Pickles, which must be fulfilled by a system of government to be democratic.

> It must, first, be able to elicit as accurately as possible the opinion of as many people as possible on who shall be their representatives and on how the country ought to be governed. Second, it must provide ways of ensuring that those chosen by the people do in fact do what the electorate wants them to do or that they can be replaced if they do not, even between decisions.[6]

Democracy, in this sense, means not only representative but also responsive government. The ideal of a democratic republic can be best explained with reference to political justice.

2.3.1 Representative Government

Direct democracy in a country of 1.35 billion people is not possible, and hence representative democracy is the best choice. It entails the free choice of representatives by all adults through fair elections. In the Western democracies, representation by election has come to be regarded as the most important form of representation, and indeed the only proper basis of a political system.[7]

In representative democracy, it is assumed that the practice of submitting certain officeholders to periodic re-election will ensure that attention is paid to the interests of those who are represented. In this sense, the people may be said to be politically sovereign, transmitting their will effectively to the government. The people are to exercise their sovereignty through the Parliament at the centre and a legislature in each state, which is to be

[5] CAD, 16 May 1949.

[6] Dorothy Pickles, *Democracy* (London: Methuen, 1971), 13.

[7] A. H. Birch, *Representative and Responsible Government* (London: Allen and Unwin, 1964), 17.

elected on adult franchise and to which the real executive, namely, the Council of Ministers, shall be responsible. Although there is an elected president as the head of the union and a governor nominated by the president as the head of each state, neither of them can exercise any political function without the advice of the Council of Ministers which is collectively responsible to the people's representatives in the respective legislatures. The Constitution holds out equality to all the citizens in the matters of choice of their representatives, who are to run the governmental machinery. Representation, however, carries with it the clear implication of delegation from the people to a legislature. The members of the legislature, thus, must owe their power directly or indirectly to the people.[8]

2.3.2 Responsible Government

Effective government requires the appointment of civil servants whose responsibility is to implement the laws. It is a necessary condition of Indian democracy that the executive should be accountable to the elected representatives of the people. In India, the responsibility of government may also be judged according to its responsiveness to public opinion and its ability to avoid irresponsible action—imprudence and inconsistency.[9] The link between representative and responsible government is to be found in the fact that the accountability of the executive to the legislature makes certain that the government is both responsive and respectable.

2.3.3 Political Justice

The ideal of political justice is to make empowerment of the people through participation in the political system. The adoption of universal adult suffrage (Article 326) without any qualification either of sex, property or the like reflects the operationalization of the popular sovereignty. Political justice has come to mean 'the absence of any arbitrary distinction between man and man in the political sphere'. Members of the legislature shall be elected by the vote of the entire adult population, according to the principle, that is, 'one man, one vote'. If any sitting member of the legislature is convicted of any of the offences mentioned in Section 8 of the Representation of the People Act, after the pronouncement of the judgement, his membership of the legislature will be held ultra vires the constitution.[10]

The fact that men and women are offered equal opportunity in the matter of public employment attests to the fact that the Constitution is maintaining its democratic ideal of keeping up with the times.

2.4 Establishment of a Welfare State

The goal envisaged by the Constitution is that of a 'welfare state' and the establishment of a 'socialist state'.[11] That the goal of the Indian polity is socialism was ensured by inserting the word

---

[8] *S. R. Chaudhari v. State of Punjab* (2001), 7 SCC 126.

[9] Birch, *Representative*, 19.

[10] *Lily Thomas v. Union of India and Others*, 2013 (8) SCALE 469, (2013), SCC 653, (2013), 7 SCC (LS) 811.

[11] The word 'socialist' was inserted in the Preamble by the 42nd Constitutional Amendment Act, 1976.

'socialist' in the Preamble by the Constitution (42nd Amendment) Act, 1976. It has been inserted 'to spell out expressly the high ideals of socialism'. It is argued that the word 'socialism' is vague. Our Supreme Court has observed that its principal aim is to eliminate inequality of income and status, and to provide a decent standard of life to the working people. Instead of a total nationalization of all property and industry, it envisages a 'mixed economy' but aims at offering 'equal opportunity' to all, and the abolition of 'vested interests'.[12] From 1992 onwards, the trend is now away from socialism to privatization. Investment in many public enterprises has been divested in favour of private persons and many industries and services which were reserved for the government sector have been thrown open for private enterprises.

While the constitutional provisions for Fundamental Rights have the objective of ensuring political and civil liberty and equality to the people, the Directive Principles of State Policy are envisaged to promote social and economic and institutional changes for building a democratic welfare state and society in the country. Article 38 in Part IV relating to Directive Principles of State Policy casts a duty on the State to 'strive to promote the welfare of the people by securing and protecting as effectively as it may a social order in which justice, social, economic and political shall inform all the institutions of national life'. It also emphasizes that the State shall strive to minimize economic and social inequalities among individuals and groups of people.

In this context, Dr Radhakrishnan has expressed the concern, 'Poor people who wander about, find no work, no wages and starve, whose lives are a continual round of sore affliction and pinching poverty, cannot be proud of the Constitution or its law'.[13]

Although the Directives are not enforceable by any court of law, the Constitutional experts point out that these are nevertheless to be treated as 'fundamental in the governance of the country' and that it 'shall be the duty of the state to apply these principles in making laws' (Article 37). Over the years, several laws have been passed by the Parliament and state legislatures in the context of these Directives. Since 1976, the apex and high courts have been attaching increasing importance to these Directives while interpreting certain constitutional provisions, particularly those relating to Fundamental Rights.

These Directive Principles of State Policy provide explicitly authoritative guidelines to the Parliament and state legislatures to enact laws to bring about substantive changes in economic sector, social sector and for introducing certain institutional reforms for promoting people's welfare.

2.4.1 Economic Justice

Economic justice aims at establishing economic democracy and a welfare state. The State shall direct its policy towards securing operation of the economic system so as not to result in concentration of wealth and means of production; distribution of ownership and control of the material resources to subserve the common good of every citizen's right to an adequate means of livelihood; equal pay for equal work; health and strength of workers (Article 39); right to work; provision of just and humane conditions of work and maternity relief; and living wages for workers and suitable conditions of work.

---

[12] The Supreme Court is also facilitating the advent of socialism by interpreting other provisions of the Constitution in the light of the word 'socialism' in the Preamble. See *Randhir v. Union of India*, 1982, SC 879 (para 8); *Nakara v. Union of India*, AIR 1983 SC 130 (paras 33–34); *Minerva Mills v. Union of India*, AIR 1980 SC 1789.

[13] Speech of Dr Radhakrishnan at the Seminar on 'Parliamentary Democracy' on 25 February 1956.

A female is entitled for 'equal pay for equal work in context to her male counterpart'.[14] Thus, there cannot be any discrimination solely on the ground of gender. Reservation of seats for women in panchayats and municipalities have been provided for under Articles 243(d) and 243(t) of the Constitution of India with a view that the women are required to participate more in a democratic set up especially at the grassroots level. The ideal of economic justice is to make equality of status meaningful and life worth living at its best removing inequality of opportunity and of status—social, economic and political.[15]

2.4.2 Social Justice

The Indian Constitution also promises social justice to the people. Social justice is now interpreted as a fundamental right.[16]

It 'shall' be the duty of the State to promote the following: securing within limits of its economic capacity the right to education and work for the people and public assistance for the needy; provision for free and compulsory education for children; promotion of educational and economic interests of Scheduled Castes, Scheduled Tribes and other weaker sections of society; raising nutrition and public health and living standards (Articles 41, 45, 46 and 47); protection and improvement of environment and wildlife (Article 48A); protection of places of historic or artistic interest (Article 49).

In one of its orders, the Supreme Court observes that the promise for social, economic and political justice to citizens made by the Constitution of India cannot condone policies that turn a blind eye to deliberate infliction of misery on large segments of our population.[17]

2.5 Promoting International Peace and Security

Apart from confronting a powerful opposition at home due to manifold grievances under the British rule lasting 200 years, the sincerity of country's pledge to contribute 'to the promotion of world peace' is reiterated in Article 51 of the Constitution. The State has been directed to endeavour to

1. promote international peace and security;
2. maintain just and honourable relations between nations;
3. foster respect for international law and treaty obligations in the dealings of organized people with one another; and
4. encourage settlement of international disputes by arbitration.

The ideal of fraternity enshrined in the Preamble is not just confined to national territory but it also overflows to reach the loftier maxim of universal brotherhood. In the Constituent Assembly, Pandit Nehru expressed:

---

[14] *Mackinnon Mackenzie and Co. Ltd. v. Audrey D'Costa*, (1987), 2 SCC 469.
[15] *Dalmia Cement (Bharat) Ltd v. Union of India* (1996), 10 SCC 104.
[16] *Ashok Kumar Gupta v. State of UP*, (1997), 5 SCC 201.
[17] *Nandini Sundar v. State of Chhattisgarh*, AIR 2011 SC 2839 (2849).

The only possible, real object that we, in common with other nations, can have is the object of co-operating in building up some kind of a world structure, call it one world, call it what you like.[18]

It may be noted that the country's sovereignty is not jeopardized by the country's role in international peace and security and security. Indian sovereignty is consistent with the concept of 'one world', international peace and amity. The International Convention and norms can be read into them in the absence of enacted domestic law occupying the field when there is no inconsistency between them.[19]

2.6 Precepts of Liberty, Equality and Fraternity

Constitutional objectives of liberty, equality and fraternity have to be secured and protected with economic, social and political justices to all the citizens under the rule of law.[20]

2.6.1 Liberty

Liberty which is professed in the Preamble is essential for a free and civilized existence. Liberty of 'thought, expression, belief, faith and worship', as mentioned in the Preamble, is now forming part of Fundamental Rights under Articles 19, 25–28.[21] These individual rights are guaranteed against all the authorities of the State by Part III of the Constitution subject, of course, to the implementation of the Directive Principles, for the common good (Article 31C) and the 'fundamental duties', introduced (Article 51A), by the 42nd Amendment, 1976.

It is also considered unmistakably that liberty is favoured more than equality. However, it is noted that liberty should be coupled with social restraint and ranked to secure common happiness.

2.6.2 Equality

The ideal of 'equality' enshrined in the Preamble can be best explained with reference to right to equality as a fundamental right. Broadly speaking, equality has come to mean 'equal protection of the laws'. It means the right to equal treatment in similar circumstances both in the privileges conferred and in the liabilities imposed by the laws.[22] This object is secured in the body of Constitution by making illegal all discriminations by the State between citizen and citizen simply on the ground of religion, race, caste, sex or place of birth (Article 15), by throwing open 'public places' to all citizens [Article 15(2)], by abolishing untouchability (Article 17), by abolishing titles

[18] CAD, 22 January 1947.

[19] Article 51(c) has the enabling power of the Parliament to enact laws for implementing the International Conventions and norms by virtue of Article 253 read with entry 14 of the Union List in Seventh Schedule of the Constitution. Refer to *Vishakha and Others v. State of Rajasthan and Others*, SCR 1997 (Supp. 3), 404. In the absence of domestic law, International Conventions and norms are significant for the purpose of interpretation of the guarantee of gender equality, right to work with human dignity enshrined in Articles 14, 15 19(I) (g) and 21 of the Constitution and the safeguards against sexual harassment implicit therein.

[20] *S. S. Bola v. B. D. Sardana*, (1997), 8 SCC 522.

[21] In a landmark judgement, a nine-judge Supreme Court bench on 24 August 2017 declared 'privacy' a fundamental right. See *The Economic Times* (Chandigarh), 25 August 2017.

[22] *John Vallamation v. Union of India*, AIR 2003 SC 2902.

of honour (Article 18), by offering equality of opportunity in matters relating to employment under the State (Article 16) and by guaranteeing equality before the law and equal protection of the laws, as justiciable rights (Article 14).

The sustenance of gender justice is the cultivated achievement of intrinsic human rights. Equality cannot be achieved unless there are equal opportunities for both men and women. In the case, *Vishaka and Others v. State of Rajasthan and Others*, the Supreme Court referred to the Convention for Elimination of all forms of Discrimination Against Women, 1979, (CEDAW) which was ratified by the Government of India (GoI) in 1993 and framed certain guidelines. Besides these provisions, Constitution seeks to achieve 'political' equally by providing for universal adult franchise (Article 326).

The Supreme Court while declaring the 'Hijra/Transgender' as 'third gender' has held that

1. Hijras, Eunuchs, apart from binary gender, be treated as 'third gender' for the purpose of safeguarding their rights under Part III of our Constitution and the laws made by the Parliament and the state legislature.
2. Transgender persons' right to decide their self-identified gender is also upheld and the centre and state governments are directed to grant legal recognition of their gender identity such as male, female or as third gender.
3. We direct the centre and the state governments to take steps to treat them as socially and educationally backward classes of citizens and extend all kinds of reservation in cases of admission in educational institutions and for public appointment.[23]

2.6.3 Fraternity

Democracy, cherished by the framers of the Constitution, will carry no meaning if it fails to generate the spirit of fraternity and brotherhood amongst all sections of the people. The fraternity will be achieved not only by abolishing untouchability amongst the different sects of the same community but also by abolishing all communal or sectional or even local or provincial anti-social feelings which stand in the way of the unity of India. The unity and fraternity of the people professing numerous faiths, religions and cultures have been sought to be achieved by enshrining the ideal of a 'secular state',[24] which means that the State protects all religions equally and does not itself uphold any religion as the State religion. The secularism is a component of the basic structure of the Constitution.[25]

The Preamble also expresses that the State, that is, India, will assure the dignity of the individual. In this context, a number of provisions have been placed in Part IV of the Constitution, exhorting the State so to shape its social and economic policies that, inter alia, 'all citizens, men and women equally, have the right to an adequate means of livelihood' (Article 39A), 'just and humane conditions of work' (Article 42) and 'a decent standard of life and full enjoyment of leisure and social and cultural opportunities' (Article 43). The Supreme Court in one of its judgements has already declared the 'right to dignity' as a Fundamental Right.[26]

---

[23] *National Legal Services Authority v. Union of India*, (2014) 5 SCC 438 AIR 2014 SC.

[24] The word 'secular' was inserted in the Preamble by the Constitution (42nd Amendment) Act, 1976.

[25] *Bommai v. Union of India*, AIR 1994 SC 1918. Also see *Sri Adi Visheshwar of Kashi Vishwanath Temp, Varanasi v. State of UP*, (1997) 4 SCC 606 (para 26).

[26] *LIC v. Consumer Centre*, AIR 1995 SC 1811.

2.7 Fundamental Duties

The Constitution of India enumerates 10 (now 11) Fundamental Duties under Article 51A (Part IVA) for every citizen of India,[27] emphasizing that each individual shall not only have the Fundamental Rights but also a corresponding fundamental duty, such as, to uphold the sovereignty, unity and integrity of the nation, to maintain secularism and the common brotherhood amongst all the people of India. It is to be noted that there is, however, no provision in the Constitution for direct enforcement of any of these duties.[28] The Supreme Court is of the concerted view that since the duties are obligatory for a citizen, it would follow that the State should also endeavour to achieve the same goal. The court may, therefore, issue appropriate directions or give effect to any of these duties.[29] For example, to give effect to Article 51A(g) read with Articles 21, 47 and 48B, the Supreme Court recognized 'Polluter Pays Principle' as part of the law of the country.[30]

Summary

It is to be noted that ideals of political, social and economic democracy with that of liberty, equality and fraternity, the Preamble seeks to establish a democratic society infused with practices of fairness, accountability and good governance. In brief, the Constitution of India promises not only political but also social and economic justice. For a proper appreciation of the ideals, aims and objectives of the Constitution, we must turn to the various expressions enshrined in the Preamble. It is critical to keep the balance between three branches of the State. Describing the balance between legislature, judiciary and executive as the backbone of the Constitution, PM Narendra Modi recently highlighted the need for the three organs of the State to remain within their limits while working to fulfil people's wishes. Addressing the valedictory session of the Constitution Day celebrations, Modi said,

> It was because of this balance that the nation survived the Emergency … Today, when we are making every attempt to build a new India, the significance of these principles has only increased. We have to fulfill the people's hopes and aspirations by remaining within our limits.[31]

The Preamble and the objects underlying the Indian Constitution emphasizes that the goal of the Indian polity is not laissez-faire, but a welfare State, where the State—government, judiciary and parliament—has a positive duty to ensure to its citizens not only social and economic justice but also good governance. Although these ideals and objects contained in the Preamble are not enforceable by the courts, yet they have been declared to be fundamental in the governance of the country, and a government that sits on popular vote can hardly ignore them.

---

[27] Inserted by the Constitution (42nd Amendment) Act, 1976. Vide the Constitution (86th Amendment) Act, 2002, the number of Fundamental Duties is increased from 10 to 11.

[28] *Ramesharan v. Union of India*, AIR 1989 SC 549.

[29] *Rural Litigation v. State of UP*, AIR 1987 SC 359.

[30] *Vellore Citizen's Welfare Forum v. Union of India*, (1996) 5 SCC 647.

[31] *The Tribune* (Chandigarh), 27 November 2017.

3 Union Executive: President and Vice-President

LEARNING OBJECTIVES

1. **To describe the role and position of the Indian president**
2. **To discuss the procedure relating to removal of the president and vice-president**
3. **To comment on the ordinance-making power of the president**

Introduction

The Indian system of government purports to be parliamentary type of executive both at the centre and in the states. In this system, the real executive power of the government is to be exercised by the Council of Ministers comprising the leadership of the political party or parties holding a majority in the legislature and collectively responsible to it in its working. The union executive is the most important government institution. The union executive consists mainly of the (a) president (and vice-president) who exercises his power on the advice of the Council of Ministers under Article 74 of the Constitution, (b) Council of Ministers headed by the PM and (c) the services (government servants to assist the Council of Ministers in the discharge of its functions). This structure, it was believed, would provide competent leadership to the Parliament in all matters—legislation, policy enunciation, finance, administration and so on. In this chapter, an attempt is made to discuss the offices of the president and vice-president. Also, the focus is on describing the status of the president and the relation with his Council of Ministers.

3.1 President

At the head of the State stands the President of India who heads the union executive. Since 1950, there have been 14 presidents of India (Table 3.1).

3.1.1 Election of President

To seek election to the president's post, the candidate must be a citizen of India, not less than 35 years of age and qualified for election as a member of the Lok Sabha. His term of office is five years. The president is elected by members of an electoral college consisting of elected members of both

Table 3.1 Presidents of India

Election Year	Name of the President	Tenure
1950	Dr Rajendra Prasad	From 26 January 1950 to 13 May 1962
1952	Dr Rajendra Prasad	
1957	Dr Rajendra Prasad[1]	
1962	Dr S. Radhakrishnan	From 13 May 1962 to 13 May 1967
1967	Dr Zakir Hussain (died in 1969)	From 13 May 1967 to 3 May 1969
	Sh. V. V. Giri	From 3 May 1969 to 20 July 1969 (acting)
	Justice M. Hidayatullah	From 20 July 1969 to 24 August 1969 (acting)
1969	Sh. V. V. Giri	From 24 August 1969 to 24 August 1974
1974	Sh. Fakhruddin Ali Ahmed (Died in 1977)	From 24 August 1974 to 11 February 1977
	Sh. B. D. Jatti	From 11 February 1977 to 25 July 1977 (acting)
1977	Sh. Neelam Sanjiva Reddy	From 25 July 1977 to 25 July 1982
1982	Sh. Zail Singh	From 25 July 1982 to 25 July 1987
1987	Sh. R. Venkataraman	From 25 July 1987 to 25 July 1992
1992	Dr Shankar Dayal Sharma	From 25 July 1992 to 25 July 1997
1997	Sh. K. R. Narayanan	From 25 July 1997 to 25 July 2002
2002	Dr A. P. J. Abdul Kalam	From 25 July 2002 to 25 July 2007
2007	Smt. Pratibha D. Patil	From 25 July 2007 to 25 July 2012
2012	Sh. Pranab Mukherjee	From 25 July 2012 to 25 July 2017
2017	Sh. Ram Nath Kovind[2]	From 25 July 2017 to date

Houses of the Parliament and legislative assemblies of the states, union territories and Puducherry and in accordance with the system of proportional representation by means of single transferable vote [Article 55(3)]. To secure uniformity among states as well as parity between the states, as a whole, and the Union, suitable weightage is given to each vote.

The number of votes which each elected member of Parliament and of the legislative assembly (MP/MLA) of each state is entitled to cast at such election shall be determined in the following manner:

$$\frac{\text{Member of the state}}{\text{legislative assemblies}} = \frac{\text{Total population of the state}}{\text{Total number of elected members in the assembly of the state}} \div 1000$$

[1] So far, only Dr Rajendra Prasad had a second term as president.

[2] Shri Ram Nath Kovind is India's 14th president, the second SC head of the State after Shri K. R. Narayanan, and the first president from the BJP fold.

$$\text{Members of the Parliament} = \frac{\text{Total value of the votes of all the MLAs}}{\text{Total number of the elected members of both the Houses of the Parliament}}$$

Then, the quota of votes a candidate needs to win the election is determined in the following manner:

$$\frac{\text{Number of votes polled}}{\text{Number of members to be returned}} + 1 = \text{Quota}$$

This system seeks to ensure that the president is a representative of the union of states as well as a representative of the people in the country. It gives recognition to the status of the states in the federal system.[3]

Further, this provision is intended to make the election broad-based and to place the president above party politics. It may be mentioned here that the elections of the president and the vice-president cannot be challenged on the ground of any vacancy in the appropriate electoral college.[4] President is also eligible to seek re-election for any further number of terms.[5]

The method of president's election has been criticized of being partially undemocratic but indirect election was supported by the framers of the Constitution on the grounds: first, that direct election by the electorates would mean a tremendous loss of time, energy and time; and second, to elect the president directly by the people would mean investing power in him which is opposed to the parliamentary system of government.

3.1.2 Impeachment Procedure

The president may (for the violation of the Constitution) be removed from office after impeachment in either House in accordance with special procedure prescribed in Article 61. Impeachment charge is preferred by a resolution initiated by not less than one-fourth of the total number of Members of the House concerned and is passed by a majority of not less than two-thirds of its total membership. Thereafter, the other House is required to investigate the charge. The president has the right to appear or to be represented at the investigation. If, as a result of this investigation, the House adopts a resolution by not less than two-thirds of its membership, the president shall be deemed to have been removed from office with effect from the date of this resolution.[6]

There is an apprehension that the president may create a series of hurdles such as by dissolving the Lok Sabha, or by dismissing the PM and installing a puppet government, or by tempting a number of MPs by dishonourable means so as to tilt the balance in his favour at the time of voting on the resolution of impeachment.[7] Since the Constitution provides the mode and ground for

[3] In the 14th presidential election, Ram Nath Kovind, BJP-led winning candidate, secured 702,044 votes by 2,930 lawmakers, in contrast to 367,314 votes by 1,844 lawmakers secured by Meira Kumar, opposition candidate, registering 65.65% of electoral college.

[4] See 11th Constitutional Amendment Act, 1961.

[5] The first President Dr Rajendra Prasad himself took initiative and did not seek re-election in 1962.

[6] The impeachment charge of violation of the Constitution has not been levelled against any president so far.

[7] See B. C. Dass, 'Impeachment of India's President', *Journal of Constitutional and Parliamentary Studies* 5, no. 2 (1971): 245–50.

removing the president, he cannot be removed otherwise than by impeachment, in accordance with the term of Articles 56 and 61.

It is curious to discuss the position of the president in view of the plenitude of powers vested in the elected president.

3.1.3 Administrative Powers

As a component and vital part of the Parliament, the president's powers and functions are comprehensive. The Constitution says, 'Executive power of the Union shall be vested in the President' (Article 53). It has several implications. The 'executive power' has come to mean as 'the power of carrying on the business of government' or 'the administration of the affairs of the state', barring legislative and judicial functions. The expression 'executive power' has been explained by the Supreme Court in *Ram Jawaya v. State of Punjab* (1955). In this case, Justice Mukherjee observed:

> It may not be possible to frame an exhaustive definition of what executive function means and implies. Ordinarily the executive power connotes the residue of governmental functions that remains after legislative and judicial functions are taken away, subject, of course, to the provisions of the Constitution or of any law. The executive function comprises both the determination of the policy as well as carrying it into execution, the maintenance of order, the promotion of social and economic welfare, the direction of foreign policy, in fact, the carrying on or supervision of the general administration of the State.[8]

But there are constitutional limitations under which he is to exercise his executive powers. First, the executive powers are to be exercised by the president in accordance with the advice of the Council of Ministers with the PM as its head.[9] But the 44th Constitutional Amendment makes it obligatory for the president to act according to the advice given to him (in the event of reconsideration of the advice).[10] Second, Article 75(1) explicitly requires that the ministers for the council (excepting the PM) 'shall be appointed by the president on the advice of the Prime Minister'.[11]

Thus, in constitutional theory all executive actions of the Union must be expressed to be taken in the name of the president [Article 77(1)]. The president shall make rules for the convenient transaction of the business of the GoI, and for the allocation among ministers of the said business [Article 77(3)]. Again all officers of the Union shall be his subordinates [Article 53(1)] and he shall have a right to be informed by the PM of the decisions of the Council of Ministers relating to the administration of the affairs of the Union and proposals for legislation [Article 78(a)].

Besides appointing the PM and other ministers of the Union (Article 75), the president has the power to appoint Attorney General of India (Article 76), Comptroller and Auditor General (CAG) of India (Article 148), judges of the Supreme Court (Article 124), judges of the high court of the states (Articles 217), governor of a state (Article 153), administrator of a union territory (Article 239), chief election commissioner and other members of the Election Commission (Article 324),

---

[8] *Ram Jawaya v. State of Punjab*, AIR 1955, SC 549.

[9] Article 74(1) (42nd Amendment Act, 1976).

[10] Refusal to act in accordance with the advice tendered after such reconsideration will render the president liable for impeachment.

[11] If the president appoints a minister other than the one advised by the PM, the president could be removed by the process of impeachment.

chairman and members of various statutory bodies such as Finance Commission (Article 280), Union Public Service Commission or UPSC (Article 316), Official Language Commission (Article 344), National Commission for the Scheduled Castes (Article 338), National Commission for the Scheduled Tribes (Article 338A), Special officer for Linguistic Minorities (Article 350B).

The administrative power also includes the power to remove (a) his ministers, individually; (b) the attorney general for India; (c) the governor of a state; (d) the chairman or a member of the public service commission of the Union or of a state, on the report of the Supreme Court; and (e) a judge of the Supreme Court or of a high court or the election commissioner, on an address of the Parliament.

3.1.4 Military Power

The president is the commander-in-chief of the armed forces. Although, supreme command of the defence forces is vested in the president, but the Constitution expressly lays down that 'the exercise of this power shall be regulated by law' [Article 53(2)].

3.1.5 Diplomatic Power

The diplomatic power is often identified with foreign or external affairs which comprise 'all matters which bring the Union into relation with any foreign country'. On the advice of his ministers, the president negotiates treaties and agreements with foreign countries subject to ratification by the Parliament.[12] Again, like the heads of other States, the president represents India in international affairs and has the power of appointing Indian representatives to other countries and of receiving diplomatic representatives of other states, as is recognized by the Parliament.

3.1.6 Legislative Powers

Like the British Crown, the President of India is an important component of the Union Parliament.[13] The legislative powers of the President of India are nonetheless comprehensive.

1. *Summoning, dissolution, sending messages:* Under Articles 85 and 108, the president has the power to summon, prorogue and dissolve the Parliament. He inaugurates the annual sessions of both the Houses (Lok Sabha and Rajya Sabha) with an address outlining the policy of the government (Article 87) or with messages either in regard to any pending bill or to any other matter, and the House must then consider the message 'with all convenient despatch' [Article 86(2)].
2. *Nominating members to the Parliament:* The president nominates 12 members of the Rajya Sabha from among persons having special knowledge of or practical experience in the fields of science, literature, art and social service (Article 80). He may nominate at the most two

[12] India ratifies the Paris Agreement in October 2016.

[13] To say that the Constitution of India follows the principle of separation of powers is partially incorrect.

Anglo-Indians to the Lok Sabha in case he finds that the community is not adequately represented in it (Article 331).

3. *Laying certain reports before the Houses:* The president is required to cause certain reports and statements to be laid before each House of the Parliament. These include (a) the Annual Financial Statement and the Supplementary Statement, if any; (b) the report of CAG of India relating to the accounts of the GoI (Article 151); (c) the recommendations made by the Finance Commission together with an explanatory memorandum of the action taken thereon (Article 281); and (d) the report of the UPSC, explaining the reasons where any advice of the commission has not been accepted (Article 323).
4. *Previous sanction to legislation*: For introducing legislation on the following matters, the president's recommendation or sanction is required for (a) formation of new states and alternation of areas, boundaries or names of existing states (Article 3); (b) acquisition of estates under Articles 31A; (c) special provision as to financial bills [Article 117(1) and 117(3)]; (d) a bill affecting taxation in which states are interested (Article 274); and (e) restriction on trade, commerce and intercourse among states (Article 304).
5. *Assent to legislation and veto:* When a bill is presented before the president after its passage by the Parliament, it will be open to the president to take any of the following three steps: (a) declare his assent to the bill; (b) declare that he withholds his assent to the bill; and (c) in the case of a non-money bill, return the bill for reconsideration of the Parliament with or without a message suggesting amendments. In this case, if it is passed again and presented to the president, it would be obligatory upon the president to give his assent (Article 111). This power is not available in the case of a money bill.

   The object of the veto power is to prevent and control hasty and ill-considered action by the Parliament. Normally, such a power will be used in the case of private members' bill. On the contrary if a government Bill has been duly passed by Parliament and the Council of Ministers resigns before it is assented by the President, the next Ministry enjoying the confidence of Parliament may advise the President to exercise his Veto power against the Bill. In such a situation, the president's veto power would not be unconstitutional.[14]

   It should be noted that a bill after its passage shall have no legal effect until the president declares his assent to it. But no time limit is imposed by the Constitution upon the president either to declare his assent or refusal or return of the bill (Article 111 uses the words 'as soon as possible'). In the absence of a time limit, it seems that the Indian president would be able to exercise something like a 'pocket veto'[15] by simply keeping the bill on his desk for an indefinite time, particularly, if the president finds that there is likelihood of the change in government or the ministry is likely to collapse.[16]

   Further, under the Article 201, the state legislature may reconsider the non-money bill, returned by the president, within six months, and if it is passed again, the bill shall be

---

[14] The president withheld his assent to the Salary, Allowances and Pension of Members of Parliament (Amendment) Bill, 1991, which was passed by the Parliament on the last day of its sitting without seeking the president's recommendations as is required under Article 117(1).

[15] Pocket veto in generally exercised by the President of USA.

[16] For example, the passage of the Indian Post Office (Amendment) Bill, 1986, by the Parliament was criticized as curtailing the freedom of the press. President Zail Singh withheld his assent to the Bill. After the assumption of power by the National Front government in December 1989, the President R. Venkataraman returned it for reconsideration of the Council of Ministers. It seems that it has been given up.

presented to the president again for his assent. But it shall not be obligatory on the part of the president to give his assent even in the case of a money bill. So, the Union's control over state legislation shall be absolute, and no grounds are limited by the Constitution upon which the president shall be entitled to refuse his assent. These powers of the president in relation to state legislation exhibit the tilt towards a unitary federation.

6. *Ordinance-making power:* The power of the union executive to legislate by ordinance under Article 123, having the force of an Act of Parliament during its recess, is historical in origin. The relevant provision in the GOI Act, 1935 was reproduced in the Constitution with certain changes. First, the power to make Ordinance is to be exercised on the advice of the Council of Ministers. Second, any ordinance issued is required to be laid before both Houses of Parliament and ceases to operate at the expiration of six weeks from the re-assembly of Parliament or earlier, if a resolution disapproving it is passed by both Houses. The president may withdraw an ordinance any time before its expiry. Third, the ordinance-making power will be available to the president only when either of the two Houses of Parliament has been prorogued or is otherwise not in session.[17]

As the former President Pranab Mukherjee gave unqualified assent to ordinances, as many times and as often presented. Not even once did he return to the Modi government for reconsideration any of the crucial recommendations, be it the frequent issue of ordinances or the imposition of president's rules. Again, the president happily sided with the government in approving the ordinance that criminalized the holding of ₹500 and ₹1000 currency notes beyond 31 December 2016.

It is interesting to note that such a legislative power of the Executive is not available in the USA owing to the doctrine of Separation of Powers. But the power to issue ordinances has been justified in India on the ground that the president cannot deal with a pressing situation by resorting to the ordinary process of law because either House is not in session. Even though the Parliament is in session, the president may promulgate an ordinance as Article 123(1) says, 'If at any time, except when both Houses of Parliament are in session, the president is satisfied that circumstances exist which render it necessary for him to take immediate action, he may promulgate such Ordinances as the circumstances appear to him to require'.

But whether such a situation has arisen warranting promulgation of an Ordinance, the sole judge is president himself. A court cannot enquire into the propriety of his satisfaction even where it is alleged that the power was not used in good faith.[18] But if promulgated repeatedly then it is regarded as the abuse of power and a fraud on the Constitution.[19]

A clause (4) in Article 123 was inserted by the 38th Amendment in 1975 (the Indira Gandhi government) laying down that the 'president's satisfaction shall be final and could not be questioned in the court on any ground'. The 44th Amendment (the Janata government) however omitted this clause (4) from Article 123 in 1978.

However, despite the court's admonitions, there have been many occasions when ordinances have been issued almost immediately after Parliament's adjournments. The Lok Sabha has made a Rule requiring that whenever the government seeks to replace an ordinance by a bill, a statement

---

[17] For example, the Land Acquisition Ordinance was promulgated thrice by the president on the recommendation of the Union Cabinet during 2014–15. It had replaced the Land Bill, which was widely dubbed as 'anti farmer' and remained stuck in the Rajya Sabha before its dilution.

[18] *State of Punjab v. Satya Pal*, AIR 1969, SC 903.

[19] See *Wadhawa v. State of Bihar*, AIR 1987 SC 579. In this case, it was established that the Government of Bihar issued 256 ordinances and kept them alive for 14 years without getting an Act passed by the state legislature in place of the expiring ordinance.

'explaining the circumstances which necessitated immediate legislation by ordinance' must accompany such bill.

In his last address to the nation on 24 July 2017, the former President Pranab Mukherjee's advice to the government was that it should 'take the ordinance route sparingly'.[20]

3.1.7 Pardoning Power

Under Article 72, the president has the power to grant pardons, reprieves, respites or remissions of punishment or suspend, remit or commute the sentence of any person convicted of any offence: (a) in all cases where the punishment or sentence is by a court martial; (b) in all cases where the punishment or sentence is for an offence against any law relating to a *matter* to which the executive power of the Union extends; and (c) in all cases where the sentence is a sentence of death. It is also given that nothing in this clause shall affect the power conferred by law on any officer of the armed forces of the Union.

The power of the president under Article 72 is independent of the judiciary. The object of conferring this judicial power upon the executive is to correct possible judicial error.

When Kehar Singh, who was awarded death sentence in the Indira Gandhi murder case, moved the Supreme Court after making petition of mercy to the president, the court ruled: (a) since the power of the president under this Article of the Constitution is of an executive character, it has to be exercised on the advice of the central government; (b) the convict, seeking pardon, has no right to an oral hearing before the president; (c) the court can go into the question of extent of the president's power under this Article, but it cannot go into the merits of the decision of the president.[21] It implies that the courts cannot interfere with the decisions of the president on merits but they can look into whether the president has taken into account all relevant materials.

Disposing mercy petitions from convicts, former President Pranab Mukherjee said that he would 'leave not a rack behind'. Contrary to many of his predecessors, Mr Mukherjee disposed of 34 petitions, rejecting 30 of them and leaving none pending for his successor.[22]

3.1.8 Miscellaneous Powers

In addition to aforementioned powers, the president is vested with certain powers that may be of residuary in nature but are equally important. Some of these are as follows:

1. The president has the power to make rules and regulations relating to the affairs of the Union (e.g., the number of members of the UPSC, recruitment and conditions of service of persons serving the Union; the procedure relating to the joint sittings of the Houses of Parliament; the manner of enforcing the orders of the Supreme Court, etc.).

[20] See *The Tribune* (Chandigarh), 25 July 2017. In his address on the eve of 66th Republic Day, former President Pranab Mukherjee said that enacting laws without discussions 'breaches the trust' reposed by people and is not good for democracy. See also *Financial Express*, 26 January 2015.

[21] *Kehar Singh v. Union of India*, AIR 1989, SC 653.

[22] See *The Times of India* (Chandigarh), 25 July 2017. Comparing pardoning powers with those of president, governor of a state under Article 161 has no power to pardon death sentences. But the governor has the power to suspend, remit or commute a sentence of death, if conferred by law. Governor has no pardoning power in respect of cases of punishment by a court martial.

2. The president is empowered to refer any question of public importance for the opinion of the Supreme Court.
3. The president has certain special powers and responsibilities in respect of the administration of Scheduled Areas and Tribes.
4. The president has the power to give instructions to a governor to promulgate an ordinance if a bill requires his previous sanction.

3.2 President's Power of Proclaiming Emergency

The emergency provisions in the Constitution are three-fold: (a) threat to security of India (Article 352); (b) failure of constitutional machinery in a state (Article 356); and (c) threat to financial stability (Article 360).

3.2.1 Threat to Security of India

The president, on the recommendation in writing of the cabinet headed by the PM, is empowered to make a 'Proclamation of Emergency' at any time (even before the actual occurrence of any disturbance), if he is satisfied that the security of India or any part thereof is been threatened by war, external aggression or armed rebellion.[23]

Effects of proclamation: If the president issues a proclamation of grave emergency which threatens the security of India or any part of the territory thereof (under Article 352), all the legislative and executive powers of the states are placed under the authority of the Union (Article 353).

Under Article 355, it 'shall be the duty of the Union to protect every state against external aggression and internal disturbance and to ensure that the government of every state is carried on in accordance with the provisions of this Constitution'.

In such an emergency, the president may even suspend the enforcement of the Fundamental Rights (except Articles 14, 20 and 21) guaranteed in the Constitution.

Further, the Parliament may, by law, extend the life of the Lok Sabha by one year at a time and not extending in any case beyond six months after the proclamation has ceased to operate.[24]

Emergency proclaimed under Article 352 has been resorted to three times: First, from 26 October 1962 to 10 January 1968 on ground of 'external aggression' (Chinese aggression in the North-East Frontier Agency or NEFA in October 1962 and War with Pakistan in August 1965); second, from 3 December 1971 to 21 March 1977 on ground of external aggression, being in war with Pakistan in December 1971; and third, from 25 June 1975 to 21 March 1977 on ground of 'internal disturbance'.[25]

---

[23] The 44th Amendment Act, 1978, substituted the words 'armed rebellion' for 'internal disturbance'. While the 42nd Amendment Act, 1976, made the president's proclamation immune from judicial review, the 44th Amendment Act, 1978, overturned the change, so that the president's propriety can be questioned in a court on the ground of *mala fide* (*S. R. Bommai v. Union of India*, AIR 1994, SC 1918).

[24] Mrs Indira Gandhi used this power in 1976.

[25] The 'internal disturbance' which was cited in the press note relating to the proclamation was that 'certain persons have been inciting the Police and the Armed Forces against the discharge of their duties and their normal functioning'. See Ministry of Information and Broadcasting, *India 1976: A Reference Annual* (New Delhi: GoI, 1976).

Mrs Indira Gandhi, then PM of India, did assert that imposition of emergency in 1975 was 'aimed at preserving the Constitution, not destroying it'.[26] Between 1971 and 1976 (during emergency period), 19 amendments to the Constitution and 463 amendments to other laws were pushed. Nearly 100 ordinances were promulgated, and as many as 114 Presidential Acts were enacted for the states under the president's rule. As many as 102 laws were added to the Ninth Schedule, taking them out of purview of 'judicial review'.

Termination of the proclamation: Until the 44th Amendment Act, there was no parliamentary control over the revocation of a proclamation once it had been approved by resolutions of each House of Parliament. After the 44th Amendment, a president's proclamation must be laid before both Houses of Parliament for its approval within one month from the date of its issue. Unless it is approved by Parliament, the proclamation shall cease to be in operation on the expiry of one month. If the Lok Sabha is dissolved at the date of issue of the proclamation or within one month thereof, the proclamation may survive until 30 days from the date of the first sitting of the House after its reconstitution, provided the Council of States has in the meantime approved it by a resolution [Article 352(4)].

A proclamation so approved shall, unless revoked, cease to operate on the expiry of six months from the date of last such resolution [Articles 352(5)]. Every such resolution under Clauses 4 and 5 of Article 352 must be passed by either House by a majority of the total membership of that House and by a majority of not less than two-thirds of the members of that House present and voting [Article 352(6)]. Under Clause 7 of Articles 352, the president must revoke a proclamation if the Lok Sabha passes a resolution disapproving or, as the case may be, disapproving the continuance in force of such proclamation. For the purpose of moving a resolution for disapproval of a proclamation not less than one-tenth of the members of the Lok Sabha may give a notice in writing to the speaker or to the president (in the absence of a session) to convene a special sitting of the House for the purpose. A special sitting of the House is required to be held within 14 days from the date on which the notice is received by the speaker/president (Clause 8 of Article 352).

3.2.2 Failure of Constitutional Machinery in a State

The president is vested with the power to make a proclamation when he is satisfied that the government of a state cannot be carried on in accordance with the provisions of the Constitution, either on the report of the governor of the state or otherwise (Article 356). Such proclamation may also be made by the president where any state has failed to comply with, or to give effect to, any directions given by the Union, in the exercise of its executive power to the state (Article 365).

Effects of proclamation: By such proclamation, the president may (a) assume to himself all or any of the executive functions of the state government or of any other authority, save the high court, (b) declare that the powers of the state legislature shall be exercisable by or under the authority of Parliament, and (c) promulgate ordinances for the administration of the state when Parliament is not in session (Article 357).

Duration and termination of proclamation: A proclamation of emergency issued under Article 356 shall be placed before each House of Parliament and shall cease to operate after two

[26] See *The Tribune* (Chandigarh), 12 December 2015.

months unless the period is extended by a resolution passed by a simple majority in both the Houses of Parliament. In case Lok Sabha stands dissolved, the period can be extended by the Rajya Sabha which shall not run beyond 30 days from the day of first sitting of the new Lok Sabha unless the reconstituted Lok Sabha within the duration passes a resolution to the same effect. The two months' duration of such proclamation can be extended by resolutions passed by both Houses of Parliament for a period of six months at a time, subject to a maximum duration of three years [Article 356 (3 and 4)].[27]

Judicial review: While the 42nd Amendment made the president's satisfaction making proclamation of failure of constitutional machinery (Article 356) immune from judicial review, that fetter has been removed by the 44th Amendment so that the constitutionality of the proclamation can be questioned in a court on the ground of *mala fides*. The use of Article 356 on numerous occasions has evoked criticism.

Now with the judgement in S. R. Bommai's case,[28] a 9-Judge Bench held that the power under Articles 356 is an exceptional power and has to be exercised only to meet the exigencies of special situations. Coming down heavily on the Centre for the 27 March 2016 proclamation under Article 356, a division bench of High Court of Uttarakhand on 21 April 2016 said that the imposition of president's rule was contrary to the law laid down by the Supreme Court. 'We are of the view that be it suspension or dissolution, the effect is troppling of a democratically elected government. It breeds cynicism in the hearts of citizens who participate in the democratic system and also undermines democracy and foundation of federalism'.

3.2.2.1 Comparison of Proclamations Under Articles 352 and 356

While two preceding proclamations under Article 352 were made on the ground of 'external aggression', the third proclamation of emergency under Article 352 was made on the ground of 'internal disturbance'.

A comparison of proclamations under Articles 352 and 356 is briefly discussed here:

1. A Proclamation of Emergency (Article 352) may be issued by the president on the ground of threat to the security of India by war, external aggression or armed rebellion. On the other hand, a proclamation of failure of constitutional machinery (Article 356) may be issued by the president on the ground of a political deadlock or the failure by a state to carry out the directions of the Union.
2. Under a proclamation of emergency (Article 352), the state executive and legislature continue in operation and retain their powers except that the Centre gets the concurrent powers of legislation and administration of the state. On the other hand, in the case of proclamation under Article 356, the state legislature stands suspended and the state executive authority is assumed by the president in whole or in part.

---

[27] The duration of a proclamation made under Article 356 beyond one year is allowed unless a proclamation of emergency under Article 352 is in operation and the Election Commission certifies that it is not possible to hold elections to the legislative assembly of the state concerned. In such case, it may be extended up to three years, by successive resolutions for continuance being passed by both Houses of Parliament (44th Amendment).

[28] *S. R. Bommai v. Union of India*, AIR 1994, SC 918.

3. When a proclamation of emergency is issued under Article 352, Parliament can legislate in respect of state subjects only by itself. While in the case of a proclamation under Article 356, Parliament can delegate its powers in respect of state subjects to the president or any other authority specified by him.
4. In the case of a proclamation of emergency (Article 352), it may be continued indefinitely as long as it is not revoked or the Parliament does not approve its continuance by resolutions, while a proclamation of failure of constitutional machinery may be extended up to three years by Parliament.

Figures indicate that until 1 March 2015, the president's rule was imposed 124 times in states and union territories.

3.2.3 Threat to Financial Stability

Under Article 360(1), the president is empowered to make a declaration that a situation has arisen whereby 'the financial stability or credit of India or of any part thereof is threatened'.[29] The object of this proclamation is to maintain the financial stability of the country.

Effects of proclamation: While the proclamation is in operation, (a) the executive authority of the Union shall extend to the giving of directions to any state to observe canons of financial propriety; (b) the union executive shall have the power to the giving of directions to any state to reduce the salary and allowances of all or any class of persons serving in connection with the affairs of a state, and to reserve all money bills for the consideration of the president after they are passed by the legislature of the state; and (c) it shall be competent for the president to issue directions for the reduction of salaries and allowances of all or any class of persons serving in connection with the affairs of the Union including the Judges of the Supreme Court and the High Court [Article 360 (4 and 5)].

Duration of proclamation: The president may at any time revoke it by making another proclamation. The proclamation of financial emergency shall remain in force for a period of two months unless it is approved by resolutions of each House of Parliament. If the Lok Sabha is dissolved within a period of two months, the proclamation shall cease to be in operation on the expiry of 30 days from the date of the first sitting of the Lok Sabha after its reconstitution unless before the expiry of that period of 30 days, it has been approved by resolutions of each House of Parliament.

3.3 President's Status and Relations with the Prime Minister

Ever since the enforcement of the Constitution, a debatable question that has been raised is whether the president is a 'mere constitutional head' or 'not a figure head'. Politicians, constitutional experts and court judges have advanced different arguments on this issue.

[29] The Financial Emergency under Article 360(1) has not been used so far.

In Ram Jawaya's case,[30] the Supreme Court ruled that the Indian president is a constitutional head of the executive such as the British Crown. Likewise in *U. N. Rao v. Indira*, a unanimous observation of the Supreme Court was 'The Constituent Assembly did not choose the Presidential system of government'.[31]

With the 42nd Amendment of the Constitution in 1976, the political controversy ended with regard to the position of the president. The amended Article 74(1) reads, 'There shall be a Council of Ministers with the Prime Minister at the head to aid and advise the President who shall, in the exercise of his functions, act in accordance with such advice'.

The Janata government, which came to power in 1977 at the central level, added a proviso to the foregoing Article 74(1). The 44th Constitutional Amendment Act, 1978, now gives the president one chance to refer the advice given to the Council of Ministers back for a reconsideration. But if the Council of Ministers reiterates its previous stand on the advice, the president in bound to act according to that advice.[32]

That the president must act only in accordance with the advice of the Council of Ministers is based on the broader background of the sovereignty of the Parliament. When the Constituent Assembly was debating on the position of the president, the law minister categorically affirmed that if the president did not act except on the advice of the Council of Ministers, it would be tantamount to a violation of the Constitution and would make the president liable to impeachment.

Articles 53 and 74(1) emphasize that the real power is vested in the Council of Ministers and not the president. As the Supreme Court has well ruled,

> In short, the President, like the king, has not merely been constitutionally romanticised but actually vested with a pervasive and persuasive role ... While he plays such a role, he is not a rival centre of power in any sense and must abide by and act on the advice tendered by his ministers except in a narrow territory which is sometimes slippery.[33]

In early 1991, the office of the president was subjected to a controversy. President's invitation to Chandra Shekhar to form government after the fall of V. P. Singh ministry, his reluctance for seven days (from 6 March to 13 March 1991) to dissolve the ninth Lok Sabha as advised by the incumbent Council of Ministers and his singing the proclamation order for dismissal of the Tamil Nadu government without the formality of governor's report are some of the developments that have forced the Presidency to be brought into public scrutiny.

Although the president is obliged to act upon the advice of his ministers, there may be a situation when the advice of a PM is not available (e.g., in case of death) or the advice given by PM is improper (e.g., when a PM defeated in the Lok Sabha requests for its dissolution). In dealing with the first contingency, it can be said that the president shall have the power of acting without ministerial advice during the time taken in choosing a new PM, who of course, must enjoy confidence in the Lok Sabha. In this situation, no Council of Ministers is in existence, that is, in the case of the death of a PM. As far as the situation arising out of a demand for dissolution of the Lok Sabha is concerned, it cannot be said that Council of Ministers does not exist. In view of the amendments of Article 74(1), the president must act on the advice of defeated Council of Ministers

---

[30] *Ram Jawaya v. State of Punjab*, AIR 1955, SC 549.

[31] *U. N. Rao v. Indira*, AIR 1971, SC 1002.

[32] Article 74(1), as it stands after the 44th Constitutional Amendment Act, 1978.

[33] *Shamser Singh v. State of Punjab*, AIR 1974 SC 2192.

even if such advice is improper, for example, on a second occasion of defeat. If, however, the PM did not, the president might exercise the power to dissolve the Lok Sabha. But the president would naturally be circumspect in taking such an important decision on his own.

The Indian Constitution, although embodied the British conception of a Cabinet form of government, curiously did not mention this word of 'cabinet' in its provisions. Thus, constitutionally, the administration of India is conducted in the name of the president, and all orders and other instruments are made and executed in his name, but the president is required to have a Council of Ministers, with the PM as its head, to aid and advise in the exercise of his functions. Although the Council of Ministers is collectively responsible to the House of the People, the Council as such does not meet together to consider any question of policy or administration. It is the Cabinet, which has evolved by convention, and is composed of ministers of the first rank, which takes decisions on all such matters without even bringing the Council into formal consultation.

In general terms, the Constitution stipulates the duties of the PM in his relations with the president. He is required to communicate to the president all decisions of the Council of Ministers, relating to the administration of the Union and all proposals for new legislation, and to furnish such information relating to administration and legislation as the president may seek. The president is also invested with the power to get a decision taken by a minister for consideration by the Council of Ministers before it becomes effective. Constitutionally, therefore, the PM is the only link between the president and the executive. No other minister can, as a matter of right, have a formal talk with the president.

The study indicates that often Articles 352 and 356 are resorted to invoke president's emergency power for political motives. It is revealed, president's power has been used 124 times until 1 March 2015 (under Article 356). When Justice J. Sinha of the Allahabad High Court held PM Mrs Indira Gandhi of corrupt electoral practices and debarred her from holding any public office for six years, she advised the president to declare emergency and he did so on 25 June 1975 by invoking Article 352 on ground of 'internal disturbance'.[34]

B. D. Jatti, the acting president, assented to the proclamation dissolving the nine Congress-ruled state assemblies after reconsideration of the Union Cabinet's advice in 1978. Here, it appeared that the president's motive was 'political'.

On the contrary, President K. R. Narayanan declined to assent the proposed proclamation of president's rule in Uttar Pradesh and sent the document back for reconsideration of the Union Cabinet on 22 October 1997.[35] Similarly, President K. R. Narayanan returned the Cabinet resolution to dismiss the Rabri Devi government on 25 September 1998, as she enjoyed a majority in the Assembly.

The Sarkaria Commission in its report opposed the dismissal of any state government that enjoyed a majority in the state assembly.[36] The unquestioned approval of president's rule by President Pranab Mukherjee, in the two opposition-ruled states of Arunachal Pradesh and

---

[34] Grounds for declaration of Emergency under Article 352 were not ripe. H. M. Seervai writes, 'There was no alarm on the economic front, law and order situation was under control, the Home Ministry had no adverse reports indicating deterioration of law and order'. See H. M. Seervai, *The Constitutional Law of India*, 3rd ed. (Bombay: Tripathi, 1988), 980. In 1975, 39th Amendment Act was passed, debarring jurisdiction of the courts to election disputes involving dignitaries such as president, the vice-president, the PM and the speaker of the Lok Sabha.

[35] On withdrawal of support to the Kalyan Singh government in Uttar Pradesh by the Bahujan Party on 21 October 1997, then Governor Romesh Bhandari recommended to the central government the imposition of president's rule despite the fact that the Kalyan government survived with a 220–0 vote on the one line 'confidence motion'.

[36] R. S. Sarkaria, *Commission on Centre-State Relations*, Report (New Delhi: GoI, 1988).

Uttarakhand, recommended by the Modi government was criticized in the press. It was finally left to the Supreme Court to right the wrong.

The 14th President Ram Nath Kovind, who was sworn in on 25 July 2017, in his maiden speech in Parliament's Central Hall, said, 'The key to India's success is its diversity. Our diversity is the core that makes us so unique. In this land, we find a mix of states and regions, religions, languages, cultures, lifestyles and much more. We are so different and yet so similar'.

Leader of the opposition in Rajya Sabha termed the new president's speech on 25 July 2017 'most unfortunate' for leaving out any mention of 'the architect of modern India', Jawaharlal Nehru, and for referring to Deendayal Upadhyay as 'father of the nation' Mahatma Gandhi.[37]

On balance, it should be noted that, despite the vagueness of the constitutional provisions, the British convention that the sovereign must act solely on the advice of the cabinet should apply equally in the exercise of powers by the President of India.

3.4 Vice-President

The Constitution provides for a vice-president under Article 63. Unlike in the US Constitution, the vice-president does not automatically become the president on that office falling permanently vacant. He acts merely as president until arrangements are made to hold an election.[38] The vice-president is, however, as in the USA, the Chairman of the Council of States (Rajya Sabha). In the event of falling vacancy by reason of death, resignation and removal of president and the vice-president, the Chief Justice of India or, in his absence, the senior most Judge of the Supreme Court available shall discharge the functions until a new president is elected.

When the vice-president discharges the functions of the president, he ceases to perform the duties of the Chairman of the Council of States [Article 65(1)] and is entitled to president's emolument.[39] The monthly salary of the President is ₹5 lakh and that of Vice-President is ₹4 lakh.

3.4.1 Election of Vice-President

The vice-president is elected by an electoral college consisting of two Houses of Parliament by a simple majority vote [Article 66(1)][40] and holds office for a period of five years. In order to be qualified to be elected as the vice-president, a person must be (a) a citizen of India, (b) over 35 years of age and (c) must not hold an office of profit, save that of president, vice-president, governor or minister for the Union or a state. Further, a person must be qualified for election as a member of the Council of States. In case a member of the legislature is elected president or vice-president, he shall be deemed to have vacated his seat in that House of the legislature to which he belongs [Articles 59(1) and 66(2)]. He may be removed by a resolution of the Council of States passed by a majority of its members and agreed to by the House of People (Article 67).

---

[37] These comments came from the mouth of Ghulam Nabi Azad. See *The Times of India* (Chandigarh), 26 July 2017.

[38] Durga Das Basu, *Introduction to the Constitution of India*, 22nd ed. (Gurgaon: LexisNexis, 2015), 193. Basu's this work has been now taken in hand by Mr Justice G. B. Patnaik and V. Das.

[39] In 1969, when on the death of Dr Zakir Hussain, the Vice-President Shri V. V. Giri resigned, the Chief Justice Shri Hidayatullah discharged the functions from 20 July 1969.

[40] The election of the vice-president, like that of the president, shall be indirect and in accordance with the system of proportional representation by means of the single transferable vote.

There is no bar for the incumbent to seek re-election to the office of the vice president, and Dr S. Radhakrishnan was, in fact, elected for a second term in 1957.[41]

3.4.2 Functions of the Vice-President

Unlike the USA, the Chairman of the Council of States (in India) has no administrative responsibilities to fulfil except when he acts as the president until a new president is elected and enters upon the office [Article 65(1)]. He shall discharge the functions of the president during the temporary absence of the president, illness or any other cause by reason of which he is unable to discharge his functions.

3.4.3 Election Dispute

By the 42nd Constitutional Amendment Act, 1976, election to the office of vice-president was made immune from the court jurisdiction. However, the 44th Constitutional Amendment, 1978, set aside this foregoing provision of the 42nd Amendment Act. Now, disputes relating to the election of president or vice-president are dealt with in Article 71 and are decided by the Supreme Court whose 'jurisdiction shall be exclusive and final' [Article 71(1)].

Summary

The powers vested in the president are extensive and comprehensive, but the president is required to have a Council of Ministers, with the PM as its head, to aid and advise in the exercise of his functions. The president's powers to make regulations for the good government of the union territories and states and to issue ordinances are unusual provisions peculiar to the Indian Constitution. There have been many occasions when ordinances (president's rule in states and union territories has been imposed 130 times until 31 March 2017) have been issued almost immediately after Parliament was adjourned. This practice is not only undemocratic but also in conflict with the spirit of the Indian Constitution.

[41] Dr Radhakrishnan remained the Vice-President of India from 13 May 1952 to 12 May 1962.

4 Union Council of Ministers and Governance

LEARNING OBJECTIVES

1. **To discuss the sources of executive power**
2. **To understand the meaning and principles of collective responsibility**
3. **To examine the powers and position of the PM**

Introduction

The Union Council of Ministers is a body closest to the points at which policy decisions are made and are expected to be executed. The Union Council of Ministers consists of senior ministers, called cabinet ministers, and junior ministers, called ministers of state.[1] According to democratic principles, government ought to be political, not administrative. A 'democracy' is government by politicians chosen by the people. Government by civil servants is called 'bureaucracy'. The Constitution of India derives its authority from the people, and it fully recognizes sovereignty of the people in the governance of the country. This people's sovereignty is exercised through Parliament, elected on adult franchise, with a responsible Council of Ministers headed by the PM as its executive instrument.

4.1 Council of Ministers

Before the solemnity of the transfer of power under the Independence Act, 1947,[2] the executive authority for the administration of India was vested in the governor general in council. The members of the executive council were appointed by the King on the recommendations of the governor general and the secretary of state. They held office during His Majesty's pleasure, but, by convention, their tenure of office was fixed for five years. The members of the executive council were given full authority to dispose of non-policy business falling in the specified portfolios given to them by the governor general who himself held the portfolio of foreign and political departments.

[1] As on 15 September 2017, the Union Council of Ministers consisted of 28 ministers of cabinet rank and 54 ministers of state. The council headed by the PM Narendra Modi took over the regime of the central government on 26 May 2014.

[2] In terms of the Indian Independence Act, 1947, His Majesty's government in the UK abrogated all responsibility for the administration of both the dominions, and sovereignty of Parliament was transferred to their respective legislatures.

The governor general had the power to override his council, but all such cases (not so delegated) had to be referred to the Secretary of State who would either confirm, reject or adapt the governor general's decisions. Thus, the GoI mainly exercised powers delegated to it by the Secretary of State, and his orders therefore had to be obtained on matters not so delegated.

It is significant to note that the executive council under the British administration was neither responsible to nor representative of the constituted legislature. It was subject to the control of the authority of the Secretary of State and was bound to carry out all his orders and directions even when these contradicted with the considered views and advice of the council on the administration of the country. The executive council did not have a common outlook or unity of purpose since its composition had both Indian politicians and civil servants appointed by the Crown with governor general as the head. The Indian members of the council used to feel aggrieved until the formation of the interim government in 1946 for they were bypassed by the governor general on many vital issues affecting the political and economic life of the country.

With transfer of power in terms of the Indian Independence Act, 1947, the executive powers were vested in the Council of Ministers contemplated in the Government of India Act, 1935. This established formally the responsibility of the cabinet in the administration of the country.[3] The Constitution enacted on 26 November 1949 embodied the British conception of a cabinet form of government, but it did not express the term 'cabinet' in its provisions, although of course, the details of working of the cabinet system had necessarily to be left to be filled up by convention.[4]

4.1.1 Appointment, Tenure and Salaries of Ministers

Article 74(1) says, 'There shall be a Council of Ministers with the Prime Minister at the head to aid and advise the President who shall, in the exercise of his functions, act in accordance with such advice'.[5] Provided 'that the president may require the Council of Ministers to reconsider such advice, either generally or otherwise, and the president shall act in accordance with the advice tendered after such reconsiderations'.[6]

The PM is appointed by the president and is, by convention, the elected leader of the majority party in the House. Other ministers are appointed by the president on the advice of the PM [Article 75(1)]. As far as the number of ministers to be appointed is concerned, it shall not exceed 15% of the total number of members of the House of the people.[7] In September 2017, the number of ministers was 82.

Further, the president on the advice of the PM determines the rank of the different ministers and also allocates business amongst them (Article 77). In a cabinet form of government, the tenure of the Council of Ministers headed by the prime minister is dependent on the will of the legislature. So far as the selection of the prime minister is concerned, he is appointed by the president and is, by convention, the elected leader of the majority party in the Lower House. A minister may be chosen from members of either House but there is no bar to the appointment of a person from outside the legislature as minister. But, he will cease to be a minister if he has not been elected or

[3] The cabinet formed on 15 August 1947 was composed of a PM, a deputy PM and 12 other ministers.

[4] *Samsher Singh v. State of Punjab*, AIR 1974 SC 2192 (para 27).

[5] Refer to the Constitution (42nd Amendment) Act, 1976.

[6] The Proviso was inserted by the Constitution (44th Amendment) Act, 1978.

[7] Article 75 (91st Amendment), Act 2003 in force from 1 January 2004.

nominated to either of the House before the expiry of six months from the date of his appointment. There is also provision for a minister to address and to take part in the proceedings of the other House, although he cannot make his record in the House of which he is not a member (Article 88). The classification of ministers has now got legislative approval. At the Union level, these are classified into (a) cabinet ministers, (b) ministers of state and (c) deputy ministers.[8] While state ministers are not members of the cabinet, they can attend its meetings only if invited. Similarly, a deputy minister does not deliberate in the meetings of the cabinet; he assists the minister in charge of a department of ministry.

For the salaries and allowances of ministers, the Parliament enacted the Salaries and Allowances of Ministers Act, 1952, under Article 75(6) which entitles the ministers to get the same as payable to MPs. In addition to this, each minister would get a sumptuary allowance at a varying scale, according to his rank and a rent-free house.

4.1.2 Individual and Collective Responsibility

The ministers in the cabinet have both an individual and a collective responsibility. The principle of 'collective responsibility' is embodied in the Constitution. Article 75(3) reads, 'The Council of Ministers shall be collectively responsible to the House of the People'. This doctrine in its application would imply that ministers should speak with one voice on questions of State policy, even when they were not in complete agreement with a particular policy. So, the Council of Ministers shall be under a constitutional discipline to resign as soon as it loses the confidence of the Lok Sabha, even though some of the ministers may not be its members. The Constitution does not, however, define either the manner in which collective responsibility is to be fulfilled or the relations of the PM with the cabinet colleagues he has chosen.

So far as the individual responsibility is concerned, the Constitution does not, however, specify the individual responsibility of a minister to the president and his accountability to Parliament for all acts of omission and commission in his departmental charge. The personal responsibility of each minister to Parliament for matters within his competence is indeed a basic principle of the British Constitution. Article 75(2) thus reads, 'The ministers shall hold office during the pleasure of the President'. This would mean that ministers shall be individually responsible to the executive head and shall be liable to dismissal even when they may have the confidence of the Parliament. Usually the prime minister exercises the power embodied in Article 75(2) against a minister to get rid of him. The one-man commission headed by Justice M. C. Chagla, appointed in January 1958 to investigate into Life Insurance Corporation's scandal, enunciated the principle of ministerial responsibility. The commission in its findings added, 'The minister must take full responsibility for the acts of his subordinates. He cannot be permitted to say that his subordinates did not reflect his policy or acted contrary to his wishes or directions'. The Railway Minister Suresh Prabhu had to resign owning moral responsibility (the PM did not accept his resignation) for the injuries and deaths of many railway passengers due to the train accident on 23 August 2017. He was however shifted to Commerce and Industry Department on 3 September 2017.

Unlike the English principle of legal responsibility under which a minister is liable in a court for his acts, the Constitution of India does not expressly say that the president can act only

[8] Section 2 of the Salaries and Allowances of Ministers Act, 1952, defines 'minister' as a 'Member of the Council of Ministers, by whatever name called, and includes a deputy minister'. A minister gets a salary of ₹250,000 per month which includes allowances per month.

through ministers and leaves it to the president to make rules as to how his orders, etc., are to be authenticated. On other hand, courts are not entitled to enquire into what 'advice was tendered by ministers to the president' [Article 74(2)]. Hence, if an order or instrument made in accordance with rules and executed in the name of the president is authenticated by the Secretary to the GoI, there is little scope for a minister being legally accountable for the order or instrument even though it may have been done on the advice of the minister [adapted under Article 77(2)]. Although the Council of Ministers is collectively responsible to the House of the People, the council as such does not meet together to consider any question of policy or administration. It is the cabinet, which has evolved by convention, and is composed of ministers of the first rank, which takes decisions on all such questions, without even bringing the council into formal consultation. Hence, the other ministers cannot function when the prime minister dies or resigns.

4.1.3 President and the Council of Ministers

From the powers which are vested in an elected president holding for a fixed term, it appears that the president of India is not a figure head; rather, he is a mere constitutional head. The Constitution has been kept deliberately vague about the powers vested in the president, particularly in defining the constitutional position in relation to his Council of Ministers. According to the Constituent Assembly debates,

> The President means the Central cabinet responsible to the whole Parliament. On the other hand … remarkably wide area of discretion makes the President far more than a nominal executive head. In practice, the President has been the head of what Walter Bagehot called 'the dignified parts' of the Constitution.[9]

The original Constitution did not provide that the president was bound to act in accordance with the advice tendered by the Council of Ministers although it was judicially established that the president was a constitutional head of the executive like the British Crown. In *Rao v. Indira*, the Supreme Court observed, 'The Constituent Assembly did not choose the presidential system of Government'.[10]

By the 42nd Amendment Act, 1976, and further by the 44th Amendment Act, 1978, it was clear that the president is just a constitutional head. He cannot go against what the Constitution says, and, in this context, the interpretation of the Supreme Court is final.

The president's new power to return the advice for reconsideration of the Council of Ministers can be exercised only once on the same matter and if the council adheres to its previous advice, the president shall have no power to act in his discretion. This definitely keeps the door open for manoeuvrability and there might arise a tendency to escape political reality under the constitutional provisions to 'preserve, protect and defend the Constitution'.

In a situation when the advice of a PM is not available (e.g., in the case of death),[11] no Council of Ministers exists or the new PM does not command majority in the House of People, the president shall have 'the power of acting without ministerial advice'.

---

[9] See Lok Sabha, *Constituent Assembly Debates*, Vol. 9 (New Delhi: Lok Sabha Secretariat, 1949), 150.

[10] *Rao v. Indira*, AIR 1971 SC 1002 (1005).

[11] *Samsher v. State of Punjab*, AIR 1974, SC 2192 (para 30).

In the second situation, when the defeated PM in the Lok Sabha successively asks for its dissolution,[12] the president must act upon the advice of the defeated Council of Ministers even if such advice is improper, for example, on a second occasion of defeat.

4.1.4 Appointment and Removal of the PM

Article 75(1) states that the 'Prime Minister shall be appointed by the President and the other Ministers shall be appointed by the President on the advice of the Prime Minister'.[13] In selecting the PM, the president is required to invite the leader of the party in majority in the House of the People or a person who is in a position to win the confidence of the majority in that House.[14]

In the event of losing majority in the Lok Sabha and resignation by a PM, the president again invites the leader of the parties who can win the confidence of the majority in the House. But where a leader of the parties fails to do so, the president exercises his discretion in selecting the new PM. The then President Neelam Sanjiva Reddy (1977–82) established certain precedents by acting in discretion in three instances: in rejecting Morarji Desai's request to form a new government after his initial resignation; in insisting that his successor Charan Singh seek a vote of confidence in the Lok Sabha by a specific date; and in his insistence, after Charan Singh's resignation, with a recommendation to call for fresh election upon consulting other party leaders before making the decision himself. Although all three actions by the president were subjected to a lot of controversy, none was inconsistent with parliamentary conventions.[15] A decade later, a comparable situation arose which had to be dealt with by the President R. Venkataraman (1987–92). In December 1989, he appointed V. P. Singh as the head of a minority National Front government, but required him to prove his majority in the Lok Sabha. In March 1991, the V. P. Singh government fell as its predecessor did twelve years earlier, and the president appointed Chandra Shekhar as a minority PM with the support of the Congress in the Lok Sabha. When differences cropped up on certain issues between the PM and the Congress leader Rajiv Gandhi, the president followed the advice of his PM and dissolved the Lok Sabha with a call for fresh election.

Similarly, after the general election in May 1996, the President S. D. Sharma invited A. B. Vajpayee as the leader of Bharatiya Janata Party and its allies (largest single party) to form the government and to seek a vote of confidence. The Vajpayee government resigned after 13 days in the event of failing to prove a majority in the Lok Sabha. The Deve Gowda (United Front) government, which was installed subsequently, had to quit in the event of losing confidence motion (April 1997) in the House following the withdrawal of Congress support. Thus, two precedents have been established with regard to the exercise of presidential power: First, the president may appoint a PM from a minority party and ask him to seek a vote of confidence;

---

[12] Ibid.

[13] The Constitution nowhere provides for the post of deputy prime minister. It is just a matter of description and does not confer on the holder any powers of the prime minister. *K. M. Sharma v. Devi Lal*, AIR 1990.

[14] If the PM is not a member of the Lok Sabha at the time of appointment, then he should become member of the House within six months as we find in the case of Mr P. V. Narasimha Rao. Mrs Indira Gandhi was appointed the prime minister in January 1966 when she was a member of the Rajya Sabha.

[15] For a contrary view, see Barun Sengupta, *Last Days of the Morarji Raj* (Calcutta: Ananda Publishers, 1979), Chapter 10.

second, the president may follow the advice of an outgoing PM in a House lacking a clear majority in dissolving the House with a call for fresh election.

As regards the removal of the PM, Article 75(2) states that 'the Ministers shall hold office during the pleasure of the President'. It implies that the president may dismiss the PM at any time. But he shall have to appoint a new PM immediately to carry on the administration of the country and in that case, new PM shall have to seek vote of confidence within one month by virtue of a convention set by president Neelam Sanjiva Reddy in 1979 or within a couple of months when the session of the Parliament shall be held.

As the PM is not elected directly, he cannot be impeached or removed by the people. The vote of no confidence generally applies to the party laying claim to a majority of the seats in the Lok Sabha. One can assume a scenario where there is a dissent in the majority party or coalition, and successive leaders lose the vote of no confidence until a suitable leader acceptable to the majority is found. If, however, the occupant is disqualified as an MP, say because he is convicted of some crime, then he would have to resign.

4.2 Prime Minister's Power and Role

In a parliamentary form of government, members of the cabinet and within that (cabinet), the PM is almost a presidential figure. What is undisputed, however, is that within the cabinet, the PM wields more powers than his team. What contributes to the present power of the PM is a debatable issue. It is difficult to analyse how much weight should be given to different factors which enhance and constrain the power of the PM.

4.2.1 Sources of Power of Prime Minister

It is often said that powers of the PM have increased in recent years to the point of calling him a dictator. Some of this argument centres on the issue of factors contributing to the present power of the PM. The functions of the PM are not detailed in the Constitution. Yet the statutory recognition to this office has only been recently accorded. First, the PM is said to obtain power from the nature of elections. It is assumed that individual MPs depend for their electoral success on the popularity of their leader of the party. A PM can therefore expect them to regard themselves as mandated to support their leader. In a parliamentary form of government, the PM exercises the power of dismissal by asking an undesirable colleague to resign, which the latter readily complies with in order to avoid the odium of a dismissal.[16]

He can also threaten dissident backbenchers with the dissolution of Parliament. MPs will step into line to avoid the facing of fresh election at which they may not win their parliamentary seats. Few ministers resign in protest against policies they do not approve because doing so would damage the credibility of the government as well as their own political careers (an instance of what happened with Arjun Singh in 1995). When ministers tender resignations, the security of the

[16] In the Hawala racket case, for example, Mr Balram Jakhar and V. C. Shukla resigned from the Union Cabinet in January 1996. Mr Chandradeo Prasad Varma, one of the accused in the multi-crore fodder scam, had to resign from the Union Council of Ministers when the PM I. K. Gujral asked him to do so in May 1977. In the Armsgate issue (*Tehelka*), George Fernandes had to resign in April 2001 on Vajpayee's request.

PM is rarely threatened. The dependence of members of the cabinet on the PM means that he must be regarded as much more than 'first among equals'. No other member of the party leadership shares much more power and status than the PM.

Second, the PM is said to exercise control over the cabinet decision-making process. Although the cabinet as a whole has to be convinced of the rightness of most decisions, the PM's view will not be ignored because of his position. He may be of crucial significance if views in cabinet are evenly divided on an issue. It is therefore no exaggeration to say that cabinet decisions are taken by the PM together with his responsible minister. Moreover, by deciding what should be on the agenda for cabinet meetings and its timings, the PM can obstruct ideas and decisions of which he disapproves. But it is now widely accepted that a PM has to obtain the support and confidence of his cabinet colleagues for his decisions. A PM who continuously defies a cabinet majority and obstructs discussions of matters which his colleagues wish to bring before the cabinet, will have to counter many problems including being forced to modify his views, compromise or even driven out of office.

Third, there is the power of patronage. The PM not only selects the other ministers and allocates portfolios amongst them but can also remove them from office and reshuffle his cabinet. As political head of the civil service, the PM controls the machinery of the government and appointments to the most senior administrative posts in the departments and public enterprises. The power to patronage enables the PM to dominate his cabinet ministers. As in England, they 'can be chopped and changed at will by the Prime Minister'. Prime minister can ensure that the senior posts in the cabinet are held by his personal supporters.[17] In this way, PM can rely on extensive support from them. But experience suggests that men of real ability and persons representing from various regions with mass popularity are being kept out on account of the personal disfavour of the PM. Some, at least, of the balance of view in the party has to be reflected in the cabinet. Dismissal of a minister is not easy unless there is a consensus in the cabinet that he is posing a threat to the government or doing a job badly involving corruption charges. It is much more dangerous for a PM to dismiss a minister who enjoys considerable support within the cabinet and party simply because he opposed the PM's stand on a certain policy issue. The possibility of resignation and therefore injury to the reputation of the government acts as a constraint on a PM in deciding how to handle different issues.

4.2.2 Functions and Position of Prime Minister

The PM has several functions to perform and is described as the 'keystone of the cabinet arch'. Harold Laski says, 'The Prime Minister is central to the life and death of the cabinet'.[18] He 'represents the whole of the executive government in a way that no single member of the Council of Ministers or even the whole of the Council of Ministers can'.[19]

Article 74(1) of the Constitution of India expressly states that the PM is 'at the head' of the Council of Ministers. The implication of this Article is that no other ministers can function when the PM dies or resigns.

Being the leader of the party in majority, the PM does not only select the ministers of his choice but can also require any of them to resign. Besides allocating business amongst them, the prime

[17] J. P. Mackintosh, *The British Cabinet*, 2nd ed. (London: Methuen, 1968), 623.

[18] Harold J. Laski, *Parliamentary Government in England* (London: Allen, 1945), 228.

[19] S. S. Khera, *The Central Executive* (New Delhi: Orient Longman, 1975), 92.

minster can transfer any of the ministers from one department to another. The power of advising the president as regards the appointment of other ministers is thus embodied in Article 75(1). As to the function of acting as the channel of communication between the president and the Council of Ministers, Article 78 provides that it shall be the duty of the PM:

1. to communicate to the president all decisions of the Council of Ministers relating to the administration of the affairs of the Union and proposals for legislation;
2. to furnish such information relating to the administration of the affairs of the Union and proposals for legislation as the president may call for; and
3. if the president so requires to submit for the consideration of the Council of Ministers any matter on which a decision has been taken by a minister but which has not been considered by the council.

Constitutionally, therefore, the PM is the only link between the president and the Council of Ministers. As a matter of fact, no other minister can have an audience with the president. Besides the sources of power that strengthen his position, the PM performs some important functions. The PM is responsible for aiding and advising the president in distribution of work of the government to various ministries and offices and in terms of GoI (Allocation of Business) Rules, 1961. The coordinating work is generally allocated to the cabinet secretariat (CS). While generally the work of the government is divided into various ministries, the PM may retain certain portfolios if they are not allocated to any member of the cabinet.

The PM represents the country in various delegations, high level meetings and international organizations that require the attendance of the highest government officer and also addresses to the nation on various issues of national or international importance. In addition to the exercise of the traditional powers of a PM in a parliamentary democracy in the selection of his colleagues, allocation of portfolios, determination of the business of the cabinet and constitution of cabinet committees and *ad hoc* committees, it is for him to nominate for the formal approval of the president, the governors of the states and the ambassadors and other diplomatic representatives of the country abroad.

The PM is in-charge of coordinating the policy of the government and has, accordingly, a right of supervision over all the departments. Article 78 defines, also in general terms, the duties of the PM in his relation with the president. The PM is required to communicate to the president all decisions of the Council of Ministers, relating to the administration of the Union, and all proposals for new legislation and to furnish such information relating to administration and legislation, as the president may call for. The president has also the right to direct that a decision taken by a minister be submitted for consideration by the Council of Ministers before it becomes effective. Constitutionally, therefore, the PM is the only link between the president and the Council of Ministers.

4.2.3 Conclusion

There is a whole range of debatable points connected with the PM's personality and style of functioning. Some PMs (for example, Mrs Indira Gandhi during the emergency period between June 1975 and March 1977) exercise considerable power, while others are surrounded by experienced and powerful men. The power of the PM is visible when he is defending his own position as the leader and determining the fate of his colleagues. The extent to which he exercises numerous

Table 4.1 Prime Ministers of India

S. No.	Name	Tenure
1.	Jawaharlal Nehru (1889–1964)	From 15 August 1947 to 27 May 1964 (died)
2.	Gulzari Lal Nanda (1898–1998)	From 27 May 1964 to 9 June 1964 (Acting)
3.	Lal Bahadur Shastri (1904–66)	From 9 June 1964 to 11 January 1966 (died)
4.	Gulzari Lal Nanda (1898–1998)	From 11 January 1966 to 24 January 1966 (Acting)
5.	Indira Gandhi (1917–84)	From 24 January 1966 to 24 March 1977
6.	Morarji Desai (1896–1995)	From 24 March 1977 to 28 July 1979
7.	Charan Singh (1902–87)	From 28 July 1979 to 14 January 1980
8.	Indira Gandhi (1917–84)	From 14 January 1980 to 31 October 1984 (died)
9.	Rajiv Gandhi (1944–91)	From 31 October 1984 to 2 December 1989
10.	Vishwanath Pratap Singh (1931–2008)	From 2 December 1989 to 10 November 1990
11.	Chandra Shekhar (1927–2007)	From 10 November 1990 to 21 June 1991
12.	P. V. Narasimha Rao (1921–2004)	From 21 June 1991 to 16 May 1996
13.	Atal Bihari Vajpayee (b. 1924)	From 16 May 1996 to 1 June 1996
14.	H. D. Deve Gowda (b. 1933)	From 1 June 1996 to 20 April 1997
15.	I. K. Gujral (1919–2012)	From 21 April 1997 to 19 March 1998
16.	Atal Bihari Vajpayee (b. 1924)	From 19 March 1998 to 22 May 2004
17.	Manmohan Singh (b. 1932)	From 22 May 2004 to 26 May 2014
18.	Narendra Modi (b. 1950)	From 26 May 2014 till date

functions on his own depends largely on his personality and standing in the party as well his image in the public opinion. It has been stated that the PM's job is to 'seek to reconcile collective rule with the individual responsibility of ministers to Parliament'. Obviously, the role and functions of the PM could hardly be explained with precise definition.

Nevertheless, in the ultimate analysis, the strength of the PM lies in popular support as PM Narendra Modi commands. Once the position has accepted that the real power of government is vested in the Council of Ministers, subject only to parliamentary control, the logical conclusion is reached that the PM is the repository of executive power. The position of the PM in the Constitution is thus unique, and his powers are more extensive than those of the president in the USA.

4.3 Union Cabinet: Power and Role

The Constitution does not express the term 'cabinet'; instead, it uses Council of Ministers. In the Indian parliamentary system, the cabinet is the most important government institution. It is the executive instrument of the Parliament, fully answerable to it for its acts of omission and commission. As it is responsible to Parliament and the presidential powers are also exercisable on the advice of the Council of Ministers (virtually the cabinet), these powers should be considered to be flowing from the authority of Parliament. While its functions and responsibilities were understood and appreciated with the transfer of power in 1947, steps had yet to be taken to develop fully a sense of collective responsibility and to secure the necessary measure of coordination in the working of machinery of government. Under the parliamentary system, the Council of Ministers is collectively responsible to the Lok Sabha (House of the People), yet it does not meet regularly to consider any question of policy or administration. On the other hand, it is the cabinet comprising ministers of the first rank, which takes decisions on all such questions without even bringing the council into formal consultation. The ministers in the cabinet, as already pointed out, have both an individual and collective responsibility. The individual responsibility of the minister to Parliament for matters within his competence is, indeed, the English principle (this principle has not been adopted in our Constitution). On the other hand, although the ministers are collectively responsible to the Lok Sabha [Article 75(3)], they are individually responsible to the Executive head and also liable to dismissal [Article 75(2)] even when they have the confidence of the Lok Sabha. The principle of collective responsibility in its application would mean that ministers should speak with one voice on the questions of State policy.

Within the government, there is a 'ranking and packing order' in general and the cabinet in particular. Some ministers are more senior and experienced than others in the cabinet. What is undisputed is that the prime minister is 'at the head' of the Council of Ministers [Article 74(1)]. Hence, the other cabinet ministers cannot function when the prime minister dies or resigns. Let us now look at the sources of cabinet power.

First, it is the constitutional task of the cabinet to decide the policies which are to be brought before the Parliament for their discussion and approval. Second, once a cabinet decision has been taken, ministers should speak with one voice or resign. The doctrine of collective responsibility usually enables the cabinet to ensure a rule of discipline. Mackintosh says, 'It is essential for a strong government to show a united front in face of criticism'.[20] Third, the cabinet is able to secure coordination in the executive through the CS. Each minister in the Council of Ministers now is enabled to receive the cabinet decisions, and it is his responsibility to see that these are complied with in so far as they need departmental action. The CS also assists the cabinet in its other functions of policy decisions.

In a parliamentary system, the control of the entire administrative system of the Union has come to be vested in the cabinet. It is the supreme executive authority being the inner body of the Council of Ministers. It is the source of political authority. The members of the cabinet are closest to the points at which policy decisions are made and much of legislation initiated. Important bills are initiated and piloted through the Parliament by the members of the cabinet. Further, it is the cabinet that coordinates the work of all ministers. All major appointments reserved for action by the president under the Constitution, for example, attorney general, members of the UPSC, chief election commissioner, judges of the Supreme Court and high courts, governors of states and so on are made by him on the recommendation of the PM and in consultation with the minister of the department concerned. This power of patronage enhances the position of executive leadership.

Although the Union cabinet has a very important and challenging role to play in the administration, it is not without shortcomings. It is argued that when the president imposed emergency on 26 June 1975 on the late PM Mrs Gandhi's advice, there was no prior consultation

[20] Mackintosh, *The British Cabinet*, 16.

with the cabinet and that it was informed only after the proclamation had been made. One MP, Madhu Limaye, states,

> The cabinet form of government was undoubtedly twisted out of shape during the Premiership of Indira Gandhi, especially after the Congress split in 1969. During the emergency, it was reduced to mockery. Rajiv Gandhi has not only eroded the cabinet Government, he has further undermined it. His cronies dominate the decision-making process from outside the cabinet; within the cabinet Ministers are afraid to speak out their mind. Cabinet meetings are not the forum of serious discussion of policies; they are the occasions for competitive adulation of the leader.[21]

However, since June 2014, there is a change for better in the functioning of the cabinet at the Union level. Once the position is accepted that real power of government is vested in the Council of Ministers subject only of parliamentary control, the logical corollary is reached that a PM has to obtain the support of the cabinet for his decisions and cannot obstruct discussion of matters which his colleagues want to bring before the cabinet. The approval by the Union cabinet to wage policy framework for Public Sector Undertaking (PSU) workers on 23 November 2017 is an example.

4.4 Central Cabinet Committees

On the analogy of the pattern evolved in the British parliamentary system, cabinet committees have been constituted at the Union level for speedy disposal of the business of the cabinet. It may be that the real business of collective decision making in central government takes place in cabinet committees rather than the full cabinet. In the words of Morrison, 'this device enables ministers to bargain and compromise with each other and thus, reduces pressure of work upon the cabinet. Consequently, the cabinet is left free to devote itself to more important matters'.[22]

The flexible system of government in committees facilitates disposal of works. An elaborate network of cabinet committees strengthens the position of individual ministers as much as, if not more than that of the PM, by increasing the flow of information and opportunity for participation in decision-making. These committees ease coordination in particular well-defined fields of administration as well as afford opportunities for reconciliation of divergence of views. Thus, ministers who are not on the cabinet are members of one or more committees.

Thus, with a view to making expeditious and efficient disposal of the innumerable and complex problems of a welfare state, it is becoming imperative to constitute various cabinet committees. The number, scope and membership of these committees varied from time to time to suit the situation confronting the PM. Usually a committee consists of 3–8 members. The chairman of a committee is either the PM or a cabinet minister. There are standings as well as *ad hoc* committees set up either by the cabinet on the proposal of the PM or directly by the PM. The committees, which function on a permanent basis, more or less are the Political Affairs Committee, Committee on Parliamentary Affairs, Appointments Committee, Committee on Accommodation and Committee on Economic Affairs.

[21] Madhu Limaye, *Cabinet Government in India* (New Delhi: Radiant, 1989), 196.

[22] H. Morrison, *Government and Parliament* (London: Oxford University Press, 1954), 7.

4.4.1 Evolution of Committees

Soon after India's independence, two standing committees, namely, the Defence Committee and Economic Committee, were set up. In due course, there were created three more Committees—the Priorities Committee, the Rehabilitation Committee and the Resources Committee. N. Gopalaswami Ayyangar, the minister without portfolio charged with the responsibility of formulating proposals for the reorganization of the machinery of government (appointed in July 1948), recommended in his report (1949) the setting up of standing committees of cabinet. The Report states,

> [I]t is essential that there should be a proper division of labour, and effective delegation within the cabinet. This need is widely accepted in principle, and is also in accord with actual development in recent years. All that is now necessary is to recognise this position, and rationalize and establish on a permanent basis, the system of delegations which is growing up.[23]

Accordingly, on the recommendation of the Ayyangar Report (1949), the union government set up in May 1950 four standing committees on defence, economic, parliamentary and legal affairs, and administrative organization, the last being set up on an *ad hoc* basis. A fifth standing committee was soon added to the list in the form of the Appointments Committee. Each committee was given adequate secretarial assistance either from the CS or from the ministry.

In 1957, these five standing committees were abolished and ten new standing committees were set up on economic affairs, heavy industry, defence, foreign affairs, rehabilitation, scientific matters, parliamentary and legal affairs, information and broadcasting, and appointments.

Finding ill functioning of the committees, Asok Chanda, the then Comptroller and Auditor General of India, in his note to the Union cabinet in 1958, made two alternative suggestions to improve the working of the committee system. A better solution, according to him, was 'to introduce decentralised coordination by grouping ministries with interrelated functions together and placing these groups under the central supervision of senior ministers without portfolio'. As an alternative, Chanda suggested the creation of a super cabinet as an emergency measure to provide 'supreme direction' to the executive. No adequate attention was paid to these recommendations. But an important committee was set up in the wake of the Chinese invasion in 1962, namely, the Emergency Committee. It consisted of the PM as the chairman and finance, home and defence ministers. In course of time, this committee, according to Brecher, 'virtually replaced the cabinet as the supreme decision-making body in the Government of India'.[24] In course of time, however, its influence waned and it lost its predominant position. The Study Team on the Machinery of GoI, in its report (March 1967) recommended its replacement by the Committee of Defence and Foreign Affairs. Commenting on the working of the cabinet committees, the Study Team of the Administrative Reforms Commission (ARC) observed:

> But such committees can provide an effective alternative only if they are operated in a manner substantially different to what is today the case. Some of the committees have hitherto not been meeting regularly, while some others have almost fallen into disuse. Most Cabinet Committees are loaded with cabinet ministers; some ministers of state do not figure at all in any Cabinet Committee, even though they are in independent charge of ministries; no deputy minister is included anywhere. Significant sections of the Council of Ministers are, therefore, excluded from the deliberative apparatus of the cabinet. The subjects covered by the cabinet

---

[23] N. Gopalaswami Ayyangar, *Report on Reorganisation of the Machinery of Government* (New Delhi: GoI, 1949), para 23.
[24] M. Brecher, *Succession in India: A Study in Decision Making* (London: OUP, 1966), 1021.

committees in existence today range from the most important (emergency and economic coordination) to the almost trivial (location of offices in Delhi). The Committee on industries consists of three cabinet Ministers and 'the minister of the ministry or department concerned'; this is an unsatisfactory method of constituting a committee. Committees are empowered to take decisions only if matters have been referred to them by order of minister concerned or by the cabinet; thus neither the Prime Minister nor the Chairman of a committee can refer a matter for decision in committee.

The ARC in its report (September 1969) made the following recommendation with a view to improving the functioning of the committees:

1. There should be set up 11 standing committees—one each for defence; foreign affairs; economic affairs; parliamentary affairs and public relations; food and rural development; transport, tourism and communications; social services (including social welfare and family planning); commerce, industry and science; internal affairs (including centre–state relations); administration; and appointments.
2. Membership of each committee should not normally exceed six and should include all ministers in-charge of subjects covered by the committee.
3. Every standing committee should be supported by a committee of secretaries which will consider in advance all matters to be taken up by the cabinet committee.
4. *Ad hoc* committees should be retained which should be confined to mere investigation and not decision-making.

Although the central government did not accept these recommendations, yet these are of immense importance to improve working of the committees. The Janata government that came to power in March 1977 made extensive use of committees, namely, Accommodation Committee, Appointments Committee, Economic Affairs Committee, Parliamentary Affairs Committee and Political Affairs Committee. Subsequently, variations in their nomenclature and membership with each major change in government were not unusual.

As on 20 March 2013, there were 10 standing committees of the cabinet. These were the Appointments Committee, Cabinet Committee on Accommodation (CCA), Cabinet Committee on Economic Affairs (CCEA), Cabinet Committee on Parliamentary Affairs, Cabinet Committee on Political Affairs (CCPA), Cabinet Committee on Prices, Cabinet Committee on Security (CCS), Cabinet Committee on World Trade Organization Matters, Cabinet Committee on Investment and Cabinet Committee on Unique Identification Authority of India related issues.

On 10 June 2014, the Modi government decided to discontinue the following four standing committees of the cabinet: Cabinet Committee on Management of Natural Calamities, Cabinet Committee on Prices, Cabinet Committee on World Trade Organization Matters and Cabinet Committee on Unique Identification Authority of India. On 19 June 2014, the GoI reconstituted six committees of the cabinet that are discussed here in brief.

1. *Cabinet Committee on Political Affairs (CCPA):* CCPA was set up in May 2014 and is chaired by the PM. It is also known as 'Super cabinet' as it is the most important of all. It deals with all policy matters pertaining to domestic and foreign affairs. Besides the PM, 10 cabinet ministers are members of the CCPA.
2. *Appointments Committee of the Cabinet (ACC):* ACC is composed of the PM (who is the chairman) and the Minister of Home Affairs. The Establishment Officer's division processes all proposals for senior appointments in the GoI that require approval of the ACC under the

GoI Transactions of Business Rules, 1961. These include board-level appointments in PSUs and appointments to the posts at the level of joint secretary. In addition, all appointments by promotion that require ACC approval are processed through the Establishment Officer's division.

3. *Cabinet Committee on Economic Affairs (CCEA):* CCEA is one of the standing committees of the cabinet constituted by GoI. It comprises the PM (chairman), minister of home affairs, minister of external affairs, minister of finance and seven more cabinet ministers.

   Some of the major functions of the CCEA are: reviewing economic trends and evolving an economic policy framework for the country; coordinating policies and activities in the economic field including foreign investment; reviewing progress of activities in rural development and fixation of prices of agriculture products; reviewing performance of PSUs and price controls of industrial raw materials and products and disinvestments matters; and facilitating finalization factual reports on the accomplishments of the ministries, agencies and PSUs involved in projects for evaluation.[25]
4. *Cabinet Committee on Parliamentary Affairs:* The Cabinet Committee on Parliamentary Affairs, headed by the home minister is mandated to recommend the dates of Parliament sessions. It has 11 members, including 3 special invitees. It also watches the progress of government business in Parliament and gives such directions as may be necessary from time to time in order to secure smooth and efficient conduct of such business.
5. *Cabinet Committee on Accommodation (CCA):* The CCA is chaired by the minister of home affairs. Besides the home minister, seven cabinet ministers are the forming part of this committee. It mainly deals with accommodation problems of the ministers and top positions in the GoI.
6. *Cabinet Committee on Security (CCS):* The CCS of the government decides on India's defence expenditure, matters of national security and makes significant appointments. CCS is chaired by the PM and comprised of the minister of defence, the minister of finance, minister of home affairs, and the minister of external affairs.

In addition to these six cabinet committees, there are *ad hoc* committees which may be set up by the prime minister to deal with problems of national importance.

4.4.2 Conclusion

The PM himself is the chairman of four out of the six committees and the home minister is a member of all the committees and the chairman of two. In every cabinet committee, there are likely to be special invitees and political leaders who may be powerful in influencing policies. An analysis of the composition of the standing committees brings out this point that appointments to these committees have been made more on personal considerations than on the consideration of bringing only the ministers concerned together in relevant committees. The purpose of forming cabinet committees for securing coordination and for reaching quick decisions might also be largely defeated since these committees now include the bulk of the cabinet ministers. Second, practically all the committees are presided over by the prime minister, and therefore the cabinet might be hesitant to function as a revisionary authority and be content to play the role of a

[25] On 12 September 2017, the CCEA, chaired by the PM, has approved the 161 km long Barabanki–Akbarpur doubling project for promoting speedy, reliable and safe service.

recording authority. It is becoming increasingly evident that a high-level comprehensive examination of the machinery of government should now be undertaken to give the administration the form and purpose necessary for the realization of the objectives of a welfare state.

4.5 Cabinet Secretariat

4.5.1 Historical Background

Cabinet secretariat (CS) is the most important institution in the structure of central administration. It is this institution which aids the cabinet in its functioning. The origin of this institution dates back to November 1935 when the private secretary to Governor General Lord Wellington (1931–36) was designated as secretary to the executive council for recording its proceedings and providing assistance to him. Shortly afterwards, the two functions, namely, acting as private secretary to the governor general and at the same time as secretary to the council, were separated and were assigned to two different persons to be appointed as secretary to the executive council. With effect from 5 September 1946, the date of formation of the interim government, an office known as the Council Secretariat came into existence. This secretariat served the executive council as also the Coordination Committee of the Council set up in 1945.

With the dawn of Independence, the existing CS was combined with the Prime Minister's Secretariat. However, these were soon separated and N. R. Pillai was appointed as the cabinet secretary in 1950. Earlier, H. M. Patel remained the cabinet secretary for a brief period. With a view of securing all relevant data from the various ministries/departments, an economic and statistical coordination unit was set up in the CS in 1948, but, in 1950, it was transferred to the newly constituted Planning Commission. In its place, a Central Statistical Unit was attached to the CS. In May 1961, with the setting up of the Central Statistical Organization, the Unit was merged with the latter.

Following the acceptance of the recommendation made by Paul H. Appleby in 'Public Administration in India: Report of a Survey' (1953), an Organization and Methods division was set up as a wing of the CS, with a view to improve administrative efficiency in all branches of government. In March 1964, a new Department of Administrative Reforms was set up in the Ministry of Home Affairs and the Organization and Methods division was transferred to this department.

Perhaps the most important change made, as a result of the recommendations of the ARC, was the creation of a central personnel agency in the CS in August 1970 and the transfer of the department of administrative reforms from the home ministry to the CS in February 1973.

The CS in June 1975 had two departments under it, namely, the Department of Personnel and Administrative Reforms and the Department of Cabinet Affairs. The Janata Party at the centre in March 1977 brought about a reorganization of the central government in the Department of Personnel and Administrative Reforms which has been attached to the home ministry. The organization of the CS and its role have been constantly shifting with the reorganization of the executive functions of the union government.

4.5.2 Functions and Role of the Central Secretariat

The CS is responsible for the administration of the GoI. It functions from the secretariat building (New Delhi) where most of the cabinet ministers work. It supervises and coordinates the functions of the cabinet ministers which constitutes the CS. The PM being the in-charge of his cabinet, the entire gamut of governmental activities comes under the purview of this organization.

Central Secretariat is a 'staff agency'. The CS is responsible for secretarial assistance to the cabinet, its committees and *ad hoc* groups of ministers, and for the maintenance of record of their decisions and proceedings. Its administrative head is 'cabinet secretary' who is charged with the responsibility for ensuring coordination at the administrative level. Important functions coming under the purview of the CS (Department of cabinet Affairs) are as follows:

1. To prepare agenda for the meetings of the cabinet
2. To maintain the records of proceedings and decisions of the cabinet and its committees
3. To monitor implementation of the decisions/directions of the cabinet/cabinet committees/groups of ministers
4. To manage the administration of the GoI (Transaction of Business) Rules, 1961, and the GoI (Allocation of Business) Rules, 1961, and facilitate smooth transaction of business in ministries/departments of the government by ensuring adherence to these rules
5. To assist in decision-making in government by ensuring inter-ministerial coordination, ironing out differences amongst ministries/departments and evolving consensus through the instrumentality of the standing/*ad hoc* committees of secretaries
6. To ensure that the president, the vice-president and ministers are kept informed of the major activities of all ministries/departments by means of monthly summary of their activities; and managing major crisis situations in the country and coordinating activities of various ministries in such a situation
7. To prepare and provide such information and material as is necessary for the deliberations of the cabinet, cabinet committees and groups of ministers

In addition, following cases are brought to the CS on which it is expected to provide assistance and information to the cabinet:

1. Cases involving legislation including the issuing of ordinances
2. Addresses and messages of the president to the Parliament
3. Proposals to summon or prorogue the Parliament or dissolve the Lok Sabha
4. Cases involving negotiations with foreign countries on treaties, agreements, and so on
5. Proposals for sending delegations of persons abroad in any capacity
6. Proposals to appoint public committees of enquiry and consideration of reports of such committees of enquiry
7. Cases involving financial implications
8. Cases that a minister puts to the cabinet for decision and direction
9. Cases of disagreements among ministries
10. Proposals to vary or reverse decisions
11. Cases which the president or the prime minister may require to be put before the cabinet

A number of development schemes are formulated by the centre, but implemented by the states. The progress of implementation of the centrally sponsored schemes is sometimes reviewed by the cabinet secretary and necessary suggestions are issued by him to the state government to improve the effectiveness and efficiency of execution of the schemes. For example, the Direct Benefit Transfer (DBT) scheme has been shifted in 2015 to Cabinet Secretariat and its implementation is being monitored by the Prime Minister's Office (PMO) so that its benefits reach out to individual beneficiaries directly.[26]

The role of the CS could be seen in operation in the case of disaster caused by Cyclone Phailin in October 2013 in Odisha when the cabinet secretary took special interest in the restoration of connectivity or telecom services. An important function of the CS is to not only communicate to the ministry concerned the decision of the cabinet or the cabinet committees and follow up its implementation but also to perform inter-ministerial coordination that involves matters relating to delay, differences and coordination of policies.

In recent years, the rise of the Prime Minister's Secretariat has become centralized, owing to the formation of a large secretariat with many whole time advisers on various issues and a host of full-time service officers in-charge of different subjects. This has caused unnecessary centralization of power and reduction of the powers of the ministers and departmental secretaries. The CS, originally conceived for securing coordination should not itself become a de-coordinating agency. It should serve the cabinet and its committees.

The Second ARC in its 13th Report on Organizational Structure of GoI (April 2009) recommended,

> There is need to ensure that the existing coordination mechanisms like the Group of Ministers and the Committee of Secretaries function effectively and help in early resolution of issues ... Unresolved issues concerning States which require Inter-Ministerial coordination in Government of India, should be placed before the Committee of Secretaries and then to the Union cabinet for resolution.[27]

As an important body of the government, the CS has to play its creative, functional, informative and coordinative role in the cabinet functioning. By preparing the agenda for cabinet meetings, taking minutes, circulating decisions and following them up to see that action has been taken in the departments, the CS appears to be running the government. Being recognized as the nerve centre of governance, the CS is responsible for translating innovative ideas coming from either the prime minister or his colleagues.

4.6 Union Cabinet Secretary

Immediately below the political head, there is the CS, headed by cabinet secretary. As the title goes, the cabinet secretary is the administrative head of the cabinet. When the Viceroy's executive council[28] was renamed as the cabinet on 5 September 1946 (on the formation of the interim government), its Secretary Sir Eric Coates became cabinet secretary who was later replaced by H. M.

---

[26] The DBT scheme was launched on 1 January 2013 with regard to 24 schemes and now its scope has been expanded to include all welfare subsidy schemes operated by the eight Union ministries and departments, such as, LPG, wages under Mahatma Gandhi National Rural Employment Guarantee Act (MGNREGA) and National Social Assistance Programme. See *Indian Express* (Chandigarh), 9 May 2016.

[27] GoI, Second ARC, *Organizational Structure of Government of India* (New Delhi: GoI, April 2009), 164–65, para 5.12.

[28] The executive council (precursor of the cabinet) of the Viceroy of India used to have a Secretariat, which was headed by the Private Secretary of the Viceroy. Initially the role of this secretariat was merely taking care of the paper work related to the executive council. As work of the individual departments (precursor of ministries) under the council increased, the work of the Secretariat too became more complex. The Private Secretary came to be known as the Secretary of the Secretariat, and this post became more powerful over time as the Secretariat's main role became coordinating work of departments. In 1946, the Secretariat became CS and the Secretary became cabinet secretary.

Patel followed by N. R. Pillai. The cabinet secretary is generally the senior most civil servant of the IAS cadre and such a status was recommended by Gopalaswami Ayyangar:

> He (the cabinet secretary) should be an administrative officer of the highest rank, selected for the office for his special qualities of tact, energy, initiative, and efficiency and he should be entrusted as head of the Cabinet Secretariat with the positive function of securing co-ordination as well as timely and effective action by all departments of the Government of India in all matters in which the cabinet as a whole or the Prime Minister is interested. He should be a person commanding the respect and confidence of all ranks of the permanent services.[29]

Although in the official Warrant of Precedence, he occupies the highest place among the civil servants, his tenure does not last more than two to three years. (In Britain, cabinet secretary holds office for nearly 10 years or even more.) The Second ARC of the GoI (April 2009) had suggested a 3–4 years tenure for cabinet secretary but, the position has not changed.

4.6.1 Functions and Role of Cabinet Secretary

By virtue of his position in the power structure, cabinet secretary exercises much more influence in the decision-making body of the cabinet than his formal position suggests. Although his function is to provide secretariat assistance to the cabinet, he sits near the PM in the cabinet meetings and briefs the PM personally. He transforms the actual proceedings of cabinet into the form of the cabinet minutes (i.e., he puts in what is better and relevant). Although he keeps an eye upon the smooth functioning of the working of the ministries and departments, he does not have supervisory function over any of them. He is the head of the civil service and ensures that the morale of the civil servants is kept high. He protects the interests of them in situations of conflict between politicians and civil servants.

Following are the important functions of cabinet secretary in brief:

1. To act as chief advisor to the PM
2. To provide assistance to the Council of Ministers
3. To act as advisor and conscience keeper of all civil servants
4. To handle senior appointments in the government sector
5. To prepare the agenda of the cabinet and attend the cabinet's meetings
6. To ensure that the cabinet decisions reach individual ministers and are implemented
7. To act as the chairman of the Chief Secretaries' Committee and Committee of Secretaries on Administration
8. To assist the CS in decision-making in government by ensuring inter-ministerial coordination, ironing out differences amongst ministries/departments and evolving consensus through the instrumentality of the standing/*ad hoc* committees of secretaries

Dwarakadas observes that 'he is a sort of advisor and conscience-keeper to all the permanent officials'.[30] In this connection, the Ayyangar Report comments:

[29] Ayyangar, *Report on Reorganisation*, 30.

[30] R. Dwarkadas, *Role of Higher Civil Service* (Bombay: Popular, 1958), 41.

> While not laying on the Cabinet Secretariat any specific functions which would impair the initiative and responsibility of heads of departments, I think, it would be desirable to establish the convention that he should be a sufficiently senior officer so as to command the confidence and respect of all heads of departments. I would further recommend that he should be ex-officio president of the committee of secretaries set up to advise the Prime Minister and other Ministers on selections for administrative appointments.[31]

The role of cabinet secretary has been very well described by Khera:

> The cabinet secretary provides the eyes and ears for the Prime Minister to keep in touch with the process of official business in the central government. But he is in no sense the watchdog or invigilator on behalf of the Prime Minister. The worst thing that could happen would be for any member of the Council of Ministers to feel that the cabinet secretary or for that matter any other official, is sent to spy on him, or that the official may have the ear of the Prime Minister to carry tales. The cabinet secretary's is a very general staff function, not a line function in relation to the Ministers. His business is to help, not to oversee ... There are two other rather out of the ordinary functions performed by the cabinet secretary. The first is when the cabinet secretary has to act on his own authority and responsibility without the benefit of resort to the Prime Minister ... [Second, the] cabinet secretary may also be called to serve on occasions as a sort of general official factotum, whom the Prime Minister deems thus to be necessary.[32]

More recently, it is observed that the senior most civil servant is not placed in the high position of the civil service structure. In 1981, Mrs Indira Gandhi appointed the new cabinet secretary a year earlier while superseding three civil servants. Rajiv Gandhi also followed the same practice in 1985. Further, in 1986, cabinet secretary was shifted when he had one more year's service left. When the National Front government came to power, V. P. Singh also superseded several civil servants while appointing a new cabinet secretary in place of the then cabinet secretary. This post must not be politicized. 'No doubt it is the privilege of the party in power, i.e., the Prime Minister to have a cabinet secretary of his choice but he cannot completely ignore the serious objections of the opposition parties, especially the main one'.

Dissatisfied with the working of the cabinet secretary, the Deshmukh Study Team observed,

> It seems to us that the forceful and steady direction that good management … requires has not been forthcoming from this apex point in sufficient measure with the result that there has been a feeling of 'helplessness' about the senior management of the Government of India. A major reason for this is that the cabinet secretary has not been allotted a clear enough role, and a strong enough position in relation to personnel administration generally and the management of senior management in particular'.[33]

The Second ARC (April 2009) suggested that the 'role of the cabinet secretary should not be limited to that of a coordinator. He should also act as the principal advisor of the Prime Minister, the cabinet and the cabinet committees on important policy matters'.[34] Thus as an important functionary of the power structure, cabinet secretary must be recognized as having a politico-administrative role in the democratic process of India.

---

[31] Ayyangar, *Report on Reorganisation*, para 44.

[32] Khera, *The Central Executive*, 181–83.

[33] ARC, *Machinery of the Government of India and its Procedure of Work*, Report (New Delhi: GoI, 1968).

[34] Second ARC, *Thirteenth Report (on) Organizational Structure of Government of India* (New Delhi: GoI, 2009), 54 (para 4).

4.7 Prime Minister's Office (PMO)

Since Independence, the Prime Minister's Secretariat (now popularly known as PMO) has grown into a high profile component of the GoI. Many a time, the PMO has usurped the powers of the CS. Often the PMO interfered with the functioning of various ministries and departments undermining the latter's position. Officials who were part of the PMO acquired power of their own in the name of the prime minister. After Jawaharlal Nehru, the first prime minister of Independent India, the successive prime ministers put in their best to reduce its size and influence, but largely they failed to do so. Michael Brecher commented, 'There is ample evidence to indicate that the PM's Secretariat through the forceful personality of L. K. Jha has become major power centre in all India politics.'[35]

It is to Nehru's credit that during his long term of prime ministership from August 1947 to May 1964, 'he had a very small personal office and the importance of the Cabinet Secretariat was in no way affected'.[36]

Recognizing the importance of the PMO, P. N. Dhar (who became the head of the PMO during Lal Bahadur Shastri's tenure) wrote,

> Increasing complexity of governance in India today, which makes the Prime Minister deal with contenders for power and deal with socio-economic and political complexities at home and abroad, cannot be dealt with by him with the help of his cabinet without a score of specialized advisors on the pattern of the US President.[37]

4.7.1 Composition of the PMO

The PMO consists of the immediate staff of the prime minister as well as multiple levels of support staff reporting to the PM. The PMO is headed by the principal secretary, supported by one additional principal secretary, one secretary, one additional secretary, five joint secretaries, two private secretaries, six directors, six deputy secretaries, one public relations officer, one information officer, four officers on special duty (OSD), one joint director, five under secretaries, one reference officer and one research officer. In addition to these personnel, there is one national security advisor to the PM.

The PMO was originally called the Prime Minister's Secretariat until 1977, when it was designated as PMO during the prime ministership of Morarji Desai (March 1977–July 1979). The PMO is a part of the GoI's structure.[38]

During the tenure of Jawaharlal Nehru as the PM, the then secretariat was headed by a joint secretary until his death on 27 May 1964.[39] It was only during Indira Gandhi's first tenure of office

---

[35] Cited in Sarla Mallik, *The Prime Minister of India: Power and Functions* (Pillai: Chinta Prakashan, 1984), 55.

[36] B. G. Deshmukh, 'Prime Minister's Office: We Cannot and Need Not Do Without It', in *Fifty Years of Indian Administration*, ed. T. N. Chaturvedi (New Delhi: IIPA, 1998), 149.

[37] Ibid., 151.

[38] The PMO located in South Block, overlooks the grandeur of Rashtrapati Bhavan. Although in the 1990s, I. K. Gujral and some of his predecessors used Prime Minister Residence (PMR), spread over a 10-acre complex, as office. It is sandwiched between the CS on one side and the Ministries of External Affairs and Defence on the other. The 20-room PMO is equipped to provide both infrastructural and manpower support to the Nations' chief executive. Hi-tech accessories and sophisticated communication devices have been installed to monitor domestic and international developments.

[39] D. S. Mehta, *Handbook of Public Relations in India* (New Delhi: Allied Publishers, 1968).

as the PM (January 1966–March 1977) that the PMO was strengthened. In fact, she depended upon this office for evolving new policies and then implementing them successfully. It was also a reflection of her personality, that she desired a strong body that would be loyal to her. For this purpose, P. N. Haksar was appointed as the secretary to the PMO. There was a momentum of the whole movement of transferring the more important activities to the PMO which then became the main centre of governmental activities.[40] It was during her regime that the office of the secretary to the PM reached 'dizzy heights of power and authority and during the internal emergency, it emerged as the real decision-making organization verily functioning as the Government of India'.[41] Haksar helped Mrs Gandhi in emerging out of the shadow of the Congress Syndicate.[42] The PMO during Haksar's tenure came to be known as the Prime Minister House (PMH).[43] The prime minister through his office coordinates with all ministers in the Union cabinet, ministers of independent charges and governors and ministers of the state. Important policy issues, which the minister concerned feels should be submitted to the prime minister for orders or information, are received at the PMO. The PM has traditionally been the minister-in-charge of the Department of Space, Department of Atomic Energy, and Ministry of Personnel, Public Grievances and Pensions.

4.7.2 Functions and Role of PMO

Broadly, there seems to be no deadline for the functions to be performed by the PMO. 'The bureaucrats manning the PMO should ideally be backroom boys',[44] but sometimes people who are part of the PMO had acquired power and authority of their own in the name of the PM.

Following are some of the important issues and matters which are submitted by the PMO to the PM for his consideration, perusal and orders:

1. Important defence-related issues
2. Decorations, both civilian and defence, where presidential approval is required
3. All important policy decisions relating to CS
4. Proposals for appointment of Indian heads of missions abroad and requests for grant of agreement for foreign heads of missions posted to India
5. Appointments to State Administrative Tribunals and the Central Administrative Tribunal, UPSC, Election Commission, appointment of members of statutory/constitutional committees, and commissions attached to various ministries
6. All policy matters relating to the administration of the civil services and administrative reforms
7. Special packages announced for states by the PM and periodical reports submitted to PM are monitored at the PMO
8. All judicial appointments for which presidential approval is required

It is noted that the PMO helps the PM in the discharge of his overall responsibility as the head of the government. This includes giving guidance to the PM in framing new policies, monitoring them

[40] Deshmukh, 'Prime Minister's Office', 152.
[41] S. R. Maheshwari, *Indian Administration* (New Delhi: Orient Longman, 1989), 26.
[42] Prabhu Chawla, 'The Power Point Men', *India Today*, 8 March 2010.
[43] Deshmukh, 'Prime Minister's Office', 153.
[44] Arijit Barman, 'Babu's Day Out', *Outlook*, 9 April 2001, 37.

and helping him in the task of work coordination. In official language, it is 'assembling ideas, collection of relevant inputs from diverse sources, formulation of issues and working out alternatives regarding matters coming up to the PM for decision'.

As P. N. Dhar observes, 'The PMO is only a transmission belt for ideas which contribute a part of the inputs that go into policy formulation'.[45] In recent times, it is observed that the PMO has overshadowed the cabinet and its Secretariat. Due to the overpowering influence of the PMO, ministers are dependent more and more on the PMO rather than the cabinet.[46] The PMO has assumed the role of the cabinet also, thereby eroding the basic premise of a parliamentary set up. It takes all decisions and thrusts them upon the ministries without as much by-your-leave. 'The immediate fallout of this is that ministers have stopped applying their minds and have begun to depend more and more on directives from the PMO'.

Following PM Narendra Modi's meeting with additional secretary- and joint secretary-level officials in September 2017, cabinet secretary circulated a directive of 39-actionable points to secretaries of union ministries with focus on how the governance needs to be revamped. The directive observes that the Central Secretariat has lost field focus, and officers need to spend 5–6 days a month in the field mandatorily. Further, cabinet secretary asked Secretaries to 'focus largely on process simplification to reduce timelines.[47]

In his contribution to the IIPA publication, B. D. Deshmukh (former cabinet secretary, and Principal Secretary to the PM) observes,

> To conclude, as the things stand today, a Prime Minister has to have a strong PMO. Yet it should only be a highly professional body, rendering free and fair advice to the Prime Minister. It is not necessary for it to bypass the system or usurp the powers of Ministries or Cabinet Secretariat. The Prime Minister will also have to be careful that no PMH is allowed to emerge. There can then be no apprehension about a PMO becoming a high profile dominating body.[48]

Summary

To bring about good governance, ministries and departments have to be goal-oriented, less procedure-bound. They have to be responsive and citizen-friendly units. As the functions of government widened and certain aspects of administration got more and more stressed, the question of manageability assumed greater significance. Institutions sometimes have been diverted from their purposes to suit some immediate but different goals. This has inhibited the growth of new administrative organizations and led to the degeneration of the existing ones. The rapid turnover in the ranks of the top political leaders, the predominance of partisan political over rational or technical criteria for the evaluation of policies and administrative inadequacies also tend to affect adversely the good governance. The test of good governance lies in the goals of a government, in its policies and programmes, in the manner of their implementation, in the results achieved and above all, in the general perception of the people about the quality of functioning of various institutions.

[45] Quoted by Barman, 'Babu's Day Out', 36.
[46] During the Indira Gandhi's regime, her son, Sanjay Gandhi, over shadowed the PMO.
[47] See *The Economic Times* (Chandigarh), 20 September 2017.
[48] Deshmukh, 'Prime Minister's Office', 155.

5 Parliament: Supremacy and Myth

LEARNING OBJECTIVES

1. **To discuss the concept of sovereignty of Parliament**
2. **To discuss the parliamentary control over administration**
3. **To examine the myth and supremacy of legislature**

Introduction

The Constitution of India (in force from 26 January 1950),[1] drafted by the Constituent Assembly between 1946 and 1949,[2] fully recognizes the sovereignty of the people in the administration of the country. This sovereignty is exercised through Parliament, elected on adult franchise, with a Council of Ministers (in a true sense, 'the cabinet') as its executive instrument.[3] This system, it is presumed, would provide competent leadership to the legislature (Parliament) in all matters—legislation, finance, policy enunciation and so forth—and would also assure responsibility of the government to the legislature (Parliament) and to the people.

5.1 Parliament: Structure and Functions

The fathers of the Indian Constitution preferred to provide a parliamentary system of government for the Democratic Republic of India despite some dissident voices among them in favour of presidential system of government. There were two main reasons advanced in favour of this preference.

---

[1] 26 January was chosen to commemorate the *Purna Swaraj* (complete independence) declaration of Independence of 1930. On 26 January 1950, the transformation of the Dominion of India into a Sovereign Democratic Republic was formally solemnized.

[2] The Constituent Assembly, which adopted the Constitution on 26 November 1949, took approximately three years to finish its work and produced a bulky constitution comprising 395 Articles and 8 Schedules (now 12). Although the Constitution-making function of the Assembly was over, it continued as the interim Parliament until general elections were held in 1952 and the new Parliament was formed.

[3] The President of India is the constitutional head of executive of the Union. Article 74(1) of the Constitution provides that there 'shall be a Council of Ministers with the Prime Minister at the head to aid and advice the president who shall, in exercise of his functions, act in accordance with such advice'. The real executive power thus vests in the Council of Ministers with the PM as its head. The Council of Ministers is collectively responsible to the House of the People (Lok Sabha).

First, the experience of British parliamentary system of government clearly indicated its utility and vitality as responsive and democratic polity. Second, the Indian political leaders and parties were accustomed to this system of government in which they had been participating increasingly since its phased development from the elementary stage in the nineties of the nineteenth century onwards.

The Parliament (India) consists of the president (for, even though he does not sit in Parliament, except for the purpose of delivering the opening address, and a bill passed by the Parliament cannot become a law without his assent) and two Houses known as Council of States (Rajya Sabha) and House of the People (Lok Sabha). Each House has to meet within six months of its previous sitting. A joint sitting of two Houses can be held in certain cases.

5.1.1 Council of States (Rajya Sabha)

The Constitution provides that the Rajya Sabha shall consist of 12 members to be nominated by the president from amongst persons having special knowledge or practical experience in respect of such matters as literature, science, art and social service, and not more than 238 representatives of the states and of the union territories. The maximum permissible strength of the council is 250 members.[4]

Elections to the Rajya Sabha are indirect.[5] Members representing states are elected by the elected MLAs of the states in accordance with the system of proportional representation by means of a single transferable vote, and those representing union territories are chosen in such a manner as Parliament may by law prescribe. It is noted that election to the Council of States is not on the basis of equality of the states, but on the basis of population. Herein lies the difference between the Constitutions of the USA and of Australia, where each constituent state is equal in every way, electing directly an equal number of representatives to the corresponding Upper House. Not only have the Indian states unequal representation in the council but also the council is not fully federal since there is a provision for nomination to it. The council, originally conceived as a check on the possible irresponsibility of a wholly elected legislature, was now retained as a 'revisionary' House. The provision for indirect election was made because it was intended that the council should come to be composed of elder statesmen, administrators and constitutional experts, and that it should exercise a moderating influence on legislative excesses. This role, however, has come to be primarily advisory, the council now having the power to block finally any legislation passed by the House.

The council is presided over by the vice-president who is its ex-officio chairman. It is not subject to dissolution, but a third of the members retire, on the expiration of every second year, although they are eligible for re-election. This provision is intended to reflect a federal character by representing the units of the federation. Second, this provision is intended to maintain continuity in legislative processes.

5.1.2 House of the People (Lok Sabha)

The House of People or the Lok Sabha is composed of representatives of people chosen by direct election on the basis of adult suffrage.[6] The maximum strength of the House envisaged by the

---

[4] See Article 80 of the Indian Constitution.

[5] For seeking election to the Rajya Sabha, a person must be a citizen of India and not less than 30 years of age.

[6] For seeking election to the Lok Sabha, a person must be a citizen of India and not less than 25 years of age.

Constitution is now 552—530 members to represent the states 20 members to represent the union territories[7] and not more than two members of the Anglo-Indian community to be nominated by the president, if, in his opinion, that community is not adequately represented in the House. The total elective membership of the Lok Sabha is distributed among the states in such a way that the ratio between the number of seats allotted to each state and the population of the state is, as far as practicable, the same for all states. The Lok Sabha at present consists of 543 members. Of these, 530 members are directly elected from the states and 13 from union territories. Following the 84th Amendment to the Constitution in 2001, the total number of existing seats as allocated to various states in the Lok Sabha on the basis of the 1971 census shall remain unaltered until the first census to be taken after the year 2026.

The term of the Lok Sabha, unless dissolved earlier, is five years from the date appointed for its first meeting. However, while a Proclamation of Emergency is in operation, this period may be extended by Parliament by law for a period not exceeding one year at a time and not extending in any case beyond a period of six months after the Proclamation is or has ceased to operate. Sixteen Lok Sabhas have been constituted so far. The term of each Lok Sabha and its speaker(s) is given in Table 5.1.

5.1.3 Functions and Powers of Parliament

Parliament in India makes the laws and legitimizes the decisions of the government. It authorizes taxation and expenditure and makes the government accountable for financial decisions. The Lok Sabha representing the people is supreme in the administration of the country. The cabinet is merely its executive instrument, fully answerable to it for its acts of omission and commission. Although it is permissible to initiate legislation other than financial bills in either House, the approval of both the Houses is required on the final form in which it emerges as a valid legal enactment. In the event of any disagreement, a joint session is convened by presidential order to resolve the differences. Decision is taken by a simple majority vote of the members of the two Houses, thus emphasizing the supremacy of the House of the People in the field of administration. A money bill can be introduced only in the House of People, and, after its passage, it is transmitted to the other House for its 'recommendations'. The bill, with the recommendations, has to be returned within a fortnight. The final right to accept or reject any or all these recommendations vests in the House of People. Similarly, the demands for grants are placed only before the House of the People on the authority of the president; a general discussion on the budget alone is allowed in the council. Besides the power to legislate, the Constitution vests in Parliament the power to initiate amendment of the Constitution.

The Constitution Act has retained the arrangement of division of legislative and executive functions between the Union and states, leaving a field for concurrent jurisdiction. Although the characteristics of a federal structure are therefore present in the Indian Constitution, there are important reservations to emphasize the supremacy of Parliament. Thus, any subject included in the State List can be temporarily transferred for a period of one year at a time to the Union List, if the Council of States, by a two-thirds majority, considers such a transfer to be in the national interest. The Parliament can, under certain circumstances, assume legislative power with respect to a subject falling within the sphere exclusively reserved for the states. It can impeach the

[7] See, Article 81 of the Indian Constitution.

Table 5.1 Lok Sabha and Its Speaker(s) from Time to Time

Lok Sabha	Date of first Meeting	Date of Dissolution	Speaker's Name	From	To
1st Lok Sabha	13 May 1952	4 April 1957	Ganesh Vasudev Mavalankar M. Ananthasayawam Ayyangar	15 May 1952 8 March 1956	27 February 1956 10 May 1957
2nd Lok Sabha	10 May 1957	31 March 1962	M. Ananthasayawam Ayyangar	11 May 1957	16 April 1962
3rd Lok Sabha	16 April 1962	3 March 1967	Sardar Hukam Singh	17 April 1962	16 March 1967
4th Lok Sabha	16 March 1967	27 December 1970	Neelam Sanjiva Reddy Gurdial Singh Dhillon	17 March 1967 8 August 1969	19 July 1969 19 March 1971
5th Lok Sabha	19 March 1971	18 January 1977	Gurdidal Singh Dhillon Bali Ram Bhagat	22 March 1971 5 January 1976	1 December 1975 25 March 1977
6th Lok Sabha	25 March 1977	22 August 1979	Neelam Sanjiva Reddy K. S. Hedge	26 March 1977 21 July 1977	13 July 1977 21 January 1985
7th Lok Sabha	21 January 1980	31 December 1984	Balram Jakhar	22 January 1980	15 January 1985
8th Lok Sabha	15 January 1985	27 November 1989	Balram Jakhar	16 January 1985	18 December 1989
9th Lok Sabha	18 December 1989	13 March 1991	Rabi Ray	19 December 1989	9 July 1991
10th Lok Sabha	9 July 1991	10 May 1996	Shivraj V. Patil	10 July 1991	22 May 1996
11th Lok Sabha	22 May 1996	4 December 1997	P. A. Sangma	23 May 1996	23 March 1998 (FN)
12th Lok Sabha	23 March 1998	26 April 1999	G. M. C. Balayogi	24 March 1998	20 October 1999 (FN)
13th Lok Sabha	20 October 1999	6 February 2004	G. M. C. Balayogi Manohar Gajanan Joshi	22 October 1999 10 May 2002	3 March 2002 2 June 2004
14th Lok Sabha	2 June 2004	18 May 2009	Somnath Chatterjee	4 June 2004	1 June 2009
15th Lok Sabha	1 June 2009	18 May 2014	Meira Kumar	1 June 2009	18 May 2014
16th Lok Sabha	4 June 2014		Sumitra Mahajan	6 June 2014	Till date

Source: India 2017: A Reference Annual (GoI).

president and remove the Judges of Supreme Court and high courts, the chief election commissioner and the CAG in accordance with the procedure laid down in the Constitution.

In addition to its legal role, it subjects administrative actions to criticism and scrutiny. It serves as a forum for public debate on issues of public policies, besides a forum for the expression of complaints and grievances. The parliamentary power increases further as fewer votes are made into votes of confidence, over which a government can fall. When a vote is not a vote of confidence, individual MPs have greater freedom to vote without threatening the continuation of their government.

New version of bill titled as 'The Right to Fair Compensation and Transparency in Land Acquisition, Rehabilitation and Resettlement (Amendment) Second Bill, 2015' was referred to the Joint Parliamentary Committee after it was introduced in the Lok Sabha on 11 May 2015. Earlier on 10 March 2015, Lok Sabha passed Land Acquisition Amendment Bill where the NDA government had majority, but it could not be passed in the Rajya Sabha where it was in minority.

5.2 Parliamentary Committees

The enlarged scope of government activity and people's pressure for high standard of living have made the Parliament's tasks more difficult. The flexible system of government works in parliamentary committees, if worked properly, and extensively facilitates quick disposal of business and reconciliation of divergence of views.

The functions of Parliament are varied in nature. The time at its disposal is limited. It cannot make every detailed scrutiny of all legislative and other matters that come up before it. A good deal of parliamentary business is therefore transacted in the committees.

In terms of functions and procedure of conducting business, both Rajya Sabha and Lok Sabha have a similar committee structure and are regulated as per rules made by the two Houses under Article 118(1) of the Constitution.

Broadly, parliamentary committees are of two kinds: standing committees and *ad hoc* committees. The former are elected or appointed every year or periodically, and their work goes on, more or less, on a continuous basis. The latter are appointed on an *ad hoc* basis as need arises, and they cease to exist as soon as they complete the task assigned to them.

5.2.1 Standing Committees

Among the standing committees, the three financial committees—Committees on Estimates, Public Accounts and Public Undertakings—constitute a distinct group, as they keep an unremitting vigil over government expenditure and performance. While members of the Rajya Sabha are associated with Committees on Public Accounts and Public Undertakings, the members of the Committee on Estimates are drawn from the Lok Sabha. These three standing committees—structure and role—would be discussed in the chapter on 'Managing Control over National Expenditure'.

5.2.1.1 Department-related Standing Committees (DRSCs)

Besides these three financial committees, 17 department-related standing committees (DRSCs) were set up on 8 April 1993. In July 2004, rules were amended to provide for the constitution of seven more such committees, thus raising the number of DRSCs from 17 to 24. The functions of these committees are (a) to consider the demands for grants of various ministries/departments of GoI and make reports to the Houses; (b) to examine such bills as are referred to the committee by the chairman, Rajya Sabha, or the speaker, Lok Sabha, and make reports thereon; (c) to consider annual reports of ministries/departments and make reports thereon; and (d) to consider policy documents presented to the Houses, if referred to the committee by the chairman, Rajya Sabha, or the speaker, Lok Sabha, and make reports thereon.

5.2.1.2 Other Standing Committees

Some of the other standing committees are as follows:

1. *Committees to Inquire*
   a. Committee on Petitions examines petitions on bills and on matters of general public interest and also entertains representations on matters concerning subjects in the Union List.
   b. Committee of Privileges examines any question of privilege referred to it by the speaker/chairman of the House.
2. *Committees to Scrutinize*
   a. Committee on Government Assurances keeps track of all the assurances, promises, undertakings and so on given by ministers in the House and pursues them until they are implemented.
   b. Committee on Subordinate Legislation scrutinizes and reports to the House whether the power to make regulations, rules, sub-rules, bye-laws and so on conferred by the Constitution or statutes is being properly exercised by the delegated authorities.
   c. Committee on Papers Laid on the Table examines all papers laid on the table of the House by ministers, other than statutory notifications and orders which come within the purview of the Committee on Subordinate Legislation.
3. *Committees Relating to the Day-to-day Business of the House*
   a. Business Advisory Committee recommends allocation of time for items of government and other business to be brought before the Houses.
   b. Committee on Private Members' Bills and Resolutions of the Lok Sabha classifies and allocates time to bills introduced by private members.
   c. Rules Committee considers matters of procedure and conduct of business in the House and recommends amendments or additions to the Rules.
   d. Committee on Absence of Members from the sittings of the Lok Sabha considers all applications from members for leaves or absence from sittings of the House.
4. *Committee on the Welfare of Scheduled Castes and Scheduled Tribes*
   This Committee (on which members from both Houses serve) considers all matters relating to the welfare of SCs and STs which come within the purview of the union government.
5. *Committees Concerned with the Provision of Facilities of Members*
   a. General Purpose Committee considers and advises speaker/chairman on matters concerning affairs of the House, which do not appropriately fall within the purview of any other parliamentary committee.

b. House Committee deals with residential accommodation and other amenities for members.

6. *Joint Committee on Salaries and Allowances of Members of Parliament*

This committee, apart from framing rules for regulating payment of salaries, allowances and pension of MPs, frames rules in respect of amenities such as medical, housing, telephone, postal, constituency and secretariat facility.

7. *Joint Committee on Offices of Profit*

This committee recommends what offices ought to or ought not to disqualify a person from being chosen as a member of either Houses of Parliament.

8. *The Library Committee*

This committee, consisting of members from both Houses, considers matters concerning the Library of Parliament.

9. *Committee on Empowerment of Women*

On 29 April 1997, a Committee on Empowerment of Women with members from both the Houses was constituted to secure status, dignity and equality for women in all field.

10. *Ethics Committees*

On 4 March 1997, an Ethics Committee for the Rajya Sabha was created. Similarly, an Ethics Committee for the Lok Sabha was created on 16 May 2000.

5.2.2 *Ad Hoc* Committees

Ad hoc committees are also constituted from time to time, either by the two Houses on a motion adopted in that behalf or by speaker/chairman to inquire into and report on specific subjects (e.g., Committees on Food Management in Parliament House Complex, Committee on Installation of Portraits/Statues of National Leaders and Parliamentarians in Parliament House Complex, etc.). Further, Select or Joint Committees on bills are appointed to consider and report on a particular bill. These are concerned with bills and the procedure to be followed by them as laid down in the Rules of Procedure and Directions by the speaker/chairman.

5.2.3 Consultative Committees

Besides parliamentary committees, the Ministry of Parliamentary Affairs under the Government of India (Allocation of Business) Rules, 1961, constitutes Consultative Committees to provide a forum for informal discussion between MPs, and ministers and senior officers of the government on the policies, principles and programmes of the government and their implementation. In total 35 consultative committees attached to various ministries were constituted for 16th Lok Sabha and 108 meetings of consultative committees were held from 1 June 2015 to 31 May 2016.

5.2.4 Analysis of Committees

The power vested in the Parliament must be decentralized if it is to give due weightage to policy proposals. To be able to discuss these genuinely, the members need to develop expertise about the issues involved in proposals. The elected members, however, can hardly be specialists on everything. Hence is need of the decentralization of parliamentary power to various committees. These committees permit each member to specialize in a few policy areas. The idea for legislative committees actually came from the British Parliament, but, in England, the committees atrophied with the growth of the cabinet government.[8] Once parliamentary committees are set up to allow more expert consideration of proposals, Parliament would show a reasonable degree of deference towards the committee's decisions. Thus, the committees are crucial in determining the fate of legislation. In the recent years, powers of decentralization have come not only from the committee chairpersons to the subcommittees but also to the individual members. Decentralization increases the number of access points that organized interests or advocates of bills on policy can have into Parliament. The pressure on parliamentary work and time is reduced by the setting up of various parliamentary committees.

In addition to decreasing the work load, decentralization would give legislators more time to contemplate the content of the policy proposals on which they must vote. More legislators in India do not however spend much time doing research and reading about legislation. Where they have to decide quickly, they are more likely to take cues from colleagues who sit on the committee in the policy in which voting takes place. Increasing time pressure and loads on legislators make them harried and further increase the power of committee members over the bills relating to their legislative areas.

5.3 Government Business in Parliament

The task of efficiently handling diverse parliamentary work on behalf of the government, in the parliament, has been assigned to the Ministry of Parliamentary Affairs. The ministry serves as an important link between the two Houses of Parliament on one hand and the government on the other in respect of government business in parliament. The minister of parliamentary affairs, being the government Chief Whip, is entrusted with the responsibility of coordinating, planning and arranging government business in both Houses of Parliament. In discharge of this function, he is assisted by two ministers of state. The minister also keeps close and constant contact with the presiding officers, the leaders as well as Chief Whips of various parties and groups in both Houses of Parliament. During the period from 1 June 2015 to 31 May 2016, the two Houses of Parliament passed 36 bills.

Parliament, on 27 April 2016, passed two bills repealing 1053 old bills which had become redundant.[9] These are Appropriation Acts (Repeal) Bill, 2015, that seeks to repeal 758 old Appropriation Acts which have lost relevance, and the Repealing and Amending (Third) Bill, 2015, that seeks to repeal 295 enactments.[10]

A 2-year review by the Committee on Subordinate Legislation has shown that 31 new Acts and 12 Amendments had not been fully or partially converted into government orders. These include

[8] Wilfred E. Binkley, *President and Congress*, 3rd ed. (New York: Vintage Books, 1962), 50.

[9] See *The Tribune* (Chandigarh), 28 April 2016.

[10] For example, the 39th Constitution Amendment Act was passed by Parliament after it was introduced in Lok Sabha on 7 August 1975 and in Rajya Sabha on 8 August. It was ratified by several states on 9 August 1975. On Sunday 10 August 1975, the president assented to it, and it was published in the Gazette on the same day. In comparison to the GST passage which took more than three years and came into force on 1 July 2017.

laws such as Whistleblowers Protection Act (passed in May 2014), the Energy Conservation Act (September 2001 and its amendments in August 2010), Central Vigilance Commission Act (September 2003), Lokpal and Lokyuktas Act (January 2014), Central University Act (March 2009) and many more.[11]

The Committee on Subordinate Legislation has recommended in its report that all ministries and departments (GoI) frame 'essential rules' at the time of the introduction of the bill while the 'rest of subordinate legislation may be framed within three months of the coming into force of the Act'.

These subordinate legislations have to be published in the gazette and laid in both Houses of Parliament for the Committee on Subordinate Legislation to examine if the rules are within the contours of the Act.

5.4 Parliamentary Realities

In a parliamentary form of government, the supremacy of the Parliament (as in the case of England) is a basic feature. Thus in law and constitutional theory, the power of the Parliament is unlimited. The courts cannot question validity of the parliamentary laws. And there is no law which Parliament could not repeal. Wade and Phillips observed, 'Neither devolution nor delegation of legislative authority infringes the supremacy of (the British) Parliament'.[12] Thus, the legislature reigns supreme because the PM is dependent on support from a parliamentary majority to remain in office. It is noteworthy to point out that no court in England since the 17th century has ever struck down an Act of Parliament for violating some fundamental principle.

On the contrary, the sovereignty of Parliament in India is, however, limited by the provision of Fundamental Rights guaranteed to the people. It is limited also by the powers vested in the judiciary. But, in certain contingencies, even these limitations can be overcome by a special parliamentary process which can give the Union the solidarity of a unitary government. The Indian Parliament shares its supremacy with the judiciary to a limited extent. It is not omnipotent like the British Parliament which can enact, amend and repeal any law.

Further, it is pointed out that it is not the strength or weakness of the Parliament which is crucial to law-making process, but the creation of alliances beforehand between different parliamentary groups or committees to influence legislation or policy decisions. The government usually does not depend on the support of the opposition. It has, however, to rely on the backbenchers to provide it with the majority necessary to run the government. Hence, the government is more afraid of its own backbenchers than the opposition members. It fears that its own backbenchers may form a majority in the opposition division lobby. Then, there is also the need to maintain the support and morale of the majority party.

However, it has been observed that most of the MPs would rather see their party in power than the opposition, even when they disagree with the leadership on particular policy decisions. The discipline which gives the parties their cohesion is more often self-imposed than enforced on frightened and reluctant backbenchers by the whips.

It is true that the amending process is not simple except for amending the transitional provisions. It needs otherwise a two-third majority of members present and voting in both the

---

[11] See *The Financial Express* (Chandigarh), 23 September 2016.

[12] E. C. S. Wade and G. G. Phillips, *Constitutional Law* (London: Longman, 1960), 49.

Houses, a simple majority of all the members and in certain cases, the consent of at least half the number of state legislatures in addition. These provisions will undoubtedly act as a restraint on legislative excesses, except when a single party commands the requisite majority in Parliament and also controls the state legislatures. This being the position today, there is the apprehension that the constitutional safeguards and fundamental rights may not enjoy the sanctity as intended by the framers of the Constitution.

Then PM of India, Mrs Indira Gandhi, did treat the Constitution as its 'private property' and took full advantage of her majority in Parliament.[13] Between 1971 and 1976, 19 amendments to the Constitution and 463 to other laws were pushed. About 100 ordinances were promulgated, and as many as 114 presidential Acts were enacted for the states under the president's rule. As many as 102 laws were added to the protective umbrella of the Ninth Schedule, taking them out of the purview of judicial review.

Vital changes were brought in by the 42nd Amendment which amended as many as 53 Articles, the Preamble and the Seventh Schedule. The words 'secular', 'socialist' and 'integrity' were added to the Preamble and there was insertion of Article 31D, which empowered penalization of 'anti-national activities' and banning of 'anti-national associations'. Other changes included making all directive principles superior to Fundamental Rights of equality and freedoms given in Article 19(1a); increasing powers of the Parliament and its term by one year; insertion of Article 51A with 10 Fundamental Duties; making the president bound by the aid and advice given by the Council of Ministers headed by the PM; exclusion of the judicial review, including denial of powers to the high court to examine the constitutionality of central laws; establishment of tribunals; no limitation on the constituent powers of the Parliament to amend the Constitution in terms of addition, variation or repeal, and so on.

Here, it may be mentioned that during the Emergency Years (1975–77), the Parliament and the Executive ruled the roost by passing 39th and 42nd Amendments, superseding three senior-most Supreme Court judges and making punitive transfers of high court judges. But after the Emergency, the Supreme Court struck back in the name of Independence of judiciary and rule of law.[14]

Probably, Indira Gandhi was not happy with the restrictions put by the 13-judge bench of the apex court on the amending powers of the Parliament.[15] In the name of supremacy of Parliament, the Congress was not willing to accept the views that Parliament through an amendment cannot destroy or repeal the Constitution or violate its basic features. The BJP's reaction to the 16 October 2015 National Judicial Appointments Commission (NJAC) decision was similar to Indira Gandhi's views on the supremacy of the Parliament. Like the NJAC, the 42nd Amendment was also passed by the Parliament with near unanimity. The Lok Sabha passed it with 366 to 4 and Rajya Sabha with 190 to no one opposing it. The NJAC had only one dissent in Rajya Sabha, with Ram Jethmalani opposing it.

Terming as 'erroneous logic', which was given by a five-judge Constitution bench that declared the National Judicial Appointments Commission Act, 2014, and the 99th Constitution Amendment

---

[13] Eminent jurist Nanabhoy Palkhivala described the extraordinary situation of the Indira government which 'treated the Constitution as its private property and dealt with Indian law as its personal backyard'.

[14] Beant Singh Bedi, 'Third, but Pyrrhic, Win for the Long Arm of Law', *The Tribune* (Chandigarh), 17 November 2015.

[15] The 13-Judge Constitutional Bench in Keshavanand Bharati case had made it clear that separation of powers is part of the basic structure of the Constitution (AIR 1973, SC 1641).

unconstitutional, Arun Jaitley (finance minister) warned that democracy would be in danger if the 'elected are undermined'.[16]

The Constitution makes Parliament not only the legislative organ of the Union but also the authority to amend the constitutional provisions. Even so, it was generally believed that the party in power would not undertake amendments light-heartedly or use of its massive majority to erode the Fundamental Rights guaranteed in the Constitution.

On 17 June 1975, the Allahabad High Court decided against Mrs Gandhi's election to the Lok Sabha, and the Supreme Court did not give her absolute stay. Her appeal was fixed for hearing before the Supreme Court on 11 August 1975. Between 7 and 10 August, the 39th Amendment Act was passed to put her election to the Lok Sabha beyond challenge. The Supreme Court by a majority held Clause 4 to be invalid on the ground that free and fair elections are a basic feature of the Constitution.[17]

In a historical judgement delivered in the case of *Minerva Mills v. Union of India* (1980), the Chief Justice Y. V. Chandrachud said that Clauses 4 and 5 added to Article 368 by the 42nd Amendment are invalid on the ground that they violate two basic features of the Constitution, namely, limited nature of the power to amend and judicial review. The courts cannot be deprived of their power of judicial review.[18]

The Indian Parliament shares its supremacy with the judiciary to a limited extent. It is not omnipotent like the UK Parliament which can enact, amend and repeal any legislation, as the exigencies of a situation may demand. As the UK has no written constitution, there are no limitations on the legislative authority of Parliament. In the analogous case of the USA, with the Bill of Rights as an integral part of its written constitution, the theory of natural rights has been developed to transfer supremacy to the judiciary. The Indian Constitution steers a middle course between parliamentary supremacy and 'judicial' supremacy. By a majority, the Supreme Court of India struck down the 99th Constitution Amendment Act, 2014, and the NJAC Act, 2014, as unconstitutional on 16 October 2015.[19]

In the PM's election case (1975), the Supreme Court had ruled that the separation of powers is a basic feature of the Constitution. This view has been reaffirmed by it in several cases, including Mumbai Port Trust (2011), yet there has been a constant turf war between the Parliament and the Executive on one hand and the Higher Judiciary on the other.

Summary

The role of Parliament in law-making and policymaking is thus understood as a procedural device for legitimizing decisions. Moreover, in a parliamentary type or executive, a mass of legislation is made under the powers delegated to the ministers by parent statutes for reasons of pressure on parliamentary time, the technical quality of legislation and the need for sufficient time to develop adequate administrative machinery. Only a small proportion of statutory instruments receive any parliamentary scrutiny at all, although whatever there is can be relatively effective. In reality, the

[16] See *The Financial Express* (Chandigarh), 19 October 2015.
[17] *Indira Nehru Gandhi v. Raj Narain*, AIR, 1975 SC 2299.
[18] *Minerva Mills v. Union of India*, AIR, 1980, SC 1789.
[19] See *The Business Standard* (Chandigarh), 17 October 2015.

bulk of delegated legislation in India does not attract the attention or the backbenchers unless it is struck down by the judiciary. As stated earlier, power as such does not reside in the Parliament but in the Council of Ministers which is able to create a majority within the Parliament and thereby succeeds in making policy decisions. Parliament is considered to be a 'constitutional procedure device' for approving the decisions of the government rather than as an independent policymaking institution. Many Policies approved by the Parliament are initiated by the members of the cabinet or Council of Ministers, having been planned within the departments or the state after consultation with affected interests.

Parliament as an institution of law-making is theoretically supreme. But it has to share its supremacy with the judiciary to a limited extent. The Indian Constitution steers a middle course between parliamentary supremacy and judicial supremacy.

6 Central Administration: Structure and Governance

LEARNING OBJECTIVES

1. To explain the role and functions of the Central Secretariat
2. To describe the relationship patterns between executive agencies and Central Secretariat
3. To suggest measures for improving the functioning of the central government departments

Introduction

With the withdrawal of British power provided in the Indian Independence Act, 1947, the executive powers were vested in the Council of Ministers contemplated in the Government of India Act, 1935. As work of individual departments (precursor of ministries), central government realized that effective public administration system was essential for socio-economic development of the country.

Any programme of social development, of improvement in education and health, and of reform in any of the public services can succeed only if it is supported by sound administrative organization and methods based on sound principles of public administration. The building up of effective administrative organizations is a major concern to a developing country such as India. At any level, administrative organization is the *sine qua non* of development. At another level, developing countries want their organizations and institutions to conform to their unique historical cultural and social milieu. Accordingly, there have been organized efforts to promote institutional development. Most countries have established organizations for policy-making, planning, budgeting, personnel administration, functional and sectoral management information gathering and other state functions at various levels—central, state and local.

In the Indian context, the Constitution has established a parliamentary form of government. Since the Indian polity is federal in character, the Constitution recognized two important levels of administration—the centre and the state. Besides, local level administration constitutes an important edifice of the Indian administration.

6.1 Organization Structure: Historical Background

The British Government took over the administration of India from the East India Company by the Government of India Act, 1858. Thereafter, the British Parliament enacted several laws for governance of India. Some of the important legislative instruments in the pre-independence period were the Indian Councils Act, 1909 (also known as the Morley-Minto Reforms) which introduced the elections of Indians to the legislative councils; the Government of India Act, 1919 (also known as the Montague Chelmsford Reforms) which introduced a dual form of government (dyarchy) for some provinces—the reserved list and the transferred list; the Government of India Act, 1935; and finally, the Indian Independence Act, 1947.

The Government of India Act, 1935, brought several changes in the system of governance in the country. It provided for the establishment of an All-India Federation and a new system of government wherein the provinces were given more autonomy. The central legislature was to comprise two Houses—the Upper House or the Council of States and the Lower House or the Central Legislative Assembly. The dyarchy which was earlier established in the provinces was abolished but was introduced in the Centre. The executive authority of the Centre was vested in the governor general (on behalf of the Crown) who had absolute power over defence and external affairs (reserved subjects). On other matters, the governor general was to act on the advice of a 'Council of Ministers'. The Act stipulated that no finance bill could be placed in the central legislature without the consent of the governor general. The Act further provided for the three Lists—Federal, Provincial and Concurrent—for division of legislative functions between the Centre and the provinces.

Government in the pre-Independence period was primarily concerned with enforcement of law, collection of taxes, defence and administration of justice. It also took up some welfare measures for society. After Independence, the Constitution provided the framework for a democratic welfare state with the Directive Principles providing the essence of good governance. In order to achieve the objectives set by the founding fathers of the Constitution, the structure of the government was recast. New departments and organizations were established to discharge various responsibilities.

With the ushering in of economic liberalization, the span of the regulatory role of the government gets reduced, while that of facilitating role is enhanced—'government need not row the ship but merely steer it'. Added to this is the use of modern technology, especially computers and communications, which have rendered old structures obsolete.

The First ARC (1966–70), while examining the role of the union government in respect of matters falling within the ambit of state governments, stated that:

> We are of the view that the role of the Centre in areas which are covered by the State List of subjects in the Constitution should be largely that of a pioneer guide disseminator of information, overall planning and evaluator. The Centre, of course, cannot give up its general responsibility of overseeing that the broad national objectives embodied in the Constitution are achieved by the States. But that does not mean that the Central Government should take upon itself task and responsibilities which properly belong to the States or duplicated their functions. Except in the most essential areas and that too for a limited duration, the Centre should not take upon itself functions and responsibilities which are legitimately those of the states.[1]

[1] ARC, *Report on the Government of India and Its Procedures of Work* (New Delhi: GoI, 1969), para 85.

The Fifth Central Pay Commission (CPC), 1994–97, in its Supplementary Report No. 1 on Improving the Motivation Level and Supplementary Report No. 2 on Cabinet Secretariat (1997) recommended certain measures. The Fifth CPC also identified the following areas as the legitimate province of the union government:

1. National security
2. International relations
3. Law and order
4. Management of economy at macro level
5. Setting up of infrastructure
6. Social services
7. Programmes for disadvantaged sections

On the issue of overstaffing, the Fifth CPC felt that the control of size of the workforce was still essential because of various measures such as rationalizing of functions, organizational restructuring and induction of modern technology. Accordingly, the Commission recommended, 'a freeze on recruitment after abolition of 3.5 lakh vacant posts, across the board 30% cut over 10 years and statutory controls over creation of new posts, etc.'[2]

Subsequently, the Expenditure Reforms Commission (ERC; 10 July 2000) recommended that an 'optimum size of government workforce is essential for its effective functioning'. The ERC recommended the rationalization of government staff strength keeping in view the 'principle of criticality of the functions to be performed with respect to the objective of the organization rather than be driven by numbers'.

The Second ARC in its 13th Report (April 2009) recommended that the union government should primarily focus on the following core areas:

1. Defence, international relations, public order justice and rule of law
2. Human development through access to good quality education and healthcare to every citizen
3. Infrastructure and sustained natural resource development
4. Social security and social justice
5. Macroeconomic management and economic policy
6. National policies in others sectors

Also, the principle of subsidiarity should be the guiding principle while deciding the level at which a particular function should be carried out.[3]

6.2 Central Secretariat

Organizational structure of GoI (mainly central ministries and departments forming as Central Secretariat) has a long history in terms of its organization and functions. Historical development

[2] Ministry of Personnel, Public Grievances and Pensions, *Report of Fifth Central Pay Commission* (New Delhi: GoI, 1997).
[3] Second ARC, *Report on Organization Structure of Government of India* (New Delhi: GoI, April 2009), 71.

of the Central Secretariat dates back to the administration of the East India Company (1600–1858). Writing about the development of this institution, B. B. Misra points out that before the year 1756, the president and the council of Fort William transacted all their business in one general department with the help of a secretary and a few assistants. The secretary used to place before the council the 'packets' received from England for orders and instructions which, when issued, were conveyed to the authorities concerned for their implementation. As far as its functions are concerned, Misra writes that 'the Central Secretariat at Fort William in Bengal was designed to furnish the requisite information for the formulation of policy and to carry out the orders of the Company's Government'.[4] In 1763, the GoI had two departments—'Public' and 'Secret'—that swelled to five in 1785. With assumption of power by the Crown in 1858, the Secretariat's functions and role increased. It coordinated and supervised four departments—Foreign, Home, Financial and Military—of the GoI. The number of departments continued to expand from 9 in the year 1909 and 1919 to 10 in 1939 and 21 in 1945 (during World War II), when subjects between the central and provincial governments were divided. Although the overall responsibility for the governance of India was vested in the governor general, assisted by his executive council, the provinces had their own governments, exercising delegated authority over a large field. On 15 August 1947, the Central Secretariat consisted of 18 ministries which subsequently increased to 20 ministries in June 1952. To cope with the increased workload, the number of ministries and departments was increased from 25 in 1957 to 81 in 2001. Presently, there are 54 central ministries and 48 departments within their fold.[5] In addition, there are two independent departments (Department of Atomic Energy and Department of Space) and four independent offices (NITI Aayog, CS, President's Secretariat and PMO). The central government is a large complex and contains within itself a lot of diversities. There is, thus, no uniform organizational pattern among various ministries, departments and offices for development administration. The secretariats of the ministries and departments of the central government together constitute the headquarters. The Government of India (Allocation of Business) Rules, 1961, was made by the President of India under Article 77 of the Constitution for the allocation of business of the GoI. The ministries/departments of the GoI are created by the president on the advice of the PM under these rules. With increase in the multiplicity of goals and activities of government in various fields, there has been a considerable increase in the volume of business transacted in the headquarter organization which is also called the 'Central Secretariat'—the Imperial Secretariat, as it was called at one time—the counterpart of white hall. The business of the GoI is transacted in the ministries/departments, secretariats and offices (referred to as 'Department')[6] as per the distribution or subjects specified in these Rules. Each of the ministry(ies) is assigned to a minister by the president on the advice of the PM. Each department is generally under the charge of a secretary to assists the minister on policy matters and general administration.

[4] B. B. Misra, *The Central Administration of the East India Company, 1773–1834* (London: Manchester Press, 1959), 65.

[5] Ministry of Information and Broadcasting, *India 2017: A Reference Annual* (New Delhi: Publication Division, GoI, 2018).

[6] See Ministry of Personnel, Public Grievances and Pensions, *Central Secretariat Manual of Office Procedure* (New Delhi: GoI, 2015).

The structure of the GoI is as follows:

President (Executive Head)

⇓

Prime Minister (Head of Council of Ministers)

⇓

Council of Ministers (Cabinet Ministers, Ministers of State & Deputy Ministers)

⇓

Secretary and Subordinate Functionaries

6.2.1 Structure of a Department

The structure in the ministries and departments emanates from the Transaction of Business Rules as well as from the Manual of Office Procedure. The Manual says, 'A department is responsible for formulation of policies of the government in relation to business allocated to it and also for the execution and review of those policies'.

Organizational structure refers to the formal and informal patterns of relationship by which an institution organizes and distributes powers. The structure of an organization has also been defined as 'the architecture both visible and invisible which connects and weaves together all aspects of an organization's activities so that it functions as a complete dynamic entity'.[7]

A department is normally headed by a secretary to the GoI who acts as the administrative head of the department and principal adviser of the minister on all matters of policy and administration within the department. For the efficient disposal of business allotted to it, a department is divided into wings, divisions, branches and sections.

Wing: In the hierarchy of organization, a wing stands next to the department. The wing is headed by a special secretary/additional secretary/joint secretary. Such a functionary is normally vested with the maximum measure of independent functioning and responsibility in respect of the business falling within his wing subject, to the overall responsibility of the secretary for the administration of the department as a whole.

Division: A wing normally comprises a number of divisions, each functioning under the charge of an officer of the level of director/joint director/deputy secretary. A division may have several branches, each under the charge of an Under Secretary or equivalent officer.

Section: A section is generally the lowest organizational unit in a department with a well-defined area of work. It normally consists of assistants and clerks supervised by a section

[7] Elizabeth Macmillan, 'Considering Organization Structure and Design from a Complexity Paradigm Perspective', quoted from the Second ARC, *Report on Organization*, 119.

officer. Initial handling of cases (including noting and drafting) is generally done by assistants and clerks who are also known as the dealing hands.

Desk: While the above represents the commonly adopted pattern of organization of a department, there are certain variations, the most notable among them being the desk officer system. In this system, the work of a department at the lowest level is organized into distinct functional desks, each manned by two desk functionaries of appropriate ranks, for example, under secretary or section officer. Each desk functionary handles the cases himself and is provided with adequate stenographic and clerical assistance.[8]

The other notable variation is the Integrated Headquarters of Ministry of Defence, where the Vice Chiefs of Staff, the Principal Staff Officers of the concerned branches and other appropriate authorities exercise the powers delegated by the defence minister through the various branches and the directorates of the Integrated Headquarters of the Ministry of Defence.

6.2.2 Functions of the Secretariat

At present, each ministry/department has a secretariat whose major role is to help the government in the tasks of formulation, preparation of policies and programmes in order to translate these policies into coordinated action and ensuring effective implementation of polices through periodic reviews. Lord Curzon in 1905 redesigned the Central Secretariat with the following functions:

1. Policy formulation
2. Framing rules and principles of procedure
3. Exercise of financial control
4. Work pertaining to legislation
5. Directing the executive agencies in the performance of their tasks
6. Evaluation of the work of the executive agencies

The Central Secretariat has two main components—the officer and the office. The former corresponds to the directing and controlling staff whereas the latter to the executive and clerical officials. Officials not only advise the minister on various policy alternatives, they also assist him in facing parliamentary criticism. They supply him with information, facts and data so that he can reply in an appropriate way. They are further concerned with justification and defence of that policy against the attacks of opposition parties, affected interest groups and the ever vigilant press.

It is through the secretariat that the central government operates. The secretariat has been divided into several ministries and departments. It is the central part of the union government, responsible for administering the subjects mentioned in the Union List, establishing coordination among multifarious activities of national importance. The secretariat performs the following functions relating to ministries and departments:

1. Assisting the minister in the process of policy making
2. Assisting in the framing of legislation, rules and regulations

[8] Ministry of Personnel, Public Grievances and Pensions, *Central Secretariat*, 14th ed.

3. Formulation of sectoral planning and programmes; budgeting and control of expenditure; according and securing of administrative and financial approval to operational programmes and plans and their subsequent modifications
4. Exercising supervision and control over the executive departments or semi-autonomous field agencies, regarding the execution of policies and programmes as well as their evaluation
5. Interpretation of policies, coordinating and assisting other branches of government and maintaining contact with state administrations
6. Initiating measures to develop greater personnel and organizational competence both in the ministry/department and its executive agencies
7. Helping the minister in the discharge of his parliamentary responsibilities

According to S. R. Maheshwari, the secretariat, being an office, is the organization that assists the government in the fulfilment of its responsibilities, and, as a concept, it has an important role to perform.[9]

6.2.3 Secretariat Staffing and Functions

Before the dawn of Independence, the secretariat consisted of departments, each administering a specified subject, forming the portfolio of a member of the executive council. The layout of the administrative cadre for the department by 1946 was as follows:

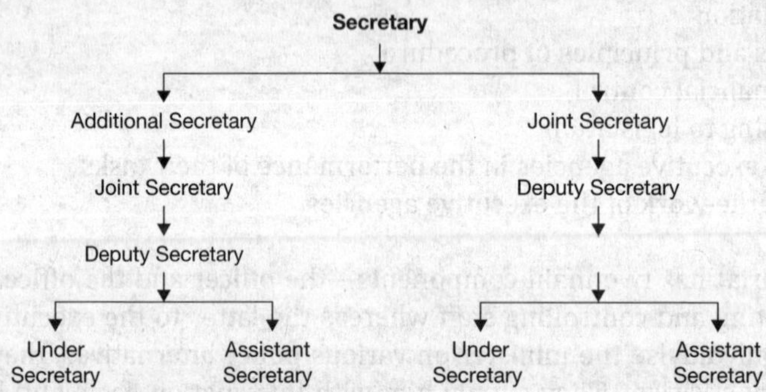

On transfer of power in August 1947, the departments were merely renamed ministries, and the hierarchy remained undisturbed. The administrative posts in the secretariat are manned by officers from (a) All India Services, (b) Central Services Group 'A' on deputation and (c) Central Secretariat Service (CSS). The CSS officers provide continuity to the work of the secretariat. The CSS officers are governed by CSS Rules of 1962 which was issued under the powers of Article 309 of the Constitution of India. As per 2016 data, its cadre size is of 11,550 members (2,471 in Group A and 9,079 Group B).[10]

Immediately below the political head, there is the secretariat organization of the department. The function of the secretariat is to provide to the minister a mature and expert advice for the

[9] S. R. Maheshwari, *Indian Administration*, 4th ed. (New Delhi: Longman, 1994), 30–32.

[10] Figures up to the year 2016.

formulation of policies and watch over the execution of these policies when they have been formulated. The secretariat may be called the brain centre of the administrative body directing and controlling the administrative activities. The head of the secretariat organization of a department is called the secretary. For the convenient transaction business, the department is further sub-divided into convenient units as mentioned in the following table.

Union Ministry (Ministers)	
Department	**Central Secretariat**
	1. Secretary
	2. Additional Secretary
	3. Joint Secretary
Wing	4. Director/Deputy Secretary
Division	5. Under Secretary
Branch	6. Section Officer
Section	7. Assistant
	8. Upper Division Clerk (UDC)
	9. Lower Division Clerk (LDC)

Taking as whole, the structure of the Central Secretariat is composed of nine grades. The functions of these levels of functionaries are described in brief.

Secretary: In the present set-up of a ministry, below the minister, secretary is the administrative head of the ministry who has been described by the ARC as the (a) 'principal adviser' of the minister on policy matters; (b) his 'chief agent' for ensuring the execution of policies and programmes; and (c) he represents the department in important national and international committees and also before the parliamentary committees. His role is therefore of a coordinator, policy guide and reviewer. On this point, Ayyangar noted:

> A Secretary should not be immersed in files and burdened with routine. It is essential that he should have time to grasp the overall picture, size up the problems facing the government in the field allotted to his charge and think and plan ahead. All these are his proper functions and must be efficiently performed. Failure to make adequate provisions in this respect cannot be compensated by mere increase in the establishment under his control.[11]

Ayyangar suggested that the secretary should not involve himself in too much of routine. He should be concerned more with the overall policy issues. He should co-ordinate and guide the work of his subordinates rather than do most of the work himself.

In a large union ministry such as the Ministry of Home Affairs (*Grih Mantralaya*), there may be six secretaries (one each heading): (a) Department of Internal Security, (b) Department of States, (c) Department of Official Language, (d) Department of Home, (e) Department of Jammu and Kashmir Affairs and (f) Department of Border Management. In such a situation, all of them are secretaries; the senior most secretary, in addition to his own work, coordinates the work of other secretaries as well.

[11] Gopalaswami Ayyangar, *Report on the Reorganization of the Machinery of Government* (New Delhi: Manager of Publications, GoI, 1949), 140.

1. *Special secretary:* This level does not find place in the normal hierarchy. However, at times, a senior officer is designated as special secretary and carries the rank of secretary itself. Such an arrangement was made for short periods in the Ministry of Agriculture and Ministry of External Affairs. However, this is an exceptional measure and tends to distort the normal functioning of the ministry/department.
2. *Additional secretary:* In the larger ministries, where the volume of work has increased, a recognizable area of work may be entrusted to an additional secretary. An additional secretary assists the secretary in sharing his workload. In most cases, the files from the joint secretary are sent to the secretary through the additional secretary concerned. However, he may be authorized (under Transaction of Business Rules framed under Article 77(3) of the Constitution) to dispose of the files.

   Originally the officer next in the hierarchy to the Secretary was the deputy secretary. But in course of time new levels of joint secretary/additional secretary and even the special secretary came into existence. Various committees have adversely commented on the interposition of these levels between the secretary and the deputy secretary. The post of additional secretary is rather more anomalous. There is no specific unit of administration of which an additional secretary is to be in-charge. Sometimes, he is placed in charge of a department and does the work of a secretary; at other time, he is placed at the head of a wing and performs the task of a joint secretary. Sometimes he helps the secretary in specific field of activity. Richard Tottenham has observed that there is no difference between the functions of a joint secretary and additional secretary to be placed in charge of some specific area of work and relieve the secretary of some of his burdens.[12] In that case, he may deal directly with the minister in respect of the particular area of work allotted to him.
3. *Joint secretary:* A joint secretary is in charge of a wing with full authority to dispose of work in his charge.
4. *Deputy secretary:* A deputy secretary controls a division consisting of two to four branches. Apart from assisting the joint secretary in the discharge of his functions, the deputy secretary has to supervise and guide the functions assigned to the under secretaries. In most departments, there are posts of director which are equivalent to those of deputy secretary.

   He should ordinarily be able to dispose of a large number of cases coming up to him on his own responsibility. However, after independence, the post has got rather devalued, and there is hardly any decision which a deputy secretary is now taking on his own. Most of the important cases are submitted to the joint secretary and even the joint secretary is not taking many decisions himself.
5. *Under secretary:* Each branch is placed under the charge of an under secretary who works as a link between the deputy secretary and the section officers under him. Generally, most of the cases dealing with policy matters in a ministry are initiated and submitted by the under secretary to the higher officers for their consideration and approval.
6. *Section officer:* In the Central Secretariat, the section is the smallest organizational unit which is headed by a section officer. The work of the section officer is mainly of a supervisory nature, supervising the works of assistants, UDC, LDC and peons.

   Section officer has to supervise the work of his staff in his section. He is also responsible for handling important cases. He distributes the work amongst the staff,

---

[12] Tottenham Committee, *Report on the Government of India Secretariat, 1945–46* (Delhi: GoI, 1946).

trains and advises them in the discharge of their duties. He is also supposed to co-ordinate the work of different functionaries in his section, and ensure prompt and efficient disposal of work. His other functions include adoption of proper methods of processing of cases, timely submission of arrears statements and other periodical reports, proper maintenance of section diary, file register, assistants' diaries and other necessary registers. He is also there to ensure strict compliance with instructions regarding treatment of secret papers.

A section officer may be designated as desk officer, who performs functions such as signing financial sanctions, affirming affidavits in court and so on, as per powers delegated by the ministries/departments.

7. *Assistant:* A section may have two to five posts of assistant. The nature of duties and responsibilities of assistant are non-supervisory in nature. It is the assistant who puts up the cases on the relevant files and does noting after examining rules and orders relating to the assigned subjects. He also assists the section officer in the discharge of his duties.
8. *Upper Division Clerk:* The Upper Division Clerks render clerical assistance at various levels of routine nature. Assistants and upper division clerks are two different categories of dealing hands, and both work under the orders and supervision of the section officer. Under clear-cut instructions of the branch officer or higher officers, they are required to prepare drafts keeping in account the following: (a) check whether all facts available for scrutiny have been correctly stated; (b) point out any mistakes or incorrect statements of the facts; (c) refer to, where necessary, precedents or Rules and Regulations on the subject; (d) suggest the Guard file, if required, and supply other relevant facts and figures; and (e) to clearly state the situation under question and suggest a course of action wherever possible.

   In an electronic environment, they may use metadata for such purposes.
9. *Lower Division Clerk (LDC) and Multitasking Staff (MTS):* Lower division clerks are generally expected to carry out work of routine nature, for example, registration of post, maintenance of section diary and file registers, indexing and recording, typing, dispatch, preparation of arrears and other statements, supervision of correction of reference books and submission of routine and simple drafts etc.[13]
10. *Personal staff members of officers (PSMs):* Staff officer/senior principal private secretary/private secretary/personal assistant/stenographer, who are personal staff members of officers, have also been prescribed such responsibilities and duties as (a) taking dictation in shorthand and its transcription and assisting in drafting and issue of all correspondences as may be directed by the officer; (b) managing of appointments/engagements; (c) attending to the telephone calls and receiving visitors; (d) maintaining the papers required to be retained by the officer; (e) destroying by shredding/burning the stenographic record of the confidential and secret letters; and (f) assisting the officer in such a manner as she/he may direct.

Thus there are many levels in most ministries and if one were to include the dealing hand (usually an assistant/UDC/LDC), the number of levels actually comprises nine. A hierarchical multi-level structure has certain strengths but several weaknesses as well. While such a system enables a vertical division of labour with extensive supervision and checks and balances at different levels, it also causes delays due to sequential examination, dilutes rather than enhances accountability, prevents

[13] Duties of untrained multitasking Staff (MTS) have been provided at Annexure-II of the Department of Personnel & Training's O.M. Retrieved from https://darpg.gov.in/sites/default/files/CSMOP-13.pdf on 21 May 2018.

an interdisciplinary approach towards solving problems and kills creativity. For routine regulatory matters such as issuing licenses/permissions and so on, such a rigid hierarchical structure with prescribed workflows and adequate delegation may be appropriate, but, for functions such as policy formulation, managing change, crafting a holistic approach on interdisciplinary matters, problem-solving and so on, it does not give optimum results and in fact could be counterproductive.

6.2.4 Tenure System, Appointment and Central Staffing Scheme

For manning senior administrative posts in the secretariat, that is, posts of and above the rank of deputy secretary, a Central Staffing Scheme was notified on 17 October 1957 which has been amended several times. Now the scheme notified in 2016 by the Department of Personnel and Training is bound by the following parameters:

1. All posts of and above the rank of under secretary in the GoI, excluding such posts of under secretary and deputy secretary as are filled by CSS officers, are filled on tenure deputation from the All India Services and Central Services Group 'A'.
2. In so far as the officers from the CSS are concerned, a specified number of posts at the levels of under secretary and deputy secretary are treated as part of their cadre, and posts over and above these are filled under the scheme.
3. Every state cadre of each All India Services provides for a central deputation quota, which in turn requires additional recruitment to be made to these services, to provide for trained and experienced members of these services to serve on posts in the central government.

6.2.4.1 Tenure System

The normal tenure for posts covered by the Scheme is given in the following table.

Post	Tenure
Under Secretary	3 years
Deputy Secretary	4 years
Director/Joint Secretary	5 years
Additional Secretary*	4 years
Secretary	No fixed tenure

Note: *In case a joint secretary is promoted as additional secretary, the tenure is 3 years subject to a minimum of 5 years and maximum of 7 years of combined as joint secretary and additional secretary.

The share of the IAS among the total posts of secretaries varies from time to time. Prior to 1947, a majority of superior posts under the central government were specifically reserved for officers of the Indian Civil Service (ICS) and even after Independence, the central government continued to depend upon the ICS and Indian Administrative Services (IAS) officers for manning the positions in the secretariat. Situation has changed somewhat over the years and members of the Group 'A' Central Services are being inducted into the secretariat. For example, on 1 March 2016, posts of deputy secretary were held by 31.9% and 36.1% by IAS and CSS respectively.

The credit for introduction of tenure system goes to Lord Curzon who never forgot 'the men in the district', and this system originated from his belief that 'India may be governed from Simla or Calcutta; but is administered from the plains'.[14] Later, the Llewellyn Smith Committee (set up in 1918) recommended the continuance of tenure system,[15] although the GoI did not agree to lengthening of the tenure office of secretary and deputy secretary from the existing 3–4 years. Commending the continuance of this practice of rotation of officers between the secretariat and the field, the Simon Commission (1930) remarked, 'It is an accepted principle that efficient Secretariat service, both in the provinces and at Delhi, depends upon a constant interchange of personnel between the districts and the Secretariat, the provinces and the centre'.[16]

The Maxwell Committee (1937), lending its support to the practice of tenure system, concluded, 'All these considerations make it most desirable that stay at headquarters should be separated as far as possible by periods to be spent elsewhere, which will increase an officer's touch with reality, widen his vision and if possible add to his technical equipment'.[17]

Similar recommendations have been made in the subsequent reports of the ARC and other commissions.

6.2.4.2 Appointment

For staffing posts of the rank of deputy secretary, director and joint secretary or equivalent, the decision is taken by the Appointments Committee of the Cabinet, assisted by (a) the Civil Services Board, consisting of cabinet secretary (chairman), secretary personnel, one secretary to the GoI, establishment officer and secretary of the administrative ministry/department, and (b) Central Establishment Board, consisting of secretary, personnel (chairman), three secretaries to the GoI and the establishment officer, which are responsible for recommending selection for appointment to all posts of and above the rank of under secretary but below the level of joint secretary.

Eligibility of officers for holding posts of the level of under secretary and above (Group 'A') is 5 years for under secretary, 9 years for deputy secretary, 14 years for director, 17 years for joint secretary, 25 years for additional secretary and 30 years for secretary.

6.3 Services Under the Secretariat

There are three services in the Central Secretariat which provides support and continuity of the governmental system in the Central Secretariat:

1. Central Secretariat Service (CSS)
2. Central Secretariat Stenographers Service (CSSS)
3. Central Secretariat Clerical Service (CSCS)

[14] Loval Frasar, *India under Curzon and After* (New York: Henry Holt, 1911), 21.

[15] Llewellyn Committee, *Report of the Government of India Secretariat Procedure Committee* (New Delhi: GoI, 1919), para 72.

[16] John Simon, *Report of the Indian Statutory Commission, Vol. I, Survey* (London: HMSO, 1930), para 315.

[17] Maxwell Committee, *Report on Organization and Procedure, 1937* (Delhi: Bengal Press, 1957), para 51–53.

The sanctioned strength of three services functioning in the Central Secretariat as on 1 July 2016 is 24,381 posts.

6.3.1 Central Secretariat Service (CSS)

6.3.1.1 Historical Background

CSS, as an organized system, is very old and its origin can be traced to the year 1919 when the Imperial Secretariat Service was constituted on the recommendation of the Llewellyn Smith Committee which had been set up on the eve of introduction of Montague Chelmsford Reforms (1918).[18]

Finding the situation then obtained in the secretariat as one characterized by 'too few officers of the right kind and too many clerks of the wrong kind', Tottenham Committee (set up in 1946) suggested that 'to improve quality and reduce quantity, each Under Secretary's Branch should contain two sections and each section should consist of one Superintendent and three Assistants. Each Superintendent should have a smaller charge, but would be expected to do much more original work'.[19]

In the year 1949, on the recommendation of Sir R. A. Gopalaswami Ayyangar, the Central Secretariat Service (Reorganization and Reinforcement) Scheme was evolved. The service under this scheme consisted of under secretary given the Grade I; superintendent of Grade II; assistant superintendent of Grade III; and assistant of Grade IV. In 1959, Grades II and III were merged on the recommendation of Second CPC.

The Bandopadhyay Committee (November 1992) did not approve the idea of elevation of section officers to Group 'A' status. It also did not justify the constitution of CSS as a Group 'A' service (CSS is not a Group 'A' central service).

6.3.1.2 Grades and Posts

The CSS has at present four grades and the number of posts held by CSS officers in each grade as on 1 July 2016 are as follows given in the following table.

CSS Grades and Posts

Grade	Sanctioned Strength
Senior Selection Grade (Director and Deputy Secretary)	600
Under Secretary	1,462
Section Officer	3,018
Assistant	6,387
Total strength	11,467

[18] Llewellyn Committee, *Report of the Government*, para 72.
[19] Tottenham Committee, *Report on the Reorganization of the Central Government* (Delhi: GoI, 1945–46).

6.3.1.3 Recruitment

Recruitment and promotion to various grades are governed by the CSS Rules, 1962, and CSS (Promotion to Grade I and Selection Grade) Regulations, 1964. The present mode of recruitment to various grades is as follows:

1. *Assistant Grade.* Recruitment to this grade is
   a. Direct—50% through an open competitive examination held by the Staff Selection Commission.
   b. Indirect—50% by promotion (from among UDCs with a five years' service).
2. *Section Officer.* Recruitment to this grade is
   a. Direct—20% through an open examination held by the UPSC.
   b. Department—40% through a Limited Departmental Competitive Examination held for assistants and stenographers Grade 'C' of Central Secretariat.
   c. Indirect—40% by promotion (from amongst assistants with an eight years' service).
3. *Under Secretary.* Recruitment to this grade is
   a. Direct—0%.
   b. Indirect—100% by promotion (from amongst section officers with an eight years' service/Group 'A' of CSSS).
4. *Deputy Secretary.* Recruitment to this grade is
   a. Direct—0%.
   b. Indirect—100% by promotion (from amongst under secretaries) having five years' service on the basis of seniority-cum-selection.

6.3.1.4 Duty and Tenure Posts

The posts of under secretary and deputy secretary held by CSS officers are 'duty posts', and, under the Centre Staffing Scheme, the posts of under Secretary and above in the Centre Secretariat (2016) are filled by drawing persons from different services without any definite quota. While the 'tenure rule' is applied to All India Services and Group 'A' Central Services, there is no tenure rule laid down for CSS officers.

6.3.2 Central Secretariat Stenographers Service (CSSS)

The CSSS is an integral part of the Central Secretariat. It was constituted in 1951 to man the posts of Stenographer III in the Central Secretariat and attached offices. Since then, its cadre structure has undergone several changes. On implementation of the recommendations of the 3rd CPC (1973), the CSSS was reorganized in four grades (A, B, C and D) of stenographers in the Central Secretariat. Later, on the recommendations of the 4th CPC, Grades 'A' and 'B' of CSSS were merged, and the posts of private secretary to secretaries to GoI and equivalent officers were upgraded to provide further avenues of promotion. With a view to provide further promotion prospects to stenographers of CSSS, posts in Grades D, C and A and B (merged) were pooled together and their strength was re-fixed in November 1993 in the ratio of 40:40:20 in each grade of the service. On 1 July 2016, the CSSS had the number of posts mentioned in the following table.

CSSS Grades and Posts

Grade	Sanctioned Strength
Senior Principal Private Secretary (SPPS)	142
Principal Private Secretary (PPS)	781
Private Secretary (PS)	2,095
Stenographer Grade 'C'	
(Personal Assistant)	2,637
Stenographer Grade 'D'	1,326
Total strength	6,981

6.3.2.1 Recruitment

Recruitment and promotion of stenographers are governed by the CSSS Rules, 1969, supplemented by the Central Secretariat Stenographers' Service (Private Secretary Grade) Rules, 1989, for promotion to the grade of principal private secretary. Personnel in this service also perform certain duties such as (a) supervision of staff in the personal section of the officer, (b) proper maintenance and custody of all housekeeping items and (c) maintenance of confidentiality of papers.

6.3.3 Central Secretariat Clerical Service (CSCS)

The CSCS was constituted with two grades along with the CSS in 1951 (but its rules came into force on 1 November 1962). The strength of the two grades and number of posts are given in the following table as on 1 July 2016.

CSCS Grades and Posts

Grade	Sanctioned Strength
Upper Division Clerk (UDC)	3,681
Lower Division Clerk (LDC)	2,252
Total strength	5,933

6.3.3.1 Recruitment

Recruitment and promotion to LDCs and UDCs are governed by the CSCS Rules, 1962. The present mode of recruitment to these two grades is as follows:

1. LDC. Recruitment to LDC grade is
   a. Direct—80% through an All India Competitive Examination held by the Staff Selection Commission.

b. Departmental—10% through a Limited Departmental Qualifying Examination.
c. Indirect—10% by promotion (from educationally qualified Group D employees on seniority-cum-fitness basis with five years' service).

2. UDC. Recruitment to UDC grade is
   a. Departmental—25% through a Limited Departmental Competitive Examination held by the SSC for LDCs with five years' service.
   b. Indirect—75% by promotion (from among LDCs on seniority-cum-fitness basis with eight years' service).

The government has decided that all the vacant posts of LDC grade (to the tune of 85% vacant posts in every select list year) be abolished, discontinuing the direct recruitment to the post of LDC. The mode of recruitment for the post of LDC would be 70% by the promotion of Group 'D' staff and 30% through Limited Departmental Competitive Examination for Group 'D' staff.[20]

6.4 Criticism and Remedial Measures of Secretariat Functioning

The situation obtaining today in the functioning of the Central Secretariat is not quite different from the one which had been observed by the study team of the ARC in 1967:

> The Secretariat at the centre is thus today encumbered with non-essential work and has, for a large part, become an unwieldy and over-staffed organization. This leads to occasional blurring of responsibilities and choking of the administrative machinery, which thus finds excuse for dilatoriness and delay. Further, the over-growth of personnel has resulted in deterioration in quality. This has inevitably meant increased burden for officers at the higher levels.

1. *Multiple layers lead to inefficiency and delays:* The Manual of Office Procedure lays down at least 7–8 levels—from the dealing hand to the Minister—through which papers usually pass before decisions are taken. It has also been observed that many of the levels do not make any significant contribution in decision-making. Multiple scrutiny inevitably leads to delays, and abdication of responsibility in the examination process in the erroneous belief that other levels would ensure adequate analysis.
2. *Fuzzy delegations:* The multiple levels, as stated before, combined with vague and/or inadequate delegation, encourage reverse delegation of work to higher levels. This is particularly because the Manual is extremely vague, as regards the specific of delegation especially at the level of under secretary/deputy secretary/director/joint secretary. In practice, however, it has been observed that many departments have not done so thus leaving it to the discretion of individual officers, whether to dispose of matters at his level or send it to the next level. Due to a pervasive culture of risk avoidance, the inevitable result is the practice of routinely sending all files upwards.

[20] Vide DOPT's Order No. 9/2/2003-C.S. 1 dated 20 April 2005.

3. *Focus on file management at the expense of outcomes:* The Manual of Office Procedure states that the ultimate objective of all government business is to meet the citizen's needs and to further their welfare without undue delay. At the same time, those who are accountable for the conduct of that business have to ensure that public funds are managed with utmost care and prudence. Even though the manual emphasizes the importance of outcomes over processes, the bulk of the stipulations are focused on file management and recordkeeping. The Manual of Office Procedure appears to emphasize the action to be taken on receipt of papers rather than on a proactive approach towards the department's priorities.
4. *Absence of team-based working:* The multiple levels along with division of task into separate units leads to the creation of quasi-independent silos within each department. Complex issues requiring a multi-disciplinary approach thus get embroiled in turf battles rather than generating a holistic approach. The need for interdisciplinary work teams for dealing with cross-cutting issues is not met due to the hierarchical and heavily segmented structure combined with procedures that constrain team efforts.

S. R. Maheshwari notes that the 'personnel in the Secretariat suffer from a certain amount of superiority, even arrogance and vanity vis-à-vis the executive agencies. Instead of assisting and encouraging the latter in the carrying out of their responsibilities, the Secretariat today acts as an inhibiting factor'.[21]

6.4.1 Remedial Measures

The secretariat is primarily a policy-making institution and therefore its focus should be on institution-building and policy-making for the nation. A new approach to policy-making would call for restructuring the design of the ministries to make them less hierarchical by creating flatter structures with team-based orientation. The ministries, as they function now, are centralized, hierarchical organizations rightly divided into many layers, boxes and silos. Much of the civil service hierarchies in the ministries continue to be structured along traditional lines of authority, carefully regulated to ensure that as few mistakes are made as possible. The staff in the ministries is more concerned with internal processes than with results. The systemic rigidities, needless complexities and over-centralization in the policy-making structures are too complex and too constraining. There are too many decision points in the policy structures, and there are a large number of veto points to be negotiated for a decision to emerge. While such hierarchical exercise of authority provides some control of quality and integrity of decision-making, it often leads to exasperating delays and takes the focus away from delivering results. It is necessary that these hierarchies should be dismantled and team-based structures be introduced.

Some remedial measures for proper functioning and structure of the secretariat are as follows:

1. *Clarity in delegation:* It has been observed that in carrying out the business in government, a scheme of delegation does exist in each department, but it is not well defined in some cases. Even though the Manual of Office Procedure (modified from time to time) states that officers at the level of joint secretary/additional secretary/special secretary are 'entrusted with maximum measure of independent functioning and responsibility in respect of all

[21] Maheshwari, *Indian Administration*, 55.

business falling within their wings'. In actual practice, it is observed more in breach than in reality. The experience has been that these officials often tend to 'play safe' and mark files to higher levels even in cases of routine issues.

2. *Streamlining levels to reduce delays:* There are at least nine levels from the dealing hand to the minister before a decision is taken on certain matters. The secretariat's functioning should be streamlined to avoid duplication of efforts and an ambiguity of policy-decision. To cure these evils, it seems desirable that (a) noting by clerks and assistants should be minimized; (b) references as they come should be assigned to the appropriate level in the hierarchy, which as a rule should not be more than two levels below that at which a decision is expected to be taken; (c) wherever possible, a senior officer should give specific directions about the manner in which a case should be disposed of; and (d) the officer should ask for the information requisite for the disposal of a reference.

   It is suggested that the central government should take a major initiative to minimize layers to improve the quality of decision-making and significantly reduce delays. In this context, the Second ARC suggested that 'the number of levels through which a file passes for a decision should not exceed three'.

   The Second ARC also recommended,

   > Departments should build an electronic database of decisions that are likely to be used as precedents. Thereafter such database should be periodically reviewed and where necessary, changes in rules introduced in order to codify them. There may also be precedents that may be the result of wrong or arbitrary decision-making which the Department would prefer not to rely on for the future. In such cases the Department would have to appropriately change its policy/guidelines and if required even the rules to ensure that these precedents are not wrongly used.[22]

3. *Emphasis on securing coordination:* There is need to ensure that the existing coordination mechanisms such as Committee of Secretaries function effectively and help in early resolution of issues. Unresolved issues concerning states which require inter-ministerial coordination in GoI should be placed before the Committee of Secretaries and then to the union cabinet for resolution. In conclusion, it is reiterated that the best way to achieve the objective of reducing delays and creating more responsive, efficient and accountable organizational structures would be by modifying the existing structure of the government departments and incorporating elements of team-based working for achieving the tasks and objectives assigned to them. As mentioned earlier, the ministries would basically concentrate on policy-making, supervision, monitoring and evaluation and budgetary processes while leaving the implementation to executive agencies.

6.5 Attached and Subordinate Offices

Each Department may have one or more attached or subordinate offices. They have distinct places in the government organization. The Manual of Office Procedure (GoI) states:

[22] Second ARC, *Report on Organization*, 164.

> Where the execution of the policies of the government requires decentralization of executive and/or direction, a department may have under it executive agencies called 'Attached' and 'Subordinate' offices. Attached offices are generally responsible for providing executive direction required in the implementation of the policies laid down by the department to which they are attached. They also serve as repository of technical information and advise the department on technical aspects of question dealt with by them.

On the other hand, 'subordinate offices generally function as field establishments or as agencies responsible for the detailed execution of the policies of government'. They function under the direction of an attached office or where the volume of executive direction involved is not considerable directly under the department. 'In the latter case, they assist the departments concerned in handling technical matters in their respective fields of specialization'.

A distinction is required to be made between 'organization of these offices and Ministry and Departments'. Usually, the head of an attached office is a technical officer called registrar, director general or chief engineer and so on. Below him, there are a few technical or non-technical officers who help him in his duties. The proportion of technical and non-technical secretariat officers differ from office to office. There is no common pattern of organization of attached offices.

As far as the functions of 'attached offices' are concerned, they provide technical information for 'the policy formulation as well as executive direction for its implementation'. Often attached offices are regarded as field organizations because they not only issue executive directions to the subordinate offices but are also responsible for its implementation. They act as coordinate mechanisms for the subordinate offices and keep the secretariat informed about the various problems faced in the implementation of the policies. The attached offices, thus, could be considered as the headquarters of the field organization rather than an extension of the secretariat.

6.5.1 Relationship Between Attached and Subordinate Offices

The subordinate offices function as field agencies, responsible for the detailed implementation of the policies and decisions of the government. They generally function under the direction of an attached office. According to the Manual of Office Procedure, the attached offices 'are responsible for providing executive direction required in the implementation of the policies laid down by the ministry to which they are attached'. In other words, such an office plays dual role that of directing the subordinate offices below and submitting proposals to the secretariat above. On the other hand, a subordinate office is a mere field agency 'responsible for the detailed execution of the decisions of the government'. The role which the subordinate offices play is very crucial being at 'the delivering of goods end'. However, it is observed that such a distinction is blurred. Even the Manual recognizes that although the subordinate offices generally function under direction of the attached offices, in some cases, they may functions directly under the ministry.

As early as 1945–46, Tottenham exclaimed in exasperation, 'No one has ever been able to arrive at a really satisfactory definition of an Attached Office'.

Tottenham, therefore, recommended the abolition of distinction between the two categories of offices. The First CPC (1946–47) also found such distinction 'artificial' and recommended its abolition. It recommended the regrouping of offices into three categories: (a) policy-making organization, that is, secretariat proper; (b) offices of the executive heads and advisory organizations and (c) offices subordinate to the above two categories. The Second CPC (1957–59) suggested a functional classification based upon two criteria:

1. Offices which were associated with the shaping of policy by furnishing technical data and advice and by giving executive directions to the field agencies and which were responsible for implementing the policies of the government should be designated as attached offices.
2. Offices mainly responsible for the execution of government policies and programmes should be called subordinate offices.

The ARC (1966–70) examined the problem in the wider context of secretariat and non-secretariat organizations and their relationship and made certain recommendations. However, despite all the aforementioned recommendations, the distinction between the two remains undefined. However it is found that while the attached offices have been able to better the conditions of service of their employees and achieve a higher status almost co-equal to that of the secretariat, the subordinate offices continue to slog in their subordinate status.

Besides the attached and subordinate offices, there are a large number of organizations which carry out different functions assigned to them.[23] These may be categorized as follows:

1. *Constitutional bodies:* Such bodies which are constituted under the provisions of the Constitution of India.
2. *Statutory bodies:* Such bodies which are established under the statute or an Act of Parliament.
3. *Autonomous bodies:* Such bodies which are established by the governments to discharge the activities which are related to governmental functions. Although such bodies are given autonomy to discharge their functions in accordance with the Memorandum of Associations and so on, but the government's control exists since these are funded by the GoI.
4. *PSUs:* PSU is that part of the industry which is controlled fully or partly by the government. These undertakings have been set up in the form of companies or corporations in which the shares are held by the president or his nominees and which are managed by Board of Directors which includes officials and non-officials.

6.6 Relationship Patterns Between Secretariat and Executive Agencies

In discussing relationship between the secretariat (mainly policy-making organization) and the executive agencies (implementing agencies), there exist a variety of structural patterns. The first pattern is an integrated pattern such as the model of the Railway Board. This pattern is suitable for organizations which are dealing with commercial functions. The second pattern is the link pattern in which a senior functionary of a ministry is head of the executive agency functioning under the concerned ministry. This dual role of a functionary sometimes leads to ambiguity. For example, the joint secretary in the Department of Labour and Employment may also be the director general

[23] Extracted from Ministry of Personnel, Public Grievances and Pensions, *Central Secretariat Manual of Office Procedure.*

of employment and training. The strength of this pattern is that it reduces the distance between the secretariat and attached office.

In the third pattern, the ministry and the executive department have separate offices but a common record or a file bureau located in the executive department. The attached office submits proposals on its own files and refers the ministry along with the papers, complete in all respects. After the proposal is disposed of by the ministry, the file is returned to the executive head. The example is Ministry of Defence and the Air Force Headquarters. The advantage of this system is that it avoids duplication of files and reduces time period. In the fourth pattern, the ministry and the executive department both have a common office, common files and a common file bureau under the control of the executive department. The advantage is that in this system, a proposal is examined only once which results in quick disposal of business and saves a lot of money. In the fifth system, an *ex-officio* secretariat status is accorded to the head of an executive agency. The example is that a textile commissioner who is ex-officio joint secretary in the Ministry of Textiles. The merits of the system are that the head of the attached office brought in closer contact with the ministry's office, gets more closely involved in policy-making and gets certain powers to take decision on certain issues. In the sixth relationship pattern, both the ministry and the executive department have distinct and separate offices and files of their own. Consultation between them takes place through self-contained communications. This system has the in-built strength of ensuring uniform polices in matters of various executive agencies of a ministry and multi-level examination of proposals. However, it has the inherent disadvantages of duplication of work being processed in two offices and delays and conflicts.

The foregoing relationship patterns between the secretariat and executive agencies have both weaknesses and strengths. They represents the attempts at bridging the gulf between secretariat and non-secretariat organizations through devices such as giving of ex-office secretariat status to the heads of the executive agencies; introduction of the single file system, placement of executive agencies and so on.

Recently after PM Narendra Modi's interaction with additional secretary- and joint secretary-level officials, the cabinet secretary issued a directive containing 39-actionable points, asking the secretaries to spend 5–6 days a month in the field as the 'Central Secretariat has lost field focus'. Further, the cabinet secretary said in the directive, 'Instead of multiple orders on the same subject, each department should undertake an annual validation of all office memorandums on the same subjects. While doing so, all earlier orders on the subject should be subsumed and only one Office Memorandum (OM) should remain current'.[24]

Summary

The Central Secretariat, called at one time the Imperial Secretariat, has a history of more than 300 years. Despite the fact that the system it has evolved is slow, cumbersome and unresponsive, the secretariat has certain inherent strengths which have helped the government to stand the test of time. It has contributed to the nation-building, maturing of democracy and ushering in an era of good governance. The structure which it has developed over the years has facilitated and contributed to the strengthening of the cooperative federalism.

[24] See *The Economic Times* (Chandigarh), 20 September 2017.

In the hierarchical structure of central administration, the Central Secretariat occupies a distinct place. It is the centre of power and its writ runs throughout the length and breadth of the country. Policies and programmes of the government originate from here, and it is the centre of conflicts and cooperation between the ministers and the civil servants. It is also the centre of all kinds of political, sectional and interest group pressures. The decisions taken by the Central Secretariat are vital for the country. Thus, the Central Secretariat is the main executive instrument of the GoI and is responsible for managing the central subjects, coordinating the multifarious activities of national importance and assisting in the formulation of foreign, economic, social and financial policies.

The Central Secretariat occupies an apex position. To quote the ARC,

> The Secretariat system of work has lent balance, consistency and continuity to the administration, and serves as a nucleus for the total machinery of a Ministry. It has facilitated inter-Ministry coordination and accountability to Parliament at the Ministerial level. As an institutional system, it is indispensable for the proper functioning of Government.[25]

Needless to emphasize that the Central Secretariat has, since Independence, evolved a pattern of administration in which continuity and specialization have their place with knowledge and administrative experience in the work and management of a department.

Annexure I

List of the Ministries/Departments (2018)

1. Ministry of Agriculture and Farmers Welfare (Krishi evam Kisan Kalyan Mantralaya)
   a. Department of Agriculture, Co-operation and Farmers Welfare (Krishi, Sahkarita evam Kisan Kalyan Vibhag)
   b. Department of Agricultural Research and Education (Krishi Anusandhan aur Shiksha Vibhag)
   c. Department of Animal Husbandry, and Fisheries and Dairying (Pashupalan, Dairy aur Matsyapalan Vibhag)
2. Ministry of Ayurveda, Yoga and Naturopathy, Unani, Siddha and Homoeopathy (AYUSH; Ayurveda, Yoga evam Prakritik Chikitsa, Unani Siddha evam Homoeopathy) (Ayush Mantralaya)
3. Ministry of Chemicals and Fertilizers (Rasayan aur Urvarak Mantralaya)
   a. Department of Chemicals and Petro-Chemicals (Rasayan aur Petro-Rasayan Vibhag)
   b. Department of Fertilizers (Urvarak Vibhag)
   c. Department of Pharmaceuticals (Aushadh Vibhag)
4. Ministry of Civil Aviation (Nagar Vimanan Mantralaya)
5. Ministry of Coal (Koyla Mantralaya)
6. Ministry of Commerce and Industry (Vanijya aur Udyog Mantralaya)
   a. Department of Commerce (Vanijya Vibhag)
   b. Department of Industrial Policy and Promotion (Audyogik Niti aur Samvardhan Vibhag)

---

[25] ARC, *Report on the Government.*

7. Ministry of Communications (Sanchar Mantralaya)
    a. Department of Telecommunications (Doorsanchar Vibhag)
    b. Department of Posts (Dak Vibhag)
8. Ministry of Consumer Affairs, Food and Public Distribution (Upbhokta Mamle, Khadya aur Sarvajanik Vitaran Mantralaya)
    a. Department of Consumer Affairs (Upbhokta Mamle Vibhag)
    b. Department of Food and Public Distribution (Khadya aur Sarvajanik Vitaran Vibhag)
9. Ministry of Corporate Affairs (Corporate Karya Mantralaya)
10. Ministry of Culture (Sanskriti Mantralaya)
11. Ministry of Defence (Raksha Mantralaya)
    a. Department of Defence (Raksha Vibhag)
    b. Department of Defence Production (Raksha Utpadan Vibhag)
    c. Department of Defence Research and Development (Raksha Anusandhan tatha Vikas Vibhag)
    d. Department of Ex-servicemen Welfare (Poorva Senani Kalyan Vibhag)
12. Ministry of Development of North-Eastern Region (Uttar Poorvi Kshetra Vikas Mantralaya)
13. Ministry of Drinking Water and Sanitation (Peyjal aur Swachchhata Mantralaya)
14. Ministry of Earth Sciences (Prithvi Vigyan Mantralaya)
15. Ministry of Electronics and Information Technology (Electroniki aur Suchana Praudyogiki Mantralaya)
16. Ministry of Environment, Forest and Climate Change (Paryavaran, Van aur Jalvayu Parivartan Mantralaya)
17. Ministry of External Affairs (Videsh Mantralaya)
18. Ministry of Finance (Vitta Mantralaya)
    a. Department of Economic Affairs (Arthik Karya Vibhag)
    b. Department of Expenditure (Vyaya Vibhag)
    c. Department of Revenue (Rajaswa Vibhag)
    d. Department of Investment and Public Asset Management (DIPAM; Nivesh aur Lok Parisampatti Prabandhan Vibhag)
    e. Department of Financial Services (Vittiya Sewayen Vibhag)
19. Ministry of Food Processing Industries (Khadya Prasanskaran Udyog Mantralaya)
20. Ministry of Health and Family Welfare (Swasthya aur Pariwar Kalyan Mantralaya)
    a. Department of Health and Family Welfare (Swastlzya aur Parivar Kalyan Vibhag)
    b. Department of Health Research (Swasthya Anusandhan Vibhag)
21. Ministry of Heavy Industries and Public Enterprises (Bhari Udyog aur Lok Udyam Mantralaya)
    a. Department of Heavy Industries (Bhari Udyog Vibhag)
    b. Department of Public Enterprises (Lok Udyam Vibhag)
22. Ministry of Home Affairs (Grih Mantralaya)
    a. Department of Internal Security (Aantarik Suraksha Vibhag)
    b. Department of States (Rajya Vibhag)
    c. Department of Official Language (Raj Bhasha Vibhag)
    d. Department of Home (Grih Vibhag)
    e. Department of Jammu and Kashmir Affairs (Jammu evam Kashmir Vibhag)
    f. Department of Border Management (Seema Prabandhan Vibhag)

23. Ministry of Housing and Urban Affairs
(Awasan aur Shahari Karya Mantralaya)
24. Ministry of Human Resource Development (Manav Sansadhan Vikas Mantralaya)
    a. Department of School Education and Literacy (School Shiksha aur Saksharta Vibhag)
    b. Department of Higher Education (Uchchatar Shiksha Vibhag)
25. Ministry of Information and Broadcasting (Suchana aur Prasaran Mantralaya)
26. Ministry of Labour and Employment (Shram aur Rozgar Mantralaya)
27. Ministry of Law and Justice (Vidhi aur Nyaya Mantralaya)
    a. Department of Legal Affairs (Vidhi Karya Vibhag)
    b. Legislative Department (Vidhayee Vibhag)
    c. Department of Justice (Nyaya Vibhang)
28. Ministry of Micro, Small and Medium Enterprises (Sukshm, Laghu aur Madhyam Udyam Mantralaya)
29. Ministry of Mines (Khan Mantralaya)
30. Ministry of Minority Affairs (Alpasankhyak Karya Mantralaya)
31. Ministry of New and Renewable Energy (Naveen aur Navikarniya Urja Mantralaya)
32. Ministry of Panchayati Raj (Panchayati Raj Mantralaya)
33. Ministry of Parliamentary Affairs (Sansadiya Karya Mantralaya)
34. Ministry of Personnel, Public Grievances and Pensions (Karmik, Lok Shikayat aur Pension Mantralaya)
    a. Department of Personnel and Training (Karmik aur Prashikshan Vibhag)
    b. Department of Administrative Reforms and Public Grievances (Prashasnik Sudhar aur Lok Shikayat Vibhag)
    c. Department of Pensions and Pensioners' Welfare (Pension aur Pension Bhogi Kalyan Vibhag)
35. Ministry of Petroleum and Natural Gas (Petroleum aur Prakritik Gas Mantralaya)
36. Ministry of Planning (Yojana Mantralaya)
37. Ministry of Power (Vidyut Mantralaya)
38. Ministry of Railways (Rail Mantralaya)
39. Ministry of Road Transport and Highways (Sarak Parivahan aur Raj Marg Mantralaya)
40. Ministry of Rural Development (Gramin Vikas Mantralaya)
    a. Department of Rural Development (Gramin Vikas Vibhag)
    b. Department of Land Resources (Bhumi Sansadhan Vibhag)
41. Ministry of Science and Technology (Vigyan aur Praudyogiki Mantralaya)
    a. Department of Science and Technology (Vigyan aur Praudyogiki Vibhag)
    b. Department of Scientific and Industrial Research (Vigyan aur Audyogik Anusandhan Vibhag)
    c. Department of Bio-technology (Biotechnology Vibhag)
42. Ministry of Shipping (Pot Parivahan Mantralaya)
43. Ministry of Skill Development and Entrepreneurship (Kaushal Vikas evam Udyamita Mantralaya)
44. Ministry of Social Justice and Empowerment (Samajik Nyaya aur Adhikarita Mantralaya)
    a. Department of Social Justice and Empowerment (Samajik Nyaya aur Adhikarita Vibhag)
    b. Department of Empowerment of Persons with Disabilities (Viklang Jan Sashaktikaran Vibhag)

45. Ministry of Statistics and Programme Implementation (Sankhyiki aur Karyakram Karyanvayan Mantralaya)
46. Ministry of Steel (Ispat Mantralaya)
47. Ministry of Textiles (Vastra Mantralaya)
48. Ministry of Tourism (Paryatan Mantralaya)
49. Ministry of Tribal Affairs (Janjatiya Karya Mantralaya)
50. Ministry of Urban Development (Shahri Vikas Mantralaya)
51. Ministry of Housing and Urban Poverty Alleviation (Awas aur Shahri Garibi Upshaman Mantralaya)
52. Ministry of Water Resources, River Development and Ganga Rejuvenation (Jal Sansadhan, Nadi Vikas aur Ganga Sanrakshan Mantralaya)
53. Ministry of Women and Child Development (Mahila aur Bal Vikas Mantralaya)
54. Ministry of Youth Affairs and Sports (Yuva Karyakram aur Khel Mantralaya)
    a. Department of Youth Affairs (Yuva Karyakram Vibhag)
    b. Department of Sports (Khel Vibhag)

Independent Departments

55. Department of Atomic Energy (Parmanu Urja Vibhag)
56. Department of Space (Antariksh Vibhag)

Apex/Independent Office

57. NITI Aayog (National Institution for Transforming India)
58. Cabinet Secretariat (Mantrimandal Sachivalaya)
59. President's Secretariat (Rashtrapati Sachivalaya)
60. Prime Minister's Office (Pradhan Mantri Karyalaya)

7 State Executive and Governance

LEARNING OBJECTIVES

1. **To evaluate the position of governors of states in the context of recent judicial pronouncements**
2. **To discuss the powers and position of the chief ministers of states**
3. **To discuss the unique position of the chief secretary as the head of state machinery**

Introduction

India, a union of states, presently comprises 29 states and 7 union territories.[1] Each state enjoys the status of being a member of the federal system and shares a distribution of powers with the Union. The seven union territories, barring Puducherry (governed under Article 239A, added in 1962) and Delhi (governed under Articles 239AA and 239AB, added in 1992), are centrally administered areas governed by the president acting through an administrator appointed by him. Administrators of Andaman and Nicobar Islands, Delhi and Puducherry are designated as lieutenant governors. The Governor of Punjab is concurrently the administrator of Chandigarh. The administrator of Dadra and Nagar Haveli is concurrently the administrator of Daman and Diu. Lakshadweep has a separate administrator.

The National Capital Territory of Delhi and Union Territory of Puducherry each has a legislative assembly and Council of Ministers. The legislative assembly of the Union Territory of Puducherry may make laws with respect to matters enumerated in List II or List III in the Seventh Schedule of the Constitution insofar as these matters are applicable in relation to the union territory. The legislative assembly of National Capital Territory of Delhi has also these powers with the exceptions that Entries 1, 2 and 18 of the List II are not within the legislative competence of the legislative assembly. Certain categories of bills, however, require the prior approval of the central government for introduction in the legislative assembly. Some bills, passed by the legislative assemblies of the Union Territory of Puducherry and national Capital Territory of Delhi, are required to be reserved for consideration and assent of the president.

[1] The states are Andhra Pradesh, Assam, Arunachal Pradesh, Bihar, Chhattisgarh, Goa, Gujarat, Haryana, Himachal Pradesh, Jammu and Kashmir, Jharkhand, Karnataka, Kerala, Madhya Pradesh, Maharashtra, Manipur, Meghalaya, Mizoram, Nagaland, Odisha, Punjab, Rajasthan, Sikkim, Tamil Nadu, Telangana, Tripura, Uttarakhand, Uttar Pradesh and West Bengal. Union territories are Andaman and Nicobar Islands, Chandigarh, Dadra and Nagar Haveli, Daman and Diu, National Capital Territory of Delhi, Lakshadweep and Puducherry.

7.1 Integration of Indian States

The present federal and unitary system under the 1950 Constitution (and subsequent amendments) has a unique background. A distinctive feature of the new Constitution is the union of some 552 Indian princely states with the rest of India. At the time of the constitutional reforms leading to the GoI Act, 1935, India was divided into parts, namely, British India (comprising of nine governors' provinces and some other areas administered by the GoI itself),[2] and the Indian states (comprising of some 600 states, which were mostly under the personal rule of the rulers).[3] About 300 of them were estates or *jagirs* granted by the rulers as rewards for services or otherwise to particular individuals or families. As these Indian states had not been annexed by the British Crown, these were allowed to remain under the personal rule of their chiefs and princes, under the 'suzerainty' of the Grown.

Here, it may be stated that the assumption of suzerainty by the Crown in 1858—the relationship between the Crown and the Indian states—came to be described by the term 'Paramountcy'. Under this paramountcy, while the Crown accepted responsibility for their external relations and defence, the Indian states were allowed to manage their internal affairs. But the Crown interfered in cases of misrule and maladministration as well as for giving effects to its international commitments. So, even in the internal spheres, the Indian states had no legal 'right' against non-interference. Nevertheless, the rulers of the Indian states enjoyed certain personal rights and privileges and normally carried on their personal administration unaffected by political events. The framers of the GoI Act, 1935, envisaged a federal structure of the whole of India.[4] Under this system, while it was compulsory for the 11 provinces and 6 chief commissioners of provinces to join the federation, it was, however, optional for the rulers of the princely states to join it. Moreover, in the case of the Indian states, the authority of the federation could be limited by the 'Instrument of Accession'. The accession of the Indian states to the proposed federation never came true, and this part of the Act of 1935 was finally given up in 1939.

The Cabinet Mission in March 1946 recommended that there should be a Union of India, embracing both British India and the states, which would deal only with foreign affairs, defence and communications, while the states would retain all powers other than these.

With the passage of the Indian Independence Act, 1947 (the bill was introduced in the House of Commons on 4 July 1947 which received the Royal assent on 18 July 1947 under which, as from 15 August 1947, two independent dominions, India and Pakistan, were created), paramountcy of the Crown over the Indian states lapsed. But soon the princely states realized that it was no longer possible for them to maintain their existence independent of and separate from the rest of the country. Therefore, all the 552 princely states (except Hyderabad, Kashmir, Bahawalpur, Junagadh and the N. W. F. States—Chitral, Phulra, Dir, Swat and Amb) had acceded to the Dominion of India by 15 August 1947.

Of the states, 216 merged states were included in the territories of the states in Part B of the First Schedule of the Constitution.[5] Total 61 states were converted into centrally administered

[2] British India was under the direct rule of the Crown through its representatives and worked according to the statutes of Parliament and enactments of the Indian legislatures.

[3] Indian states were also known as princely states. Suzerainty was assumed over the entire territory of India when the Crown took over authority from the East India Company in 1858.

[4] Refer to the GoI Act, 1935.

[5] The process of merger started with the merger of Odisha and Chhattisgarh states with the then Province of Orissa on 1 January 1948, and the last instance was the merger of Cooch–Behar with the state of West Bengal in January 1950.

areas and included in Part C of the First Scheduled of the Constitution. The third form of integration was described as union of states, incorporating groups of states into new viable units.[6] Under this form, 275 states were integrated into 5 unions, namely, (a) Madhya Bharat, (b) Patiala and East Punjab States Union (PEPSU), (c) Rajasthan, (d) Saurashtra and (e) Travancore-Cochin. These were included in the states in Part B of the First Schedule. Jammu and Kashmir acceded to India on 26 October 1947 and was included as a state in Part B, but its accession was confirmed in November 1956 on the recommendation of the constituent assembly.[7] Hyderabad initially did not accede to India, but finally it was included as a state in Part B by the ratification of the constituent assembly of the state. Mysore was also included in Part B of the First Schedule.

It may be pointed here that there was a formal agreement between the GoI and rulers of each of the states by which they voluntarily agreed to the merger and ceded all powers for the governance of the states to the Dominion of India, keeping a few personal rights and privileges for themselves. Further, it is to be noted that the Rajpramukhs of the five unions as well as the rulers of Hyderabad, Mysore, Jammu and Kashmir adopted the Constitution of India by presidential proclamations. With the legislation of the Constitution (7th Amendment) Act, 1956, Part B states as a class was merged with Part A states. Consequently, the Indian states (erstwhile princely states) lost their identity and became part of one uniform political organization embodied in the Constitution of India.[8]

Broadly speaking, the political structure of government in the states is the same as that for the Union, namely, a parliamentary system of government with a constitutional head and with ministerial responsibility to the popular House of the legislature (the governor acts according to the advice of Council of Ministers except in matters in respect of which the governor is empowered under Article 163(1) to act in his discretion).

7.2 Governor of the State

The governor is the head of the state just as the president stands at the head of the executive power of the Union of India and all executive action of a state has to be taken in the name of the governor (Article 154).

7.2.1 Selection Process and Removal

The governor is not elected by the process of direct or indirect voting (like the chief minister or the president). The governor of a particular state is appointed directly by the President of India for a period of five years unless he resigns office but he holds office at the pleasure of the president (Article 156). He can be reappointed and the term does not cease on its end. The security of the

[6] The first union formed was the Saurashtra Union consolidating the Kathiawar States and many other states (15 February 1948), and the last one was the Union of Travancore–Cochin, formed on 1 July 1949.

[7] Special provisions were made only for Kashmir under Article 370 in view of its special position and problems. The states of Jammu and Kashmir, which is an integral part of India, is the only state which has acquired the distinction of having a separate Constitution for the administration of the state in place of the provisions of Part VI of the Constitution of India which govern all the other states.

[8] The Constitution (26th Amendment) Act, 1971, abolished the Privy Purse granted to the rulers of the former Indian states and certain other personal privileges with effect from 28 December 1971.

tenure has little meaning as he may be removed by the president at any time.[9] For appointment of the governor, (a) he must be a citizen of India; (b) he must have completed 35 years of age; (c) he must not hold any other office of profit; and (d) he must not be a member of the legislatures of the Union or any other state (Article 158).[10] It may be of interest to note that the original plan in the Draft Constitution was to have elected governors, but, in the constituent assembly, it was replaced by the method of appointment by the president. The following was the argument advanced in the constituent assembly:

> When the whole of the executive power is vested in the Council of Ministers, if there is another person who believes that he has got the backing of the province behind him and, therefore, at his discretion he can come forward and intervene in the governance of the province, it would really amount to a surrender of democracy.[11]

The governor might consider himself to be superior to the chief minister if he were to be elected by direct vote, and this might lead to frequent friction between the governor and the chief minister.[12]

7.2.2 Salary and Privileges

The governor is entitled to a monthly salary of ₹3.5 lakhs, free official residence and also such allowances and privileges as are specified in the governor's (Emoluments, Allowances and Privileges) Act, 1982, as amended in 2009 (w.e.f. 1 January 2006). Under Article 158(3) and (4), it is provided that these cannot be changed to the detriment of an incumbent during his term of office. Article 159 requires the governor or the person discharging the functions of a governor to take an oath to faithfully execute the office and to preserve, protect and defend the Constitution and the law. Further, no criminal proceedings, including proceeding for his arrest or imprisonment, can be instituted against the governor during his term of office.

7.2.3 Position Comparison of Governor and President

The powers of the governor are analogous to those of the president except that he has no military or diplomatic powers. While both the President of India and the governor of a state stand at the head of the executive power of the Union and state respectively, there are some fundamental differences in their position. First, the president, unlike the governor, is elected, and unlike the governor who holds office at the president's pleasure, the president can be removed only by the difficult process of impeachment (Article 56). Second, while the president is bound by the advice of the Council of Ministers in the discharge of his functions (Article 74), the governor may in certain situations act in his discretion (Article163).

---

[9] See, for example, *Surya Narain v. Union of India*, AIR 1982, Rajasthan. On the advice of the National Front PM V. P. Singh, the president in December 1989 asked all the governors to resign simply because another party had come to power at the Centre.

[10] The Supreme Court in *Hargovind v. Raghukal* (AIR 1979 SC 1109) held that the governor's office was not an office of profit under the government.

[11] *Constituent Assembly Debates*, vol. VII, 455.

[12] Active politicians from the ruling party are often appointed as governor.

7.2.3.1 Executive Powers

The governor is the head of the executive power of a state and all executive actions of the state have to be taken in the name of the governor. The governor is required to frame rules of business allocating work to different ministers. A decision of the Council of Ministers does not become operative as a government order unless expressed in the governor's name (Article 166).

The chief minister is appointed by the governor, while other ministers are appointed by the governor on the advice of the chief minister. The Council of Ministers shall be collectively responsible to the legislative assembly of the state and individually responsible to the governor (Article 164).[13] The governor also appoints the advocate general and members of the State Public Service Commission (Articles 165 and 316). While the ministers as well as advocate general hold office at the pleasure of the governor, the members of Service Commission can be removed only by the president on the basis of enquiry report of the Supreme Court. Apart from the power to appoint the judges of subordinate courts (Articles 233 and 234), the governor is entitled to be consulted by the president in the appointment of judges of the state high court [Article 217(1)]. Like the president, the governor under Article 333 (23rd Amendment Act, 1969) has the power to nominate one member of the Anglo-Indian community to legislative assembly if he feels that the community is not adequately represented in the assembly. Like the president, the governor has the corresponding power to nominate one-sixth members to the legislative council (where the Upper House of the state legislature exists) from among 'persons having special knowledge or practical experience in respect of matters such as literature, science, art, co-operative movement and social service' [Article 171(5)].

The governor also exercises power in the appointment of vice chancellors in universities in the states of which he is the chancellor. This is not a power which he has to exercise on the advice of the Council of Ministers but one where he exercises some discretion in choosing a person of his choice from the given list.

7.2.3.2 Legislative Powers

Just as the president is an integral part of the Parliament, the governor is a part of the legislature of the state (Article 168). He has the power to summon and prorogue the two Houses of the state legislature[14] and can dissolve the legislative assembly of the state (Article 174). He has a right of addressing and sending messages to the legislature (Articles 175 and 176). Under Article 200, the governor is empowered to reserve a bill passed by the state legislature for the assent of the president. The objective of this provision is to ensure that even if the state legislature passes any bill which is not in the national interest, such a bill could be prevented from becoming a law by the action of the governor. All money bills can be introduced in the legislature only with his consent and he has the right to reserve it for the consent of the president.

The governor also possesses the power of causing to be laid before the state legislature the annual financial statement (Article 202) and of making demands for grants and recommending money bills (Article 207), annual reports of the State Public Service Commission (Article 323), Auditor General (Article 151) and State Finance Commission [Article 243-1(4)].

---

[13] *Manoj Narula v. Union of India*, AIR 2014, SCC (9)1.

[14] States of Bihar, Andhra Pradesh, Maharashtra, Karnataka, Uttar Pradesh, Tamil Nadu and Telangana have two Houses known as 'legislative council' and 'legislative assembly'. To these must be added Jammu and Kashmir, which has adopted a bi-cameral legislature, by its own state constitution.

7.2.3.3 Ordinance-making Power

Just as the president under Article 123, the governor under Article 213 possesses the power to promulgate ordinances having the force of an Act of the state legislature in the following respects:

1. The governor shall exercise this power only when the state legislature is not in session.
2. The power shall be exercised with the aid and advice of the Council of Ministers, or governor must be convinced that circumstances exist which render it necessary for him to take immediate action.
3. The governor himself is competent to withdraw the ordinance at any time.
4. The ordinance must be placed before the state legislature within six weeks from the date of its re-assembly and shall cease to operate on the expiry of six weeks.

The governor's power of promulgation of ordinances is confined to the subjects in List II (6l subjects) and List III (52 subjects) of Seventh Schedule of the Constitution.

The distinctive feature of ordinance-making power of the governor is that he is barred from promulgating an ordinance without instructions from the president if (a) a bill containing the same provisions would have required president's prior sanction for its introduction in the legislature; (b) a bill containing the same provisions would have been reserved by the governor for the consideration of the president; and (c) an Act of the state legislature containing the same provisions would have been invalid without the assent of the president.

It may be of peculiar interest to note that the governor's ordinance will prevail notwithstanding repugnancy with a union law relating to a concurrent subject if the ordinance has been made in pursuance of 'instructions of the president'. The misuse of ordinance-making power of governor surfaced in *D. C. Wadhava v. State of Bihar*.[15] The governor of Bihar promulgated a total of 256 ordinances which were repeatedly promulgated during 1967–81. The court ruled that it was a 'subversion of the democratic process' and a 'fraud on the Constitution'. The ordinance-making power must not be resorted to serve political ends and be sparingly used only to meet extraordinary circumstances.

In another case pertaining to the appointment of teachers in Bihar by taking the ordinance route four times, the Supreme Court on 2 January 2017 said that re-promulgation of an ordinance 'was a fraud on the Constitution and the satisfaction of the president or the governor to promulgate an ordinance was not immune from judicial review' if the satisfaction had an oblique motive.[16]

7.2.3.4 Power of Veto

After the passage of the bill by the state legislature, the governor may (a) give his assent to the bill; (b) withhold his assent to the bill; (c) reserve the bill for the consideration of the president; (d) seek certain clarifications or information; and (e) return the non-money bill with a message. If a bill is returned by the governor to the state legislature with a message, it will be considered accordingly; and if passed again with or without amendments, it shall receive the governor's assent (Article 200). In the case of a money bill, so reserved, the president may give or withhold

[15] *D. C. Wadhava v. State of Bihar*, AIR 1987 SCC 378.

[16] See *The Tribune* (Chandigarh), 3 January 2017.

his assent. But in the case of a bill other than a money bill, the president may direct the governor to return the bill to the state legislature for reconsideration. If it is passed again, the bill shall be presented to the president again (Article 201). The bill shall have no legal effect until the president declares his assent, meaning, thereby, that he can keep the bill of the state legislature pending for an indefinite period of time. Alternatively, the president may, as in the case of the Kerala Education Bill, refer the bill to the Supreme Court for its advisory opinion under Article 143, if it appears to the president that the bill in question requires consideration of the Supreme Court.

7.2.3.5 Pardoning Power

The governor is vested with the power to grant pardons, reprieves, respites or remission of punishment or to suspend, remit or commute the sentence of any person convicted of any offence against any law relating to a matter to which the executive power of the state extends (Article 161). Although the governor has the power to grant a full pardon at any time even during the pendency of the case in the Supreme Court, he cannot exercise the power of suspension of the sentence for the period when the Supreme Court is taking care of the case.[17]

7.2.3.6 Emergency Powers

Unlike the president, the governor of a state (except the Governor of Jammu and Kashmir who has the power to impose governor's rule under Section 92 of the Constitution of Jammu and Kashmir) has no emergency powers to impose governor's rule. However, he has the power to recommend to the president whenever he is satisfied that a situation has arisen in which the government of the state cannot be carried on in consonance with the provisions of the Constitution (Article 356), and, in such a situation, president's rule can be imposed on the state and the governor then acting as the representative of the president assumes the functions of the government of the state.

7.2.4 Discretionary Functions and Special Responsibilities

In contrast to the president's power under Article 74, the governor is empowered to exercise functions in his discretion (Article 163). In the exercise of discretionary functions, he will not be required to act according to the advice of the Council of Ministers. Where the governor is required by the Constitution to act in his discretion, the validity of anything done by the governor shall not be called into question [Article 163 (2)].

Besides this, the functions which are specially required by the Constitution to be exercised by the governor in his discretion include the following:

1. Making rules of business [Article 166 (3)]
2. Reserving a bill for the consideration of the president (Article 200)
3. Making a report about the failure of constitutional machinery in the state [Article 356 (1)]

[17] In a significant case pertaining to release of one convict tried under the then *Terrorists and Disruptive Activities* (Prevention) Act (TADA), the Supreme Court on 29 June 2016 set aside a Punjab and Haryana High Court order and ruled that terrorists had no right to seek parole or premature release, citing human rights. See *The Tribune*, 30 June 2016.

4. Administering the union territory independently of his Council of Ministers when appointed as the administrator by the president [Article 239 (2)]
5. Determining the amount payable by the state of Assam to the district council as royalty accruing from licences for minerals [Paragraph 9(2) of the Sixth Schedule]

In addition to these discretionary functions, the governor has to discharge certain special responsibilities according to the directions issued by the president from time to time, which practically means that he is to act 'in his discretion'. Such responsibilities include the following:

1. Maintaining law and order by the Governor of Nagaland so long as internal disturbances caused by the hostile Nagas in the state continue 371A(1)
2. Securing by the Governor of Manipur the proper functioning of the committee of the legislative assembly consisting of the members elected from the Hill Areas of Manipur [371 C(1)]
3. Exercising individual judgement by the governor with respect to law and order in the state of Arunachal Pradesh (371H)
4. Ensuring by the Governor of Karnataka for '(a) establishment of a separate development board for Hyderabad–Karnataka region, (b) equitable allocation of funds for developmental expenditure over the said region, (c) equitable opportunities and facilities for the people belonging to the said region in matters of public employment, education and vocational training' (371J)

Likewise, in the Sixth Schedule, which applies to tribal areas of Assam, Meghalaya, Tripura and Mizoram, as specified in Para 20 of that schedule, discretionary powers are given to governor in matters relating to sharing of royalties between district council and state government. The Sixth Schedule vests additional discretionary powers in governors of Mizoram and Tripura in almost all their functions (except approving regulations for levying taxes and money lending by non-tribals by district councils) since December 1998. In Sikkim, the governor has been given special responsibility for peace and social and economic advancement of different sections of population.

It is here clarified that the governor while discharging such constitutional functions as appointments of chief minister of a state or sending a report to the president about the failure of constitutional machinery in a state or in respect of matters relating to assent to a bill passed by legislature exercises his own judgement.

7.2.5 Discretion in Practice

Article 163(2) imposes a duty on governor to act without ministerial advice in certain other matters, according to the circumstances, even though they are not specifically mentioned in the Constitution as discretionary functions.[18] For example, where one ministry has resigned and another alternative ministry cannot be formed, the making of a report under Article 356, thus, must be regarded as a function to be exercised by the governor in the exercise of his discretion. The Proclamation as to failure of the constitutional machinery in the state made by the president on the recommendation of the governor under Article 356(1) is judicially reviewable to the extent

[18] *Samsher v. State of Punjab*, AIR 1974 SC 2192, para 47, 88, 153.

of examining whether it was issued on the basis of any material at all or whether the material was relevant or whether the Proclamation was issued in the malafide exercise of power. The Supreme Court or high court can strike down the proclamation if it is found to be malafide or based on wholly irrelevant or extraneous grounds.[19]

The governor of a state may reserve any bill for the consideration of the president (under Article 200). Bills relating to subjects such as compulsory acquisition of property, measures affecting powers and position of high courts and imposition of taxes on storage, distribution and sale of water or electricity in inter-state river or river valley development projects should necessarily be so reserved. No bills seeking to impose restrictions on inter-state trade can be introduced in a state legislature without previous sanction of the president. Governor's action may be justified when he considers that the Bill in question would affect the powers of the Union or contravene any of the provisions of the Constitution. Governor is free from accountability. On the other hand, he will be under the complete control of the president for his exercise of discretion and performance of activities. And then he remains in office at the president's pleasure under the Article 156(1).

After the emergency, the Janata Party government summarily dismissed all the Congress-appointed governors. On return to power, the Congress did a repeat for Janata-appointed governors. In 2004, the UPA government sacked four NDA-appointed governors of Uttar Pradesh, Gujarat, Haryana and Goa.

The Constitution provides a five-year tenure for a governor, but he holds office at the president's pleasure. His position is very insecure as compared to other constitutional authorities. The Sarkaria Commission reports says that between 1967 and 1986, some 298 governors were appointed and of them, only 18 could complete their full five-year term.

In a path-breaking judgement, the Supreme Court ruled, 'A governor cannot be removed on the ground that he is out of sync with the policies and ideologies of the union government, nor can he be removed on the ground that the Centre has lost confidence in him'.[20] At the 11th meeting of the Inter State Council (ISC), which was held after a gap of 10 years on 16 July 2016, the then Bihar chief minister went to the extent of demanding abolition of the office of governor.

> However, if it is not possible to do away with it, then our opinion is that provisions relating to the appointment of governor must be clearly defined and made transparent....[21]

The Punchhi Commission report (2010) too had recommended that for a chief minister's removal, the governor must give the leader of the House an opportunity to prove his majority through a floor test'.

7.2.6 Conclusion

A sharp controversy has of late arisen upon the question whether a governor is an agent of the Centre. In actual working, it may be briefed that in states where one party has a clear majority, the

[19] *S. R. Bommai v. Union of India*, AIR 1994 SC 1918. See also the judgement of Uttarakhand High Court quashing the proclamation of president's rule in the state and asked the congress government headed by Harish Rawat to prove his majority in the assembly on 29 April 2016, which he did. See *The Financial Express*, 22 April 2016.

[20] See *The Tribune* (Chandigarh), 8 May 2010.

[21] At the 11th ISC meeting, Chief Ministers Nitish Kumar (Bihar), Mamata Banerjee (West Bengal) and Manik Sarkar (Tripura) were critical of the role of governor and the Centre's repeated move to usurp powers of the state in the name of internal security. See *The Tribune* (Chandigarh), 17 July 2016.

part played by the governor has been that of a constitutional head; however, in those states where there are different parties with little control over the legislative assembly, the governor has acted as a mere agent of the Centre in various matters such as inviting a person to form a ministry or removing the chief minister having the confidence of the legislative assembly by means of a report under Article 356. K. V. Rao, a noted constitutional expert is critical of the manner in which the governor is appointed. Rao says:

> Today at the root of all troubles is the simple fact that the Head of the State is neither chosen by that State nor is he responsible to it, nor removable... By the very method of appointment and removal, the Governor becomes subordinate to the President and events prove that he cannot disobey him.

Rao distinguishes between his role as a 'link' and that of an 'agent'. His role as a link is more positive than an agent. He 'cannot be both these things at the same time. He should be a reflection of the state government ... but not its antithesis nor a spy of the Centre.[22]

Despite the controversy over his role, there is one aspect in which the system of appointing an outsider by the Centre has proved to be beneficial, and that is the prevention of disruptive and separatist forces from impairing the national unity and strength. It might otherwise have been possible without the knowledge of the Centre, under a locally elected governor. In certain circumstances, he exercises powers on behest of the Centre, which in many cases cause encroachment on the legislative and executive powers of a state.

7.3 Council of Ministries

At the state level, the real executive is the Council of Ministers headed by the chief minister. The chief minister has similar functions in the state analogous to those of the PM at the Centre.

7.3.1 Appointment and Removal

Chief minister is appointed by the governor who also appoints other ministers on the advice of the chief minister (Article 164). The Council of Ministers with the chief minister as head, aids and advises 'governor in exercise of his functions except in so far as he is by or under the Constitution required to exercise his functions or any of them in his discretion' (Article 163).

The convention has it that the leader of the party in the assembly having absolute majority is invited to form the government. Only when the governor finds that no party has a clear majority in the assembly can he exercise any discretion in the choice of the chief minister. Generally, in such a situation, the governor asks the leader of the single largest party to form the government.

It is quite possible that some parties may reach some sort of understanding and then stake a claim to form the government on the basis of having the largest number of seats in the state assembly. For example, the governor of Uttar Pradesh accepted the argument of Mulayam Singh Yadav that he is the leader of Samajvadi Party and enjoys the support of Bahujan Samaj Party and

[22] K. V. Rao, 'Role of the State Governor in India', in *Essays on Indian Government and Politics*, ed. Varinder Grover (New Delhi: Deep and Deep, 1988), 159.

then appointed him the chief minister, although the Bharatiya Janata Party was the largest party in the state assembly. When invited minorities to form the government, the governor has got into controversies. This happened in the case of Tamil Nadu Governor S. L. Khurana who invited the faction of the All India Anna Dravida Munnetra Kazhagam (AIADMK) headed by Mrs Janaki Ramachandran to form the government after Mr M. G. Ramachandran's death as the Janaki government was never able to prove its majority in the state assembly. Such instances of the governor's discretion in the choice of the chief minister (generally the leader of the party) to form the government do arise occasionally and despite many efforts, no definite guidelines have been laid down for the guidance of a governor in such situations.[23]

The Council of Ministers is collectively responsible to the state legislative assembly under Article 164(2) and (ministers) individually responsible to the governor. The chief minister may demand the resignation of any member of the Council of Ministers who has lost his confidence (even on the ground of ill health, inefficiency or corruption) and if the member does not resign, the chief minister can request the governor to dismiss him which the latter does so. As regards the removal of the chief minister, Article 164(1) maintains that he holds office at the pleasure of the governor. This Article read with Article 164(2) has implication that so long as the chief minister enjoys the support and confidence of the assembly, he cannot be removed by the governor. In actual working, the removal of the chief minister is done on the Centre's directive to the governor.[24]

7.3.2 Composition of the Council of Ministers

Like the Council of Ministers at the union executive, ministers at the state level are ranked as (a) cabinet ministers, (b) ministers of state, (c) deputy ministers and (d) parliamentary secretaries. While cabinet ministers and ministers of state usually hold independent charge of their portfolios, the deputy ministers and parliamentary secretaries are expected to assist the former in their running of the administration of the state.

The governor allocates and reallocates portfolios among ministers on the advice of the chief minister with a view to making political adjustments as well as enhancing administrative effectiveness. A strong chief minister can exercise much more control over his council but if his position in the party is weak, he has to cater to the demands of the various factions in the party. It has been observed that where coalition government exists, the chief minister is, in many situations, not able to assert himself in relation to the ministers belonging to different coalition parties. Such a state of affairs weakens not only the political system of the country but also affects the administration of the state.

In this context, the (First) ARC of the GoI (1966–70) had suggested that a ministry in a state should not have more than 10% of the members of the party in power in the state assembly.[25] This suggestion has not been observed in practice. The Second ARC in its 15th Report recommended

---

[23] In June 2018, JD(S) H.D. Kumaraswamy was appointed CM of Karnataka as he enjoyed support of Congress–BSP parties since B.S. Yeddurappa failed to win vote set by SC judge for floor test on 19 May 2018, although BJP was single largest party.

[24] The proclamation of president's rule, imposed in Uttarakhand on the recommendation of the state governor, was quashed by the state high court on 21 April 2016 and the former Chief Minister Harish Rawat was asked to prove his majority in the assembly on 29 April 2016. Justice K. M Joseph said the imposition of president's rule was contrary to law laid down by Supreme Court.

[25] ARC, *Report on State Administration* (New Delhi: GoI, 1969), 1.

that the maximum size of the Council of Ministers should not exceed 10% where membership of the assembly is more than 200 and a maximum of 15% where membership of the assembly is less than 200.[26]

7.3.3 Functions of the Council of Ministers

As already stated, the Council of Ministers under Article 163(1) aids and advises the governor in the exercise of his functions. In practice, however, the government of the state is carried on by the Council of Ministers headed by the chief minister. The Council decides on policies concerning the governance of the state (with reference to subjects mentioned in the State and Concurrent Lists). It is responsible for the functioning of all state departments and government undertakings. In general, the Council deals with the following matters:

1. Formulation, implementation, monitoring and evaluation of state policies, programmes and plans
2. Preparation of the governor's address to the legislative assembly
3. Presentation of bills, including proposals for budgetary demands and fresh legislation in the state legislature
4. Recommendation of the appointment of the members of the Public Service Commission, the advocate general, judges of the subordinate courts and so on
5. Advising the governor to summon, prorogue or dissolve the legislative assembly and so on
6. Union–state and inter-state relations, changes the administrative system of the state
7. Answering questions raised in the legislature during the question hours, call attention motions and adjournment motions regarding the functioning of their departments and public undertakings
8. Any matter referred to it by the governor either for consideration or seeking clarification
9. Rendering advice to the governor on all important administrative matters of the state

Thus the Council of Ministers is responsible for the governance of the state.

7.3.4 Relationship Between the Governor and the Council of Ministers

As has already been maintained, the governor is a constitutional head of the state executive. He is discharging his functional responsibility in accordance with the prescriptions of the constitutional provisions. The provisions relating to the governor's Council of Ministers are similar to those of the president's Council of Ministers, subject to certain exceptions.

While the Constitution does not empower the president to exercise any function 'in his discretion', it authorizes the governor to exercise some functions 'on his discretion'. In this respect, the principle of cabinet responsibility in the states differs from that in the Union. Article 163(1) says,

[26] Second ARC, *Report on State and District Administration* (New Delhi: GoI, 2009).

> There shall be a Council of Ministers ... to aid and advise the Governor in the exercise of his functions, except insofar as he is by or under this Constitution required to exercise his functions or any of them in his discretion.

It is because of this discretionary jurisdiction of the governor that no amendment was made by the 42nd Amendment Act in Article 163(1) as in Article 74(1), which we have discussed in earlier chapter. It is to be noted that in the exercise of the functions which the governor is empowered to exercise in his discretion, he will not be required to act according to the advice of his ministers or even to seek such advice. Further, with regard to any matter for which

> Governor is required by the Constitution to act in his discretion, the decision of the Governor shall be final, and the validity of anything done by the Governor shall not be called into question on the ground that he ought or ought not to have acted in his discretion.[27]

7.3.5 Cabinet and Its Power

Cabinet, within the Council of Ministers, is a policy or decision-making body. Members of the cabinet, including the chief minister, are closest to the points at which policy decisions are made. Functioning of the state cabinet reveals that it exercises constitutional and extra-constitutional powers.

The first source of cabinet power is the rights conferred upon its members by the constitution. It is the task of the cabinet to decide policies which are to be placed before the state legislature for its discussion and approval.

The second source of cabinet power is unity. It is a rule that once a cabinet decision has been taken, ministers must be prepared to defend it or resign.[28] In a parliamentary form of government, this rule is called 'collective responsibility'.

Third, the cabinet as an institution secures control and coordination among the functions assigned to the executive. Each minister now receives the cabinet decisions and it is his responsibility to instruct his departments for departmental action.

And finally, exercise of whip secures party unity as a function of discipline. The dependence of members of the Council of Ministers on the chief minister means that he must be regarded as a leading member not only of party in power but also of the government which he heads.

Within the Council of Ministers, the cabinet has an important role to play in the decision-making of the state government. On an approval of the chief minister, a letter is issued by the chief secretary which informs all the cabinet ministers about the time, venue and agenda of the meeting. Ministers of state may also be invited to the meeting by the chief minister. Generally, a cabinet meeting presided over by the chief minister is held at a two-day notice, but it can be summoned at a shorter notice as well. Its deliberations are conducted with great care and in case of differences of opinion, the chief minister has to iron them out. In addition to a formal meeting, the chief minister may seek the opinion or decision on a certain urgent item by circulating it among the ministers. Such a decision, taken by circulation, requires the formal approval of the next cabinet

---

[27] See Article 163 (2) of the Constitution.

[28] Recently, deputy chief minister and some other members of the Council of Ministers had to resign from the Nitish Government in Bihar (July 2017).

meeting. The chief minister can himself take a decision and then place it for endorsement by the cabinet.

The chief secretary or special secretary (cabinet) reads out the summary of the cabinet memo regarding the case on which a decision is required to be taken. The effectiveness of the chief minister and the collaborative spirit among his colleagues influences the total outcome of a cabinet meeting. The chief minister's role is crucial in guiding the decisions and evolving a consensus. Although, in principle, all policy decisions should be taken by the cabinet, in practice, at times, the chief minister can take policy decisions on his own also and report it and that becomes, through due process, the decision of the cabinet as such. A decision of the cabinet may be released at a public or press meeting or announced on the floor of the legislature. The minutes of the cabinet meeting which are prepared by the chief secretary or the special secretary (cabinet) are sent to all the ministers, the secretary to the governor and other secretaries after their approval from the chief minister. In the CS, a register is maintained for the purpose of recording the progress made in regard to various decisions of the cabinet.

7.4 Chief Minister

The chief minister heads the Council of Ministers and is regarded as 'the leader of the state'. It is the chief minister on whose advice the ministers of the council are appointed, removed and dismissed. His resignation or dismissal means the fall of the Council of Ministers. He allocates and reallocates the portfolios to his colleagues who must enjoy his confidence. The chief minister decides about the size of the Council of Ministers and presides over the meetings of the cabinet. He determines the time, place and agenda of cabinet meetings. In case of differences of opinion in the cabinet, the chief minister has to iron them out. He coordinates and supervises over the government policies and working of different ministries.

The chief minister acts as a coordinating link between the government and the Council of Ministers. Under Article 167, duties of the chief minister of a state (other than the state of Jammu and Kashmir) are as follows:

1. To communicate to the governor of the state all decisions of the Council of Ministers relating to the administration of the affair of the state and proposals for legislation
2. To furnish such information relating to the administration of that affairs of the state and proposals for legislation as the governor may call for
3. If the governor so requires, to submit for the consideration of the Council of Ministers any matter on which a decision has been taken by a minister but which has not been considered by the Council

The following cases have to be submitted to the chief minister (e.g., in the case of Punjab) for orders, by the minister concerned:

1. Proposals for the grant of pardon or commutation of sentence in pursuance of Article 161
2. Cases raising questions of policy and cases of administrative importance
3. Cases which affect or are likely to affect peace and tranquillity of the state

4. Cases which affect or are likely to affect the interests of Scheduled Castes, Scheduled Tribes and backward classes
5. Cases which affect the relations of the state government with the GoI, any other state governments, the Supreme Court or a high court
6. Constitution of an Advisory Board under Article 22(4a) for the detention of persons without trial
7. Proposals for the prosecution, dismissal, removal or compulsory retirement of any gazetted officer
8. Proposals for the appointment and posting of such officer as (a) chief secretary, secretaries and joint secretaries; (b) heads of department; (c) district judges; (d) deputy inspectors general of police; (e) deputy commissioners or collectors; (J) superintendents of police; and (g) superintending engineers
9. Proposals to nominate members of the legislative councils (where these exist)
10. Proposals for the provisions of representation to the Anglo-Indian community
11. Any communication from the Election Commissions
12. Cases or questions as to disqualification of members of a house of legislature

Above these prescribed functions, the chief minister has to maintain informal or formal contacts with the people at large. He has to keep a watchful eye on the media and public opinion when he is considering policy proposals.

7.4.1 Position of the Chief Minister

The position of the chief minister of the state is analogous to the PM at the centre. But he is not the PM of the nation. He is just one among equals of the status of chief ministers of the nation. What contributes to the image and personality of a chief minister is a debatable point. Whether his power represents something significantly different from the past political experience. It is extremely difficult to know how much weight should be assigned to the different factors which enhance and constrain the power of a chief minister.

First, the chief minister is said to obtain power and position from the nature of contemporary elections. Individual MLAs depend for their electoral success on the popularity of the party leadership and their leaders. A chief minister can therefore expect MLAs or members of the government to regard themselves as mandated to support their leader. These MLAs will step into line rather than face of prospect of an election when the chief minister threatens dissident members with the dissolution of the legislative assembly. This is a rather extreme view of the relationship between a chief minister and his colleagues. It ignores the fact that the electoral choice is based on the image of the party and the record of the previous government.

Secondly, the chief minister's hand is strengthened by the control he exercises over the cabinet's decision-making. By deciding what should be on the agenda and interpreting the sense of the meeting, the chief minister can obstruct ideas and decisions of which he disapproves. But the cabinet as a whole has to be persuaded of the rightness of most decisions. It depends upon the knowledge and ability of the chief minister to modify those decisions. Moreover, there is nothing unusual about a chief minister being forced to modify his views or compromise in the course of cabinet discussions. To carry on as leader, the chief minister must retain the confidence of his colleagues, which means that he cannot dictate to it. The chief minister can be overruled by their cabinet ministers and even driven from office.

The chief minister's position is quite eminent when his party commands a clear majority in the state legislature. But when he heads a coalition government, it becomes difficult for the chief minister to ensure the rule of collective responsibility. Much of the energy and time of the chief minister will, in that situation, be wasted on keeping his team united and adequately disciplined.

Being the leader of the ruling party, the chief minister maintains the discipline in the party and as long as he enjoys the confidence of the legislature, he can retain his position. At times, particularly at the time of selection of his ministers, he has to face the pressure of the party MLAs. The dissidents are sometimes appointed chairmen of various public undertakings, cooperative institutions or expelled from the party. Party MLAs also put pressure on the chief minister, particularly in matters of development works and posting and transfer of officials in their constituencies. The chief minister has therefore to play an effective and constructive role in the party politics. In case the chief minister belongs to the ruling party at the Centre, he has to depend to a large extent on the advice of the PM or the party leadership. Most chief ministers of the ruling party have behaved like messengers of the PMs. A critic has observed, for example,

> Under Mrs. Gandhi and under Rajiv Gandhi, Chief Ministers have generally come to be nominated primarily by the Prime Minister and their survival has hinged more on the Central party backing than on the legislative majority of the State Congress units. Most Chief Ministers are allowed by the central leadership to have a pliant or, at any rate, a cooperative Pradesh Congress President in the interest of government stability and containing factionalism.[29]

The chief minister has to interact with several union ministers, the Finance Commission, NITI Aayog members and other bodies for financial assistance and project's clearance. In matters of financial grants, especially when required during emergency crises, the chief minister's influence and rapport with the union ministers play an important role. He has also to take cognizance of the PM's letters relating to the problems of the state. The ISC of which he is the member provides an opportunity to plead the state's case for more financial grants and increased central assistance for the policies, programmes and projects of the state. The chief minister discusses with NITI Aayog Members for the plans for socio-economic development of the state.

It is therefore no exaggeration to say that the decisions of the government are taken by the chief minister together with the responsible minister so that the chief minister is 'in' all important decisions. The dependence of members of the council on the chief minister means that he must be regarded as much more than first among equals.

7.5 State Civil Secretariat

In a federal structure, the constitution provides for a separate system of administration for the Union and its units, namely, the states. But in practice, the state governments follow the pattern of the union government in their systems of governance. On the pattern of the central secretariat, each state has its own Civil Secretariat to assist the Council of Ministers in the discharge of its

[29] M. P. Singh, 'The Congress Centennial: A Retrospect and Prospect', *The Indian Journal of Political Science* 46, no. 4 (1985): 521.

responsibilities.[30] The Civil Secretariat is the highest echelon of the state administrative organization. It is the nerve centre of the state government and its writ runs throughout the length and breadth of the state. It is at this level that all policies and programmes of the state government get formulated and executive orders originate. It is here that the relationship between the ministers and civil servants is face to face and confrontation direct. Not only this, the secretariat is subject to all sorts of lobbying by pressure groups. It is expected to serve as a buffer and a shock absorber of conflicting pressures.

7.5.1 Structure

As an organization, the State Civil Secretariat consists of a political head (chief minister, assisted by the Council of Ministers), the secretaries, financial commissioners and their staff. While the political executive (Council of Ministers) which changes from time to time reflects public opinion in the state and lays down policy, the civil service is tasked to execute that policy.

The expression 'secretariat' means the office of the secretary. The secretary, being the principal adviser to the minister, needs to be equipped with an office to help him in the discharge of his responsibilities. The word 'secretariat' is conglomeration of various departments which are politically under the control of the ministers.

> The existence of a Secretariat in the government organization arises from the need for separating questions of policy from current administration so that the latter is entirely handed over to a separate agency which enjoys a certain amount of freedom in the field of execution.[31]

The secretariat consists of several departments. These departments aid the political executive in the formulation of policy as well as monitoring of its execution through direction of the working of the various directorates and through periodic review of programme implementation. The number of secretariat departments is usually more than the number of secretaries.

The chief secretary is the head of the entire state secretariat while secretary is a head of one or two departments. The secretary is a senior administrative officer of generalist category. The secretary is the secretary to the state government as a whole and not to the individual minister concerned. The number of secretariat departments vary from state to state and may range from 15 to 40. For example, the state secretariat (*Maharashtra*) of consists of 37 departments (figures for 2017).[32]

---

[30] D. D. Basu, *Introduction to the Constitution of India*, 22nd ed., as updated by G. B. Patnaik and Yasobant Das (Gurgaon: Lexis Nexis, 2015), 255.

[31] Government of Bombay, *Report of the Administrative Enquiry Committee* (Bombay: Government of Bombay, 1948), Para 91.

[32] Maharashtra Mantralaya consists of 37 departments: (i) General Administration, (ii) Revenue, (iii) Home, (iv) Forest, (v) Agriculture, (vi) Agriculture, Animal Husbandry, Dairy, (vii) School Education and Sports, (viii) Urban Development, (ix) Public Works, (x) Finance, (xi) Industrial, (xii) Medical Education and Drug, (xiii) Water Resources, (xiv) Law and Judiciary, (xv) Rural Development and Panchayat Raj, (xvi) Food Civil Supply and Consumer Protection, (xvii) Social Justice and Special Assistance, (xviii) Water Conservation and EGS, (xix) Housing, (xx) Water Supply and Sanitation, (xxi) Public Health, (xxii) Tribal Development, (xxiii) Environment, (xxiv) Cooperation, Marketing, (xxv) Textile, (xxvi) Higher and Technical Education, (xxvii) Energy, (xxviii) Marathi Language, (xxix) Tourism and Cultural Affairs, (xxx) Minority Development, (xxxi) Skill Development and Entrepreneurship, (xxxii) Transport, (xxxiii) Women and Child Development, (xxxiv) Parliamentary Affairs, (xxxv) Labour, (xxxvi) Information Technology and (xxxvii) Planning.

The normal practice is that one secretary may be in charge of more than one department, although in case of major departments, such as, finance and home, the secretary has only single charge. The minister in charge of the departments is primarily responsible for the disposal of the business pertaining to that department. In the case of Punjab, there were 29 additional and special chief secretaries, financial commissioners and principal secretaries and 61 administrative secretaries belonging to IAS cadre.[33]

A line of distinction has to be made between a secretariat department and an executive department. The latter is the executive organization of the government and has at its top a functionary, generally known as the head of the department (e.g., Director of Public Instruction—a specialist incumbent in most departments at the state level) who is subordinate to the former (secretary to the government, e.g., education secretary, a generalist incumbent). The head of the department is concerned primarily with a single secretary to the state government and a single minister for his orders and the funds which he has to spend. All secretariat departments do not have 'executive departments'.

Some of them, such as, departments of finance, personnel, planning, administrative reforms, laws and so on, offer advice. The head of the department may be a specialist and the secretary a generalist but no hard and fast rules exist in this regard. The merger and bifurcation of departments is a prerogative of the cabinet, and it is a continuous process as per policy requirements of the government. In addition to the functional departments, the state secretariats have staff organizations such as chief minister's secretariat, cabinet secretariat and CS office which act as policymaking centres with powers of coordination and control.

7.5.2 Hierarchy in Structure

Next to the chief secretary at the administrative level is the additional or special chief secretary who is vested with important policy matters and administrative functions which are not dealt with by the chief secretary.

Usually a principal secretary or secretary of the department is assisted by a hierarchical team of several junior officials called as special secretary/additional secretary, joint secretary, deputy secretary, under secretary and assistant secretary. The office component of the secretariat consists of superintendent (or section officer), assistant superintendents, upper division clerks, lower division clerks, steno-typists and typists and manual workers.

The principal secretary (as in Punjab Government) or the secretary heads the department and acts as a principal adviser of the minister on administrative and policy matters. He is personally responsible for the observance of rules of business and other activities of his department. He represents his department and can be called a link with other departments of the government. The secretary also issues instructions and orders distribution of work among the staff and is responsible for the organization and efficiency or the department. The additional secretary may function as secretary in relation to subjects allotted to his charge. He is the de facto head and deals directly with the minister. The deputy secretary acts on behalf of the secretary. Next in hierarchy is the under secretary who has the responsibility of submitting all relevant materials to his seniors. The under secretary initiates actions on all communications and examines the

[33] Figures of secretaries of Punjab as on 15 September 2017.

papers under disposal and submits the case to the deputy secretary for his perusal and consideration.

It may be added here that secretarial officials are subject to tenure system and are appointed for a fixed term. They are drawn from the field and revert to the field after secretariat tenure and most of them belong to generalist services. The state secretariat like any other secretariat is a repository of authority of state government. It serves as a think tank and a coordinating and controlling nodal organization.

Needless to say that the responsibility for execution of the policies is entrusted to the heads of departments and their subordinate field staff including technical experts.

7.5.3 Functions of the Secretariat

While the governor and the chief minister enjoy a constitutional status under the Constitution of India, the chief secretary, his secretariat and state services have been created to make the state government function on the pattern of secretariat of the union government. The Shiv Charan Mathur (former chief minister of Rajasthan) Commission (1999–2003) identified specific functions of the state secretariat in Rajasthan. Some of the following functions are usually performed by most of the state secretariats:

1. Obtaining decisions on policy matters and enunciating the policy decisions in clear language
2. Assisting the minister in the discharge of his policymaking and legislative functions
3. Overall planning and finance (budgeting and control of expenditure)
4. Legislative business (framing legislation, rules, etc.)
5. Personnel management policies (initiating steps to develop greater personnel and organizational competence)
6. Legal advice
7. Coordination and cross-clearance among the administrative departments in the secretariat
8. Communication with the central and other state governments and the central institutions, such as NITI Aayog, Finance Commission
9. Overall evaluation, supervision and control and coordination of work being done by the field departments

7.5.4 Areas of Problems and Suggestions

The First ARC in its report on state administration in 1969 identified following as areas of problems:

1. Inordinate delay in decision-making
2. Interference of secretariat officials in executive affairs for their non-secretariat activities
3. Irrational grouping of subjects in department
4. Lack of field experience of senior officials working under tenure system
5. Outdatedness of allocation of subjects
6. Failure to adapt with the change of new governments in the states

Remedies have to be found for the following defects in the functioning of the secretariat:

1. *Improper assumption of departmental work:* The secretariat, in most states, has improperly assumed work which does not belong to it. To some extent, the constant interference both from the level of the ministers and from the secretariat officers in the functioning of the departments leads to calling up a large numbers of files unnecessarily to the secretariat. Such interference has, in many cases, led to the practice of departments making a reference to the secretariat in proposals in which they are otherwise themselves qualified or competent to take action. Also, the assumption of departmental work by the secretariat resulted in killing of the initiative of the heads of department and led to an unhealthy relationships between the secretaries and departmental heads. The proper job of the secretary should be to encourage and assist in the development of greater organizational and personnel competence in field departments. The secretary should help the heads to attain programme targets, anticipating difficulties in implementation and pre-planning remedial measures.
2. *Faulty financial procedures:* The present way of functioning of the finance department is found to be obstructive of effective action. In actual practice, the officials of the finance department continue to indulge in petty objections and queries causing national waste and delays, and hindering the tempo of progress. There is clearly the need for reduction of post-budget scrutiny by the finance department.
3. *Faulty methods of work:* Under the present system, the first scrutiny of a proposal is made by the assistant. Thereafter, the superintendent or section officer adds a note. The upper levels, that is, of the under secretary and the deputy secretary, do likewise until the papers reach the secretary, who passes final orders or submits the file to the minister. The assistant, as in the case of Punjab Civil Secretariat, who prepares the first note, has little idea, usually, of the practical aspects of problem in the field. Second, there is often too much inconsequential and repetitive noting causing delays and frustration on the part of heads of department. The files get needlessly bulky and tend to obstruct rather than hasten the decision. All this happens even when a departmental proposal has been discussed and approved in principle at the top layer of the secretariat.

> The overgrowth of staff and accelerated promotions have resulted in the dilution of the quality of the services at all levels. The staff seek more to secure security, emoluments and promotional avenues than to shoulder legitimate duties and responsibilities. These tendencies have, instead of improving the quality of work, caused undue delay in disposal of government work and frustration to the people.[34]

Then there is the confusion in regard to jurisdiction between the secretariat and the field departments. The officers have developed an attitude of evasion of responsibility. They are not certain whether their decisions would stand and in case of reversal of decisions by the superior officers, they would themselves not come into trouble. Consequently, the method of working in the secretariat has easily lent itself to pushing up papers for orders. The result is inefficiency, frustration and evasion of responsibility. The job of an administrative secretary is to facilitate the working of departments in the field by providing them with various

[34] R. Sapru, 'Punjab and Haryana', in *State Administration in India*, vol. 2, ed. A. P. Padhi (New Delhi: Uppal, 1988), 427.

administrative aids and facilities. He should devote much more time to general policies, plans and programmes.

4. *Insufficient delegations to departmental heads:* Many cases relating to gazetted officials and non-gazetted civil servants too are coming up to the secretariat for orders of the minister or secretary. Cases relating to such matters as deputation terms, transfers, advances from provident fund, earned leave where clear norms and policies have been laid down and a large number of precedents exist, are all being referred to government. There is considerable scope for administrative delegations to the heads of department. Administrative delegations should be made side by side with further delegations of financial powers.

   As to the working of the secretariat, a committee observed,

> The heads of departments seem to feel that instead of creating conditions which will facilitate the smooth carrying out of the work, the secretariat creates hurdles in their way, which results in considerable delays. Since the secretariat is the repository of all the power and authority of government, the lack of proper delegation to lower authorities is also a charge at its door. Sanctions of government are even today necessary for trivial matters ... Some of the senior secretaries agreed that while the proper function of the secretariat was to deal with policy matters, at least forty per cent of the time of the secretariat was spent on routine matters like sanctioning small amounts of expenditure, considering service problems of individuals etc. The secretariat is not in touch with the field organization sufficiently closely with the result that what is happening in the field is not often known to the secretariat accurately.[35]

In brief, remedies have to be found for the following defects in the secretariat: over-staffing; faulty methods of work; too many levels of noting; overlapping and duplication of work between and among departments, particularly between planning and finance departments; faulty and excessive financial procedures; lack of administrative and financial delegations to departmental heads; lack of proper selection and observance of tenure of secretariat officers; and interference in day-to-day administration of field departments.

There is no uniformity of delegation of authority to executive heads of departments. The ARC struggled with it and suggested workable measures. To quote the ARC:

1. 'Due to the dominant position of the secretariat appointments are considered prestigious. A secretariat posting ensures an officer's stay in the state capital. Moreover, he escapes the pressures and tensions of the field which are enormous in a functioning democracy. A stay in the secretariat assures the officials a cosy existence with many social amenities of life. He functions in close proximity to ministers and senior colleagues which helps in winning promotions and better postings. It should change.
2. There are too many levels and functionaries involved in the secretariat leading to delays in the transactions of public business. The cell system can be a good example of innovative reform.
3. There is the problem of over administration. The need for a bigger administrative apparatus will be left with the diversification of the functions of the government and the result is the expansion of the secretariat activities. Moreover it is easier to create new positions in the secretariat, as the persons with decision-making authority are all located in the secretariat and the human factors influence the decision'.[36]

---

[35] Quoted by S. R. Maheshwari, *State Administration in India* (New Delhi: Macmillan, 1979), 65.

[36] Ibid.

7.5.5 Conclusion

The civil secretariat in a state is an organization intended in the main to assist the Council of Ministers in the discharge of its responsibilities. Ministers do not usually have more than the broad guidelines of the policies and programmes which they want to carry out. These have to be worked out in detail. All the implications, including financial, have to be studied and necessary additions or modifications have to be proposed by the secretariat, after obtaining the relevant data and suggestions from the concerned departments. It may be mentioned here that the implementation of policies is the job of field departments and other agencies. So far as the secretariat is concerned, its job is to facilitate this implementation by adequate transmission to the field and to keep a record of progress made, for the use of the ministers, through such reports, returns and other methods that may be evolved. It is further contended that if effective delegations, both administrative and financial, are made to the heads of department, and if unnecessary interference in the working of departments from the ministry and secretariat is given up together with the undesirable dominance of the secretariat over the field departments, the existing unhealthy relations between the two can be remedied.

7.6 State Chief Secretary

In each of 29 component states, there is the office of the chief secretary. The chief secretary is the head of the administrative machinery. He is the kingpin of the state secretariat. As he is the chief of the secretaries in the state, the post of the chief secretary is considered to be of critical importance to the functioning of the state administration. That is why the chief minister is very particular in the choosing of the chief secretary from amongst senior administrators.

7.6.1 Appointment and Tenure

The chief secretary belonging to the IAS cadre is chosen by the chief minister, usually from the first seven senior IAS officers of the state cadre. Since 1973, by virtue of his unique position, the chief secretary's post has been equated with that of the secretary to the GoI. In general, three main considerations guide in the choice of a chief secretary: seniority, service record and the chief minister's confidence. There is no fixed tenure for the incumbent to the chief secretary's post. In this context, the ARC, in its report on state administration in 1969, had recommended that a chief secretary should have a minimum tenure of 3–4 years.[37] This suggestion has, however, not been accepted and has not been considered feasible either because, in that case, a chief minister may find himself laden with a chief secretary appointed by his predecessor.

7.6.2 Functions

The Constitution of India is silent as to the duties and functions which the chief secretary has to discharge. His functions are enumerated in the rules of business framed by the state governments.

---

[37] ARC, *Report on State Administration* (New Delhi: GoI, 1968), 26.

To some extent, the office of the chief secretary has assumed additional burdens by taking up new work in view of its urgency and then letting it remain there. Generally speaking, chief secretary performs the following functions:

1. Being principal adviser to the chief minister, the chief secretary tenders advice on all state functions and matters on which advice is sought.
2. He exercises general supervision and control over the entire secretariat.
3. Being the secretary to the cabinet, the chief secretary, prepares the agenda for cabinet meetings and drafts their minutes.
4. Being the chief of the civil service, the chief secretary deals with all matters relating to appointment, transfer, placement, promotion and retirement of personnel of the higher civil services.
5. Being the chief of all secretaries, he presides over a large number of committees.
6. He is the main channel of communications between the state governments and GoI.
7. He looks after all other matters not falling within the responsibilities of other secretaries.

Roles performed by the chief secretary are discussed in brief in the following subsections.

7.6.2.1 As a Policy Advisor

By virtue of his unique position as advisor to the cabinet, and the head of the official machinery, the chief secretary exercises much more power in the formulation of public policies than the formal description of his responsibilities suggests. He can advise authoritatively from experience on the practicability of different policy choices. He advises chief minister to take decisions that arise within the framework of existing policy but which cannot be dealt with by routine administration. He is further involved in decision-making when preparing explanatory material for ministerial use on the operation of current policy, when answering legislative questions and when generally aiding the Council of Ministers to account for the operation of the state departments. Much of the legislation, which the cabinet is willing to formulate, come from the chief secretary's administrative experience. New policy emerges as he brings ideas to bear on problems which the chief minister or ministers wish to solve. He also advises on the financial and administrative implications of different policy alternatives.

7.6.2.2 As a Coordinator of Administration

Although each department is under the control of a secretary to the government, the chief secretary, who is also a secretary to the general administration department and ex-officio secretary to the cabinet, has the overall authority. Another important role which chief secretary plays is to secure administrative coordination at intra-state, inter-state and Centre–state levels. Apart from attending to the work of the departments which are directly under him, he is expected to bring about effective coordination of work of different secretariat departments and to ensure that there is a certain degree of uniformity in the policies adopted by the state government with respect to different departments.[38] As the head of the secretariat, he supervises the work of different

[38] ARC, *Report on State Administration*, 26.

departments, resolves inter-departmental disputes and promotes coordination in the state administration. The chief secretary further acts as a coordinating officer by presiding over the meetings of the secretaries and heads of different departments and helps resolve inter-departmental differences and issues relating to boundaries, sharing of electricity and river waters. The coordinating role of the chief secretary in state administration was well brought out in the report of the study team of the ARC on state-level administration in the following words:

> But the Secretariat organisation itself needs co-ordination and discipline. This can be achieved by strengthening the position of the Chief Secretary, who is to function as the chief co-ordinator under the Chief Minister. Being the captain of the team of secretaries to government, the Chief Secretary should be senior person of outstanding ability. He should not only command respect and confidence of all the services in the state ... The Chief Secretary by his tact, experience, ability and seniority, has to so manage things that the political leadership keeps to its essential task of laying down policies and programmes and of co-ordinating the work amongst the ministers themselves. This requires a person of high calibre and tact.[39]

Through his participation in the Zonal Council, Chief Secretaries Conference and in other conferences invited by the central government, the chief secretary can bring about better coordination between the state and Centre and among the states themselves.

7.6.2.3 As an Administrative Head of Certain Departments

The chief secretary is not only the head of the civil secretariat department but also of departments such as general administration, personnel, administrative reforms, grievance and so on. Consequently, the importance of the post of the chief secretary has increased. General administration, including establishment questions, which forms part of the usual charge of the chief secretary is now a difficult and important job and requires experience, concentrated attention and sound balancing of the pros and cons involved. The skills and knowledge derived from his administrative experience enable him to argue from position of great strength about the administrative difficulties raised by proposals and the political repercussions likely to be encountered from the interests most affected. According to the rules of business of the state governments, the chief secretary is also the secretary to the cabinet. All important questions are taken up to the cabinet and various government departments. Only the senior-most administrative officer, that is, the chief secretary, can be in a position to render correct advice to the cabinet and to provide suitable guidance to the departments of the state government.

Further, being the chief of the civil service and in-charge of the Department of Personnel, the role of the chief secretary has considerably increased. He is seized with all important matters relating to appointment, transfer, placement, seniority, promotion, training and retirement of personnel of the higher civil services. Most of personnel policies, conditions of service and staff relations are shaped by his intervention.

In view of the enormous responsibilities that the chief secretary has to undertake, he has to be sensitive to issues arising from political and administrative systems of the state.

[39] ARC, *Report of the Study Team on State Administration* (New Delhi: GoI, 1968), 33.

7.6.3 Evaluation of Role Performance

The chief secretary occupies a position of eminence in the structure of state administration. In fact, he is the real executive. The role of the chief secretary in the state differs from time to time and leadership of the chief minister. Often, he has provided effective leadership in the administration of the state. In some states, he is credited to have initiated policies of development and welfare for the weaker sections to the community. In others, he has failed to restore law and order and take the state towards new horizons of socio-economic development. He is also charged for 'neglecting files and causing delay in the implementation of some vital decisions'.[40] Another senior secretary said that 'we had to wait for weeks to have a meeting with the chief secretary and urgent government business suffered'.

Most chief secretaries are often too hard-pressed by day-to-day cases and workloads to be able to reflect adequately on new policies. The administration of existing policies generally occupies most of their time. Forecasting expenditure, preparing explanatory briefs on current policies, negotiating with interest groups and administration of subordinate personnel have led to the neglect of the policymaking function by the chief secretaries. Apart from this their frequent transfers and stay for a year or so means that the average time for the cabinet secretariat is less than the average time required for a programme or policy to be planned, implemented and assessed. Their work of coordinating policies and bringing about an integrated approach in the programmes and policies of the state government has become more onerous in the context of divergent ideologies among the members of the Council of Ministers. Despite all these, chief secretary exercises much more influence and powers than his formal position suggests.

What Mangat Rai views about the chief secretary's role and position is aptly briefed: 'The Chief Secretary's job is not a technician's or even a professional's he is not a knowledgeable engineer, nor even a first class magistrate, he is part of the process of government and in a democratic republic, part of the human process'.[41] In a shocking incident on 20 February 2018, the Delhi Chief Secretary lodged an FIR for an alleged assault on him by ruling Aam Aadmi Party MLAs at CM residence.

7.7 State Executive Departments

The work of a state department is generally distributed into (a) policymaking wing and (b) policy-executing wing. The overall responsibility of both wings is entrusted to a secretary to the state government who acts as the administrative head of the department and principal adviser of the minister on all matters of policy and administration within the department. The administrative secretary and the head of the department are just two functionaries of the department.

The second wing (policy-executing wing) comprises a number of divisions each functioning under the charge of an officer of the level of director/joint director/deputy secretary. A division may have several branches each under the charge of an under secretary or equivalent officer.

---

[40] See *India Today*, 30 June 1982, p. 32.

[41] E. N. Mangat Rai, *Commitment My Style: Career in the Indian Civil Service* (New Delhi: Vikas Publishing, 1973), 243.

7.7.1 Executive Department Defined

In simple words, an executive department is a branch of government charged with the executive and enforcement of laws and policies and the administration of public affairs. In the words of Simon Commission, the executive department

> is an administrative unit, separate from the Secretariat, which reaches its apex usually in the single officer like the Inspector-General of Police or the Chief Conservator of Forests, outside the Secretariat altogether such a head of department will usually be concerned principally with a single Secretary to Government and a... single Minister, for his orders and the funds which he has to spend.[42]

It is generally noted that each administrative department of the secretariat has a corresponding executive department in the field. Most executive departments divided on functional basis are located at the state capital. They provide executive directions required in the implementation of policies and programmes laid down by the administrative departments. They serve as repository of technical knowledge and advise the secretariat departments on technical aspects of questions involved. About 50% of these posts are held by the specialists. Powers of the head of the executive department, both administrative and financial are defined in the financial and civil service rules, budget manual and under executive orders. These rules indicate the category of cases they have to be referred to the head of the department for final decisions. The head of the department has the responsibility to set its machinery in order and keep his staff in good spirit so that the desired goals and objectives are achieved. Thus, the responsibility for the execution of policies devolves on heads of departments and their field personnel who include technical experts.

Where the execution of the policies of the government requires decentralization of executive action, a department may have under it executive agencies called 'attached' and 'subordinate' offices. Attached offices are generally responsible for providing executive direction required in the implementation of the policies to be laid down by the department to which they are attached.

Subordinate offices generally function as field establishments or as agencies responsible for the detailed execution of the governmental policies or programmes. They function under the direction of an attached office, or where the volume of executive direction involved is not considerable, directly under a department. In the latter case, they assist the departments concerned in handling technical matters in their respective fields of specialization.

The number and size of executive departments vary from state to state. For example, in Punjab, there are at present 50 heads (mostly specialists) who are in charge of various executive departments (e.g., director, hospitality, excise and taxation commissioner, chief conservator of soils, DGP; inspector general of prisons, registrar of cooperative societies, chief engineer, river water resources and so on are given the designation of heads in the Government of Punjab). Thus, there is no common nomenclature for the heads; moreover, differences exist between the position, pay scales and roles of the heads of executive departments.

In the case of Maharashtra, there are 37 departments (within these there exist 176 sub-departments). As far as the internal administration of a directorate is concerned, it follows the usually hierarchical pattern comprising director, additional director, joint director, deputy director and assistant director. A section is generally the lowest organizational unit in a department with a well-defined area of work. It normally consists of assistants and clerks supervised by a section

---

[42] Great Britain, *Report of the Indian Statutory Commission, vol. I*, Survey (London: HMSO, Cmd. 3568, 1939), Para 312.

officer. Initial handling of cases (including noting and drafting) is generally done by assistants and clerks who are also known as the dealing hands.

7.7.2 Functions of the Head of the Department

Being the in-charge of the department, the head has enormous financial and administrative powers which he exercises under the departmental rules. Generally the head is responsible for the following functions:

1. Advising the administrative department (secretariat department) to which the head is associated on the technical aspects of the policy in question
2. Implementing, monitoring and evaluating the policies, programmes and plans
3. Exercising control and supervision over the field personnel
4. Formulating the budget proposals and schemes for the department
5. Allocating grants and budgetary funds
6. Dealing with personnel matters relating to transfer, promotion, posting, confirmation, training, appointment and so on of subordinate staff
7. Advising public service commission concerning vacancies, promotions and disciplinary actions

7.7.3 Problem Areas and Remedial Measures for Improvement

Remedies have to be found for the following defects in the functioning of executive departments:

A distressing situation in relationship: One of the glaring defects which remains to be remedied relates to the relationship between the secretariat and the executive departments. The difference between what the secretariat and executive departments are doing has been allowed to get blurred. There is a tendency among the secretariat officers to extend direct control over departmental work which does not belong properly to the secretariat. A distressing feature is that the heads of departments are not being given the recognition due to them. They and their associations regret that engineers and members of specialist class are not generally given full responsibility and opportunities nor the corresponding authority. Because of the position of subservience thrust upon the head, he has also become an automation 'drifting at the mercy of external stimuli'. In the course of his work experience, he has also lost his initiative and the will to work. This inertia has affected down to the lowest functionary in the department. This appears to be a highly distressing situation.

Lack of delegation: It has been observed that most powers belong to the government both in the financial and administrative spheres. The Heads of the departments have been delegated certain powers but it seems that delegations are made with mental reservation and, quite often, convey in their wording an element of 'humiliation'. For example, in emergency circumstances, stores (not exceeding ₹5,000 in cost) can be purchased directly by the Administrative Department without exhausting all possible channels. But the head of department does not have any such power so that it is implied that if there is a real emergency, the head concerned must come up to the administrative department. Further, there is a tendency on the part of the government to intervene even in the delegations given to the heads in matters of postings and transfers. This is because of the pressure, in some form or the other, exerted on the political masters. Often, it is seen that the officials themselves approach MLAs and ministers in order to secure a better station or a more furnace. In the process, the heads enjoy little or no control over personnel in matters of their postings and transfers. Thus, insufficient administrative and tardy financial delegations exist in favour of the heads of the departments.

The utility of delegation for removal of delay and tension is recognized. Much of the time of the head of department could be saved by clear and adequate administrative and financial delegations to him. He is seen devoting much of his time in sending up cases for financial sanctions, administrative approval for transfer of staff. If he has himself the powers for final disposal, he could devote more time to implementing schemes. Further, administrative delegations in personnel matters would result in the increase of departmental efficiency.

Irrational system of reports and returns and meetings: The head of the department has not only to contend with tardy financial delegations but is also subjected to numberless checks and cross-checks which take so much of his precious time and energy. Agriculture, for example, is of critical importance to the economy of the state in Punjab, but its director has to collect data from the field and submit approximately 700 reports and returns in a year to the administrative department, the planning department, the finance department, ICAR and a host of other authorities. And, not to mention reports that are asked for by the secretaries on the spur of the moment. While some of the statements are of some importance, many do no serve any useful purpose. Presently although the prescribed reports and returns are sent to the administrative secretariat, yet when the time comes for the utilization of any particular data, the same data may be again called for by separate individual references and the head of department is summoned personally to clarify what the data means and to explain how the data has been used by him in the formulation of proposals or schemes.

Besides transmission of reports and returns, the precious time of the head goes away in petty discussions, meetings and other gatherings. For an approval of a proposal or sanctioned scheme, he has to discuss it from the level of an under secretary to the administrative secretary. The proposal is again discussed with the minister in the presence of the secretary and again with the planning department and, if financial implication, with the officials of the finance department, who normally insist on technical scrutiny. Consequently, enough time is not left to the head to supervise his staff and supervise the implementation of the schemes.

In this context, much of the time and energy of a head or a director could be saved by rationalization of the system of reports and returns. Further, adequate and clear financial and administrative delegations would relieve head of the tardy procedures. One way of ensuring delegation is to confer on him appropriate secretariat status where he does not assume himself the responsibility of the secretary of the department.

Certain problems of technical departments: Most departments at the directorate level are technical in nature and consequently each faces a different type of problems. In their case, lack of clear and adequate delegations, insufficient control over the departmental personnel and too much waste of time in discussions, preparation of reports and returns impede the tempo of progress of the departmental schemes. It is often said that initiative, enthusiasm and vigour have been gradually drained out of the technicians and specialists because of the tardy controls, supervision, checks, crosschecks and other forms of continuous humiliation meted out to them.

Although the administrative secretary and the head of the department are just two functionaries of the Department, there has been a growing tendency on the part of secretaries to regard themselves as government and to treat the heads as subordinates. The authority assigned to the secretary to record remarks at all, is irksome and creates a feeling of subordination and, therefore, of resentment in the head leading to unhealthy relationship between himself and the administrative secretary.

It is important that heads of technical departments and specialists are given the recognition and acknowledgement due to them. A suggestion as already made in the various reports of commissions that, as in the case of IAS, there should be an all India service for engineering, education, agriculture, health and medicine. Recently, the Ministry of Human Resource Development of the GoI has started the process for formulating the New Education Policy which includes a key proposal of creating an All India Education Service.[43]

Summary

The improper assumption of departmental work by the secretariat has led in course of time to an unhealthy relationship between the administrative secretaries and departmental heads. The remedy to this ailment lies in allowing the heads of the departments to carry out programmes and policies without unnecessary interference of the administrative secretaries. The administrative secretary should be concerned only to examine the comparative necessity of a scheme put forward by a departmental head, its financial aspects and repercussions, if any, on the public in the event of the scheme being accepted and implemented. The proper job of a secretary is to devote much more time to general policies, plans and programmes and to development of organizational and personnel competence in field departments. He should work in close association with the Head to attain programme targets, anticipating difficulties in implementation and pre-planning remedial measures. For expediting the implementation of departmental schemes and programmes, the administrative secretary should render assistance to the head by resolving problems and removing bottlenecks. It is further suggested that if adequate and clear delegations both administrative and financial are given to the head, and if unnecessary interference in the working of the department from the government or the secretariat is given up together with the pose of dominance of the administrative secretary with respect to the head of department, the existing unhealthy relations between the two can be remedied.

As stated in the beginning, the Constitution of India provides for a federal government, having separate systems of administration for the union and states. The Constitution also contain provisions for the governance of the union, states and union territories. It provides for a uniform structure for all 29 states (except in certain matters of Jammu and Kashmir). Broadly speaking, the pattern of government in the states is similar to that of the union, namely, a parliamentary system in which the executive head, being a constitutional authority, acts on the advice of the Council of Ministers responsible to the state legislature.

[43] See *Times of India* (Chandigarh), 28 May 2016.

8 Administering Federalism and Intergovernmental Relations

LEARNING OBJECTIVES

1. **To understand the relationships and interactions among two or more units of government**
2. **To study legislative and administrative arrangements for intergovernmental relations (IGR)**
3. **To discuss the importance and role of the Inter-State Council (ISC) in the context of federal system of governance**

Introduction

Administration of a policy or programme in a federal polity like ours (India) often involves interactions among two or more units of government (Union, state and local). The relationships and interactions among them are called IGR. These relationships are also called federalism when applied to the union government's relations with the state governments and the states' relationships with each other. Administering IGR has become all the more important in the wake of cooperative federalism. They involve consultation, cooperation and coordination of the relationships among governments for the purpose of achieving specific policy goals or programme's objectives.

William Anderson, who popularized the term 'intergovernmental relations', designates it as 'an important body of activities or interactions occurring between governmental units of all types and levels within the federal system'.[1] Consequently, 'IGR is generally characterized by reciprocal activity and interdependent choices among multiple governmental units and political interests'.[2]

In brief, the study of IGR is concerned with how the multiplicity of types of governmental units interact with one another. IGR involves a series of political, administrative and financial relationships among all units of government that possess varying degrees of authority and jurisdictional autonomy.

IGR includes relations between (a) the national (usually called central or federal) government and local units of government, (b) two or more states, (c) each state and its own subordinate

[1] William Anderson, *Intergovernmental Relations in Review* (Minneapolis, MN: University of Minnesota Press, 1960), 3.

[2] D. Krane and D. S. Wright, 'Intergovernmental Relations', in *International Encyclopedia of Public Policy and Administration*, Vol. 2, ed. J. Shafritz (Boulder, CO: Westview Press, 1998), 1168–76.

(local) governments and (d) two or more governments at the local level. Regardless of the country, the design of IGR has important implications for the public policy. Framers of the Indian Constitution deliberately omitted the word 'federation' apprehending that it would pose a serious challenge to the unity and integrity of the country.[3]

The subject matter of channels of IGR includes: (a) legislation and policymaking area, (b) administration, (c) fiscal adjustment (which is a crucial area in most multi-sphere political systems) and (d) information gathering (information exchange or joint collection). Tensions between centre–state and local level officials may not be inevitable but may result when federal or central programme requirements and regulation interfere with the policy and political preferences of diverse state and local unit constituencies. Greater IGR between union, state and local results from several factors, some of which are as follows:

1. Conflict of interest among federal units
2. Unavoidable interdependence and interpretation between levels
3. Increased role of government at all levels

Effective IGR is required particularly where the constitution provides that a considerable portion of central legislation is to be executed or administered by the states as in India. Hence in a federal country such as India, there is the need to make provisions for IGR. Experience of IGR in many federations points to the existence of a variety of arrangements (constitutionally prescribed, established by legislation, government resolution and so on). Specifically, IGR is desirable as to

1. coordinate national and state policies in areas where jurisdiction is shared (concurrent subjects);
2. improve the information base in order to better policy-making and to reconcile policy differences;
3. attain national objectives in social and economic policy areas of state and local jurisdiction;
4. work towards a coordinated approach in the implementation of public policies at the national, state and local levels;
5. accommodate differences among states in policy capacity and fiscal resources for the exercise of their jurisdiction;
6. enable state and local governments to meet the specific needs of their people; and
7. contribute to stability through alternative channel of policymaking.

Thus, by way of idealizing IGR, differences in policy areas can be ironed out. In this context, Henry observes,

> All in all, federal systems of government and decentralized governance appear to be less corrupt, more efficient, less costly, more responsive, more innovative, and have more trusting citizens than do unitary systems and centralized governance.[4]

[3] Dr Ambedkar, the chairman of the Drafting Committee for the Constitution stated that 'although its constitution may be federal in structure', the committee had used the term 'Union' because of certain advantages. See *Draft Constitution*, 21 February 1948, p. iv. Article 1 of our Constitution says, 'India, that is Bharat, shall be of Union of States'. As such states have no freedom to secede from it. Moreover, the federation is not outcome of an agreement by the Units (states). The concept of 'federation' was introduced by the GoI Act, 1935 (see Section 5 of the Act).

[4] Nicholas Henry, *Public Administration and Public Affairs*, 12th ed. (New Delhi: PHI Learning, Indian reprint 2012), 412.

The constitutional system of India is practically federal, but with striking unitary features.[5] In an influential case, the Supreme Court observed that the Indian Constitution is basically federal in form and is marked by the traditional characteristics of a federal system.[6] A federal structure involves the following features that differentiate from the unitary system: (a) separate national and state identities, (b) distribution of jurisdictional powers, (c) integrating nation and states and (d) Supreme Court's power of interpreting the Constitution and nullifying government's action which violates the Constitution.

8.1 Legislative and Administrative Arrangements for IGR

Law-making and policy implementation in a system of multi-level government confront a basic problem of governance: How to resolve policy conflicts and competing claims between and among central, state and local governments? The basic question is: How to relate area and function? The link between constitutional arrangements (policy requirements) and intergovernmental unit implementation (administration) is primarily an issue of IGR or federation.

8.1.1 Separate National and State Identities

Structurally, India is a union of states (Article 1 of the Indian Constitution) but organized on federal lines[7] with power vertically divided between the union, state and local governments. The Constitution also contains detailed provisions governing IGR which would promote harmonious functions of the whole political structure—Union, state and local governments.

In the federal structure of India, the nation is divided into 29 states and 7 union territories.[8] The latter are administered as if they were parts of a unitary state. Predominantly, therefore, India is federal. In certain circumstances, federalism may be suspended by the imposition of the president's rule. Although in normal times, the Centre has more authority than the states, the spheres of both are clearly demarcated in such matters as legislation, policymaking, administration, finance, trade and commerce. Like the Centre, the states have their own governmental machinery—legislature, executive and services—functioning within the sphere guaranteed to them.

---

[5] *S. R. Bommai v. Union of India*, AIR 1994, SC 1918.

[6] The American federation has been described by its Supreme Court as 'an indestructible Union composed of indestructible States'. See *Taxas v. White* (1869), 7 Wall. 700.

[7] The term 'federation' has not been used in the Indian Constitution as the erstwhile semi-autonomous provinces (later designated as states) were merged together by the decision of representatives of people in the constituent assembly to form the Union. There was therefore no formal agreement among these entities to form any federation. The constituent units of the Union have therefore no constitutional right for secession. The Union has both federal as well as unitary features. No state save Jammu and Kashmir has a right to determine its own constitution.

[8] The number of states within the Union has increased from 14 in 1950 to 29 at present. This has been mostly due to reorganization of boundaries of the states and upgrading political status of the union territories. The erstwhile princely states were also merged into these states. There are also at present seven union territories under the direct control of the union government. Two of these, namely, Delhi and Puducherry, have a higher political status than the other territories. Articles 371F, 371G, 371H, 371I and 371J make certain provisions for the states of Sikkim, Mizoram, Arunachal Pradesh, Goa and Karnataka, respectively, in the Constitution.

8.1.2 Distribution of Jurisdictional Powers

The Indian Constitution distinguishes national and state responsibilities by enumerating legislative subjects. The Constitution has divided powers between the Union and the states (Articles 245–52 and Seventh Schedule). Three lists of powers and functions have been constitutionally prescribed. The Union List now comprises 100 subject matters after a gain of three entries (addition of entries 2A, 92A, 92B, 92C and deletion of entry 33) during recent years. These subject matters are considered to be of national importance or scope, for example, defence, international relations, major means of transport and communication, credit institutions and currency and so on. The Union Parliament may legislate on these subject matters and the union government may exercise executive powers in co-extension with the legislative powers. The State List now includes 61 subject matters after deletion of 5 entries over the years. These matters are considered to be of regional and local concern, for example, public order, public health, agriculture, water supplies and so on. The state legislature may make laws in respect of these subject matters. The executive power of the state also extends to such matters. The Concurrent List now contains 52 subject matters after a gain of five entries during the past few years.[9] These matters are considered to be both national and regional interest and scope. Both, the Union Parliament and state legislature, may make laws in respect of these, for example, population control, criminal law and procedure, economic and social planning, education, electricity, factories and so on. The executive power in regard to these matters normally belongs to state government, but it is subject to being limited by any law specifically passed by the Parliament for this purpose (Article 162). In case of any inconsistency between laws and policy made by Parliament and the ones made by state legislatures in respect of these matters, normally the former would prevail.[10] Only if the state law has acquired the assent of Parliament when reserved for its consideration, the state law would prevail. But Parliament may pass a new law for amending or repealing the state law concerned (Article 254).

The Constitution vests the residuary power (i.e., the power to legislate with respect to any matter not enumerated in any of the three lists) in the Parliament (Article 248) and the final determination as to whether a particular matter falls under the residuary power or not is that of the courts.[11]

8.1.3 Proliferation of the Union Legislative Powers

The Parliament may assume powers on certain occasion to make laws in regard to subject matters included in the State List. The Council of States (Rajya Sabha) may pass a resolution by a two-third majority if it is necessary in national interest for Parliament to pass such law or laws. The resolution is to remain in force for a period not exceeding one year (Article 249). Second, two or more

[9] Addition of 5 entries are administration of justice, population control, weights and measures, forests and education.

[10] The notification creating 92 universities by the Chhattisgarh state under Entry 32 of List II was quashed by the Supreme Court as the State Act undermined the University Grants Commission Act, 1954. See *Dr Yashpal v. State of Chhattisgarh*, 2005(5) SCC 420.

[11] The residuary powers are reserved to the states under the American Constitution. The Indian Constitution has followed the Canadian Constitution in vesting the residuary powers in the union government.

state legislatures may pass a resolution inviting the Parliament to pass a law in respect of a specified state subject matter. This law can also be extended to other states if their legislatures pass resolutions to that effect (Article 252). Examples are The Water (Prevention and Control of Pollution) Act, 1974, and The Transplantation of Human Organs Act, 1994.

Third, the Parliament is competent to enact laws in respect of any matters included in the State List for the whole or part of the country if a Proclamation of Emergency has been put into operation. Such laws are to cease to operate within a period of six months after the expiry of the Emergency Proclamation (Article 250). If there is any inconsistency between law made by the Parliament during Proclamation of Emergency or in accordance with Rajya Sabha resolution and the law made by state legislatures, the former is to prevail.

The Parliament may pass an amendment bill for making a change in any of the three Lists in the Seventh Schedule. But it has to be ratified by the legislatures of not less than one-half of the states before being made into law after receiving the president's assent. The Parliament has been constitutionally empowered (Article 3) to admit or establish new states and reorganize and rename the existing ones.

8.1.4 Strong Central Bias

The states are to ensure compliance with the Union laws within their respective territories (Article 256). The union government is competent to issue directions, if need be, for this purpose. Also, states are not to impede or prejudice exercise of the Union executive powers. Directions can be given by the union government if necessary in this connection (Article 257). Moreover, the Union can issue directions to a state on certain other matters as protection of railways, construction and maintenance of means of communication of national importance (Article 257), implementation of Scheduled Tribe Welfare Schemes (Article 339), development of Hindi language (Article 351), provision of adequate primary education facilities in mother tongue to linguistic minorities (Article 350A) and more importantly, that the state government is carried on in accordance with the provisions of the Constitution (Article 355).

It is to be noted that the Constitution prescribes a coercive sanction for the enforcement of the directions (Article 365) issued by the union government during the Proclamation of failure of constitutional machinery in a state (Article 356) and during a Proclamation of Emergency under Article 353. Further, during a Proclamation of Financial Emergency, state governments are required to observe canons of financial propriety, as may be specified in the directions under Article 360.

8.1.5 Single Citizenship

In contrast to double citizenship as in the USA—an American is a citizen not only of the state in which he resides but also of the federal structure of the USA—the Indian Constitution, like the Canadian one, confers on an Indian status of single citizenship, that is, the citizenship of India (Article 5).

8.1.6 Mutual Delegation of Executive Functions

Besides the division of powers between the Union and states, the Constitution makes certain provisions for coordination between the Union and states and also among the states. There can be mutual delegation of executive functions between the Union and states. With the consent of a state government, president may entrust to that government or its officers any executive functions of the Union. Parliament may also do the same when making a Union law applicable to a state (Article 258). Similarly a state government with the consent of union government may entrust certain state functions to that government (Article 258A). Also, Parliament may make financial grants to give financial assistance to a state in need of it.

8.1.7 Creation of All India Services

Administrative coordination between the states and the Union is also being promoted by the constitutional provision for All India Services. These services are common to both the Union and states and are moved between them. At present, there are three such services in operation. These are IAS, Indian Police Service (IPS) and Indian Forest Service (IFS). More services can be created, if need be, according to the Constitution (Article 312).[12] The objective behind the provision for the All India Services is to impart a greater cohesion to the federal system and to maintain standards of administration throughout the Union.

8.1.8 Local Government System

The country has local government system in the urban areas (municipalities) and in rural areas (panchayats). These are governed by laws passed by the state legislatures and function under the supervision of state governments. Article 40 in the Constitution on Directive Principles of State Policy has directed the state to organize village panchayats and empower them to function as units of self-government. Panchayat institutions and municipalities have expanded considerably in number and spatial coverage. With the 73rd and 74th Constitution Amendment Acts, 1992, these local governing institutions have been accorded constitutional status. The state governments have now passed new laws or are amending existing ones in context of these new provisions incorporated in Parts IX and IXA of the Constitution on account of these Acts. The Eleventh Schedule (Article 243G) and Twelfth Schedule (Article 243W) of the Constitution provide 29 and 18 subjects to the panchayats and *nagar palikas* (town municipalities) respectively, which may be considered by a state legislature for devolution to the panchayats and the municipalities respectively.

[12] Until 1961, no additional All India Services were created, but several new services have been added to the list of All India Services, namely, the Indian Engineering Service, the Indian Forest Service and the Indian Medical Service. See the All India Services (Amendment), Act, 1963. The Supreme Court has directed the GoI in 1992 for the setting up of an All India Judicial Services, but so far this service remains uncreated. On 30 January 2017, the Supreme Court questioned the feasibility of the All India Judicial Services saying how could the power of high courts to appoint judicial officers in trial courts be taken away. Recently, a committee on National Education Policy which submitted its Report to the HRD Ministry (GoI) on 27 May 2016 recommended the creation of an All India Education Service. But so far this service has not been created.

Article 243ZD mandates the constitution of a District Planning Committee to consolidate the plans between those prepared by the panchayats and municipalities in the district and to prepare a draft development plan for the district as a whole. Under Article 243ZE, Metropolitan Planning Committee would prepare a draft development plan for metropolitan area as a whole. Further, a State Finance Commission has been provided in every state for reviewing financial position of the panchayats and municipalities and making recommendations to the state government concerned for strengthening it (Articles 243I and 243Y).

8.1.9 Unified System of Judiciary

The Constitution also makes provision for a unified system of judiciary. In the hierarchy of courts, there is Supreme Court at the apex, high courts at state level and subordinate courts at the lower level. The Constitution stipulates the main provisions for their organization, jurisdiction and powers.

The Supreme Court has original, appellate and advisory jurisdictions. The original jurisdiction relates to determination of a dispute between the GoI and any state/s on one side and one or more states on the other or among two or more states (Article 131). However, any disputes regarding treaty and foreign arguments and so on as well as certain other matters (e.g., river water dispute) are excluded from its jurisdictions. The original jurisdiction of the court also covers cases of violation of Fundamental Rights of individuals. The Supreme Court is the highest court of appeal from all courts in the country. Its appellate jurisdiction covers cases involving interpretation of Constitution and civil and criminal cases. Further, on a reference by president, it may be asked to express its opinion on a question of law or fact of public importance (Article 143).

In the hierarchy of judicial system, a high court is constituted in each state or else a common high court may be constituted for two or more states as decided by Parliament. The high court has appellate jurisdiction in civil cases from the decisions of district judges and subordinate judges. It has also appellate jurisdiction in appeals from the decisions of session judges, additional and assistant session judges and in certain cases from decisions of judicial or metropolitan magistrates. It also exercises superintendence in relation to all district and subordinate courts and tribunals other than military tribunals, which are under its jurisdiction.

At the district level, the district and sessions judges are the top judicial authority in both civil and criminal matters in a district. They try serious criminal cases and hear appeals from the decisions of magistrates and subordinate civil judges.

The judiciary (through the functioning of the Supreme Court and high courts) has been playing an active role as the guardian of the Constitution. Judiciary is vested with the power of judicial reviews and has struck down several laws as violative of the Constitutions. It has declared several cases of legislative action as unconstitutional or illegal. For example, for higher judiciary appointments (judges of the high courts and the Supreme Court), the Supreme Court on 16 October 2015 struck down the National Judicial Appointments Commission Act, 2014, (99th Constitutional Amendment) as 'unconstitutional and void' and restored the 22-year-old collegium system.

Also the judiciary decides all disputes arising between the Union and the states and between different states, and generally among different units of the constitutional edifice. The Supreme Court and the high courts decide on the constitutionality of issues brought before them, besides interpreting specific provisions of a statute or an executive order. Judicial decisions provide legitimacy to policies of the government. For example, in a landmark judgement, the Supreme Court held on 10 July 2013 that—Parliament has exceeded its powers conferred by the Constitution in enacting Sub-Section (4) of Section 8 of the Representation of the People Act, 1951 that protected the sitting lawmakers against immediate disqualification upon conviction—from 10 July 2013 onwards, MPs, MLAs and MLCs would automatically lose their membership if sentenced to jail for not less than two years by the trial court.[13] The Supreme Court in 2002, and subsequently in 2003, made it mandatory for all candidates contesting elections to disclose criminal, financial and educational background prior to the polls by filling an affidavit with the Election Commission. In a significant verdict, the apex court on 16 April 2017 ruled that candidates availing of the age relaxation under reserved category for government jobs cannot claim the right of be appointed under the general category.[14]

8.2 Drivers and Agencies for Federalism

Federalism of the most devolved and decentralized variety should be the choice that focuses on the creation of healthy relations between the federal structure and its units. A few non-statutory and statutory bodies (through constitutional prescriptions or parliamentary legislation) have been established for one purpose or the other of common interest for the Union and status. Apart from extra-constitutional agencies, such as the NITI Aayog, set up by the union government which further the coordination of state policy and eliminate difference as between the states, the Indian Constitution establishes Finance Commission (under Article 280) for facilitating intergovernmental financial cooperation and Inter State Council or ISC (under Article 263) for investigating and discussing subjects of common interests between and among states and the Union. Administrative coordination between the states and the Union is also being promoted by the constitutional provision under Article 312 for All India Services. These services are common to both the Union and states and are moved between them. Recently the Goods and Services Tax Council (GSTC) has been set up on 16 September 2016 under Article 279A for improving tax compliance and effecting governance of cooperative federalism.

8.2.1 Policy-planning Machinery

The Indian Constitution originally did not contain any provisions relating to the planning machinery, such as the Planning Commission (established in 1950) and the National Development Council (NDC; established in 1952). Nor were these agencies established under a statute.[15] Planning Commission, seen as an extra constitutional and non-statutory body was set up by a resolution on 15 March 1950 of the union cabinet by PM Jawaharlal Nehru with himself as its first

[13] The Supreme Court verdict came on two PILs filed by Lily Thomas and Lok Prahari (NGO) challenging the provision saying it was against the constitutional provisions under Article 102(1) relating to Parliament and Article 191(1) pertaining to legislative assemblies and Councils of States.

[14] See *The Tribune* (Chandigarh), 17 April 2017.

[15] The 74th Constitutional Amendment Act provides for the setting up of District Planning Committees and Metropolitan Planning Committees at the local level. In his first Independence Day address, PM Narendra Modi had announced that a new institution would be created to replace the Planning Commission in order to respect the country's federal structure.

chairman to formulate an integrated Five Year Plan for economic and social development. From the terms of reference, it will be apparent that the Planning Commission was thought of as a staff agency to prepare national plans for social and economic development within the framework of a federal state, a parliamentary democracy and a welfare state. The commission was to suggest, co-ordinate and evaluate policies and programmes, although the final responsibility to the people's representatives and to the people remained with the political institutions. Although the states had no planning commissions of similar status, they had special planning departments and boards (advisory boards) to do the planning work. The 74th Constitutional Amendment Act, 1992 (w.e.f. 1 June 1993) provides for setting up of district planning committees and metropolitan planning committees (Articles 243ZD and 243ZE).[16] These committees are now being associated with the formulation and implementation of plans within the range of responsibilities assigned to them.

On 13 August 2014, the union cabinet of the Modi government approved the repeal of the cabinet resolution of 15 March 1950 by which the Planning Commission was set up. Speaking at his first meeting with chief ministers on 7 December 2014, PM Narendra Modi stressed that 'it was impossible for the nation to develop' unless states develop and have a greater role in the new body (think tank) which reflects the true spirit of 'cooperative federalism'. To Modi, the Planning Commission symbolized centralized planning of the Nehruvian Era and ruled out incremental steps and proposed a 'bottom to top' approach in policy planning to be implemented by a 'think tank'. Experiences by several state governments had shown that the Planning Commission and the union cabinet exercised greater control over the formulation of policy in the state sphere than the Constitution warranted.

A 14th Finance Commission (FY 2015–20) member Govinda Rao remarked, 'Centrally planning is a negation of federalism, nor does it make any sense for approving the plans of the states'. In its first meeting with the chief ministers on 7 December 2014, the PM Narendra Modi, citing remarks of former PM Manmohan Singh towards the end of his term on 30 April 2014, said, 'Dr Singh, who had been associated for a long time with the Planning Commission, had noted the body has no futuristic vision in the post-reform period and that it would have to reinvent itself to remain more effective and relevant in the present situation'.[17] The PM Modi ruled out incremental steps and called for a total replacement of the Planning Commission by a 'think tank' of independent experts, chief ministers and the prime minister.

India's Finance Minister Arun Jaitley made the following observation on the necessity of creating NITI Aayog:

> The 65-year-old Planning Commission had become a redundant organization. It was relevant in a command economy structure, but not any longer. India is a diversified country and its states are in various phases of economic development along with their own strengths and weaknesses. In this context, a 'one-size-fits-all' approach to economic planning is obsolete. It cannot make India competitive in today's global economy.[18]

The Planning Commission was finally scrapped on 13 August 2014 by a union cabinet decision, and it was replaced by a new body called the NITI Aayog (National Institution for Transforming India).

---

[16] The states have agreed to the union government's suggestion that these planning committees would also include representatives of district panchayats and deal with subject matters of common interest and concern to municipalities and panchayats.

[17] See *The Triune* (Chandigarh), 8 December 2014.

[18] 'We Will Use Every Provision in the Constitution to Push Reforms', *OPEN Magazine*. http://www.openthemagazine.com

8.2.1.1 NITI Aayog

NITI Aayog was created through a union cabinet resolution on 1 January 2015 in place of the Planning Commission.[19] The NITI Aayog is tasked to serve as a policy 'think tank' of the government as a 'directional and policy dynamo' and would provide the governments at the centre and in states with strategic and technical advice on key policy matters including economic issues of national and international importance.

As per the policy statement of the government, NITI Aayog will create a knowledge, innovation and entrepreneurial support system through a collaborative community of national and international experts, practitioners and partners. It will offer a platform for resolution of inter-sectoral and inter-departmental issues in order to accelerate the implementation of the development agenda. In addition to being the incubator of ideas for development, the NITI Aayog will provide a critical directional and strategic input into the development process. Noting that progress is not possible without all states advancing in tandem, Modi called upon chief ministers to work with the Centre to forge a model of 'cooperative federalism', hereby the Centre and the states can come together to resolve differences. He termed this partnership as 'Team India'.[20] Through the mechanism of the NITI Aayog, India would move away from 'one-size-fits-all' schemes and forge a better match between various schemes and the needs of states. One of the objectives of and NITI Aayog will be to ensure that the interests of the national security are incorporated in economic strategy and policy.

8.2.1.2 Organization of the NITI Aayog

The NITI Aayog comprises the following:

1. PM of India as the chairperson.
2. Governing council comprising the chief ministers of all the states and union territories with legislatures and lieutenant governors of other union territories.
3. Regional councils will be formed to address specific issues and contingencies impacting more than one state or a region. These will be formed for a specified tenure. The regional councils will be convened by the prime minister and will comprise of the chief ministers of states and lieutenant governors of union territories in the region. These will be chaired by the chairperson of the NITI Aayog or his nominee.
4. Experts, specialists and practitioners with relevant domain knowledge as special invitees nominated by the prime minister.
5. Full-time organizational framework (in addition to prime minister as the chairperson) comprising
   a. Vice chairperson—a full-time member of eminence;
   b. Members—two full-time experts;
   c. Part-time members—maximum of two from leading universities, research organizations and other relevant institutions in an ex officio capacity. Part-time members will be on a rotational basis;
   d. Ex officio members—maximum of four members of the Union Council of Ministers to be nominated by the prime minister;

[19] See *The Financial Express* (Chandigarh), 2 January 2015.

[20] *The Tribune*, Chandigarh, 9 February 2015.

e. Chief executive officer—to be appointed by the prime minister for a fixed tenure, in the rank of secretary to the GoI; and
f. Secretariat, as deemed necessary.[21]

According to a statement, the regional councils will be formed to address specific issues and contingencies impacting more than one state or a region. These will be formed for a specified tenure. The regional councils will be convened by the PM and will comprise the chief ministers of states and lieutenant governors of union territories in the region. These will be chaired by the chairperson of the NITI Aayog or his nominee.

The NITI Aayog will also have experts, specialists and practitioners with relevant domain knowledge as special invitees nominated by the prime minister. The two part-time members of the new body would be from leading universities and research organizations. Figure 8.1 shows the structure and composition of the NITI Aayog, replacing Planning Commission.

Explanatory Notes:
NITI Aayog has been set up on 1 January 2015.

- PM is the chairman; vice chairman is appointed by PM; CEO is an officer of secretary rank.
- Members include (a) 4–5 domain experts to assist vice chairman, (b) 2 part-time members from institutes/universities, appointed on rotational basis and (c) 4 council ministers (ex-officio) nominated by PM.

Figure 8.1 Structure and Composition of NITI Aayog

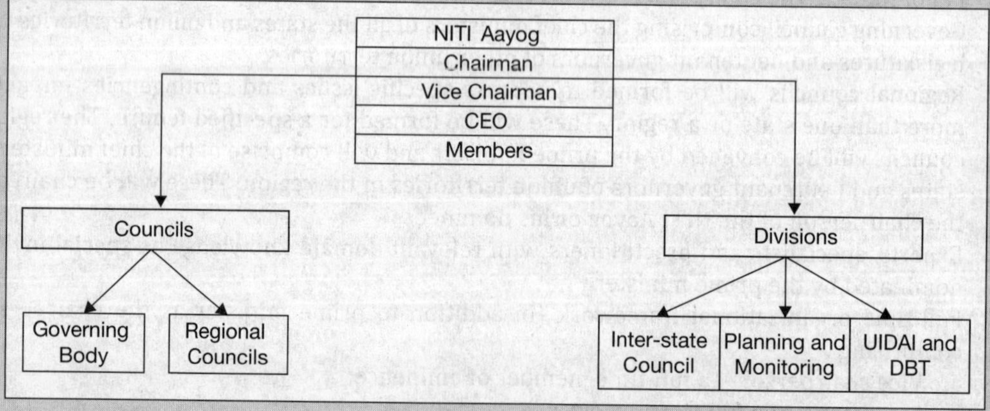

Source: NITI Aayog (GoI), New Delhi.

[21] 'Cabinet Resolution for NITI Aayog', *Gazette of India*, Retrieved 10 January 2015, http://www.egazette.ni.in/WriteReadData/2015/162317.pdf. Mr Arvind Pangariya was appointed as the first vice chairperson of NITI, who resigned in August 2017 and was replaced by Dr Rajiv Kumar.

- Governing council comprising all state chief ministers and lieutenant governors of union territories (headed by PM) to ensure genuine and continuing partnership of all states in policymaking.
- Regional councils to address specific issues within a specific time frame.
- ISC will carry the development agenda to the states forward to finance and other central ministers (headed by a secretary). It will move from home ministry to Yojana Bhawan to oversee development works by the states. Thus, the states will have a greater role in planning.
- The planning and monitoring division will work on a long-term plan for the government and evaluate the flagship social sector schemes (headed by a secretary).

8.2.1.3 Objectives and Functions of the NITI Aayog

The NITI Aayog (established on 1 January 2015) will serve as a 'think tank' of the governments as 'a directional and policy dynamo' and would provide the governments at Centre and in states with strategic and technical advice on key policy matters including economic issues of national and international importance.[22]

> NITI Aayog will seek to provide a critical directional and strategic input into the development process. The centre-to-state-one-way flow of policy, that was the hallmark of Planning Commission era, is now sought to be replaced by a genuine and continuing partnership of states.

NITI Aayog will merge as a 'think tank' that will provide governments at the central and state levels with relevant strategic and technical advice across the spectrum of key elements of policy.

The NITI Aayog will also seek to put an end to slow and tardy implementation of policy by fostering better inter-ministry coordination and better centre–state coordination. It will help evolve a shared vision of national development priorities and foster cooperative federalism, recognizing that strong states make a strong nation.

The NITI Aayog will develop mechanisms to formulate credible plans to the village level and aggregate these progressively at higher levels of government. 'It will ensure special attention to the sections of society that may be at risk of not benefiting adequately from economic progress'. The NITI Aayog will 'create a knowledge, innovation and entrepreneurial support system through a collaborative community of national and international experts, practitioners and partners'. It will 'offer a platform for resolution of inter-sectoral and inter-departmental issues in order to accelerate the implementation of the development agenda' (http://niti.gov.in/content/functions, accessed on 21 May 2010).

In addition, the NITI Aayog will monitor and evaluate the implementation of programmes and focus on technology upgradation and capacity building. Through this, the NITI Aayog will aim to accomplish the following objectives and opportunities:

- An administration paradigm in which the government is an enabler rather than a 'provide of first and last resort'.

[22] See *The Financial Express* (Chandigarh), 2 January 2015. While chairing the first session of the NITI Aayog on 8 February 2015, the PM Narendra Modi said, 'We will move away from "one-size-fits-all" schemes and forge a better match between these schemes and the needs of states'.

- Progress from 'food security' to focus on a mix of agricultural production as well as actual returns that farmers get from their produce.
- Ensure that India is an active player in the debates and deliberations on the global commons.
- Ensure that the economically vibrant middle class remains engaged, and its potential is fully realized.
- Leverage India's pool of entrepreneurial scientific and intellectual human capital.
- Incorporate the significant geo-economic and geo-political strength of the Non-Resident Indian community.
- Use urbanization as an opportunity to create a wholesome and secure habitat through the use of modern technology.
- Use technology to reduce opacity and potential for misadventure in governance.

The NITI Aayog aims to enable India to better face complex, challenges, through the following:

- Leveraging of India's demographic dividend and realization of the potential of youth, men and women, through education skill development, elimination of gender bias and employment.
- Elimination of poverty and the chance for every Indian to live a life of dignity and self-respect.
- Redressal of inequalities based on gender bias, caste and economic disparities.
- Integrate villages institutionally into the development process.
- Policy support to more than 50 million small businesses, which are a major source of employment creation safeguarding of our environmental and ecological assets.

The NITI Aayog is quite different from the Planning Commission. Two key activities of the commission had been to prepare and implement the Five Year Plans and to allocate financial resources to states. However, neither of these activities forms a part of the mandate of NITI Aayog. The 12th Five Year Plan which ended on 31st March 2017 was India's last Five Year Plan.

The 14th Finance Commission raised the shares of states in the divisible pool from 32% to 42%, leaving no additional funds for allocation to states through NITI Aayog.[23] Likewise, the annual resource allocation exercise that brought state chief ministers to the doorstep of the Planning Commission is now no more. PC is now abolished.

It is observed that among many functions that NITI Aayog performs three stand out notably: '(a) promotion of cooperative and competitive federalism, (b) assisting the central government in policymaking and (c) serving as the governments think tank'.[24]

The governing council of NITI Aayog on 8 February 2015 appointed three subgroups of chief ministers to advise the central government on the subjects of 'Centrally Sponsored Schemes', 'Skill Development' and 'Swachh Bharat Mission'. It also set up two task forces at the Aayog on 'Agricultural Development' and 'Elimination of Poverty', with parallel task force on each subject constituted in the states and union territories. The NITI Aayog is also in process of bringing out the 15-year Vision, 7-year Strategy, and 3-year Action Plan documents.

---

[23] See *Times of India* (Chandigarh), 2 January 2017.

[24] See *The Financial Express* (Chandigarh), 29 July 2016.

The second meeting of governing council of the NITI Aayog called by the PM Narendra Modi on 15 July 2015, who sought support for rural development through the passage of the Land Acquisition Bill, 2015, was boycotted by over a dozen chief ministers. The Union Finance Minister Arun Jaitley observed, 'An overwhelming section said either the Centre must build a consensus and pass amendments … quickly or give flexibility to states to make their own laws'.[25] The PM Modi said, 'The political deadlock over land acquisition is seriously impacting rural development, including the creation of schools, hospitals, roads and irrigation projects'. The fourth meeting of NITI Aayog Governing Council on 16 June 2018 focused on issues such as doubling of farmers' income, development of aspirational districts, Ayushman Bharat, Mission Indradhanush and Nutrition Mission.[26]

At the first National Conference of Chief Secretaries which was also attended by the NITI Aayog vice chairman and CEO, the PM Narendra Modi urged the top bureaucrats of all states and union territories 'to remain ever mindful of the credo of competitive cooperative federalism'.[27]

Earlier, NITI Aayog has identified 5 states (Madhya Pradesh, Odisha, Chhattisgarh, Jharkhand and Andhra Pradesh) in education sector and five states (Uttar Pradesh, Bihar, Assam, Karnataka and Gujarat) in the health sector to assist them in bringing about a transformational change in sectors in a fixed span.[28] At the fourth meeting, Chief Ministers of non-BJP ruled states said that Centre should follow cooperative federalism.

8.2.1.4 A Critical Evaluation of Policy Planning Machinery

The government's move to replace the Planning Commission with a new institution called 'NITI Aayog' was criticized by opposition parties of India. The Congress sought to know whether the reform introduced by the BJP-led government was premised on any meaningful programme or if the move was simply born out of political opposition to the party that ran the Planning Commission for over 60 years. 'The real issue is do you (the government) have a substantive meaningful programme to reform the Planning Commission?' Congress spokesperson Abhishek Manu Singhvi said:

> If you (the BJP government) simply want to abolish it (the commission), because it is something which (Jawaharlal) Nehru created for this country and you don't like Nehru or simply because it was run by the Congress for 60 years and you don't like the Congress, that is pitiable.[29]
>
> The idea to create an institution where states' leaders will be part and parcel of the collective thinking with the Centre and other stakeholders in formulating a vision for the development of the country is right on as compared with the previous structure, where a handful of people formulated the vision and then presented it to the National Development Council (NDC). This was not entirely absorbed and adopted by the latter.[30]
>
> In fact, a recent survey of expert opinions in the magazine *Business World* shows that either a very clear distinction of roles of NDC, Governing Council and Inter State Council or a merger of one or two with a vibrant and functional ISC can serve the two key goals of such forums: policy development and conflict resolution.[31]

[25] *The Hindustan Times* (Chandigarh), 16 July 2015.

[26] See *The Financial Express* (Chandigarh), 16 July 2015.

[27] See *The Economic Times*, 12 July 2017.

[28] See *The Tribune* (Chandigarh), 16 June 2017 and 17 June 2018.

[29] IANS, 'NITI Aayog Critics Ignorant of Facts: Sitharaman', *Business Standard*, 4 January 2015. http://www.business-standard.com/article/news-ians/niti-aayog-critics-ignorant-of-facts-says-sitharaman-115010400455_1.html

[30] ET Bureau, 'Planning Commission is Now "NITI Aayog"', *The Economic Times*, 2 January 2015.

[31] C. K. Sharma, 'NITI's Destiny and the Federal Question', *Business World*, 8 April 2015.

The thrust behind the setting up of the NITI Aayog is to coordinate states for identifying specific problems and devising mechanisms to resolve them through the spirit of cooperative federalism.[32] Sharma in his writing on federalism, makes a strong case for collaborative federalism but also adds that this outcome can be realized only in the context of 'a balanced, transparent and distortion free system of intergovernmental fiscal relations'.[33]

With a view to seeing that this NITI Aayog plays an effective intergovernmental policymaking and conflict resolution role among and between Union and state governments, it is important for the union government to ensure that this institutions is insulated, from partisan pressure. In an article, Rao argues that the 'NITI Aayog be given statutory status and powers', if it has to play an effective 'role in promoting intergovernmental bargains, resolving issues and coordinating policies between the Union and states in the spirit of cooperative federalism'.[34]

According to NITI Aayog CEO, a lot of programmes have been laid out by the NDA-led government, but 'states have to be key drivers to implement these programmes and hence the Prime Minister is driving competitive federalism'.[35]

8.2.2 National Development Council (NDC)

NDC was set up as an extra-constitutional and non-statutory body by a cabinet resolution on 6 August 1952, on the initiative of the first PM Jawaharlal Nehru. In the first meeting of the NDC held on 8–9 November 1952, PM observed that the NDC was essentially a forum for intimate cooperation between state governments and the central government for all the tasks of national development. Following functions were assigned to the NDC[36]:

1. To review the working of the National Plan from time to time
2. To consider important questions of social and economic policy affecting national development
3. To recommend measures for the achievement of the aims and targets set out in the National Plan

In 1967, the functions of the NDC were redefined to include the following:

1. Prescribing guidelines for the formulation of the national plan
2. Considering the national plans as formulated by the Planning Commission
3. Assessing resources required for implementing the plan and to suggest ways and means for raising them

The NDC, as reconstituted in 1967 on the acceptance of the ARC's recommendations (1967), is composed of the PM (as chairman) all union cabinet ministers, chief ministers of all states, chief

[32] Union Finance Minister Arun Jaitley's comments on the nature of NITI Aayog. See *The Financial Express* (Chandigarh), 9 February 2015.

[33] C. K. Sharma, 'Reimagining Federalism in India: Exploring the Frontiers of Collaborative Federal Architecture', *Asia-Pacific Social Science Review* 15, no. 1 (2015).

[34] M. Govinda Rao, 'Getting NITI Aayog to Work', *The Financial Express* (Chandigarh), 21 July 2015.

[35] See *The Economic Times*, 12 July 2017.

[36] http://planningcommission.gov.in/reports/genrep/50NDCs/vol1_1to14.pdf (accessed on 21 May 2018).

ministers/administrators of all union territories and the members of the Planning Commission (now replaced with NITI Aayog on 1 January 2015).

Apart from conferences held on specific problems, there are annual conferences at the highest level, such as the Conference of Governors, the Chief Ministers' Conference, the Law Ministers' Conference, the Chief Justices' Conference, which are of no mean importance from the standpoint of the state as well as interstate relations. As Appleby observed:

> The power that is exercised organically in New Delhi is the uncertain and discontinuous power of prestige. It is influence rather than power. Its method is making plans, issuing pronouncements, and holding conferences. Any real power in most of the development field is the personal power of particular leaders and the informal, extra-constitutional, extra-administrative power of a dominant party, coherent and strongly led by the same leaders. Dependence of achievement, therefore, is in some crucial ways, apart from the formal organs of governance, in forces which in the future may take quite different forms.[37]

8.2.2.1 A Critical Evaluation of NDC

The NDC appeared to be a useful instrument of intergovernmental policy cooperation. It served as an apex forum not only for the approval of the Five Year Plans but also for achieving policy coordination on the matters of national significance. However, of date, it has become a body of partisan forum. In this context, Santhanam observed, 'The position of NDC has come to approximate to that of a super cabinet of the entire Indian federalism, a cabinet functioning for the Government of India and the governments of all the States'.[38]

The Sarkaria Commission (1988) lamented that the NDC had not been able to act as an effective instrument for developing consensus and commitment to national policies. It recommended that it should be renamed as National Economic and Development Council.

8.3 Fiscal Federalism

Granting of funds by one government to other governments for the purpose of achieving specific goals is called fiscal federalism. This may take the form of grants-in-aid or a conditional gift from one government to another. Intergovernmental financial relations are critical to the financial health of the country. The degree to which three spheres of government—central, state and local—can perform their constitutional responsibilities effectively depends upon the financial resources available to them. Here, there are both vertical and horizontal dimensions. There is the vertical distribution of revenue raised nationally to match the expenditure responsibilities of central, state and local spheres of governments. There is also the horizontal dimension of the allocation of equitable spheres of financial resources to each state and local government taking account of disparities in resources and needs. Articles from 264 to 290 govern the financial relations between the Union and the states.

After making provisions for the transfer of resources from the Union to the states in the form of shared taxes and the grants, the Constitution provided for the constitution of a Finance

[37] Paul H. Appleby, *Public Administration in India* (New Delhi: Cabinet Secretariat, 1953), 22.

[38] K. Santhanam, *Union–State Relations in India* (Bombay: Asia Publishing House, 1960), 47.

Commission at five-year intervals (Article 280) to suggest the principles and the amount of such sharing. Other similar matters could also be referred to such a commission by presidential order.[39]

A State Finance Commission has been provided for in every state for reviewing financial position of the panchayats and municipalities and making recommendations to the government concerned for strengthening it (Articles 243I and 243Y). These financial commissions operating at the central and state levels facilitate intergovernmental financial cooperation.

Among the objectives for the operations of the Finance Commission that need to be emphasized is the desirability of focusing on maximizing the scope for economic growth and minimizing complexities that would arise from the inevitable pressures to consider every possible variable. To secure healthy cooperation among all the three spheres of government, it is necessary to devise some procedures for consultation between governments prior to financial transfers from central tax revenue to state and local spheres of government in order to support their constitutional expenditure responsibilities. The Punchhi Commission (2010) recommended the introduction of Goods and Services Tax (GST) to be levied by the Centre and states. The GST Act has been in operation since 1 July 2017.

By means of grants-in-aid under Article 275, the Union would be in a position to correct inter-state disparities in financial assistance. Special grants may be given for promoting the welfare of the STs and for raising the level of administration of the Scheduled Areas. Under Article 282, the Union or a state gives grant for any public purpose, such as, National Literacy Mission, Polio Eradication and so on. Besides, under Members of Parliament Local Area Development (MPLAD) Scheme, a member of parliament is allowed to recommend expenditure every year up to the ceiling fixed for any work for public purpose.[40] The Union has claim to immunity in respect of its property (Article 285). Analogous to this, the property and income of the state is exempt from Union taxation. The Centre may also relax norms under the Fiscal Responsibility and Budget Management Act to increase the state's borrowing limit.[41]

8.4 Inter State Council (ISC)

Conflicts of interest and disputes between two or more states are inevitable. Although states have their own sphere of powers and enjoy a certain degree of independence, yet they cannot remain in complete isolation from each other. Accepting the recommendation of the first commission on centre–state relations (the Sarkaria Commission which submitted its report in January 1988), the GoI constituted an ISC under Article 263 on 28 May 1990.

---

[39] The First Finance Commission was constituted in 1951 with Sri K. C. Neogy as the chairman and the 14th Finance Commission has been constituted in 2012 whose operational duration is 2015–20. The duty of the FC is to make recommendations to the president as to (a) distribution of taxes between the Union and the states, (b) principles governing the grants-in-aid of revenues of the states, (c) measures needed to augment the consolidate, fund of the state for supplementing the resources of the panchayats and municipalities in the state and (d) any other matter that may be referred by the president.

[40] The Supreme Court held that MPLAD Scheme is constitutional under Article 275 and 282. Refer to *Bhim Singh v. Union of India*, 2010 (5), SCC 538.

[41] For example, the Punjab government's borrowing limit was enhanced by ₹10,000 crore by Union Finance Ministry to enable the state to rescue its debt-ridden farmers. See *The Tribune*, 18 August 2017.

The composition of the council as per the presidential order dated 28 May 1990 is as follows:

1. PM as the chairman
2. Chief ministers of all states
3. Chief ministers of union territories having a legislative assembly and Administrators of union territories not having a legislative assembly
4. Six ministers of cabinet rank in the Union Council of Ministers to be nominated by the prime minister

The second ARC (2005–2009) recommended that the ISC must be given the power to resolve inter-state and union–state conflicts. However, it also recommended that the Council need not exist in perpetuity. It should be constituted as and when the need arises.

The Punchhi Commission on centre–state relations (2010) recommended functional independence and quasi-judicial status for the ISC. It also recommended that ISC should be made a vibrant negotiating forum for policy development and conflict resolution.

The Constitution of India empowers the President of India to establish a constitutional body for inquiring into and advising upon inter-state disputes under Art 263 (a) and for achieving better coordination of policy and action under Article 263 (b) and (c), regarding subjects of common interest to some or all of the states, or the Union and one or more of the states.[42]

However, the following issues may not be brought up before the Council:

1. Any issue which can be resolved at the official/ministerial level
2. Any issue which has to be dealt with by the NDC, the National Integration Council (NIC), and the Finance Commission
3. Any issue which is sub judice or is under consideration in either House of Parliament
4. Any other issue the discussion of which may, in the opinion of the chairman, create discord between the states or otherwise be against the public interest or against the interests of the sovereignty or integrity of India, the security of the state, friendly relations with foreign state or public order

It is mentioned here that there is no provision that makes it mandatory for the Council to hold its meetings on a regular basis with a constitutionally specified frequency. Ten members, including the chairman, form the quorum for a meeting of the Council. The union government on 1 November 2017 reconstituted the ISC, the mandate of which is to investigate and advise on disputes between states, with PM Narendra Modi being its chairman and six union ministers and chief ministers of all states and union territories having legislative assemblies. Eight other union ministers have been made permanent invitees to the council. They represent Ministries of Commerce, Food, Food Processing Industries, Tribal Affairs, HRD, Petroleum, Railways and Home. In another notification, the government reconstituted the standing committee of the ISC under the chairmanship of Home Minister Rajnath Singh. Four union ministers and seven chief ministers are

[42] Article 263 of the Indian Constitution. It may be mentioned here that ISC has not been assigned the function envisaged in clause (a) of Article 263 as recommended by the Sarkaria commission. In exercise of this power, the president has so far established a Central Council of Health, a Central Council of Local Self-Government, and a Transport Development Council for the purpose of coordinating the policy of the states relating to these matters.

members of the new standing committee of the council. The job of the standing committee will be to monitor the implementation of decisions taken on the recommendations of the council and consider any other matter referred to it by the council.[43]

The National Commission to Review the Working of the Constitution (NCRWC) 2002 (under Justice M. N. Venkatachaliah) as well as the Second Commission on Centre–State Relations 2010 (under Justice M. M. Punchhi) in their respective reports recommend that the ISC need to be substantially strengthened and activized as the key player in IGR. The Punchhi Commission also suggested equal representation of states, small or big, in the Rajya Sabha to alter the balance of power in favour of smaller states in federal governance. It strongly expressed itself in favour of removal of 'factors inhibiting the composition and functioning of the Second Chamber as a representative forum of states' by constitutional amendment.

Coordination between states: The power of the president to set up ISC may be exercised not only for advising upon disputes but also for the purpose of investigating and discussing subjects in which some or all of the states of the Union and one or more of the states have a common interest. In exercise of this power, the president has already constituted the Central Council of Health, the Central Council of Local Self-Government, the Central Council of Indian Medicine and the Central Council of Homeopathy. In this connection, it should be mentioned that advisory bodies to advice on inter-state matters have also been established under statutory authority.

In the 11th ISC meeting which was held on 16 July 2016, some chief ministers expressed flagging concerns over centre–state relations. For example, Karnataka Home Minister said, 'The States should have greater autonomy in respect of subjects in the State List and the Union should be extremely restrained in asserting parliamentary supremacy over them. Harmonious operation of the Concurrent List could be considered as cooperative federalism at its best'. The deputy chief minister of Punjab accused the Centre of reducing states to the status of mere beggars. The chief minister of Bihar went to extent of demanding abolition of the post of governor.

In his concluding remarks at the 11th meeting of the ISC, the PM Modi said, 'There should be better coordination between the police department of the states. For this the focus should be on technology and training of the police personnel, particularly in matters related to cybercrime'.[44]

The ISC is the only constitutional body to deal with federal disputes in a comprehensive manner. It has a high potential to strengthen vertical and horizontal cooperation in Indian federalism. However, this potential remains untapped. It was made to languish while the Planning Commission flourished. But it is only the 'constitutional entity for harmonizing the actions of the Centre and states. Its effective utilization would lend legitimacy to cooperative federalism'.[45]

8.5 Goods and Services Tax Council (GSTC)

To secure healthy cooperation among all the three spheres of government, it is necessary to devise some procedures for consultation between governments prior to financial transfers from central tax revenue to state and local spheres of government in order to support their constitutional expenditure responsibilities. The Punchhi Commission (2010) recommended the introduction of

[43] See *The Tribune* (Chandigarh), 2 November 2017.

[44] See *The Economic Times* (Chandigarh), 17 July 2016.

[45] N. K. Singh, 'An Unfinished Agenda of Federalism', *Indian Express*, 4 November 2015.

GST to be levied by the Centre and states. And after a strenuous effort, the Modi government at the union level succeeded in the enactment of GST bill.

On 8 September 2016, the Constitution (101st Amendment) Act, 2016, received the assent of the President of India for the introduction of GST in the country (the notification for bringing into force Article 279A(1) with effect from 12 September 2016 was issued on 10 September 2016. On 12 September 2016, the union cabinet approved the creation of GSTC and its secretariat, and, on 16 September 2016, the GSTC was set up under Article 279A of the Indian Constitution. GSTC is an institutional mechanism comprising a chairperson (union finance minister) and one member nominee from each state government as members. The union minister of state in charge of revenue or finance is also a member. Nominee ministers from the state governments have been given power to choose 'one amongst themselves' a vice chairperson of the council 'for such period as they may decide', allowing rotation if needed. One-half of the total number of members of the GSTC is the determined quorum as its meetings, and every decision is to be taken by a majority of not less than three-fourth of the weighted votes—central government has one-third weightage of the votes cast and state governments taken together, two-third—members present and voting at the meeting. As the GSTC is mandated to be

> guided by the need for a harmonized structure of goods and services tax and for the development of harmonized national market for goods and services, the Council has to recommend the following:
>
> 1. the taxes, cesses and surcharges levied by the Union, the States and the local bodies which may be subsumed in the goods and services tax;
> 2. the goods and services that may be subjected to, or exempted from goods and services tax;
> 3. model Goods and Services Tax Laws, principles of levy, appointment of Goods and Services Tax levied on supplies in the course of inter-State trade or commerce under Article 269A and the principles that govern the place of supply;
> 4. the threshold limit of turnover below which goods and services may be exempted from goods and services tax;
> 5. the rates, including floor rates, with bands of goods and services tax;
> 6. any special rate or rates for a specific period, to raise additional resources during any natural calamity or disaster;
> 7. special provision with respect to the States of Arunachal Pradesh, Assam, Jammu and Kashmir, Manipur, Mizoram, Nagaland, Sikkim, Tripura, Himachal Pradesh and Uttarakhand; and
> 8. any other matter relating to the goods and services tax, to be decided by the GST Council.
>
> GST rates have been finalized with a four-tier structure of 5, 12, 18 and 28 per cent while basic consumption items such as foodgrains will be taxed at zero percent. With President's assent given to four parliamentary legislations namely, Central Goods and Services Tax Act, the Goods and Services Tax Compensation to States Act, the Integrated Goods and Services Tax Act, and the Union Territory Goods and Services Tax Act on 13 April 2017. GST regime was rolled out on 1 July 2017.[46]

GSTC has the mandate to recommend to the legislature implications of the GST on (a) tax structure, (b) tax incidence, (c) tax consumption, (d) tax payment, (e) compliance, (f) credit utilization and (g) reporting, and it also has in its zone of consideration business-process implications in terms of (i) pricing of product and services, (ii) supply chain operations, (iii) realistic accounting

[46] See *The Tribune* (Chandigarh), 2 July 2017.

and (iv) e-governance. After receipt of the GSTC recommendations, legislative action is taken in the Parliament of India.

Recently, the union government has decided to refund its share of 58% of the taxes of the Centre would collect under the GST as part of the deal to promote industrial units in Himachal Pradesh, Jammu and Kashmir, north eastern states, including Sikkim and Uttarakhand, until March 2027.[47] Within the framework of GST Act, each industry will be entitled to its own refund mechanism during this period. By reimbursing 42% tax claims of these units, all that the hill states would get in return is possible employment for local youth.

It may be mentioned here that under the GST regime rolled out on 1 July 2017, there is no provision for exemptions. Central or state governments, however are empowered to refund their portion of tax. Rajeev Dimri, a leader of Indian Tax BMR and Associates said that 'by reaching a consensus on the contentions issue of dual control, the GST Council had taken a significant step towards the implementation of GST'.[48]

The Economic Survey (2016–17) released on 31 January 2017 in the Parliament by the Union Finance Minister indicated, 'The GST will create a common Indian market, improve tax compliance and governance, and boost investment and growth; it is also a bold new experiment in the governance of India's cooperative federalism'.[49] Furthermore, Economic Survey observed, 'Fiscal gains from implementing the GST and demonetization, while almost certain to occur, will probably take time to be fully realized'.

In this connection, the editorial page of the *Economic Times* writes that GST is the biggest move to end black money. Further, it is said that 'adoption of the goods and services tax would create a seamless common market'.[50] The GST would subsume and eliminate the previous cascade 17 central and state taxes and 23 cesses, leading to efficiency gains and lowering retail prices.

It may be mentioned here that the GSTC has been constituted as a fully discursive body in the spirit of cooperative federalism. It is not merely a forum of compensation-seekers, but apex recommendatory constitutional entity. The voting pattern of the GSTC is such that the states will play a major role with a two-third share, and though the central government with a one-thirds share has veto power, decisions are taken by a three-fourth majority.

8.6 National Integration Council (NIC)

NIC is a non-constitutional body to address problems of communalism, casteism and regionalism. As a forum, the NIC was created by the Nehru government in the backdrop of the Chinese aggression in 1962 that goes beyond the intergovernmental scope and includes nongovernmental agencies also. The NIC is a 103-members forum of union ministers, chief ministers, political leaders, heads of national commissions and eminent public figures. The body can be used to gauge broader

[47] The union cabinet cleared the CGST refund scheme with a budgetary allocation of ₹27,413 crore which will come as a great relief to sectors such as pharma, automobiles and FMCG. However, this central decision may not be appreciated by the non-hill states, which are struggling to bring in new units and woo the existing ones with sops, including subsidized power and tax incentives. See *The Tribune* (Chandigarh), 18 August 2017.

[48] See *The Tribune* (Chandigarh), 17 January 2017.

[49] Economic Survey, 2016–17. See *The Tribune* (Chandigarh), 1 February 2017.

[50] *The Economic Times* (Chandigarh), 3 July 2017.

opinion of the intelligentsia on sensitive matters. It discusses such issues as banning on extremist organizations, communal violence, imposition of Article 356 in the state and related matters.

The 15th meeting of the NIC held in New Delhi on 10 September 2011 reiterated the declaration of objectives, adopted by the NIC in 1968 which is as follows:

> The foundation of our national life is common citizenship, unity in diversity, freedom of religions, secularism, equality, justice—social, economic and political—and fraternity among all communities.[51]

In 2009, the central government set up a National Investigation Agency to deal with terror across the country.[52]

8.7 Extra Judicial Tribunal

Since the states, in every federation, normally act as independent units in the exercise of their internal sovereignty, conflicts of interest between the units are sure to arise. Hence, in order to maintain the strength of the Union, it is essential that there should be adequate provision for judicial determination of disputes.

While Article 131 provides for the judicial determination of disputes between states by vesting the Supreme Court with exclusive jurisdiction in the matter, Article 262 provides for the adjudication of one class of disputes by an extrajudicial tribunal. Under the Article, the Parliament has enacted the Inter-State Water Disputes Act, 1956, to provide for adjudication of disputes relating to waters of inter-state rivers and river valleys.[53] Under the aforesaid Act, the union government has constituted several water disputes Tribunals.

The NCRWC noted that on several occasions, the parties to the disputes approached the Supreme Court for judicial review both against the interim orders of the Tribunal as also against the final decision.[54] Further, in the implementation of decision of the Tribunal, the oustees seek financial compensation and often resort to agitation for enforcing their Fundamental Rights under Article 21 of the Constitution consequent on the submergence of their lands due to construction of reservoirs.

In the context of the water disputes involving one or more states, the NCRWC made certain suggestions. First, it observes that it is not necessary to exclude inter-state water disputes from the original jurisdiction of the Supreme Court under Article 131. Second, the NCRWC has recommended that appropriate parliamentary legislation should be made for repealing the River Boards Act, 1956, and replacing it by another comprehensive enactment under Entry 56 of List 1. Third, the NCRWC is of the view that as water disputes are important, they should be heard and

---

[51] See http://mha.nic.in/NIC-List 290811.pdf

[52] The union ministry has taken the decision after the Supreme Court ruled that the Kerala government has no jurisdiction to prosecute the two Italian marines—Massimiliano Lattore and Salvatore Girone—allegedly involved in the killing of the fishermen.

[53] The process under the Act including the giving of the award by the Tribunal takes normally 7–10 years. The delay at times has been causing bitterness and friction between the states involved in the disputes.

[54] On the recommendations of the Sarkaria Commission, the ISC and the Ministry of Water Resources, Section 6 of the Inter-State Water Disputes Act, 1956, has been amended to provide that the decision of The Tribunal, after its publication in the official gazette by the central government shall have the same force as an order or decree of the Supreme Court.

disposed by a bench not less than three judges and if necessary, a bench of five judges of the Supreme Court for the final disposal of the suit. A draft National Policy Guidelines for water. Allocation of inter-state rivers has been prepared and considered by the National Water Resources Council which referred it to the National Water Board for review and for arriving at a consensus draft.

The president can establish an ISC for enquiring into and advising upon inter-state disputes, if at any time it appears to him that the public interest would be served by the establishment of such a council under Article 263(a). On 18 December 2016, the Centre decided to set up a single, permanent tribunal to adjudicate all inter-state river water disputes subsuming existing tribunals in order to resolve grievances of states in a speedy manner.

8.8 Inter-state Commerce Commission

For promoting coordination between states in public interest, Article 307 of the India Constitution provides for appointment of an authority. The NCRWC and the Second Commission on Centre–State Relations (constituted on 27 April 2007 under the chairmanship of Justice M. M. Punchhi) recommended the setting up of an Inter-state Trade and Commerce Commission under Article 307, read with Entry 42 of the List I for carrying out objectives of Articles 301 to 304 and other purposes relating to the needs of inter-state trade and commerce.

As a constitutional body and similar to the Inter-State Commerce Commission in the USA for regulating trade and commerce throughout the territory of India, no such commission has been constituted so far.

8.9 Zonal Councils

Five Zonal Councils—Northern, Southern, Eastern, Western and Central—have been established under the States Reorganisation Act, 1956, to advise on policy and matters of common interests (economic and social planning, border disputes and inter-state transport and the likes) to each of the five zones into which the territory of India has been divided. If properly worked, these councils would foster the federal sentiment by resisting the separatist tendencies of linguism and provincialism.

Besides the five Zonal Councils, there is a North Eastern Council established under the North Eastern Council Act, 1971, to deal with the common problems of Assam, Meghalaya, Manipur, Nagaland, Tripura, Arunachal Pradesh and Mizoram. Even these regional councils representing the common interests in their dealings with the union governments have failed in this task.

8.10 Policy and Administrative Implications of IGR

As a framework, Inter-governmental relations are diverse and multi-theoretic. IGR designates an important body of activities in all federal and unitary systems of the world. But they have several policy and administrative implications. A major issue relates to provision of IGR. The issue is whether provision of IGR should be constitutionally prescribed, established by legislation or left to be developed by practice and convention? It is observed that practically in all constitutions where there has been multi-sphere governments, constitutional provisions for some basic intergovernmental institutions and processes have been made, although rarely in detail.

The Indian Constitution specifically contains several provisions governing IGR but does not specify the scope or timing of such implementation. A second issues is whether different forms of IGR should be in terms of encouraging centralization or overemphasizing the states? This will depend on the extent to which IGR are based on mutual agreement or are used as a vehicle for imposing views by one sphere on another. A third significant issue is who manages or controls IGR? What are the appropriate roles of legislature, executive, judiciary and independent commissions in facilitating intergovernmental coordination? This will depend on the extent to which IGR are managed or controlled by these bodies.

A fourth important issue is how to relate IGR to democratic accountability? Often complex arrangements for intergovernmental coordination and decision requiring consultation and negotiation between governments dilute or undermine the democratic accountability of each government. Some mechanisms have to be devised for linking IGR to democratic accountability. A fifth issue is how to secure balance between intergovernmental coordination on one hand and the diversity and policy state initiatives on the other?

Many systems of IGR focus just on two tiers of spheres, leaving local government totally within state or provincial jurisdiction. The Indian Constitution has accorded constitutional status to the local governing institutions (under the 73rd and 74th Constitution Amendment Acts, 1992; inserted on 1 June 1993). The Indian Constitution in Parts IX (Panchayats) and IXA (Municipalities) appropriately recognizes the importance of local government as a third sphere, but this does make IGR more complex and give to them a triangular rather than hierarchical character.

Given predominant role to executives in parliamentary form, administrative channels of IGR are crucial for achieving effective cooperative government in policy areas. But despite constitutional provisions in respect of union–state relations, some problems continue to persist in policy and governance areas. For example, while states in India raise issues of law and order as being their subject, terrorism operates in a seamless world and states do not have the wherewithal to deal with the situation. States turn to the Ministry of Home Affairs (GoI) which deploys central forces and at times calls in the army to deal with such situations. Large-scale deployment of central forces leads to complaints of human rights violations.[55]

The 15th Finance Commission (FC) of India has been constituted on 27 November 2017 to give recommendations for five fiscal years commencing on 1 April 2020. The main tasks of the FC are to 'strengthen cooperative federalism, improve quality of public spending and help protect fiscal stability'.

This unique system of political organization as envisaged in the Indian Constitution, it is believed, would promote IGR and thereby facilitate cooperative and competitive policymaking. But at the same time, the Constitution makes the Centre more powerful than the states in legislation and policymaking. As stated already, in the case of division of powers, the Constitution ensures the Union's legislative supremacy over the Union list, Concurrent list and the residuary legislative jurisdictions. Over the State List, the Parliament can legislate in specified and exceptional circumstances as per Article 249. It ensures the supremacy of Parliament in matters of taxation,

[55] There is a demand for repeal of the Armed Forces Special Power Act as issues to which solutions have not been found in Jammu and Kashmir and Northeast (except Tripura). See *The Tribune*, 12 July 2015.

constitutionally anticipated emergencies, judicial administration, in constitutional amendments and so on. In practices, analysis of the application of emergency provisions of the Constitution India, role of the state governor and financial dependence of the states upon the centre endorse the unitary tilt to federalism in India. This creates conflicts and tensions in the functioning of the states and local-level machinery. There are also disputes within and outside public sector entities. For example, in a dispute between the Indraprastha Gas Ltd. (IGL) and the Petroleum and Natural Gas Regulatory Board (PNGRB) over gas price fixation, the Supreme Court on 1 July 2015 pronounced its verdict upholding the Delhi High Court order (2013) ruling in favour of IGL. The apex court says, 'The PNGRB has no power to fix or regulate the maximum retail price at which gas is sold by city gas distribution entities'.[56]

Although the ISC is constitutionally sanctified, the presidential order setting up the ISC reduced its full constitutional mandate by omitting Clause (a) of Article 263, which would have changed it with the duty of 'inquiring into and advising upon disputes which may have arisen between states'. This was in conformity with the recommendation of the Sarkaria Commission Report on Centre–State Relations (1988). This obviously diverts such disputes to other political or judicial forums such as tribunals or courts of laws. Conference of Governors or Chief Justices of high courts, chaired by the president or Chief Justice of India, respectively, also occasionally takes place, but these forums deal with constitutional or legal issues rather than political matters in the IGR.

A survey conducted by C. K. Sharma shows that there is an overwhelming consensus that the Finance Commission and the ISC are the two constitutional bodies which have the potential to strengthen federalism in India.[57] The NITI Aayog is specifically designed to promote cooperative federalism.

Such bodies as discussed facilitate cooperation and interaction between intergovernmental agencies. The interaction and recommendations reached help in the formulation of policies governing IGR. These must ensure that changes envisaged in policy matters are brought about smoothly, and that national and regional interests do not clash with each other. This relationship has certain dimensions in legislative laws and policymaking, that is, legislative, administrative and financial.

8.11 Conditions for Effective IGR

The study of intergovernmentalism has been equally significant as a line of inquiry for both federal and unitary states in recent decades. The subject of IGR has, however, gained grounds among governments especially experiencing federation. The federal structure of governance in India may become democratically unsustainable if the union government fails to ensure a decisive role for state governments in the framing of policies and implementation of development programmes. As such there is the need for examining conditions required for effective IGR.

A first condition for effective intergovernmental interaction and cooperation is the constitutional provision. But experience suggests that more than legal provisions, there are two fundamental prerequisites for effective IGR. The first is the establishment of a political culture of cooperation, mutual respect and trust. And to develop a sense of trust requires tolerance towards diversity and

[56] See *Financial Express* (Chandigarh), 3 July 2015.

[57] Sharma, 'Reimagining Federalism'; also see Sharma, 'NITI's Destiny'.

a willingness to consult and take account of the concern of other state governments before policymaking. Imposed relations do not work and breed resentment and distrust.

Speaking at the first meeting of the chief ministers chaired by the PM Narendra Modi on 7 December 2014, Punjab Chief Minister Parkash Singh Badal welcomed and said that the 'plan panel had been imposed on country's constitutional structure through an administrative order violating the federal spirit, as it placed excessive powers regarding planned development in the hands of centre'.[58]

Second, a political culture fostering cooperation requires recognition of the need for intergovernmental consultation and interaction in a political partnership emphasizing mutual assistance and support, regular exchange of information and consultation, cooperation and coordination in areas of overlapping and complementary jurisdiction. In his first meeting with chief ministers on 7 December 2014, PM Narendra Modi said that 'states must have a greater role in the "think tank" and reflect the true spirit of cooperative federalism'.[59]

A second condition for effective IGR is the development of capacity within each government in terms of human and financial resources and technological facilities. The three All India Services—IAS, IPS and IFS—have been constitutionally accepted in India to engage effectively in IGR. These services are expected to coordinate developmental activities in the states and the Centre and keep divisive forces, if any, at bay.[60] An important task will be to develop the All India Services through training programmes enabling them to preserve administrative unity and uniformity in the country's governance. The Supreme Court in India has directed the GoI for the creation of an All India Judicial Services on the lines of IAS and IPS. But several states were apprehensive about its viability, mainly citing the need for using regional languages in lower court proceedings.[61]

For effective IGR between all levels of government in the polity, there would be the need for provision of adequate financial resources and communication and e-governance infrastructure to enable frequent informal exchange of views. A scholar in the study of IGR urges 'the need to install and improve mechanisms for dissemination of information about service delivery and development of a Database and Research Cell to assist intergovernmental interactions'.[62]

Much more attention has to be paid towards improving the functioning of mechanisms engaged in IGR. Constitutional and institutional bodies such as the Finance Commission (Article 280), ISC (Article 263), NITI Aayog, Central Council of Health, Transport Development Council, NIC and so on should hold meetings annually or more frequently to share information, discuss problems and contemplate joint action. They are expected to sustain relationships, recommend policy measures and facilitate intergovernmental legislative cooperation. In this way, federal structure of governance will become democratically sustainable.

---

[58] See *Hindustan Times* (Chandigarh), 8 December 2014.

[59] *The Financial Express* (Chandigarh), 8 December 2014.

[60] U. C. Agarwal, 'Public Services in India: Achievements and Disappointment', *Indian Journal of Public Administration* LII, no. 3 (2006): 308.

[61] See *The Tribune* (Chandigarh), 8 April 2013. A Joint conference of chief ministers and Chief Justices on 7 April 2013 failed to arrive at a consensus on the creation of an All India Judicial Services.

[62] C. K. Sharma, 'Intergovernmental Coordination Mechanisms in India', *South Asian Journal of Socio-political Studies* 15, no. 2 (2015): 48.

Summary

Functioning of various constitutional bodies and executive-created institutions facilitating IGR in most federal countries including India indicates that they do contribute to the policymaking process. However, it is observed that the development of a political culture of cooperation, mutual respect and trust is much more important to effective IGR than the establishment of formal structures and legal procedures.[63] In this way, danger of monopoly to the policymaking in a federation can be warded off. If we try to temper with the federal structure as envisaged in the Indian Constitution, unity of the Indian states will be in danger.

In step with the times, both the Parliament and the intergovernmental forums (especially the ISC under Article 263) in their respective domains must ensure opportunity of deliberative as well as participating democracy. This can be achieved by expanding the scope and practice of interaction with the civil society, the media and all the stakeholders in the processes of policy management and federal governance.

The system of triple government—union, state and local—set up by the Constitution requires for its smooth working, mutual delegation of functions and mutual understanding. It is because the Indian Constitution is 'neither purely federal nor purely unitary but is a combination of both. It is a Union or Composite State of a novel type'.[64] Of course, the country has a federal system of governance, or at the most, the country is moving towards a strong federal structure. It is important and critical to keep the balance between functioning of the union and state governments. People's hopes and aspirations for good governance and development can be fulfilled if the interdependence among the union, the state and local governments is preserved.

[63] D. S. Wright and C. L. Cho, 'State Administration and Intergovernmental Interdependency', in *Handbook of State Government Administration*, ed. J. J. Gargin (New York: Marcel Dekker, 2000), 33–66.

[64] Granville Austin, *The Indian Constitution* (New Delhi: Oxford University Press, 1966), 186.

9 Administration of the Civil Service

LEARNING OBJECTIVES

1. **To analyse the role of the senior civil servants in a setting of societal transformation**
2. **To examine the unifying role of the All India Services in the whole administrative system of the country**
3. **To highlight importance of recruitment and in-service training for the civil services**
4. **To discuss the ways of ensuring the independence of the state Public Service Commission**

Introduction

For the running of administration (now broadly called governance) of the country, the government—legislative, executive and judicature—needs the executive instrument expressed as civil service. It is this 'civil service' which serves as an art and craft of the state. Before we discuss structure, recruitment, training and role of the civil service, it is appropriate to give an explanation as to origin and meaning of the civil service.

The origin of the concept of 'civil service' is traced to the establishment of the East India Company (EIC) on the last day of the year 1600. The term 'civil service' was coined by it and 'applied to that part of the service of the East India Company carried on by the covenanted servants who did not belong to the Army and Navy'. As the activities of the EIC increased in size by reasons of its appointment as the dewans (as collectors of land revenue) of the Mughal emperors in Bengal, the officials or servants of the Company came to be invested gradually with administrative and judicial functions. The transformation of the 'writers' into administrators led to the formation of a constituted service. But the word 'civil service' gained popularity in the middle of the 19th century when the British rulers decided to hold competitive examinations to select candidates for higher posts in India. It was called civil to differentiate it from the military, which had its own separate identity and establishment. Later, when in 1854 the British government adopted the practice of holding competitive examinations for filling posts under the government at home as well, the recruited persons began to be referred to as 'civil servants'. Sir Charles Trevelyan, brother-in-law to Lord Macaulay, who commenced his brilliant administrative career in India, was responsible for popularizing the civil service as a description of officials serving the state in a professional capacity other than those exercising military or judicial functions.

The term 'civil service' is used here broadly to include all those personnel who are employed in a civil capacity by government (central/state/local), typically excluding those belonging to political, judicial and legislative offices and those employed in public enterprises and regulatory agencies which operate independently of the statutory civil service. As for the term 'higher civil servants' or senior administrators, it refers to a larger strata of above-middle-rank officials. When considering the concept 'top administrators', it refers to the highest levels of line civil servants in governmental positions below the politicians.

Civil service is an important asset. It is considered to be the fourth branch of the government, the other being legislature, executive and judicature. The civil service is an integral part of the development process and has a significant role to play in this task. It would be a mistake if the importance of the civil service were not fully recognized by those involved in the development effort. By virtue of its security of tenure and because of its crucial place in the power structure, the civil service maintains continuity in government. The civil servants, especially the higher civil servants, are the link between the successive ministries and repository of the principles and practices which endure while ministers come and go. The civil service is, therefore, an indispensable part of the government.

9.1 All India Services

The nature of the All India Services (AIS) is unique to the civil service system in India. It has a long history. It has prospered slowly and steadily first under the rule of EIC (1601–1858)[1] and later under the British Crown (1858–1947) and finally under the Indian Constitution Act, 1950. The constitutional and statutory provisions and administrative arrangements that evolved from time to time invested the civil services especially the superior civil services with enormous prestige and gave these significant power in the governance of the country.

9.1.1 Services Under the EIC

With the grant of Dewani of Bengal, Bihar and Orissa in 1765 by the hands of the Emperor, the company emerged as a political entity.[2] As a result of this, the servants of the Company started asserting their right to collect revenue. Warren Hastings, who assumed the governorship of Bengal in 1772, laid the foundation in India of a civil service in the modern sense.[3] Gladden writes, 'He (Warren Hastings) reorganized the revenue administration, remodelled the judicial system and freed trade from its existing abuses'. O'Malley attributed the creation of the civil service to the worth of both Warren Hastings and Lord Cornwallis. He writes, 'The former laid the foundation on which the latter built up a superstructure'.[4]

Warren Hastings divided the covenanted civil service into two categories. One was concerned with 'purely commercial functions', and the other with 'general administration'. In each district, a civil and criminal court was set up. While the civil court was presided over by the collector who was the Company's servant, the criminal court was presided over by a native judge. However, the proceedings of the court were subject to inspection and control by the collector of the civil court.

[1] The EIC (originally a trading organization) was incorporated by Queen Elizabeth on 31 December 1600.
[2] B. B. Misra, *The Bureaucracy in India* (Delhi: Oxford University Press, 1970), 45.
[3] E. N. Gladden, *A History of Public Administration*, vol. 2 (London: Frank, 1972), 246.
[4] L. S. S. O'Malley, *The Indian Civil Service, 1601–1930* (London: John Murray, 1931), 23.

The Regulating Act, 1773, which forbade civil servants from accepting gifts from the natives of India, the Pitt's India Act, 1784, and the Charter Act, 1793, together with Lord Cornwallis' reforms lent statutory recognition to the importance and service conditions of the employees of the company.[5] Looking at the necessity of training to be imparted to the Company's civil servants in India, Lord Wellesley (1798–1805) founded the college at Fort William at Calcutta in August 1800 (abolished in January 1802) but subsequently a training institution at Haileybury in England replaced it in 1806, which too was abolished in January 1858. The key to the selection of the civil servants in India from 1793 to 1854 to the covenanted service was made on the basis of nominations by the Directors of the EIC but with the passage of the GoI Act, 1853, and submission of the Macaulay Report in November 1854, the system of competitive examination was put into operation from 1855. (The first successful Indian candidate for the covenanted service was Mr Satyendranath Tagore who gained his place in 1864.) Thus, the ICS owes its origin to the Macaulay Report.

9.1.1.1 Services Under the British Crown (1858–1919)

The EIC's rule came to end with the assumption of suzerainty by the Crown in 1858. Since a very few natives were successful in getting into the civil services, the need for the Indianization of the ICS was felt. The GoI Act, 1870, and subsequently rules were framed in 1879 which provided that about a sixth of the posts reserved for covenanted services should be filled by the natives.

The Aitchison Commission (1887): The Commission recommended reduction in the cadre of covenanted civil services (the government did not reduce the cadre) to an elite cadre. On the recommendation of the Aitchison Commission, the civil services in India were divided into three categories.

1. Imperial Services. This comprised of ICS, IPS, IMS, IFS and other AIS, the officers of which were appointed and controlled by the Secretary of State for India in England.
2. Provincial Services. This comprised of less important covenanted services and important non-covenanted services.
3. Subordinate Services. This comprised of less important non-covenanted services.

The Islington Commission (1912–15): The Commission observed in its report in 1917 that out of a total of 1371 members of the ICS, only 63 were Indians (4.5% of the total strength). The total strength of ICS in 1913 is as follows:

Europeans	1,305
Eurasians	3
Hindus	41
Parsis	6
Muslims	9
Indian Christians	7
Total	**1,371**

Source: Islington Commission Report, 1917, p. 511.

[5] R. K. Sapru, *Civil Service Administration in India* (New Delhi: Deep Publications, 1985), 109–10.

The 'historic Declaration' of 20 August 1917 and the recommendations of the Islington Commission (1917) had envisaged acceleration of process of Indianization of higher civil services. Among other things, the Islington Commission had suggested that in future, only 75% of the vacancies in the premier civil service, called the ICS, should be filled in England by recruitment through open competitive examination, and the remaining 25% be filled in India by nomination.[6] The Commission tried to justify its preference for nomination as against competition as a means of recruitment in India on the ground that minorities, particularly the Muslims, were educationally far behind the majority community (i.e., the Hindu).[7] The Commission also recommended the classification of services into four categories: Imperial, Central (Class I and Class II), Provincial and Subordinate.

The Montford Report (1918): The Montagu–Chelmsford Report (1918), besides stressing healthy relationship between the superior civil servants and ministers, recommended that 33% of the superior posts should be recruited in India and that the quota be increased by 1.5% annually 'until a new Commission (Indian Statutory Commission) is appointed to examine the whole subject'.[8]

9.1.1.2 Civil Services Under the GoI Act, 1919

The GoI Act, 1919, authorized the Secretary of State in Council to make rules for appointment to the higher civil services 'by nomination of persons domiciled in India'.[9] The Act also authorized the Secretary of State in Council to make rules for regulating the civil services in India, the methods of recruitment, the conditions of service, pay and allowances and discipline and conduct.[10] The Act also provided for the creation of a Public Service Commission (PSC) in India, which was set up in 1926.

On the eve of the GoI Act, 1919, nine AIS existed (see Table 9.1). The sanctioned strength and the actual position of personnel of each service are given in Table 9.1.

The last to be added to the list of AIS was the Indian Agriculture Service in 1906. All these services were grouped into Security AIS—ICS and IP and other AIS. Appointment and control of these services rested with the Secretary of State as it was thought necessary to keep British control over the country, despite the fact that the GoI Act introduced decentralization of administration.

As a result of reforms (in 1918 and 1919), the first ICS examination was held in 1922 at Allahabad. From 1915 to 1922, the GoI made 291 appointments to the ICS cadre out of which 84 candidates were recruited through open competition held in London, while all the rest were nominated.[11] But intensification of national movement, growing demand for Indianization of higher civil services and introduction of dyarchy (which promised progressive realization of

[6] GoI, *Report of the Royal Commission on Public Services in India*, vol. I (Islington Commission), 29.
[7] Ibid., 30.
[8] GoI, *Montford Report 1918*, para 317.
[9] The GoI Act, 1919 (Consolidated), Section 97(6).
[10] GoI, *Report of the Royal Commission on Superior Services in India* (Lee Commission, 1924), 4.
[11] See the Memorandum submitted in 1928 to the Indian Statutory Commission, Vol. XV, 197.

Table 9.1 The All India Services as on 1 January 1924

Services	Sanctioned Strength	Actual Numbers
1. Indian Civil Service	1,350	1,290
2. Indian Police Service	732	739
3. Indian Forest Service	399	348
4. Indian Educational Service (Men)	379	309
Indian Educational Service (Women)	42	36
5. Indian Agriculture Service	157	109
6. Indian Veterinary Service	54	38
7. Indian Forest Engineering Service	18	17
8. Indian Medical Service (Civil)	420	373
9. Indian Service of Engineers	728	736
Total	**4,279**	**3,975**

Source: Lee Commission Report, 1924.

responsible and self-government in India) in the post-1919 period brought about many changes in AIS. Criticism of the individual members of the services by questions in the provincial and central legislatures, the 'ignominy' of working under Indian ministers in provinces, the non-cooperation movement of 1920–22 and the breach of covenant between the Secretary of State and the civilian by the introduction of dyarchy resulting in insecurity of tenure and so on left a dampening effect on the attraction of AIS. Accordingly, about 200 European officers who had joined the AIS before 1 January 1920 were allowed to retire prematurely between 1 April 1920 and 31 December 1921.[12] Further, it was found that Indians accounted for only 13% of the ICS.

9.1.1.3 Effect of the Lee Commission Report (1924)

On the basis of the recommendations of the Lee Commission, the recruitment and control of central services was delegated to the GoI. Further, the Lee Commission recommended that no further recruitment be made by the Secretary of State to the Indian Educational Service, the Indian Agriculture Service, the Indian Veterinary Service, the IFS in Mumbai and Burma and the Indian Service of Engineers in the Roads and Buildings Branch of the Public Works Department. This was expected to lead automatically to the gradual reduction of Europeans in these services. All these

[12] Great Britain, *Report of the Indian Statutory Commission*, vol. I (London: His Majesty's Stationery office, 1930), para 294.

Table 9.2 Position of Indians vis-à-vis Europeans in the All India Services

(As on 1 January 1933)

Name of the All India Service	European	Indians	Total
1. Indian Civil Service	819	478	1,297
2. Indian Policed Service	505	160	665
3. Indian Forest Service	203	96	299
4. Indian Service of Engineers	304	292	596
5. Indian Medical Service (Civil)	200	98	298
6. Indian Educational Services	96	79	175
7. Indian Agriculture Service	46	30	76
8. Indian Veterinary Service	20	2	22
Total	**2,193**	**1,235**	**3,428**

Source: Report of the Joint Parliamentary Committee for Indian Constitutional Reforms, 1933, p. 174.

services were to be converted as provincial services. The Commission recommended that the provincial governments be authorized to make rules for the regulation of those services which were to man the transferred departments. Regarding AIS, it recommended that 20% should be filled from the provincial services by way of promotion and the rest should be recruited through a competitive examination on a basis of a parity between British and Indian candidates. However, entry on the basis of a 'parity' could not be achieved. The position of Indians vis-à-vis Europeans in the composition of the AIS in 1933 is given in Table 9.2.

Earlier, a committee appointed by the United Provinces Legislative Council asserted, 'We hold the retention of these services (i.e., AIS) in a system of full provincial autonomy would unnecessarily complicate matters'.[13] Shiva Rao said, 'I do not think it would be satisfactory to work these services on an All India basis and at the same time ensure a proper relationship between the services and the Ministry'.[14] Bheem Rao Ambedkar also said, 'No Province can be deemed to have provincial autonomy, if it has not the right to regulate the civil services that is going to work in its area'.[15] In 1933–34, in the Joint Committee on Indian Constitutional Reforms, some leaders again urged the provincialization of AIS but it did not accept it, because it regarded the need for a regular supply of officers, both Indian and British, of the highest quality as vital to the stability of the proposed Constitution itself.[16]

[13] GoI, *Report of the Committee Appointed by the United Provinces Legislative Council to Cooperate with the Indian Statutory Commission* (Allahabad: Government Press, 1929), 104–105.

[14] B. Shiva Rao, *Indian Round Table Conference: Proceedings of the Sub-committee, vol. VIII* (Calcutta: Central Publication Branch, 1931), 54.

[15] Rao, *Indian Round Table Conference*, p. 55 (ibid., proceedings).

[16] Great Britain, *Report of the Joint Committee on Indian Constitutional Reforms, vol. I, part I* (London: His Majesty's Stationery office, 1934), para 286.

9.1.1.4 Civil Services Under GoI Act, 1935

The GoI Act, 1935, had envisaged a federation of the British Indian Provinces (compulsory) and the Indian states (optional) with more powers to the central government. However, the Act made certain provisions relating to the civil services which were contained in Chapter 11, starting from Article 119 onwards. It defined the rights and status of the personnel of the AIS in the proposed federation and provinces and guaranteed the existing privileges regarding pay, promotion, leave, pension and so on. The Act also made provision for the setting up of a PSC in each province and a Federal Public Service Commission. The GoI, 1935, quickened the pace of Indianization of the higher civil services.

The GoI Act,, 1935, specifically mentioned the functions of the Commission relating to recruitment, promotion, transfer and disciplinary matters. Consequently, the recruitment of Indian candidates continued both by selection and competitive examination held in Delhi, the last being in 1943. During 1941–42 and 1942–43, only 50% of the posts were held reserved, to be filled after the war by candidates with war service. The result was that the Indians in ICS scored over the Europeans. This is clear from Table 9.3.

From Table 9.3, it will be seen that in less than three years after the start of the Second World War, the number of Indians increased from 587 to 625 while that of Europeans in the ICS fell from 599 to 573.

GoI Act, 1935, allowed the continuance of only three AIS, namely, ICS, IPS and Indian Medical Service (Civil). Other services were not abolished abruptly or altogether. Only fresh recruitment into these services was discontinued, thus enabling its painless extinction through the natural process of retirement, resignation and casualties of its members.

Table 9.3 Europeans and Indians in the ICS, Including List Posts

(As on 1st January)

	1941			1942		
Province	**Indian**	**Europeans**	**Total**	**Indian**	**Europeans**	**Total**
Madras	106	81	188*	109	81	191*
Bombay	84	66	150	87	65	152
Bengal	111	96	208*	113	93	207*
UP	109	105	214	108	104	212
Punjab	78	103	181	76	100	176
Bihar & Orissa	67	63	130	68	60	128
CP and Bihar	46	46	93*	47	46	94*
Assam	16	25	41	17	24	41
Total	**617**	**585**	**1,205**	**625**	**573**	**1,201**

Source: GoI, Home (Estts.) File No. 35/15/42, pp. 4–5.
Note: *One unclassified persons.

With the withdrawal of British Power under the Indian Independence Act of 1947, 'the authority of the civil service was progressively whittled away; but, nevertheless, it retained its premier position'.[17]

9.1.1.5 State of Civil Services During 1947–50

When freedom was achieved, a question arose as to whether the AIS be disbanded or retained. Jawaharlal Nehru, the first PM of Independent India, and Pt G. B. Pant were not in favour of continuation of the AIS. Nehru, for example, wrote in his autobiography:

> But of one thing I am quite sure that no new order can be built up in India, so long as the spirit of ICS pervades our administration and public services. That spirit of authoritarianism is the ally of imperialism and it cannot co-exist with freedom. It will either succeed in crushing freedom or will be swept away by itself. Only with one type of State, it is likely to fit in and that is the Fascist type. Therefore, it seems quite essential that the ICS and similar services must disappear completely as such before we can start real work on a new order.[18]

Sardar Patel, the then union home minister, on the contrary, felt the necessity of AIS. While presiding over a Provincial Premiers Conference in October 1946, he said,

> They (officers of the AIS) will also serve as liaison between the Provinces and the Government and introduce certain amount of freshness and vigour in the administration, both at the Centre and in the Provinces. Therefore, my advice is that we should have an All India Service.[19]

Again speaking in the constituent assembly, he warned,

> There is no alternative to this administrative system … The Union will go, you will not have a united India, if you have not a good All India Service, which has the independence to speak out its mind, which has a sense of security that you will stand by your work.[20]

Despite resistance from national leaders such as Pt Nehru and Pt Pant and a few states such as Punjab, West Bengal and Jammu and Kashmir, Sardar Patel succeeded in securing an agreement for two AIS. Further, it was decided not to make further recruitment to the ICS and IPS but two new analogous services called IAS and IPS were established in 1949.

9.1.1.6 AIS Under the Indian Republic

In the beginning, a distinction is required to be made between AIS and Central Civil Service (CCS). The CCSs are concerned directly with the administration and permanent bureaucracy of GoI. The Central Service is an expression which refers to certain services under the Union, maintained on All India basis, for services throughout the country, for instance, the Indian Foreign Service, the

---

[17] Asok Chanda, *Indian Administration,* 2nd ed. (London: George Allen and Unwin, 1967), 98.
[18] Jawaharlal Nehru, *An Autobiography* (London: The Bodley Head, 1953), 443.
[19] Sardar Patel, *Proceedings of Premiers' Conference* (October 1946).
[20] *Constituent Assembly Debates,* vol. X, no. 3, 10 October 1946.

Indian Audit and Accounts Service (IAAS),[21] Indian Economic Service (IES) and the like.[22] The expression 'All India Services', on the contrary, is a technical one, used by Constitution to indicate only IAS, IPS and IFS and such other services which may be created in the manner provided by Article 312 of the Constitution. Article 312(1) states that

> [I]f the Council of the States has declared by resolution supported by not less than two-thirds of the members present and voting that it is necessary or expedient in the national interest so to do, Parliament may by law provide for the creation of one or more All India Services, including an All India judicial service [common to the Union and the states].[23]

In accordance with this provision, and seeing the need of the day, the Rajya Sabha, on 6 December 1961, adopted a resolution for creating the following three AIS on technical side:

1. Indian Service of Engineers
2. Indian Medical and Health Service
3. Indian Forest Service

Out of these three, only one service, that is, IFS, came into existence from 1 July 1966. Others could not make it because the state governments of Tamil Nadu, Kerala, Karnataka, Punjab, West Bengal, Jammu and Kashmir, Assam and Himachal Pradesh revised their stand mainly on the ground of state autonomy. Subsequently, Parliament altered the All India Services Act, 1951.

The All India Services Act, 1951, originally provided only for two services, namely, IAS and IPS. This Article was amended in 1963 to provide for the creation of three more services in the fields of 'forestry' 'medicine and health' and 'engineering'. Of these, only one, namely, the IFS, was constituted. The remaining proposed services relating to 'medicine and health' and 'engineering' have not been constituted so far.

The Indian Medical and Health Service was constituted on February 1969, but recruitment to this service could not be taken up by the GoI, although the Government of Haryana had already agreed to constitute cadres of strength. The service could not be constituted as the governments of Jammu and Kashmir, Maharashtra and Tamil Nadu have resiled from the earlier stand and are still reconsidering the matter.

Similarly, the Indian Service of Engineers (which was created as a result of the All India Services Act, 1951, as amended in September 1963) could not be constituted, although 19 out of the 22 states have agreed to participate in the services. The governments of Jammu and Kashmir and Tamil Nadu are still reconsidering the matter. The basic idea for establishing AIS is to make possible the creation of services which have common and uniform administrative standards in all the states.

The AIS—IAS, IPS and IFS—serves the purpose of meeting the manpower requirements of the state governments for higher posts in the states and also the central government for posts of the level of under secretary and above. Each AIS is divided into a number of state cadres, including one for union territories, and each state cadre has a central deputation quota consisting of an aggregate

[21] At the top of IAAS structure is Comptroller and Auditor General (CAG).

[22] Chief Economic Advisor is at head of the IES.

[23] The Supreme Court on 30 January 2017 questioned the feasibility of the All India Judicial Service saying how could the power of the high courts to appoint judicial officers in trial courts be taken away. See *The Times of India* (Chandigarh), 31 January 2017.

number of senior posts (IAS) under the Centre likely to be manned by the members of the AIS of that state cadre. A common unique feature of the AIS is that the members of these services are recruited by the Centre but their services are placed under various state cadres and they have the liability to serve both under the state and the central governments. This aspect of AIS strengthens the unitary character of the Indian federation.

The examination for recruitment of IAS and IPS, conducted by the UPSC (Union Public Service Commission), is a common annual civil service examination. IFS recruitment examination is held separately on annual basis. The recruited officers are trained by the central government and upon completion of the training period, they are allotted to different state cadres. The cadre controlling authority for the IAS is the Ministry of Personnel, Public Grievances and Pensions, while the Ministry of Environment, Forest and Climate Change is for the IFS and the Ministry of Home Affairs is for the IPS. There are now 26 state cadres including two joint cadres: (a) Assam and Meghalaya, and (b) Arunachal Pradesh, Goa, Mizoram and the union territories (AGMU). The authorized cadre strength of AIS as on 1 January 2017 was 14,355.

When members of these services serve the central government, they continue to be borne on the state cadre to which they belong and their term of services under the centre is treated as on tenure deputation.

So far as the conditions of service of the AIS are concerned, the members are governed by All India Services Act, 1951, and the rules framed by the central government in consultation with the states which apply to all the three AIS. However, in respect of other conditions such as dearness allowances, house rent allowance, travelling allowance, city compensatory allowance and so on, the members are governed by the rules and regulations framed by the state government in which they serve. The cadre strength of the three AIS in all the states and union territories is given in Table 9.4.

There are state cadres, and the officers of AIS—IAS, IFS and IPS—are divided into state cadres. When on probation, the AIS officers are allocated to their states. Officers of AIS working with the union government are posted on deputation for some years. The AIS officers in a state cadre may be original residents of that state but almost two-thirds of all officers are from outside the state. The AIS officer cannot demand his home state cadre but may put in request for being considered for the home cadre. Once allotted to a state cadre, an officer generally continues with that state cadre during his/her whole service. Selected candidates are appointed to different state cadres and as when required, they also move to union government jobs on deputation. A brief discussion is put down here regarding performances of functions and responsibilities of the AIS.

Table 9.4 Authorized and Actual Strength of AIS Officers

Service	Authorized	Actual	Shortage
Indian Administrative Service	(6,077) 6,396	(4,356) 4,926	(1,721) 1,470
Indian Police Service	(4,720) 4,802	(3,393) 3,894	(1,327) 908
Indian Forest Service	(3,079) 3,157	2597	560

Notes: Figure as on 1 January 2017. Figures in brackets as on 1 January 2011.

Indian Administrative Service (IAS): Functionaries of the IAS are trained to handle government affairs. They are not specialists. But by virtue of their training and experience gained during their services, they become capable of handling all sorts of jobs. Every functionary is assigned to a particular office which deals with policy matters pertaining to that area. The policy matters are framed, modified, interpreted in this office under the direct supervision of the administrative officer in consultation with the minister. The implementation of policies is also done on the advice of the officer. The cabinet secretary stands at the top of the government machinery, involved in policymaking, followed by secretary/additional secretary, joint secretary, director, under secretary and junior scale officers in that order. These appointments are filled by civil servants according to seniority in the civil services. In the process of decision-making, a number of officers give their views to the minister who weighs the matter and makes a decision, considering the issue involved. Implementation of policies and programmes is the main job of the IAS. The implementation process involves supervision and touring. The allocation of enormous funds to and by the field officers calls for supervision and the officials concerned have to reply to queries made in the Parliament for which they must remain well informed. When on an official tour in a foreign country, at the level of deputy secretary, he is even authorized to sign agreements on behalf of the government. An IAS officer begins his career in the state with two years in probation. This period is spent at training schools, secretariat, field offices or in a district magistrate's office. He is given the position of sub-divisional magistrate and has to look after the law, order and general administration including developmental work in the area under his charge. After the probation and two years of services as a junior scale officer, the officer is put in the senior scale. Then he may function as a district magistrate, managing director of a public enterprise or director of a department. Senior scale comprises the senior time scale (joint secretary), junior administrative grade (additional secretary) and the selection grade (special secretary). Selection grade is given on promotion after 13 years of regular service. The next promotion within the state is that of a commissioner-cum-secretary after 16 years. This promotion also entitles them to the super time scale. Then after 24 years of regular service, he may be promoted to above super time scale who is designated as principal secretaries/financial commissioners in some states. Some appointments of secretaries are considered more prestigious than others, for example, the finance secretary, development commissioners and home secretary, and hence they enjoy the salary of a principal secretary. The chief secretary in the state is the top ranking civil servant and may be assisted by additional chief secretaries.

At district level, when he is appointed as the district magistrate (Uttar Pradesh) or deputy commissioner (in Punjab), his role is to oversee law and order and general administration and development work.

Indian Police Service (IPS): With the Independence on 15 August 1947, the Imperial Police (IP) was replaced by the term the IPS in 1948. The IPS is the only service which stands next to IAS in terms of power, authority and promotion. An IPS officer takes charge as an Assistant Superintendent of Police of a Sub-division after probation of 2 years. The next appointment is as Superintendent of Police or Deputy Commissioner of Police after 4 years; in Junior Administrative Grade after 9 years; in Selection Grade in 13 years; and then as Deputy Inspector General of Police or Additional Commissioner of Police in 14 years; as Inspector General of Police in 18 years; Additional Director General of Police in 25 years. Finally, the next promotion is as Director General of Police, after 30 years of service.

The Director General of Police and Commissioner of Police is the head of the entire police force of the State or a metropolitan city (like Kolkata, Delhi, Mumbai, Chennai etc.) and the Additional DGP/Special Police Commissioner reports to him. Specialised police forces like criminal Investigation Department, Special Branch, etc. are headed by the Inspector General or Joint Commissioner of Police.

An IPS officer has vast opportunities to work in several international organizations such as Interpol, International Cricket Council, the United Nations, Consulates (Foreign Missions) and embassies all over the world in various capacities such as first secretary, consul, consul general, deputy high commissioner, high commissioner and ambassador and so on. Besides, IPS officers also work in national government agencies such as Intelligence Bureau, Research and Analysis Wing, Central Bureau of Investigation, and in several PSUs such as GAIL, SAIL, Indian Oil Corporation Limited and so on. Senior positions are also held by IPS in Border Security Force, Central Reserve Police Force and Central Industrial Security Force and so on. The roles of the district magistrate (IAS) and senior superintendent of police (IPS) are well defined in Police Regulations and other relevant Acts. Turf wars will not help them run an India that has 21st century aspirations, with a 19th century bureaucracy. In this way, an IPS officer is no less important in the structure of Indian administration.

Indian Forest Service (IFS): Indian Forest Act, 1927, provides the legal framework for the protection and management of forest and the transit of forest produce. In 1864, the British Rule established the Imperial Forest Department and consequently in 1867, the Imperial Forestry Service was organized.[24] Persons appointed in this service were given training in forestry management. By the GoI Act, 1935, the forestry items were transferred to the provincial list, and recruitment to the Imperial Forestry Service was subsequently discontinued.

After Independence, under the All India Services Act, 1951, the modern IFS was established in 1966 for protection, conservation and regeneration of forest resources. Ranks of the IFS are as follows: assistant conservator of forests—a probationary officer; divisional forest officer; deputy conservator of forests; conservator of forests (CFs), chief conservator of forests (CCFs); additional principal chief conservator of forests (Add. PCCFs), principal chief conservator of forests (PCCF) and head of forest force (HoFF)—highest post in a state. Director general of forests (India) is the highest post at the centre, selected from among the senior-most PCCFs of states.

Besides getting entrusted with senior positions in the Central Secretariat, State Secretariats and various assignments under the Central Staffing Scheme, the IFS officers also work in various international and national organizations related to management of forests, wildlife and environment such as Food and Agricultural Organization (FAO) of the United Nations, International Centre for Integrated Mountain Development (ICIMOD), SAARC Forestry Centre, Forest Survey of India, Wildlife Institute of India, Indian Council of Forestry Research and Education (ICFRE), Indira Gandhi National Forest Academy (IGNFA), Directorate of Forest Education, Wildlife Crime Control Bureau (WCCB), etc. The implementation of the National Forest Policy which aims to preserve one-third of the total land area has been a big responsibility of the IFS.

[24] Besides the Indian Forest College that was established at Dehradun in 1938, an Imperial Forest Research Institute was also established in Dehradun in 1906.

Objectives and Rationale Behind AIS

The main objectives of the founding fathers in providing for the AIS were as follows:

1. Facilitating liaison between the Centre and the states
2. Maintaining a certain level of uniformity in standards of administration
3. Enabling the administrative machinery at the union level to keep in touch with the ground realities in the states
4. Helping the state administrative machinery to acquire a broader outlook and exposure, and provide them with the best possible talent for manning senior positions
5. Ensuring that political considerations, either in recruitment or in discipline and control were reduced to the minimum, if not eliminated altogether

B. B. Misra felt concerned at the abolition of other AIS. He said,

> It was the ICS and IP that remained unaffected and continued to act as unifying force. Most of the other All India Services were abolished. Considerations of national unity, the positive need of India's all round development and the attainment of a minimum uniform standard in administration were allowed to go by default.[25]

The ARC in its Report on Personnel Administration also observed,

> The intention of having All India Services was mainly to ensure uniformly high standards of administration in all States in key activities, to provide for interchange of experience between the States and the Centre, and to obtain, where needed, the experience of State administration at the decision-making levels at the Centre.[26]

The Sarkaria Commission's Views

The Commission on Centre–State Relations (Sarkaria Commission) in 1983 also focussed on the AIS and stated emphatically as under:

1. 'The All India Services are as much necessary today as they were when the Constitution was framed … The members of the All India Services have shown themselves capable of discharging the roles that the framers of the Constitution envisaged for them'.[27]
2. The AIS should be further strengthened and greater emphasis laid on the role expected to be played by them through well-planned improvements in selection, training, deployment, development and promotion policies and methods.
3. There should be regular consultation on the management of AIS between the union and state governments (through creation of an Advisory Council for Personnel Administration of AIS).

The Sarkaria Commission, invoking the recommendations of the Estimates Committee of the Lok Sabha, recommended that the union government might persuade the state governments to agree

---

[25] B. B. Misra, *Administrative History of India 1834–1947* (London: OUP, 1970), 143.
[26] ARC, *Report on Personnel Administration* (New Delhi: ARC, 1969), 7.
[27] GoI, *Commission on Centre–State Relations, Report, Part I* (Delhi: Controller of Publications, 1989), 224.

to the Constitution of the Indian Service of Engineers, the Indian Medical and Health Service and an AIS for education.[28] As regards constituting AIS in other sectors, such as agriculture, cooperation, industry and so on, the Commission recommended (a) to begin with, a pool of officers drawn from the union and the various state governments may be created in a sector; (b) these officers may be made available for posting for fixed tenures and with attractive special pays in governments other than their own; and (c) after the pool system has worked successfully for a few years, steps may be taken to constitute an AIS in that sector.

Thus the existing system of AIS is unique in its approach to deal with administration of the country. Although, for instance, the IAS is considered a direct descendant of the fabled ICS, there is considerable difference both in concept and design between the two. The ICS was set up to run a revenue-oriented routine administration under colonial decree, whereas the IAS was constituted to give a development-oriented democratic administration to the country in response to the will of the people. Although the IAS officers have manfully toiled on, it is felt that the steel frame is losing its 'steel'. Being less amenable to pressures, they have now become centre of politics. A major onslaught, especially on the IAS and IPS castigates their generalist character, while their central counterparts, both in the civil services and in the central police organizations, are said to be specialists in their respective fields. The continuance and rationale of AIS has been justified on the grounds discussed as under:

Holders of nation unity and integrity: In the AIS, the Constitution makers had reposed much faith and confidence. Gopalaswami Ayyangar, a distinguished member of the constituent assembly, had envisaged 'the higher services consisting of the best material available in the country' would stand up for certain basic values and standards and would not waver whatever the political climate may be. These erudite men spearheaded by Sardar Vallabhbhai Patel had foreseen convulsions and aberrations setting in the body-politic of the country in the initial decades of Independence. The IAS along with its sister service, the IPS, was expected to weather the storm and sustain the nation on an even keel. To ensure this, the founding fathers covenanted the AIS into the constitution, thereby giving them protection against political vicissitudes.

The Sarkaria Commission warned that any move to dilute their structure, network or authority under any mistaken notion should be regarded as retrograde and harmful. The Fifth CPC (January 1997) strongly felt the continuance of the AIS. The Commission writes, 'Only a network of AIS can insure us against disintegration'.[29]

The AIS can promote the unity and solidarity of the country by combating parochial attitudes of the states. Because the officers of these services are generally posted in states other than their own, they are less susceptible to local and regional influences than officers from within the state would be.

Ideal for a federation: India has come a long way since the dawn of Independence and opted for a federal system of government. The officers of these services can be and are rotated between the Centre and states, thereby, facilitating liaison between the two. Moreover, wide and varied background from which members of this service are recruited, after training and orientation, the postings and assignments, the intimate knowledge of the people gained through exposure and experience in far-flung areas give them a rare insight into agonies and aspirations of the people.

[28] Lok Sabha (7th), *Estimates Committee, Report* (New Delhi: Lok Sabha Secretariat, April 1984).

[29] Central Pay Commission, *Report of the Fifth Central Pay Commission*, vol. I (New Delhi: AIRF, January 1997), 514.

In a federal system, differences on many issues arise between the union and state governments, which can be evened out by the AIS officers as these are controlled by the union government.

Instrument of change and administrative efficiency: Further the officers of the AIS are supposed to have acquired adequate knowledge and experience which make them capable to deal with diverse nature of problems. With all the stresses and strains, trials and turbulations, pulls and pressures, if this country is today functioning in one piece, a large measure of credit must go to the AIS. If the fruits of economic and social development achieved over the last 70 years have reached almost every nook and corner of this vast and varied land of ours, at least in small measure, it is mainly due to the administrative set up manned by the members of these services. If there is one single group of men who have direct access to the problems of the common man and the policies of the government, it is the members of these services.

Independent in outlook: The members of the AIS hold key posts in the states, and they can give independent advice to the state ministers, which the officers of state services would hesitate to do. Further, the responsibility for the administration of a state, in the event of the breakdown of the constitutional machinery, is vested in the president, the existence in the state of a certain number of officers of AIS occupying key posts in the administration will certainly be helpful to him. He can count more on the cooperation of officers, who, in the last analysis, are union government's employees, than on the officers of state government.[30]

9.1.1.7 Need for More AIS and Strengthening Its Character

The Sarkaria Commission (1988), the ARC (1966–68), the Fifth CPC (1997), all have stressed the importance, need, expansion and strengthening of the AIS with a view to meeting the growing aspirations of the people. The Fifth CPC recorded to have stressed by stating, 'But it is the country's larger interests to have more AIS. To begin with, we have recommended two-Indian Medical Service and Indian Engineering Service'.[31] Similarly, the Constitution also envisages an All India Judicial Service which has not been constituted so far.

The CPC (1997) also emphasized strengthening of the all India character of AIS. In this context, the Fifth CPC recommended the following:

1. Allotment of state cadres should be done in a transparent manner at the time of appointment itself.
2. When officers are promoted to AIS, 50% of them should be allotted to contiguous states of the same region and the balance 50% to their own state.
3. All AIS officers should be compelled to do at least one stint of deputation with the centre during the first 15 years of their service.
4. The central government should have the authority to change the state of allotment for any officer, if there is evidence to show that he has developed a close nexus with either the politicians or other elements in a slate.
5. There should be a minimum tenure for every post. A premature transfer should be effected only when the procedure enunciated is followed.

[30] B. Shiva Roa, *The Framing of India's Constitution*, vol. IV (Bombay: N. M. Tripathi, 1968), 332–33.
[31] Central Pay Commission, *Report*, 514.

6. No transfer should be based on the recommendations, verbal or written, of anyone except the designated authorities in the civil service.
7. State governments should not have power to place an AIS officer under suspension.
8. No IAS officer should be posted as a district collector unless he has completed nine years of service.

9.1.1.8 New Cadre Policy for AIS (2017)

A new policy for cadre allocation has been finalized by the central government for officers of AIS—IAS, IPS and IFS—aimed at ensuring national integration in the top bureaucracy.[32] Now under this policy, officers of AIS are required to choose one cadre from a set of five zones instead of one cadre from 26 states/cadres. They may be posted on central deputation during the course of their service after fulfilling certain eligibility conditions. Zone I has seven cadres: AGMU, Jammu and Kashmir, Himachal Pradesh, Uttarakhand, Punjab, Rajasthan and Haryana. Zone II consists of Uttar Pradesh, Bihar, Jharkhand and Odisha, while Zone III comprises Gujarat, Maharashtra, Madhya Pradesh and Chhattisgarh. West Bengal, Sikkim, Assam, Meghalaya, Manipur, Tripura and Nagaland constitute Zone IV, while Zone V has Telangana, Andhra Pradesh, Karnataka, Tamil Nadu and Kerala.

Candidates appearing for the CSE will have to first give their choices in a descending order of preference from among the various zones, as per the new policy. The preferences for the zones will remain in the same order and no change will be permitted there. Under the new policy, candidates can only select one state/cadre from a zone as their first choice. Their second, third, fourth and fifth choices have to be from the different zones. 'If a candidate does not give any preference for any of the zones/cadres, it will be presumed that he has no specific preference for those zones/cadres', says the policy. The policy also suggests that 'if candidates are not allocated any one of the cadres for which they have indicated a preference, they shall be allotted, along with other candidates, any of the remaining cadres, arranged in an alphabetical order, where there are vacancies'. Candidates will be allotted their home cadre on the basis of merit, preference and vacancy in the category, it said. One of the officials said that the policy is likely to be put into effect from the year 2018.

9.2 Central Civil Services (CCS)

The expression 'central services' refers to certain services under the union, maintained on an all India basis, for service throughout the country. They are under the control of the central government alone. But as the AIS are common to both centre and states, these are under their joint control.

As earlier stated, with the enactment of the GoI Act, 1919, the Imperial Services headed by the Secretary of State for India were split into two—AIS and central services. The All India and central services (Group A) were designated as Central Superior Services in as early as 1924. From 1924 to 1934, Administration in India consisted of 10 AIS and 5 central departments, all under the control of Secretary of State for India, and 3 central departments under joint provincial and

[32] See *The Tribune* (Chandigarh), 24 August 2017.

imperial control. On the other hand, the central services were headed by the viceroy and governor general of India.

Now, Group A officers are appointed by the president and appointments to Group B are made by the authorities specified by a general or special order of the president.

As on 3 April 2017, there were 61 Group A services, out of which, 52 services were declared as organized.

9.2.1 Genesis of Service Classification

The genesis of classification of services designated as Classes I, II, III and IV lay in the recommendation of the Islington Commission (1912–15). The Second CPC (the Das Commission, 1957–59) recommended its abolition on the ground that 'it served no practically purpose', and, subsequently on the recommendation of the Third CPC (the Dayal Commission), Classes I, II, III and IV were re-designated as Groups 'A', 'B', 'C' and 'D'. The Fourth CPC recommended its continuance.

Looking at the international practices, it is found that most countries have evolved their own system of classification of personnel. The civil service in England is divided into a large number of classes, the main components of which are (a) the administrative class, (b) the executive class, (c) the clerical class and (d) the messengerial class. Besides, there are other classes such as the work groups of professionals, economists and statisticians, scientific and medical officers. In Canada, Australia and USA, the whole service is divided into hundreds of occupational groups comprising individual posts at various levels. The latter are placed in one or other of 18 grades common to the whole service in the USA. In West Germany, civil employees are classified into four classes of service, namely, the higher, the elevated, the middle and the simple. The division is however, based on occupational differences, methods of recruitment and the pay scales admissible to each service.

The Fifth CPC (1997) recommended the abolition of classification of services into Groups 'A', 'B', 'C' and 'D' and proposed reorganization of various grades into 'levels', comprising (a) top executives, (b) senior executives, (c) executives, (d) supervisory staff, (e) supporting staff and (f) auxiliary staff. The Fifth CPC also recommended the discontinuance of gazetted status. The commission observes that 'the existing classification serves no practical purpose. The time has come to give a decent burial to the present system and to make it a true representatives of futuristic working environment in the government'.[33]

The public services of the central government may be classified into (a) civil services and (b) defence services of the central government. The civil services of the central government comprise the following:

1. AIS (IAS, IPS and IFS (Group 'A')
2. CCS (Group 'A' and Group 'B')
3. Professional and technical services (engineering, scientific, medical and para medical services)
4. CCS (Group 'C' and Group 'D' Staff)

Broadly, the 'civil services' at the centre are organized into four groups, namely, Group 'A' (which includes all India and central services), Group 'B', Group 'C' and Group 'D'. This classification

[33] Central Pay Commission, *Report*, 463.

broadly is based on the rank, status and degree of responsibility attached with the posts. Group 'A' posts carry higher administrative and executive responsibilities and include senior management positions in ministries/departments and field formations. The junior level of Group 'A' along with Group 'B' constitute the middle level in the government. Group 'C' staff performs certain supervisory as well as operative tasks and also renders clerical assistance. Group 'D' posts are meant for carrying out routine duties and other supporting functions. The functions performed by the Groups B, C and D officers and staff are varied and range from general administration to specialized and technical functions. There are also intra-group variations in each of these categories depending on the ministry, department or organization they are working for, and this is reflected in different designations and functions within each group. Further, some ministers have large departments and specialized/technical services attached with them, others are, however, in the nature of nodal, policy formulating ministries that have only general administration staff working under them.

9.2.2 Central Civil Services (Group A)

The number of Central Civil 'Group A' Services has been increasing from 30 in 1971 to 61 in 2017 (with around 56,000 civil servants currently in service).[34] Some of the known central services are Indian Foreign Service, Indian Information Service, IES, Indian Defence Accounts Service and the like. Further, CCS are broadly classified into (a) technical services (which include engineering and scientific services) and (b) non-technical services (which are meant to administer non-technical areas of administration such as audit, income tax and railways.

Following are the organized Group 'A' central services (including two AIS) through the UPSC civil service examination conducted every calendar year. Since the examination is a single window entry to the numerous services under various categories, it gets allotted as per the merit list ranking based or candidate's final score.

All India Services (Group A)

- Indian Administrative Service (IAS)
- Indian Police Service (IPS)

Central Services (Group A)

- Indian Audit and Accounts Service (IAAS)
- Indian Civil Accounts Service (ICAS)
- Indian Corporate Law Service (ICLS)
- Indian Defence Accounts Service (IDAS)
- Indian Defence Estates Service (IDES)
- Indian Foreign Service

[34] Union government approved formation of Indian Skill Development Service, https://timesofindia.indiatimes.com/good-governance/centre/Govt-gives-nod-for-Indian-Skill-Development-Service/articleshow/49266707.cms (accessed 8 October 2015). The government also approved the formation of Indian Enterprise Development Service in 2016. https://timesofindia.indiatimes.com/india/government-clears-formation-of-indian-enterprise-development-service/articleshow/56100072.cms (accessed on 8 January 2017).

- Indian Information Service (IIS)
- Indian Ordnance Factories Service (IOFS)
- Indian Postal Service (IPoS)
- Indian Post and Telecommunication Accounts and Finance Service (IP&TAFS)
- Indian Railway Accounts Service (IRAS)
- Indian Railway Personnel Service (IRPS)
- Indian Railway Traffic Service (IRTS)
- Indian Revenue Service (IRS-IT)
- Indian Revenue Service (IRS-C&CE)
- Indian Trade Service (ITS)
- Railway Protection Force (RPF)

9.2.2.1 Mode of Recruitment

The recruitment of the CCS (Group A) is made through Combined Defence Services Examination, CSE, Engineering Services Examination, National Defence Academy Examination, Combined Geo-Scientist and Geologist Examination, Naval Academy Examination, IES/ISS Examination, Railway Apprentice Examination, Combined Medical Services Examination, IFS Examination and Central Armed Police Forces Examination.

All promotions of empanelment in the CCS are either by the Civil Services Board or by Appointments Committee of the Cabinet.

9.2.2.2 Cadre Structure of Central Civil Services

Group 'A' CCS has a cadre structure which is in the form of a pyramid. This starts with junior time scale which is generally a probation-cum-training grade for direct recruits and passes through senior time scale, junior administrative grade and senior administrative grade (SAG). Generally, all the Group 'A' service cadres have posts in higher grades.

Further, organized Group 'A' cadre consists of two components—(a) regular duty posts and (b) reserves regular duty posts (core of the cadre)—that are meant for performing the functions for which the service has been constituted. In addition, the reserves are of four types: (a) probationary reserve, (b) leave reserve, (c) training reserve and (d) deputation reserve.

Another problem relating to Group 'A' service cadres is that of long delays in the Departmental Promotion Committee (DPC) procedures for filling vacant posts. The Fifth CPC recommended that the DPC involving consultation with the UPSC should be held for promotion to SAG-level posts only. For functional promotion to grades below SAG level, an interdepartmental screening committee may be constituted to clear such promotion cases within time.

9.2.2.3 Method of Removal and Disciplinary Proceedings

Article 311(1) says that a member of an AIS, or of any civil service under the union, shall not be dismissed or removed by an authority subordinate to that by which he was appointed. Article 311(2) lays down the procedure for his removal. Clause 2 of this article lays down that no such civil servant shall be dismissed or removed or reduced in rank except after an enquiry, in which he has been informed of the charges against him and given a reasonable opportunity of being heard in respect of these charges. And, where it is proposed, after such an enquiry, to impose on him any such penalty, it will be done only on the basis of the evidence adduced during such inquiry. However, this clause does not apply to a public employee on the ground of conviction on a criminal charge, or where it is not reasonably practicable to hold enquiry, or where president/governor is satisfied that such an enquiry is not in the interest of the security of the state.

9.2.3 Central Civil Services (Group B)

The junior level of Group A along with Group B constitute the middle level in the government. Group B services stand second in the pyramid structure of the CCS. In this, some of them are regular Group B services and others are isolated posts in Group B scales of pay. Presently, there are 29 CCS in Group B.

9.2.3.1 Recruitment at Group B Level

For Group B posts, the combined graduate level examination (CGLE) is conducted by the Staff Selection Commission (SSC). All appointments to Group B are made by the authorities specified by a general special order of the president.

There is no direct recruitment at present at the Group B (gazetted) level for either the general administration services or for the specialized services, and employees reach this level only by promotion. This is cutting edge or the visible face of government for most cadres. For the taxation departments, Group B officers are the income tax officers, excise and customs superintendents and customs appraisers. (These were earlier recruited directly, however, the practice has recently been discontinued.) Similarly, in the case of railways, Group B posts are entirely by promotion. In the general administration set up, the key Group B officer is the section officer and here also the earlier practice of recruiting them directly has been discontinued. Since all these officers, as mentioned earlier, function at the cutting-edge level and have frequent interface with civil society, it is necessary to ensure that the most suitable persons hold these posts. In this context, Second ARC recommended that a certain percentage of vacancies (say 25% every year) at the level of section officer as well as for other specialized Group B posts should be filled through 'direct recruitment'.

As far as their career progression is concerned, some Group B services are feeder in the AIS. For example, the Income Tax Department and the Customs and Central Excise Department are feeder services to the corresponding Group 'A' services. The All India Services (Appointment by Promotion) Rules provides for a promotion quota of 33.3% of senior duty posts plus central deputation reserves for the respective feeder cadres.

9.2.4 Central Civil Services (Group C)

Initially, recruitment for Group C (non-technical) posts was being done by the SSC which was constituted in 1977 on the recommendations of the First ARC.[35] This SSC has a nationwide network

[35] The Estimates Committee of Parliament in its 47th Report (1967–68) recommended the setting up of a Service Selection Commission for taking over recruitment to lower category of posts from the UPSC. Subsequently, the First ARC also recommended the setting up of a recruitment board.

of nine regional/sub-regional offices. The regional offices are located at Allahabad, Bangalore, Chennai, Guwahati, Kolkata, Mumbai and New Delhi, and two sub-regional offices are located at Chandigarh and Raipur. After its constitution in 1977, the SSC has been also entrusted with the recruitment for Group C (non-technical) and Group B (non-gazetted, both technical and non-technical) posts in various ministries/departments of GoI and their attached and subordinate offices except those for which recruitment is made by the Railway Recruitment Boards.

The SSC conducts recruitment to various categories of posts for which candidates are required to possess a graduation degree. The SSC holds CGLE for various Groups B and C posts such as income tax inspectors, central excise inspectors, CBI inspectors, assistants, customs appraisers and so on. A preliminary examination in the optical mark recognition (OMR) format is held, followed by a main written examination of 3–5 papers. The screened candidates are called for an interview. The process of examination from the date of advertisement to the final selection takes more than a year. The reason attributed to the long process is the number of stages in which the examination is conducted. Further, data of the past few years shows that for this examination about 10 lakhs candidates appear in a year, out of which the selected candidates are in the range of 10,000 and 30,000. In addition, the SSC conducts three separate examinations for the posts of sub-inspectors in Central Police Organization, tax assistants in the Income Tax Department and section officers (audit) in the office of the CAG, respectively, for which the candidates have to be at least graduates.

Besides, the SSC also conducts recruitment of junior engineers (in Central Public Works Department; technical Group C posts), Jr Hindi translators, statistical investigators and so on for which the eligibility is a graduation degree.

The Second ARC in its 10th report recommended, 'There is no need to conduct separate examinations for posts (Group "B" non-gazetted and Group "C") which require a graduate degree. There should be a common examination and thereafter, the candidates should be allowed to apply for various posts with this examination score'.[36]

9.2.4.1 Recruitment to the LDC Grade

Recruitment to the LDC grade although is being phased out as per central government decision,[37] still they are being recruited in some departments and organizations. The SSC holds an annual matric-level examination for LDCs and stenographers. The prescribed qualification for candidates is matriculation or equivalent and, on an average, more than 5 lakh candidates appear for this examination. The candidates are first screened through a preliminary examination in an OMR format and those who qualify it appear for a written test. Candidates who have cleared the written test appear for a skills test whose contents vary according to the post for which they have applied. Interviews are not a part of this process. This entire process takes more than a year. The Second ARC recommends:

> In case it is felt necessary to recruit LDCs in certain organizations/departments, especially in field offices, their recruitment should be done through the Staff Selection Commission. The existing recruitment process needs to be modified on the following lines: (i) The minimum qualification should be class 12th pass or

---

[36] Ibid., 321.

[37] GoI, Department of Personnel and Training, OM No. 3/12/97 – CS II dated 28 February 2008.

equivalent. (ii) The test should comprise of objective type questions. (iii) Short listed candidates should be administered a skills test. This should be conducted on computers so that the capability of the candidates to use word processing softwares also assessed.[38]

9.2.5 Central Civil Services (Group D)

As on 31 March 2016, the total number of group 'D' employees in the central government (also employed in workshop) aggregated to 4.90 lakh. Group 'D' civilian staff on the central pay roll constitutes an integral component of the CCS. A large number of Group 'D' posts in the non-workshop categories bear designations, such as, peon, *daftary* (someone who maintains official documents and papers), *jamadar* (someone who sweeps and cleans office premises), *safaiwala* (cleaner; sweeper), record sorter and so on, which are indicative of functions or occupations. Direct recruitment to these posts is generally made in the new scale. While no specific and essential educational qualifications have been prescribed for recruitment to the posts of *safaiwala*, *farash* (housekeeping attendant or dusting man) and *chowkidar* (watchman) because of the nature of their duties and activities, education up to middle school level is required for the other Group 'D' posts in the non-workshop categories because of their responsibilities and having paper work.

The Fifth CPC recommended that the entire 15% of the vacancies should be filled only on the basis of the results of a limited departmental competitive examination so as to ensure that only those fulfilling certain minimum standards are promoted to the clerical cadre. Elsewhere it is emphasized that employees in the Group 'D' and Group 'C' need special training in the face of new environment. The thrust of training for Group 'C' and Group 'D' employees which form a bulk of the workforce will have to be towards multi-skilling. The Fifth CPC stresses that 'all group "D" staff should be trained in different skills so that they can simultaneously perform various functions presently being carried out by a plethora of auxiliary staff'.[39]

9.2.5.1 Pattern of Civil Services Examination

As earlier stated, the AIS and the central services in India are recruited on the basis of open national level competitive examinations conducted by the UPSC. There is a provision for the reservation of posts to the extent of 50% in all categories of the civil services for those belonging to the SCs, STs and OBCs. The officers of the AIS serve the central government, union territories as well as state governments. But IAS is the most important among all the services in the country.

To become a part of the Indian Civil Service (ICS), the candidate has to be an Indian. The age limit for ICS as on January 2017 was 21–32 years and the upper age limit was relaxed for SC/ST candidates by five years.[40] The pattern of CSE had been undergoing changes ever since it was introduced by the British rule in India.

The CSE is a nationwide competitive examination in India conducted by the UPSC for recruitment to various civil services of the GoI, including the IAS, Indian Foreign Service and IPS

[38] Second ARC, *Report on Organization Structure*, 163.

[39] Central Pay Commission, *Report*, 179.

[40] The UPSC is planning to shrink the upper age limit to 21–26 from 21–32 for CS examination, to isolate the candidates who are presently preparing for the India's most prominent examination. Anyhow, there would not be any reduction in upper age limit for the candidates who belong to community category SC/ST which is 37 years (2017).

among others. It is conducted in three phases—a preliminary examination consisting of two objective-type papers (general studies and aptitude test), a main examination consisting of nine papers of conventional (essay) type and a personality test (interview).

Preliminary Examination

The pattern of the preliminary examination up to 2010 was based on the recommendations of the Kothari Commission (1979). It included two examinations, one on general studies worth 150 marks, and the second on 1 of 23 optional subjects worth 300 marks. Until 2011, when it was revamped, the preliminary pattern was sustained with only minor changes once every 10–15 years.

From 2011 onwards, the preliminary examination, now popularly known as the Civil Services Aptitude Test (CSAT)—officially it is still called General Studies Paper l and Paper 2—intends to focus on analytical abilities and understanding rather than the ability to memorize. The new pattern includes two papers of two hours duration and 200 marks each, both papers have multiple choice objective type questions only. They are as under:

- *Paper 1* tests the candidate's knowledge on current events, history of India and Indian national movement, Indian and world geography, Indian polity, Panchayati Raj system and governance, economic and social development, environmental ecology, biodiversity, climate change and general science and art and culture.
- *Paper 2* tests the candidate's skills in comprehension, interpersonal skills, communication, logical reasoning, analytical ability, decision-making, problem solving, basic numeracy, data interpretation, English language comprehension skill and mental ability.

In August 2014, the centre announced that English marks in CSAT 2 will not be included for gradation or merit and 2011 candidates may get a second chance to appear for the test next year.

In May 2015, the GoI announced that Paper 2 of the preliminary examination will be qualifying in nature, that is, it wouldn't be graded for eligibility in main examination and a candidate needs to secure at least 33% marks in order to be eligible for graded on the basis of marks of Paper 1 of the preliminary test.

Main Examination

The civil services main examination consists of a written examination and an interview. The written examination consists of nine papers, two qualifying and seven ranking in nature. The range of questions may vary from just 1 mark to 60 marks, 20 words to 600 words answers. Candidates who pass qualifying papers are ranked according to marks and selected number of candidates are called for interview or a personality test at the commission's discretion

According to the new marks allocations in CSE 2013, there are some changes made in the examination according to the suggestion of the Nigarvekar Committee.[41] However, after some controversy, the qualifying papers for Indian languages and English were restored to the examination. For the new format of CSE, see Table 9.5.

[41] Government rolls back changes to UPSC mains examination.

Table 9.5 Civil Services New Main Format

Paper	Subject	Marks
Paper A	One of the Indian languages listed below, to be selected by the candidates (from the languages listed in the English Schedule to the Constitution of India) (Qualifying)[a]	300
Paper B	English (Qualifying)	300
Paper I	Essay	250
Paper II	General Studies I (Indian heritage and culture, history and geography of the world and Society)	250
Paper III	General Studies II (Governance, constitution, polity, social justice and international relations)	250
Paper IV	General Studies III (Technology, economic development, bio-diversity, environment, security and disaster management)	250
Paper V	General Studies IV (ethics, integrity and aptitude)	250
Papers VI, VII	Two paper on subjects to be selected by the candidates from the list of optional subjects below (250 marks for each paper)[b]	500
Sub Total (Written Test)		1,750
Personality Test (Interview)		275
Total Marks		2,025

Notes: [a] The examination is offered in Assamese, Bengali, Bodo, Dogri, English, Gujarati, Hindi, Kannada, Kashmiri, Konkani, Maithili, Malayalam, Manipuri, Marathi, Nepali, Oriya, Punjabi, Sanskrit, Santhali, Sindi, Tamil, Telugu and Urdu languages.

[b] Optional Subjects: Paper 1 is theoretical but Paper 2 is often dominated by current affairs and application-based questions. Agriculture, animal husbandry and veterinary science, anthropology, botany, chemistry, civil engineering, commerce and accountancy, economics, electrical engineering, geography, geology, history, law, literature of any one of the non-English languages (out of 23 mainly Indian), management, mathematics, mechanical engineering, medical science, philosophy, physics, political science and international relations, psychology, public administration, sociology, statistics and zoology.

Interview Test

Starting with the examination of 1993, the interview carries 275 marks, with no minimum qualifying marks.[42] The candidate has the option to answer questions related to personality test in any of languages specified in the Eighth Schedule of the Indian Constitution or in English. Candidates, obtaining the minimum qualifying marks in the written part as may be fixed by the UPSC, are called for an interview test.

Officially called the 'Personality Test', the objective of the interview is to assess the personal suitability of the candidate for a career in public service by a board of competent and 'unbiased' observers. The test is intended to evaluate the mental calibre of a candidate. In broad terms, this is really an assessment of not only a candidate's intellectual qualities but also social traits and

[42] On the recommendation of the Satish Chandra Committee (set up in 1988) the marks for interview test were increased from 250 to 300 with effect from examination 1993. Presently (2018), marks for interview test are 275.

interest in current affairs. Some of the qualities to be judged include mental alterness, critical powers assimilation, clear and logical exposition, balance of judgement, depth of interest, ability for social cohesion and leadership, and intellectual and moral integrity.

The total number of marks in the papers and the interview (after deleting the marks of Papers and A and B) comes to 2025. The marks thus obtained in the main examination (written and interview) determine candidate's ranking.

9.3 Public Service Commission: Union and State

9.3.1 Introduction

The statutory provisions and administrative arrangements evolved from time to time during the British Rule in India invested the recruiting agency (e.g., Public Service Commission [PSC]) with enormous prestige and gave it significant authority in the government structure. Recruitment to the superior services continues to be on the British administration pattern even after India's Independence.

For long, it has been realized that for good governance, a body of competent and dedicated civil servants recruited purely on criterion is essential. Inevitably, it is increasingly recognized that only through the institution of the PSC, working as an independent and impartial authority, that it can play a dynamic role in the selection of persons of such a high calibre. For such selection, it does not only ensure a good opportunity for all citizens to participate in administration of their own country but also increases public confidence in the administrative machinery.

9.3.2 Origin

The origin of the PSC can be traced to the provision made in the GoI Act, 1919.[43] Section 96(c) of the Act provided for the establishment of a PSC in India,

> consisting of not more than five members, of whom one shall be a chairman, appointed by the Secretary of State in Council. Each member shall hold office for five years, and may be reappointed. No member shall be removed from office before the expiry of his term of office, except by order of the Secretary of State in Council.[44]

The commission was given, in regard to recruitment and control of the public services, such functions as may be assigned to it by the Secretary of State in Council in accordance with rules made under this section.

Following the recommendation of the Royal Commission on the Superior Civil Services (Lee Commission) in 1924, a Central Public Service Commission (consisting of a chairman and four other members that assumed office on 1 October 1926) was set up under this section in 1926. Its role was limited to all India and higher services. Following the recommendations of the Simon

[43] Earlier in 1855 a Civil Service Commission was set up for holding competitive examinations for the civil services on the Macaulay Committee's (1854) recommendation, but the examinations were conducted in England, not in India.

[44] Section 38 of GoI Act, 1919.

Commission, the GoI Act, 1935, provided in section 264 for the establishment of a Federal Public Service Commission which came into being in 1937.

9.3.3 Composition and Terms of PSC Members

The present Constitution under Article 315 makes provision for a PSC for the union and states or a Joint PSC for a group of states (the Parliament can set up a Joint PSC in pursuance of a resolution of the state legislatures concerned. On request by the governor of the state and approval of the president, the UPSC may perform the functions of the State Public Service Commission or SPSC).

The number, appointment and conditions of service of members of the PSC (on 31 March 2017, the UPSC consisted of the chairman and nine members against the sanctioned strength of one chairman and ten members) are determined (a) by the president in the case of the union/joint commission and (b) by the governor of the state in the case of a SPSC. Further, half of the members of a PSC shall be persons who have held office under the GoI or of a state for at least 10 years (Article 316). Provisions regarding governing the UPSC and SPSC are briefly discussed in Table 9.6.

Table 9.6 Provisions Governing PSC (Union and State)

	UPSC/Joint PSC	SPSC
Appointment Article	315	315
Number of members and their conditions of services (Article 318)	Determined by the president	Determined by the governor of state
Term of services of a member (Article 316)	6 years or until he attains the age of 65 years	6 years or until he attains the age of 62 years
Termination of a member's office (Article 316(2))	(i) by resignation addressed to the president (ii) by removal by the president	by resignation addressed to governor by removal by president
Grounds for removal of a member (Article 317)	(i) (a) adjudged insolvent (b) engages in paid employment outside the duties (c) declared infirm in mind or body by the president (ii) found guilty of misbehaviour by the Supreme Court's inquiry on a reference by the president	Same as prescribed for a UPSC members except the governor's power of a member's suspension pending the president's final order
Reasons for guilty of misbehaviour (Article 317(4))	(i) involved or interested in any government contract (ii) participates in profit of government contract	Same as prescribed for a UPSC member
Expenses of the Commission and its staff (Article 322)	Charged on the consolidated fund of India	Charged on the consolidated fund of the state

9.3.4 Independence of the PSC

The Constitution of India seeks to ensure the functioning of the PSC free from the political executive in the following ways:

1. The PSC is a constitutional body.
2. The chairman and the members of the PSC cannot be removed except in the manner and for the grounds enumerated in the Constitution.
3. The conditions of service of a member of the PSC cannot be varied to his disadvantage after his appointment (Article 318).
4. The expenses of the PSC are charged on the Consolidated Fund of India or of the state (Article 322) and the same are not votable by the Parliament or the state legislature concerned.
5. Certain disabilities are imposed on the chairman and members of the PSC with respect to government employment in the future. The Constitution specifies such disabilities as
    a. the chairman of the UPSC shall be ineligible for further employment either under the GoI or under the government of a state;
    b. the chairman of a SPSC shall be eligible for appointment as the chairman or any other member of the UPSC or as the chairman of any other SPSC, but not for any other employment either under the GoI or under the government of a state;
    c. a member other than the chairman of the UPSC shall be eligible for appointment as the chairman of the UPSC or as the chairman of a SPSC, but not for any other employment either under the GoI or under the government of a state;
    d. a member other than the chairman of a SPSC shall be eligible for appointment as the chairman or any other member of the UPSC as the chairman of that or any other SPSC, but not for any other employment either under the GoI or under the government of a state.

Thus while the chairman of the UPSC is barred against further employment in the government, the chairman of the SPSC or the other members of the union or state commissions have scope of employment in a higher post within the PSC but not outside. A PSC member is ineligible for re-appointment on the expiration of his term of office.

9.3.5 Functions of Public Service Commission

The functions of the PSC are prescribed under Article 320 of the Constitution which are as follows:

1. It shall be the duty of the Union and the SPSC to conduct examinations for appointments to the services of the union and the services of the state respectively.
2. It shall also be the duty of the UPSC, if requested by any two or more states so to do, to assist those states in framing and operating schemes of joint recruitment for any services for which candidates possessing special qualifications are required.
3. The UPSC or the SPSC, as the case may be, shall be consulted
    a. on all matters relating to methods of recruitment to civil services and for civil posts;

b. on the principles to be followed in making appointments to civil services and posts and in making promotions and transfers from one service to another and on the suitability of candidates for such appointments, promotions or transfers;
c. on all disciplinary matters affecting a person serving under the GoI or the government of a state in a civil capacity, including memorials or petitions relating to such matters;
d. on any claim by or in respect of a person who is serving or has served under the GoI or the government of a state or under the Crown in India or under the government of an Indian state, in a civil capacity, that any costs incurred by him in defending legal proceedings instituted against him in respect of acts done or purporting to be done in the execution of his duty should be paid out of the Consolidated Fund of India, or, as the case may be, out of the Consolidated Fund of the state;
e. on any claim for the award of a pension in respect of injuries sustained by a person while serving under the GoI or the government of a state or under the Crown in India or under the government of an Indian state, in a civil capacity and any question as to the amount of any such award, and it shall be the duty of a PSC to advise on any matter so referred to them and on any other matter which the president, or, as the case may be, the governor of the state, may refer to them, provided that the president as respects the all-India services and also as respects other services and posts in connection with the affairs of the union, and the governor as respects other services and posts in connection with the affairs of a state, may make regulations specifying the matters in which either generally, or in any particular class of case or in any particular circumstances, it shall not be necessary for a PSC to be consulted.

4. Nothing in Clause (3) shall require a PSC to be consulted as respects the manner in which any provision referred to in Clause (4) of Article 16 may be made or as respects the manner in which effect may be given to the provisions of Article 335.
5. All regulations made under the proviso to Clause (3) by the president or the governor of a state shall be laid for not less than 14 days before each House of Parliament or the House or each House of the legislature of the state, as the case may be, as soon as possible after they are made, and shall be subject to such modifications, whether by way of repeal or amendment, as both Houses of Parliament or the House or both Houses of the legislature of the state may make during the session in which they are so laid.

9.3.5.1 PSC Advisory Role

As stated earlier, the function, of the UPSC is to advise unless it is sought. The Constitution has no provision to make it obligatory upon the government to act upon the advice of the Commission in any case.[45] This is because of the fact, that under the Parliamentary system of government, it is the Cabinet which is responsible for the proper administration of the country, and its responsibility is to the Parliament. The Cabinet cannot, therefore, abjure this ultimate responsibility by binding itself by the opinion of any other body of persons. On the other hand, in matters relating to the recruitment to the services and the likes it would be profitable for the ministers to take the advice

---

[45] *D'Silva v. Union of India*, AIR, 1962, SC 1130.

of a body of experts. It is in this context that the Secretary of State for India Sir Samuel Hoare justified the parallel provisions as to the PSC in the GoI Act, 1935:

> Experience goes to show that they are likely to have more influence if they are advisory than if they have mandatory powers. The danger is that if you give them mandatory powers you then set up two governments.[46]

It has been held by the Supreme Court[47] that if the government fails to consult the PSC with respect to any of the specified matters, the resulting act of the government is not invalidated by reason of such omission, and no individual who is affected by such act can seek redress in a court of law against the government for such irregularity or omission. The government is also not bound to accept the Commission's advice where it is sought on cases referred to the Commission under Article 320. For example, during the year 1997–98, there were 16 such cases of non-acceptance of the UPSC's advice (3 promotions cases, 3 recruitment cases, 3 transfer and deputation cases and 7 disciplinary cases).[48] Similarly in 2009–10, there were 15 cases in which the advice of the UPSC was not accepted by the central government. R. C. Sarkar, a former chairman of the UPSC, comments that it should be made obligatory for the government to accept the recommendations of the UPSC.[49]

9.3.5.2 Power to Extend Functions of PSC

Further under Article 321, functions of the UPSC or SPSC may be extended by an Act of Parliament or the state legislature in respect of the service of the union or the state or any local authority or other body corporate constituted by law.

9.3.5.3 Reports of PSC

In addition under Article 323(1)/323(2), it shall be the duty of the UPSC/SPSC to present annually to the president/governor a report as to the work done by the Union/state commission, and on receipt of such report, the president/governor shall cause a copy thereof together with a memorandum explaining, as respect the cases, if any, where the advice of the commission was not accepted, the reason for such non-acceptance, to be laid before each House of Parliament/state legislature.

9.3.6 Functions of the UPSC

The functions of the commission fall broadly under two categories: (a) the provisions of the Constitution and the Acts, Rules and Regulations made thereunder and (b) the conventions and special orders issued by the government.

---

[46] U. K. Parliament Debate, Vol. 300, C. 858.

[47] *Ram Gopal v. State of Madhya Pradesh*, AIR 1970, SC 158.

[48] UPSC, *Annual Report, 1997–98* (New Delhi: UPSC, 2000), 30.

[49] R. C. Sarkar, 'UPSC: Erosion of Authority', *The Statesman* (New Delhi), 27 April 1974.

Under Article 320 of the Constitution, the Commission is required to advise the government on the following:

1. All matters relating to framing of recruitment rules, principles to be allowed in making appointments, promotions and transfers from one service to another and, in respect, disciplinary matters affecting civil servants. Further, the Commission is consulted in matters relating to grant of injury pension as well as in certain cases of re-imbursement of legal expenses.
2. To conduct examinations for appointment to the service of the Union of India; recruitment to the AIS and central services is made through the CSE, Engineering Services Examination, Combined Medical Services Examination and so on. The Commission also holds examinations for admission to the National Defence Academy and the Indian Military, Navy and Air Force Academies.

Under the provisions of Article 321 of the Constitution, the Commission is consulted in respect of appointments to certain categories of posts under the Municipal Corporation of Delhi, Employees State Insurance Corporation, the Employees Provident Fund Organisation. Certain categories of posts under the New Delhi Municipal Council are also now required to be filled in consultation with the Commission as per the provisions in the NDMC Act, 1994.

Further, the UPSC is required to be consulted in the matter relating to proposals for amending the UPSC (Exemption from Consultation) Regulations, 1958: proposals for upgrading a Group 'C' post or downgrading a Group 'B' post, recruitment to which was made without consulting the Commission; association of the chairman or a member of the Commission in DPC constituted for promotion by selection to and within Group 'A' services/posts; Special Recruitment Board for making selections for the scientists pool and the likes; principles for the determination of seniority; interpretation of existing conditions of service; proposal regarding withholding or withdrawing the whole or part of pension permanently or for a specified period due to gross misconduct, negligence during the service.

The posts and services which have been excluded from the Commission's purview from time to time, after the issue of the UPSC (Exemption from Consultation) Regulations, 1958, and which remain excluded, are enumerated in Appendix I.

9.3.7 ARC Recommendations

The Administrative Reforms Commission (ARC) in its Report on Personnel Administration (1969) made certain recommendations regarding the composition and powers of the PSCs which are as follows:

1. a. In appointing members of SPSC, the governor should consult the chairman of the UPSC and also the chairman of the SPSC.
   b. In appointing members of the UPSC the chairman of the UPSC should be consulted (even when the appointment deals with his own successor).
   c. Not less than two-thirds of the members of the UPSC should be drawn from among the chairmen and members of the SPSCs.
   d. At least one of the members of a SPSC should belong to a different state.
   e. The minimum academic qualification for a member of the Commission should be a university degree.

f. Only a secretary or head of a department or person holding a post equivalent to this rank or a comparable post in the institution of higher education should be eligible for selection out of government officials.
g. Members selected from non-officials should have practised at least for 10 years in any of the recognized professions, namely, law, medicine, engineering, science, technology, accountancy or administration.

2. a. The Commission should be consulted by the government before keeping certain matters regarding consultation with it beyond its purview.
b. The UPSC should be associated with the selection of personnel, and their promotion, within the quasi-government bodies entirely or substantially financed by government.
c. SPSCs should be equipped with similar powers over quasi-government institutions falling within the jurisdiction of their respective state governments.
d. Research cells should be set up in the PSC to appraise the effectiveness of recruitment by follow-up studies and to analyse trends in the skill market and in the educational sphere and to provide data for determining the recruitment policies.

9.3.8 Criticism of PSC Functioning

The independence of the PSC has been a subject of much controversy. It is observed that the appointment of the members to the PSCs, especially the SPSC, have been made largely on political considerations. The Law Commission of India in its Fourth Report observed,

> We are constrained to state that the personnel of the PSC in some of the States was not such as could inspire confidence from the points of view of either efficiency or impartiality. There appears little doubt that in some of the states appointments to the Commissions are made not on considerations of merit but on grounds of party and political affiliations.[50]

An ex-chairman of the Madhya Pradesh PSC said,

> The constitutional independence given to the Commission is largely vitiated by vesting the appointment of members in the hands of the Governor, (i.e., the Chief Minister in actual practice). The Chief Minister often appoints persons on political, communal, regional and other grounds, and not solely on merit, such persons usually find it difficult to resist ministerial pressure and influence in carrying out their duties in an independent and impartial manner.[51]

In Maharashtra, a deputy minister was appointed a member of the Commission from the quota reserved for civil servants. According to B. A. V. Sharma,

> Although the appointment serves to fulfil the legal niceties it was clearly against the spirit of the Constitution. There cannot be a worse example of a party government ruthlessly seeking to promote its interests and that of a party member in total disregard of constitutional propriety.[52]

[50] *Law Commission of India, 4th Report*, Vol. I, 171.

[51] D. V. Rege, 'The Public Service Commission: Its Powers and Functions—A Critical Assessment', in *Studies in State Administration*, ed. G. S. Halappa (Karnatak University, 1963), 134.

[52] B. A. V. Sharma, 'Public Service Commissions in India', in *Studies in Indian Democracy*, ed. S. P. Aiyar and R. Srinivasan (Bombay: Allied Publishers, 1965), 227.

What is shocking is the widespread public belief that money factor or other means of corruption do play important role in the selection of candidates. For example, a special court on 15 January 2018 sentenced former Punjab Public Service Commission Chairman Ravinderpal Singh Sidhu to seven years of rigorous imprisonment in a disproportionate assets case. Earlier, in 2015, a Patiala court had sentenced Sidhu to seven-year rigorous imprisonment in connection with the 2002 cash-for-job scam.

The UPSC in its 47th report observes in connection with its independence,

> Since the efficiency of the Civil Services is dependent, to a great extent, on the quality of the manpower selected, the Commission have been taking meticulous care to ensure selection of persons of high calibre through a transparent, fair and objective selection process. The systems, procedures and methods for recruitment to the Civil Services are being constantly reviewed for tapping the best talents available. There is a firm recognition that the quality of the public services in India—and the quality on the whole remains high—has been maintained only because the Commission have so steadfastly adhered to the principle of merit.[53]

The government is under an obligation while presenting the Commission's report in the Parliament/state legislature to explain the reasons why in any particular case the recommendation of the Commission has been overridden by the government. Notwithstanding the safeguard, there is also criticism about the functioning of the PSC.

1. One of the criticisms is the system of making ad hoc appointments for a temporary period without consulting the PSC and then approaching the Commission to approve of the appointment. From the monthly returns received from about half of the central departments/ministries, the UPSC observed that 173 fresh ad hoc appointments to Group 'A' posts and 68 to Group 'B' posts were made during the year 1997–98.[54]
2. There is also the trend on the part of the union ministries/departments to send proposals to withdraw requisitions for recruitment even after they had been notified by the PSC. This creates problems for smooth functioning of the PSC.
3. There are also delays in holding the DPCs for the confirmation of officers and obtaining the Commission's approval to the recommendations of such DPCs. For example, during 1997–98, the cases of 574 officers were referred to the DPCs for confirmation after delays of more than two years. The UPSC in its 1999–2000 report observed that officers should not be made to wait for such long periods for their confirmation.
4. Often the rules laying down the qualifications for the office to which such appointment has been made are changed retrospectively to fit in the appointee. Further, long delays continue to occur in notifying the Recruitment Rules approved by the UPSC. For example, during 1997–98, there were 290 cases pending for notification, out of which 88 cases were more than 3-year old.
5. Another criticism is that sometimes annual reports are presented to the Parliament/state legislature long after the year under review. Often 2–3 years are taken for presenting the reports in the legislature after their receipt by the president/governor. 'If the Legislature slumbers, the entire machinery of Parliamentary government will succumb, not to speak of any particular object of scrutiny by the Legislature'.

[53] UPSC, *47th Annual Report 1996–97* (New Delhi: UPSC, 2000), V.

[54] UPSC, *48th Report* (New Delhi: GoI Press, 2000), 2.

9.3.9 Conclusion

The question of appointment to high offices is of critical importance to the functioning of the machinery of the government. PSCs both at the state and central levels should function as independent and constitutional authorities. They should act fearlessly and should not succumb to any political or administrative influences. Only persons of high integrity and calibre should be appointed as members to the PSCs.

9.4 UPSC Committees on Civil Service Reforms

9.4.1 The Kothari Committee (1975–76)

To improve the recruitment methods, the UPSC set up a committee under the chairmanship of D. S. Kothari in 1975. Its recommendations (report was submitted in 1976), which were put into implementation from 1979 examinations, related to (a) civil services (preliminary examinations; objective type) for the selection of candidates for main examination and (b) civil services (main) examinations (written and interview) for the selection of candidates for the various services and posts. It also made recommendations regarding the answering of questions in language (as included in Eighth Schedule) and a list of subjects for the preliminary as well as main examinations.

9.4.2 The Satish Chandra Committee (1988–89)

In September 1988, another committee under the chairmanship of former UGC chairman, Professor Satish Chandra, was set up by the UPSC to review and recommend the recruitment procedure for all India and Class I and Class II central services. On Committee's recommendations, which were implemented from 1993 examinations, an essay paper of 200 marks was introduced in the civil services (main) examination besides raising marks from 250 to 300 for the interview test. It also made recommendations concerning deletion and addition of optional subjects for the preliminary as well as main examinations.

9.4.3 The Alagh Committee (2000–2001)

In the current phase of globalization and liberalization, the need was felt to amend the current practices of selecting cadres for the higher civil services. Accordingly, the UPSC appointed in July 2000 a nine-member committee headed by Y. K. Alagh to examine the present schedule of CSEs and recommend changes. The Alagh Committee has been asked to evaluate the effectiveness of the scheme and review the rules for the examinations, apart from studying the feasibility of adopting an improved method of allocation of services. It has also been asked to examine the present practices of a common main written examination and the differential assessment of candidates by an interview board personality test to determine the relative suitably of candidates for different service is a viable mechanism. Besides, it has been asked to suggest modifications, additions or deletions in the subjects of the preliminary or main examinations. Further, the Committee has been asked to examine the desirability of associating the UPSC with assessment of officers in terms of satisfactory completion of their induction training in training institutions.

Based on the Alagh Committee's recommendations and the government's approval, the UPSC finally decided to change the pattern of tile preliminary examination. This entrance test was to be rechristened 'Civil Service Aptitude Test' (CSAT) and would be in practice from the year 2011–12. In the new scheme, there would be two objective papers in the prelims—(a) general studies (already in practice) and (b) aptitude test—each carrying 200 marks and of two hours duration. However, there would be no optional subject-based paper, and the new scheme would now test the candidates on their aptitude, decision-making skills and analytical abilities rather than their memorizing abilities.

9.4.4 The Hota Committee (2003–2004)

Under the chairmanship of P. C. Hota, a former, chairman of the UPSC, a Committee on Civil Services Reforms was set up in 2003. This was yet another initiative by the government to examine the whole gamut of a civil service reform. The Committee made the following important recommendations:

1. Age for entrants to the civil services should be 21–24 years for general candidates with a five years age concession to members of SC/STs and three years for OBCs.
2. Annual performance plans for officers.
3. After 15 years of rigorous review, if an officer is not found honest and performance oriented, he be weeded out of the service.
4. The duties, functions and responsibilities of all senior posts are to be laid down and publicized.
5. Article 311 of the Constitution to be amended to enable the president/governor to dismiss/remove public servants in case of corrupt practices/having assets disproportionate to known sources of income.
6. Antiquated rules and procedures in the government must be discarded and new simplified ones put in place.
7. E-governance to be encouraged to augment efficiency and ensure transparency in government.
8. Civil servants should be encouraged to move laterally to non-governmental organizations.
9. To increase the representation of women in the civil services, it is proposed that within 15 years, at least 25% members of the higher civil service should be women as against 13% women at that time.[55]

Important Recommendations of the Second ARC on Refurbishing Personnel Administration (November 2008):

1. Establishment of the National Institutes of Public Administration to run bachelor's degree courses.
2. Reduction in age for appearing in CS examinations (21–25, 21–28 and 21–29 for general, OBC and SC/ST candidates, respectively).

[55] UPSC, Committee on Civil Service Reforms (P. C. Hota), *Report 2003–04* (New Delhi: UPSC, July 2004), 15.

3. Conducting of the preliminary and main examinations on 2–3 consecutive days. Preliminary examination should consist of an objective type test having one or two papers on general studies. Main examination should consist of two papers in compulsory subjects and one separate essay paper.
4. Induction of officers of the state civil services into AIS on the basis of a common examination, and promotion into Group 'A' on consideration of annual confidential reports (ACRs) and examination.
5. Supervision by UPSC of the functioning of DPCs.
6. As a capacity-building measure, every government servant should undergo mandatory training at the induction stage and also periodically during his/her career.
7. A CCS authority to be set up which, among other things, would formulate guidelines for appointments at the 'senior management level' in the GoI.
8. Developing Institute of Secretariat Training and Management (ISTM) as a nodal agency for design and delivery of common foundation courses for Groups B and C central services.
9. For Group B, 25% vacancies every year should be filled through 'direct recruitment'.
10. Phasing out of the practice of recruitment of LDCs.
11. Posts of assistants under CCS should be filled in the ratio of 40% by promotion from UDCs, 40% by direct recruitment and 20% through Limited Departmental Competitive Examination.
12. CCS authority should be assigned the responsibility for the placement of officers at middle management level who would have completed the minimum qualifying years of service.
13. Permitting civil servants to go on deputation.
14. Making performance appraisal system consultative and transparent.
15. Evolving in-house mechanisms for rewarding good performance.
16. Establishment of a system of two intensive reviews—one on completion of 14 years of service, and another on completion of 20 years of service—to assess the fitness of the government employees.
17. Evolving a system of disciplinary proceedings as per constitutional requirement.
18. Safeguarding the political neutrality and impartiality of the civil services.
19. Drafting and enactment of a Civil Services Bill incorporating Civil Services Values and the Code of Ethics.
20. Amending the new Cadre Allocation Policy, 2008, for the allocation of cadre to candidates selected for the AIS.

9.5 Training in the Civil Services

9.5.1 Introduction

Explaining the importance of training, as a contributory factor to raising the competence of the civil service, Marquis Wellesley (1760–1842) on 10 July 1800 said,

> How was this empire to be governed on a permanent footing? The answer lay … in a civil service capable of an inexhaustible supply of useful knowledge, cultivated talents and disciplined morals.[56]

[56] Quoted in B. B. Misra, *Central Administration of the East India Company, 1733–1834* (Bombay: Oxford University Press, 1959), 386.

The fact is that civil service training refurbishes the personnel with mental calibre and competence so that they are able to perform jobs of higher responsibility.

The civil service is an important government institution. It is one of the most live elements in the edifice of the government. As a matter of fact, the image of a government in the minds of the people is, to a large extent, formed on the basis of day-to-day performance of the administration. The achievements of a government, whatever its purposes or tasks, depend considerably on the conduct and effectiveness of civil servants. Ability is a pre-requisite to achievement, but unless this ability is built in, motivated, schooled and properly guided towards specific objectives, achievement will not be possible. Development of the civil servants has, therefore, become an integral part of the national development. The basic issue today is the question of coping with the growing demands and challenges of the country with added manpower. It is, therefore, necessary and desirable that all conceivable steps are taken to build up the ability and effectiveness of the civil service. National development is thus largely dependent on the civil servants who are prepared through training to perform the tasks that the state demands. Hence, the power and influence of the training function has increased considerably in recent years. Today good training is viewed 'as an investment in human resources'.[57] It is one of the most important and yet the least developed resources in the civil service. Thus, training, in the broadest sense, is an important element contributing to national development. It helps in raising one's performance capability and the level of organizational productivity as well. Emphasizing the need and importance of training in the public service, Y. B. Chavan, a former minister of home affairs, GoI, in his inaugural address to the conference on training sponsored by the training division of the Ministry of Home Affairs and organized by the Indian Institute of Public Administration (IIPA) at New Delhi, said, 'All jobs in public administration, whether high or low, involve an element of skill and if they are to be performed at optimum efficiency, such skills have to be methodically and systematically cultivated'.[58]

Definition: Training is the process by which an individual is made fit to perform certain functions. The basic objective of training is to provide appropriate management and working knowledge and skills so as to boost a civil servant's efficiency and effectiveness to the highest level. It is oriented to develop the state of mind of a civil servant so that he may perform his duties efficiently and enthusiastically and exercise his authority properly. Training has been broadly defined as 'purposeful development of human resources'. This definition is not sharply different from other aspects of learning of education.

Indian administration had a unique tradition of paying attention to administration. We come across minute details of administration in the old manuscripts and manuals. We find that there was a tradition of choosing individuals even for minor jobs with great care. After the meticulous manner in which assessment was made of the individual's personality for selection, he was attached to experienced persons who would give him the necessary training for the purpose for which he was recruited. In the early period of the British establishment in India, youths going into the EIC service received commercial training at Christ's Hospital.

The available literature indicates that during the 18th century, there was no systematic provision for training the civil servants, either in India or in England. However, a scrutiny of the

---

[57] ARC, *Report on Personnel Administration*, 62.

[58] Y. B. Chavan, 'Training and Reorientation of Civil Service Attitude', *The Indian Journal of Public Administration* XV, no. 1 (January–March 1969): 1.

available literature on this subject reveals that a working knowledge of accounts was considered essential. To quote Philip Woodruff, 'Sometimes they [civil servants] had been sent for a few months to a commercial office, but there they learnt only what would fit them for the... unprofitable duty of mere copying clerks'.[59] Lord Wellesley, who became governor general in 1798, embarked on a policy of territorial expansion. He founded a college called College of Fort William at Calcutta in August 1800 for training of covenanted services.[60]

But six years later, Haileybury college was established in England as a training college for the EIC's covenanted servants who were nominated either by the directors or the Board of the Control. The enactment of the Charter Act in 1853 made appointment to the covenanted civil service open to competition among national subjects of Her Majesty. In 1855, the Haileybury College was shut down. The first competitive examination was held in 1855 in London on the basis of the Report of the Macaulay Committee (1854).

Lord Macaulay proposed that the age limit for new recruits should be 18–25 years and the period of training should be 1–2 years. He proposed teaching four papers, that is, history, geography, jurisprudence, financial and commercial sciences and oriental languages, especially Sanskrit language.

Training for the civil servants recruited in the United Kingdom was of two years—one year in England and one year's district training in India. For those recruited in India, the training spell in the United Kingdom was of two years. Training in England was imparted in the four British universities of Oxford, Cambridge, Dublin and London. The subjects that were taught were classical and provincial languages, Indian law, history, economics, British history and constitutional law. At the end, there was an examination and the probationer was sent to India for field training.[61] At the district level, the trainee was attached to the district collector and given a thorough grounding in magisterial work, administration of revenue laws and survey and settlement. After this spell, the trainee received his first posting.

The Islington Commission (1912–15), in its report, recommended that the training in British universities be increased to three years, with emphasis on legal training. The Commission, for the first time, talked of interchange of ideas among trainers 'by letting the men see on the spot, each other's training methods'.[62]

It is noted that any necessary development and improvement would follow from his experience within the civil service rather than by formal training. L. S. S. O'Malley wrote in 1930:

> The real training of a young civilian begins in India with practical work in different branches of the administration. On arrival he is made an Assistant Magistrate with powers of the lowest class and is posted to the headquarters of a district to learn his work under the supervision of a collector.[63]

Practical training was given in a number of fields, including land survey and settlement.

The question of the training of civil servants was reviewed in a comprehensive way by the Assheton Committee in 1944. In accordance with the recommendations of this committee, a

---

[59] Philip Woodruff, *The Men Who Ruled: The Founders* (London: Jonathan Cape, 1935), 279.

[60] A covenanted service consisted of all superior posts and was meant only for the Britishers. The College was abolished on 27 January 1802 due to differences of opinion between Lord Wellesley and the Court of Directors.

[61] See B. N. Puri, 'The Training of Civil Servants Under the Company', *Journal of LBS National Academy of Administration* 12, (July 1967).

[62] S. R. Maheswari, *The Evolution of Indian Administration* (Agra: Lakshmi Narian Agarwal, 1970), 74.

[63] O'Malley, *The Indian Civil Service*, 256.

directorate of training and education was created in the treasury. Earlier arrangements had been introduced in the departments for the development of the techniques of organization and methods. A central school was also established in 1945 for giving initial training to the administrative class, but this arrangement was short-lived and was the first causality in the economic campaign of 1951. Thereafter, training became once again a departmental responsibility as before.

9.5.2 Civil Service Training After Independence

With the dawn of Independence on 15 August 1947, the country was confronted with numerous problems, including the problem of rehabilitation of nearly 20 million refugees who were torn from their hearths and homes as a result of the partition of the country. The preoccupation with the immediate objectives resulted in the neglect of training. When the two AIS, namely, IAS and the IPS, were reconstituted under the able guidance of Sardar Patel, arrangements were also made for their training. The stress in the post-Independence training institutions had been nevertheless different; instead of making agents to serve the Empire, the objective now was to produce good patriotic Indians who might cope with the growing demands on the administration. With the increase in the functions of government following the adoption of the socialist pattern of society as a goal, it had become imperative for the government to plan suitable training programmes for the civil servants. It is well to look at the following observation of the Planning Commission in this context:

> Next to recruitment the training of personnel has considerable bearing on administrative efficiency. Each type of work in the government requires a programme of training suited to it. In general, in all branches of administration, it is necessary to provide for the training of personnel at the commencement of service as well as at appropriate intervals in later years. In this connection, we would emphasize the importance of careful grounding in revenue and development administration for recruits to the Indian Administrative Service.[64]

The need for training has been emphasized in the successive Five Year Plans. The Second Five Year Plan (1956–61) stressed the need for 'organising large-scale training programmes in all fields, and mobilising the available training resources, including public and private institutions, industrial and other establishments, apprenticeship and in-service training'. In the context of programmes for the training of manpower, the Third Five Year Plan (1961–66) laid emphasis on

> the reorganisation and expansion of existing institutions, development of large numbers of new institutions, special measure for obtaining and training teachers and instructors, introduction of new techniques for intensifying training and shortening the periods needed, expanding facilities for imparting practical training, and developing new ways of making use of trained personnel as a scarce key resources.[65]

The ARC (India) also recommended that the 'government should, with the assistance of experienced administrators and experts in training techniques, formulate a clear-cut and far-sighted

[64] India, Planning Commission, *Administration and Public Cooperation* (Delhi: Manager of Publications, 1954), 121.

[65] Third Five Year Plan (1961–66), GoI, https://archive.org/stream/in.ernet.dli.2015.223422/2015.223422.Third-Five_djvu.txt

national policy on civil service training, setting out objectives and priorities and guidelines for preparation of training, plans'.[66] A scheme for 'Training of Personnel for Development Administration' was included in the Fifth Five Year Plan (1974–79). Subsequent Five Year Plans also emphasized the importance and need of training for the civil servants in India.

Since training came to be considered an essential part of the human resources development programme, the government in the post-Independence period set up many institutions for training in the civil service. The IAS Training School at Metcalfe House, New Delhi, was established in 1947 to provide training to the members of IAS. Another IAS Staff College was set up at Shimla in 1955 to provide in-service training and to meet the training requirements of those selected through special recruitment processes in addition to the annual intake. On 9 September 1958, these two institutions were merged to form, what is known as the National Academy of Administration at Mussoorie. The GoI also set up the Central Training Division in the Ministry of Home Affairs in 1968. Earlier on the recommendation of the Appleby Report of 1953, the IIPA was set up in 1954 which later on was converted into a training-cum-research institution. The establishment of the Department of Personnel in 1970 and the creation of the new Ministry of Personnel, Public Grievances and Pensions with the Department of Personnel and Training in 1985, training in the civil service acquired increasing attention.

The Second ARC in its 10th Report said, 'All Civil servants should undergo mandatory training before each promotion and each officer/official should be evaluated after each training programme'. On the pattern of 'Common Foundation Course' for all Group 'A' services, the ARC recommended that for 'Groups "B" and "C" services, the Institute of Secretariat Training and Management (ISTM) may be developed as the nodal agency for design and delivery of Common Foundation Courses'.[67]

9.5.3 National Training Policy (1996)

The National Training Policy (NTP) was formulated in 1996. It stipulates that training programmes should focus on evolving the attributes of commitment, responsiveness, awareness and accountability. For the purpose of imparting appropriate training, the civil services are divided into the following three levels:

1. The lower level functionaries of Group 'D' and the lower stages of Group 'C' services.
2. The supervisory and the middle management/administrative level (Group B; lower stage of Group 'A' and higher stage of Group 'C').
3. Group 'A' services and the AIS comprising the administrative and managerial levels.

The NTP envisages that each department should spend 1.5% of its annual budget on training.

In 2010, a revised Draft NTP was prepared which envisages the appointment of training manager as the nodal person for training in each ministry/department. It has revised the minimum expenditure on training from 1.5–2.5% of the annual budget of each government ministry/department. It also prescribes the creation of a National Training Council, chaired by the minister of state for personnel, public grievances and pensions.

[66] ARC, *Report on Personnel Administration*, 62–63.

[67] Second ARC, *Report on Organization Structure*, 320.

9.5.4 National Training Policy (2012)

With a view to transforming civil service, it is essential to develop human resource management system. As civil service is a vital force in the governance, it should be developed and motivated. Within this transformational process, it is imperative to match civil servants' competencies with the jobs they have to do and bridge competency gaps for current and future roles through training.

9.5.4.1 Training Objectives of the NTP 2012

The objective of training will be to develop a professional, impartial and efficient civil service that is responsive to the needs of the citizens. In doing so, care shall be taken to emphasize the development of proper ethics, commitment to work and empathy for the vulnerable sections, as differently abled, senior citizens, SCs, STs, etc. The competency framework will be used to ensure that civil servants have the requisite knowledge, skills and attitude to effectively perform the functions they are entrusted with. The success of training will be in actual improvement in the performance of civil servants.

9.5.4.2 Training Targets

All civil servants will be provided with to equip them with the competencies for their current or future jobs. Such training will be imparted: (a) at the time of their entry into service, and (b) at appropriate intervals in the course of their careers. Such training will be made available for all civil servants from the lowest level functionaries to the highest levels.

The opportunities for training will not be restricted only at ministerial points in a career but will be available to meet needs as they arise through a mix of conventional courses, distance and e-learning. Further, priority will be given to the training of front-line staff, including training on soft skills, so as to improve customer orientation as well as quality of service delivery to the citizens.

9.5.5 Training and Development Institutions

The training effort to produce civil service personnel of the requisite capacity necessitated the designing of training programmes and establishment of training institutes. A few in this direction are discussed in the following pages.

9.5.5.1 Induction Training for All India and Central Services

The Lal Bahadur Shastri National Academy of Administration located at Mussoorie is the national apex institution responsible for imparting 'induction training' to the members of the AIS and central services (Group A) recruited through CSE conducted by the UPSC. The 'induction training' comprises (a) foundational course followed by (b) a professional course imparted at the National Academy.

1. *Foundational course:* The idea underlying the foundational course is that officers of the AIS and central service Group 'A' should acquaint themselves with the machinery of the government and the broad principles of public administration. It is designed to promote a common outlook and understanding and to build-up right attitudes and values among them. They should acquire 'an understanding of the constitutional, economic and social framework within which they have to function, as these largely determine the policies and programmes towards the framing and execution of which they will have to make their contribution'.[68]

   The foundational course is also intended to cover such matters as aims and obligations of the civil service, and the ethics of the profession objectivity, integrity, thoroughness, impartiality and so on.

   Since the probationers are drawn from diverse disciplines, and since many of them do not have detailed knowledge about the country and its administration, they are taught subjects which include (a) Constitution of India and political system of the country (b) administrative tribunals and civil and criminal courts (c) public administration (d) social administration (e) management theories and practices (f) finance and financial administration (g) Indian economy and economics (h) knowledge of history, culture, fine arts, music and so on, and (i) computers and use of communication technology.

   As for the activities organized during the foundational course for the IAS, there are three types of activities.

   a. *Village visit programme.* This one week programme is designed to sensitize the officer trainees to the reality of rural India, through a structural study of a village.
   b. *Trek in the Himalayas.* This component of training is designed to inculcate the spirit of adventure, team working, positive group affinity, better Interpersonal relations, endurance and love for nature.
   c. *Extra-curricular activities.* These include cultural programmes and zonal days and is designed to develop a holistic personality of a training officer.
2. *Professional course:* After completing the foundational course lasting for about 17 weeks, the probationers of the services (central services Group A, and IPS and IFS) other than the IAS go to their respective training institutions for professional course, as given in the following table:

1. Indian Police Service	Sardar Vallabhahai Patel National Police Academy, Hyderabad
2. Indian Forest Service	Forest Research Institute, Dehradun
3. Indian Revenue Service (Income Tax)	Revenue Service Staff College, Nagpur
4. Indian Postal Service	Post and Telegraph Training Centre, Saharanpur
5. Indian Audit and Accounts Service	National Academy on Audit and Accounts, Shimla
6. Indian Railway Service	Railway Staff College, Baroda

   Professional course for the IAS probationers: The IAS probationers continue to stay at the National Academy of Administration (Mussoorie) for undergoing a further course of

[68] GoI, *Report on Indian and State Administrative Services and Problems of District Administration* (New Delhi: Planning Commission, 1962), 14.

institutional training. On the recommendation of the ARC and also on the active consideration of the GoI, since 1969, the government has introduced a new pattern of training called the 'sandwich post-foundational institutional training' for the IAS. Under this scheme, new recruits to the IAS undergo two spells of training at the Academy. At the end of the first spell of institutional training, the IAS probationers are sent to the state (to which they are allotted) for undergoing field training for 12 months. Apart from conducting programme for fresh IAS probationers, it runs refresher courses for senior IAS officers. A week long vertically integrated training is also being imparted annually to all IAS officers.

The training programme for the IAS probationers in a state is given in Table 9.7.

In most states, district training lasts for 52 weeks. The IAS probationer during this spell is under the supervision of a district collector and regularly reports to him and corresponds about his progress with a specified member of the faculty at the Academy. The probationer is required to prepare a detailed plan of his attachments with several district-level functionaries. The idea is to acquaint him with field administration and the officers he is most likely to interact with.

Table 9.7 Training Programmes for the IAS Probationers in the State

	Areas	Duration of Training	Period
1.	Field Training	12 months	From April to March
	A. Institutional Training	4 months	From April to July
	B. District Training	8 months	From August to March
2.	Preliminary attachment with the Deputy Commissioner	1 week	1st week
3.	Development and Panchayat Training	4 weeks	2nd week to 5th week
4.	Police Training	2 weeks	6th week and 7th week
5.	Jail and Treasury Training	1 week	8th week
6.	Local Government Training	1 week	9th week
7.	Attachment with other District Officers, namely, Public Works, Education and Health	1 week	10th week
8.	Agriculture Training	2 weeks	11th and 12th week
9.	Training regarding Cooperatives	1 week	13th week
10.	Revenue Training	10 weeks	14th week to 23rd week
11.	Attachment with the Sub-Divisional Officers (Civil)	4 week	24th week to 27 weeks
12.	Training in District Office	4 weeks	28th week to 31st week
13.	Attachment with the Deputy Commissioner	3 weeks	32nd week to 34th week

The institutional field training break-up can be explained by taking Rajasthan as an example.[69] The Government of Rajasthan has made the following arrangement for the district training of IAS Probationers:

1.	Attachment with Tehsil	1 week
2.	Attachment with BDO and VLW	1 week
3.	Attachment with Zila Parishad	2 days
4.	Attachment with SDO	1 week
5.	Attachment with Superintendent of Police	2 days
6.	Attachment with District Judge, CJM and other District Level Officers (e.g. PWD, Irrigation, Forests, RTO, DSO, Animal Husbandry, Education, Health, etc.)	2 weeks
7.	Attachment with DRDA and Special Development Projects	1 week
8.	Attachment with Police Station	2 days
9.	Attachment with Municipality	2 days
10.	Independent charge of BDO	4 weeks
11.	Independent Charge of Tehsildar	4 weeks
12.	Settlement Training	1 week
13.	Institutional Training at RIPA (I Phase)	3 weeks
14.	Institutional Training at RIPA (II Phase)	4 weeks
15.	Debriefing Sessions	3 days
16.	Independent charge as Assistant Collector and Magistrate	28 weeks

The probationers at the district study the district administration, both developmental and regulatory, including the maintenance of law and order. After this, they report back at the Academy to round off their second phase of the professional training for a period of three months.

The district training is designed to acquaint the IAS officers with the working of the totality of government at the district and local levels. To this effect, they are placed under a senior colleague—a district collector/deputy commissioner—for the practical understanding of the administration in action, of the complex problems involved, of dealing with people, subordinates, colleagues and seniors.

The institutional training at the district consists of (a) under study period, (b) on the job training, (c) attachment to district and lower-level officers and (d) institutional training.

After undergoing 12 months' field training in the state, the IAS probationers again return to the Academy for a second spell of training (for about 4 months) when the emphasis is on discussing the various administrative problems. This part of institutional training is largely problem-oriented and based on experience and observations of the trainees in the state.

In his Report (1981–85), L. K. Jha (chairman of the Economic ARC) made suggestions for a change in the existing procedure for recruitment to various branches of the AIS, including the IAS. He is of the opinion that the present insistence on a university degree as the

[69] Ramesh K. Arora and Rajni Goyal, *Indian Public Administration, 3rd ed.* (New Delhi: New Age International, 2013), 536–37.

minimum qualification for candidates competing for these services should be given up and that our IAS probationers should be selected after they have completed the 10+2 stage of education. This, Jha thinks, would save the country's future administrators from having to go through a course of academy training which is not necessarily suited to their professional responsibilities.[70] Instead, he has proposed intensive training for the successful candidates chosen under the proposed method at an administrative college where they would be taught subjects closely related to their future duties. The emphasis would be on selective rather than general education, and the stress would be in favour of a version of technical training for the purposes of running the administration. These proposals of his have been criticized on a number of grounds. G. D. Khosla (former chairman of ICS and retired Chief Justice of the Punjab High Court) says, 'I do not favour the selection of IAS probationers at the plus two stage of education and then giving them an intensive training in administrative work'.[71] In fact, this would make the IAS less acceptable. S. D. Bhambri (a former Chief Secretary to the Government of Haryana) says that there is ample scope for all types of skills to be made use of in present-day development administration.[72]

What is needed is that the training of the IAS recruits should be made more vigorous and comprehensive. Induction training to the higher civil servants is of great value. P. R. Dubhashi (a former Director of the IIPA) says that the induction training has to be so structured that

> it provides a broader view of the environment and administrative set-up so that it widens the horizon and perspective of officers. There should be adequate stress on intellectual accomplishment and building up of sound character. It should also be as comprehensive as possible to provide knowledge and skills for specific jobs which these officers will be required to hold in the coming years.[73]

3. *In-service training programmes:* Under the direction of late PM Rajiv Gandhi, a meaningful programme of training for IAS officers has been drawn in three phases by the Ministry of Personnel, Public Grievances and Pensions. The first phase is the early nine or ten years when the officers have to work in the field implementing various programmes. The course designed for this phase is for a period of three weeks. It aims to equip the participants, by upgrading their knowledge, skills and behavioural understanding, to handle the existing job better and handle likely job assignments in the coming five years. These assignments include collectors, district development officers, project officers, heads and additional heads of departments, officers in autonomous bodies, public sector enterprises and state/central secretariat. For modules, namely, the organizational behaviour, the financial management and decentralized planning, the computer training and knowledge/skills in other areas have been designed. For the second phase, with 10–18 years of service, the main thrust is on the aspects of modern management concepts and decision analysis, with particular focus on management in governments as well as in the public sector. This is to help the officers to go in for specialization in selected areas in a later stage of their career. Finally, at the beginning of the senior phase of career, when the IAS officers start getting

[70] See *The Tribune*, 1 July 1981.

[71] G. D. Khosla, 'Restructuring the IAS', *The Tribune*, 2 July 1981.

[72] *The Tribune*, 3 July 1981.

[73] P. R. Dubhashi, *Recent Trends in Public Administration* (Delhi: Kaveri Books, 1995), 214.

opportunities to contribute to the policymaking process, they will undergo training programmes related to policy analysis for a period of three weeks.

The IIPA, the National Academy of Administration (Mussoorie), Administrative Staff College (ASC) of India (Hyderabad) and National Institute of Public Finance Policy (New Delhi) run a number of in-service programmes for senior officers. These are not just refresher courses but also advanced programmes keeping in view the progress of modern management techniques, impact of science and technology on administration and development of behavioural sciences relevant to public services.

9.5.5.2 Training of Group 'A' Officers of IAAS

The officers of the IAAS recruited through the CSE are initially placed on probation, and they undergo a 17-week foundation course along with the officers of other Group 'A' civil services. Subsequently, they are imparted intensive professional training at the National Academy of Audit and Accounts, Shimla, and at National Institute of Financial Management, Faridabad. The professional course covers accounting and auditing (both governmental and commercial), financial management, central service rules and regulations, cost and management accounting, management concepts, quantitative techniques and electronic data processing. During this period, the officers are also given general exposure to public finance and fiscal policy, centralized economic planning, project appraisal and management, commercial law, organizational behaviour and structure and functioning of audit organizations. This is supplemented by practical training in one of the department's field offices, namely, Accountant General, Himachal Pradesh, also located at Shimla, as well as attachment to district treasuries, public works divisions, Reserve Bank of India, Controller General of Accounts (the accounting authority for the union government), and Bureau of Parliamentary Studies in the Lok Sabha Secretariat. This part of the course covers two phases of 51 weeks and 10 weeks. Between the two phases of institutional training, the probationers are attached to various field formations throughout the country, for gaining practical experience in accounting and auditing. They are also required to pass a two part departmental examination.

The officers promoted to the IAAS from the cadres of accounts officers and audit officers also go through an intensive orientation course. The course exposes the officers to concepts of general management and electronic data processing and prepares them to adapt to their changed job requirements and additional responsibilities.

The National Academy of Audit and Accounts, Shimla, organizes several in-service training courses for officers at various levels. These include advanced programmes in accounts and project accounts, financial management, audit methodology, economic and fiscal management, public finance and so on.

9.5.5.3 Training for the Indian Foreign Service

The members of the Indian Foreign Service recruited through the CSE initially undergo a 17-week foundational course. On completion of the course, they have to attend separate training courses and institutions where they undergo training for learning of some foreign languages, subjects related to diplomatic techniques and procedures as well as international affairs. They also get practical administrative training at the district and secretariat levels.

9.5.5.4 Training in Local Self-government

The Panchayati Raj institutions and municipal bodies in the wake of 73rd and 74th Constitutional Amendments in 1992 acquired increasing importance. Local governments responsible to the local people are in a better position to the local needs of the people. Their employees account for more than two million persons. As compared to higher civil servants, very little attention and resources have been devoted for training the local government employees. They have to be trained to line up to the responsibilities of the modern local government.

At present, the National Institute of Rural Development (NIRD) located at Hyderabad is the national apex organization for training, research and consultancy in rural development. It has a regional centre in Guwahati to cater to the needs of the north-eastern region. The NIRD is imparting training on all relevant rural development issues covering watershed management, participatory rural appraisal, role of NGOs, development of SCs/STs, financial management of District Rural Development Agencies (DRDAs), decentralized planning and so on. It has commenced from 1994 a series of high-intensity, short-duration programmes popularly known as banner programmes, for important district-level functionaries such as collectors and project directors of DRDAs. Further, in order to improve quality of training, NIRD has been organizing training of trainers, supplying training modules and also organizing off-campus training programmes.

With the enactment of the Constitution (73rd Amendment) Act relating to the setting up of Panchayati Raj Institutions, there is an imperative need to train a large number of Panchayati Raj functionaries within a short span of time. State Institutes of Rural Development, along with the Extension Training Centres (ETCs)/Panchayati Raj Training Centres, constitute the only training hierarchy to reach down to the village level. Hence, there is an urgent need to strengthen/augment the existing training infrastructure through a selective approach covering those states which would require training for Panchayati Raj functionaries in the near future.

The ETCs have been assigned the task of imparting training to village/block level rural development functionaries. Considering the increase in the number of development functionaries and rural organizations and the rejuvenation of the Panchayati Raj System, the role of ETCs has acquired added importance.

For municipal employees in India, there are a few institutes for their training. The All India Institute of Local Self Government has done pioneering work in the field of municipal training. It was established in 1951 having its headquarters in Mumbai; it conducts various training programmes regularly at its different centres providing its training services to people from all the parts of the country.

The central government has also established a Centre for Training and Research in Municipal Administration with the objective of stimulating and strengthening municipal administration. Besides a Centre for Research and Training in Municipal Administration at the national level, the central government has established four regional centres in places such as Kolkata, Mumbai, Hyderabad and Lucknow for imparting training to the municipal personnel in these regions.

Mention may be made of the National Institute of Urban Affairs (NIUA) which organizes training programmes for functionaries engaged in the planning, implementation and management of Urban Basic Service Programme. The NIUA, set up in 1976, imparts training in human settlement planning, and holds urban development workshops. For the municipal services, the Centre for Urban Studies of the IIPA, New Delhi, organizes training courses in urban and municipal administration besides undertaking research in municipal affairs. The Centre also collaborates with other regional centres and academic institutions in training and research in urban administration.

9.5.5.5 Institute of Secretariat Training and Management

The old Central Secretariat Training School set up in 1948 in New Delhi was renamed as ISTM. It is a training institution for the different grades of officials working in the central secretariat and its attached offices up to middle management level as well as government employees of lower levels in state and union territories and autonomous organizations. Its training courses could be broadly grouped as follows: foundational and refresher programmes, management programmes, specialized programmes, training of trainers' programmes, secretariat programmes and behavioural science programmes. The thrust in courses includes organization and methods, office procedure, financial rules and regulations and so on.

9.5.5.6 Administrative Staff College

The ASC located at Hyderabad was established in 1957 on the recommendation of the All India Council for Technical Education and is patterned on ASC at Henley in Britain. The college provides 'a course of studies which investigates the principles and techniques of organization and administration in civil life … (and) seeks to bring together experienced executives of proved administrative capacity and gives them an opportunity of examining different administrative practices in order to prepare them for still higher responsibilities in future'.

9.5.5.7 Indian Institute of Public Administration

The IIPA, New Delhi, was established in 1954 on the recommendation of the Appleby's Report of a Survey on Public Administration in India (1953). The Ford Foundation played an important role in setting up the Indian School of Public Administration in 1958 which was modelled on the Littauer Centre at Harvard and the Maxwell School at Syracuse. The School was abolished in 1968 and today the IIPA has become a premier institution in the country for the training of senior-level civil servants of both central and state governments and executives of PSUs. Its training courses could be broadly grouped in two categories.

1. *Sponsored Programmes:* The IIPA conducts training programmes which are sponsored by (a) the Department of Personnel and Training of the Union Ministry of Personnel, Public Grievances and Pensions and (b) other ministries and agencies such as the Department of Rural Development and Bureau of Police Research and Development (GoI).
2. *Fee-Charged Programmes:* The IIPA also conducts training programmes on its own and for which participation fee is charged. As a whole the IIPA conducts about 50–60 courses (e.g., rural development administration, personnel administration, environment conservation management and financial administration) every year with 1,200–1,500 participants. The training programmes at the IIPA are designed in a pragmatic way to see that the course content is closely related to the problems of the day-to-day working of the participants. The training methodology and techniques include lectures, discussions, workshop sessions,

presentation of case studies and discussion thereon, library work and so on. Full interaction among academics, policymakers and administrators in an objective environment of the Institute is a special feature of the training programmes. These programmes are designed to secure effective administration. In recent years, the IIPA has undertaken the initiative and responsibility for conducting courses on policy formulation for members of the IAS in pursuance of the direction of the PM that the civil servants of all categories must compulsorily go in for training courses.

9.5.5.8 Specialized Training Institutions

Besides, there are a large number of specialized training institutions in the country to meet its training needs. Some of them are National Institute of Financial Management, Faridabad; National Institute of Public Finance and Policy, New Delhi; Institute of Economic Growth, New Delhi; Institute of Development Studies, Kolkata; Management Development Institute, Gurugram; V. M. National Institute of Cooperative Management, Pune.

For example, the Institute of Government Accounts and Finance, Kolkata, (set up in February 1992) imparts in-service training on government accounting, financial management, administrative and establishment matters and allied matters to officials working in the central government ministries/departments.

9.5.5.9 Department of Personnel and Training

At present the Department of Personnel and Training is under the control of Ministry of Personnel, Public Grievances and Pensions. The training division was established in April 1968 in pursuance of the recommendation made by the committee on administration dealings with the progress of implementation of the cabinet decisions on administrative improvements. Since then, the functions and responsibilities of the training division have grown manifold. The ARC in its report on personnel administration made strong recommendations concerning training. It observed that training of the various functional cadres should be the responsibility of the individual departments and ministries. However, the training division should have the overall responsibility for training in headquarters work as well as preparing personnel for entry to senior management.

The Department of Personnel and Training has now the functional responsibility of formulating a national policy for civil service training and of ensuring its implementation.

9.5.5.10 State Training Institutes

On the central pattern, most states in India have set up training institutions for the training of state civil services and members of the IAS on the state centre. The Haryana Institute of Public Administration, Gurugram, and the Punjab State Institute of Public Administration, Chandigarh, for examples, arrange training programmes in professional and general courses for their Class I and Class II employees.

In addition, most states have secretariat training centres or cells which provide working knowledge of the secretariat to the new recruits and assistants. This training is intended to introduce to the new recruits the rules, regulations and procedure relating to the work of the secretariat. For imparting in-service training in accountancy, there is the Accounts Training Institute in Panchkula, Haryana.

The subordinate staff (Class III and Class IV employees), which constitutes 97% of the state government personnel, has not been favourably treated from the standpoint of training. As compared to higher civil servants (Class I and Class II), very little attention and resources have been devoted to train the subordinate staff in the lower echelons of the hierarchy. It has been estimated that about 80% of Class III and 95% of Class IV personnel are not trained.

The NTP 2012 emphasized that training institutions should play an important role to achieve the objectives of the NTP 2012. For this, they have to keep track of international trends in training and development and assimilate them in Indian context. Further, training institutions are required to upgrade the skills of trainers/faculty members in the new and emerging training techniques and methodologies to take account of training feedback and the needs of clients. They should conduct evaluation studies to assess the impact of training programmes conducted by them on organizational performance.

9.5.6 Role of Ministry/Department

Under the NTP 2012, each ministry/department is required to adopt a systematic approach to training and shall do the following:

1. Develop a Training Management Information System (TMIS) to facilitate training and development activities of the Ministry/Department.
2. Undertake benchmarking/evaluation study of training institutions under the control of Ministry/Department to mould them as Centre of Excellence.
3. Commission surveys/studies to measure the clients'/customers' satisfaction level on the services delivered by the Ministry/Department.
4. Review the implementation of the Annual Training Plan, Cadre Training Plan and the functioning of Training Institution(s) under the Ministry/Department (including attached/subordinate offices) and in particular to look at the:
   a. Utilization of training capacity;
   b. Quality of training conducted;
   c. Adequacy of the physical and training infrastructure, faculty, finances and delegation of powers for carrying out the institute's mandate;
   d. Training of the Group B and C staff, particularly those at the cutting-edge level (as may be applicable); and
   e. Proper selection and development of faculty, incentives for them and stability of their tenure. The conduct and character of the selected faculty should be demonstrative of the ethics and values taught in the classroom.[74]

[74] GoI, Ministry of Personnel, Public Grievances and Pensions, Department of Personal and Training Division, *National Training Policy 2012* (New Delhi: Training Division, 2012), 11.

9.5.7 Inadequacy and Effectiveness for Training

From the foregoing discussion, it is clear that, although training in the civil service in India has acquired relative importance, it is, in fact, faced with a large number of complex problems. The main reason for this is that training is considered an important mechanism of change. And change in the civil service inevitably results in disturbing the established practices and methods that civil servants have been using for most of their lives. They can accept new techniques and methods, but these offer resistance to changes in their own areas of work, especially when these are proposed by people who are less familiar with the business in hand. Training must, therefore, refurbishes personnel with mental calibre and competence.

It is important to relate training to jobs and careers. For this, jobs should first be analysed into a series of activities; second, necessary skills and methods should be identified to conduct these activities; and third, steps should be taken to impart training to the employees who need to know more to do these jobs. This sort of job-oriented training, although neglected to a large extent, may be supplemented by career or development training with a view to fitting the right civil servant into the right job. This is the most important guiding principle of the civil service training. To quote from a United Nations publication: 'Training can be effective only if the knowledge and skills acquired by the trainees can be and actually are used for performance improvement and also if successful training is really helping the trainees in their career development'.[75] It is also very important to determine the needs of the training of civil servants and the appropriate selection of them (employees). It has been found that most departments have been sending those employees who are likely to receive only minimal benefit from the training because they are the ones who can least upset developmental work. On the other hand, in many cases, departments have declined to send nominations for various training and development courses on the ground that their limited manpower did not permit them to do so. It is suggested that departmental heads should develop a more positive attitude towards training and development of their personnel. They should send only those employees who have requisite potential for development and who are most likely to benefit from participation in the training.

The research reveals that adequate financial and staff resources are not invested on training programmes. The availability of sufficient fund and competent training staff has always been a problem in the civil service. Since the money spent on training programmes is investment,[76] it will be of great disadvantage in the long run if financial considerations are allowed to abridge the scope and effectiveness of such programmes.

To ensure better performance of training programmes in the civil service, a good deal of emphasis should be laid on employing competent and experienced staff to direct them. The civil service should develop adequate training programmes to meet the needs of all parts of it and all levels. A survey of the training programmes arranged in the civil service reveals that such programmes are lopsided and uneven. While civil servants in some departments have the benefit of training and development opportunities, in other departments similar opportunities are not offered. An excessive dependence upon external resources will contribute little to developing internal resources of the departments concerned in the long run.

---

[75] United Nations, Department of Economic and Social Affairs, *Development Administration: Current Approaches and Trends in Public Administration for National Development* (United Nations Publication, Sales No. E.76 II, H.I.), 97.

[76] N. K. Bhojwani, 'Training of Public Servants in a Developing Economy', *Indian Journal of Public Administration* 3, no. 4 (October–December 1961): 447.

The study also indicates that most of the training programmes are arranged for higher civil servants (Classes I and II). Training for subordinate class, which constitutes 97% of the government personnel, is largely neglected. It has been roughly estimated that about 85% of the Class III and 95% of Class IV personnel are presently untrained. Again, these programmes are incapable of providing the degree of flexibility required to cater to individual needs. The training of civil servants of those at junior levels is stressed particularly those who are generally at the cutting-edge of the administration.

Finally, the study indicates that there is the continuing problem of lack of professional courses in Hindi. At present, most of the training and development programmes conducted by departments and agencies are only in English. It goes without saying that until the civil service in India is able to remove this shortcoming and provide all of its training and development programmes both in English and Hindi, the government's goal of promoting the regional language of Hindi in the public administration will remain unfulfilled. Also, the syllabi and methods of training need to be revamped and modern techniques and audio-visual aids introduced in order to keep them abreast of the changing needs. In this connection, Mertin Heper very rightly remark:

> It is without doubt that the public administration training programmes should be coupled with changes in the overall bureaucrat milieu if one does not want to nullify the positive contributions of education. Otherwise not only are the trainees frustrated, and inclined to indifference and cynicism, but the purpose of the whole enterprise may be grossly displaced.[77]

To sum up, training has become an important aspect of administration, acquiring increasing support at all levels of government and requiring adequate resources both in man and material. It has assumed far-reaching importance for its role in the improvement of administrative capability.[78]

9.6. Indiscipline in Civil Services

Since the advent of Independence, there has also bean cases of indiscipline in almost all ranks of the civil service. This affects adversely on the efficiency of administration. It is observed that the procedural requirements are so stringent that there is always a reasonable chance of the civil servant getting off lightly. Further, it is noticed that ministerial intervention or some other political influence is invoked to lighten the disciplinary action. Although such intervention is based, primarily on misplaced compassion, it undermines the discipline.

The service rules and provisions in the code of conduct state clearly that no government employee should approach authorities outside the proper official channel for any help in service matters. In fact, however, such approaches are being reported daily, and it is becoming difficult to take notice of the violation of rules on the subject. This practice is encouraging indiscipline. Unless this practice is discouraged that any intervention outside the official channel will be ignored, it is very difficult to arrest the growth of indiscipline.

---

[77] Mertin Heper, 'Public Administration Training for Potential Bureaucratic Elites' in *Development Digest* 15, no. 4 (October 1977): 21.

[78] Radhakrishnan Sapru, 'Development Administration: An Approach to Administrative Capability for Development', *Administrative Science Review* 9, no. 3 (Dacca: BIPA, September 1979): 45–46.

It is equally important to provide that representations of grievances are dealt with effectively and efficiently. In dealing with the question of disciplinary action, it is equally necessary to balance the requirements of natural justice and security on the one hand, with the need for speedy and effective action on the other. Discipline should, therefore, be given a new thinking. The rules and the procedure prescribed for disciplinary action are designed to make the delinquent afford the maximum opportunity of pleading and clearing himself. But the process is dilatory and cumbersome. Disciplinary proceedings are both protracted and involved. Higher officials invariably, therefore, overlook minor lapses, rather than initiate distasteful time-consuming departmental proceedings.

The Second ARC recommended that 'the minimum statutory disciplinary and dismissal procedures required to satisfy the criteria of natural justice should be spelt out leaving the details of the procedure to be followed to the respective government departments'. Further, it recommended that 'no penalty of removal and dismissal should be imposed, except by an Authority, which is at least three levels above the post which the government is holding'.[79]

It is therefore imperative to simplify the procedure appropriately, but without compromising the essentials of natural justice. Based on the recommendation of the Committee on Prevention of Corruption (1964), headed by K. Santhanam, the CCS (Conduct) Rules 1964 were revised and notified laying down the code of conduct for central government employees. The Second ARC in its report recommended that the following should be included in the code of ethics for civil servants:

1. *Integrity:* Civil servants should be guided solely by public interest in their official decision-making and not by any financial or other consideration either in respect of themselves, their families or their friends.
2. *Impartiality:* Civil servants in carrying out their official work, including functions like procurement, recruitment, delivery of services and so on should take decisions based on merit and free from any partisan consideration.
3. *Commitment to public service:* Civil servants should deliver services in a fair, effective, impartial and courteous manner.
4. *Open accountability:* Civil servants are accountable for their decisions and actions and should be willing to subject themselves to appropriate scrutiny for this purpose.
5. *Devotion to duty:* Civil servants should maintain absolute and unstinting devotion towards their duties and responsibilities at all times.
6. *Exemplary behaviour:* Civil servants should treat all members of the public with respect and courtesy and at all times should behave in a manner that upholds the rich traditions of the civil services.[80]

9.7 Senior Civil Servants: Challenges and Role

Specific rationality, which was Weber's ultimate criteria for efficiency,[81] could be obtained through the exercise of control based on knowledge. Weber put it as, 'Bureaucratic administration means

---

[79] Second ARC, *Report on Organization Structure*, 328–29. The Union Finance Ministry dismissed 72 tax officers and prematurity retired another 33 Indian Revenue Service Officers for non-performance and on disciplinary grounds. See *Business Standard* (Chandigarh), 12 May 2016.

[80] Second ARC, *Report on Organization Structure*, 331.

[81] R. M. Weiss, 'Weber on Bureaucracy: Management Consultant or Political Theorist', *Academy of Management Review* 8, no. 2 (1983): 242–48.

fundamentally the exercise of control on the basis of knowledge'.[82] This is its specifically rational character, and 'bureaucratic authority is specifically rational in the sense of being bound to discursively analysable rules'.[83]

Pfiffner and Presthus defined bureaucracy as 'the system of authority, men, offices and methods, that government uses to carry out its programmes'.[84]

The term 'bureaucracy' may be defined as an administrative organization consisting of a legal body of non-elective employed officials and organized hierarchically in departments in accordance with rules governing their employment conditions.

Higher Civil Servants: As for the term 'higher civil servants', it is defined as 'the relatively permanent top group of civil servants' who are placed between the political decision-makers and the rank-and-file bureaucracy and who share, in different degrees, the task of directing the various administrative agencies.[85]

9.7.1 The Challenge Before Civil Services

Here is an attempt to analyse the role of the bureaucrats or civil servants or administrators—call it what you like—in a setting of societal transformation of a developing country with special reference to India. The desirable roles that administrators play is a subject receiving growing attention in developed as well as developing countries. Accepted patterns of recruitment, training and careers of administrators, especially senior ones, are increasingly recognized as inadequate for meeting new challenges. A few illustrations from increasingly recognized inadequacies of them are given below:

1. Despite enormous progress over the past generation, more than 30% of the people in developing countries, including India, still live in acute poverty and suffer grossly inadequate access to such resources as education, health services, infrastructure, land and credit. The primary obstacles to development are administrative, rather than economic. Most administrators lack the administrative capability for implementing development policies and programmes.
2. Relationships between senior administrators and political elites are unsatisfactory, mainly due to lack of cooperation between operationalization of initiatives on policies by politicians and working them out by senior administrators.
3. Advances in science and technology and their far-going consequences for all aspects of society pose complex issues requiring professional inputs for their comprehension which the present senior officials are not qualified to provide. David C. Potter discovered that bureaucracy could not easily cope with problems requiring innovation, specialist expertise and responsiveness to local demands.[86]
4. Senior administrators in the newly independent developing countries have grave difficulties in handling changing interfaces between governments and citizens. For example, S. R.

---

[82] Max Weber, *The Theory of Social and Economic Organization*, 339.

[83] Ibid., 361.

[84] John M. Pfiffner and Robert V. Presthus, *Public Administration, 4th ed.* (New York: Ronald Press, 1960), 40.

[85] Hahn-Been Lee, 'The Role of the Higher Civil Service Under Rapid Social and Political Change', in *Development Administration in Asia*, ed. Edward W. Weidner (Durham: Duke University Press, 1970), 108.

[86] David C. Potter, *Indian Political Administrators, 1919–83* (Oxford: Clarendon Press, 1986), 236–45.

Maheswari points out that under the Constitution of Independent India, 'the administrative system was called upon to undergo an attitudinal change' in order to serve the people. But such a transformation could not be accomplished. For under the British regime, 'it was aloof, distant, domineering, even haughty in its relationship with the people'.[87]

5. There seems to be little doubt that under conditions of widespread corruption, administrative performance and economic development decline below optimal levels and thus lower general welfare. K. R. Hope explains, 'In developing states bureaucratic administration has been transformed into an institution that emphasizes the sovereignty of politics rather than the supremacy of administration'.[88]

O. P. Dwivedi has rightly stated that

> For politicians, expediency circumventing the established administrative norms, and blatant use of power and authority for personal benefit have become the necessary instruments of governance. Naturally, in such an environment, many administrators get coopted or join the venal group in order to avail themselves of similar privileges and wealth. This unholy partnership is frightening those administrators who are unable to stand against such activities because of the fear of being transferred to remote postings, harassed, or even punished on flimsy grounds.[89]

Legitimacy of public administration is being challenged in the context of privatization of public enterprises. In Stever's view, 'Public administration must appear to both elected officials and the public as a crucial function to the maintenance of society. Furthermore, the civil servant must achieve a certain mystique in the performance of these crucial functions'.[90]

In brief, the rise in aspirations of the people in India has compelled the centre and state governments to adopt policies for alleviating poverty and improving the quality of life of all sections of society. But the machinery of government and the procedures which have hitherto been followed are not always in consonance with the growing needs. With the increase in the size and complexity of government operations, greater responsibilities are being placed on senior administrators. Their role is becoming more complex and it has to combine a variety of skills and capabilities. They are being called upon to respond dynamically to the processes of economic and social change. They are expected to be less legalistic and more result-oriented in their developmental approach. They are being asked to place priority on productivity, development of human resources, return on investment and capacity utilization. Hence, the role of senior administrators has come to be recognized universally as part of a strategic effort in the modernization of national administrative systems for development.

---

[87] S. R. Maheshwari, 'Strengthening Administration Capabilities in India', *Public Administration and Development* 4, (1984): 50.

[88] K. R. Hope, 'Administrative Corruption and Administrative Reform in Developing States', *Corruption and Reform* 2, no. 2 (1987): 128.

[89] O. P. Dwivedi, 'Administrative Heritage, Morality and Challenges in the Sub-continent since the British Raj', *Public Administration and Development* 9, no. 3 (June–August 1989): 250.

[90] J. A. Stever, *The End of Public Administration* (New York: Dobbs Ferry, 1988).

9.7.2 The Role of Senior Civil Servants

The term 'senior administrators' has been used more often than commonly understood. While the definition of senior administrators varies depending upon the system of public service a country has adopted, there are certain elements which generally characterize them.

First, structurally, senior administrators hold posts in the top three grades of the public service, although they may be assigned to different levels of administration.

Second, in terms of functions, senior administrators are officials responsible for the management of a major function of government, ranging from law and order to national development.

Third, from the point of view of power, senior administrators have statutory authority which is used for influencing decisions including those concerning the allocation of human and physical resources.

Numerically, senior administrators represent a small group in the public service, largely drawn from members of the generalist administrative cadre of the career civil service, who have come up through competitive examinations after formal education and training at successive levels. They constitute an important component of governance. They exercise much more power than their formal authority suggests. By virtue of their functions, senior administrators enjoy considerable influence, power and prestige in society. The development roles of the higher-level bureaucracy (senior administrators) can be divided into five major categories.

9.7.2.1 Role in Policy Formulation and Implementation

In most developing countries, the political leadership which took over administration from a colonial power was preoccupied with several problems other than economic and social development. Some of them continue to be preoccupied with internal political tensions. In many cases, the political leadership lacks the required expertise and professional skills for development planning. Under these circumstances, the role of senior administrators in the formulation of development policy becomes all the more important.

The functions of senior administrators, as conventionally recognized, encompass the formulation of policy, coordination and improvement of administrative machinery and the exercise of general administrative control over departments of public services. Further, senior administrators are required to assist in the preparation of legislative measures and to ensure that government decisions are properly implemented. They also advise on the financial and administrative implications of different policy alternatives. In many instances, their 'advisory' role transforms itself into virtually the most effective factor in the determination of policies.

Besides participation in making policies, senior administrators are involved in implementing them and giving directions to the lower levels of bureaucracy for this purpose. They also monitor the implementation process.

For successful implementation of policies, administrators are responsible for mobilization and managing of resources required to carry through these policies. They translate the general policy and its objectives into operational targets.

9.7.2.2 Advice on Financial and Administrative Implications

The senior administrators have the responsibility of advising on the financial and administrative implications of different policy alternatives. Being more aware than the politicians about the financial resources and possible expenditure involved, administrators determine the allocation of funds for the implementation of plans according to priorities. At times in India, this major task has led to the selection of public servants as political leaders for financial policy.

9.7.2.3 As an Agent of Change

Senior administrators have the responsibility to work as agents of change. Exhorting the civil servants to be 'agents of change' and work as a team aiming to 'reform, perform and transform', PM Modi said on 21 April 2016 that over the years, the scope of a civil servant's task had changed from a regulator to administrator to controller to one with keen managerial skills. 'Often senior civil servants are too tired of work, leading to interruptions and implementation of government schemes they have to be cautious against this tired attitudes'.[91]

9.7.2.4 Training Function

Once a policy has been made, it becomes the responsibility of senior administrators to interpret it to the lower levels of bureaucracy and to train the latter in the methods to be adopted to achieve its goals. This major task is performed through training institutes, conferences and communication media. Senior administrators are expected to devote some time in training junior administrators working under them.

It is equally important that senior officials also learn from the knowledge of their juniors who probably know better ways to do a task.

9.7.2.5 Political Dimension to the Role

A large number of politicians in India however project a different view of the role of senior administrators. By and large, they tend to regard them as instruments for facilitating and carrying out political dictates, and thus may even use them as scapegoats for achieving certain political ends.

Students of public administration view the role of senior administrators in terms of dimension of power and authority in order to get things done. They may exercise the authority of expertise. Some senior administrators exhibit more preoccupation with intra-administrative matters of personnel and finance and less with policy and plan issues.

9.7.3 Conclusion

In essence senior administrators are responsible for policy analysis and advice, for the management of the department or offices entrusted to them, as well as for the implementation and monitoring of programmes, for mobilization of resources and provision of leadership for the realization

[91] See *The Times of India* (Chandigarh), 22 April 2016.

of certain goals. With the tasks of the public service being more numerous, complex and varied, there is now need for competent and achievement-oriented senior administrators to cope with the changing needs of society.

PM Modi, in his meeting with the senior and middle-level bureaucrats of eight states (Gujarat, Haryana, Himachal Pradesh, Jammu and Kashmir, Punjab, Rajasthan, Punjab and Uttarakhand), advised them to 'be quick in making decision and keep the common Indian in mind when you do so. Be truthful, work without fear and bring in the same energy and enthusiasm that you had when you joined the IAS Academy'.[92]

9.7.3.1 Constraints in Role

1. *Disagreement with political leadership:* Despite their vast experience and a near monopoly of knowledge, senior administrators are often not in agreement with the political leadership on several issues. Such disagreements can force them to become yes-men. Navanit Sinha observes that all India civil servants cease to be civil. 'They almost become integrated into the political set-up sharing the spoils when in power; and if suffering deprivations, they shift their loyalties to new political elites well in time'.[93]
2. *Resisting new ideas and innovations:* Most senior administrators often tend to resist new ideas and innovations suggested by foreign experts or their own junior officials who have been educated and trained in modern skills. Such resistance stems from their unwillingness as well as fear that technically qualified junior persons may oust them from the chairs of power and authority they hold.

   Further, those who were trained under the traditional operations approach (maintaining law and order, provision of some limited services) of the colonial rule found themselves inadequate in dealing with the processes of economic and social change. In this context, Kuldeep Mathur observes, 'In the day-to-day administration, in the development tasks, and in the nation-building activities, the task of reorienting the administrative ethos has not been an easy one. Disillusionment with administrative performance stems from this perceived failure'.[94]
3. *Supremacy of superiority but lack of commitment*

Senior officials are able to argue from positions of great strength due to their seniority and high salary. A closer analysis will generally prove that many of them occupy higher positions not necessarily because of special skill or technological expertise, but because of seniority and even patronage. Having entered the AIS at an early age (between 21 and 25), many have come to the top by length of service or promotion, but at the same time may not take interest in developmental activities. Senior bureaucrats possess more substantive interests in maintaining the status quo and do not wish to stretch their authority to see that proper implementation takes place.[95]

---

[92] See *The Economic Times* (Chandigarh), 6 April 2017.

[93] Navanit Sinha, 'Role and Rational of All India Service', *The Indian Journal of Public Administration* 37, no. 1 (January–March 1991): 103.

[94] Kuldeep Mathur, 'Bureaucracy in India: Development and Pursuit of Self-interest', *The Indian Journal of Public Administration* 37, no. 4 (October–December 1991): 640.

[95] India, Planning Commission, *Report on Agrarian Relations* (New Delhi: Planning Commission, 1973), 9.

Some of them are inefficient and unresponsive in the face of new challenges and some enjoy political patronage. Prem Latha Bansal, in her study of the IAS, concludes that

> the ability of the Indian administrative system to carry out a planned programme of socio-economic development has been limited, perhaps partly due to lack of commitment to the ultimate goals of society, and partly due to its inability to mobilise enough public support for developmental programmes, because of its authoritarian attitude.[96]

Further, it has been argued that the administrators of the post-Independence India were as elitist and west-oriented as their counterparts during colonial rule. Many of them continued to be alienated from the poor sections of the community and did not possess requite behavioural traits to administer the development tasks initiated by the government.

Summary

Good governance and sustainable development have come to be recognized as goals of government of our country. These cherished goals need to be translated by the joint efforts of executive, legislature, judiciary, civil service, private sector and active participation by the civil society. Technically, public organizations manned by personnel have the major responsibility to implement, execute and enforce development goals and governing laws and policies. Democracy flourishes and citizens gain the fruits of good governance when government institutions are goal-oriented and people-centred.

Civil services have an added responsibility for this institution is involved not only in the formulation of public goals but also in taking decisions and implementing them. Resources (personnel, finance, equipment or enforcement assignments) must be given to the civil servants to carry out their implementation tasks. In fact, resources are critical inputs between public policymakers and civil servants. For the civil service is an indispensable component of the government.

Recently, in a major push to bring in "fresh energy and idea" in formulating and implementing public policies, the Centre has decided to allow private sector specialists to have lateral entry into the government at the joint secretary level.[97]

---

[96] Prem Latha Bansal, *Administrative Development in India* (New Delhi: Sterling Publishers, 1974), 136.
[97] See *The Tribune* (Chandigarh), 11 June 2018.

Appendix I

List of Posts/Services Excluded from the Purview of the Union Public Service Commission since the Issue of the UPSC (Exemption from Consultation) Regulations on 1 September 1958

Schedule I

(Posts excluded for the purposes of Article 320(3)(a) and (b) of the Constitution.)

S. No.	Designation of the Posts/Services	Date from which Excluded
1.	All Civil and Criminal judicial posts in Union Territories under the control of a High Court or a Court of a Judicial Commissioner, other than those included in Item (7).	1.9.1958
2.	Posts in the secretariat and personal staff of the president and the vice-president.	26.3.1962
3.	Posts in Government Hospitality Organisation under the Ministry of External Affairs.	26.3.1962
4.	Posts of National Research Professor under the Ministry of Education.	25.3.1963
5.	Posts of Consultant and Chief Consultant in the Planning Commission.	25.4.1964
6.	Posts of Private Secretary to the Solicitor General of India and the Additional Solicitor General of India.	14.4.1965
7.	Judicial Commissioners, Additional Judicial Commissioners, District Judges, Session Judges, Additional District Judges and Additional Sessions Judges in Union Territories.	9.3.1966
8.	All the Services and Posts under or connected with the organization dealing with external intelligence in the Government of India vide the UPSC (Exemptions from Consultation) Supplementary Regulations, 1970.	14.8.1970
9.	Group 'B' Ministerial posts in the Intelligence Bureau other than the posts of Section Officer.	12.2.1973
10.	All technical and administrative posts in or under (a) the Department of Space and (b) Space Commission.	14.11.1974
11.	All technical and administrative posts in under (a) the Department of Electronics and (b) Electronics Commission.	13.8.1975
12.	Recruitment/Promotions of scientific and technical personnel in the Defence Research and Development Organisation (DRDO) under the Ministry of Defence.	18.5.1985
13.	All Group 'A' and Group 'B' posts in or under the Central Administrative Tribunal.	10.1.1986

(Continued)

(Continued)

S. No.	Designation of the Posts/Services	Date from which Excluded
14.	Scientific posts in the Ministry of Science and Technology, Department of Ocean Development, Department of Non-Conventional Energy Sources and the Department of Environment, Forests and Wild-Life, as specified in the Annexure to the DOP&T Notification No. 390l/2/96 Estt. B dated 1.4.87 except in respect of appointment to be made thereto by promotion through the DPC\Amendment vide DOP & T Notification No. 39018/96 Estt. B dated 6.5.96.	6.5.1996
15.	Group 'B' (Non-Gazette) posts of Assistants and Stenographers Grade 'C' to be filled by direct recruitment through open competitive examination.	7.9.1989
16.	Post of Advisers and equivalent in the Planning Commission in the scale of ₹5,900–8,000 except where they are required to be filled under the Senior Starting Scheme or those included in any organized service.	7.9.1989
17.	Group 'B' Non-gazetted posts in the Department of Telecommunications.	29.12.1989
18.	Group 'B' non-gazetted posts under the Andaman and Nicobar Islands and Lakshadweep Administration.	18.9.1990
19.	Posts/Services to the exclusion of which the Commission agreed under Item (20) of the Schedule to the UPSC (Exemption from Constitution) Regulations:	1963–64
	i. Posts connected with the Special Border Security Scheme under the Ministry of External Affairs.	22.7.1960
	ii. Posts in the Central Reserve Police and the Indo-Tibetan Border Force.	4.8.1988
	iii. Posts in the High Commission of India, London and in other Indian Missions abroad to which recruitment is made locally by the respective Indian Missions.	
20.	Post of Examiner of Patents and Designs, Assistant Controller of Patents and Designs, Deputy Controller of Patents and Designs, Joint Controller of Patents and Designs, Sr. Joint Controller of Patents and Designs, Deputy Chief Executive Officer, Senior Documentation Officer, Senior Reprography Officer. Junior Documentation Officer, Reprography Officer and Senior Programmer in the Patent Office under the Department of Industrial Development, Ministry of Industry.	6.7.1999
21.	Post of Lt. General, Scientist 'H' Major General, Scientist 'G' Secretary, Addl. Secretary, Joint Secretary, Director, Deputy Secretary, Under Secretary, Principal Private Secretary, Senior System Analyst, Research Officer, Private Secretary Section Officer, Protocol Officer, Research Assistant, Personal Assistant, Protocol Assistant, Senior Librarian and Information Assistant and Draftsman Grade 'I' in the National Security Council Secretariat, Cabinet Secretariat.	31.1.2001

S. No.	Designation of the Posts/Services	Date from which Excluded
22.	Professor of Law, Lal Bahadur Shastri National Academy of Administration, Mussoorie.	31.1.2003
23.	All posts under the National Technical Research Organisation	14.7.2005
24.	Posts of Director Generals of the Archaeological Survey of India, New Delhi, the National Archives of India, New Delhi and the National Museum, New Delhi and the posts of Directors of the National Gallery of Modern Art, New Delhi, the Anthropological Survey of India, Kolkata, the National Library, Kolkata, and the National Research Laboratory for Conservation of Cultural Property, Lucknow and the post of the Librarian in the Central Reference Library, Kolkata, under the Ministry of Culture.	30.04.2009
25.	Post of Chief Economic Adviser, Department of Economic Affairs.	22.7.2009

Source: UPSC, Sixtieth Annual Report 2009–10 (New Delhi, 2011).

Schedule II

Posts Excluded for the Purposes of Article 320(3) (b) of the Constitution of India

S. No.	Designation of the Posts/Services	Date from which Excluded
1.	Group B Non-gazetted posts under the Ministry of Water Resources.	13.11.1991
2.	Direct recruitment to all Group B posts in the various ministries/departments of the Government of India and their attached and subordinate offices and which are in the scale of pay, the maximum of which is below ₹10,500/-	21.5.1999
3.	Direct recruitment to all non-gazetted posts carrying the pay scale of ₹6,500–10,500/-.	29.9.2005
4.	Post of Special Director of Enforcement in the Enforcement Directorate in the pay scale of ₹16,400–20,000/-.	1.6.2006
5.	Post of Deputy Secretary in the pay band – 3 of ₹15,600–39,100/- with grade pay of ₹7,600/- and Director in the pay band – 4 of ₹37,400–67,000/- in the grade pay of ₹8,700/- of Central Secretariat Services (CCS).	30.7.2008
6.	Recruitment on deputation basis as may be made at any time within a period of three years to the post of Superintendent of Police (non-IPS), Additional Superintendent of Police, Deputy superintendent of Police, Deputy Legal Advisor, Senior Public Prosecutor, Public Prosecutor, Senior System Analyst, Programmer, Assistant Programmer, Network Administrator, Senior Private Secretary, Stenographer Grade-C/Personal Assistant, Assistant and Accountant in the National Investigation Agency under the Ministry of Home Affairs, for full deputation tenure	6.1.2010

Source: UPSC, Sixtieth Annual Report 2009–10 (New Delhi, 2011).

10 District Administration: Governance Practice

LEARNING OBJECTIVES

1. **To highlight the purposes and role of district administration**
2. **To analyse the role of DC after India's Independence**
3. **To examine the relationship between the DM and the district SP**

Introduction

Government goals and strategic directions towards governance carry meanings when they really contribute to the common man's prosperity and happiness. It is this 'governance' that the common man feels when he comes into direct contact with the administration at the district level—village, town or sub-urban. Before we discuss the purposes and role of district administration and its functionaries (deputy commissioner, sub-divisional officer or SDO, village headman, mainly charged with responsibility of general affairs of the government), it seems imperative to define what we mean by the term 'district administration'.

District is the basic territorial unit of administration in India, and district administration is the 'total functioning of government in a district'.[1] Potter defines 'district administration' as 'the total action of government in an area specified as a district by a state government'.[2] *Oxford Dictionary* defines 'district administration' as the 'territory marked off for special administrative purpose'. District administration, broadly, is the management of affairs within a basic territorial unit called 'district'.

As of January 2018, there are a total of 712 districts, up from 640 in the 2011 Census of India and 593 recorded in the 2001 Census of India.[3] The formation or reorganization of a new district is the subject matter of state administration. District being the territorial unit of administration is created by the state government, and its boundary can be altered by the government for administrative convenience.

---

[1] S. S. Khera, *District Administration*, 2nd ed. (New Delhi: National, 1979), 79.
[2] D. C. Potter, *Government in Rural India* (London: G. Bell & Sons, 1964), 8.
[3] Telangana state, which was carved out of Andhra Pradesh on 11 October 2016, has 31 districts (2017).

Origin of District Administration

District administration, as it stands today, has a long history. Its origin can be traced to the territorial structure of administration of the Mauryan Period. The unwieldy Mauryan Empire had to be split up into territorial units of administration of manageable size and placed under the charge of *rajuka* (provincial official) who corresponded to the present-day deputy commissioner. Although essentially a revenue official, the *rajuka* also exercised judicial functions, carried on public works, such as irrigation, roads and so on. In the Mauryan Period, revenue villages were called *gramas*, a group of revenue villages was called *stana* or *taluk*, several *stanas* were called *aharas* or *district*, a group of districts was called a *pradesh* or the region (state) and several *pradesh* were called the *janapada* or a province.

During the times of the Guptas, the Empire was divided into provinces, probably known as *desas*, the province into *bhuktis*, which were about the size of a commissioner's division, and the *bhuktis* into *visayas*, roughly corresponding to a modern district. The *visaya* was placed in charge of a *visayapati*, who was responsible for maintenance of law and order and the collection of taxes and revenues.

Similar territorial units of district administration existed under the *mohammadan* rulers. Under the Delhi Sultanate, the Empire was divided into provinces, the provinces into *shiqs* which were put under *shiqdars*. Sher Shah Suri divided the Empire into *sarkars* and the *sarkars* into *parganas*. The latter became the basic unit of administration and was administered by an *amin*, a revenue official, who was assisted by a *fotadar*, a treasurer, and a *shiqdar*, who was a military officer. This system served as a model to Akbar's revenue minister, Raja Todar Mal, and may also be regarded as forming the basis of the British system of revenue administration.

Mughals also followed the system of district administration. The Empire was divided into *subas*, the *subas* into *sarkars* and *sarkars* into *parganas*. The *sarkar* was the counterpart of the modern district. The *sarkar* was placed in charge of a *faujdar*, a military officer, whose duties were to maintain peace and order, keep the army well-equipped and read for service and to assist the *amalguzar*, the collector of revenue of the *sarkar*, in revenue collection.

The British adopted Mughal patterns, spread the system throughout the country, and adapted its operating mechanisms to suit the imperial need. The *diwani* grant to the EIC in 1765 by the effete Mughal Emperor led the British Government in the realization of the two objects it had in view, namely, the collection of revenue and the consolidation of its authority in an alien land. Consequently in 1772, the Governor General Warren Hastings dismissed the Indian *naib diwans* (for collection of revenue) and posted the EIC's servants to the charge of fiscal district as collectors. The official was invested with civil jurisdiction under the 'judicial plan' of 1772, but this arrangement was short-lived. However, in 1786 (the district was made the basis of Indian administration in 1786), a decentralized system was evolved under which the collectors were charged with the civil administration of the district exercising revenue, judicial as well as magisterial powers.[4] This involved the division of the provinces of Bengal, Bihar and Orissa into small districts, each under the charge of a collector who was also made the judge and magistrate.

This combination of judicial and executive functions in one functionary was altered in 1793 by Governor General Lord Cornwallis, who separated the two. The revenue functions were assigned to the collector and general administration, police, civil-judicial and criminal judicial functions to

[4] Haridwar Rai, 'The Changing Role of the District Collector', in *District Administration*, ed. T. N. Chaturvedi and R. B. Jain (New Delhi: IIPA, 1980), 17.

a judge-magistrate. In 1839, there were three top officers in the district, namely, DM for law and order, the DC for revenue collection and district judge for civil and higher criminal cases.

In contrast to the Cornwallis system was the Monro School of district administration, which evolved in the first decade of the 19th century in the provinces of Madras, Bombay and North-West Frontier Province (NWFP). Under this system (built on the ancient custom), the officer responsible for collection of revenue was vested with extensive judicial authority as well. The DC became the real head and effective ruler of the district and exercised wide discretionary power. He was responsible for the welfare of the people and the general administration of the district. This was the paternalistic or the patriarchal system of district administration under which the conception of the duties of the district officer was comprehensive, requiring the constant exercise of his faculties and making him active, alert and dynamic.

After the Sepoy Mutiny in 1857, two offices of collector and magistrate were reunited in provinces administered under the Cornwallis system. The collector-magistrate became the head of the district in 1859. The years between 1857 and 1909 witnessed strong concentration of powers in the hands of the collector. Macaulay is reported to have observed, 'Such a power as that collectors in India have over the people of India is not found in any other part of the world possessed by any class of functionaries'.[5] O'Malley in his work, *The Indian Civil Service*, pointed out that the functions and powers which were concentrated in the office of the collector made him an overburdened official.[6] District work was essentially autocratic, involving very little consultation among equals.

The Royal Commission on Decentralization (1907–1909) and the GoI Act, 1919 did not undermine the collector's authority in any way. The Simon Commission (1930) also disapproved of the weakening of the collector's position. The GoI Act, 1935, however, diluted the collector's authority in the sense that he had now to work in collaboration with the elected ministers. Provincial authority granted under this Act did not last long and the beginning of the Second World War (1939–45) put an end to this short-lived experiment. This system with concentration of powers (DM for law and order, DC for revenue collection and district judge for civil and criminal cases) in one person for running of the district administration continued and remained basically unaltered until the end of the British Administration in India in 1947. In the1970s, judicial powers were taken away from the DM and given to the district judge.

10.1 Purposes and Role of District Administration

There are, broadly speaking, three purposes of district administration, of which maintenance of law and order is the top most. The other two are (a) revenue and land records administration and (b) promotion of public welfare.

For D. C. Potter, the purposes of district administration are to (a) maintain the district in a state of law and order, (b) ensure that justice shall be done and rule of law shall prevail, (c) assess and collect a number of taxes, that is, land revenue, irrigation rates, agricultural income tax and so on, (d) ensure that the land which is the major sources of the people is properly administered,

---

[5] British Parliament, *Parliamentary Debates*, 3rd Series, CXXVIII (24 June 1853), 745–46.

[6] For more details, see L. S. S. O'Malley, *The Indian Civil Service 1601–1930* (London: John Murray, 1934), 111.

(e) exercise various regulatory and control functions of the government and (f) take immediate action in case of a calamity or disaster and the like.[7]

District administration, in order to be effective, must have a unity of purpose and singularity of approach which is often found missing.[8] The second PM of India, Lal Bahadur Shastri, said,

> The entire team in a district has to work with a sense of dedication in the same manner as a soldier on the battle front. The district officer should regard himself in all humility as a commander who has to organize this drive and achieve the target which must be clearly laid down.[9]

With the withdrawal of power under the Independence Act, 1947, the focus of district administration shifted to welfare and developmental activities. The introduction of Panchayati Raj institutions in the rural district clipped the role of the DC. The reorganization of the district administration, integration of the activities of various developmental agencies, and linking up of local self-governing institutions with the state administrative departments strengthened the functions and role of the district officers. The organizational dimension of district administration with the 73rd Constitutional Amendment acquired greater complexity. With the introduction of decentralization of administrative machinery, the provisioning of adequate coordinating mechanisms at the local level and involvement of people at every state of planning and implementation of development programmes, the district-level administration acquired greater complexity in recent years.

Recently, the cabinet secretary of the GoI has circulated a 39 actionable points directive to all secretaries of all ministries asking them to spend 5–6 days a month in the field.[10] The directive is largely on 'how the governance needs to be revamped to give it a human touch and an efficient turnaround'.

10.1.1 Structure and Functionaries

The district is further divided into levels at division, sub-division, tehsil, pargana[11] and village. Mainly the structure of administration at the district level consists of district (as a whole), sub-division (revenue division), tehsil (consisting of 200–600 villages), pargana (a circle in Punjab and Maharashtra, pargana in Uttar Pradesh and *firka* in Tamil Nadu) and village (lowest unit for all administrative and fiscal purposes). The representative of the government in the village is the *patwari* (a government official who keeps records regarding the ownership of land) who is considered to be 'eyes and ears' of the collector. He holds an important position in the lower level of bureaucracy. The DC through the Zila Parishads, blocks and gram panchayats carries out development programmes.

In addition to the DC, there are many other functionaries at the district level which include SP, chief medical officer, district and sessions judge, executive engineer, district education officer, district food and supply officer, district social welfare officer, district development officer (DDO)

---

[7] Potter, *Government in Rural India*, 15–20.

[8] P. R. Dubashi, *Essays in Public Administration* (New Delhi: NBO Publishers, 1985), 54.

[9] Cited in P. K. Dave, 'The Collector, Today and Tomorrow', in *District Administration*, ed. T. N. Chaturvedi and R. B. Jain (New Delhi: IIPA, 1980), 39.

[10] See *The Economic Times* (Chandigarh), 20 September 2017.

[11] *Pargana* is a group of villages or a subdivision of a district.

and a host of other officers. These officers keep the DC informed of their activities and report any serious matters connected with law and order to him.

Since India's Independence, there have been radical changes in the fundamental purposes of district administration. Its role has widened to include proper administration of all socio-economic programmes for the development of the district and the empowerment of people, particularly those belonging to the weaker sections of the community. The importance of good district administration has been well emphasized in various administrative reports. As per these reports, good district administration is not only essential for the speedy and proper implementation of all programmes for the development of the district, and the welfare of people, particularly those living in the rural areas, but it can also make or mar the prestige of Government.

It is at the tier of district administration that the common man comes into direct contact with the administration. Almost all the departments of state government have their field agencies in the district headquarters where people come into contact. The district is thus a multipurpose unit having vast number of officials who administer the affairs of the government. The people approach the district functionaries for various purposes, such as registration of property rights, obtaining licences and permits, obtaining general or specific services, redressal of grievances and so on. Thus, for a common man, the district administration is the government.

It is the at the district level that the policies of the state or central government are intended to be implemented. Social and economic welfare programmes set out in the state and central plans are administered by the district and local officials. Therefore, the success of any popular government depends on how its programmes, plans and policies are implemented by the district administration.

The responsibility for administration of law and order, including the protection of the life and property of the people, devolves upon the district administration. The district administration can get all departments to work harmoniously and as a team, for the welfare and the development of the people and the development of the district as a whole. It can bring about the closest possible contact and understanding between the government and people.

The district, indeed, is an image of total government writ small. Many British and Indian men of public life, who later rose to high positions in the state or central government, gained their training in the districts. It is one thing that districts taught techniques of authoritarian government. The district administration, however, was efficient and responsive to central control, if not so readily responsive to local needs. The 73rd and 74th Constitutional Amendments altered the structure of the district administration.

10.2 District Collector/Deputy Commissioner

The district is the basic unit of administration in the state. It is placed under the charge of a district officer, called DC. At the head of the district administration, the DC plays an important role in the hierarchy of state administration.

The institution of the 'DC', also called the deputy commissioner (Haryana, Punjab, Assam, Jammu and Kashmir and Karnataka) and DM (Uttar Pradesh and West Bengal), is very old and has undergone a radical change since India's Independence. As already mentioned, the office of the collector was created on 14 May 1772 by Warren Hastings for the dual purpose of collecting revenue and dispensing justice. The district was made the territorial unit of administration in 1786. In 1790, the DC was vested with the responsibility of magistracy (i.e., law and order).

However, Lord Cornwallis in 1793 withdrew judicial powers from the magistrate-collector and gave them to the judge-magistrate of the district. In 1831, powers of the DC were again increased to enable him not only to collect the revenue and maintain law and order but also to decide lower criminal cases. In 1839, three top officers in the district were entrusted with different tasks, namely, DM for law and order, the DC for revenue collection, and district judge for civil and higher criminal cases. This trifurcation of responsibility for district administration continued for over a century until the judicial powers were taken away from the DM and given to the district judge in the early 1970s.

10.2.1 District Collector: A Representative of British Empire

During the British Rule in India, the DC held a position of great importance. 'In one capacity or another, he possesses all the authority necessary to make him in the eyes of the people, the representative of the Executive Government'. Sir William Hunter described the multifarious functions and position of the district officer in 1892 as follows:

> The district officer, whether known as Collector-Magistrate or Deputy Commissioner, is the responsible head of his jurisdiction. Upon his energy and personal character depends ultimately the efficiency of our Indian Government. His own special duties are so numerous and so various as to bewilder the outsider; and the work of his subordinates, European and native, largely depends upon the stimulus of his personal example. His position has been compared to that of the French prefect, but such a comparison is unjust in many ways to the Indian district officer. He is not a mere subordinate of a central bureau, who takes his colour from his chief and represents the political parties or the permanent officialism of the capital. The Indian collector is a strongly individualized worker in every department of rural well-being, with a large measure of local independence and of individual initiative. As the name of Collector-Magistrate implies, his main functions are two-fold. He is a fiscal officer, charged with the collection of the revenue from the land and other sources. He is also a revenue and criminal judge, both of first instance and in appeal. But his title by no means exhausts his multifarious duties. He does in a smaller local sphere all that the Home Secretary superintends in England, and a great deal more; for he is the representative of a paternal and not a constitutional Government.[12]

In his account, Woodruff says that the collector was the 'imperial government embodied'.[13] On the other hand, O'Malley points out that the collector was overburdened with work.[14] Ramsay McDonald went to the extent of describing the position of the DC as 'the tortoise which supports the elephant upon which the Indian Government rests'.

Indeed, before the Montford Reforms, the deputy commissioner was an Olympian God in the district, the locus of all authority. 'He was just as mush the eyes, ears and arms of the Provincial Government as when functioning as revenue officer or district magistrate ... A single will operate in all spheres of activities in the district'.[15]

The introduction of dyarchy on 3 January 1922 in eight provinces contemplated under the Act of 1919 and provincial autonomy under the Act of 1935 diluted the collector's authority and power. Except in the spheres of law and order and collection of revenue, the deputy commissioner

[12] Quoted by S. R. Maheshwari, *Indian Administration*, 6th ed. (New Delhi: Orient Black Swan, 2013), 575.
[13] Philip Woodruff, *The Guardians* (London: Jonathan Cape, 1959), 58.
[14] O'Malley, *The Indian Civil Service*, 111.
[15] Great Britain, *Report of the Indian Statutory Commission* (London: HMSO, 1930), 301.

assumed increasingly the role of coordinator. Nevertheless, until the end of the British Rule, the DC continued to be main prop of the Indian administration.

The other side of the picture painted by some eminent writers is quite interesting and thought provoking. Referring to acts of benevolence by some collectors, Woodruff writes, 'There was Brown whose hobbies were tigers and embankments, Smith who ... planted all the roads in every district he was ever in with double avenues of trees and Jones who was building hospitals where he wasn't pigsticking'.[16]

10.3 Role of the Collector After Independence

After India's Independence, the role of the DC underwent a substantial change.[17] Main factors contributing to the emergent role are democratic decentralization, decline of administrative and moral values, political apathy, public consciousness and role of mass media and so on.

Independence brought new challenges to district officials. No longer was it considered adequate for a DC and other district officers to administer benevolently over a *status quo* society and economy. As the welfare state got underway, the collectors were asked to supervise and encourage the improvement and development of the countryside. Plans and programmes, in bits and pieces, flew out of the state governments' offices, and the collector had his hands full passing out administrative orders and forms for completion by his subordinates. Coordination, if any existed, was left to the Collector's mind. Collector's role and responsibilities in various capacities have been discussed in the following sections.

10.3.1 DC as Head of Land and Revenue Administration

Of various functions entrusted to the office of the deputy commissioner, revenue administration is probably of critical importance. Revenue administration is an important component of district administration of which the collector is the key official. In this capacity, he possesses the power of general supervision and control of the land records and their staff. The DC is responsible for collection of land revenue. He supervises collection of nearly all the government dues, which include government loans, exercise revenue, cooperative loan, agricultural dues, water rates and so on. When these dues cannot be realized, certificate proceeding course is adopted. The hallmark of any administration is its capacity to collect the dues and enforce the claims. Unfortunately, certificate proceeding is a cumbersome exercise and is the most neglected item of work in the office of the DC. It is largely experienced that collection of *taqavi* loan, agricultural or cooperative loan is very poor.

Besides being collector of government dues, the DC is the head of the revenue administration, and he is the kingpin of the relief operations in the district. In times of drought and flood, the DC is the supreme head at the district level and he is fully responsible for the relief work in the district. Of course, the distribution of relief operation has become a politically significant matter.

---

[16] Woodruff, *The Guardians*, 96.

[17] Being the key official in the District, the DC belongs to the IAS and is appointed under the land revenue code. The IAS officer may be a direct recruit or a promotee from the state civil services.

Relief funds are seldom utilized to the full. It is generally diverted to routine items of general administration thereby reducing the impact of relief operations.

The DC is the custodian of the land records which consist of basic village records, village maps, nature of the soil and so on. The collector is responsible not only for the maintenance of these records and settlement operations but also for the implementation of land reform laws. Further, he is also responsible for the acquisition of land for public purposes (housing schemes, slum clearance, etc.). He is also the head of the treasury. The treasury officers of the district work under his supervision. The power to grant licences for arms, cinemas, driving and so on brings the DC in contact with the public. He also hears appeals in revenue cases against the orders of the lower courts.

It may be briefed that the revenue work is a colossal task and, therefore, he is assisted in this function by SDOs, *naib tehsildars* (tax officer), *patwaris* and *kanungos* (subordinate to a *patwari*). Some states, such as, Andhra Pradesh, have another IAS officer designated as the district revenue officer in district to assist the DC.

10.3.2 DC as District Magistrate

The official heading the district was the collector (under the Land Revenue Code) for land purposes, and DM for the overseeing of law and order functions. The DM as the chief executive at the district is primarily responsible for maintaining law and order of the district. In normal times, the SP looks after the law and order situation and the DM's role is confined to general supervision of the law and order situation. People may approach the DM about the lapses of the police or about failures in bringing the criminal to book. Before separation of the judicial functions in 1970s the DM exercised control over the criminal administration. Now his control is only minimal. It times of emergency, however, when the law and order situation breaks down, the control of DM over the police force is closer. The police is directly concerned with the law and order situation and have to tackle the agitationists and law-breakers. The police, since it is directly involved, may adopt a hostile attitude in tackling such situations or may adopt a soft approach in order to avoid confrontation and responsibility. The DM has, therefore, to take stock of the situation and supervise the preventive actions that are taken.

Over the last five decades, it is widely felt that law and order situation in most districts have steadily worsened. Frequent and high incidence of communal tension, caste feuds, increasing poverty at the lower strata of society, lack of respect for law, ever-increasing terrorism and the rivalry between the magistracy and the police are manifestations of this deterioration. Lacking the moral strength and stature to resists political pressures, DMs are manipulated to serve individual and sectarian interests, as opposed to the welfare of the majority of the people of the district.[18]

But it would be totally wrong to blame the DM for the state of lawless and disorder situation at the district. In 1995, the gruesome lynching of the DM of Gopalganj in Bihar spoke of the decline of his prestige and authority. During the British Rule, the DM was 'the eyes and ears of the government'. He was not only the principal head of the revenue and law and order administration

[18] For example, an Amnesty International report slammed the Government of Uttar Pradesh for delay of nearly 14 months in the registration of an FIR and recording the statements of seven gangrape survivors of the Muzaffarnagar riots in 2013. In three cases, survivors turned hostile in the face of constant threats and intimidation. See *The Times of India* (Chandigarh), 10 February 2017.

but the general administration of the district as a whole. He was the primus inter pares among the district-level officers including the SP.

In many district states, the DM acts as an agent of the judiciary. The execution of the *writs* of civil and criminal courts is his responsibility. He can hear cases under the preventive section of the Code of Criminal Procedure, and exercises powers under Section 144 in case of disturbance to peace within his jurisdiction.

The deputy commissioner is also associated with supervisory functions of the district jail including the welfare of the inmates of the jail. He confirms the execution of capital sentences of prisoners who are condemned.

10.3.2.1 Relationship with Police

Relationship between the DM and the district SP has always been a sensitive issue. After Independence, the police has resented its subordinate role in law and order administration. The SP in practice is the head of the criminal administration and the real boss of the police force in the district. A practice has been evolved by which the DM and the SP submit joint report on incidents of police firing and other matters affecting law and order. The incidence of suspension of two DSPs and three other personnel of the Chandigarh Police in May 1999 by the Home Secretary, Chandigarh Administration, was resented by the then IG of Police Kiran Bedi. She added that the head of the department had to be trusted. 'Hierarchy has not been followed while passing the orders'.[19]

Police excesses are increasingly becoming a source of immense embarrassment to government. The senior police personnel including the IG of police are unable to impose discipline. The DM is reduced to a mere spectator and often has to bear the brunt of lapses of the police. There are scathing attacks on the police for its rude behaviour and excesses in the legislature and, on most occasions, the government parries the problem by holding inquiries. But there is no doubt that there is little control of the DM over the police. The work of police is technical in essence. The senior police officers, such as IG, DIG and SSP, have started resenting the authority of the DM in law and order matters. After the autonomy of the police in the district was accepted by the government, the subordinate staff in the police force started taking advantage of the politician–criminal nexus and challenged, in practice, the authority of their own superiors.

For example, after a clash between two communities during a Muharram procession, the DM of Kanpur used Section 144 of Code of Criminal Procedure, prohibiting unlawful assembly of people and carrying of weapons in order to restore normalcy.[20]

10.3.3 DC as Coordinator

During the British times, the collector decided most of the maters. He was the governor of local affairs. After Independence, several departments were set up at district level, such as, agriculture, public health, public works, irrigation, education and cooperation, whose officials and workers

[19] *The Tribune* (Chandigarh), 12 May 1999.

[20] See *The Economic Times* (Chandigarh), 3 October 2017. A day after two Kanpur villages witnessed violence, locals blamed the ensuing local body election for the 'unnecessary communal tension created to polarise people and draw political mileage'. See *The Tribune* (Chandigarh), 3 October 2017.

maintained liaison with the collector but who were not directly subordinate to him. Using technical and departmental lines of communications, these departments managed to escape coordination by the collectorate. For rural development, these uncoordinated departmental representatives have proved to be blockage to effective planning and development. So it was the collector, in the end, who disposed of problems, for he was the advisor upon whom all depended. As all developments and plans take the district as the major operational unit, the coordinating role of the collector becomes vital and recognized. The old administrative pattern was accepted more or less intact. The second PM of India Lal Bahadur Shastri remarked,

> The entire team in a district has to work with a sense of dedication in the same manner as a soldier on the battle front. The district officer should regard himself in all humility as a commander who has to organize this drive and achieve the target which must be clearly laid down.[21]

10.3.4 DC as Development Officer

In the past, the deputy commissioner and his field agents worked effectively for a good many years as far as law and order was concerned. They travelled periodically through the district territory, listening to complaints, hearing appeals against previous local judgements, having an opportunity to anticipate social and economic crises. The villages themselves, as social and economic units were not seriously affected by the collector's attention.

Independence, however, brought new challenges to districts of India. No longer was it regarded adequate for DC and other district officials to administer benevolently. As the welfare state got underway after enunciation of Directive Principles of State Policy in the 1950 Constitution, the DC's role underwent substantial changes. When in 1952 a new and all-pervasive Community Development Programme and National Extension Service was launched to revitalize rural India, to increase agricultural productivity and bring the benefits of national and state legislation to the grassroots, collectors in 1955 were given charge of all development functions within their districts.[22] It was hoped that by this change in policy, collectors would be encouraged to devote their lost energies to economic and social change and would give less time to revenue and law and other functions. In the wake of acceptance of the ideology of the welfare state, the deputy commissioner became the district development commissioner. He was saddled with varied responsibilities for administration of policies and programmes in land reforms, social justice, community development, cooperation, public distribution and poverty alleviation.

In 1978, the government launched the Integrated Rural Development Programme (IRDP) for improving the economic and social status of the rural people in the country. Some schemes such as Desert Development Programme (DDP), Training the Rural Youth for Self Employment (TRYSEM) and National Rural Employment Programme (NREP), Development of Women and Children in Rural Areas (DWCRA) acquired growing importance in the 1970s. In the task of socio-economic development, the role of the deputy commissioner was as a leader between different development departments. The emphasis was on his leadership role in the socio-economic development at the district. It may be mentioned here that there is no uniformity in the states. For

---

[21] Cited in Dave, 'The Collector', 39.

[22] A. Dunham and R. N. Paul, 'Community Development: A Working Bibliography', *Community Development Review* 4, no. 1 (March 1959).

example, in Gujarat and Maharashtra, all developmental activities have been entrusted to the DDO, who is also an IAS Officer, and the DC's role in development administration is only marginal. These DDOs were officers of revenue service and were made to perform the duties of additional district magistrate (ADM) also, which indicates the suspicion that they were to be used mainly as ADMs as reflected from their qualifications and nature of service. In the beginning, the developmental activities were not part of the normal administrative functions and the district administration was more or less kept insulated. All development projects and their execution were under a development commissioner. This parallel line approach hampered developmental work, for example, a minor irrigation project could not take-off because the required land-acquisition work was held up. The deputy commissioner who was busy in his regulatory functions of election, law and order, revenue collection and so on, did not find time to process the case of land acquisition. After some prolonged hit-and-miss trials, the single line arrangement was evolved in which the DC was made the coordinator of all activities in the district. The DC opines that with the district-level officer treating his head of department as the real boss and the DC as the dummy boss, development activities suffer. Often the situation is so bad that not only there is lack of coordination and cooperation but there is also marked hostility. Some DCs begin with a commitment to improving the welfare of the people but soon learn that translating this commitment into reality not only requires time and energy but also invites opposition from vested interests.

10.3.5 73rd and 74th Constitutional Amendments and Role of the DC

The 73rd and 74th Constitutional Amendments, 1992, empowered the local bodies to improve the quality of living of the local people. The main features of the Acts (1992) include the provisions comprising the mandatory constitutional framework for panchayats and municipalities, uniform five-year terms for both these institutions, 33% reservation for women and establishment of a state-level election and finance commission and district planning committees. After the empowerment of local government institutions, the role of the DC changed immensely.

It may be stated that relationships and powers of the DC vis-à-vis local government institutions vary from state to state. Mainly two different patterns have emerged in the context of panchayats.

First, where people's representatives enjoy greater power. For example, in Andhra Pradesh, the chairman of the Zila Parishad is permitted to exercise administrative control over the chief executive officer who is equivalent to an IAS or DM, for the purpose of implementation of the resolution of the Zila Parishad or any standing committee. Similarly, in Uttar Pradesh and Madhya Pradesh, the Zila Panchayat has the power to control and supervise the administration of the DRDA within its jurisdiction. The Karnataka model shows that the collector, who until now enjoyed powerful position, performs limited functions. The whole planning process came to be integrated at the district level and the DRDA was merged with the Zila Parishad.[23] Further, under the constitutional provisions, the state finance commission has also curtailed the jurisdictions of the collector in the financial matters. The adoption of democratic decentralization as a policy has divested the collector of certain responsibilities in some states. On the contrary, there is another

[23] P. Singh, *Legislative Status of Panchayati Raj in India* (New Delhi: IIPA, 1997), 557.

pattern of relationships between the collector vis-à-vis local government institutions. In this model, the DC has got a dominating role.

For instance, the Karnataka Panchayati Raj Act, 1993, not only provides the power of supervision along with the control over execution of all works of the zila panchayat by the commissioner but also the power to dissolve the gram panchayat. Similarly, the Bihar Panchayati Raj Act, 1993, provides the power of control to the state government over the PRIs in many areas. In the Act of 1993, the state legislature has been empowered to use emergency power against the panchayats, which is exercised through the collector at the district level. Likewise, in Andhra Pradesh, the *sarpanch* (head of a village) and *upsarpanch* (immediate subordinate of *sarpanch*) can be suspended if, in the opinion of the collector, they abuse the power vested in them.

Despite the fact, the constitutional provisions strengthen the local government bodies, state governments (through collectorate as the district representative of the state) still continue to exercise power to control, monitor and even to recommend suspension and dissolution. While local bodies have been given 29 programmes on which they only can plan, the final authority for implementation of these programmes is vested in the hands of bureaucracy.

The recommendations of the Second ARC (2009) envisaged a new role for the collector vis-à-vis local government institutions. The commission felt that that there was need to redefine the role and responsibilities of the collector in a clear manner. His job profile needed to consist of (a) well-defined set of exclusive activities both statutory and non-statutory as a functionary of the state government and (b) the general work of coordination with various departments/agencies of the state and the union governments at the district level.[24]

The main functions of the collector, Second ARC suggests, should include the following:

1. Land and revenue administration, land acquisition, custodian of government lands and properties, registration, recovery of public demand
2. Executive magistracy and maintenances of law and order, internal security, prison, remand and juvenile homes
3. Licensing and regulatory functions with respect to various laws pertaining to arms, explosives, cinemas and so on
4. Disaster management
5. Civil supplies, public distribution and social welfare
6. Excise
7. Transport
8. Mining
9. Labour laws
10. Elections
11. Legal affairs
12. Census
13. Protocol, general administration
14. Treasury management/district accounts related works
15. Public Relations Department, NIC and other miscellaneous functions assigned by the state government, coordination with civil society
16. Coordination with line departments/other agencies of the state and union governments

[24] Second ARC, *Fifteenth Report on State and District Administration* (New Delhi: ARC, April 2009), 71.

From the list of functions suggested by the Second ARC, it becomes difficult to make a distinction between regulatory and the developmental aspects of subjects such as mining and transport and of the coordination with the executive departments and agencies of the state and central governments.

In the interim period until the time the local elected institutions matured into district governments, the Second ARC envisages that each district will have a district council comprising representatives of both rural and urban bodies. The DC would act as the chief officer of this council. Thus, the DC-cum-chief officer would exercise a dual responsibility and would be fully accountable to the elected district government on all local matters.

Today, the DC is seen obsessed with prestige and indifference to public welfare. Social graces are less important. The DC must win the confidence of villagers, knowledgeably discuss plans and programmes relating to development of villages with panchayat leaders and work in harmony with MLAs and MPs.

10.3.5.1 Constraints to the Functioning of DC's Institution

1. *Political interference:* Local politicians, now-a-days, have not only started acting as ventilators of popular grievances and articulators of the people's need but also pressurized local officers, not excluding the DM, for a particular decision in a particular case or for posting a particular officer in a particular place. This sort of political interference in administration increasingly has become the order of the day, making a mockery of the 'rule of law' and subverting democratic governance. The entire district administration has been, of late, subjected to party political influence. In addition to such interference, many district officers are impressed upon to issue gun licences, permits for scarce supplies such as sugar and cement, and to give preferential treatment in transfers and posting to certain government officials within their jurisdictions.
2. *Criminalization of politics:* A new phenomenon called 'criminalization of politics' has started vitiating district administration. The influence of criminals have grown so much that since late 1980s, criminals have gained in strength and managed to sit in various elective bodies of decision-making. Indirectly, this trend has led to the decline of the values and behaviour pattern of the DM. The decline in the authority and prestige of the DC is not an isolated phenomenon but is part of an all-round decline of institutions and professions caused by the gradual decline of value system.[25]
3. *Uncertainty of tenure:* Presently, the DC is so uncertain of his stay in any district that he has no motivation to organize developmental activities on a long-term basis. As previously noted, most DCs complained of political interference as a major constraint to doing their tasks effectively. In addition to the brief tenure, a number of other factors work against his becoming an effective agent of socio-economic change. Protocol requires the DC to receive, be available to and see off ministers. Such frequent interruptions of their developmental work are common and time consuming. In some cases, where DCs really tried to serve as catalysts of change, as a result of their actions, they either were ridiculed or were removed from the district.

[25] V. Subramaninam, 'Changing Administrative Values in India', *Indian Journal of Public Administration* 43, no. 3 (July–September 1997): 269–73.

The climate of uncertainty of tenure in a district, created by political reality, has not only demoralized the DC, but is also seen as having an adverse effect on the performance of his duties as an agent of change.

10.3.5.2 Future of District Magistrate and Suggestions

In the context of 73rd and 74th Constitutional Amendments and politico-administrative experiences since India's Independence, the role and responsibilities of the DM have to be redefined. In this context, what Mukhopadhyay feels is quoted here:

> The existing system of posting young IAS officers at the helm of district administration and that too for a brief period is not conducive to promoting quality of governance in the districts where bulk of the population lives and the majority of development projects are implemented. Senior officers having adequate exposure in the secretariat should be considered for posting as District Magistrate because the new role envisaged for such an officer in the changed context of democratic decentralization should be intrinsically different from that of a junior officer always looking for a berth in the secretariat or something higher up in course of career advancement. A mature officer, sufficiently senior in comparison with the mandarins in the secretariat, would be in a better position to serve the nation well by his administrative knack and capability of resisting unhealthy local political pressure and tendering well-informed advice in a dignified manner to the elected leaders in-charge of district administration and development activities. The politician and the administrator on the spot can still evolve not rivalry but good partnership. The political and administrative systems should succour each other as they survive in uneasy coexistence.[26]

The deputy commissioner is the key official in the district. Although his responsibilities have increased, the authority has declined since independence. It is generally felt that the deputy commissioner is a much overworked and harassed official and that no improvement in this state of affairs is possible unless

1. there is substantial decentralization of powers to SDOs;
2. better office accommodation and arrangements for the disposal of business are provided;
3. he is relieved of the time-wasting protocol duties which he is expected to perform at all odd hours of the day and night;
4. there is less interference with his authority, particularly in transfers and disciplinary action initiated by him against officials under his administrative control;
5. he has a more effective control over the issue of licences, permits and quotas;
6. conditions for systematic and uninterrupted touring of the district are created;
7. there is reduction in the number of committees which he has to preside over, the meetings he has to attend both within and without his district and extraneous activities connected with sports, culture, welfare and so on, which he is required to promote.

[26] A. Mukhopadhyay, 'Changing Role of District Magistrate', in *Fifty Years of Indian Administration*, ed. T. N. Chaturvedi (New Delhi: IIPA, 1998), 441–42.

10.4 District Administration at Sub-division Level

The district is geographically divided into a number of sub-divisions (in Uttar Pradesh and Madhya Pradesh) or revenue divisions (in Tamil Nadu) or *prants* (in Maharashtra). The official-in-charge of this division is called SDO (in Uttar Pradesh and Punjab) or sub-divisional magistrate (SDM) or revenue divisional officer or sub-collector (in Tamil Nadu) and *prant* officer (deputy collector or assistant collector in Maharashtra). Like the DC, the SDO is a generalist area administrator. He is a link between the DC and the *tehsildar* in revenue matters. He is a valuable field aide to the DC and is an integral part of the district administration. His functions are similar to those of the DC but are confined to the sub-division. He is the principal assistant to the deputy commissioner and is responsible to him for the maintenance of law and order. The office of the SDO provides a training ground for the new recruits to the IAS.

The SDO is vested with both revenue and magisterial functions. The SDO generally belongs to the state executive and is appointed by the state government which controls him. Like the deputy commissioner, he is an all-purpose officer at the sub-divisional level.

> The sub-divisional officer is an overall (Revenue, Magisterial and Executive) officer in the sub-division. He is territorial officer like collector in the district and tehsildar in the tehsil, where he performs a number of functions and duties and emerges as the chief executive officer and representative of government in his area.[27]

The SDO (civil) occupies an important position in the administrative hierarchy of the state administration. With decentralization to the sub-division, he is expected to play vital role in maintaining law and order, collection of revenue and other social and economic development functions.

10.4.1 SDO and Panchayats

The SDO should be invested with necessary powers if decentralization is to be effective. With the 73rd Constitutional Amendment, the SDO has a different role to play in the functioning of panchayats in the sub-division under his administration. A different approach is needed whereby the SDO helps the panchayats at the intermediate level in matters of planning and administration. He should refrain from exercising excessive control over functioning of panchayats. It is however in the interests of the people's welfare that the experience, prestige and advice of the local SDO are fully utilized. Unfortunately, the decentralization has not been effective and even where there has been decentralization, it has proved ineffective because of constant interference from higher authorities and encouragement given to disgruntled persons to approach higher authorities, for either a stay of an adverse order or for its reversal. There must be substantial decentralization to the sub-divisions and to make such decentralization effective, the SDO should be equipped with the necessary powers and given the necessary staff.

As the SDO is to play a bigger role and will have to tour more extensively, he must be provided with adequate and competent staff. In the bigger sub-divisions, it may be necessary to give him an assistant commissioner or extra assistant commissioner as his deputy so that the work at headquarters does not suffer or accumulate while he is on tour.

[27] J. D. Shukla, *State Administration in India* (New Delhi: IIPA), 107.

10.4.2 Role as Coordinator

Just as the DC is expected to act as coordinator at district level, the SDO has a similar role. The view is whether he is at a position to play this role properly. There is a tendency on the part of departments to resent his role as a coordinator. Coordination is essential, and the SDO is the only official who can bring this about. To enable him to perform this role effectively, he should be authorized, in case an official is not cooperative, to place on record his views on the annual report on the offending official.

10.4.3 SDO and Law and Order

As mentioned earlier, the SDO is also SDM for the maintenance of law and order, although the judiciary has been separated from the executive, the trial of some security cases under Criminal Procedure Code continues to be responsibility of the SDOs and executive magistrates.

As regards his relations with the police, it is a fact that complaints against police excesses, acts of omission and commission, harassment and so on are made to him by people and that he also receives such complaints from higher authorities for enquiry and report. In this context, SDO's responsibility for maintenance of law and order is paramount, and, therefore, it is important that he works in close association with DSP, inspector and station house officer serving in the sub-division.

10.4.4 Conclusion

As an important functionary at the sub-division level, the SDO has an important role to play in matters such as the following:

1. Coordination of department activities
2. Maintaining law and order
3. Promoting general welfare of the rural population
4. Revenue collection
5. Supervising the field staff under his administrative control
6. Helping and promoting the implementation of programmes and plans coming under the purview of the panchayats in his sub-divisional area

10.5 District Administration at Tehsil and Lower Levels

A tehsil (taluk in Assam, Bihar, Odisha and West Bengal) is under the charge of a *tehsildar* who is a member of the state civil service cadre. He and his assistants (*naib tehsildars*) and *patwaris* have jurisdiction over nearly 400 villages in day-to-day revenue affairs and other matters. His principal duties are to see that the local revenue and other governmental dues are collected in time and in full, to keep in safe custody all governmental money and property entrusted to him, to supervise the land record work in his tehsil, to see that *patwaris* and other revenue personnel perform their duties properly and to report to his immediate superior (usually the SDO in most cases) any unusual occurrence.

Tehsildar has also certain magisterial powers and works closely with the police in the area. He is required to tour for at least one-third of his working time in most states and submits the tour diary every month to the collector.

10.5.1 District Administration at *Pargana* Level

The next lower units in revenue administration is known as *pargana* in Uttar Pradesh, circle in Maharashtra and *firka* in Tamil Nadu. The head of this unit is called supervisor *quanungo* in Uttar Pardesh, circle inspector in Maharashtra.

The *kanungo* is a peripatetic officer who inspects the work of 30–50 patwaris that he has in his charge. The village accountant, called *karnam* in Tamil Nadu, *karkun* or *kulkarni* in Maharashtra and *patwari* in Northern India, is the representative of the government in his charge of one or several villages. He is aptly described as 'the eyes and ears' of the collector. He is a salaried government employee. His primary duty is to keep up-to-date the land records initially prepared at the time of settlement. He also prepares and files at the tehsil office data based on his intimate knowledge such as area under cultivation and yield per acre which are later compiled at the district, state and even national levels. Additionally, he reports on matters relating to police work, agriculture, irrigation and public health. He is a repository of information about his circle of one or more villages. He is a multipurpose functionary at the lowest rung of revenue administration ladder, but his role is of crucial importance in the entire hierarchy.

10.6 Districts Administration at Village Level

District administration at village level in the lowest unit in the hierarchy of administration which is administered by a village establishment headed by a village headman. The village headman, called *patel* in the southern states, *lambardar* or *numbardar* in the northern states tries petty criminal cases and as village *munsif*, has also petty civil jurisdiction. He collects the land revenue and sends it to the taluk treasury. He maintains order and reports the occurrence of crime to higher authorities. In addition, he is the custodian of all government property in the village. In view of his multifarious activities, village headman is the most powerful government functionary at the village level.

10.7 Shortcomings and Measures for Improving District Administration

10.7.1 Defects and Shortcomings in the District Administration

District administration, as at present, suffers from a number of serious defects and shortcomings. Most of these defects are common to all areas of administration. Those which are peculiar to district administration are as follows:

1. Delays in the disposal of government business
2. Corruption at lower and middle levels
3. Inefficiency and confusion in the administration
4. Unsatisfactory outlook and general apathy of the official
5. Indiscipline in the services and administration

10.7.2 Measures for Improving District Administration

The Planning Commission in its First Five Year Plan emphasized the role to be played by the district administration and suggested the following:

> In brief, from now, the primary emphasis in district administration has to be on the implementation of development programs in cooperation with the active support of the people. The reorganization of district administration has to provide for (a) strengthening and improving the machinery of general administration; (b) integration of activities of various development departments in the district and the provision of common extension organization; (c) linking up, in relation to all development works, of local self-governing institutions with administrative agencies of the state government; (d) regional coordination and supervision of district development programmes.

Certain radical measures are needed to be taken to improve the district administration. Some of the measures suggested are as follows:

1. All district offices should be housed in one well-designed building to avoid much trouble to the people.
2. The deputy commissioner should be relieved of a substantial part of his current protocol duties. To reduce delay, and inefficiency, there should be substantial delegation and decentralization of work to SDO.
3. There should be no interference with the DC's authority in transfer and disciplinary action of his subordinates.
4. There is the need of creation of Public Grievances Cell in the DC Office.
5. A good deal of emphasis has to be on securing coordination as several departments are headed by specialists, each enjoying a high degree of autonomy but with a little coordinated approach.
6. Creating a simplified, responsive, effective and transparent environment, aimed at time-bound delivery of services. For implementing the initiative, digitization of office records of all departments, computerization of offices through software use is required.
7. Second ARC suggests that in every office of the DC, there should be adequate system of management information systems (MIS), information technology, e-governance, performance management, outcome evaluation, process reengineering and innovativeness in systems and procedures in order to enhance the effectiveness of district administration.[28]

[28] Second ARC, *Fifteenth Report*, 434.

8. Introduction of citizen-centric governance system which addresses concerns of citizens. In this system, administration has to reflect the features of accountability, accessibility, transparency and efficiency.

Summary

Before India's independence and over the centuries from the Mughal times to the end of the British Rule in August 1947, the district administration headed by the collector or deputy commissioner remained more or less intact. The independent India adopted the British pattern of the institution of collector to suit the country's need for tighter bonds between central, state and local powers. He is still collector for land revenue purposes, and DM for overseeing law and order functions. In 1947, Sir Edward Blunt wrote, 'And for many years to come by whatever Constitution of India may be ruled, no government will be able to do without the District Officer'.[29]

[29] E. A. H. Blunt, *The Indian Civil Service* (London: Faber and Faber, 1937).

11 Decentralization and Rural Local Governance

LEARNING OBJECTIVES

1. To examine the role of local self-government after the 73rd Constitutional Amendment Act
2. To discuss the meaning and significance of decentralization of governance
3. To elaborate state government control over panchayats

Introduction

'Decentralization' is recognized not only as an important component of local governance but also as a base for democracy. It is universally acknowledged that certain functions of government are best administered at the local level for the reason that decentralizing the provision of public services such as sanitation, water supply, health and social welfare maximizes welfare by responding efficiently to public needs. Local governments responsible to the local people are in a better position to meet the local needs of the people than governments functioning from a distance. From the viewpoint of administration, decentralization of the powers and functions of central or state government, which underlines the rationale for federalism, helps to improve the administrative machinery. In the context of development, local government can make significant contributions to planning and implementing programmes in such sectors as agriculture, minor irrigation, cottage industry, animal husbandry, environment protection and public works, apart from delivering social services in the areas of sanitation, health, education, nutrition and housing. Further, the real grassroots democracy and development can take place only with the active participation of the local people. Participatory government and development make it possible to mobilize resources to which centrally administered revenue instruments cannot reach. Above all, meaningful participation helps to impart a sense of responsibility among the people and thereby strengthens the foundation of a democratic polity. These considerations reflect the recognition that decentralization is an answer to many problems. Despite recognition of its merits, the process of decentralization has yet to acquire fuller meaning and strength in local governance.

Decentralization has its own importance and role, but it is not free from dangers of social disparity, economic exploitation, patronage politics and fiscal deficiency. Before we discuss certain issues of local governance in rural and urban India, it is imperative to understand what we mean by the term 'decentralization'.

What Is Decentralization?

Decentralization is the process of transferring or dispersing functions from the central authority to the regional or local authority. Cheema and Rondinelli defined 'decentralization' as 'transfer of planning, decision-making or administrative authority from the central government to its field organizations, local administration units, semi-autonomous and parastatal organizations, local governments or NGOs'.[1]

The term 'decentralization' is interchangeably used with terms such as de-concentration, devolution and delegation, although they have different connotations. Decentralization refers to 'transfer of authority away from the national capital whether by decentralization, that is delegation, to field officers or by devolution to local authorities or other local bodies'.[2] In the words of L. D. White, 'The progress of transfer of administrative authority from a lower to a higher level of government is called "centralization"; the converse, decentralization'.[3] Further, decentralization is a method 'embracing both processes of de-concentration and devolution'.[4] While de-concentration stands for the 'delegation of authority adequate for the discharge of specified functions to staff of a central department who are situated outside the headquarters and devolution is the legal conferring of powers to discharge specified or residual functions upon formally constituted local authorities'.[5]

Columbia University's Earth Institute identified one of three major trends relating to decentralization as 'increased involvement of local jurisdictions and civil society in the management of their affairs, with new forms of participation, consultation and partnerships'.[6]

Decentralization in any area is a response to the problems of centralized systems. It is often linked to concepts of participation in decision-making, democracy, equality and liberty from higher authority.[7] It can lead to local efficiency, equity and development.[8] Decentralization has been described as a 'counterpart to globalization'. Cornell University's project on 'Restructuring Local Government' by Warner states that decentralization refers to the 'global trend' of devolving responsibilities to regional or local governments. To him, decentralization 'enhances the democratic voice'.[9]

According to a 1999 United Nations Development Programme report:

> A large number of developing and transitional countries have embarked on some form of decentralization programmes. This trend is coupled with a growing interest in the role of civil society and the private sector as partners to governments in seeing new ways of service delivery.

---

[1] G. S. Cheema and D. A. Rondinelli, eds., *Decentralization and Development: Implementation in Developing Countries* (Beverly Hills, California: SAGE, 1983).

[2] United Nations, *Decentralization for National and Local Development* (New York: United Nations, Technical Assistance Programme, 1962), 3.

[3] L. D. White, *Introduction to the Study of Public Administration* (New York: Macmillan, 1955), 37.

[4] H. Maddick, *Democracy, Decentralization and Development* (Bombay: Asia Publishing House, 1963), 23.

[5] Ibid., 23.

[6] Earth Institute of Columbia University (EICU), *A History of Decentralization*. http://www.ciesin.org/decentralization/English/General/history_fao.html (accessed on 4 February 2013).

[7] Subhabrata Dutta, *Democratic Decentralization and Grassroots Leadership in India* (New Delhi: Mittal Publications, 2009), 5–8.

[8] J. Ribot, 'Democratic Decentralization of Natural Resources', *Public Administration and Development* 23, (2003): 53–65.

[9] Mildred Warner, *Restructuring Local Government Project* (Cornell University). http://www.mildredwarner.org/restructuring (accessed on 4 February 2013).

Decentralization of governance and the strengthening of local governance capacity is in part also a function of broader societal trends. These include, for example, the growing distrust of government generally, the spectacular demise of some of the most centralized regimes in the world (especially the Soviet Union) and the emerging separatist demands that seem to routinely prop up in one or another part of the world.

Heller argues that strengthening and empowering local government has been justified not only on the grounds of making government more efficient but also on the grounds of increasing accountability and participation.[10]

Significance of Decentralization

1. Decentralization of governance is useful for heterogeneous regions. It is a means of overcoming the severe limitations of centrally controlled schemes and programmes.
2. Decentralization of governance can safeguard against fraud, misuse of resources and proper execution of programmes.
3. By decentralizing functions and by making use of local knowledge, good governance is assured. It ensures closer interaction between governmental officials and the local population. e-Panchayat is one of the Mission Mode projects (MMPs) being implemented by the Centre. Computerization is in full swing at panchayat levels in Kerala, Karnataka, Madhya Pradesh, Gujarat, West Bengal, Andhra Pradesh and Goa. The decentralized governance can strengthen the state's monitoring mechanism.
4. Decentralization can allow for better political and administrative penetration of national governmental policies into remote areas. As social audit is carried out by the people who must reap the planned benefits of government programmes, the implementation gap can be abridged to a great extent by eliminating leakage, diversion and misuse of government funds.
5. If people are encouraged to participate in the development programmes and policies, most of the apprehensions expressed by the father of the Constitution of India, B. R. Ambedkar, about the dominance of the affluent and the upper caste people in the rural areas would disappear.

Centralization and Decentralization Aspects of Administration

Centralization and decentralization are the two types of structures that can be found in the organization, government and management. Centralization of authority means the power of planning and decision-making are exclusively in the hands of top management. It alludes to the concentration of all the powers at the apex level. On the contrary, decentralization refers to the dissemination of powers by the apex-level management to the middle or low-level units. It means delegation of authority, at all the levels of management.

Arguing for a decentralized administration, Cheema and Rondinelli wrote,

---

[10] Patrick Heller, 'Moving the State: The Politics of Democratic Decentralization in Kerala, South Africa, and Porto Alegre', *Politics & Society* 29 (2001): 131–63.

Decentralized helps in institutionalizing the participation of citizens in development planning by creating alternative means of decision-making. It leads to a more flexible, innovative and creative administration that reduces the cost of planning and increases the number of public goods. It also ensures political stability by increasing the participation of local people in decision-making.[11]

11.1 Government Decentralization

Scholars have described the functioning of governments in terms of centralization and decentralization. Rising governing expenditures, poor economic performance and the rise of free market economy have convinced and forced governments of both developed and developing countries to decentralize their operations, to induce competition within their services, to contract out to private firms operating in the market and to privatize some services and functions. Obviously, decentralization is not only a device for the delegation or dispersal of administrative authority, but it is also a democratic means of devolution of political authority. Here in this chapter, the focus would be on political, administrative and fiscal decentralization.

11.1.1 Political Decentralization

Political decentralization implies the creation of new levels of government or local authorities. Political decentralization aims to give citizens or their elected representatives more power. It may be associated with pluralistic politics and representative government, but it also means giving citizens, or their representatives, more influence in the formulation and implementation of laws and policies.

11.1.2 Administrative Decentralization

Administrative decentralization may be geographical or functional. In geographical or territorial decentralization, the powers and functions of headquarters are decentralized to the field agencies for effective performance. Four major forms of administrative decentralization have been described.

1. *Decontraction:* It is the weakest form of decentralization that shifts responsibility for decision-making, finance and implementation of certain public functions.
2. *Delegation:* Delegation transfers responsibility for decision-making, finance and implementation of certain public functions to semi-autonomous organizations not wholly controlled by the central government, but ultimately accountable to it.
3. *Devolution delegation:* Devolution delegation passes down responsibility for decision-making, finance and implementation of certain public functions to the sub-national level, such as a regional, local or state government.
4. *Divestment delegation:* Divestment delegation is also one of the forms of administrative delegation. It is also called privatization. It may mean merely contracting out services to

[11] Cheema and Rondinelli, *Decentralization and Development.*

private companies. Or it may mean relinquishing totally all responsibility for decision-making, finance and implementation of certain public functions.[12]

11.1.3 Fiscal Decentralization

Fiscal decentralization is quite important. On it depends the success and failure of local government. Fiscal decentralization means decentralizing revenue raising and/or expenditure of moneys to a lower level of government while maintaining financial responsibility.[13] Fiscal decentralization can be achieved through user fees, expansion of local property or sales taxes, intergovernmental transfers of central government grants and loans, etc.

11.1.3.1 Criticism

As mentioned in the beginning of the chapter that decentralization is not free from disadvantages. Factors impeding decentralization include weak local administration or technical capacity which may result into poor delivery services. Second, inadequate financial resources available to perform new local responsibilities can hinder the functioning of local governments. Third, decentralization can make national policy coordination too complex. It may allow corrupt local elites to capture local power. Further, local cooperation may be undermined by any distrust between private and public sectors. Fourth, decentralization may result in higher enforcement costs and conflict for resources if there is no higher level of authority.[14]

Fifth, decentralization may not be as efficient for standardized, routine, network-based services as opposed to those that need more complicated inputs.[15] Sixth, patronage politics becomes quite possible in local administration. This will become rampant and often civil servants feel compromised.

In summary, it is noted that while decentralization may increase 'productive efficiency', it may undermine 'allocative efficiency' by making redistribution of wealth more difficult. Decentralization will cause greater disparities between the rich and the poor regions, especially during times of crisis when the national government may not be able to help regions needing it.[16]

11.2 Pre-Conditions for Effective Decentralization

Local governance assessment is useful at national level in order to avert the dangers of decentralization. While centralized power centres can find reasons to frustrate decentralization, it has been found that decentralization causes greater disparities between the rich and poor regions. A balance approach is needed to ensure good governance for the local regions.

[12] Janet Kodras, 'Restructuring the State: Devolution, Privatization, and the Geographic Redistribution of Power and Capacity in Governance', *Urban Affairs Annual Reviews* 48, (1997): 68–79.

[13] Different forms of decentralization. See EICU, *A History*.

[14] UN, 'Environment in Decentralized Development', *UN Food and Agriculture Organization*. http://www.fao.org/docrep/005/y4256e/y4256e00.htm (accessed on 23 February 2013).

[15] See EICU, *A History*.

[16] See Remy Prud'homme, 'The Dangers of Decentralization', *World Bank Research Observer* 10, no. 2 (1995): 201.

Chanchal Sharma identified eight essential conditions for successful decentralization in order to avert the so-called dangers of decentralization[17]:

1. Social preparedness and mechanisms to prevent elite capture
2. Strong administrative and technical capacity at the higher levels
3. Strong political commitment at the higher levels
4. Sustained initiatives for capacity building at the local level
5. Strong legal framework for transparency and accountability
6. Transformation of local government organizations into high performing organizations
7. Appropriate reasons to decentralize—intentions matter
8. Effective judicial system, citizen's oversight and anticorruption bodies to prevent decentralization of corruption

11.3 Decentralized System for Rural Local Government

History of Local Department in India is very old. In this section, an effort is made to discuss the decentralized system for local government in the ancient and medieval period. Besides, the progress that was witnessed during the British period is also analysed in this section.

11.3.1 Ancient and Medieval Period

India, among the developing countries, is the largest democracy characterized by parliamentary system and federal structure of government. Besides the union government, there are 29 constituent state governments, 6 union territory administrations and one National Capital Territory government. Local government is under the control of state governments and union territory administrations. The central government provides general direction and support (including finance) to state governments regarding local government.

The institutions of local government in India have flourished since time immemorial. During ancient period, about which some information is available in the Rig Veda (1200 BC) and a few later sources, the panchayats or village governments as they were called functioned in self-sufficient villages spread in several kingdoms and principalities in the Indian sub-continent. The self-government set up comprised a village assembly and in course of time, its standing committee, the panchayat. The village elders belonging to various households constituted the assembly and some, among them chosen by consensus, comprised the panchayat. This village government took decisions and actions based upon religious precepts and customs and traditional conventions with respect to various matters such as village defence and law and order, maintenance and utilization of commercial assets and certain amenities, inter-personal or inter-household disputes and allied matters. It was also responsible for the collection of tax or financial levy and payment to the central government of the kingdom or principality and also performance of any duty

[17] C. K. Sharma, 'Governance, Governmentality and Governability: Constraints and Possibilities of Decentralization in South Asia, Keynote Address', International Conference on Local Representation of Power in South Asia, organized by the Department of Political Science, G. C. University, Lahore, (Pakistan), 12 November 2014.

assigned sometimes by the latter. This general pattern of self-government underwent adaptations over different places and times.

Writing about these village communities in 1830, Sir Charles Metcalfe stated,

> This union of the village communities, each one forming a separate state in itself, has, I conceive contributed more than any other cause to the preservation of the people of India through all the revolutions and changes which they have suffered, and is in a high degree conductive to their happiness, and to the enjoyment of a great portion of freedom and independence.[18]

Sharma is of concerted view that democratic decentralization is a necessary condition for achieving empowerment of people. But simultaneously, he argues that decentralization must vigorously pursue the creation of supportive conditions for meaningful engagement of informed citizenry.

Coming to the medieval period of Muslim and especially of Mughal Rule in India, a feudalistic system of governments emerged in which government began to have major responsibility for the maintenance of law and order, local defence, higher judicial functions and tax administration. A new class of feudal chiefs and revenue collectors (zamindars) emerged between the rulers and the village people. This tended to cause erosions in self-government in villages.

11.3.2 Progress of Local Government During British Period

The present statutory system of local government in the sense of 'a representative organization' responsible to a body of electors, enjoying wide powers of administration and taxation and functioning both as a school for training in responsibility and a vital link in the chain of organization that make us the government of the country, is no doubt a British creation.[19] But it was not any policy of the British rulers to confer local autonomy on the people of India that prompted them to introduce local government. The Taxation Enquiry Commission as rightly observed:

> It was the need for the decentralization of administration and the connected need for the association of Indians with administration (in order for one thing, that taxes could be more easily imposed and collected) that prompted the early British Indian administration to embark on the introduction of local self-government institutions in this country. The resolution of Lord Mayo (1870) on financial decentralization also visualized the development of local self-government institutions; but this was subordinate to the need for tapping local sources of revenue of effecting economy by decentralized administration.[20]

The policy of setting up local self-governing bodies in urban and rural areas during the British regime marked the process of decentralization. The first municipal corporation created in India was that of Madras (now Chennai) in 1687 followed by presidency towns of Calcutta (now Kolkata) and Bombay (now Mumbai) in 1792 and 1793 respectively. Lord Mayo in 1870 in a resolution adopted financial decentralization with respect to sanitation and public works. The

---

[18] M. Elphinstone, *The History of India* (London: John Murray, 1905), 68.

[19] GoI, *Memoranda Submitted to the Indian Statutory Commission by the Government of India, vol. V* (Calcutta: GoI, 1930), 105.

[20] Ministry of Finance, *Report of the Taxation Enquiry Commission (TEC), 1953–54, vol. III* (Delhi: GoI, 1955), 336.

publication of Lord Mayo's Resolution on provincial finance which, in providing for a measure of decentralization from the centre to the provinces, emphasized the ideal of increased association of Indians in the administration and indicated the extension of municipal self-government as the most promising field for its attainment. The Resolution encouraged the general application of the principle of election with the avowed object of developing self-government.

However, the cause of decentralization of administration was strongly pleaded by Lord Ripon in his historic resolution issued on 18 May 1882. Ripon's reform laid the foundation of local self-government in India which served as the groundwork of democratic institutions in higher spheres. That is why Lord Ripon is regarded as the father of local self-government in India. Through his resolution, Ripon emphasized the training and political participation of Indians in the art of governance.

The practical changes which the resolution inaugurated may be summed up as follows: It advocated (a) the establishment of a network of local self-government institutions, especially in rural areas; (b) the reduction of official element in local bodies to not more than one-third of the whole; (c) the exercise of control from without and not from within; (d) a large measure of financial decentralization; (e) the adoption of election as a means of constituting local bodies wherever possible; and (f) preference for a variety of systems of rigid uniformity. While insisting carefully on a unity of aim, the emphasis now was on the 'self-government' rather than on the 'local' aspect of local self-government.[21]

It may be noted that the British administrators were not happy with Ripon's resolution as they feared a general weakening of field administration under a local self-governing rule. However, under political pressure generated by the national freedom struggle and administrative convenience, the British Government had to concede Ripon's thesis of decentralization.

11.3.3 Royal Commission on Decentralization, 1907–1909

The government system of financial control, financial inadequacy and poor representation of Indians on local bodies were reasons which, particularly under Lord Curzon, compelled the British Government to appoint the Royal Commission on Decentralization in 1907. The Commission made certain recommendations about reorganization and reinvigoration of the local self-government. As regards rural local self-government, it recommended revamping of sub-district and district boards and also setting up of a network of village panchayats with informally elected members and with village headman as its chairperson. The panchayat was to be empowered not only to provide elementary civic service but also to perform minor judicial functions. The Commission recommended a three-tier rural bodies system by addition of village panchayats to the sub-district and district boards already in existence in provinces. The Decentralization Report which came out in 1909 however failed to advance the cause of local self-government. The GoI Resolution of 1915 attributed its failure to financial inadequacy, want of public spirit, the apathy of respectable Indians towards election and sectarian animosities. There was no attempt to relax centralized control which stifled the growth of self-governing institutions.[22]

---

[21] Ministry of Finance, *Report of the Taxation*, 334.

[22] Quoted by Misra, *Administrative History*, 610–11.

Later, the British policy towards 'progressive realization of responsible government in India' declared on 20 August 1917 by Montague (Secretary of State for India) coupled with GoI Resolution of 1918 strengthened further the cause of decentralization of administration.

Consequently, a highly centralized structure of British Rule was gradually decentralized at the provincial level with the GoI Acts of 1919 and 1935. Under the GoI Act, 1919, as a sequel to the Montague–Chelmsford Reforms, 'dyarchy' was introduced. Under dyarchy (1921–37), certain departments were for the first time put in charge of elected ministers responsible to the legislature, and the remaining departments were kept in change of the members of the governor's executive council (government officials). The GoI Act, 1935, strengthened the process of decentralization by the introduction of 'provincial autonomy' in the provinces which reflected the federal nature of the constitution. During the last phase of British Rule (1919–47) both rural and urban local bodies were put under the charge of provincial ministers who were appointed as a result of constitutional reforms of 1919 in the country and were given enhanced administrative powers in respect of local government under the provincial autonomy and up to 1947.

To briefly mention, when India achieved Independence on 15 August 1947, it inherited local government structure whose impact can be seen even today. But the local government did not blossom sufficiently. One scholar observed:

> The record of working of large majority of the reorganised rural local bodies however was rather unsatisfactory, by and large. The elected representatives and chairmen in local bodies needed positive guidance and appropriate support from the government to perform their duties properly. This was not forthcoming adequately most of the time. Instead, ministers tended to exploit the local bodies for gaining political support.[23]

The state of bureaucracy did not shed its rigid adherence to red tape in dealing with working of local bodies instead of motivating and guiding them to perform their responsibilities properly in the interest of local people. Second, local factionalism, elite domination, widespread poverty and illiteracy did not provide a congenial environment for flourishing of the representative local bodies still in their political adolescence.

Third, failure of local bodies to raise substantial income locally and meagreness of government grants to them resulted in a serious financial constraint on the scope and quality of their working as well as in creating dependency complex within them. Fourth, there was not, by and large, satisfactory arrangements for provision of suitable and accountable administrative personnel to local bodies. The government departments were reluctant to transfer their field officers and staff so as to work under the direction of the rural local bodies to perform the duties assigned to them. Fifth, there was very inadequate coordination between local bodies and district administration in the provision of civic services, improvement of local infrastructure and rural development in regard to which both had been assigned respective responsibility. Also, growing communalism and political agitations in the country for one purpose or the other had an adverse effect on the appropriate functioning of local bodies. The whole issue of democracy and development did not receive much attention. Thus, the Independence of the country ushered in a new period in the history of local government in India.

---

[23] B. S. Khanna, *Rural Local Government in India and South Asia* (New Delhi: Deep Publication, 1999), 10–11.

11.4 Development in Rural Local Government Before Constitutional Amendment

After India's Independence, there was radical change in the system of local government. The first PM of Independent country, Jawaharlal Nehru, took keen interest in the furtherance of participation and control of governance by the people of the country at the local level. To Nehru 'local self-government is and must be the basis of any true system of democracy'.[24]

To restructure the existing system of government was a debatable point before the Constitution makers of the free India. The Indian National Congress, which was the major political party at the time of independence, was committed to a strong central government despite Mahatma Gandhi's vision of future India in which economic and political power would be decentralized and each village would be economically self-reliant. The other consideration was the fear of presence of fissiparous tendencies, and so it was felt that decentralization could not be permitted beyond a point because of the risk of instability. B. R. Ambedkar argued in the constituent assembly that the Indian social structure at the village level was hierarchical, oppressive and insensitive to change. He opposed giving powers to the prevailing rural power structure (panchayats which would work to the detriment of the *harijans* and the rural poor). However, the emphasis on democracy and country's linguistic, cultural, ethnic and geographical diversity necessitated some autonomy for regional government. The balance of these considerations gave rise to the present three-tier system of centre, state and local governments.

In the beginning, two provisions relating to local bodies were adopted in the 1950 Constitution. Article 40 (adopted in deference to wishes of Mahatma Gandhi) in the chapter 'Directive Principles of State Policy' says, 'The State shall take steps to organize village panchayats and endow them with such powers and authority as may be necessary to enable them to function as units of self-government'. Among the division of powers, it is included in the State List empowering the state governments to constitute local governments and other local authorities for the purpose of local self-government or village administration.

During the first decade in Independent India, fresh laws on panchayats were passed by the state governments of Uttar Pradesh (1947), Bihar (1947), Madras (1950), Punjab (1952), West Bengal (1957), Bombay (1958) and in several of the new states created as a result of the territorial reorganizations initiated in the country. Article 40 of the Constitution regarding panchayats was an important authoritative affirmation and impetus for these laws passed in states under general guidance of the union government. Although there were variations in the provisions of these laws, their main purpose was to strengthening structure and powers of village panchayats.

All India Council of Local Self-Government (including the ministers of local self-government) was created in 1948. Jawaharlal Nehru, who inaugurated the first meeting of the council remarked,

> Local self-government is and must be the basis of any true system of democracy. We have got rather into the habit of thinking of democracy at the top and not so much below. Democracy at the top may not be a success unless you build on this foundation from below.[25]

---

[24] Quoted in S. R. Maheshwari, *Local Government in India* (Agra: Lakshmi Narain Agarwal, 2009), 23.

[25] Quoted in R. C. Agarwal, *Political Theory (Principles of Political Science)* (New Delhi: Chand and Company Ltd), 399.

In view of financial constraints faced by local governments in the states, the union government set up the Local Finance Committee in 1951 to study and make recommendations about the improvement of finances of local self-government institutions. Two years later (1953–54), another body appointed by it, called Taxation Enquiry Commission, also made some recommendations regarding improvement of local finances which constituted one of critical factors in appropriate performance of functions by these institutions. As the result of stepping up of adoption of administrative measures, the number of village panchayats began to rise. It increased from 83,087 in 1935–36 to 117,593 by 1956–57.[26]

Local government structure in rural India was extremely varied before 1957. The publication of the Report of the Study Team on the Community Development Projects and National Extension Service (under the chairmanship of Balwantrai Mehta).[27] Sponsor by the Planning Commission and the Second Five Year Plan gave a boost to local self-government by stressing 'the need for creating within the district and local levels, a well-organised democratic structure of administration in which the village panchayats will be organically linked with popular organisations at higher levels'.[28] The report of the Balvantray Mehta study team was followed by the introduction of a somewhat standardized panchayat system consisting of a three-tier structure of village panchayats, panchayat samitis at the block/taluk (village cluster) sub-division level, and Zila Parishads (district boards/councils) at the district level.

The new three-tiered rural local bodies system was named as Panchayati Raj on the suggestion of the then PM Jawaharlal Nehru. The lead in establishment of the Panchayati Raj was taken by the states of Rajasthan (2 October 1959), Andhra Pradesh and Tamil Nadu in 1959. The Panchayat Samiti was the key level in the scheme of decentralization. The Samiti's jurisdiction was to be conterminous with that of a community development block, the members being directly elected. This system envisaged that the pradhans of the panchayat samitis would together constitute the Zila Parishad with the collector/deputy commissioner as the chairman. The Parishad was visualized as an advisory body at the district level. The village panchayats would constitute the lowest level in the three-tier structure. Accordingly, most of the states had enacted their legislation on Panchayati Raj. While the Balvantray Mehta pattern was generally followed in most states, there were some local variations in accordance with the local needs and perceptions. For example, Maharashtra and Gujarat gave primacy to the district tier by having strong Zila Parishads with considerable administrative powers. Nevertheless, the idea of decentralization of political and administrative powers did get across the decision-makers.

Since the end of 1959, a network of Panchayati Raj institutions (PRIs) began to be built up by most state governments. By 1964–65, the Panchayati Raj began to function in rural areas of 12 out of 15 states and one (Himachal Pradesh, then a union territory) out of seven union territories in India.

The state governments made an increasing allocation of grants-in-aid to PRIs over the years to augment their finances for expenditure on promotion of local services and development. Besides providing these various types of support, the Directorate of Panchayats scrutinized resolutions and budgets of panchayats and rescinded any resolution or financial provision if it was not considered in conformity with the Panchayat Act.

---

[26] Now the number of gram panchayats has risen to 250,000 (Approximately, 2017 data).

[27] Committee on Plan Projects, *Report of the Team for the Study of Community Project and National Extension Service* (New Delhi: GoI Publishers, 1957).

[28] Planning Commission, *Report on Second Five Year Plan* (New Delhi: GoI), chapter 7.

The district collector was also empowered in many states to conduct inspection of working of a PRI and recommended to the state government any corrective action, if needed. Several members and chairmen of the PRIs in various states however complained from time to time that the state government concerned was not adopting appropriately supportive and rational policy or action in its dealings with the institutions. During the next two decades, Panchayati Raj began to stagnate in first few years (1965–70) and then started declining in efficacy of its role for promotion of development programmes in rural areas.

In this context, the Asoka Mehta Committee Report on PRIs observed, 'Panchayati Raj institutions are dominated by economically and socially privileged sections of society and have as such facilitated the emergence of oligarchic forces yielding no benefits to weaker sections'.[29] The concept of Panchayati Raj has been far from clear, and as the committee commented, 'Some would treat it just as an administrative agency; other as an extension of democracy at the grassroots level; and still others as a charter of rural local government'. The Committee also observed,

> The activities of Panchayati Raj were meagre, their resource base weak and the overall attention given to them niggardly. As if this was not enough, some of the state governments would postpone the holding of elections or supersede some of the important tiers of Panchayati raj institutions for one reason or the other… In the ultimate analysis, all this led to a weakening of political support to Panchayati raj institutions and of administrative will to work through them.[30]

The committee came out strongly in support of the PRIs and pleaded, 'If PRIs were involved in the development process, planning will be realistic, programming will cater to the felt needs and the priorities of the people and implementation would evoke people's involvement and participation'. The committee recommended a two-tier system of PRIs with one body at the district level (Zila Parishad) and another for a cluster of villages below the district-level body (known as mandal panchayat).

The committee made recommendations for the reform and revitalization of Panchayati Raj which were as follows:

1. Panchayati Raj should be viewed as local government and genuine and effective devolution of powers to it should take place.
2. Primary unit in Panchayati Raj system should be Zila Parishad and not the Panchayati Samiti, as the Parishad had better leadership and resources (administrative and financial) to play a substantial development role.
3. The mandal panchayat with appropriate powers and resources and covering a smaller area than development block and larger one than that of village panchayat, should replace the panchayat samiti and the panchayat as it would be more effective in management of civic services and developmental schemes.
4. Administrative wing of Zila Parishad in particular and also that of the mandal panchayat should be suitably staffed and appropriately headed by well qualified civil servants.
5. Below the mandal panchayat there should be a village committee, including substantially weak sections of people, to perform functions allocated to it by the mandal panchayat.

---

[29] GoI, *Report of Committee on Panchayati Raj Institutions* (New Delhi: Ministry of Agriculture and Irrigation, 1978).
[30] Ibid., 6.

6. There should be direct election of members of the Zila Parishad and the mandal panchayat with provisions for reservation of seats for the SCs and STs in proportion to their population as well as reservation of two seats for women.
7. In order to provide appropriate coordination between rural development and urban development, municipal bodies should have representation in Zila Parishad and the mandal panchayat.
8. Political parties should be free to take part in the elections to Panchayati Raj and participate in its working as this would energize it and make its working cogent and coherent.
9. For improving capabilities and reorienting attitudes of people's representatives and of bureaucracy within Panchayati Raj, a massive programme of education and training should be set up in place of existing limited one.

It may be mentioned here that the recommendations of the committee were not accepted by the union government due to the change of the ruling party within it.

Reorganization of the Panchayati Raj was undertaken in a few states, such as Karnataka (1987), Andhra Pradesh (1987) and Madhya Pradesh (1990). Particularly in Karnataka and Andhra Pradesh, by and large, reorganization bore the imprint of the recommendations made by the Asoka Mehta Committee in 1978 which had remained almost ignored by the successive union governments.

In Karnataka and Andhra Pradesh, mandal panchayats were set up in place of panchayat samitis respectively. Age of voters was reduced from 21 to 18 years. Very substantial increase in reservation of seats in PRIs was made for socially weak sections of people. In Karnataka, to a large extent, and in Andhra Pradesh, to a substantial extent, devolution of powers took place from the state governments to PRIs. In both these states, however, Panchayati Raj institutions were dissolved by the Congress Party in 1992.

11.5 Empowerment of Panchayats Through Constitutional Act

While there has been marked trend towards centralization in economic matters, especially with the mechanism of planning, it cannot be denied that the centre's intervention has effected decentralization of provision of basic public services. However, the process of devolution since 1950 has not helped the local governments as much as it should have. There is no sign of reduction of inequalities and abatement of poverty. Looking at the languishing of grassroots democracy, the G. Y. K. Rao Committee on Administrative Arrangements for Rural Development stressed the importance of local initiative in local development and recommended revitalization of the PRIs. The committee came out with a blueprint of a decentralized system of field administration with Panchayati Raj playing the vital role in local planning and development. Another committee under the chairmanship of L. M. Singhvi, deploring the languishing of popular institutions at the grassroots level, observed, 'The Panchayati Institutions have become moribund and … they have been denuded of their promise and vitality. The committee recommended that local self-government should be constitutionally recognised, protected and preserved by the inclusion of a new chapter in the Constitution'.[31]

On 15 May 1989, a Constitution (64th Amendment) Bill was introduced by the Rajiv Gandhi government in the Lok Sabha to grant constitutional status to local government units, but it failed to become an Act for the want of necessary support from Rajya Sabha. The ruling party hailed the Bill as the *Magna Carta* of democratic decentralization. On the contrary, the opposition parties criticized the Bill as a calculated attempt 'to overturn the federal constitution' and also an attempt to forge a direct link between the centre and the PRIs. E. M. S. Namboodiripad is reported to have said, 'What is attempted in this bill under cover of giving more and more power to the Panchayati Raj institutions' is empowering the central government to decide 'What should be their composition, how they are to be elected, etc. The central government decides everything. This is the negation of decentralisation, a further dose of centralization'.

To grant constitutional status to local self-government, the Constitution (72nd Amendment) Bill, 1991, was introduced in the Lok Sabha in September 1991 and was referred to a Joint Committee of Parliament. On the basis of their report, the Lok Sabha passed the Bill on 22 December 1992 and the Rajya Sabha passed the Bill on the following day. After ratification by the legislatures of more than half the states, the president gave his assent to the Bill on 20 April 1993. The Act was brought into force on 24 April 1993 as the Constitution (73rd Amendment) Act, 1992. It has incorporated a new Part IX regarding panchayats, including a new Eleventh Schedule of subjects related to which the implementation of schemes for economic development and social justice may be entrusted to the panchayats. The Act enjoins upon the state governments to adopt a more or less uniform pattern of structure of PRIs across the country.

Following the passage of the 73rd Constitutional Amendment Act, legislatures of the various states have enacted detailed laws according to guidelines provided by the constitutional provisions (Part IX relates to the panchayats, containing Articles from 243 to 243-O).

11.5.1 Distinctive Features of New System

It may be pointed out that 'local government', including self-government institutions in both urban and rural areas, is an exclusive state subject under Entry 5 of List II of the Seventh Schedule, so that the Union cannot enact any law to create rights and liabilities relating to these subjects. The new system contained certain novel provisions, for example, direct election by the people in the same manner as at the Union and state levels; reservation of seats for women; an election commission to conduct election; and a finance commission to ensure financial viability of these institutions. In addition to these features, respective state legislatures are required to supplement by laws within Constitutional Amendment Act which will define the details as to the powers and functions of the various organs of local government.

It may be noted that these amendments do not apply to Jammu and Kashmir, Meghalaya, Mizoram, Nagaland and certain other areas as specified in the Article 243M.[32] These areas include scheduled areas under Article 244(1), tribal area under Article 244(2), hill areas of Manipur for

[31] Committee on Revitalisation of Panchayati Raj Institutions for Democracy and Development, under the chairmanship of L. M. Singhvi, New Delhi, 1986.

[32] By 83rd Constitution Amendment Act, 2000, reservation in panchayats need not be made in favour of the SCs in Arunachal Pradesh, wholly inhabited by tribal population.

which District Councils Act exists, and the district of Darjeeling in the state of West Bengal for which Darjeeling Gorkha Hill Council exists.

The main features of the Constitution (73rd Amendment Act, 1992), which would be legislated upon in all the states are discussed in brief in this section.

11.5.1.1 Three-tier System

The Constitution under Part IX envisages a three-tier system of panchayats: village panchayat, intermediate panchayat (where the population is above 20 lakhs) and district panchayat.[33] Smaller states with population below 20 lakhs will have option not to have intermediate level panchayat.

11.5.1.2 Composition of the Panchayat

Seats in panchayats at all three levels shall be filled by direct election. In addition, chairpersons of village panchayats can be made, members of the panchayats at intermediate level and chairpersons of panchayats at intermediate level can be members of panchayat district level. MPs, MLAs and MLCs could also be members of panchayats at the intermediate or the district level (on the decision of state legislature).

The electorate is called 'gram sabha' consisting of persons registered in the electoral rolls relating to a village comprised within the area of a panchayat. This gram sabha shall perform such functions and exercise such powers as may be entrusted to it by the state legislatures.

11.5.1.3 Reservation of Seats for SC/ST and Women

Article 243D provides reservation of seats for SCs and STs in proportion of their population.[34] If, for example, the SCs constitute 40% of the population and the STs 20%, then 40% and 20% seats shall be reserved for them respectively. Out of the seats so reserved, not less than one-third of the seats shall be reserved for women belonging to SCs and STs respectively. In addition, not less one-third of the total number of seats to be filled by direct elections in every Panchayat shall be reserved for women. A state may make provision for similar reservation of the offices of chairpersons in the panchayats at the village and other levels.

Legislature of the state shall be at liberty to provide reservation of seats and offices of chairpersons in panchayats in favour of backward class of citizens.

11.5.1.4 Duration of Panchayat

Every panchayat shall have a uniform five-year term and elections to constitute new bodics shall be completed before the expiry of the term. In the event of dissolution, elections will be compulsorily held within six months. The reconstituted panchayat will serve for the remaining period of

[33] Panchayat means an institution of self-government constituted under Article 243B for the rural areas. There are nearly 2.55 lakh elected panchayats in the country (June 2018).

[34] These reservations favouring the SCs and STs shall cease to be operative when the period specified in Article 334 (at present 70 years, i.e., up to 24 January 2020).

five-year term. It will not be possible to dissolve the existing panchayats by amendment of any Act before the expiry of its duration.

11.5.1.5 Qualification for Membership

Article 243F provides that all persons, above the age of 21 years, and who are qualified to be chosen to the state legislature shall be qualified to be chosen as a member of a panchayat.

11.5.2 State Election Commission

Article 243K provides for the constitution of a State Election Commission consisting of a state election commissioner (SEC) to be appointed by the governor for superintendence, direction and control of the electoral process including preparation of electoral rolls. To ensure the independence of the commission, it is laid down that SEC can be removed only in the same manner and on the same grounds as a judge of a high court. Further, it is laid down that courts shall have no jurisdiction to examine the validity of a law, relating to delimitation of constituencies or the allotments of seats, made under Article 243K.

11.5.3 Setting up of District Planning Committees

Article 243ZD of the Constitution mandates the setting up of District Planning Committees in every district, to consolidate the plans prepared by the panchayats and municipalities in the district and to prepare the draft development plan for the entire district.

11.5.3.1 Powers and Responsibilities of Panchayats

Article 243G provides that state legislatures have the legislative power, to confer on the panchayats such powers and authority as may be necessary to enable them to function as institutions of self-government. They may be entrusted with the responsibility of (a) preparing plans for economic development and social justice, (b) implementation of schemes for economic development and social justice and (c) in regard to matters listed in the Eleventh Schedule, containing 29 items.[35]

11.5.3.2 Powers to Impose Taxes and Financial Resources

Under Article 243H, a state may by law authorize a panchayat to levy, collect and appropriate taxes, duties, tolls and fees. The panchayat will receive adequate funds for carrying out their

[35] Eleventh Schedule (Article 243G) lists following items:

(i) Agriculture, (ii) land improvement, (iii) minor irrigation, (iv) animal husbandry, dairying and poultry, (v) fisheries, (vi) social forestry, (vii) minor forest produce, (viii) small-scale industries, (ix) khadi collage industries, (x) rural housing, (xi) drinking water, (xii) fuel and fodder, (xiii) roads, bridges, waterways, (xiv) rural electrification, (xv) non-conventional energy sources, (xvi) poverty alleviation programme, (xvii) education, including primary and secondary schools, (xviii) technical training and vocational education, (xix) adult and non-formal education, (xx) libraries, (xxi) cultural activities, (xxii) markets and fairs, (xxiii) health and sanitation, including primary health centres and dispensaries, (xxiv) family welfare, (xxv) women and child development, (xxvi) social welfare, (xxvii) welfare of the weaker sections, (xxviii) public distribution system, (xxix) maintenance of community assets.

functions. Grants from state government will constitute an important source of funding, but state governments are also expected to assign the revenue of certain taxes to the panchayat.

11.5.4 Constitution of Finance Commission

The Constitution further provides that State Finance Commissions (SFCs) be constituted every five years. SFCs are to make recommendations to the governor regarding the distribution between the state and panchayats of the net proceeds of taxes, duties, tolls, fees and so on, the determination of taxes, duties, tolls and fees, which may be assigned to, or appropriated by, the panchayats, and grants-in-aid to the panchayats from the Consolidated Fund of State, as well as measures needed to improve the financial position of the panchayats.

The report of the commission, together with a memorandum of action taken on it, shall be laid before the state legislature.[36]

11.6 Implementation of the Amendment Act, 1992

The 73rd Constitutional Amendment Act providing constitutional status and framework for the panchayats in India is a positive and a significant step towards making panchayats vibrant local democratic institutions, contributing significantly to ongoing process of democratization and development among rural people which constitute very large majority in this country. Yet it has to be seen whether it is being implemented in the spirit of framers of the Constitutional Amendment Act. Both the union and the state governments have been taking specific steps, although rather slowly by the latter, towards implementation of the Amendment Act.

11.6.1 Union Ministry of Panchayati Raj

As far as union ministry is concerned, it has been playing the role of a motivator, guide and supporter for the implementation of the Amendment Act in states and union territories. The Ministry of Panchayati Raj (MoPR) was created in 2004. It has the primary objective to ensure the compliance of the provisions of Part IX of the Constitution, provisions regarding the district planning committees as per Article 243ZD and Panchayat Extension to Scheduled Areas Act (PESA), 1996.

Today, there are more than 2.55 lakh panchayats in the country, which include 248,263 gram panchayats, 6,610 block panchayats and 595 district panchayats. There are more than 30 lakh panchayat representatives which also include nearly 14.37 lakh Elected Women Representatives. 'Panchayat' is a state subject and MoPR promotes Panchayati Raj through its schemes, advocacy with states, and by creating and sharing knowledge about Panchayati Raj.

Further, since majority of elected three million representatives in the panchayats lack adequate knowledge and experience about working of panchayats, orientation and training for them on large scale are needed. MoPR is trying to help the state governments financially and otherwise to

[36] These provisions are modelled on Article 280 which contains provisions regarding appointment of a Finance Commission for distribution of finances between the union and the states.

improve and expand requisite training programmes for these representatives and officers of panchayats.

Rajiv Gandhi Panchayat Sashaktikaran Abhiyan (RGPSA): To improve the functioning of PRIs, the MoPR implemented the RGPSA in the 12th FYP period. The RGPSA addressed the major constraints of inadequate devolution of powers, lack of manpower, inadequate infrastructure and limited capacity in the effective functioning of panchayats by providing manpower, infrastructure, training and promotion of devolution of power to panchayats and put in place structures of accountability. From 2015–16, the provision of funds to the states under the scheme was transferred to them. Nearly ₹200 crore were provided to the state governments to meet their capacity-building obligations under Fourteenth Finance Commission (FFC) Award, particularly to support training for Gram Panchayat Development Plan (GPDP).

Rashtriya Gram Swaraj Abhiyan (RGSA): A new restructured scheme, namely RGSA, to help PRIs to develop governance capabilities to deliver on the sustainable development goals (SDGs) was announced in 2016. RGSA has the following sub-schemes: (a) capacity building, (b) MMP on e-panchayat, (c) ATM services in panchayat bhawans and (d) incentivization of panchayats.

Besides, the FFC award (for the period of 2015–20) has created an opportunity for convergent plans at the local level and leadership by panchayats in providing basic amenities and services to the people. The thrust of the new scheme will be on the lines of the Gramoday se Bharat Uday programme which focuses on social empowerment, economic empowerment and enabled gram sabhas through, convergence of resources at the panchayat level. MoPR has supported states to develop state-specific guidelines for GPDP which converge all the resources over which the panchayats have command including FFC funds, MGNREGA funds, Swachh Bharat funds and so on.

Initiatives, undertaken by the MoPR for capacity building include support for training of all stakeholders of local governance; support for building training capability—infrastructure and human resources for training; support for providing computers and e-governance tools for information capture and governance support for strengthening governance in PESA villages; supporting material and guidelines have been prepared and disseminated to the states and training institutions.

e-Panchayat Initiatives: The MoPR is also working with the state governments towards automating internal workflow processes of nearly 2.5 lakh panchayats across the country, benefitting approximately 30 lakh elected members and about 10 lakh PRI functionaries and improve local governance and make democracy work effectively at grassroots level. In this regard, e-panchayat is one of the Mission Mode Projects (MMPs) under the Digital India programme of GoI. The project seeks to completely transform the functioning of PRIs, making them more transparent, accountable and effective as organs of decentralized self-governing institutions. This will make democracy truly decentralized. The states are also being provided financial support for manpower, computers and capacity building for the implementation of e-panchayat through the ministry's umbrella scheme, RGSA, under its restructuring. Under e-panchayat MMP, a suite of core common applications has been developed to address various aspects of panchayats' functioning, including planning, budgeting, implementation, accounting, monitoring, social audit and delivery of citizen services such as issue of certificates, licenses and so on.

11.6.2 State Governments and Union Territory Administrations

Both state governments and union territory administrations have taken steps towards passing of fresh panchayat laws or amendment to the existing ones in conformity with the Constitution (73rd Amendment) Act, 1992.

Within this broad framework, as local government is a state subject, state legislatures have a critical role in determining various aspects of Panchayati Raj in their states. Panchayats are to function as institutions of local government and prepare plans and implement schemes for economic development and social justice, but the precise devolution of powers and authority to panchayats is left to the states. The state legislatures are to decide on the nature of devolution to the panchayats, including the 29 matters illustratively set out in the Eleventh Schedule. Thus, states play a critical role in building panchayat capacities and in creating an appropriate framework for accountability and transparency.

11.6.3 Recommendations of Fourteenth and Fifteenth Finance Commissions

Under the FFC award for the period 2015–20, grants to the tune of ₹200,292.20 crore are being devolved to gram panchayats in the country, constituted under Part IX of the Constitution for 26 states to ensure stable flow of resources at regular intervals which will augment resources available with them to discharge their statutorily assigned functions.[37]

To facilitate better monitoring of the release and utilization of grants, including FFC grants, an online system (MIS) has been developed. PRIASoft (web-based panchayat accounting software) and PlanPlus (web-based participatory planning software) have also been developed by the ministry for adoption by the states. The 15th FC has been constituted on 27 November 2017 to strengthen cooperative federalism and protect fiscal stability.

11.7 Government Control and Accountability of PRIs

The objective of the 73rd Constitutional Amendment was to ensure that the panchayat system functions as the institution of democratic decentralization. But this objective has not been fully translated. As has been found in many research studies, the state governments treat the PRIs as organs of political power. Instead of assigning functions to the PRIs through statute, they have chosen to delegate legislation in the form of rules and executive orders. 'The task of assigning functions to the panchayats was given to the state legislature, but the same seems to have been usurped by the state governments'. In other words, like before the passing of the 73rd Constitutional Amendment, empowerment of panchayats still remains at the mercy of the government. The government in almost all states continues to function as symbols of centralized forces.

[37] It may be pointed out that the FFC has not recommended grants to non-Part IX areas under Sixth Schedule in Meghalaya, Mizoram, Tripura and Assam, the areas in the hill districts of Manipur, rural areas of Nagaland and Mizoram.

Some of the traditional methods of supervision and control are as follows:

1. Powers of sanction of budget
2. Powers of suspension and cancellation of resolution and orders
3. Powers of suspension and removal of chairpersons, vice-chairpersons and members
4. Powers of suspension and supersession of PRIs

The adoption of undemocratic method to suspend or remove elected members of the panchayats by the executive on its own judgement is relic of the colonial practice. This is a highly coercive instrument at the hands of the state government. The point is that there should be provisions and procedure in the State Panchayat Acts as to how elected persons or body as a whole could be suspended or removed from the office. But the coercive power to supersede the elected local body at the hands of the state government is exercised on the basis of political considerations. The state government should be taken to the task at the appropriate judicature.

Besides this, issues of accountability and transparency of panchayats are of serious concern. The state governments need to design the components of accountability of the PRIs. These are as follows:

1. Integrity in the use of resources and preventing rent-seeking tendencies of public officials/ representatives
2. Adherence to the rule of law in conducting public affairs
3. Exercise of administrative powers of officials and political executives in fair manner
4. Responsiveness of the PRIs to the urgent needs of the people
5. Performance of the PRIs in terms of efficiency and effectiveness.

11.8 Functioning of the Panchayati Raj System

Since the passage of the 73rd Constitutional Amendment Act, 1992, there have been significant improvements in the functioning of PRIs. In some states, panchayats are functioning as institutions of local government and prepare plans and implement schemes for economic development and social justice. In some states, however, they have failed, largely to meet the rural peoples' aspirations. The point is that there are positive as well as negative aspects revealed by the various studies on working of the panchayats system.

11.8.1 Positive Aspects and Contribution of the Panchayat System

One striking aspect of functioning of the revamped panchayat system is that it has been contributing more substantially than the preceding one to ongoing process of democratization among people. This is partly on account of the enlarged participation of women and socially backward classes in panchayat elections and their growing interest in panchayat activities, as they have been guaranteed increased representation in elected offices of members and chairpersons in panchayats. Moreover, rural people have now more intercommunications and interactions with the panchayat administration than with the district administration. They therefore tend to be increasingly vocal about their local needs and views. This tends to stimulate public response and public responsibility of the panchayats.

Second, there is a positive trend in the growth of panchayats in the countryside. As noted earlier, there are currently more than 2.55 lakh Panchayats (including 248,263 Gram Panchayats, 6,618 Block Panchayats and 595 District Panchayats). Panchayats are now more functionally active and are providing increased opportunities for development of rural leadership as elected panchayat members and in particularly as chairpersons. This leadership tends to be less conventional and more progressive than other local leadership. Their role is expected to contribute appropriately to socio-economic development in villages.

Third positive aspect is that although there are large variations in actual devolution of powers, functions and resources upon panchayat system across the states and union territories, on the whole, its functional role has become more substantial and spatially enlarged. For example, a new restructured, scheme, namely, RGSA is helping PRIs to develop governance capabilities to deliver on the Sustainable Development Goals (SDGs). This scheme, which includes sub-schemes such as e-panchayat and ATM services, is playing a critical role in building panchayat capacities.

Fourth, revamped district planning committees are now preparing composite rural and urban development plans. The panchayats and the municipalities are to collaborate jointly for this purpose. This has greatly lessened unnecessary dichotomy in development planning.

Further, it is noted that manpower support and assistance is being extended by the panchayat system to various state governments in the implementation of family planning/welfare programmes and for the protection and improvement of environment. These two national issues are very challenging, and mobilization of people support partly through the panchayat system for dealing with these is proving useful.

In some states such as Karnataka, Tamil Nadu, Andhra Pradesh and Maharashtra, gram panchayats are playing a significant role in the beneficiary-oriented programmes such as National Rural Drinking Water Programme, Swachh Bharat Mission (Gramin), education, women empowerment , etc.

11.8.2 Shortcomings in the Panchayat System

Decentralized governance, to be effective, has to ensure that citizens become the central focus in designing service delivery. But careful working of the panchayat system reveals that the PRIs suffer from several weaknesses.

First, many panchayats in several states have rather small population and therefore do not have even the minimum resources of their own to undertake basic services and activities autonomously. Their heavy dependence, financial and administrative, upon the state governments not only dilutes their appropriate autonomy but also introduces an element of uncertainty in their proposed programmes of activities. Most PRIs do not get financial resources from their respective governments in sectors of education and health.

Second, continuous partial paralysis in working of the gram sabhas in many villages in several states weakens people participation in panchayat affairs. Elected members, especially women members, lack a participatory approach. They hesitate to come forward to participate in socio-economic activities.

Third, substantial percentage of the elected members and chairpersons of the gram panchayats in particular are uneducated or semi-educated. As such their functional role is weak. This tends to depress efficiency and probity in standards which are already not satisfactory in many panchayats in several states.

Fourth, actual devolution of statutorily specified powers and functions along with transfer of requisite finances and administrative personnel to the panchayat system in a phased manner in many states has been inadequate so far. This is tending to cause frustrations among majority of chairpersons of the panchayats in several states.

A micro-level study on PRI reveals that

> [t]he authority of the Panchayati Raj System is limited to the District level only. The power of the administrative authority lies in the hands of the Bureaucrats. Out of 29 subjects in Eleventh Schedule, five departments are partially transferred to Panchayats in A&N Islands.[38]

Although the departments are transferred to the PRIs, most of the departments are still lying with the parent departments.

Fifth, panchayat administration has been deficient in requisite standards of efficiency, probity and social equity and pubic accountability. This has been partly on account of absence of well-organized panchayat administrative services and too much dependence of the panchayat upon the state government for deputed state personnel and also some dependence upon adhocism in recruiting their own personnel. Moreover, inadequacy of requisite understanding of their respective role by officials and the elected representatives within many panchayat system result in frictions between the two. This tends to create administrative distortions and malpractices in the functioning of many panchayats. Also, within several panchayat systems, selfish nexus between the officials and the elected chairpersons is resulting in nepotism and corrupt practices.

Sixth, within a district, there is dichotomy between the functioning of two wings of local government, panchayats and municipalities. This deprives them of beneficial coordination in provision of basic and welfare services quite often. In addition, the coordination between the panchayat system and the district administration offices or government field offices tends to be weak or fractional. This dilutes the local support system for active functioning of panchayats in several districts.

Seventh, it is pointed out that 'political parties have been taking part in Panchayat election and functioning in recent years particularly. But many of them have not as yet developed any policy guidelines or strategies to enable them to contribute to proper working of Panchayat system in various States'.[39] Particularly during the election time, 'the PRIs become arenas of political conflict'.[40]

---

[38] K. Mondal and A. Banerjee, 'Finances of PRI in the Absence of Legislature: A Micro-level Study in A&N Islands', *South Asian Journal of Socio-Political Studies* 16, no. 1, (July–December 2015): 66.

Five departments are agriculture, public works, fisheries, road development and electricity.

[39] Khanna, *Rural Local Government*, 88.

[40] R. K. Arora and R. Goyal, *Indian Public Administration, 3rd ed.* (New Delhi: New Age International Publishers, 2013), 434.

It would not be out of place that the 73rd Constitutional Amendment has not significantly altered the functional domain of the panchayats at various tiers. One of the serious concerns has been that the panchayats have been marginalized by the centre and the states by sponsoring schemes for rural areas without associating these bodies in their planning and implementation. The centrally sponsored schemes for provision and improvement of civic services have not been transferred to the local bodies for grassroots-level planning and implementation. Thus the major constraints are inadequate powers, lack of manpower, inadequate infrastructure and limited capacity in the effective functioning of panchayats.

Summary

Some important issues that need to be addressed in the context of decentralization and rural governance are summarized here.

First, panchayat system, in order to be rural-oriented governance, needs administrative and considerable support and safeguards from the states and central governments. Moreover, PRIs need mechanisms to ensure high levels of participation in the design and monitoring of the rural programmes. People must be empowered to participate in decision-making processes, enjoying equality, liberty, fraternity, fundamental rights and basic human needs. They should be involved in 'designing appropriate village development plans, preparation of people's budget with prioritization and allocation of resources based on their needs'.[41]

And second, as rural upliftment programmes need adequate financial resources and as the locally raised revenues are insufficient, the PRIs' prosperity and progress depend on the financial support of the state and central governments. With a view to strengthening these institutions from the financial point of view, setting up of SFCs every five years in order to provide an institutional basis for the fiscal relationship between the state and local bodies would have to be ensured. As far as possible, their financial dependency from the state and central governments does not come in the way of progressive realization of self-government objectives.

The third important issue relates to the need for strengthening administrative and managerial capabilities in the PRIs. PRIs need the administrative capacity for large-scale decentralization. The emphasis has to be on administrative skills in financial management, public communications and community relations.

The fourth issue is about elite capture of the PRIs. Nearly 80% of all PRIs have become victims of powerful elites. Given the unequal power structure that is a characteristic feature of most Indian villages, we have to ensure that the process of democratic decentralization is not made to subserve the vested interests of the rich and powerful in rural India to the detriment of the poor and the marginalized.

And, fifth issue relates to the need for resolving social fragmentation and conflict at the local level. At the each level of PRIs, there is the need for forums for mediating inter-group rivalries and forging cross-cutting ties among diverse competing groups. Good governance in the rural countryside requires institutions of conflict resolution. In order to create a functioning society, we need the PRIs to be institutions of conflict mediation and resolution.

---

[41] K. P. Shashidharan, 'Towards a Grassroots Democracy', *Financial Express* (Chandigarh), 2 June 2016.

Further, the panchayats can also arrange interaction of the service providers with the beneficiaries to create an enabling environment for better performance. As opposed to centralization, democratic decentralization can greatly enhance state capacity to quicken the pace of local development, be it social, economic or political. For this, state government (also union territory administration) should give more powers to PRIs to strengthen their wings. At the same time, there has to be introduction of social audit to keep a check on the functioning of panchayats. Proper social audit would help in creating a positive impact upon local governance.

12 Urban Decentralization and Local Governance

LEARNING OBJECTIVES

1. **To discuss the historical perspectives of urban decentralization**
2. **To examine the impact of the 74th Constitutional Amendment Act on the structure of urban governance**
3. **To discuss the laws and powers of the state government regarding control over urban local bodies**

Introduction

'Local governance', in recent years, has attracted the attention of social scientists, policy-makers as well as public mangers. But it is a complex issue and poses a formidable challenge in today's public management in our country. Within local government, urban governance is of critical importance as the happiness and prosperity of the local people depends on it.

What Is Urban Decentralization?

Decentralization as a major issue in the study of metropolitan growth has focused on a variety of phenomenon, such as the redistribution of people, employment and commerce. It has been established that metropolitan areas or big cities have changed from uninodal into multimodal cities. A conceptual discussion of the term 'urban decentralization' is presented here.

Urban decentralization may be defined as consisting of a movement of the residential population away from commercial and financial complex to areas on the outer edge of the city. Muller asserted that urban decentralization 'refers to the specific relocation of people and activities from city suburbs'.[1] Another definition is offered by Berry and Kasarda who used the term urban decentralization 'to denote the process whereby a suburban ring grows faster, either in relative percentage rates or in absolute numbers than the central city'.[2]

[1] P. O. Muller, *Contemporary, Suburban America* (Englewood Cliffs, NJ: Prentice Hall, 1981), xi.

[2] B. J. L. Berry and J. D. Kasarda, *Contemporary Urban Ecology* (New York: Macmillan, 1977), 180.

Implications of Local Governance

A democratic government believes in good governance practices, ethics and accountability to promote and meet the aspirations and expectations of the people. As such in governance practice, local government, operating at either the rural or the urban areas, lays emphasis on conducting its affairs within the framework of policies, internal and external regulations, in a transparent and responsible manner. After discussing the conceptual issues related to urban decentralization, we turn to discussion on empowerment of the local people and urban governance.

Since the enactment of the 74th Constitutional Amendment in 1992 (in force from 1 June 1993), there have been significant improvements in functioning of the municipalities. Yet, there is considerable ambiguity about the role the urban local bodies (ULBs) have to play in the overall urban governance system of the country. The subject of urban governance becomes more important when we consider the magnitude of problems arising from urbanization and unprecedented growth of the cities.

It is universally recognized that certain functions of government are best administered at the local level for the reason that decentralizing the provision of public services such as sanitation, water supply, health and social welfare maximizes welfare by responding efficiently to public needs. Municipal governments responsible to the people of municipalities are in a better position to cater to the local needs of the people than governments—centre or state—functioning from a distance. Before we talk about the structure and functioning of the municipalities in India as local government institutions, it is important to look to its past.

12.1 Historical Perspective of Urban Decentralization

12.1.1 Pre-Independence Period

Although local government in India has its roots in ancient and medieval times, in its present structure and style of functioning, it owes its origin to the British system of administration in India. Municipal government was first introduced in India in 1687 in Madras, now Chennai. An order of the court of directors enjoined the formation of a corporation composed of European and Indian members of the city of Madras for the purpose of local taxation. The experiment had a brief and unsuccessful trial. A charter of 1726 superseded the corporation by a mayor's court, which was more a judicial than an administrative body. No further mention of municipal legislation is to be found in any presidency for the next 50 years.

The Regulating Act, 1773, was the first Parliamentary legislation under which the governor general of British India was authorized to establish municipal administration in the three presidency towns, now called Chennai, Kolkata and Mumbai (erstwhile Madras, Calcutta and Bombay), by appointing justices of peace in these towns. Besides these presidency towns, Acts were passed for Bengal in 1842 and for the whole of British India in 1850 permitting the formation of local committee (based on the application of the inhabitants), to make better provision for public health and convenience and to raise tax in pursuance of this object. Following the report in 1863 of the Royal Army Sanitary Commission, highlighting unhealthy conditions of towns, action was taken by the different provincial governments to pass various municipal Acts (e.g., Bengal Municipal Act,

1884). The publication of Lord Mayo's Resolution on provincial finance which, in providing for a measure of decentralization from the centre to the provinces, emphasized the need of increased association of Indians in the administration. Lord Mayo's Resolution on financial decentralization of 1870 was responsible for the incorporation of the principle of election in the municipal law of provinces where it was not already recognized. By 1870, there were about 200 municipalities throughout British India.[3] The famous Ripon Resolution of 1882, which emphasized political education through introduction of local government to replace 'the more autocratic system' operating under district administration, could not however enthuse Indians in municipal administration. The result of the resolution in urban areas was a series of Provincial Acts providing for the following:

1. Election of members of municipal bodies to the number of half to three-fourths in each case
2. Grant to them the privilege in many cases of electing their chairman or vice-chairman
3. Enlargement of functions so as to include various aspects of public health, medical relief and education
4. Increase in powers, financial responsibilities and financial resources

Poor representation of Indians on local bodies and too much centralization, particularly under Lord Curzon, compelled the British Government for the appointment of the Royal Commission on Decentralization in 1907. Following the Decentralization Commission Report (1909) and the Montagu–Chelmsford Report (1918), under the GoI Act, 1919, municipal bodies were released from the control of the district officers. Local self-government became a transferred subject under the charge of a popular minister of the provincial legislature.

In the GoI Act, 1935, the power to enact legislation was specifically given to the provincial legislature by Entry 12 in the Provincial Legislative List. By virtue of this power, new Acts were enacted by many other provinces, vesting powers of administration in the hands of local government. However, with the introduction of provincial autonomy under the GoI Act, 1935, the interest of Indian nationalists in municipal affairs became less and political participation at the provincial legislatures took the shift.

12.2 Urban Decentralization After Independence and Before 74th Amendment

Under the 1950 Constitution of India, urban local government (ULG) is placed as a state subject. Entry 5 of the List II of the Seventh Schedule says, 'Local government, that is to say, the constitution and powers of municipal corporations, improvement trusts, district boards, mining settlement authorities and other local authorities for the purpose of local self-government or village administration'.

The Central Planning Commission in its Five Year Plans also highlighted the problems of ULBs and outlined strategies for overcoming these problems. Further, the central government has, from time to time, set up the following committees to improve the structure and functioning of ULBs:

[3] H. Tinker, *The Foundations of Local Self-government in India, Pakistan and Burma* (London: Athlone Press, 1954).

1. Local Finance Enquiry Committee, 1951
2. Committee on the Training of Municipal Employees, 1963
3. Committee of Ministers on Augmentation of Financial Resources of Urban Local Bodies, 1963
4. Rural–Urban Relationship Committee, 1966
5. Committee on the Service Conditions of Municipal Employees, 1968
6. Committee on Budgetary Reform in Municipal Administration, 1974
7. Study Group on Constitution, Powers and Laws of Urban Local Bodies and Municipal Corporations, 1982
8. The National Commission on Urbanization (NCU), 1988

12.2.1 Ministry of Urban Development and Central Council of Local Government

The Central Council of Local Government was set up in 1954 (erstwhile Central Council of Local Self-Government) as an advisory body to deal with problems of both rural and ULG. Since 1958, it deals with ULG body.

In addition, there is the Union Ministry of Urban Development, set up in 1985, which has the responsibility of broad policy formulation and monitoring of programmes in the area of urban development.

12.2.2 The National Commission on Urbanization

In 1988, in its report, the NCU expressed its concern thus:

> The inefficiency of our cities and towns is being perpetuated by obsolete, rigid and inefficient laws, regulatory provisions and norms. The urban centres, with their concentration of diverse activities, should be generators of wealth; instead, they have degenerated into parasites looking elsewhere for support. This is a perversion of the economic system, because logically it is the urban markets which should trigger off prosperity in rural areas. Instead, the cities claim that they cannot even pay for their own upkeep, and constantly hanker for subsidies. This distorts profoundly the basic relationship which should exist between the rural and the urban sectors of our economy.[4]

12.2.3 Constitution Amendment Bill, 1989

Complementary to the 64th Constitution Amendment Bill ensuring devolution of power of Panchayats, the 65th Constitution Amendment Bill was introduced in the Parliament to revamp the municipal government in India. The amendment sought to ensure that municipal bodies were invested with necessary powers and authority to enable them to function effectively as units of local government. Three types of *nagar palikas* (municipalities) were envisaged: nagar panchayats for population between 10,000 and 20,000; municipal councils for urban areas with a population between 20,000 and 300,000; and municipal corporations for urban areas with a population

[4] Extract from Second ARC, *Sixth Report on Local Governance* (New Delhi: GoI, 2007), 203–204.

exceeding 300,000. The 65th Constitution Amendment Bill could not be passed in the Rajya Sabha when it was introduced in October 1989. The moribund nature of municipal affairs has been indicated by the Bill as follows:

> In many states, local bodies have become weak and ineffective on account of a variety of reasons, including prolonged supersession's and inadequate devolution of powers and functions. As a result, Urban Local Bodies are not able to perform effectively as vibrant democratic units of self-government.[5]

12.3 74th Constitutional Amendment Act

When the country liberalized its economy in the early 1990s, it also took steps to amend its Constitution to provide for decentralized elected local governments. The Narasimha Rao government introduced the Constitution Amendment Bill (based on the 65th Amendment Bill) pertaining to municipalities in the Lok Sabha on 16 September 1991, which was finally passed by both the Houses in December 1992. After the Bill was ratified by a resolution of at least half the number of state legislatures, it received the assent of the president on 20 April 1993 (w.e.f. 1 June 1993) and was published as the Constitution 74th Amendment Act, 1992.[6] This Amendment Act (forming Part IX A of the Indian Constitution) gives a constitutional status to the municipalities, and its provisions are applicable to all states and union territories except the scheduled and tribal areas governed by Article 244(1 and 2).

12.3.1 Structure of Urban Governance

The structures required for civic governance are complex. While there is no uniformity in the pattern, all states have ULBs as institutions of decentralization which usually provide services of a purely local nature. These are created in designated urban areas as defined by the census and also for areas of special importance decided by the state/central government authorities. The small towns are covered under the discretionary criteria of urban settlement until these reach the required population threshold of 10,000 for municipalization with fully elected councils. Again, when a municipal area covers the population of about 300,000, the status of municipal corporation is generally accorded.

12.3.2 Different Types of Urban Local Governments

The 74th Constitutional Amendment lays down three types of municipal bodies:[7]

1. *Nagar panchayat* (by whatever name called)*:* This is for a transitional area, which is transforming itself from being a rural area into an urban area.

[5] India, 'Statement of Objects and Reasons', *Bill no. 159 of 1991 on Municipalities* (New Delhi: Lok Sabha Secretariat, 1991).

[6] Ministry of Urban Dévelopment, *Power to People: The Nagar Palika Act* (New Delhi: GoI, 1993).

[7] The term Urban Local Body (ULB), municipal body, municipal council in a generic sense and ULG have been used interchangeably in the report.

2. *Municipal council:* This is for 'a smaller urban area'.
3. *Municipal corporation:* This is for 'a larger urban area'.

Implicit in this classification of ULGs is the recognition of the need for variation in the functional domain and requirements depending on the size of the population they need to serve. The state government would decide the criteria for different types of municipal bodies apart from constituting industrial townships outside these three categories which need not be the elected bodies. The positions of the cantonments are left unaffected by the 74th Amendment Act.

12.3.3 Composition of Municipalities

The members of a municipality would generally be elected by direct election. The legislature of a state may by law provide for representation in a municipality of:

1. persons having special knowledge or experience in municipal administration;
2. members of Lok Sabha, state assembly, Rajya Sabha and legislative council; and
3. the chairpersons of committees constituted under Clause 5 of Article 243S.

12.3.3.1 Ward Committees

The 74th Amendment Act has also provided for the creation of elected ward committees and zonal committees in the big cities (with a population of 300,000 and more) and representation of their chairpersons in the city councils. In doing so, the elected ward councillors are given primacy in area-level decision-making. Further, it is open for the state legislature to constitute committees in addition to the ward committees.

12.3.3.2 Reservation of Seats for SCs/STs and Women

In municipalities, seats would be reserved for SCs and STs in proportion to their population and one-third of the total number of seats would be reserved for women. This includes the quota for women belonging to SCs and STs.[8] All reservations in favour of SCs and STs shall come to an end (on 24 January 2020) with the expiry of the period specified in Article 334. It has been left to the state legislature to prescribe by law the manner of reservation of the offices of the chairpersons of municipalities.

12.3.3.3 Duration of Municipalities

Article 243U prescribes that every municipality shall continue for five years from the date of its first meeting. But it may be dissolved earlier according to law. Article 243U further prescribes that, before dissolution, a reasonable opportunity of being heard must be given to the municipality. A municipality constituted after its dissolution shall continue only for the remainder of the term. But if the remainder of the period is less than six months, it shall not be necessary to hold elections.

[8] It is permissible for a state legislature to make provisions for reservation of seats or offices of chairpersons in favour of backward classes.

12.3.3.4 Qualification for Membership

Article 243V provides that all persons who have attained the age of 21 years and are qualified to be chosen to the state legislature shall be qualified to be chosen as a member of a municipality. Age for election to state legislature is 25 years (Article 173).

12.3.3.5 Powers and Responsibility of Municipalities

Legislatures of states have been conferred the power (Article 243W) to confer on the municipalities all such powers as may be necessary to enable them to function as institutions of self-government. They may be given the responsibility of:

1. preparing plans for economic development and social justice;
2. implementing schemes (poverty alleviation); and
3. implementing matters contained in the Twelfth Schedule which contains 18 items.[9]

However, major functions that the municipal bodies handle are (a) public health and sanitation, (b) water supply and drainage, (c) public works and roads, (d) primary education and (e) health clinics and maternity homes. The usual practice is to divide the state functions into various sub-functions and delegate some of these to the municipalities.

12.3.4 Finance and State Finance Commission

The legislature of a state may by law authorize a municipality to levy, collect and appropriate taxes, duties, tolls and fees. It can also assign to a municipality various taxes, duties and so on collected by the state government. Further grants-in-aid may be assigned to the municipalities from the state consolidated fund.

The SFC appointed under Article 243-I under Panchayat Finance Commission shall also review the financial position of the municipalities and make recommendations to the governor for the following:

1. The principles which should govern
   a. the distribution between the state and the municipalities of the net proceeds of the taxes, duties, tolls and fees leviable by the state and the allocation between the municipalities at all levels;

[9] Items listed in the Twelfth Schedule, Article 243W of the 74th Amendment: (i) urban planning, (ii) regulation of land use and construction of buildings, (iii) planning for economic and social development, (iv) roads and bridges, (v) water supply for domestic and commercial purposes, (vi) public health, sanitation and solid waste management, (vii) fire services, (viii) urban forestry, protection of the environment, (ix) safeguarding the interests of weaker sections including the handicapped and mentally retarded, (x) slum improvement and upgradation, (xi) urban poverty alleviation, (xii) provision of urban amenities and facilities such as parks, (xiii) promotion of cultural, educational and aesthetic aspects, (xiv) burials, cremation grounds and electric crematoriums, (xv) cattle ponds, prevention of cruelty to animals, (xvi) vital statistics including registration of births and deaths, (xvii) public amenities including street lighting, parking lots, bus stops and public conveniences and (xviii) regulation of slaughter houses and tanneries.

   b. the determination of the taxes, duties, tolls and fees which may be assigned to the municipalities; and
   c. the grants-in-aid to the municipalities from the consolidated Fund of the state
2. The measures needed to improve the financial position of the municipalities
3. Any other matter that may be referred to FC by the governor

The FC appointed under Article 280 would also make recommendation in regard to the measures needed to augment the Consolidated Fund of State to supplement the resources of the municipalities in the state on the basis of the recommendations made by the state.

12.3.4.1 Election to Municipalities

The State Election Commission constituted under Article 243K shall have the power of direction and control of (a) the preparation of electoral rolls for and (b) the conduct of all elections to the municipalities. The courts are debarred to examine the validity of a law relating to delimitation of constituencies or the allotment of seats made under Article 243 ZA.

12.3.4.2 Constitution of District and Metropolitan Committees

The 74th Amendment also provides for creation of the following:

1. District Planning Committee (243ZD), which shall prepare and forward the development plan to the state government
2. Metropolitan Planning Committee (243ZE), which shall prepare a development plan for the whole metropolitan area and forward to the state government

The composition of the committees and the manner in which chairpersons are to be chosen and seats are to be filled are to be provided by a law to be made by the state legislature. But it has been laid down that

1. in case of the District Planning Committee, at least four-fifth of the members shall be elected by the elected members of the district-level panchayat and of municipalities in the district from amongst themselves. Their proportion would be in accordance with the ratio of urban and rural population of the district; and
2. in case of Metropolitan Planning Committee, at least two-thirds of the members of the committee shall be elected by the members of the municipalities and chairpersons of the panchayats in the metropolitan area form amongst themselves.

With respect to functions that are to be performed by the district committee and Metropolitan Planning Committee (to prepare a development plan for the whole metropolitan area), the state legislature would by law make provisions including functions relating to planning and coordination for the metropolitan area.

12.4 Some Recent Programmes of Urban Governance

12.4.1 Union Ministry of Urban Development

The Ministry of Urban Development has the responsibility of broad policy formulation and monitoring of programmes in the area of urban development. Urban development is a state subject but the GoI plays a coordinating and monitoring role and also supports urban development through centrally sponsored schemes. The ministry addresses various issues of urban sector through policy guidelines, legislative guidance and sectoral programmes.

12.4.2 Smart Cities Mission

The Smart Cities Mission was launched by the central government in 2015. Smart Cities Mission is based on the idea of developing the entire urban ecosystem on the principles of complete and integrated planning.

The Mission is operated as a centrally sponsored scheme. The central government has announced the list of first 20 urban areas that will be developed as smart cities. They are Ahmedabad, Belagavi (Belgaum), Bhopal, Bhubaneshwar, Chennai, Coimbatore, Davanagere, Guwahati, Indore, Jabalpur, Jaipur, Kakinada, Kochi, Ludhiana, New Delhi, Pune, Solapur, Surat, Udaipur and Vishakhapatnam. The money is to be released for the Mission from the centre, and states would be part of this exercise.[10] GoI selected 27 more cities for conversion as smart cities.

In the approach of the Smart Cities Mission, the objective is to promote cities that provide core infrastructure and give a decent quality of life to its citizens, a clean and sustainable environment and application of 'smart' solutions. 'The focus is on sustainable and inclusive development and the idea is to look at compact areas, create a replicable model which will act like a lighthouse to other aspiring cities'. The core infrastructure elements in a smart city would include (a) adequate water supply; (b) assured electricity supply; (c) sanitation, including solid waste management; (d) efficient urban mobility and public transport; (e) affordable housing, especially for the poor; (f) robust IT connectivity and digitalization; (g) good governance, especially e-governance and citizen participation; (h) sustainable environment; (i) safety and security of citizens, particularly women, children and the elderly; and (j) health and education.

12.4.3 Atal Mission for Rejuvenation and Urban Transformation

The Atal Mission for Rejuvenation and Urban Transformation (AMRUT) was launched in 2015. The objective of the Mission is to improve basic urban infrastructure in 500 cities/towns which would be known as Mission cities/towns. The Mission is being operated as a centrally sponsored scheme. It aims to cover all cities and towns with a population of over one lakh with notified municipalities, including Cantonment Boards (civilian areas) and certain other cities such as capital towns, some cities on stem of main rivers and tourist and hill destinations.

[10] The deadline for commencing the execution of Smart Cities Mission was 25 June 2016.

The purpose of AMRUT is to (a) ensure that every household has access to a tap with assured supply of water and a sewerage connection; (b) increase the amenity value of cities by developing greenery and well maintained open spaces (e.g., parks); and (c) reduce pollution by switching to public transport or constructing facilities for non-motorized transport (e.g., walking and cycling). AMRUT makes states equal partners in planning and implementation of projects, thus actualizing the spirit of cooperative federalism. As of now, 497 cities/towns have been selected under this mission.

12.4.4 Urban Infrastructure and Governance

The extended phase of Urban Infrastructure and Governance (UIG) sub-component of Jawaharlal Nehru National Urban Renewal Mission (JNNURM) concluded in 2014. In the initial phase of project implementation under UIG sub-component, 538 projects at a total cost of ₹60,200.78 crore was sanctioned.

Out of the total 538 projects sanctioned earlier under UIG sub-mission, 243 projects have been completed till December 2014, and 295 projects are reported to be in various stages of implementation.

In addition to this project, there is an extended phase of Urban Infrastructure Development Scheme. The extended phase of Urban Infrastructure Development Scheme for Small and Medium Towns (UIDSSMT) sub-component of JNNURM concluded in 2014. Under the first phase of UIDSSMT, 801 projects at a total cost of ₹13,866 crore have been sanctioned. Of 801 projects taken up under UIDSSMT sub-mission, 454 projects have been physically completed until December 2014 and 347 projects are under various stages of implementation.

12.4.5 Scheme for UID in Satellite Towns Around Seven Mega Cities

Ministry of Urban Development is implementing a pilot scheme for urban infrastructure development in satellite towns around seven mega cities. The objectives of this scheme are as follows:

1. To develop urban infrastructure facilities such as drinking water, sewerage and solid waste management and so on at satellite towns around the seven megacities and to channelize their future growth so as to reduce pressure on the mega cities.
2. To implement reforms such as e-governance, property tax, double entry accounting, creation of barrier free environment, structural safety norms in compliance with the national building code, water and energy audit of water and wastewater utilities and implementation of service level benchmarks.
3. Strengthening implementation of reforms such as levy of reasonable user charges, earmarking of budgets for basic services and at least 10–15% of housing sites for the urban poor, formulation of byelaws to incorporate provisions for disaster management, water harvesting and reuse and recycle of waste water and implementation of public private partnership (PPP) projects.

12.4.6 Urban Transport

Significant improvement in public transport, pedestrianization and ion-motorized modes are a critical requirement for improving mobility in urban areas and thereby facilitating economic growth. Such improved mobility would also have a beneficial impact on the urban poor by improving their access to employment, education and health care. For urban planning, it is necessary to give attention to an appropriate policy for the integration of transportation and traffic plans with land use plans for every urban agglomeration.

A National Urban Transport Policy (NUTP) has been formulated by the GoI. The focus of the policy is to 'move people not vehicles'. This policy envisages integrated land use and transport planning, significant improvements in public transport, encouragement of non-motorized modes of travel, provision of adequate parking spaces as also a comprehensive set of measures for capacity building in urban transport planning.

12.4.7 National Heritage City Development and Augmentation Yojana

The National Heritage City Development and Augmentation Yojana (HRIDAY) was launched in 2015 with an initial coverage of 12 cities. The scheme is aimed at preserving and revitalizing the soul and unique character of the heritage cities in the country. The Mission is being operated as a central sector scheme and is initially being implemented in 12 identified cities, namely, Ajmer, Amaravati, Amritsar, Badami, Dwarka, Gaya, Kanchipuram, Mathura, Puri, Varanasi, Velankanni and Warangal.

12.4.8 Jawaharlal Nehru National Urban Renewal Mission

JNNURM was launched in 2005. It is a reform-driven, fast-track programme to ensure planned development of cities/towns with focus on efficiency in urban infrastructure/service delivery mechanisms and through community participation and enhanced accountability of ULBs/parastatal agencies towards citizens. Under JNNURM, priority has been accorded in sanctioning of projects for water supply, sewerage and drainage sectors. Also, projects have been sanctioned for urban transport sector which include construction of roads, flyovers, bus rapid transport system. The Mission has already sanctioned projects for 65 select cities across the country. Out of these 65 cities, 35 cities are with a million plus population and other 30 cities are either state capitals or cities of heritage and tourism importance, totalling 55 mission cities under UIG. This central government scheme has not been accepted favourably in many states.

12.5 State Government Control Over Urban Local Bodies

The law governing ULBs as prevalent in the states contains various provisions prescribing measures regarding governmental control over these bodies. Such controls are in the form of the following:

1. Necessity to seek approval of major projects by the state governments
2. Power of the state government to require production of documents
3. Power of the state government to inspect the offices or works of the ULBs
4. Power of the state government to issue directions to the ULBs
5. Power of the state government to suspend or cancel any resolution(s) passed by the ULBs
6. Power of the state government to dissolve or supersede the ULBs

Such powers are exercised through the district collector, the municipal commissioner and other officials of the state government.

For illustration, in the context of 'Dissolution of Corporation', the Punjab Municipal Corporation Act, 1976, lays down:

1. If in the opinion of government, a corporation is not competent to perform its duties or persistently makes default in the performance of duties imposed on it by or under this Act or any others law for the time being in force or exceeds or abuses any of its powers, the government may, by an order published, along with the reasons thereof, in the Official Gazette, dissolve such corporation; provided that the Corporation shall be given a reasonable opportunity of being heard before its dissolution.
2. When a Municipal Corporation is dissolved under Sub-section (1):
   a. all Councillors of the Corporation shall vacate their offices forthwith;
   b. all powers and duties of the Corporation during its dissolution shall be exercised and performed by such person or authority, as the government may, by notification, appoint in this behalf; and
   c. all property in possession of the Corporation shall be held by the government (Section 407).

Similarly, the state government has the power to call for records. For example, the Kolkata Municipal Corporation Act, 1980, prescribes that the state government may at any time require any municipal authority:

1. to produce any record, correspondence, plan or other documents;
2. to furnish any return, estimate, statement, accounts or statistics; and
3. to furnish or obtain any report, and thereupon such authority shall comply with such requirement (Section 113).

In this context, the Second ARC (2007) in its *Report on Local Governance* recommends the following:[11]

1. Municipal governments should have full autonomy over the functions/activities devolved to them.
2. If the state government feels that there are circumstances that make it necessary to suspend or rescind any resolution passed by the ULBs or to dissolve or supersede them, it should not do so unless the matter has been referred to the concerned local body ombudsman and the ombudsman recommends such action.

---

[11] Second ARC, *Sixth Report*, 309.

3. If, on any occasion, the state government is in the possession of records or has adequate reasons to initiate action against the ULBs or its elected representatives, it should place the records before the local body ombudsman concerned for investigation.

The Second ARC (2007) set up by the GoI in its *Report on Local Governance* is of the view that since

> local bodies (both urban and rural) constitute the third tier of governance, they must have full autonomy in the areas assigned to them. At the same time, it should also be the responsibility of the State Government to ensure that the local governments carry out their activities in accordance with law. But this should not translate into State Government exercising day-to-day control over the functioning of local governments. Thus, a balance has to be struck between the functional autonomy of the local governments and the State Government's responsibility to ensure proper governance under law. The powers of the State Government should be confined to a few items like suspension or cancellation of any resolution and dissolution or supercession, of the local body under special circumstances. But even such powers should be used sparingly and only after a report from the local body Ombudsman.[12]

In case of resolutions passed by the ULBs which are considered by the respective state government to be beyond their purview or where the state government is of the opinion that on grounds of absolute breakdown of the administrative machinery or financial bankruptcy or entrenched corruption, etc. the ULBs needs to be dissolved or superseded, it should place the records before the body ombudsman concerned for investigation.

12.6 Function of Local Government: An Appraisal

In a developing country such as India, rapid urbanization, caused by population growth and migration of people from rural areas, has been taking place unaccompanied by modernization in terms of infrastructure and good governance. There is a growing concern about the issues connected with urbanization, such as, environment pollution, slum settlements, poverty and inadequate amenities and services. This rate of urbanization is posing a threat to not only the natural environment but also to the achievement of the better quality of services. As the country continues to urbanize, with greater percentage of its people migrating from rural areas to urban areas, an integrated and decentralized approach to managing existing city resources and effectively planning for urban governance will be critical to the well-being of increasing numbers of its population.

The legislation of the 74th Constitutional Amendment in 1992 (w.e.f. 1 June 1993) has added a new dimension to the decentralization process in the country by assigning a constitutional status to ULBs. This Constitutional Amendment is aimed at gradual transfer of powers and authority of state legislatures to ULBs so that they function as institutions of self-government.

In addition, this Constitutional Amendment provides for the demarcation of ULBs' responsibilities under the Twelfth Schedule of the Constitution and the formation of SFCs to identify avenues for municipal finance and recommend criteria to devolve resources from the states to ULBs.

---

[12] Ibid., 308.

It is pointed out that these provisions, although not fully implemented, provided functional and financial autonomy within the framework of a democratic government structure, and made ULBs directly accountable to their citizens. But the exact demarcation of powers, functions and finances between the state government and ULBs is left to be determined by the state governments.

The appropriate structure of local finance—the mix of taxes, user charges and transfers—is critical to ensure that ULBs have access to the financial resources that they deserve, given the functions that are being devolved to them. However, revenue sources are hardly commensurate with their responsibilities. Two major tax revenue sources are property taxes and fees, fines and rent. Invariably, the expenditures are met to a great extent out of grants and loans given by the state government. In several instances, the state government is only the disbursing agency in the sense that it receives funds from the centre or international funding agencies to distribute among ULBs. Furthermore, the power of these bodies to tap resources is severely limited, as the state governments usually do not allow them to raise loans directly from the market. Even borrowings from financial institutions are usually required to be approved by the state government, apart from exercising controls on the tax powers of the local bodies.

Unfortunately, 25 years after the 74th Constitutional Amendment, ULBs find themselves in a financially precarious situation on all fronts—own revenues through taxes and non-tax sources, transfers as well as grants. As a result, ULB finances are in a mess. This has serious repercussion for how municipalities will finance their capital investments that are desperately required. Hence, what is required is action to improve the state of municipal finances in the country.

As far as the municipal functions are concerned, municipal bodies although constitutionally possess legally powers, in practice, this has not happened, and 'the state governments continue to intrude into the municipal domain through parallel legislations or executive decisions. The unlimited encroachment into the municipal domain by the states has affected the attainment of governance goals'.[13]

The 74th Constitutional Amendment provides for the creation of wards committees but leaves it to the states to determine their composition. Sadly, most states have not constituted these committees so far. And where they have been constituted, they are typically formed through nominations, usually of favourites of the local councillor or member of the legislative assembly. Three states, namely, Haryana, Karnataka and Tamil Nadu, which are fast urbanizing, present contrasting styles of functioning of local governments while pretending to abide by constitutional mandates. In the state of Haryana (Gurugram's city being near to the capital of India), urban development model raises some disturbing questions. Does in the city of Gurugram the collection of gated communities, malls and offices constitute a city? In this city environment pollution, slum settlements and transport system are causing health problems to the people.

As in most states, the state of Tamil Nadu functions 'as no more than extensions of state departments. Yet, it is claimed that, local governments in the state run relatively better even in the absence of devolution'.[14] Both Karnataka and Tamil Nadu have also not constituted metropolitan planning committees for the Bangalore and Chennai metropolitan areas in consonance with the mandatory provisions of Article 243ZE of the Constitution.[15]

---

[13] M. R. Biju and M. R. B. Padmanabha, 'Governance of Small Cities in India: Issues and Challenges', *South Asian Journal of Socio-Political Studies* 16, no. 2 (January–June 2016): 65–71.

[14] T. R. Raghunandan, 'Urban Decentralization: The Forsaken Opportunity', *Livemint*, 30 April 2013.

[15] Urban Planning is in the hands of institutions such as the Chennai Metropolitan Development Authority or the Bangalore Development.

In the state of Karnataka, there was a tendency to delay in holding panchayat and municipal elections. On the initiative of the SEC, the Supreme Court passed a stinging order directing the state to give full cooperation in holding elections for ULBs.

Despite a federal structure and a long tradition of village democracy, the aims of decentralization, however, do not seem to have materialized. Decentralization does not seem to have made much headway beyond the level of the federating states. Given the framework, it appears that the local bodies still derive their powers and functions by delegation from the states and have a limited functional or fiscal jurisdiction of their own. The urban local institutions still continue to depend heavily on the state governments for their funds. The authority of local bodies has been undermined by various means, such as, keeping the elections in abeyance and by financial control over them.

Consequent upon the 74th Amendment Act, with certain mandatory and enabling provisions, one can assert that certain uniformities of structure have emerged across the country for decentralization of power. The uniformities are in terms of tiers in consonance with the 73rd and 74th Amendments. Wherever enabling provision exists, like mode of elections to different posts, periodicity of meetings of various bodies or percentage of reservations for standing committees, different states have adopted different provisions in their respective Acts. The 73rd and 74th Amendment Acts, indeed, have created local government structures (panchayats and municipalities) 'necessary for decentralization' of power. Further, constitution of finance commission for resource allocation and creation of separate election commission to conduct elections to local bodies will ensure continuance and healthy functioning of municipalities in the country. However, for truly democratic decentralization of power, these bodies should be given enough powers. It is doubtful whether all the state governments have done enough to these bodies.

An important factor impeding the process of decentralization is the adoption of centralized planning as a strategy of development. Under the 73rd and 74th Amendment Acts, there is an obligation on the states to endow local governments with adequate functional and fiscal powers.

While in the last ultimate analysis, there is no substitute for local self-government, there are certain advantages in having certain governmental functions taken up at a unified higher level. What is needed to effect the necessary decentralization is the political will on the part of the centre and states, and this has to be created through consultation rather than confrontation. Accordingly, constitutional status and legal backing to local governments would provide a much needed stimulus for decentralization in India.

12.7 Suggestions for Improvement of Local Government

For ensuring success of reforms, several issues need suitable attention and action by the governments and other organizations concerned. These are summed up here.

1. State government should adopt more positive policy than hitherto towards local government. Support and guidance rather than expediency, *ad hocism* and partisanship should be the basis of this policy.

2. The existing separate Department of Urban Local Government and of Rural Local Government and their respective directorates need to be consolidated into one composite Department of Local Government and directorate to ensure a well-integrated policy and coordinated support in regard to local government functioning in urban and the rural areas. Also, the consolidated department should have appropriate expertise and constructive attitude within it to provide support and guidance to local government to improve considerably its functional capabilities.
3. The Central Council of Local Government set up under Article 263, which now reviews working of only ULG and advises union and the state governments, should be empowered, as earlier, to take within its purview rural local government as well. This would facilitate coordinated policy and action in regard to both wings of local government.
4. There should also be a standing consultative committee, comprising representatives of local governments and state governments in every state to discuss issues and problems of local government and advise both the state government and local government institutions, accordingly for appropriate action.
5. Small local government institutions (panchayats and municipalities) should be consolidated into medium sized ones so as to be financially and administratively viable.
6. Further delays in devolution of powers and finances to local governments should not take place any longer so as to avoid general frustrations among people and their elected representatives.
7. Management system in local government needs to be appropriately overhauled as at present it lacks adequate efficiency, professional integrity and public relations.
8. Suitable orientation of very large number of the elected representatives and training of local government bureaucrats should be improved and enlarged considerably to be more effective than hitherto.
9. Political parties should pay more attention to revamping of their role in working of local government and developing appropriate programme agendas for this purpose.
10. The media and nongovernment organizations (NGOs) and social scientists and intelligentsia need to play a more positive role in guiding and helping local governments to deal with their problems or constraints.

At present, people's expectations about reformed and revitalized local government aiming at contributing to processes of democratization and development suitably and vigorously are very high. However, much depends upon the union government, state governments, elected local government representatives as well as political parties for playing their appropriate role vigorously and meaningfully for increasing success of the reformed panchayats and municipalities in the length and breadth of this socially and economically diverse and vast country. It is encouraging to find that the union government is showing a good deal of earnestness in providing increasingly positive support for this purpose. Certain state governments also seem to be enthused making efforts for increasing success of the reformed system of local government.

Summary

Local governance is a critical factor to the citizen's overall development. But it poses a formidable challenge to the government. In order that fruits of good governance reach the citizens, democratic institutions such as municipal governments and panchayats need careful nurturing, abundant resources and functional autonomy. But transfer of power from the state authority is difficult. Despite 74th Constitutional Amendment in 1992, ULBs (municipalities) find themselves in a financially precarious situation on all fronts. This has seriously affected the functioning of the local government institutions. There are no signs of gradual transfer of powers and authority of state legislatures to ULBs. These bodies do not function as institutions of self-government. What is required is action to improve the state of municipal finance in the country. Such a transformation in the role of states vis-à-vis local governments is critical. At the same time, local government empowerment must ensure better quality of governance. The existing processes of service delivery and governance need to be improved at the local level.

13 Managing Control Over National Expenditure

LEARNING OBJECTIVES

1. **To discuss the system of parliamentary control over national expenditure**
2. **To discuss the role of the union finance ministry in the socio-economic development of the country**
3. **To bring out the role of the CAG as an independent authority**

Introduction

Public money, acquired through taxation and cess, sales of goods and services, confiscation and fines and by some other regulatory and legal means, must be used for purposes approved and within the amounts appropriated. In other words, there has to be the necessity of justifying the public expenditure by government departments. This calls for the establishment of institutions that are tasked to exercise control over national expenditure. Mainly, there are three types of controls by the constitutional bodies:

1. Parliamentary Control
   a. Committee on Public Accounts (1952)
   b. Committee on Estimates (1950)
   c. Committee on Public Undertakings (1964)
   d. Standing Committees (1993)
2. Treasury Control
   a. Finance Ministry
3. Audit Control
   a. Comptroller and Auditor General

13.1 Parliamentary Control

Parliament, which is the legal body of representatives of the people, is recognized as an important institution of control over national expenditure. Parliamentary control establishes the democratic principle that taxes cannot be imposed nor money spent without the approval of the parliament.

Article 113(3) of the Indian Constitution stipulates that 'no demand for a grant shall be made except on the recommendations of the president'. It is the function of the parliament not only to vote grants of public expenditure but also to ensure that the grants made by it are spent legally and prudently. All receipts and disbursement of the union are kept under the following:

1. Consolidated Fund of India (forming of receipt of revenues and raised loans) from which money cannot be withdrawn except under Parliament's authority (Article 266)
2. Public Account of India (forming receipts such as deposits, service funds and remittances) from which disbursements are not subject to the vote of Parliament (Article 284)
3. Contingency Fund of India which has been set up under Article 267(1) to meet unforeseen needs not provided in the Annual Appropriation Act

The Parliament gets the opportunity of control over the political executive not only at the budget sessions but at other times as well. The control which parliament exercises is briefed here.

13.1.1 In-built Techniques of Control

1. *President's address:* MPs, after the president's address to the new session, get an opportunity to criticize the government for its alleged acts of omission as well as commission.
2. *Budget discussion:* During the general discussion on the Finance Bill, Submission of Demands for Grants, and discussion during the passage of the Appropriation Bill, the intervening period provides ample opportunities to the members of both the houses of Parliament to discuss the budget proposals and general policy of taxation. The estimates of expenditure charged on the Consolidation Fund of India are subject to discussion but not to a vote of Parliament,[1] while on the rest of the expenditure, the Lok Sabha has the power to assent, to reject or reduce but not to increase, the amount of any demand.[2] The Lok Sabha, thus, has limited power to change the demands. Members of the Lok Sabha can move three kinds of cut motions to assent, reject or reduce the amount of a demand. The Rajya Sabha members cannot move these motions. The cut motions are given here.
   a. *Policy Cut Motion*. 'That the amount of the demand be reduced to Rupee 1', indicating disapproval of the policy underlying the demands. It is known as 'Disapproval of Policy Cut'.
   b. *Economy Cut Motion*. 'That the amount of the demand be reduced by a specific amount' to project economy that can result from the suggestion of the member.
   c. *Token Cut*. 'That the amount of the demand be reduced by ₹100 to ventilate a specific grievance'.

   These cut motions serve no useful purpose as the cabinet enjoys the support of the majority of the members of the Lok Sabha.
3. *Question Hour:* The first hour forms the most valuable part of the day's proceedings, and is reserved for raising starred and unstarred, supplementary and short notice questions by the members of the Parliament. It serves the purpose of asserting the supremacy of Parliament (Doklam stand-off with China raised in Parliament Monsoon Session 2017).

---

[1] *Constitution of India* (1950), Article 113 (1).
[2] *Constitution of India* (1950), Article 113 (2).

Besides question hour, financial matters are also discussed during the *Zero Hour* discussion (India's innovation since 1962), Adjournment Debates (discussion on a definite matter of urgent public importance with the consent of the speaker) and *No Confidence Motions* (Rule 198 of the Rules of Procedure provides an occasion when the entire or part of the government policy is criticized).

In addition, there are three parliamentary committees—Public Accounts Committee (PAC), Estimates Committee (EC) and Committee on Public Undertakings (CPU)—which have an important role to play in the control of public expenditure.

13.1.2 Committee on Public Accounts

The Committee on Public Accounts (often called Public Accounts Committee) was created in 1923 on the suggestion of the Montford Reforms (1918) and also on the recommendation of the GoI Act, 1919, for finding out financial irregularities.[3] When it was constituted at the Centre in 1923, it had 12 members—8 non-officials elected by assembly members and the remaining 4 officials, nominated by the governor general. The finance member acted as its chairman. The auditor general under the GoI Act, 1919, used to assist the committee. His reports became important documents for the investigation by the PAC.

> From its very inception, the Central Public Accounts Committee became a major force in the legislative control of public expenditure. Despite the limitations of its constitution and the restrictions on its authority, it exercised enormous influence in bringing pressure to bear upon Government to enforce economy in the expenditure of public moneys.[4]

In its very first report, the PAC observed:

> The Departments of the Government of India will realize that they are now, for the first time, being brought face to face with the necessity of justifying their expenditure in detail to a responsible body of representatives of the Indian tax-payer. By realizing this, they will be led, naturally, as expenditure is incurred during the course of the year, to keep in mind and devise machinery for the task of justifying their expenditure before the Assembly.[5]

Initially, the PAC consisted of 15 members elected by the Lok Sabha from among its members every year. Later, its membership was increased to 22 in 1953 to provide representation to the Council of States. At present, as constituted, the committee consists of 22 members—15 from Lok Sabha and 7 from Rajya Sabha. Members are elected by the parliament every year from among its members according to the principle of proportional representation by means of a single transferable vote to enable all parties secure due representation on it. The term of office of the members is only one year but by convention, members are re-elected for another year. The chairman of the

[3] In the UK, PAC of the House was constituted in 1866 to consider the report of the CAG to examine official witnesses, usually permanent secretaries of departments on matters relating to their charges, and to make thereafter such recommendations as it considered necessary to the House.

[4] Asok Chanda Roy, *Indian Administration*, 2nd ed. (London: George Allen and Unwin, 1967), 172–73.

[5] Ibid., 173.

committee is appointed by the speaker from amongst its members.[6] The chairman has a casting vote in case of a tie. The quorum for a meeting is four members.

13.1.2.1 Functions

Article 308 of the Rules of Procedure and Conduct of Business in the Lok Sabha prescribes the functions and duties of the PAC. The committee, as embodied in the Rules of Procedure, is to satisfy itself

1. that the moneys shown in the accounts as having been disbursed were legally available for and applicable to the service or purpose to which they have been applied or charged;
2. that the expenditure conforms to the authority which governs it; and
3. that every re-appropriation has been made in accordance with the provisions made in this behalf under rules framed by competent authority.

It shall be also the duty of the committee

1. to examine the statement of accounts showing the income and expenditure of the state corporations, trading and manufacturing schemes and projects, together with the balance sheets and statements of profit and loss accounts which the president may have required to be prepared or are prepared under the provisions of the statutory rules and the report of the CAG thereon;
2. to examine the statement of accounts showing the income and expenditure of autonomous and semi-autonomous bodies, the audit of which may be conducted by the CAG of India either under the directions of the president or under a statute of the Parliament;
3. to consider the report of the CAG in cases where the president may have required him to conduct an audit of any receipts, or to examine the accounts of stores and stocks; and
4. if any money has been spent on any services during a financial year in excess of the amount granted by the House for that purpose, the committee shall examine, with reference to the facts of each case, the circumstances leading to such an excess and make such recommendation as it may deem fit.

The main function of the PAC is to examine the reports of the CAG with a view to ascertaining that the money granted by the parliament has been used by the government 'within the scope of the demand'. This phrase demands that expenditure should not merely not exceed the appropriations made with parliamentary approval but also that the nature of items of expenditure compiled against a grant should warrant their being so recorded. In this connection, it is clarified that PAC is not concerned with the question of policy; rather, it is only concerned with the policy of the method of expenditure. As a rule, it expresses no opinion on points of general policy, but the question whether there is any extravagance or waste in carrying out that policy is within its field of inquiry. The PAC concentrates more on a general control of economy and leaves questions of internal administration to the minister in charge of the department. It considers itself justified,

[6] Since 1967, the chairman of the PAC is selected from the opposition. None of the 22 members shall be a minister in government.

however, in calling attention to weak points in the administration itself, leaving the department to remedy them.[7]

13.1.2.2 Role and Evaluation of the PAC's Functioning

The foregoing discussion on the charter of the PAC would indicate that the committee has a useful role to play in focusing attention on instances of wasteful expenditure, malpractices and serious financial irregularities. Its role is quite significant in the sense that it has kept the executive accountable to Parliament and thereby considerably improved, and lent a new dimension to the country's fiscal policies. Notwithstanding the fact that the committee has no power to compel any administrative action to be taken on its recommendations, its power is indirect and lies nominally in the potential results of its reports and in the publicity which it is able to give to the questions it examines and in the 'moral effect of its criticism'.

The examination of the committee extends, to use an oft-quoted remark, 'beyond the formality of the expenditure, to its wisdom, faithfulness and economy'. The purpose of this comprehensive review is to ascertain whether the executive has observed the principle of prudent housekeeping in national expenditure.

By convention, the government invariably accepts the committee's recommendations. If, in an individual case, the government feels that the recommendation is unacceptable or inappropriate, it makes a representation to the committee for a reconsideration. If the committee reaffirms its earlier recommendation, the ultimate decision must rest with the Parliament. In actual practice, however, such a situation is not allowed to develop and differences are resolved by a process of consultation.

In 2011, the PAC probed the 2G spectrum scam which brought the committee to public attention. Similarly, the PAC headed by senior Congress leader K. V. Thomas took a serious note on the demonetization (8 November 2016) impact and started probing the move wherein it decided to call RBI Governor Urjit Patel, Finance Secretary Ashok Lavasa and Economic Affairs Secretary S. Das, and a decision was taken unanimously by all members of the PAC committee.[8]

The PAC of the Parliament also resolved on 27 May 2016 to take up the CAG report on the Augusta Wasteland issue for examination that rocked the Parliament throughout first week of May 2016.[9]

All the recommendations have a positive impact on the government administration in general and on different sectors of the economy in particular. Highlighting the importance and impact of the PAC, S. K. Mehta writes in the *Indian Journal of Public Administration*:

> During the period of its existence, the Committee has given ample proof of what is required of a Parliamentary Committee which is charged with the responsibility of seeing that the Executive acts in financial mattes within the parameters assigned to it by the Parliament, both as regards raising revenue and spending it.[10]

[7] The members of the committee may ask any question that has a financial bearing on the expenditure in the accounts under consideration. The committee, however, as a whole has no power, even after the minutest examination and on the clearest evidence, to disallow any item of expenditure. It can only comment on that item.

[8] See *EconomicTimes.com*. https://economictimes.indiatimes.com/news/economy/policy/demonetisation-public-accounts-committee-to-call-rbi-governor-in-january-to-review-economic-impact/articleshow/55724523.cms (accessed on 27 February 2017).

[9] See *The Indian Express* (Chandigarh), 28 May 2016.

[10] S. K. Mehta, 'Impact of PAC on Executive: A Case Study', *Indian Journal of Public Administration* 35, no. 1 (1989): 40.

Notwithstanding the fact that the committee has no power to compel any administrative action to be taken on its observations, this has not affected the effectiveness of the committee's recommendations.

It may be concluded that the PAC is an important institution tasked with the responsibility of assessing the financial irregularities caused by administrative action. Moreover, the conventions developed by the PAC conform to the highest traditions of a parliamentary democracy.

13.1.3 Committee on Estimates

The Committee on Estimates (often called Estimates Committee or EC) assists the Parliament in the exercise of its control over national expenditure. The EC was constituted on 10 April 1950 after the enactment of the Constitution Act in November 1949. But before this, there was an elected Standing Finance Committee, attached to the finance department. But, it had hardly any of the attributes of the present EC.

It had long been felt that to make parliamentary control over expenditure fuller and more comprehensive, it was also necessary to subject the estimates presented to the Parliament to a detailed examination in order to secure possible economies in the execution of plans and programmes. Parliamentary control over expenditure can be regarded as complete only when both of these functions—utilization of appropriations prudently and detailed examination of the estimates—have been properly carried out. In the case of second function, it was felt that a revision of estimates before their presentation to the Parliament would dilute ministerial and treasury responsibility and would also commit the Parliament to the proposed estimates.

In order to overcome this difficulty, a provision was made for the scrutiny of these estimates after they have been voted by Parliament, so that its recommendations could be embodied in the estimates of subsequent appropriations. It was acknowledged that this arrangement would not only leave the responsibilities of the ministers, departments and the treasury undisturbed, but would also secure effective parliamentary control over future estimates.

In proposing the constitution of an EC, Dr John Mathai, the then union finance minister, hoped that the committee would exert a healthy influence upon the course of public expenditure in two directions. In the first place, the committee's suggestions and criticisms would give very useful guidance to the government in the matter or regulating expenditure. Secondly, the knowledge that the expenditure of the government and of the various departments of government would be examined in detail by an independent authority would act as a deterrent to extravagance in public expenditure.

13.1.3.1 Composition and Functions of the EC

Estimates Committee was constituted on 10 April 1950. It is elected every year from amongst the members of the House of the People only, according to the principle of proportionate representation by means of a single transferable vote. The membership of the committee was initially fixed at 25, but was increased to 30 later in 1956, to facilitate the constitution of sub-committees to undertake an intensive examination of the estimates over a wider field.[11] The chairman is selected

[11] A minister cannot be elected as a member of the committee.

by the speaker from amongst the members of the committee. Although the tenure of the committee is only one year, the maintenance of continuity is sought by a convention according to which only one-third of the members retire every year.

The EC examines the estimates referred to it by Lok Sabha or the speaker and the estimates which it may deem fit with a view to:

1. 'report what economies, improvements in organisations, efficiency and administrative reforms, consistent with the policy underlying the estimates may be effected;
2. suggest alternative policies in order to bring about efficiency and economy in administration;
3. examine whether the money is well laid out within the limits of the policy implied in the estimates; and
4. suggest the form in which estimates can be presented to Parliament'.[12]

On election, the EC undertakes the review of selected estimates after having collected the necessary and relevant material from departments concerned. The material assembled forms the basis of a subsequent examination of the estimates. As the first step, the questionnaire, is transmitted to the ministries which are required to furnish full and complete answers to the points raised, supplemented by any additional material or any representation which they may choose to make. These are then studied in committee or sub-committee, as the case may be, as a prelude to an examination of the departmental officials. Before the conclusions are finally embodied in a report, the convention is for the chairman of the committee to discuss these informally with the minister concerned, but only when the committee is unable to agree fully with the policy reflected in the estimates. The draft reports are then finally considered and the majority view is presented as the unanimous recommendation of the committee; no notes of dissent are permitted. A copy of the report, as adopted by the committee, is sent to the ministry for factual verification before presenting it to the House. The reports, which are in form of recommendations, are then submitted to the Lok Sabha.

Although the report of the EC is not discussed in the House, it is open, however, to any member to refer to the report at the time of the general discussion on thc budget. As it is a parliamentary committee, the recommendations of the EC are given due weight by the government. If, in an individual case, the government feels that the recommendation is inappropriate or unacceptable, it makes a representation to the committee for its reconsideration. The committee reviews the position and may reaffirm the previous recommendation. If, after these processes, the differences still remain unresolved, it is for the Parliament to take a final decision. In practice, however, differences are sorted out by a process of consultation. The report contains following three types of recommendations:

1. For improving the organization
2. For securing the economy
3. For providing guidance in the presentation of estimates

[12] Lok Sabha Secretariat, *Rules of Procedures and Conduct of Business in the Lok Sabha*, 9th ed. (New Delhi: Author, 1957), 310.

13.1.3.2 Role and Evaluation of EC's Functioning

The EC devotes a great deal of attention to the organizational aspect and to measures which would, in its opinion, provide that the money voted by the Parliament was better spent. In its very first report, it touched upon the efficiency and organization of the ministry which it had taken up for examination. The second report was entirely devoted to the reorganization of the secretariat of the departments of government. Since then, almost every report has touched upon the question of efficiency and administrative reorganization. Its Ninth Report was devoted entirely to questions of administrative, financial and other reforms. Similarly, the Sixteenth Report dealt with the organization and administration of nationalized undertakings.

Since its inception in April 1950, the committee has presented 964 reports, covering almost all the ministries/departments of GoI. Out of these, 496 are the original reports and 468 are reports on action taken by the government on earlier reports of the committee as on 10 December 2010.

These activities of the EC have not been adequately regarded by the secretaries to government. A great deal of their time is certainly lost in trying to defend the policies of government and the present structure and functions of their departments. This practice of the committee has created an embarrassing situation for the permanent officials of the departments who are required to defend before a parliamentary committee the policies of government. But, in a democracy, it is the responsibility of the ministers to justify on the floor of the House the policies of government, if challenged by the opposition. The EC cannot be the forum for discussion of policy, nor can officials be counsels for defence.

Moreover, a committee with a floating membership can hardly be sufficiently familiar with the administrative processes and problems to be able to make any significant contribution towards administrative reorganization. Its activities thus encroach indirectly on the policymaking functions of government and its reproaches undermine public confidence in the government administration.

Like the PAC, the EC has played an important role in focusing attention on instances of wasteful expenditure and serious financial irregularities. The EC makes a detailed analysis of the estimates of the ministers and examines to what extent the government policies have been carried out in the most efficient and economical manner.

The recommendations of the EC have touched on matters of administrative reorganization, departmental working and effecting economy. The committee has provided guidance to general aspects of estimates presentation. Its recommendations are of considerable value in respect of functional and economic classification of budgets.

However, despite severe criticisms levelled against the EC, it is performing a useful role in the Indian administrative system. It keeps the machinery of administration under parliamentary scrutiny which is a very healthy feature. It acts as a standing committee on administrative improvement by highlighting the shortcomings and mistakes of public organizations. Its role is quite significant as the government accepts almost all its recommendations.

A modification of the terms of reference of committee, more on the lines of its counterparts in other parliamentary democracies, will not only enhance its usefulness as an effective mechanism of parliamentary control but will also remove the possibility of interference with the functions of other constitutional and established authorities.

13.1.4 Committee on Public Undertakings

13.1.4.1 Composition and Functions of the CPU

The CPU, set up by the Parliament in May 1964, is a financial committee of the Parliament. It consists of 22 members—15 elected by the Lok Sabha and 7 by Rajya Sabha, from amongst their members, according to the principle of proportional representation by means of a single transferable vote. The chairman is appointed by the speaker from amongst the members of the committee. A minister is not eligible to become a member of the committee. The term of the committee does not exceed one year.[13]

The CPU is essentially an important institution of parliamentary financial control over public enterprises and thereby exercising control over public expenditure. With the increase in the number and massive investments of public funds in the public enterprises, it was felt that a separate committee of the Parliament for public undertakings be set up on the pattern of the Select Committee on Nationalised Industries in Britain. (It has been now abolished and replaced by a new separate departmental select committee with terms of reference covering its departments' associated public bodies, including nationalized industries.) Referring to the urgency of the creation of a control mechanism, Asok Chanda writes,

> Parliament could hardly rest content with the dwindling opportunities of reviewing the working of state enterprises. Massive investments of public funds made in their creation and the unceasing complaints of their inefficient and wasteful management had also disturbed Parliament and made it feel that it should be better informed about the state enterprises and be able to make constructive suggestions for improving their performance.[14]

13.1.4.2 Functions

The committee which was formed during the budget session on 1 May 1964 has been given the following functions:

1. To examine the reports and accounts of the public undertakings specified in the schedule
2. To examine the reports, if any, of the CAG on the public undertakings
3. To examine in the context of the autonomy and efficiency of the public undertaking whether the affairs of the public undertakings are being managed in accordance with sound business principles and prudent commercial practices
4. To examine such other functions vested in the public accounts and the EC in relation to public undertakings specified in the schedule or under the Rules of Procedure and Conduct of Business of this House, as are not covered by clauses (a), (b) and (c) and as may be allotted to the committee by the speaker from time to time

The committee is not to examine and investigate the following:

1. Matters of major government policy as distinct from business or commercial functions of the government

[13] The CPU was set up in May 1964 on the recommendation of the Krishna Menon Committee.
[14] Asok Chanda, *Indian Administration*, 198.

2. Matters of day-to-day administration
3. Matters for the consideration of which machinery is established by any special statute under which a particular public undertaking is established

13.1.4.3 Working and Procedure of the CPU

In the first instance, the CPU selects such public undertakings or subjects that may deem fit and fall within their terms of reference. The ministry/undertaking concerned is asked to furnish necessary material relating to those subjects for the information of the members of the committee.

From time to time, the CPU may appoint one or more study groups for carrying out detailed examination of selected subjects. If it appears to the committee that it is necessary for the purpose of its examination that an on the spot study should be conducted, the committee undertakes tours to examine other relevant undertakings. Notes relating to the undertakings to be visited are called for in advance from the ministry/undertaking concerned and circulated to the members of the committee. These form the starting point for the informal discussion which the committee holds at the project site or place of visit. The members of the committee, while on tour, may also meet informally the representatives of the Chambers of Commerce and Industry, non-official organizations and bodies which are concerned with the subject under its examination.

Later, in the light of these informal discussions, the memoranda and other information received, non-official and official witnesses are invited to give evidence at formal sittings of the committee held at appropriate place, usually in New Delhi. All discussions held by the CPU with the representatives of the undertaking or ministry or department, non-official organizations, labour unions and so on are to be treated as confidential.

The observations/recommendations of the committee are embodied in their reports which are presented to both the Houses of Parliament. After a report has been presented to the House, the ministry or undertaking concerned is required to take action on various observations and recommendations contained in the report. The replies of the government are examined by an action taken sub-committee/committee, and an action taken report is presented to the House.

It is observed that since its inception, the various committees have from time to time presented 585 reports until the end of the Fifteenth Lok Sabha (May 2014). Of these, 293 are original reports and 292 are reports on action taken by the government on original reports of the committee. Out of 293 original reports, 38 are in the nature of horizontal studies on various aspects of working of the public undertakings.[15]

It is worth and important to study and analyse comments, as an example, on National Highway Authority of India (NHAI) projects.

Long delays have become a hallmark of NHAI projects, with just 55 out of total 388 such works getting completed on or before time between 1995 and 30 June 2016, the CPU said in its report tabled in Parliament (August 2017). It attributed the delays to problems related to land acquisition and regulatory hurdles. The CPU said that it has been confirmed that 'a decision has since been taken by NHAI that henceforth no project would be awarded unless 80% of land is available with

[15] 'Data to this effect (May 2014) is available with the Lok Sabha Secretariat. The government will now nudge state-run banks to present potential targets for merger and acquisitions after putting in place a procedure for quick decisions on such consolidation proposals, and lenders have been told to identify synergies across platforms including business operations and geographical spread', a senior finance ministry official said. See *The Economic Times* (Chandigarh), 25 August 2017.

the Authority with requisite forest clearance'.[16] Stressing that such a decision should have been taken by the NHAI long back, the CPU expressed hope of better outcome following implementation of favourable policies.

13.1.4.4 Exchange Traded Fund

In his February 2014 budget speech, the union finance minister had said that a new Exchange Traded Fund (ETF) with diversified stocks of central public sector enterprises (CPSE) and other government holdings would be set up.[17] The government has said that it will maintain at least 51% stake in central public sector units and at least 52% in state-run banks. The first CPSE–ETF was set up in 2014 by the Department of Investment and Public Asset Management (DIPAM). This new ETF, presently comprised of 10 companies—Oil and Natural Gas Corporation, Coal India, Indian Oil Corporation, GAIL (India), Oil India, Power Finance Corporation, Bharat Electronics, Rural Electrification Corporation, Engineers India Ltd and Container Corporation of India.

Although ETFs are technically mutual funds, they are bought and sold on the stock exchanges like company stock. In August 2017, the Indian Government announced the launch of 'Bharat 22' ETF, which holds 22 stocks including those of public sector enterprises and banks.[18]

13.1.4.5 Role and Evaluation of CPU's Functioning

The committee which came into existence in 1964 decided to take up about 6–7 undertakings for detailed examination every year and to review in addition one aspect or another common to all undertakings. But not all the undertakings scheduled come under the audit scrutiny of CAG. Moreover, not all public undertakings have been placed under the purview of this committee. Similarly, there may be no audit comments on some of the undertakings taken up for examination by the committee. In this situation, its control may prove, as elsewhere, to be more potential than real.

Second, audit comments will have the impact only on those undertakings which are taken up for examination. Audit comments on the remaining undertakings, however serious they may be, will not receive attention until such time as they are selected for detailed examination. In such a situation, there is likely to be wasteful expenditure and consequently, corrective measures may be correspondingly delayed. This is largely defeating the purpose for which the committee has been constituted.

A reorientation of policy is needed which would give a large autonomy to the undertakings, secure greater efficiency in their management and fulfil the objectives of accountability in a better way. This implies public sector units require not only substantial financial resources but also a corps of competent administrative and technical personnel. The country is admittedly deficient in both. What is more important is that reorientation of policy should bring greater realism in planning competence and wider interests in management, and should, lastly, give the public a

[16] *PTI News*, 2 August 2017.

[17] A type of investment fund that is traded on a stock exchange.

[18] The Bharat-22 ETF also has three stocks which are not PSUs. These are Axis Bank, ITC and L&T. The government holds these stocks because they were part of the investment portfolio of the old Unit Trust of India (UTI). See *The Economic Times* (Chandigarh), 25 August 2017.

feeling of partnership and confidence in the ability of the state enterprises to make a significant contribution towards building a new India, industrially strong and economically efficient.

13.1.5 Department-related Standing Committees

Besides these three financial committees, the Rules Committee of Lok Sabha recommended setting up of 17 department-related standing committees (DRSCs). Accordingly, 17 DRSCs were set up on 8 April 1993. In July 2004, rules were amended to provide for the constitution of seven more such committees, thus raising the number of DRSCs from 17 to 24.[19] The functions of these committees are as follows:

1. To consider the demands for grants of various ministries/departments of GoI and make reports to the Houses
2. To examine such bills as are referred to the committee by the chairman, Rajya Sabha, or the speaker, Lok Sabha, and make reports thereon
3. To consider annual reports of ministries/departments and make reports thereon
4. To consider policy documents presented to the Houses, if referred to the committee by the chairman, Rajya Sabha, or the speaker, Lok Sabha, and make reports thereon

These standing committees examine bills that are referred to them. They also examine the expenditure plans of ministries in the Union Budget. In addition, they may examine the working of the departments and various schemes of government.

Under Rule 268, a DRSC consists of not more than 31 members—10 members nominated by the chairman from Rajya Sabha and 21 nominated by the speaker of Lok Sabha.[20]

Of the 24 committees, 16 are administered by Lok Sabha and 8 by Rajya Sabha. The chairpersons of these committees are from the respective House. Political Parties are allocated chairs based on their strength in the Parliament. Some committees, such as, those for home affairs, finance and external affairs, are customarily chaired by a senior member of the opposition party. In the first instance, the committee invites comments and suggestions from the public on bill. The committee then will examine the written memorandum. It will also invite some experts and stakeholders for oral evidence. Based on its examination, the committee will prepare a report with its recommendations on the various provisions of the bill. The report will be tabled in Parliament, and the committee tries to form a consensus while preparing the report. However, if some members do not agree on any point, they may add a dissent note. For example, the Committee on Civil Liability for Nuclear Damages Bill had dissent notes written by MPs from Left parties.

It may be noted that the committee system was formed recognizing that the Parliament does not have the time for detailed examination and public feedback on all bills. The Parliament, therefore, delegates this task to the committee which reports back with its recommendations and move appropriate amendments. Following this, the Parliament can vote on these amendments, and finalize the bill in question.

---

[19] DRSCs are on finance; agriculture; HRD; IT, rural development; labour; chemicals; health; coal and steel; science and technology; social justice; energy; industry; urban development; food; personnel; home affairs; railways; defence; water; external affairs; petroleum; commerce; and transport.

[20] Final membership is decided based on the MP's area of interest as well as their party's decision on allocation of seats.

Most bills are referred to such committees but this is not a mandatory requirement before passing a bill.[21] In some cases, if a bill is not referred to a committee and passed by one house, the other house may constitute a select committee for detailed examination.[22]

The standing committee provides equal opportunity to everyone to write in their memoranda. It also allows parliamentarians to devote a significant amount of time to understand the nuance of a bill and make appropriate modifications. Thus, the standing committee system is an opportunity to strengthen legislation in an informed and participatory manner.

Subhash Kashyap argues that these standing committees should embrace the entire spectrum of administration. They should provide (a) close pre-budget scrutiny of all estimates and expenditure being voted (as was done for the demands for grants for 1995–96); (b) non-partisan examination of functioning of government departments; (c) monitoring and evaluation of performances and examination of supplementary estimates; (d) feedback to the Parliament and government on economic proposals; (e) close scrutiny of legislative proposals; (f) review of the implementation of laws passed by the Parliament in respect of subject areas; (g) development of leadership, including its second line, in the Parliament; and (h) development of specialization and expertise among members.[23]

Indeed, one may say that the best way to ensure a representative system is to remove the anti-defection law, minimize the use of whips, and let MPs vote according to what their conscience says. That may give us a more accountable government in a democratic polity.

13.2 Treasury Control: Finance Ministry

13.2.1 Introduction

In the government structure, the union finance ministry occupies an important place. It is mainly concerned with the economy of the country. In particular, it concerns itself with taxation, financial legislation, financial institutions, capital markets, union and state finances, and Union Budget.[24] The parliamentary system of government entrusts this union ministry to take legislative authorization of income and expenditure from the Parliament through budget and to see to it what public expenditure disbursement reflects the wishes of the people.

The union finance ministry plays a critical and crucial role in the socio-economic development of the country. It is responsible for the sound administration of the finances of the union government and, to a large extent, of the state governments as well. It mobilizes resources, exercises control over public expenditure and regulates the transfer of funds from the union to the states. In the ultimate analysis, its approach and decisions affect practically the whole economy of the country. Highlighting the important place the Ministry of Finance occupies in the government system, the Haldane Committee (1918) observed,

[21] For example, the Standing Committee on Science and Technology examined the Civil Liability for Nuclear Damages Bill. The Committee made several recommendations, some of which increased the potential liability of suppliers of nuclear equipment in case of an accident.

[22] Examples include such select committees formed by the Rajya Sabha on the Wakf Amendment Bill and the Prevention of Torture Bill.

[23] S. C. Kashyap, 'Standing Committees Must Learn to Run', *Times of India* (New Delhi), 20 May 1995.

[24] The first Union Budget was presented on 26 November 1947.

> The Department of Finance must necessarily have an exceptional position among all the State Departments. The service which it has to perform—that of supervising and controlling all operations of government in so far as they affect the financial position—involves not only the direct administration of taxation and other branches of revenue, but also the control of all forms of expenditure, including the incurring of obligations or liability to expenditure.[25]

Sir Ivor Jennings also remarked that the Treasury 'must be a prime element in co-ordination. For every government activity involves finance; and unless an effective check is imposed and co-ordination provided for, the financial consequences of departmental action cannot be foreseen'.[26]

13.2.2 Organization and Functions of Finance Ministry

The union finance ministry comprises five departments, namely, (a) Department of Economic Affairs, (b) Department of Expenditure, (c) Department of Revenue, (d) Department of Investment and Public Asset Management and (e) Department of Financial Services (DFS).

13.2.2.1 Department of Economic Affairs

The Department of Economic Affairs is the nodal agency of the union government to formulate and monitor country's economic policies and programmes having a bearing on economic management including, prices, credit, fiscal and monetary policy and investment regulations. The divisions of the Department of Economic Affairs are (a) Integrated Finance Division, (b) Budget Division, including Fiscal Responsibility and Budget Management (FRBM), (c) Financial Market Division, (d) Bilateral Cooperation Division, (e) Multilateral Institutions Division, (f) Multilateral Relations Division, (g) Aid Accounts and Audit Division, (h) Economic Division, (i) Investment and Currency Division and (j) Infrastructure and Energy Division.

The Department of Economic Affairs is also responsible for the preparation and presentation of Union Budget to the Parliament and the budget for the state governments under president's rule and union territory administration.[27]

The Directorate of Currency has the administrative control of the Security Printing and Minting Corporation of India Limited (SPMCIL), a wholly owned GoI corporation that manages GoI mints, currency presses, security presses and security paper mill.[28]

---

[25] Great Britain, *Report of the Machinery of the Government Committee* (London: HMSO, 1918), CD 9230, 17.

[26] Sir Ivor Jennings, *Cabinet Government* (Cambridge: Cambridge University Press, 1969).

[27] Along with the presentation of the Union Budget (including the Railway Budget), the finance minister also presents Annual Financial Statement (estimated receipts and expenditure of GoI) and a Finance Bill (detailing the imposition, abolition, remission or regulation of taxes proposed in the budget). A Finance Bill is any Bill which relates to revenue or expenditure but does not receive the speaker's certificate. On the contrary, a Money Bill shall bear the endorsement of the speaker when it is transmitted to the Council of States or is presented for the assent of the president.

[28] Recently, the union finance ministry allowed the RBI for the distribution of ₹200 denomination currency notes. See *The Economic Times* (Chandigarh), 24 August 2017.

13.2.2.2 Department of Expenditure

The Department of Expenditure is the nodal department for overseeing the public financial management system in the central government and matters connected with state finances. The principal activities of the department include pre-sanction appraisal of major schemes/projects, handling the bulk of the central budgetary resources transferred to states, implementation of the recommendations of the Finance and Central Pay Commissions, overseeing the expenditure management in the central ministries/departments through the interface with the financial advisors and the administration of the financial rules/regulations/orders through monitoring of audit comments/observations, preparation of central government accounts, managing the financial aspects of personnel management in the central government, assisting central ministries/departments in controlling the costs and prices of public services and so on.

The business allocated to the Department of Expenditure is carried out through its Establishment Division, Plan Finance I and II Divisions, Finance Commission Division, Staff Inspection Unit, Cost Accounts Branch, Controller General of Accounts and the Central Pension Accounting office.

13.2.2.3 Department of Revenue

The Department of Revenue exercises control in respect of revenue matters relating to direct and indirect union taxes. The department is also entrusted with the administration and enforcement of regulatory measures provided in the enactments concerning central sales tax, stamp duties and other relevant fiscal statutes. Control over production and disposal of opium and its products is also vested in this department.

The department, in coordination with the states, is also facilitating taxation reforms in the indirect taxes sector for goods and services. In this department, tax policies are formulated in order to mobilize financial resources for nation, achieve sustained growth of the economy, macroeconomic stability and promote social welfare by providing fiscal incentives for investments in the social sector.

13.2.2.4 Department of Investment and Public Asset Management

The Department of Disinvestment was set up as a separate department in 1999 and was later renamed as Ministry of Disinvestment in 2001. From 2004, the Department of Disinvestment is one of the departments under the Ministry of Finance. The Department of Disinvestment was later renamed as DIPAM in 2016.

The mandate of the department includes all matters related to management of central government investments in equity, including disinvestment of equity in central PSUs. Decisions on the recommendations of administrative ministries, NITI Aayog, etc., for disinvestment including strategic disinvestment.

DIPAM also looks after financial policy concerning the utilization of the proceeds of disinvestment channelized into the National Investment Fund.

13.2.2.5 Department of Financial Services

The Department of Financial Services (DFS) is mainly responsible for policy issues relating to public sector banks (PSBs) and financial institutions including their functioning, appointment of chairman, managing director and chief executive officers (MD and CEOs), executive directors (EDs), chairman-cum-managing directors (CMDs), legislative matters, international banking relations. Appointment of governor/deputy governor of Reserve Bank of India, matters relating to National Bank for Agriculture and Rural Development (NABARD), Agriculture Finance Corporation, co-operative banks, regional rural banks (RRBs) and rural agriculture credit. The department also administers the financial inclusion programme of the government, social security schemes and other targeted schemes aimed at facilitating flow of credit, matters relating to insurance sector and performance of public sector insurance, companies, and administration of various Insurance Acts. Matters relating to Insurance Regulatory and Development Authority of India (IRDAI) and matters relating to pension reforms including the New Pension System (NPS), legislative and other issues regarding the Pension Funds Regulatory and Development Authority (PFRDA), etc.

13.2.3 Basic Principles of Financial Control

The basic principles of financial control are as follows:

1. All revenues are required to be credited to a central fund as 'a fund into which shall flow every stream of the revenue, and from whence shall issue the supply for every public service'.
2. That money should be 'appropriated to various heads of expenditure and accounted for under those heads'. That is no diversion of funds from one head to another being impossible.
3. 'Introduction of the principle of annuality in budget grants' and unspent balances at the end of year were required to be surrendered to the Consolidated Fund.[29]
4. That 'the Treasury must approve all estimates before these were presented to the House', and also approve all expenditure in excess of the estimates or outside the scope of estimates.
5. That the appointment under the Act of 'the Comptroller and Auditor General of India (should) be responsible to Parliament and not to the executive branch of the government'. His function is to assure the Parliament that grants were utilized for the purposes made and within the scope of the grants and with efficiency and economy.

13.2.4 Process Control of Expenditure

The finance ministry's control of expenditure is a necessary requirement of parliamentary control, but it is a continuous control operating both before and after parliamentary approval of estimates.

[29] The Constitution Act of 1950 created a consolidated fund into which all revenues received by the Union are required to be credited.

The process of control is initiated when departmental estimates embodying departmental plans and policies are submitted to the Ministry of Finance for examination and acceptance. This affords the ministry not only the opportunity to assess these individually but also to have a broad view of the policy of the departments as a whole.

It is at this stage that financial control over policy becomes operational and the role of finance minister as coordinator of financial and economic policies comes into play. Further, the Ministry of Finance has got to resolve any conflict between departmental policies, assess the relative importance of competing policies in the national economy and effect such economies as are feasible in the estimates of expenditure before their presentation to the House. The Constitution Act of 1950 also created a 'contingency fund' for the purpose of meeting unforeseen expenditure, pending subsequent authorization of the expenditure by Parliament. Here, it may be mentioned that the Ministry of Finance is not the final arbiter of policy and, in the event of difference between a departmental minister and the finance minister, an appeal may be made to the cabinet where both ministers will have the opportunity of explaining their points of view. In the final analysis, it is the cabinet which decides policy, but this does not detract from the finance minister's role and authority in the field of financial management.

The financial control by the Ministry of Finance is of stringent nature. The control continues to be exercised even after the Parliament has voted the appropriations. Departments have no authority to incur expenditure on any new item, any new service or even any approved scheme, if its scope comes to be modified to raise a current or contingent liability beyond the sanctioned amount.[30] In all these matters, the ministry has to satisfy itself that the changes are economic in themselves and that they are necessitated by new developments which have emerged since parliamentary approval was given before it will allow supplementary demands to be presented to the House.

There was time when the Ministry of Finance exercised stringent expenditure control, extending to an itemized scrutiny of departmental expenditure within the scope and amount of appropriations voted. Gradually, there was the realization that this somewhat undefined duality of control was encouraging irresponsibility and improvidence in the departments. This was not only in the preparation of thc cstimates but also in the subsequent regulation of the flow of expenditure. As Maulana Azad observed,

> When Liaquat Ali Khan became the Finance Minister, he obtained possession of the key to the Government. Every proposal of every Department was subject to scrutiny by his Department. In addition, he had the power to veto. Not a *chaprasi* could be appointed in any department without the sanction of the Finance Ministry.[31]

In the interim government, Liaquat Ali Khan presented a budget (in February 1947) which attempted to impose draconian measures of taxation to 'crush the power and influence of the business community which was dominated by the Hindus'. This budget had a socialistic orientation, designed to reduce, in the words of Finance Member, 'the glaring disparity between the income and standard of life of the wealthy classes and the vast multitude of poverty-stricken masses'.[32]

---

[30] Union Food and Public Distribution Minister Ram Vilas Paswan assured Chief Minister Capt. Amarinder Singh that he would make a recommendation to the Ministry of Finance about reviewing the state's debt burden of ₹31,000 crore, incurred on the purchase of foodgrains for the central pool. See *The Tribune* (Chandigarh), 23 August 2017.

[31] M. A. K. Azad, *India Wins Freedom* (New Delhi: Orient Longman, 1959).

[32] The imposts proposed for the purpose 'were construed as a mischievous attempt on the part of the League to undermine India's industrial strength and progress'.

Now there is a pronounced trend, away from meticulous control of details, in favour of greater delegation to departments, combined with the use of methods which will enable the treasury to be content that the standards of prudent housekeeping are being observed. With some changes in the structure of the Ministry of Finance, it is found that the policy and the financial consequences of that policy go hand in hand.

The Constitution Act of 1950 deprived the Council of States (Rajya Sabha) of its financial authority, although providing for a general debate on the estimates in the council. Second, it established the supremacy of the Lok Sabha by deleting the provisions investing the head of the state with special powers.

Third, the Constitution created a Consolidated Fund into which all revenues received by the central government and all loans raised by the issue of finance ministry's bills, and all moneys received by it in repayment of loans were required to be credited. All the moneys received by or on behalf of the union government will be credited to either of the funds—the Consolidated Fund of India or the 'Public Account of India'.[33]

Besides the revenues received by the union government under Consolidated Fund (Article 266 [1]), all other public moneys received by or on behalf of the union government shall be credited to the Public Account of India (Article 266 [2]), for example, moneys received by an officer, or court in connection with affairs of the union (Article 284).

Fourth, the Constitution Act of 1950 also created a 'contingency fund' for the purpose of meeting unforeseen expenditure, pending subsequent authorization of the expenditure by the Parliament (Article 267). The amount of the Fund, at the disposal of the executive, is subject to be regulated by the appropriate legislature.

Fifth, the Act of 1950 introduced the provision for a 'vote on account' to enable the Parliament to consider the estimates more carefully over an extended period of time. Under Article 116, the executive is given an advance grant to meet its temporary and other running expenditure until the demands are voted by the Parliament. The executive responsibility for fulfilling these enlarged parliamentary requirements devolved upon the Ministry of Finance.

13.2.5 Review of Organization and Methods

Invariably, it is argued that the interests of the tax payers cannot be wholly entrusted to the spending departments without a measure of control and co-ordination by the finance department. But the system of control has to be adjusted to take account of the pattern and purpose of the administration. This means, there has to be financial delegation to the administrative departments. The extent to which financial authority can be delegated to a department must necessarily depend on the ability of its controlling personnel to exercise this authority competently. The delegations have, therefore, to be determined largely by the organization of the administrative services and by the arrangements in force to make their members conversant with both financial and administrative principles and processes.

Because of limitations inherent in the administrative setup of various departments have led to an excessive concentration of authority in the finance department, not merely for the evolution and application of general financial and economic policies and principles but also for the exercise

[33] All payments out of Consolidated Fund services are discussed in the House, not merely the withdrawals for the supply services.

of control, in meticulous details, over items of expenditure appertaining to estimates which have already been accepted and approved by the Parliament.

Thus, even after so many years since the country's independence, the conception of departmental responsibility for financial administration has not, as yet, been adopted or introduced. Delegations to departments have been neither significant nor extensive because of the limitations of administrative structure. Second, as already observed in the preceding pages, the control exercised by the finance department in matters of technical details of developmental schemes and works programmes is vehemently criticized. It is mainly because the finance department is not properly equipped for this purpose.

For example, the role of the Ministry of Finance was subjected to scathing criticism in the context of the great security scam involving an amount of over ₹8,000 crores which came to light in the early months of 1992 with the reports of the Joint Parliamentary Committee (JPC) headed by Ram Nivas Mirdha. The JPC strongly indicted the Ministry of Finance for not exercising proper control over the working of banks, RBI as well as the performance of the stock exchanges. The JPC observed, 'The seam was basically a deliberate and criminal misuse of public funds through securities transactions funded by illegally siphoning off funds of banks and PSUs to selective brokers for speculative high rates of return'.

In its final report, placed in the Parliament on 20 December 1992, the JPC indicted the Ministry of Finance. The opposition parties held the ministry responsible for this seam and demanded the resignation of the Minister of Finance Manmohan Singh. Singh, however, disagreed with the opposition demand and refuted this allegation saying that it was caused by 'systems' failure and not due to his ministry's negligence. Although Dr Singh submitted his resignation on 24 December 1992, he withdrew it at the request of the PM, who, looking at the concern of the business organizations, feared that Singh's exit would severely retard the progress of economic reforms.

As a result, the objections raised are often elementary and uninformed in character. This not only acts as an irritant but is also time consuming. Ultimately, it is observed that objections mostly come to be waived, but often only after discussions. The problem is how these aspects of control can be abridged, abated or more intelligently applied in the interests of greater speed in the execution of schemes. The transfer of financial responsibilities to administrative ministries, by divesting finance of a corresponding measure of responsibility, may be a simple enough process. But it is more difficult, without organizational changes, to ensure that these would be reasonably exercised to justify national expenditure. The purpose should be to promote economy consciousness and a sense of financial responsibility throughout all administrative departments.

Further, there is a common problem of delay in executing projects and the large-scale annual surrender of funds appropriated for their execution. This has attracted attention and criticism both in the Parliament and the Press. The delay in the execution of projects is, however, more fundamental and requires a more radical approach for solutions. Unspent appropriations result in immobilizing resources which could, with advantages, be utilized either on projects other than those included in the year's budget estimates or in assisting a more needy execution of projects included in the estimates.

The inability of an administrative ministry to spend up to the budgetary demands arises not so much from any difficulty in the scheme of implementation as from the tendency of the ministry to inflate, deliberately, the budget allotments it asks for. This tendency to overestimate spending capacity arises from two reasons: first, it is assumed that the Ministry of Finance will in any case reduce the allotment requested, and therefore it is better to ask for more; and second, the inclusion of schemes and large provisions creates both politically and administratively an impression of efficiency and energy in the sponsoring department or a ministry. It is, however, possible largely to eliminate the first cause and also the second to the extent that it is administrative, by suitable changes in the present relations between the administrative and finance ministries.

Besides the central projects, the assisted projects of the state governments also figure in the central budget, to the extent of the assistance to be given, whether in the shape of grants or loans or both. These allotments frequently remain unused by the states and contribute towards widening the gap between sanction of money and its utilization. Under the present system, where the centre accepts 50% of liability on all the approved schemes, work starts perhaps on all of them, but progress is disappointingly slow, and even halted, because of lack of resources. There is the attendant risk of the centre's financial liability being substantially increased if the projects are to be completed.

For example, the central government decided to reduce the centrally sponsored schemes to 27 from 72. Of the 27 centrally sponsored schemes, the centre would fully fund 10 schemes and provide 60 percent of the funds for the 17 others.[34]

The administrative ministries are responsible for drawing up their plans and estimates with such resources of financial experience and technical advice as are available to them within the ministry. On the other hand, the Ministry of Finance is responsible not only for the allotment of funds but also for satisfying itself in sufficient details that the schemes for which the allotments are made have no undesirable features and that they are financially sound. Often when the schemes are accepted for inclusion in the budget, the administrative ministry, at various stages, keeps on approaching the Ministry of Finance for sanctions. The result of all this is that the implementation of the scheme is often badly held up and that appropriations made on the basis of the tentative schemes lapse. If financial examination is carried out properly, administrative problems could be averted. The system is wasteful because, at present, schemes are drawn up without sufficient technical financial advice and are, therefore, from that point of view, immature.

It would expedite matters if, at the stage of obtaining the Ministry of Finance's approval, the administrative ministry was not required to give complete details of a scheme but only adequate details to enable the Ministry of Finance to take a view of the scheme as a whole and its cost. The Ministry could then sanction the scheme on that basis, and then the administrative ministry could furnish details of both staff and expenditure within the sanctioned scheme. Overall, financial control, with reference to financial policy and principles, may continue to be vested in the Ministry of Finance, but details scrutiny of proposals at expert level is vested in the administrative ministry. It is obvious that it is in the interests of the Ministry of Finance that the administrative ministries should develop a high sense of financial responsibility and that they should be equipped with financial branches that are able to shape the departmental schemes and programmes by informed and constructive criticism. It is essential that there be a complete identity of interest between the administrative and finance ministries for the speedy execution of schemes with due regard to national economy. The railway budget has been amalgamated with the Union Budget. But the merger would not deprive the Railways of its functional autonomy.[35]

---

[34] See *Business Standard* (Chandigarh), 9 November 2015.

[35] The NDA government at the centre took a decision to end the practice of presenting the Annual Railway Budget starting financial year 2018. It is now merged with the Union Budget. The government decided to supplant the plan/non-plan division of expenditure in Budget.

In respect of the assisted state schemes as well, there is a substantial concentration of central control. Consequently, there is a lack of adequate local planning, which hampers the growth of responsibility. It would be more suitable to require the states to submit their schemes in broad detail only, and that these schemes should be examined by the administrative ministries concerned in collaboration with the NITI Aayog or union finance ministry. Thereafter, financial provision should be made after a broad review, but mainly on the recommendation to be given by the state finance department that the schemes are for the welfare of the weaker sections of the society. The evaluation in terms of execution of projects and sanctioned money should be at regular intervals, perhaps every quarter of year. Such a systematic review and analysis of expenditure should make it possible to take corrective measures wherever necessary, ensure an even flow of expenditure and avoid the present hasty and injudicious spending in the last quarter of the financial year to prevent the lapse of funds. This would also provide material for the Ministry of Finance to assess the technical and financial competence of the ministries and to base future allotments on their performance.

Presently, the Ministry of Finance is confronted with challenges of great magnitude which relate to massive mobilization of financial resources in a non-inflationary manner, checking effectively unproductive expenditure, strengthening the balance of payments position and accelerating economic reforms of far-reaching significance. In view of these challenges and the prospects of a faster development economy, it is imperative that the Ministry of Finance needs to be revitalized, and its methods of working should be continuously modernized so that it performs its vital role satisfactorily.

To conclude, it is important to recognize the complementary roles of the Centre and the states and to give to the states the required measure of confidence and responsibility. The paternal attitude of the Centre, a heritage of the past, must give way to a new relationship of partners in a common endeavour, if the purposes of a welfare state, as embodied in the Indian Constitution, are to be achieved.

13.3 Audit Control: Comptroller and Auditor General

13.3.1 Introduction

The makers of the Indian Constitution fully recognized the importance and role of the CAG in the financial and economic administration in Independent India. While discussing the position of the CAG, Dr B. R. Ambedkar, the chairman of the Drafting Committee of the Constitution of India, observed,

> I am of the opinion that this dignitary or officer is probably the most important officer in the Constitution of India. If this functionary is to carry out his duties, and his duties, I submit, are far more important than the duties of judiciary, he should have been certainly as independent as the judiciary.

This recognition was but a reflection of the importance which they attached to financial administration of the country. With the enforcement of the Indian Constitution (with effect from 26 January 1950), the CAG, constitutionally speaking, acts as the guardian of the purse of the country and is the pivot of the system of parliamentary control over public expenditure. Like judiciary, the institution of the CAG is an independent authority.

13.3.2 A Brief History of CAG Under British Rule

Although the present office of the CAG of India is 140 years old, its origin can be traced to the establishment of the Indian Audit and Accounts Department in 1753. Later in 1857, the office of the auditor general was set up by Lord Canning. In 1860, an Audit Board, comprising the auditor general and the chief of the military finance department, was constituted which was subsequently abolished in 1865 with a view to centralizing the administration of the entire public accounts in the comptroller general. In 1882, the comptroller general was given the designation of CAG, who was assigned the supervision of the accounting system and conducting of an appropriation audit. The GoI Act, 1919, however, used the designation 'auditor general' and made his office an independent authority. His appointment was made by the secretary of the state in council. The Act of 1935 further enhanced his status and importance and he was equated with a judge of the federal court as far as his removal from office was concerned.

13.3.3 Constitutional Provisions for the CAG

With the enactment of the Constitution in 1950, the Auditor General of India was designated as the CAG of India. It is noteworthy that the new office is largely modelled upon the provisions of the Act of 1935. While the 1935 Act had made provision for the appointment of independent auditors general for each of the provinces, the Constitution Act recognized the authority of a single officer to act as the CAG at the union and state levels.[36] The independence of the CAG is secured by the provisions of the Constitution: First, although appointed by the president, the CAG does not hold office at the pleasure of the president unlike other civil servants, and can be removed from office only on an address from both the Houses of Parliament and supported by a two-third majority on the grounds of 'proved misbehaviour' or 'incapacity' (Article 148). And, second, his salary and conditions of service shall be statutory[37] and shall not be liable to variation to his disadvantages during his term of office (the term is six years or up to the age of 65 years). After retirement, he is disqualified for any further government office. In other matters, his conditions of service shall be determined by the Rule applicable to the rank of secretary of GoI.

Thus, the designation of the CAG is like the judge of the Supreme Court, except that the CAG has no power of appointment and disciplinary control over his subordinates. He has no power to get his decisions executed as a judge can do through the instrument of contempt of court. Lately, 'there has been considerable decline in the standard of financial discipline and probity of public officials'.[38]

[36] The CAG is ranked ninth, and it enjoys the same status as a Judge of the Supreme Court in Indian order of precedence.

[37] See the CAG Act, 1971 which was amended in 1976, 1984, 1987 and 1994. His salary and pension benefits are as per the Supreme Court Judges. His salary and the administrative expenses of his office shall be charged on the Consolidated Fund of India.

[38] B. P. Mathur, 'Public Audit and Financial Control', in *Fifty Years of Indian Administration*, ed. T. N. Chaturvedi (New Delhi: IIPA, 1998), 212.

13.3.4 Duties and Powers of the CAG

Article 149 of the Constitution reads, 'The Comptroller and Auditor General shall perform such duties and exercise such powers in relation to the accounts of Union and of the states as may be prescribed' by Parliament.

In exercise of this power, the Parliament has enacted the CAG (Duties, Powers and Conditions of Service) Act, 1971, which, as amended in 1976, relieves him of his pre-Constitution duty to compile the accounts of the union.[39]

The above parliamentary legislation prescribes the following duties for the CAG:

1. To audit and report on all expenditure from the Consolidated Fund of India and of each state and each union territory having a legislative assembly as to whether such expenditure has been in accordance with the law
2. To audit and report on all expenditure from the Contingency Funds and Public Accounts of the union and of the states
3. To audit and report on all trading, manufacturing, profit and loss accounts, and so on, kept by any department of the union or a state
4. To audit the receipts and expenditure of the Union and of each state to satisfy himself that the rules and procedures in that behalf are designed to secure an effective check on the assessment, collection and proper allocation of revenue
5. To audit and report on the receipts and expenditure of (a) all bodies and authorities 'substantially financed' from the union or state revenues, (b) government companies and (c) other corporations or bodies, when so required by the laws relating to such corporations or bodies[40]

Thus, the CAG's statutory duties and powers cover both the audit and accounting of all the financial transactions of the union and the states. In the matter of accounting, his responsibilities are well defined. But, as an auditor, his authority and functions are wider and more comprehensive than those exercised by professional auditors. He is free to bring to the notice of the Parliament the impropriety of any executive action, even when its legality is not in question. The special provisions incorporated in the Constitution make him powerful in the sense that he can review the financial administration of the country as a whole.

It is emphasized that in a parliamentary form of government, the executive (Council of Ministers) is accountable to the Parliament. But this accountability in the field of financial administration is secured through the reports of the CAG, who is rightly described as 'the guide, philosopher and friend', of the parliamentary committee on public accounts. Audit of public accounts by an independent authority is an essential component of parliamentary control over national expenditure.

Late President R. Venkataraman observed, 'Audit is the watchdog of the nation against executive extravagance and inefficiency'.[41] Others have described him as the Parliament: 'Parliament only

---

[39] The accounts of the state governments continue to be compiled by the CAG.

[40] As on 31 March 2015, there were 570 central government public sector enterprises under the audit jurisdiction of the CAG. These included 390 government companies, 174 government-controlled companies and 6 statutory corporations.

[41] M. S. Ramayyar, *History of Indian Audit and Accounts Department* (New Delhi: Indian Institute of Public Administration, 1967), 10.

works through him'. His functions are not merely to ensure that the appropriations made by the Parliament have not been exceeded or that the expenditure conforms to rules but also to satisfy himself, on behalf of the Parliament, as to its economy.

His constitutional responsibility imposes duty on him to uphold the Constitution and the laws in the field of financial administration, and therefore to disallow any expenditure which in his opinion violates and fringes the laws. But a wider and more important responsibility is the examination of sanctions accorded by competent authorities so as to satisfy himself that these are proper and fulfil purpose for which the sanctions have been accorded. The CAG is competent, therefore, to challenge any improper exercise of discretion and also to comment on the propriety of sanctions and expenditure.

13.3.5 Comptroller and Auditor General and Public Accounts Committee

CAG's reports are discussed by the legislature through the PAC and the CPU. It is good that timely actions are taken. But inordinate delay in deliberation of the reports of CAG of various states frustrates the very purpose of the audit. The faults highlighted in these reports loose significance with the passage of time and the chance of eradication of irregularities and malpractices becomes remote.

13.3.6 CAG and Administration

Over the past five decades, it is observed that CAG's relations with the administration have tended to develop on somewhat unusual lines. While the role assigned to the CAG in the Indian Constitution is similar to that in other parliamentary democracies, it is sad that the administration does not cooperate in furnishing records and information required for examination by the CAG. One former CAG observed in an article, 'The deliberate delay and occasional refusal by the executive to furnish records effectively dilutes the powers of CAG to examine crucial transactions. The provisions of 1971 Act does not provide adequate deterrence against the constraint'.[42]

In all democratic governments, the audit is looked upon as a valued ally which brings to notice technical irregularities and lapses on the part of the administration. For example, Audit Report no. 34 of 2017 contains the results of compliance audit of loans to independent power producers by Rural Electrification Corporation (REC) Limited and Power Finance Corporation (PFC) Limited over the period from 2013–14 to 2015–16. The audit report that was tabled in the Parliament on 10 August 2017 pointed out that both REC and PFC 'did not conduct appropriate due diligence during credit appraisal and in the process assumed higher risks on the loan accounts'.[43] In most developed countries, irregularities are rectified and disciplinary action initiated in the course of a current audit itself. For instance, the CAG in 2G Spectrum Allocation probity estimated that there was presumptive loss of ₹1,766 billion to the national exchequer. On 2 February 2012, the Supreme Court on a public interest litigation (PIL) declared the allotment of spectrum as

---

[42] V. K. Shunglu, 'Role of Comptroller and Auditor General in India', in *Fifty Years of Indian Administration*, ed. T. N. Chaturvedi (New Delhi: IIPA, 1998), 202.

[43] Paragraph 2.1 of the Executive Summary taken from Report No. 34 of 2017 of the CAG (GoI).

'unconstitutional and arbitrary' and quashed all the 122 licenses issued in 2008 during the tenure of A. Raja (then minister for communications and IT). The government said it had the authority to allocate coal blocks by a process of competitive bidding, but chose not to.[44] As a result, both public sector enterprises and private firms paid less than they might have otherwise. Its final report tabled in the Parliament pointed out that the 'windfall gain' to the allocatees was ₹1,856 billion.[45]

In another financial irregularity, the CAG, in its report tabled in the Parliament on 21 July 2017, said its audit indicated that the six private telecos, including Reliance Communications, Bharti Airtel, Vodafone India and Idea Cellular, understated revenues to the extent of ₹61,064.56 crore during 2010–11 and 2014–15, leading to a 'short payment' of ₹7,697.62 crore to the government.

Thus the lapses of a department, as embodied in the audit reports, more particularly when endorsed by the PAC, are regarded by the public as a virtual inducement of the department. This, in itself, acts as an effective deterrent in the commission of irregularities and secures their immediate rectification when they are brought to notice. Unfortunately, this conception of complementary relationship has yet to be evolved.

But the government departments resent on the ground that such interference is incompatible with their responsibility for the administration. This view has been supported by Appleby, according to whom, the question of economy is inseparably connected with the efficiency of the administration.[46]

It is important that the CAG works in close cooperation with the government concerned with a view to ensuring both propriety and regularity in the public expenditure. In this connection, A. C. Roy, a former CAG of India, has rightly said that the roles of

> Audit and Administration are really complementary to each other, they are never intended to act in opposition to one another. The purpose of both is the same, namely, to obtain the optimum results by the outlay of limited resources in carrying out our plans and programmes.[47]

In the ultimate analysis, audit and administration are the components of the machinery of government. 'It is only when these components are properly synchronized in operation that the optimum result can be obtained. The need for a reorientation of the attitude and re-adjustment of the relations between Audit and Administration has thus assumed paramount importance'.[48]

Thus, an abridgement of the functions of the CAG is looked upon as an encroachment on the autonomy of the Parliament which exercises control over national expenditure. To improve the functioning of audit performance, the CAG should take steps to strengthen and develop necessary competence and expertise.[49]

The attitude of Audit necessitates reorientation. What is more important is that these components, namely, audit and administration, should understand each other's points of view. There should be a positive approach to bring audit and administration closer and to facilitate coordinated and concerted action for the removal of irregularities and malpractices. As this

[44] CAG Report No. 7 of 2012–13 for the period ended March 2012.
[45] See *The Wall Street Journal*, 21 March 2017.
[46] Quoted by Shunglu, 198–203.
[47] Appleby, *Public Administration in India: Report of a* Survey, 27–28, 42–43.
[48] Asok Chanda, 243–44.
[49] D. Krishna, 'Role of Audit in Improving Financial Administration', *Indian Journal of Public Administration* 35, no. 4 (1989): 967–76.

dignitary takes on sensitive issues of high-level political and bureaucratic corruption and malpractices, the CAG becomes vulnerable to criticisms of exceeding his authority, his competence and even of partisan attitude. But as a constitutional functionary, he enjoys more prestige than any other officer in the Constitution.

Summary

Good governance and development is dependent on many factors, of which, availability of finance is of critical importance. Finance is a means to achieving human development and country's progress. As such, the government must devote much of its attention to creating, organizing and utilizing financial resources in a sustainable and prudent manner. The management of finance is, therefore, of great significance. In fact, there is a close relationship between finance (as a fuel) and administration (as a means to governance). Administration is becoming more responsive to and more appreciative of the role of Ministry of Finance and the CAG.

14 Administering Law and Order

LEARNING OBJECTIVES

1. **To discuss the role of central agencies in the maintenance of law and order**
2. **To examine the position of law and order machinery at the state level**
3. **To examine challenges arising out of criminalization of politics in the state**

Introduction

Despite impressive achievements on many fronts, law and order machinery in India remains under severe criticism at both the state and union levels. For the past 70 years, the graph shows that crime has perhaps gone up by a frightening 500% compared with the rise of population. As of today, over three crore cases, both civil and criminal, are pending with the courts in India. Expressing concerns over the arrears of court cases, the former Chief Justice of India, A. S. Anand, remarked, 'The lack of speedy dispute resolution system has a direct impact on the level of lawlessness in our society. A peaceful society is a necessary precondition for any kind of development'.[1]

A report published by the National Crime Records Bureau (NCRB) compared the crime rates of 1953 and 2006. The report noted that burglary (known as house breaking in India) has declined over a period of 53 years by 79.84%, from 147,379, a rate of 39.3/100,000, in 1953 to 91,666, a rate of 7.9/100,000 in 2006; murder has increased by 7.39%, from 19,803, a rate of 2.61/100,000 in 1953, to 32,481, a rate of 2.81/100,000 in 2006; kidnapping has increased by 47.80%, from 5,261, a rate of 1.40/100,000 in 1953, to 23,991, a rate of 2.07/100,000 in 2006; robbery has declined by 28.85%, from 8,407, a rate of 2.24/100,000 in 1953, to 18,456 in 2006; and riots have declined by 10.58%, from 20,529, a rate of 5.47/100,000 in 1953, to 56,641, a rate of 4.90/100,000 in 2006. In 2006, some 5,102,460 cognizable crimes were committed, including 1,878,293 Indian Penal Code (IPC) crimes and 3,224,167 Special and Local Laws (SLL) crimes, with an increase of 1.5% over 2005 (5,026,337). IP crime rate in 2006 was 167.7 compared to 165.3 in 2005, showing an increase of 1.5% in 2006. SLL crime rate in 2006 was 287.9 compared to 290.5 in 2005, showing a decline of 0.9% in 2006.[2]

---

[1] A. S. Anand, 'Indian Judiciary and Challenges of 21st Century', *The Indian Journal of Public Administration* 45, no. 3 (1999): 300.

[2] Ministry of Home Affairs, *Crime in India 2006* (New Delhi: NCRB, 2007). All figures relating to crimes are drawn from the NCRB. NCRB set-up in 1986 functions as a repository of information on crime and criminals.

According to data of 2016 by the NCRB, 4,831,515 cognizable crimes, comprising 2,975,711 IPC and 1,855,805 SLL crimes, were reported in 2016, showing an increase of 2.6% over 2015 (4,710,676 cases).

Rape cases recorded an increase of 12.4%, from 34,651 cases in 2015 to 38,947 in 2016. Murder cases decreased by 5.2%, from 32,127 cases in 2015 to 30,450 cases in 2016. Cases of kidnapping and abduction have shown an increasing trend with the increase of 6% (88,008) cases in 2016 over 82,999 cases in 2015. The total number of crimes against children in 2016 was 106,958, which is 13.6% more than 2015 (94,172 cases). Atrocities have also increased by 5.5% (40,801 case) in 2016 over 2015.

The NCRB reveals that a crime against a woman is committed every 3 minutes, a woman is raped every 29 minutes, and a dowry death occurs every 77 minutes and one case of cruelty committed either by husband or by relative of the husband occurs every 9 minutes.[3]

Administration of 'law and order' has been increasingly recognized as an important aspect of public administration. It has acquired a new dimension in the context of good governance and socio-economic development. The maintenance of law and order is the major task of the government. Due to massive population growth, increasing unemployment, poverty and inequality, and breaking up of social structure, law and order problem has become more complex and serious in a developing country like ours.

Definition

The phrase 'law and order' is very wide, and it is necessary to define it. Law, according to Austin, is 'the command of the sovereign', while T. H. Green regards it as 'the system of rights and obligations which the state enforces'. Under Article 13(3)(a) of the Constitution of India, 'law' includes 'any ordinance, order, bye-law, rule, regulation, notification, custom or usage having in the territory of India the forces of law'.

'Order' is a prerequisite to a progressive society. Law is indispensable to order, and enforcement is essential to law. In reference to 'public order', it signifies the state of tranquillity prevailing among the members of a society.

Constitutional Jurisdictions

The subjects—'public order' (Entry 1), 'police, including railway and village police' (Entry 2), 'procedure in revenue courts' (Entry 3) and 'prisons' (Entry 4)—included in List II fall within the jurisdiction of a state. The union has a duty to protect states against external aggression and internal disturbance under Article 355, and, under Article 356, the President of India can supersede a state government when he is satisfied that the government of the state cannot be carried on in accordance with the provisions of the Constitution.

[3] In case of Chandigarh (UT), for example, 141 cases of crimes—murder (22), murder attempt (22), rape (50), dacoity (11) and heist (36)—were registered until 11 October 2017; Uttar Pradesh reported the highest number of cases of murder, that is, 4,889, which come to 16.1% of the total such cases in the country, followed by Bihar with 2,581 cases (8.64%). See *PTI News*, 30 November 2017; See *Times of India* (Chandigarh), 22 October 2017.

14.1 Historical Background

> The police is the primary constitutional force for the protection of the individuals in the enjoyment of their legal rights, designed to stand between the powerful and the weak, to prevent oppression, disaster and crime, and to represent the cause of law and order at all times and in all places. In every court and alley, the policeman stands for good citizenship. He is a reality to comprehend, and upon his impartiality, efficiency and intelligence depends the estimation in which law is held by the masses.[4]

From time to time, there have been people's police and the ruler's police in India. The essence of the people's police is that 'police is the public and public is the police'. The police possesses only those powers that have been conferred on them by the public, and they are no more than a body of civil officers whose duties are to preserve order, prevent and detect crime and enforce laws on behalf of the community as a whole. In sharp contrast to this is the ruler-appointed police. It is mainly in the interest of the ruler, whether he be a monarch or a dictator, that the laws are enforced.

So, the duty of enforcing law and preventing crime is only a by-product of the main task of the police, acting as a 'peace force', to maintain and uphold the legal and constitutional rights of the people.

The present system of police and its administration in India has evolved over several centuries. Kautilya's *Arthashastra* (written around 310 BC) contains references about investigation patterns, punishment agencies and control devices during the Mauryan and Gupta periods. According to him, law and the State were inseparable. The objective of *dharma* was the preservation of moral order and securing of effective governance as also sovereignty of the nation.[5]

In the Mauryan times, when India was united through an empire, people could travel in the country freely. Infractors of law were severely punished. Megasthenese wrote in his recollection that in Patliputra (with four thousand people), the daily average theft totalled around only 100 units of local currency. In the 5th century AD, the famous Chinese traveller Fa-Hien faced no harassment. On the other hand, another Chinese traveller Hieun Tsang, who moved from the northwest of India to Assam, was robbed more than once. It seems law and order had deteriorated since the Gupta times. During the period of Sultanates, the law and order situation was indeed very bad. Sher Shah Suri restored some degree of order with a firm hand in a short 4-year period of his rule. The position was further consolidated during Mughal times. However, after the death of Aurangzeb (in March 1707), the Mughal Empire weakened and ultimately collapsed.

The Muslim rulers in India had developed some kind of police system.[6] The empire was divided into *subas* (provinces) under the charge of *subedars* (governors), sub-division under the charge of *fauzdars* and *thanas* (police station) under the charge of *thanedars* (station house officers or SHOs). *Fauzdar* was an official who acted as a 'collector' as well as a 'superintendent of police'. In the large towns and cities, *kotwal*, assisted by a number of *darogas*, had the responsibility of maintaining law and order and for arranging night patrolling. The *daroga* system of the Mughals functioned under remote control and had come to be thoroughly unreliable, inefficient and oppressive towards the end of that era. The movement for a reform of the system started with Cornwallis taking over the administration of the police and criminal justice into British hands in 1792–93.

---

[4] W. L. Melville, *A History of Police in England* (London: Methuen, 1901).

[5] R. P. Kangle, *The Kautilya Arthashastra* (New Delhi: Motilal Banarsidass, 1972).

[6] J. N. Sarkar, *Mughal Administration* (Calcutta: M. C. Sarkar, 1935), 23.

When the British gradually started taking over power in India, they found in the country an indigenous police system based on mutual security, each villager providing security to his neighbours, and, at the top an enforcement police responsible for controlling crime and disorder. The system had worked well under the Mughals, but as the Mughal hold on government started weakening, this village police was seized by the *zamindars* at many places, and often utilized for their own benefit. In order to improve the police administration, the British abolished this indigenous system, based on mutual security, and replaced it by a ruler-appointed police with a magistrate in charge of a district and a *darogah* under him in charge of large areas (400 to 500 sq. miles). The British did this, no doubt, with the good intention of curbing the tyrannical power of the *zamindars*, but, in trying to get rid of the evil, they also swept out with the same broom all that was good in the old system. Thus a predominantly people's police gave place to a ruler-appointed police owing allegiance to a foreign power. The first break with the public occurred then and the breach has continued.[7]

14.1.1 Police Reform

Police is one of the important institutions of the government and a pillar of democracy. It has to ensure order and good stability in the society. It is because of the dependence of the society on the police and the expectations from it to safeguard its interests that the governments at both the levels, state and union, have taken initiatives to reform the police.

Earlier the GoI appointed an all India Police Commission (under presidentship of M. H. Court) in 1860 to inquire exhaustively into the police needs of the country. The recommendations of the commission led to the enactment of the Indian Police Act of 1861 and the procedures for its operations were laid down in the Criminal Procedure Code, first enacted in 1861 (the code was amended in 1898 and subsequently in 1973) and the Indian Evidence Act, 1872.

The organizational structure and the working of the police in our country, with minor variations, have largely been based on the Indian Police Act, 1861.[8] A significant landmark in the growth and attempt at reform of the police has been the India Police Commission of 1902–1903 (was set up by Lord Curzon) with A. H. L. Fraser. Subsequently, with the changing times, many committees and commissions have been set up, sometimes to look into specific aspects and more often to review the overall working of the police by the provincial and later by the state governments, as they came to be known after the promulgation of the Constitution. The attainment of freedom with its growing political articulation and the consciousness of the necessity to redefine the police and functions of the law enforcement agencies in the changed political context led to the establishment of committees and commissions in various states which submitted valuable reports. From time to time, action has been taken on the recommendations and suggestions for improved police working by these august bodies. Although law and order is a state subject, during the last seven decades, the union government has provided financial and administrative support as well as expertise and guidelines for a more effective police force. In 1971, the GoI set up a committee on police training under the chairmanship of M. S. Gore. The report of the committee, while having training as its main focus, has covered a wider ground, such as, the role of the police in the social context, police–citizen relationship, the determinants of police efficiency other than training and so on.

[7] Ibid.

[8] B. B. Misra, *The Administrative History of India* 1834–1947 (Delhi: Oxford, 1970), 538.

On 15 November 1977, the GoI, Ministry of Home Affairs, appointed National Police Commission (NPC) under the chairmanship of Dharam Vira to review at the national level of the police system. The NPC produced nine reports (between 1979 and 1981), although only scanty attention was paid to them. The police force continues to be far from efficient. It is generally regarded as corrupt and oppressive and has utterly failed to secure the goodwill of the people.

In addition to these commissions (first in 1860, second in 1902 and third in 1977), many states appointed commissions and committees to go into issues of police reforms. To cite a few are Kerala Police Reorganisation Commission, 1959; the West Bengal Police Commission, 1960–61; the Delhi Police Commission, 1968; the Tamil Nadu Police Commission, 1971; and Uttar Pradesh Police Commission, 1981. Most of these were able to pinpoint the weaknesses of the policing system, such as, domination of party politics in the states, incessant political interference in the functioning of police and general lowering of the image as well as effectiveness of this force. During the dark period of Emergency, in the mid-1970 s, brutalities of the police force came into limelight.

14.1.2 Police Reform Committees (1998–2005)

Ribeiro Committee (1998–99): It was formed by the GoI on the directive of the Supreme Court to review the NPC's recommendations. The Ribeiro Committee produced two reports.

Padmanabhaiah Committee (2000): In 2000, the GoI set up a third committee on police reform under K. Padmanabhaiah (former union home secretary) which released its report in the year 2000.

Malimath Committee Report (2003): The Malimath Committee, which submitted its report in March 2003, observed that the success of the whole process of criminal justice administration depended completely on the proper functioning of the police organization, especially at the investigation stage.

Soli Sorabjee Committee (2005): The Soli Sorabjee Committee submitted a Model Police Act to the union government in late 2006.

14.1.3 Supreme Court Bench Instructions (2006)

In 2006, a bench of the Supreme Court consisting of Justice Y. K. Sabharwal, Justice C. K. Thakkar and Justice P. K. Balasubramanyan identified several reforms in police force to be implemented by state governments as necessary to professionalize the police in India; some of them are as follows:

1. A mid- or high-ranking police officer must not be transferred more frequently than every 2 years.
2. The state government cannot ask the police force to hire someone, nor can it choose the director general of the state police.
3. There must be separate departments and staff for investigation and patrolling, which will include the creation of (a) a State Security Commission for policies and direction, (b) a Police Establishment Board, which will decide the selection, promotions and transfers of

police officers and other staff and (c) a Police Complaint Authority to inquire into allegations of police misconduct.

Since most state governments failed to comply with the Supreme Court's orders, it asked for their explanation.[9] Later, most of the state governments took measures to reform the police forces and gave them the operational independence they needed for fearless and proper law enforcement.[10]

Again in October 2012, a Supreme Court bench asked all the state governments and union territories to inform about compliance of its September 2006 judgements.[11] However, many of the reforms (ordered by the Supreme Court) have now been implemented by many state governments.

14.2 Crimes, Communal Violence and Insurgency

Former Chief Justice of India A. S. Anand noted in an article that

> when the judicial administration enters the 21st Century, in not too distance a future, the first thing to be kept in view by all concerned is that the arrears of court cases which have mounted till not get eradicated at the earliest. The consumer of justice wants unpolluted, expeditious and inexpensive justice.[12]

Nearly 20 years have passed since he voiced his concern about the pendency of cases before courts in India. As on 4 February 2018, over 4.2 million cases are pending in HCs.

14.2.1 Rise in Violent Crimes

For maintenance of law, public order and peace, the IPC, 1860, the Indian Evidence Act, 1872, and the Code of Criminal Procedure, 1898, as amended in 1973, were enacted. After Independence, several laws have been enacted from time to time to meet the growing crime prevention needs. Still there has been an almost unrelenting upward trend in the rise of crimes in India. According to figures of *Crime in India 2016*, a total of 4,831,515 cognizable crimes were committed, including 2,975,711 IPC crimes and 1,855,804 SLL crimes.[13] The violent crimes increased substantially to 335,901 in 2015, which included cases of dowry deaths (7,634), murder (32,127), rape (34,651), kidnapping and abduction (82,999), dacoity (3,972), riots (65,255) and robbery (36,188). In addition, there were cases of crimes against women (327,394), children below 18 years (94,172) and senior citizens (205,232) and cases of child trafficking (3,490). The situation is further aggravated by militant violence in Jammu and Kashmir (infiltration by Pakistan), insurgency in the

[9] 'Compliance with Supreme Court Directives'. http://humanrightsinitiative.org/old/programs/aj/police/exchange/Compliance%20with%20SC%20directives%20-%20Jan%2007.pdf. Archived from the original on 6 March 2013.

[10] 'The Supreme Court Takes the Lead on Police Reform', *Prakash Singh v. Union of India*. http://humanrightsinitiative.org/old/programs/aj/police/exchange/Compliance%20with%20SC%20directives%20-%20Jan%2007.pdf. Archived from the original on 25 September 2009.

[11] 'SC Asked States to File Affidavit on Police Reforms', *Hindustan Times*, 16 October 2012.

[12] A. S. Anand, 'Indian Judiciary and Challenges', 299.

[13] Ministry of Home Affairs, *Crime in India 2016* (New Delhi: National Crime Branch Bureau, GoI, 2017).

north-eastern states and Leftist extremist violence in parts of Bihar, Andhra Pradesh, Maharashtra and Madhya Pradesh.

According to data, Kerala has the highest cognizable crime rate of 723.2/100,000 persons as of 2015, with 50.9% of the cases filed under 'causing injuries under rash driving/road rage', while Nagaland recorded lowest rates of 55.1/100,000 persons.

An interesting feature of the crime statistics in the country is the increasing number of complaints received against police personnel. There were total 54,916 complaints reported in the country in the year 2015, according to the NCRB (Ministry of Home Affairs), from which only 16,308 inquiries were instituted and only 5,526 cases were registered against them, and only 1,122 police personnel were sent up for trial, from which, only 25 police personnel were convicted. NCRB reports that there were 30 deaths in police custody in 2015 and 67 deaths of people who were in police custody without judicial sanction.[14] Both under the constitutional provisions and statutory law, the police only have a maximum of 24 hours in which they can keep someone in custody without magistrate's order and continued scrutiny. Deaths in police custody are already a major source of concern, and it is shocking that there were even higher numbers of deaths in potential cases of illegal custody by the police.

The cases of violence and riots were reported in Bhagalpur (1989), Bombay (1992–93), Tripura (2004), Deganga (2010), Fatehpur in Uttar Pradesh (2016), Malda in West Bengal (2016), Ramganj in Rajasthan (2016), Hangal in Karnataka (2016), Imphal in Manipur (2016), Roorkee in Uttarakhand (2016), Chhapra in Bihar (2016), Haryana (2017) and in many other town.[15]

There had been serial bombings in Tamil Nadu and even anti-Christian incidents in several parts in the country between the years 1998 and 2000.

14.3 Role of Central Agencies in Maintenance of Law and Order

Makers of the Indian Constitution did not envisage any central machinery for the maintenance of law and order. Although one member, Brajeshwar Prasad, sought to give the Centre the power for the protection of public order. The states are in sole charge of public order and the protection to central property in the states is the responsibility of state governments (centre is vested with the power to give guidance and assistance to the states). 'Police' and the 'public order' are subjects under the State List. The only fetter on state autonomy in this regard emanates from centre's directive power. A few important central agencies having responsibility for law and order and police administration are discussed in the following sub-sections.

14.3.1 Union Ministry of Home Affairs

Under the federal structure, the Constitution imposes certain responsibilities in regard to the police on the central government. The latter, through the Ministry of Home Affairs, monitors

[14] Ibid.

[15] On 7 January 2017, Minister of State for Home Affairs, Kiren Rijiju, during his briefing to the Parliament, stated that 278 communal clashes took place in the first five months of the year 2016.

trends and developments in the law and order situation and matters relating to communal harmony and internal security of the country. The ministry provides guidance and assistance to the states as and when necessary. It has the total responsibility for the administration of law and order of union territories.[16]

The Ministry of Home Affairs is also the cadre controlling authority for the IPS, Delhi, Andaman and Nicobar Islands Police Service (DANIPS), and Delhi, Andaman and Nicobar Islands Civil Service (DANICS). Police I division of the ministry is the cadre controlling authority in respect of the IPS; whereas, the union territories division is the administrative division for DANIPS and DANCIS and the All India Services officers posted and working in the AGMUT (Arunachal Pradesh, Goa, Mizoram and Union Territories) Cadre.

14.3.2 Central Armed Police Forces

The Central Armed Police Forces (CAPF) refers to uniform nomenclature of five security forces in India under the authority of Ministry of Home Affairs. They are the Border Security Forces (BSF), Central Reserve Police Force (CRPF), Central Industrial Security Force (CISF), Indo-Tibetan Border Police (ITBP) and Sashastra Seema Bal (SSB).

Each of the five CAPFs—BSF, CRPF, ITBP, CISF and SSB—has its own cadre of officers, but they are headed by the IPS officers. The higher echelons in these organizations, including the head of the organizations, designated as director general, is reserved by the Ministry of Home Affairs for IPS officers. The directorate generals of those five CAPFs were upgraded following the 6 CPC the apex scale, a grade held by directorate generals of various state police.

As far as recruitment of the forces is concerned, it is conducted mainly in three modes.

Gazetted officers in CAPFs are recruited through CAPF (assistant commandants) examination conducted by UPSC. They are appointed as assistant commandants and are gazetted officers, generally referred as DAGOs (directly appointed gazetted officers). DEGOs (departmental entry gazetted officers) are the ones who have been promoted through departmental examination conducted internally for subordinate officers. Subordinate officers such as sub-inspectors are recruited through competitive examination conducted by Staff Selection Commission and they are referred as DASOs (directly appointed subordinate officers). DESOs (departmental entry subordinate officers) are the ones who have been promoted through departmental examination conducted internally for constables, head constables and assistant sub-inspectors.

Constables are recruited through competitive examination conducted by Staff Selection Commission. Apart from these modes, CAPFs conduct recruitment for specialized posts such as engineers, doctors, etc., among DAGOs, and wireless operators, technicians, nursing staff, etc., among subordinate officers, and constables directly under their own authority.

[16] The Ministry of Home Affairs has the following constituents departments: (a) Border Management, (b) Internal Security, (c) Jammu and Kashmir, (d) Home, (e) Official Language and (f) States. There are organizational divisions of the ministry itself, without the splitting into specialized departments; these are (a) Administration Division, (b) Border Management Division, (c) Centre–State Division, (d) Coordination Division, (e) Disaster Management Division, (f) Finance Division, (g) Foreigners Division, (h) Freedom Fighters & Rehabilitation Division, (i) Human Rights Division, (j) Internal Security Division I, (k) Internal Security Division II, (l) Jammu and Kashmir Division, (m) Judicial Division, (n) Left Wing Extremism Division, (o) North East Division, (p) Police Division I, (q) Police Division II, (r) Police Modernisation Division, (s) Policy Planning Division and (t) Union Territories Division.

14.3.3 Central Reserve Police Force (CRPF)

CRPF, formerly known as the Crown Representative's Police was first raised in 1939 with a force of one battalion for helping the former rulers of Indian states to maintain law and order. After Independence, the central government enacted CRPF Act in 1949. Under this legislation, no part of the country is free from its jurisdiction. Pursuant to the powers conferred by Section 18(1), the union government made rules known as the CRPF Rules, 1955. Rule 25(a), which lays down the 'primary duty' of CRPF, states, 'Members of the force may be employed in any part of the Indian union for the restoration and maintenance of law and order, and for any other purposes as directed by the central government'. Thus CRPF has been assigned a wide field of operation. The Centre then has the unfettered right to deploy CRPF in any constituent state. Moreover, it is the discretion of the central government to determine the purpose for which CRPF may be used.

The CRPF Act, 1949, spells out the two main functions of this force. First, the GoI may send it to those trouble spots where the central government has a special responsibility to discharge and, where the situation warrants, deploy armed police. Second, the GoI may send CRPF to any part of the country to supplement the local police.

CRPF today comprises 243 battalions, including six mahila battalions, and has a sanctioned strength of 313,678 personnel.[17] The Central Reserve Police includes (a) the Rapid Action Force (RAF), a 15 battalion anti-riot force trained to respond to sectarian violence; (b) the Commando battalion for Resolute Action (COBRA), a 10 battalion strong anti-Naxalite/COIN force, 5 signal battalion; 1 Special Duty Group, 1 Parliament Duty Group of 1200 constables each.[18]

Two factors have helped to enlargement to CRPF and their deployment throughout the country. First, the states were increasingly finding their meagre resources inadequate for augmenting their own police force to cope with emergency law and order situations such as widespread linguistic agitations and communal disturbances and later political movements. Naturally, they encouraged the Centre to increase the strength of CRPF so that their own police force might be supplemented. Their motive was to shift in this way to the central exchequer a portion of their police expenditure. The Centre, also to prevent the involvement of the army, except for strictly defence purposes, came to support the idea of the proliferation of their police force. Second, the uni-party rule all over the country served to bring about and identify of their views. Any significant dilution of state autonomy was not controverted because at that time, both the central and the state governments were part of a single, unified political machine.

The mission of CRPF is to enable the government to maintain rule of law, public order and internal security effectively and efficiently to preserve national integrity and promote social harmony and development by upholding supremacy of the Constitution.

Besides law and order and counter-insurgency duties, the role of CRPF in the general elections, held repeatedly during the past few years, has been very significant and vital. This is especially true for the trouble-ridden states of Jammu and Kashmir, Bihar and in the northeast. During the parliamentary elections of 2014, CRPF played a major role in the security arrangements. Of late, CRPF contingents are also being deployed in UN missions.

---

[17] Ministry of Home Affairs, *Annual Report 2016–17* (New Delhi: GoI, 2017). The Ministry of Home Affairs plans to raise 12 new battalions including a Mahila Battalion by 2019.

[18] 'COBRA Sector', retrieved from crpf.nic.in

14.3.4 Border Security Force

To replace the multiplicity of state police forces guarding the borders, the Border Security Force was raised in 1965 with a strength of 25.5 battalions. The present strength of BSF is 186 battalions with a sanctioned strength of 257,363 personnel, including an expanding air wing, marine wing, artillery regiments and commando units.[19] It currently stands as the world's largest border guarding force. BSF has been termed as the First Line of Defence of Indian Territories.[20]

BSF has been assigned the role of promoting a sense of security amongst the people living in the border areas and preventing trans-border crimes such as smuggling, infiltration/exfiltration and other illegal activities. BSF has also been deployed to fight terrorism/militancy in the state of Jammu and Kashmir and insurgency in the eastern sector.[21]

BSF had played a very important role in the liberation of Bangladesh which Indira Gandhi and Sheikh Mujibur Rehman had also acknowledged. Besides, it played a remarkable role in Operation Vijay, Kargil War (1999), Bangladeshi–Indian Border skirmishes (2001) and India–Pakistan Border skirmishes (2013–17).

BSF, long considered a male bastion, has now deployed its first batch of women personnel at the border to carry out regular frisking of women as well as other duties performed by their male counterparts, including guarding the border. Over 100 women have been deployed on the highly volatile Indo-Pak border, while around 60 are deployed on the Indo-Bangla border. More women constables are being deployed on the borders.

Keeping in view the versatile role in BSF, the central government broad-based the training programme for its personnel. The battalions earmarked for induction in Jammu and Kashmir for fighting militancy are imparted pre-induction training to give them the necessary orientation to deal with the difficult task of fighting militancy. Adequate care is also taken in this pre-induction training towards human rights aspects.

14.3.5 Central Industrial Security Force (CISF)

CISF was set up under an Act of the Parliament of India on 10 March 1969 with a strength of 2,800 personnel. It was subsequently made an armed force of the Republic of India by another Act of Parliament passed on 15 June 1983. Its current active strength is 144,418 personnel.[22] In April 2017, the government raised the sanctioned strength from 145,000 to 180,000 personnel.[23] CISF is headed by an IPS officer with the rank of director general, assisted by an IPS officer in the rank of additional director general. The force is divided into seven sectors—Airport, North, Northeast, East, West, South and Training—and also has a Fire Service Wing.

CISF provides security coverage to 300 industrial units, government infrastructure projects and facilities and establishments located all over India such as atomic power plants, space installations, mints, oil field and refineries, major ports, heavy engineering, steel plants, barrages, fertilizer units, airports and hydroelectric/thermal power plants owned and controlled by central PSUs and currency note presses producing Indian currency. In addition to that, with the passage of the CISF

[19] 'Former D. G.' retrieved from crpf.nic.in

[20] Ministry of Home Affairs, *Annual Report 2015–16* (New Delhi: GoI, 2016), 172.

[21] K. F. Rustamji, from IPS, was the first director general of BSF.

[22] Ministry of Home Affairs, *Annual Report 2016–17*.

[23] 'Press Information Bureau'. http://pib.nic.in/PressReleseDetail.aspx?PRID=1516122 (accessed on 29 April 2017).

(Amendment) Bill, 2008, (w.e.f. 25 February 2009), CISF has started providing security to private and cooperative establishments across the country, such as, the Infosys, Bengaluru, Reliance Refinery, Jamnagar and the Delhi Metro Airport Express Line, for a fee. Besides, CISF also provides consultancy services to private industries as well as other organizations within the Indian government.

Among others, its clients include TISCO, Jamshedpur; SEBI Headquarters, Mumbai; Vidhan Sabha, Bengaluru; and Odisha Mining Company, Bhubaneshwar. The role of CISF has undergone a diversification and it now also protects airports, seaports, metro rail networks, government buildings, heritage monuments (including the Taj Mahal and Red Fort), opium and alkaloids extractions, nuclear power plants and space installations. It also specializes in VIP security as well as disaster management.

14.3.5.1 Special Security Group

In 2006, CISF, on the basis of recommendations of the Intelligence Bureau, raised a special unit called Special Security Group (SSG) to provide security cover to persons nominated by the Ministry of Home Affairs. It came into existence on 17 November 2006. This unit is responsible for providing physical protection, evacuation, mobile and static security cover to persons who have been nominated by the ministry.

14.3.6 Indo-Tibetan Border Police (ITBP)

ITBP was raised in October 1962 under the CRPF Act in the wake of the Chinese aggression to mount vigil on the Indo-Tibetan Border. ITBP is one of the five CAPFs of India. In September 1996, the Parliament of India enacted the ITBP Force Act, 1992, to 'provide for the constitution and regulation' of ITBP 'for ensuring the security of the borders of India and for matters connected therewith'.[24]

ITBP, which started with 4 battalions, has since restructuring in 1978 has undergone expansion to a force of 56 battalions as of 2017 with a sanctioned strength of 89,432.[25] Instead of one inspector general in 1983, ITBP now has 16 director generals/inspector generals, and over 40 deputy inspector general of police.[26] ITBP personnel have been deployed abroad in UN peacekeeping missions in Bosnia and Herzegovina, Western Sahara, Sudan, Afghanistan and elsewhere.

14.3.6.1 Functions

ITBP is a multidimensional force which primarily has following five functions:

1. Vigil on the northern borders, detection and prevention of border violations, and promotion of the sense of security among the local populace

[24] *The Indo-Tibetan Border Police Force Act, 1992*. http://itbpolice.nic.in/itbpwebsite/somepdfs/itbp_act_rules.pdf (accessed on 29 September 2014).

[25] Ministry of Home Affairs, *Annual Report 2016–17*.

[26] Ibid.

2. Check illegal immigration and trans-border smuggling
3. Provide security to sensitive installations and threatened VIPs
4. Restore and preserve order in any area in the event of disturbance
5. To maintain the peace

14.3.6.2 Training Centres

ITBP training centres develop among the trainees the qualities such as professional skills, *esprit de corps* and leadership. They are taught the values of integrity, impartiality and respect for all castes, creeds and religions. Maintaining the highest tradition of supreme sacrifice in the service of motherland, the Himveers are also taught to function effectively while always keeping in mind human rights and the codes of war which always guide their conduct. The Basic Training Centre at Bhanu, ITBP Academy at Mussoorie, and the Mountaineering and Skiing Institute at Auli run the training programmes and conduct indoor and outdoor training activities in pursuance of this mission.

The motto of ITBP, '*Shaurya, Dridata, Karm Nishtha*' (valour, determination, devotion to duty) has always inspired its men in accepting challenges to bring glory to the nation and honour to the force. Presently, battalions of ITBP are deployed on border guard duties from Karakoram Pass in Ladakh to Diphu La in Arunachal Pradesh, covering 3,488 km of the India–China borer. Manned border posts are at altitudes as high as 21,000 feet (6,400 m) in the western, middle and eastern sector of the border. ITBP is a mountain-trained force and most of the officers and men are professionally trained mountaineers and skiers.

14.3.7 National Security Guard (NSG)

The National Security Guard (NSG) was raised as a Federal Contingency Force in 1984 to meet emerging threats of terrorism in the country. NSG is a unique force trained and designed to take high risk, counter-hijack and counter-terrorist operations. NSG has also been assigned the task of providing mobile security to 'Z' plus category VIPs. The NSG personnel are often referred to in the media as Black Cats because of the black dress and black cat insignia worn on their uniform.[27]

NSG is under the authority of Ministry of Home Affairs. However, it is not categorized under the uniform nomenclature of CAPF. It has a special forces mandate, and its core operational capability is provided by the Special Action Group (SAG) which is drawn from the Indian Army. The Special Rangers Group (SRG), the police component of NSG, which also handles VIP security, is composed of personnel on deputation from other CAPF and state police forces.[28]

As a specialized counter terrorism force, it is intended for use 'only in exceptional situations' and not meant to take over the 'functions of the state police forces or other para military forces'.[29] Yet, over the years, its role has vastly expanded to provide personal security to influential politicians quite independent of the real threat that they face. The strength of the SAG is estimated to be 9,000 personnel.

---

[27] Jugal R. Purohit, 'No Choppers, No Training, No Men: National Security Guard', *Daily Mail*, 18 April 2013.

[28] Sixth Central Pay Commission (March 2008), *Report* (New Delhi: Ministry of Finance, 2008), 455.

[29] 'National Security Guard', Ministry of Home Affairs. Retrieved from nsg.gov.in

The NSG is headed by the director general who is selected by the union home minister. The director general is assisted by four IPS officers for administrative matters of whom two are inspector generals each for administration and headquarters, who in turn are assisted by deputy inspector generals.[30] The financial advisor of the NSG is an Indian Revenue Service (IRS) officer of the rank of joint secretary and also has deputy advisors from the Indian Audit and Accounts Service (IAAS) and Indian Civil Accounts Service (ICAS). The NSG's headquarter is located at Mehram Nagar, Palam (New Delhi).

14.3.7.1 Operation and Training

Operations and training is under senior army officers on deputation to NSG. A major general of Indian Army, on deputation, designated as inspector general (operations), is responsible for planning and conduct of operations. Training is under another major general (training), located in Manesar, Gurugram. They are further assisted by two brigadiers on deputation from Indian Army as deputy inspector general (operations) and deputy inspector general (training).[31]

A new training centre has been set up at Ibrahimpatnam, Hyderabad, to train commandos. In response to criticism of the time taken by NSG units to arrive in November 2008 Mumbai attacks, from their base in Manesar, Haryana, the Ministry of Home Affairs decided to deploy NSG contingents in major cities across India such as Mumbai, Kolkata, Hyderabad and Chennai.[32]

14.3.7.2 Special Ranger Group (SRG)

The NSG has three SRGs, each with a strength of battalion, approximately total 900 all ranks. SRG personnel are drawn on deputation from CAPF and state police forces. There are three SRGs—11, 12 and 13.[33] Initially SRG's mandate was to render logistical support to the SAGs during operations and are deployed for guarding high-risk VIPs/VVIPs. However, Since 2013, 11SRG is converted into a regular SAG unit for undertaking specific counter-terror operations.[34] The SAG is the main offensive or the strike wing of NSG.

14.3.8 Assam Rifles

Assam Rifles, raised initially as Cachar Levy in 1835, is the oldest para military force in the country. In the northeast, its men are fondly called 'Friends of Hill People'.[35] Over the course of its history, the Assam Rifles and its predecessor units (Assam Military Police, Assam Frontier Police) have served in a number of roles, conflicts and theatres including I World War and II World War,

[30] See mha.nic.in. Ministry of Home Affairs (GoI).

[31] See *Hindustan Times.* https://www.hindustantimes.com/india/nsg-gets-3-army-officers-for-terror-ops-training/story-K2YX6fUNTfpjRZg4Z59U2J.html (accessed on 3 February 2015).

[32] See *The Indian Express*, (Chandigarh), 1 December 2008.

[33] See *The Times of India.* https://timesofindia.indiatimes.com/india/Learning-with-the-Times-NSG-a-federal-force-set-up-in-1984/articleshow/3806266.cms (accessed on 1 July 2012).

[34] See *Times of India.* http://epaperbeta.timesofindia.com/Article.aspx?eid=31808&articlexml=NSG-withdraws-600-men-from-VIP-security-duty-15022016009030 (accessed on 3 February 2015).

[35] Since 1835, the Assam Rifles have undergone a number of name changes—the Assam Frontier Police (1883), the Assam Military Police (1891) and Eastern Bengal and Assam Military Police (1913)—before finally becoming the Assam Rifles in 1917. See A. K. Sharma, 'The Assam Rifles: Sentinels of the East', *Frontier India*, 16 May 2008.

where they served mainly in Burma. Now, the Assam Rifles is under the control of the union Ministry of Home Affairs and they perform many roles including the provision of internal security under the control of the army through the conduct of counter insurgency and border security operations, provision of aid to the civil power in times of emergency, and the provision of communications, medical assistance and education in remote areas. In times of war, they can also be used as a combat force to secure rear areas if needed. Since 2002, it has been guarding the Indo-Myanmar barrier as per the government policy of 'one border one force'.

From a force of five battalions in 1947, the Assam Rifles has grown substantially over the years. In 1960, there were 17 battalions; in 1968, there were 21; and today, there are 46 battalions. In addition, the force has several area headquarters, a training centre that processes up to 1,800 recruits at time, and a number of logistics units. There are currently 46 battalions of Assam Rifles with a sanctioned strength of 63,747 personnel.[36]

As the number of the force and the number of battalions gradually increased, the rank of the force commander was also upgraded until now it is that of lieutenant general.

14.3.9 Railway Protection Force (RPF)

Besides the state railway police, which is controlled by the state government and is responsible for preventing and investigating crimes committed on the railways, there is the RPF under the central government to guard and protect railway property, tracks and property entrusted to railways.

The genesis of the present RPF can be traced to the year 1854 when the railway companies employed certain staff designated as 'Railway Police'. Later, under the Police Act, 1861, the Company deployed a contingent staff for security of the railways. In 1872, on the recommendation of the Railway Police Committee, Railway Police was organized into 'Government Police' (the precursor of Government Railway Police or GRP) for law enforcement and 'Company Police' (the precursor of RPF) for watch and ward duties (a *chowkidar* system) in the Railways. This watch and ward organization continued up to 1954. The 'Company Police' evolved into present RPF in 1957 with the passage of RPF Bill by the Parliament (29 August 1957). RPF Rules were made on 10 September 1959 and RPF Regulations were formulated in 1966. The RPF Act, 1957, was modified by the Parliament vide Act No. 60 of 1985 on 20 September 1985 for the constitution and maintenance of the force as an armed force of the union. For carrying out the purposes of the Act, RPF Rules, 1987, was framed.

The present RPF is the arm of the CAPF which has the power to arrest, investigate and prosecute criminals. Personnel strength of RPF is about 80,000. As on 1 January 2018, sanctioned strength of Group 'A' officers in RPF is 441, including 127 officers recruited through CSEs of UPSC. RPF is headed by the director general.

For the safety of the railway passengers and railways property, the RPF has the following objectives:

1. Carry on an unrelenting fight against criminals in protecting railway passengers, passenger area and railway property
2. Facilitate passenger-travel and security by removing all anti-social elements from trains, railway premises and passenger area

[36] Ministry of Home Affairs, *Annual Report* 2016–17.

3. Remain vigilant to prevent trafficking in women and children and take appropriate action to rehabilitate destitute children found in Railway areas
4. Co-operate with other departments of the railways in improving the efficiency and image of the Indian Railways
5. Act as a bridge between the GRP/local police and the railway administration
6. Adopt proactively all modern technology, best human rights practices, management techniques and special measures for protection of female and elderly passengers and children, in the pursuit of these objectives

RPF is a security force of India entrusted with protecting railway passengers, passenger area and railway property of the Indian Railways. It is under the authority of the Ministry of the Railways.

14.3.10 The Special Protection Group (SPG)

SPG is the executive protection agency of the GoI. It is responsible for the protection of the PM of India, and his/her immediate families. The force was established in 1985 after the assassination of Indira Gandhi. It provides the security 24×7 all over India to the PM, including ex-PM and their family members at any location across India.

14.3.11 Sashastra Seema Bal (SSB)

SSB, formed in the year 1963, is one of the five main CAPFs, which is deployed at the Indo-Nepal and Indo-Bhutan borders. SSB is a dedicated CAPF having more than 82,000 personnel. SSB personnel are trained in the fields of law and order, military tactics, jungle warfare, counter insurgency and internal security. SSB personnel also serve in the Intelligence Bureau, Research and Analysis Wing (RAW), SPG, NSG, etc., on deputations. Officers start from the level of an assistant commandant, equivalent to the DSP in a state and retire at the rank of inspector general.

14.3.12 Central Investigation and Intelligence Bureau

Besides the aforementioned agencies, there are other agencies maintained by the central government which assist in the investigation of crime and providing information useful for maintenance of internal security.

1. *Central Bureau of Investigation (CBI):* CBI is India's premier investigative agency, responsible for a wide variety of criminal and national security matters. CBI was formed by a mere resolution of the central government than by a parliamentary legislation. Despite the fact that the CBI lacks legislation, it is a formal and authorized agency of the central government to carry out policing all across the nation. It is controlled by the Department of Personnel and Training in the Ministry of Personnel, Public Grievances and Pensions of the union government, usually headed by a union minister who reports directly to the PM. It is India's official Interpol unit. CBI draws its officers from the best IPS and IRS officers around the country. It is responsible for investigation into various crimes and national security matters.

2. *Directorate of Criminal Investigation (DCI):* DCI is headed by the director general of intelligence (income tax) which was created to tackle the menace of black money with cross-border ramifications. The revamp is aimed at launching 'un-intrusive' investigations against 'persons and transactions suspected to be involved in criminal activities having cross-border, inter-state or international ramifications, that pose a threat to national security and are punishable under the direct tax law'.
3. *Directorate of Revenue Intelligence (DRI):* DRI is an intelligence-based organization responsible for the co-ordination of India's anti-smuggling efforts.
4. *Central Economic Intelligence Bureau (CEIB):* This CEIB is an Indian intelligence agency responsible for gathering information and monitoring the economic and financial sectors for economic offences and warfare.
5. *Directorate General of Central Excise Intelligence (DGCEI):* DGCEI, earlier known as the directorate general of anti-evasion, is an intelligence-based organization for the detection of tax evasion cases related to central excise duty and service tax.
6. *Narcotics Control Bureau (NCB):* NCB is responsible for anti-narcotic operations all over the country. It checks the spread of contraband as well as the cultivation of drugs.
7. *National Investigation Agency (NIA):* NIA is the central agency to combat terror in India. The agency is empowered to deal with terror-related crimes across states without special permission from the states. The NIA was created by an Act of Parliament in 2009 in response to the November 2008 Mumbai terror attacks, as need for a central agency to combat terrorism was found. It also deals with drug trafficking and currency counterfeiting.
8. *Bureau of Police Research & Development (BPR&D):* BPR&D was set up on 28 August 1970 in furtherance of the objective of the central government for the modernization of police forces. Besides, it is involved in the research pertaining to problems that the police faces, the training of police personnel and the introduction of scientific technology at both central and state levels.
9. National Crime Records Bureau (NCRB)*:* NCRB was created in 1986 on the recommendation of the NPC (1979). It was formed by the amalgamation of the Directorate of Coordination Police Computers, Central Finger Print Bureau, Data Section of Coordination Division of Central Bureau of Investigation and Statistical Section of the Bureau of Police Research and Development.
10. *Central Forensic Science Laboratory (CFSL):* CFSL is a wing of the union Ministry of Home Affairs, which fulfils the forensic requirements in the country. At present, there are seven central forensic laboratories located in Hyderabad, Kolkata, Bhopal, Chandigarh, Pune, Guwahati and New Delhi, which are undertaking forensic activities.
11. *LNJN National Institute of Criminology and Forensic Sciences (LNJN-NICFS):* Lok Nayak Jaya Prakash Narayan NICFS (formerly the 'Institute of Criminology and Forensic Science') came into existence on 4 January 1972 on the recommendations of a committee appointed by the University Grants Commission (UGC) to look into the applied aspects of education, training and research in the fields of criminology and forensic science to commensurate with the growing needs of the country in general and the criminal justice system in India in particular. In September 1979, the institute was constituted as a separate department under the Ministry of Home Affairs which was headed by a full-time director. It is headed by senior IPS officers. The Institute conducts research in various aspects of criminology and forensics, including cyber forensics.

14.3.13 Conclusion

Notwithstanding constitutional provisions, the Centre has come to play a significance role in the law and order sphere of the states. First, the centre has an important coordination role. The centre monitors trends and developments in the law and order situation and matters relating to communal harmony and internal security of the country. Second, the centre has an important development role. Besides research on the organization of policing, the centre assists the states in modernization and development of their police forces. Third, the centre has set up its own para military forces to perform police functions. The centre assists the state and union territory administrations by providing central para military forces to maintain law and order. The consistent increase in deployment, according to a report (June 2018), is leading to a situation whereby over-deployment is likely to affect anti-insurgency and border-guarding operations, besides affecting their personnel needs.

14.4 Role of State Agencies in Maintenance of Law and Order

14.4.1 Introduction

Maintenance of law and order is primarily the responsibility of the state governments, and, to achieve this goal, they have their own organizations.

At the state level, the home department is politically headed by the chief minister or home minister, and administratively by the additional chief secretary (home) or principal secretary (home). Generally an IAS officer acts as the agency executive of the state home department. The home department is responsible for law and order and is concerned with policy decisions regarding police administration in the state. The home secretary or principal secretary (home) aids and advises the minister in the discharge of his duties and controls, coordinates and supervises the varied aspects of police administration in relation to the directives of the central government and the activities of the officials who are below him in the hierarchy.

Under the administrative control of the home department comes the police department, headed by the DGP or inspector general of police, drawn as a rule from the IPS. Operationally, he is in charge of police force activities including its discipline, training and deployment. Several high-ranking officers such as inspector general, deputy inspector general, assistant inspector general, SSP, etc., assist the DGP in his line and staff function. In the maintenance of law and order in the state, he acts as a principal advisor to the state government and executes its policy decisions and directives.

The Police Act of 1861 established the fundamental principles of organization for police forces in India, and, with minor modifications, continues in effect. Consequently, although state-level police forces are separate and may differ in terms of the quality of equipment and resources, their patterns of organization and operation are markedly similar.

Under the inspector general police are a number of police 'ranges', composed of 3–6 districts that are headed by deputy inspectors general. District police headquarters are commanded by superintendents. District superintendents have wide discretionary powers and are responsible for overseeing subordinate police stations as well as special elements, such as, criminal investigation detachments, equipment storehouses and armouries and traffic police. Many large districts also have several assistant district superintendents.

Most preventive police work is carried out by constables assigned to police stations. Depending on the number of stations, a district may be subdivided and, in some states, further divided into police 'circles' to facilitate the supervision from district headquarters. Most of the major metropolitan areas such as Mumbai, Kolkata and Chennai have police commissionerates, working under the state police, headed by commissioners. Police in the states and union territories are assisted by units of Indian Home Guard volunteers, maintained under guidelines formulated by the Ministry of Home Affairs.

Some cities in India follow the police commissionerate system such as Barrackpore Police Commissionerate, Kolkata. The chief of police commissionerate is the police commissioner. Reporting to the police commissioner are the joint police commissioner, deputy commissioner of police and assistant commissioner of police. Commissioner of police and his deputies are empowered as executive magistrates and hence, are empowered to promulgate Section 144 and grant arms licence. In metropolitan cities of Kolkata, Mumbai, Delhi and Chennai, since 1978, the responsibility for law and order vests with the police commissioner and the DM has no say in this regard.

14.4.2 Organization of Police Wing at the State Level

In most of the states and union territories, the pattern of organization of the police wing is as follows:

1. State police is headed by an IPS officer in the rank of DGP who is assisted by two or more additional DGPs.
2. State forces are organized into zones which consist of two or more ranges, and each zone is headed by an inspector general of police.
3. Further, ranges consist of several districts, and each range is headed by a deputy inspector general of police.
4. District of more importance is headed by a Senior Superintendent of Police, while other districts are headed by a superintendent of police. In case SSP is heading the district, s/he is assisted by one or more superintendents of police. If superintendent of police is heading the district, then s/he is assisted by one or more additional superintendents of police.
5. Each district is divided into subdivisions or circles and will be under the command of a DSP.
6. Each subdivision is made up of several police stations under the command of an inspector of police, who, in turn, is assisted by sub-inspectors and assistant sub-inspector. As per the various Indian laws, sub-inspector (and above) are the only officers who can file a charge sheet in the court.

14.4.3 Recruitment and Training

Each state and union territory administration has its own system of recruitment and training. The recruitment process differs according to the level of the position, and direct entry (where an applicant does not have to start at the lowest level) is possible. The educational requirements increase with recruitment for higher posts.

The DSPs or Assistant Commissioners of Police (ASPs) are recruited every year by the UPSC through an extremely competitive examination and are appointed into the IPS. IPS officers are then assigned to a state police force. Superintendents of police undergo rigorous training for 44 weeks. The training programme also involves external invitees such as lawyers and management consultants. At the end of probation, they undergo an orientation training of few weeks at the assigned state's police academy.

Lower, non-managerial positions are selected by the state or central government and are trained at Police Recruit Schools. The duration of training for inspectors is roughly a year, and for constables is nearly nine months. The training staff for these schools are drawn from the police force itself. Police are trained in basic law, self-protection, weapon handling and so on. From recruit stations, best recruits are taken into special forces where they undergo special training.

The basic unit of law and administration is the police *thana* headed by the SHO who in his duties is assisted by a complement of inspectors, sub-inspectors, head constables and constables. The SP or SSP, in-charge of the district police, is an important functionary in the police hierarchy. Officers in charge of sub-units within a district such as subdivisions, circles and police stations are subordinated to the SSP/SP.

SP/SSP, in some states, works under the overall supervision of the DM and looks through the problems of law and order and of administration of crime in the district. He is empowered to take all sorts of preventive measures if a breach of peace is apprehended in the district. He advises the DM to impose prohibitory orders and even curfew. In the event of breach of law, s/he makes adequate police arrangements to meet the situation.

14.4.4 Role of District Magistrate in Maintenance of Law and Order

It may be emphasized that administration of law and order is not the exclusive responsibility of the police. In all emergencies, there is no one else except the district collector/deputy commissioner, drawn from the IAS, to whom the state government and the public turn. The DC by virtue of his position as representative of the government, vested with a variety of legal, statutory and administrative powers is the only person who can be expected to handle maintenance of law and order. For the administration of law and order in the district, the DC exercises general control over the district police. This is for the reason that the DC is in charge of the entire district.[37] A social order such as ours cannot survive if a balance is not built into the system which can only be through the recognition and reinforcing of the significant role of the DM in the police system. Thus the SP/SSP at the district level is subjected to two kinds of control: (a) operational control by officers in the police and (b) a hierarchical control by the DM. The DM (when he acts in the field of law and order) can inspect the police stations and ask for information, record and register dealing with crime. It is the responsibility of the SP/SSP to inform the DM of any apprehension of the breach of law and order. He may order the prohibition of the performance of any objectionable play and seize the material under the National Security Act, 1980. Specifically, authorized DM/commissioner of police can issue orders of detention of a person if his/her activities are considered prejudicial to the defence, security or maintenance of public order.

DSPs are not empowered as executive magistrates in a district. The DM, who is an IAS officer, exercises these powers, such as, promulgating Section 144 and granting arms licences. The DM can call for armed forces to aid the civil administration to deal with any abnormal situation. He can

[37] S. S. Khera, *District Administration in India* (Bombay: Asia Publishing House, 1974), 33.

ban the assembly of five or more persons if it is likely to cause danger to peace, apart from imposing curfew in particular area for a specific period.

14.4.5 Issue of Relationship Between DM and SP/SSP

There has been yet another controversy as to the relationship between the DM and the SP at the district level. The Indian Police Commission of 1902–1903 recommended a relaxation of the control of SP and asked the DM not to interfere in matters of departmental management and discipline. The Royal Commission on Decentralization (1907–1909) however suggested that the powers of the DM vis-à-vis the police be increased. The report of the working group of the ARC was of the view that promulgation of orders under Section 144 of the Criminal Procedure Code (1973) should be given to the police on whom rests the principal duty of maintaining law and order. It is argued that the subordination of the police has increased the volume of paper work without leading to any better performance of duties.

The NPC (set up on 15 November 1977) in its eighth report suggested the enactment of a new Act to replace the Indian Police Act, 1861, which could meet the present-day needs. The commission also proposed that the police should be made solely responsible for the maintenance of law and order to the exclusion of the DM.

Along with this controversy of subordination of police must also go the interference by ministers and politicians. It is true that very few police officials have been bold enough to make open complaints against the pressures frequently put on them to do things which are either against the law and rules or which they would not have done left to themselves. But the truth is that such meddling has been and is taking place almost in every state in the country.

The police officials, including the SHO/SP/SSP know the consequences of ministerial displeasure such as transfer to inconvenient places, adverse remarks in confidential sheets, denial of promotion and so on. There is no question that his interference by ministers and politicians is also one of the main reasons for the fall in police efficiency and their poor image among the public.

Summary

Law and order coupled with fundamentalism and insurgency pose a serious threat and promise little respite. With the exception of some of the central police organizations, state agencies for maintenance of law and order need professional and managerial competence which includes education, training and leadership qualities. The police officers need professional training and be given a wider exposure. Police should pay greater attention to and emphasize on justiciability of their action. There should not be any attempt to reject any allegation of violation of human rights against members of the police force. Police administration need to be based on probity and accountability. The police has to be initiated in developing an attitude of promptness and effectiveness in its working.

If the police is to become an effective, impartial, friendly force for the protection of the citizen, it is not only desirable but essential that force is insulated from incessant and unreasonable pressures of those who exercise power, authority and influence in their own interest. It is unfortunate that the police force has become politicized and, therefore, the inevitable consequence has been the shattering of command lines and the breeding of indiscipline.

The union Ministry of Home Affairs issued guidelines in 1985 prescribing for all members of police, fruitful allegiance to the Constitution of the country, upholding of the rights of citizens, firm and impartial enforcement of laws, using persuasion and warning before using force, preventing crimes and disorders rather than let these happen, behaving like responsible citizens, seeking public cooperation, being helpful and sympathetic to people, placing duty before self, maintaining the highest standards of discipline and honesty and being free of any religious or social prejudices. 'Important test for police will be to build mutual trust with people and to act as People's Police'.[38]

State law and order administration of public administration is an important dimension of public administration. On it depends the socio-economic development of the country. The policeman is an agent of the state and 'the long arm of the law' for preserving order in society and providing citizens with a sense of security. The role played by both the central and state agencies in the maintenance of law and order has not been commendable. The union Ministry of Home Affairs (Department of Internal Security) has assumed considerable powers of direction and control relating to law and order of states. *The Annual Report* of the union Ministry of the Home Affairs admits that the ministry 'monitors trends and developments in the law and order situation and matters relating to communal harmony and internal security' and keeps a watch on the administration in the states to 'see that it is carried on in accordance with the provisions of the Constitution'. Moreover states are also increasingly finding their meagre resources inadequate for augmenting their own police force to cope with emergency law and order situations such as widespread linguistic agitations and communal riots. On the contrary, the role played by the central agencies in law and order administration has been regarded as a direct encroachment on states' jurisdiction and a violation of the federal constitution.

The state law and order machinery has, over the years, lost much of its credibility. Its methods of investigation and handling law and order problem are crude. Complaints of physical torture, ill-treatment and harassment by police officials are read in the daily newspapers. There is appreciable evidence of successful political intervention in police affairs, some of which has produced injustices and weakened the morale of the force. Anyway, the fact remains that 'at present the police is at the disposal of the executive which can employ the way it wants'. The criminalization of politics and the politicization of criminals has aggravated the law and order situation in the country. Kidnapping and killing of law enforcement officials, journalist and even witnesses have created lawlessness, and the public trust in government has been completely lost. The gradual loss of moral and ethical values and integrative forces have brought about a situation in which violence, conflict and lawlessness among various segments of society prevail.

There have been many recommendations for administrative and police reforms but scanty attention has been given to modernize the police force in the context of liberal democracy. Maybe the police officers are efficient and dutiful, but the environment within which they have to handle complexity of law and order administration is so extremely intricate that it is doubtful whether these officials would be able to protect the citizens or individuals in the enjoyment of their rights.

[38] K. M. Mathur, 'Fifty Years of Indian Police—A Reappraisal', *Indian Journal of Public Administration* 44, no.1 (1998): 68.

15 Social Welfare Administration

LEARNING OBJECTIVES

1. **To learn the concepts of social welfare and social welfare administration**
2. **To enumerate the constitutional provisions dealing with social welfare aspects**
3. **To discuss policies and programmes for the welfare of children and women at national level**
4. **To discuss policies and programmes for the SCs and STs in India**

Introduction

India's Constitution of 1950, embodying the concept of a welfare state, has given a new purpose and role to the administration. But without a reorganization of the civil services and machinery of the government, it would be difficult to secure the fulfilment of the purposes of a welfare state. The government of a welfare state must pay attention to the social welfare needs of the masses rather than concerning itself merely with the maintenance of law and order. The whole purpose of government and its administrative arm has to be reoriented.

The regulatory state has become the welfare state, which, in addition to playing the regulatory role, has accepted the challenge of performing wide-ranging services for its citizens. The modern state has assumed the role of an agent of socio-economic change. The necessity for the state to assume a dominant role in welfare field was recognized in the First Five Year Plan, which pronounced: 'As the social structure becomes more complex, the state is called upon to play an increasing role providing service for the welfare of the people'.[1] In fact, this welfare function absorbs a steadily growing share of the resources of the state. It is therefore not surprising that welfare administration has evolved into a distinct part of public administration, which is commonly labelled as social administration.

Concepts of Social Welfare and Social Welfare Administration

Encyclopaedia Britannica defines 'social welfare' as 'a system of laws and institutions which a government attempts to protect and promote the economic and social welfare of its citizens

[1] Planning Commission, *First Five Year Plan 1951–56* (New Delhi: GoI, 1951).

usually based on various forms of social insurance against unemployment, accident, illness and old age'. Friedlander defines 'social welfare' as

> the organized system of social services and institutions, designed to aid individuals and groups to attain satisfying standards of life and health, and personal and social relationships which permit them to develop their full capacities and to promote their well-being in harmony with the needs of their families and the community.[2]

To Heywood, social welfare promotes the economic well-being of the individuals with the basic needs necessary for a healthy life. Heywood puts forward following reasons for the strengthening of the social welfare system:

1. 'It promotes social cohesion and national unity, in that it gives all citizens a "stake" in society and guarantees at least some basic social support.
2. It enlarges freedom in the sense that it safeguards people from poverty and provides conditions in which they can develop and realize their potential.
3. It ensures prosperity by countering the effects of social deprivation and helping those who cannot help themselves.
4. It serves as a redistributive mechanism that promotes greater equality and strengthens a sense of social responsibility'.[3]

As far as definition of 'social welfare administration' is concerned, it is the process of providing resources and services to meet the social needs of the individuals, families and communities. Social needs may encompass medical care, food, clothing, housing and right to security in the wake of unemployment, sickness, disability, widowhood, old age or other lack of livelihood.

According to John C. Kidneigh, social welfare administration is 'the process of transforming social policy into social services—a two-way process: transforming policy into concrete social services and the use of experience in recommending modification of policy'.[4]

With a view to realizing aims and objectives of social welfare, the government formulates social policies and programmes (relating to health, education, social needs of the people, etc.) and in pursuance thereof enacts social laws, allocates financial assistance and provides organizational and administrative linkages. Invariably, the government also seeks the help and cooperation of non-governmental organizations and voluntary sector for the effective implementation of various social laws and programmes.

Jawaharlal Nehru, the first PM of India, observed that the welfare must be a common property of everyone in India and not monopoly of a privileged group, as it is today. In particular, those who are underprivileged today and have no opportunities of growth and progress must be brought within its field. He further added,

> The core idea of social welfare is the human well-being in its each and every respect and a welfare state must ensure minimum opportunities for the physical and social well-being of all citizens, it would eliminate exploitation, disparities and thus would provide for the self-development of the individual.[5]

---

[2] Walter A. Friedlander, *Introduction to Social Welfare* (New Delhi: Prentice-Hall, 1967), 4.
[3] Andrew Heywood, *Key Concepts in Politics* (New York: Palgrave Macmillan, 2005), 152.
[4] John C. Kidneigh, 'Social Work Administration', *Social Work Journal* 31 (April 1959): 58.
[5] Planning Commission, *First Five Year Plan* (New Delhi: GoI, 1951).

In an effort to establishing an effective system of welfare, the complexity of this field of administration has to be fully appreciated. No universal classification of welfare system has been so far accepted. It would appear that the organization of this great complex of services requires extremely careful analysis. Such services demand a setting where a great diversity of specialists and supporting workers can do complicated tasks.

Principles of Social Welfare Administration

Some significant principles of social welfare administration which are recognized and practised in the area of social welfare have been enumerated by Trecker in his work *Social Group Work*. He grouped these principles into three broad blocks for the sake of understanding.[6]

1. **Principles related to professional values**
   a. *The principle of social work values:* The values of the profession are the foundation of social welfare.
   b. *The principle of community and client needs:* The needs of the community are the basis for the existence of social agencies.
   c. *The principle of cultural setting:* The culture of the community must be understood in as much as it influences the way needs are expressed.
   d. *The principle of purposeful relationship:* Effective purposeful working relationship must be established between the administration and the constituency.
   e. *The principle of professional responsibility:* The administrator is responsible for the provision of high quality professional services.
   f. *The principle of participation:* Appropriate contributions of administration and constituency must be utilized through dynamic participation.
   g. *The principle of evaluation:* Continuous evaluation of processes and programmes is essential to the fulfilment of the agency's objectives.
2. **Principles related to administrative functions**
   a. *The principle of agency purpose:* The social purpose of the agency must be clearly formulated, understood and utilized.
   b. *The principle of planning:* The process of continuous planning is fundamental to the development of meaningful services.
   c. *The principle of organization:* The work of people must be structured so that responsibilities and relationships are clearly defined.
   d. *The principle of delegation:* The delegation of responsibility and authority to other professional persons is essential.
   e. *The principle of communication:* Open channels of communication are essential to the complete functioning of people.
   f. *The principle of coordination:* The work delegated to many people must be properly coordinated.
   g. *The principle of resource utilization:* The resources of money facilities and personnel must be carefully fostered, conserved and utilized in the agency.

[6] H. B. Trecker, *Social Group Work: Principles and Practices* (New York: Association Press, 1972).

h. *The principle of leadership:* The administrator must carry major responsibility for the leadership of the agency in terms of goal attainment and the provision of professional services.

3. **General principles**
   a. *The principle of agency totality:* The agency must be understood in its totality.
   b. *The principle of change:* The process of change is continuous, both within the community and within the agency.
   c. *The principle of growth:* The growth and development of all participants is furthered by the administrator who provides challenging work assignments, thoughtful supervision and opportunities for individual and group learning.

15.1 Constitutional and Legal Provisions for Welfare

The Constitution of India contains several provisions dealing with social welfare aspects. India is a welfare state, committed to the welfare and development of its people in general and of vulnerable sections in particular. Preamble, Directive Principles of State Policy, Fundamental Rights and specific sections, namely, Articles 38, 39 and 46, in the Constitution of India stand testimony to the commitment of the State to its people. As a matter of strategy, the GoI has resorted to human development for minimizing inequality in income, status and opportunities for its people. This strategy is directed to secure distributive justice and utilization of economic resources to subserve common good. Programmes are directed to promote educational and economic interests of weaker sections in general and those of SCs, STs, backward classes and minorities, in particular, to avoid injustice and exploitation.

15.1.1 Preamble

The Preamble to the Indian Constitution reflects the nature of the State in India. Initially it declares India to be a 'sovereign' 'democratic' and 'republic'. But with the 42nd Constitutional Amendment in 1976, the State's outlook has been broadened to include elements of 'secular' and 'socialist'. The Preamble envisages securing for all its citizens:

> Justice, social, economic and political; Liberty of thought expression, belief, faith and worship; Equality of status and of opportunity; and to promote among them all; fraternity assuring the dignity of the individual and the unity and integrity of the Nation.

The Preamble thus reflects all the attributes of a welfare State.

15.1.2 Fundamental Rights

Part III of the Constitution provides for a set of six Fundamental Rights to all the citizens (and in a few cases to non-citizens also). These include Right to Equality; Right to Freedom; Right Against Exploitation; Right to Freedom of Religion; Cultural and Educational Rights; and Right to Constitutional Remedies. All these rights are also available to the persons with disabilities even though no specific mention of such persons appears in this Part of the Constitution.

In particular, Article 15 is of relevance. This Article of the Constitution prohibits discrimination on grounds of religion, race, caste, sex and place of birth. Article 16 provides for the equality of opportunity in matters of public employment. In particular, in pursuance of Article 17 of the Constitution of India, the Untouchability (Offences) Act, 1955, was enacted, and, subsequently, it was amended in the year 1976 as the Protection of Civil Rights Act, 1955. The Act extends to the whole of India and provides punishment for the practice of untouchability.

15.1.3 Directive Principles of State Policy

The Directive Principles of State Policy have been incorporated in Part IV from Article 36 to Article 56 of the Constitution. Even though non-justiciable, these have been declared as fundamental in the governance of the country. These principles are intended to be the imperative basis of state policy. These are really in the nature of instructions issued to future legislatures and executives for their guidance. Article 41, Right to work, to education and to public assistance in certain cases, provides, 'The State shall, within the limits of its economic capacity and development, make effective provision for securing the right to work, to education and to public assistance in case of unemployment, old age, sickness and disablement and in other cases of undeserved want'. Article 38 says, 'The State shall strive to promote the welfare of the people by securing and protecting as effectively as it may, a social order in which justice, social, economic and political, shall inform all the institutions of the national life'. Article 42 directs the State to make provision for securing just and humane conditions of work and for maternity relief. Article 46 says, 'The State shall promote with special care the educational and economic interests of the weaker sections of the people, and, in particular, of the Scheduled Castes and the Scheduled Tribes, and shall protect them from social injustice and all forms of exploitation'. Likewise, Article 47 says, 'The State shall regard the raising of the level of nutrition and the standard of living of its people and the improvement of public health as among its primary duties'.

15.1.4 Certain Constitutional Provisions for Welfare of Weaker Sections

A major concern of the framers of the Constitution has been the welfare and development of the weaker sections of society and, among them, more especially, that of SCs, STs and the denotified, nomadic and semi-nomadic tribes, who constitute nearly one-quarter of the total population. These groups have, for historical reasons, remained socially and economically backward. The Constitution in its Part XVI makes special provisions relating to certain classes. For example, some of these are mentioned here:

1. Article 330 (Reservation of seats for Scheduled Castes and Scheduled Tribes in the House of the People) and Scheduled Tribes in autonomous districts of Assam
2. Article 332 (Reservation of seats for Scheduled Castes and Scheduled Tribes in the legislative assemblies of the states)
3. Article 335 (Claims of Scheduled Castes and Scheduled Tribes to services and posts)
4. Article 338 (National Commission for Scheduled Castes) and 4A. 338A (National Commission for Scheduled Tribes)

5. Article 339 (Control of the Union over the administration of Scheduled Areas and the welfare of Scheduled Tribes)
6. Article 340 (Appointment of a commission to investigate the conditions of backward classes)
7. Articles 341 and 342 specification of Scheduled Castes and Scheduled Tribes, respectively.

Besides, Eleventh Schedule to Article 243G and Twelfth Schedule to Article 243W, which pertain to the powers and responsibilities of the panchayats and municipalities respectively with respect to implementation of schemes for economic development and social justice, which also include welfare and safeguarding the interests of persons with disabilities among other weaker sections of the society. The relevant extracts of the said schedules are reproduced here. Eleventh Schedule to Article 243G: 'Social welfare, including welfare of the handicapped and mentally retarded (Entry No. 26)'. Twelfth Schedule to Article 243W: 'Safeguarding the interests of weaker sections of society, including the handicapped and mentally retarded (Entry No. 9)'.

15.1.5 Other Social Legislative Measures

As some of the social legislative measures are still in pipeline, and others have already been implemented. Some of these are as follows:

1. Protection of Civil Rights Act, 1955 (amended in 1976)
2. Mental Health Act, 1987
3. Rehabilitation Council of India Act, 1992
4. National Commission for Minorities (NCM) Act, 1992
5. National Commission for Backward Classes (NCBC) Act, 1993
6. Persons with Disabilities (PwD) Act, 1995
7. Wakf Act, 1995
8. National Commission for Scheduled Tribes Amendment Act, 2003
9. Scheduled Castes and Scheduled Tribes (Prevention of Atrocities) Amendment Act, 2015

15.2 Legislative Welfare Measures for Women and Children

Women and children constitute roughly two-thirds of India's total population (1,210.9 million of which 587.6 million are females, as per the census 2011). The development of women and children is of great significance as it sets the pace for national development.

15.2.1 Ministry of Women and Child Development

The Ministry of Women and Child Development came into existence in January 2006 with the prime objective of addressing gaps in state action for women and children and for promoting inter-ministerial and inter-sectoral convergence to create gender equitable and child centred legislation policies and programmes. Earlier to this year, the Department of Women and Child Development was merged Ministry of Human Resource Development after bifurcation of the erstwhile Ministry of Welfare in 1985–86. The ministry has a major responsibility which includes formulation of plans, policies and programmes for women and children, enactment and amendment of legislations related to them, and overall guidance and coordination of efforts of governmental organizations and NGOs working in the field of women and child development.

The ministry has a vision of empowered women living with dignity and contributing as equal partners in development in an environment free from violence and discrimination. Its mission for children is to ensure development, care and protection through policies and programmes, enabling them to grow and develop to their full potential.

15.2.2 Legislative Measures Relating to Women and Children

Apart from constitutional provisions, the central government has enacted various legislative measures which are related to women and children. The Ministry of Women and Child Development is in charge of the administration of the following Acts relating to women and children[7]:

1. The Immoral Traffic (Prevention) Act, 1956 (as amended in 1986)
2. The Indecent Representation of Women (Prevention) Act, 1986 (60 of 1986)
3. The Dowry Prohibition Act, 1961 as amended in 1986
4. The Commission of Sati (Prevention) Act, 1987 (3 of 1988)
5. The Prohibition of Child Marriage Act, 2006 (notified in January 2007)
6. Protection of Women from Domestic Violence Act, 2005
7. National Commission for Women Act, 1990
8. Infant Milk Substitutes, Feeding Bottles and Infant Food (Regulation of Production, Supply and Distribution) Act, 1992 (41 of 1992)
9. Commission for Protection of Child Rights Act, 2005
10. Juvenile Justice (Care and Protection of Children) Amendment Act, 2011
11. The Protection of Children from Sexual Offences Act, 2012
12. Sexual Harassment of Women at Workplace (Prevention, Prohibition and Redressal) Act, 2012

15.3 Policies and Programmes for the Welfare of Women

15.3.1 National Policy for Women

The National Policy for Empowerment of Women (NPEW), 2001, is being replaced by the new National Policy for Women (NPW), 2016, which has been unveiled by the Ministry of Women and Child Development on 17 May 2016.[8]

[7] Under the Juvenile Justice Act, 2015, the age of children is between 16 and 18 years for trial of an offence.

[8] NPW (2016) is under consideration for the union cabinet approval.

Some of the salient features of NPW:

1. To create a society with women as equal partners
2. To make cyber space a safe place for women and to address a redistribution of gender roles, review of personal and customary laws in accordance with the constitutional provisions
3. To review the criminalization of marital rape keeping women's right in mind
4. To ensure health and education of women
5. To improve access to pre-primary education, enrolment of adolescent girls
6. To carry out skill development and provide equal employment opportunities
7. To provide suitable benefits related to maternity and childcare services
8. To increase women's participation in political, administration, civil services and corporate arena
9. To address all forms of violence against women
10. To improve child sex ratio
11. To prevent trafficking at source, transit and destination areas

Operational strategies include the following:

1. To enable safety and security of women with the help of 'One Stop Centres, Women Helpline, Mahila Police Volunteers, Reservation of Women in Police force, Panic buttons in mobiles, surveillance mechanisms in public places'
2. To create eco-systems to encourage entrepreneurship amongst women through podium's such as Mahila, e-Haat and the likes
3. Aiding women in workplace through flexi timings, increased maternity leave, provision of child care/crèches at workplace, building for women youth through gender champion initiative, frontline workers, women sarpanches and all officials dealing with policy and delivery systems impacting women

15.3.2 National Commission for Women

The National Commission for Women (NCW) is a statutory body of the GoI, generally concerned with advising the government on all policy matters affecting women. It was established in January 1992, under the provisions of the Indian Constitution as defined in the 1990 NCW Act. The objective of the NCW is to represent the rights of woman in India and to provide a voice for their issues and concerns. The subjects of their campaigns have included dowry, politics, religion, equal representation for woman in jobs, the exploitation of women, police abuses against women and so on. The commission continues to pursue its mandated activities, namely, review of legislation, interventions in specific individual complaints of atrocities and denial of rights.

15.3.3 Scheme for Adolescent Girls (Sabla)

Sabla was introduced in the year 2010–11 and is operational in 205 selected districts on a pilot basis. It aims at all round development of adolescent girls of 11–18 years (with a focus on all out-of-school). Sabla is being implemented through the state governments/union territories with cost sharing ratio between the center, the states and the UTs (with legislation) in the ratio of 50:50 for nutrition and 60:40 for rest of the components. Anganwadi Centre (AWC) is the focal point for the delivery of the services.

15.3.4 Pradhan Mantri Matru Vandana Yojana

Government announced Pan India implementation of maternity benefit programme to eligible pregnant women and lactating mothers. The programme was named as Pradhan Mantri Matru Vandana Yojana (PMMVY). The PMMVY is a centrally sponsored scheme under which the grant-in-aid is being released to states/UTs in cost sharing ratio between the centre and the states and UTs with legislature as 60:40, for north-eastern states and Himalayan states it will be 90:10 and 100 per cent for union territories without legislature. The scheme envisages providing cash incentive amounting to ₹5,000 directly to the bank/post office account of PW and LM in DBT mode.[9]

15.3.5 Swadhar and Short Stay Homes

The Swadhar Scheme was launched in 2001–2002 as a central sector scheme for providing holistic and integrated services to women in difficult circumstances and without any family, social and economic support, such as destitute widows deserted by their families, women prisoners released from jails, trafficked women, victims of terrorist violence without any means for survival, mentally challenged women and so on. The package or services made available under the scheme include provision for food, clothing, shelter, healthcare counselling and legal support, social and economic rehabilitation through education, awareness generation and skill upgradation. The scheme is implemented through Social Welfare, Women and Child Development Department, Women's Development Corporation, urban local bodies, and voluntary organizations, etc.

The scheme of Short Stay Homes provides for 6 months to 3 years temporary accommodation, maintenance and rehabilitative services through voluntary organizations to homeless women and girls. Children accompanying the mother or born in the home are permitted to stay in the home up to age of 7 years, after which they may be referred to children's institutes.

15.3.6 Ujjawala

Launched in 2009, Ujjawala is a comprehensive scheme for prevention of trafficking, with following five specific components:

1. *Prevention*, which includes formation of community vigilance groups
2. *Rescue*, for safe withdrawal of the victim
3. *Rehabilitation*
4. *Reintegration*, for restoring into family/community
5. *Repatriation*, to provide support to cross-border victims for their safe repatriation to their country of organ

A comprehensive legislation on trafficking (2017) has been drafted by WCD Ministry.

[9] All organized sector women employees are excluded from the scheme as they are entitled for paid maternity leave.

15.3.7 Gender Budgeting Initiatives

The Ministry of Women and Child Development of the GoI has been undertaking several initiatives, including advocating for setting up of gender budgeting cells (GBCs) in all ministries and departments, strengthening internal and external capacities and building expertise of GBCs to undertake gender mainstreaming of policies and programmes so as to ensure that benefits of development reach women.

15.3.8 National Mission for Empowerment of Women

National Mission for Empowerment of Women (NMEW), a centrally sponsored scheme, was launched by the GoI in 2010 with an aim to achieve empowerment of women by securing intersectoral convergence of programmes of different ministries/departments of central and state governments. It has the mandate to strengthen and facilitate the process of coordinating all the women's welfare and socio-economic development programmes.

The mission has an executive director and experts in various fields. The women centres at the village legal, the first point of contact for women, are known as *Poorna Shakti Kendras*, which is the focal point for action on ground through which the services to grassroots women would be facilitated. In addition, the NMEW is made as the nodal agency for addressing the issue of declining child sex ratio.[10]

15.3.9 Beti Bachao, Beti Padhao Campaigns

In the backdrop of a trend of declining sex ratio in the age group up to five years, the GoI has introduced a new scheme called 'Beti Bachao, Beti Padhao' scheme in 2014 with the twin aim of not only improving the adverse sex ratio but also to ensure that girls are educated. 'Mass communication campaign on Beti Bachao Beti Padhao aims at ensuring girls are born, nurtured and educated without discrimination to become empowered citizens of this country'. The campaign interlinks national-, state- and district-level interventions with community-level action in 100 districts, bringing together different stakeholders for accelerated impact.

15.3.10 Sukanya Samriddhi Account

Along with the Beti Bachao, Beti Padhao scheme, the government also launched the 'Sukanya Samriddhi Account' programme. Despite being a small savings scheme, the Sukanya Samriddhi Account has the potential to have a phenomenal impact on the lives and self-esteem of young girls in the country. The scheme aims to ensure a bright future for the girl children by facilitating their education and marriage expenses.

Under the scheme, a parent or legal guardian can open an account in the name of girl child until she attains the age of 10. The maximum amount of ₹150,000 or minimum amount of ₹1,000 per

[10] Against a sex ratio of 871 women per 1,000 men in 2014, sex ratio in Haryana has climbed to 899 in 2016. See *The Tribune* (Chandigarh), 16 December 2016.

year can be deposited in any post office branch or any public sector bank. The account will be valid for 21 years from the date of opening, after which it will mature and the money will be paid to the girl child in whose name the account had been opened. The account will also automatically close if the girl child gets married before the completion of the tenure of 21 years. Premature withdrawal of 50% money can be made when the girl child attains the age of 18 years for the education or her marriage.

15.3.11 Rashtriya Mahila Kosh (National Credit Fund for Women)

The National Credit Fund for Women (Rashtriya Mahila Kosh or RMK) was set up under the Societies Registration Act, 1860, on 30 March 1993 with corpus fund of ₹31 crore to meet the credit needs for poor women. The RMK has pioneered an alternate credit delivery mechanism in the country by advancing micro-credit to the self-help groups (SHGs) of poor women through a diverse range of intermediary organizations working at the grassroots level, such as, NGOs, women federations, cooperatives, urban women cooperative banks and so on. To be eligible for a loan from RMK, the intermediary micro-financing organizations (IMOs) should have experience in thrift and credit management of 3 years or more and must not work for profit. The partner organizations that take loans from RMK are instructed to impart literacy, education, awareness on health, hygiene, nutrition, HIV/AIDS, legal rights and so on to the women SHG members. RMK has extended micro-credit across 27 states and 7 union territories.

15.3.12 Scheme of Central Social Welfare Board

The Central Social Welfare Board (CSWB) was set up in August 1953, which further sets up Family Counselling Centre (FCC). Through these centres, counselling, referral and rehabilitative services are provided to the women who are victims of atrocities, family maladjustment and social ostracism.

The FCCs work in close collaboration with the local administration, police, courts, legal aid cells, medical and psychiatric institutions, vocational training centres, short stay homes and so on to provide referral and rehabilitative services.

Many state governments have declared FCCs as service providers and counsellors as protection officer under the Protection of Women from Domestic Violence Act, 2005.

In addition, the CSWB initiates condensed courses of education for adult girls/women who could not join mainstream education and who were dropouts from formal schools. The scheme aims to provide educational opportunities to girls/women above the age of 15 years along with additional inputs of skill development at different levels—primary, middle/high school and matric/secondary levels.

The CSWB also organizes awareness generation programme/scheme. This scheme aims at empowering women by providing knowledge through organizing awareness generation camps and to enhance their participation in development process and decision-making.

15.3.13 Suggestions for Women Development

It is important to recognize the women's role in national development. The general development programmes for women should reflect greater gender sensitivity. The flow of benefits to women in education, health and employment need to be monitored. Women must be enabled to function as equal partners and participants in development and not merely as beneficiaries of various schemes. Socio-cultural and administrative constraints to the realization of women's full potential need to be removed and there has to be greater social awareness of their contribution to national well-being. The media, both mass and folk, must be assigned an important role. Voluntary agencies should be supported in their advocacy and social activism programmes for gender equality and prevention of atrocities on women. PRIs should be involved in the designing and implementation of women's programmes.

A major thrust in the strategy for women's development should be on the formation and strengthening of grassroots level women's groups which will articulate local women's needs and play an important role in decentralized planning and implementation of programmes. Services for women under various programmes of employment, education, health care, family welfare, drinking water and nutrition should be made available at the grassroots level in the form of a package through convergence and integration.

Adolescent girls, out of the school system, have been a neglected category in the matter of reach of social services. Their developmental needs will require special attention in order to prepare them for adult roles. Special programmes should be developed for adolescent and young girls as these groups have generally suffered on account of poor nutrition, lack of health care, education and training and restrictive social customs and practices.

The existing legal safeguards for women against injustice and atrocities need to be reviewed, loopholes removed and their implementation monitored. One of the basic requirements for improving the status of women is to bring about changes in the laws relating to inheritance of property. Laws must protect the interests of women and enable them to get an equal share in the parental property, whether inherited or self-acquired. Social legislations for women should be effectively enforced with the help of women's groups. The National Commission on Women has an obligation to act as a watchdog body on matters concerning women.

15.4 Policies and Programmes for the Welfare of Children

Children are the integral component of the human resources. They are the asset to the country's development. They need to be developed. The central as well as state governments have launched several programmes for their development. The Ministry of Women and Child Development has taken several programmes and initiatives for the child development.

15.4.1 National Policy for Children (2013)

The government adopted a National Policy for Children in April 2013. The new policy reaffirms the government's commitment to the realization of the rights of all children of 18 years as children. The policy recognizes childhood as an integral part of life with a value of its own. The policy has identified survival, health, nutrition, education development, protection and participation as the undeniable rights of every child, and has also declared these as key priority areas that need to be given a good deal of attention by the governmental and non-governmental agencies.

As children's needs are multisectoral, interconnected and require collective action, the policy aims at purposeful convergence and strong coordination across different sectors and levels of governance; active engagement and partnerships with all stakeholders; setting up of a comprehensive and reliable knowledge base; provision of adequate resources; and sensitization and capacity development of all those who work for and with children. To deal with child abuse case, government has brought a special law, the Protection of Children from Sexual Offences Act, 2012. The act defines a child as any person below eighteen years of age.

Being gender neutral, the definition of 'child' provides equal protection to both the male and the female child. The Act provides for stringent punishments which range from simple to rigorous imprisonment of varying periods. The Act provides for the establishment of special courts for trials of offences under the Act, keeping the best interest of the child of paramount importance at every stage of the judicial process. The National Commission for the Protection of Child Rights (NCPCR) and State Commissions for the Protections of Child Rights (SCPCRs) have been made the designated authorities to monitor the implementation of the Act.

15.4.2 National Nutrition Policy

The National Nutrition Policy was formulated in 1993, and, as a follow up, the National Plan of Action was developed in 1995. The National Plan of Action identified the different sectors in the government for taking up coordinated action to combat malnutrition.

Demonstrations for the promotion of low-cost nutritious recipes are held to facilitate adoption of means to achieve better nutrition. Linkages with ICDS are maintained for better quality of supplementary nutrition, health and nutrition education are maintained. For the promotion of infant and young child feeding practices, focus on appropriate feeding and implementation of IMS Act are undertaken.

There is also the Food and Nutrition Board in the Ministry of Women and Child Development which is involved in policymaking, strategy development as well as identifying innovative measures for the improvement of the nutritional status of the people of our country.

15.4.3 Integrated Child Protection Scheme (ICPS)

Ministry of Women and Child Development is implementing this comprehensive centrally sponsored scheme since 2009–10 through the state governments/UT administrations on a predefined cost-sharing financial pattern. The objectives of the scheme are to contribute to the improvement in the well-being of children in difficult circumstances as well as reduction of vulnerabilities to situation and actions that lead to abuse, neglect, exploitation, abandonment and separation of children from parents. ICPS provides preventive, statutory care and rehabilitation services to children who are in need of care and protection, children in conflict with law as defined under the Juvenile Justice (Care and Protection of Children) Act, 2000, and its Amendment Act, 2015, and any other vulnerable child. It provides financial support to state governments/UT administrations for running services for children either by themselves or through suitable NGOs. These services include (a) homes of various types for children, (b) emergency outreach service through childline, (c) open shelters for children in need of care and protection in urban and semi-urban areas and (d) family-based non-institutional care through sponsorship, foster care and adoptions.

As reported by the state governments/UT administration, 619 Child Welfare Committees and 618 Juvenile Justice Boards have been set up across the country so far to ensure effective implementation of the scheme and provide quality services to children.[11]

15.4.4 National Crèche Scheme

Rajiv Gandhi National Crèche Scheme provides day-care facilities to the children in the age group of 0–6 years from families with specific monthly income. In addition to being a safe space for the children, the crèches provide services as supplementary nutrition, pre-school education and emergency health care and so on. The scheme is presently being implemented through the Central Social Welfare Board (CSWB) and Indian Council for Child Welfare (ICCW).

15.4.5 Childline Services

Childline is a 24-hour toll-free emergency outreach telephone service (1098) for children in distress. At present, Childline is functioning in over 300 cities and districts. The basic objectives of childline are to (a) respond to the emergency needs of the children in difficulty, (b) provide a forum for networking among government agencies and non-government agencies dedicated to child care and protection, (c) sensitize hospitals, medical personnel, police, municipal corporations and so on towards needs of children, (d) ensure protection of rights of the child and (e) provide an opportunity to communities to respond to the needs of children in difficult circumstances.

15.4.6 Scheme for Welfare of Working Children in Need of Care and Protection

The scheme is being implemented since January 2005 with the objective of providing non-formal education, vocational training and so on to working children to facilitate their entry/re-entry into mainstream education in cases where they have either not attended any learning system or where, for some reason, their education has been discontinued, with a view to prevent their future exploitation. Under this scheme, financial assistance is provided to NGOs by the Ministry of Labour and Employment for setting up composite centres of working children in the areas that have not already been covered. At present, the Ministry of Women and Child Development is assisting 116 projects of 100 children each under this scheme in 14 states/union territories.

15.4.7 Integrated Child Development Services (ICDS)

With the announcement of National Policy for Children in 1974, an ICDS was initiated with 33 ICDS blocks/projects in 1975–76. The ICDS is one of the flagship programmes of the government

[11] Figures up to June 2016.

which represents one of the world's largest and unique programmes for early childhood development. The programme aims at addressing health, nutrition and the development needs of young children, pregnant and nursing mothers. National Institute of Public Cooperation and Child Development (NIPCCD) has been functioning as an apex institution for the training of the ICDS functionaries since 1975. As a nodal resource agency, the institute has also been entrusted with the responsibility of training and capacity building of functionaries at the national and regional level, under the ICPS. The scheme provides an integrated package of services comprising supplementary nutrition, immunization, health check-up, referral service, pre-school non-formal education and health and nutrition education for mothers. The target groups are children in the age group of 0–6 years and expectant and nursing mothers.

The NIPCCD is currently focusing on gender planning and mainstreaming, gender budgeting, economic and political empowerment of women, prevention of sexual harassment at workplace, prevention of gender-related violence such as female foeticide, female infanticide, trafficking of women and children, child marriage and so on. In addition to these, the institute provides technical advice and consultancy to government and voluntary agencies in promoting and implementing policies and programmes for women and child development and voluntary action.

15.4.8 National Commission for Protection of Child Rights

A National Commission for Protection of Child Rights was set up in March 2007 in accordance with the provisions of the Act (NCPCR), 2005, for proper enforcement of children's rights and effective implementation of laws and programmes relating to children. Its mission is to protect, promote and defend child rights in India. Its mandate is to ensure that all laws, policies, programmes, practices and administrative structure in the country are in consonance with the child rights perspective as enshrined in the Constitution of India and also in the UN Convention on the Rights of the Child (UNCRC). Under the provisions of the Act, state commissions have been set up in many states and union territories. The NCPCR, along with the state commissions, have a specific role for the implementation of the Rights of Child to Free and Compulsory Education Act, 2009. The State Commissions for Protection of Child Rights have also been entrusted with the task of monitoring the implementation of the Protection of Children from Sexual Offences (POCSO) Rules, 2012.

15.4.9 National Institute of Public Cooperation and Child Development

NIPCCD, New Delhi, is an autonomous organization functioning under the aegis of the Ministry of Women and Child Development. The objectives of the institute are to develop and promote voluntary action in social development; to take a comprehensive view of child development and to promote relevant need-based programmes in pursuance of the National Policy for Children; to formulate national policy for empowerment of coordination between governmental and voluntary action in social development; to evolve framework and perspective for organizing programmes related to women and children through governmental and voluntary efforts; and to establish liaison with international and regional agencies, research institutions, universities and technical bodies engaged in activities similar to those of the institute.

15.5 Welfare of Scheduled Castes

Of all, the sections of the 'Shudras' (once placed on the lowest rung of the social hierarchy; menials and the servants) were destined to suffer all types of deprivations. These 'untouchables' and depressed classes came to be labelled as SCs. The term scheduled castes or SC first appeared in the GoI Act, 1935. In pursuit of this Act, the British government had issued the GoI (Scheduled Castes) Order, 1936, specifying certain castes, races and tribes as SCs in the then provinces of Assam, Bengal, Bihar, Bombay, Central Provinces and Berar, Madras, Orissa, Punjab and United Provinces.

15.5.1 Current Status of Scheduled Castes and Scheduled Tribes

SCs are specified in accordance with Article 341 of the Constitution; according to this article, certain communities, suffering from the social disabilities including untouchability, have been specified in the states and union territories as SCs. About 475 castes fall in the category of SCs, of which Chamars, Adi Dravida, Balmikis and Dhobi constitute a major chunk. Population-wise, SCs constitute a major portion of our total population. They number, according to 2011 census, nearly 20 crores, which is 16.6% of the country's total population (121 crores).[12]

About 44% of the SC population is living below the poverty line. The main reason for the socio-economic backwardness of the SCs is the age-old practice of untouchability due to which they have been deprived of economic opportunities in the society.

15.5.2 National Commission for Scheduled Castes

The National Commission for Scheduled Castes and Scheduled Tribes which was set up under Article 338 of the Constitution in 1990 was bifurcated into two Commissions, namely, National Commission for Scheduled Castes and National Commission for Scheduled Tribes (NCST), after the 89th Constitutional (Amendment) Act, 2003. The National Commission for Scheduled Castes is responsible for monitoring the safeguards provided for SCs and also to review issues concerning their welfare. The commission consists of a chairperson, vice chairperson and five other members. Their tenure is of three years duration from the date of joining. The main functions of the commission, as enumerated in the Article 338(5) of the Constitution, are as follows:

1. To investigate and monitor all matters relating to the safeguards provided for SCs in the Constitution
2. To enquire into specific complaints with respect to the deprivation of rights and safeguards of the SCs
3. To participate and advise on planning processes and the socio-economic development of SCs

[12] As per census 2011, in Uttar Pradesh alone, there are 41 million people who belong to SC category, representing 20.7% of the total population of the state.

4. To present to the president, annually and at such times as the commission may deem fit, reports on the working of those safeguards
5. To make recommendations in terms of the measures that should be taken by the union or any state for the effective implementation of those safeguards and other measures for the protection, welfare and socio-economic development of SCs
6. To discharge such other functions, in relation to the protection, welfare and development and advancement of SCs as the president may subject to the provisions of any law made by the Parliament[13]

15.5.3 National Commission for Safai Karamcharis and NSKFDC

National Commission for Safai Karamcharis (NCSK) as an Indian statutory body was established on 12 August 1994 under National Commission for Safai Karamcharis Act, 1993. The NCSK has been given extension of tenure for three years beyond 31 March 2016.[14]

NCSK seeks to study, evaluate and monitor the implementation of Safai Karamcharis as an autonomous organization and to provide redressal of their grievances as well. The NCSK has been entrusted with the following functions:

1. To recommend to the central government the specific programmes of action towards elimination of inequalities in status, facilities and opportunities for *safai karamcharis* (sweepers) under a time-bound action plan
2. To study and evaluate the programmes and schemes relating to the social and economic rehabilitation of *safai karamcharis* and make recommendations to the central and state governments for better coordination and implementation of such programmes and schemes
3. To investigate specific grievances and take into *suo moto* notice of matters relating to non-implementation of (a) programmes or schemes in respect of any group of *safai karamcharis*, (b) decisions, guidelines or instructions, aimed at mitigating the hardship of *safai karamcharis*, (c) provisions of any law in its application to *safai karamcharis* and (d) take up such matters with the concerned authorities or with the central or state governments
4. To make periodical reports to the central and state governments on any matter concerning *safai karamcharis*, taking into account any difficulties or disabilities being encountered by safai karamcharis
5. To take up any other related matter which may be referred to it by the central government

In the discharge of its functions, NCSK is empowered to call for information with respect to any matter related to Safai Karamcharis Act from any government or local or other authority.

Further, a National Safai Karamcharis Finance and Development Corporation (NSKFDC) was incorporated in January 1997 under Section 25 of the Companies Act, 1956. NSKFDC is an apex corporation under the Ministry of Social Justice and Empowerment, GoI. The target groups of the

[13] The Commission is given the powers of a civil court trying a suit while making enquiry and monitoring matters related to safeguards of SCs.

[14] Shri Manohar Valji Bhai Zala (as the chairman) along with two members, Smt. Manju Diler and Shri Dalip Kallu, have been appointed to the NCSK on 16 March 2017.

Corporation are 'scavengers' who are engaged or employed by an individual or a local authority or a public or private agency for manually cleaning, carrying, disposing of, or otherwise handling in any manner, human excreta.

15.5.4 Scheduled Castes and Scheduled Tribes (Prevention of Atrocities) Act, 2015

The Scheduled Castes and Scheduled Tribes (Prevention of Atrocities) Act, 1989 (PoA Act) came into force with effect from 1990. This legislation aims at preventing commission of offences by persons other than SCs and STs against these castes and tribes. This Act was amended in 2015 and 2016, looking at the continuing high incidence of offences against members of SCs and STs.

15.5.4.1 Education Development for the SCs

Some significant measures have been taken by the union Ministry of Social Justice and Empowerment to alleviate sufferings of the SC students on educational front.[15] Under Pre-Matric Scholarship Scheme for SC students, 100% central assistance for expenditure is implemented by the state governments and UT administrations. Similarly, National Overseas Scholarship (NOS) Scheme for SC students provides for fees charged by institutions as per actual, monthly maintenance allowance, passage visa fee and insurance premium, annual contingency allowance, incidental journey allowance and so on. Only two children (below the age of 35 years) of the same parents/guardians are eligible to get the benefits under this scheme. Financial assistance under the scheme is provided for a maximum period of 4 years for PhD and 3 years for Master's programme.

In addition, there is Rajiv Gandhi National Fellowship scheme for SC students. The scheme provides financial assistance to SC students for pursuing research studies leading to MPhil, PhD and equivalent research degree in universities, research institutions and scientific institutions. UGC is the nodal agency for implementing the scheme. About 2,000 Junior Research Fellowships (JRF) per year are awarded to SC students. Under the Babu Jagjivan Ram Chhatrawas Yojana, the objective is to provide hostel facilities to SC boys and girls studying in middle schools, higher secondary schools, colleges and universities. The state governments/UT administrations and the central and state universities/institutions are eligible for central assistance, both for fresh construction of hostel buildings and for expansion of the existing hostel facilities while NGOs and deemed universities in the private sector can avail the benefit only for expansion of their existing hostel facilities.

15.5.4.2 Economic Empowerment Measures for the SCs

Some of the economic empowerment measures taken for the SCs are as follows:

1. Under the Special Central Assistance scheme, 100% grant is given to the states/union territories, as an additive to their Scheduled Castes Sub-Plan (SCSP). The main objective is

[15] Literacy in India is a key for socio-economic progress and the literacy rate has grown to 74% in 2011 from 12% at the end of British rule in India in 1947.

to give a thrust to family-oriented schemes of economic development of SCs below the poverty line.

2. In 1979, a centrally sponsored scheme for participating in the equity share of the Scheduled Castes Development Corporation (SCDC) in the ratio of 49:51 (central–state) was introduced. The main functions of SCDCs are identifying eligible SC families and motivating them to undertake economic development schemes. At present, SCDCs are functioning in 27 states and union territories which are providing credit and inputs by way of margin money loans and subsidy to the target group.
3. There is also a National Scheduled Castes Finance and Development Corporation (NSFDC) which was set up in February 1989 under Section 8 of the Companies Act 2013. The broad objective of NSFDC is to provide financial assistance in the form of concessional loans to SC families, and skill-cum-entrepreneurial training to the youth of the target group, living below double the poverty line for their economic development.

15.6 Welfare Measures for the Tribal Communities

Population-wise, STs constitute 104 million of the total population that is nearly 8.6% of the country's total population (1201 million, as per 2011 census). The tribal population in the country presents varied picture of race, language and culture. The culturally diverse tribal communities who inhabit different habitats of the country, show divergence of not only habits and customs but also personality and innate motives on which they are nourished. The level of literacy among the STs is nearly 35%, compared to 74% of the general population in 2011. Economically, STs form the lowest strata of the society. An estimated 50% of the ST population is still living below the poverty line.

The union Ministry of Tribal Affairs was set up in 1999 after the bifurcation of Ministry of Social Justice and Empowerment with the objective of providing more focused approach on the integrated socio-economic development of the STs, the most underprivileged of the society, in a coordinated and planned manner.

The Constitution of India provides various safeguards for the protection and promotion of the interests of the tribal communities. Some of the significant Articles in this regard are Articles 19, 46, 244, 330, 332, 334, 338A, 339 and 342.

15.6.1 Scheduled Areas and Tribal Areas

In order to protect the interests the STs with regard to land alienation and other social factors, provisions of the Fifth Schedule and Sixth Schedule have been enshrined in the Constitution. The Fifth Schedule under Article 244(1) of the Constitution defines 'scheduled areas' that the president may by order declare to be scheduled areas after consultation with the governor of the state. The Sixth Schedule under Article 244(2) of the Constitution relates to those areas in the states of Assam, Meghalaya, Tripura and Mizoram which are declared 'tribal areas' and provides for district councils and/or regional councils for such areas. These councils have been conferred with wide ranging legislative, judicial and executive powers.

In terms of Article 342(1), the president may, with respect to any state or union territory, and, where it is a state, after consultation with the governor thereof, notify tribes or tribal communities or parts thereof as STs. The criteria generally adopted for specification of a community as a ST are (a) indications of primitive traits, (b) distinctive culture, (c) shyness of contact with the community at large and (d) geographical isolation, that is, backwardness.

15.6.2 National Commission for Scheduled Tribes

NCST was carved out of a statutory multimember National Commission for Scheduled Castes and Scheduled Tribes on 19 February 2004 by amending Article 338 and inserting a new Article 338A in the Constitution through the Constitution (89th Amendment) Act, 2003.[16]

15.6.3 Tribal Sub-Plan

Tribal Sub-Plan (TSP), which has been adopted since Fifth Five Year Plan, is based on the twin objectives: (a) protection of interests of tribals through legal and administrative support and (b) promotion of development efforts through plan schemes to raise their level of living. The salient features with respect to TSP for states are as follows:

1. The funds provided under the TSP of the state have to be at least equal in proportion to the ST population of each state or union territory.
2. Tribals and tribal areas of a state or union territories are given benefits under the TSP, in addition to what percolates from the overall Plan of a state/UT.
3. TSP should (a) identify the problems and need of tribal people and critical gaps in their development, (b) identify all its available resources, (c) prepare a broad policy framework for development, (d) define a suitable administrative strategy for its implementation and (e) specify the mechanism for monitoring and evaluation.

15.6.4 National Scheduled Tribes Finance and Development Corporation

With a view to pay a focused attention and accelerate the pace of economic development of STs, a separate National Scheduled Tribes Finance and Development Corporation (NSTFDC) was set up in April 2001 (the Ministry of Tribal Affairs) under Section 25 of the Companies Act.[17]

In order to achieve the mandate set for the NSTFDC (for undertaking self-employment ventures/activities), financial assistance is extended by NSTFDC to the STs with an annual family income of up to double the poverty line. NSTFDC also provides financial assistance as grant for skill and entrepreneurial development of the target group. Further, NSTFDC provides financial assistance for procuring and marketing minor forest produce so as to avoid the distress sale of produce/products by STs.

---

[16] Since the needs and problems of STs and the solutions required were quite different from those of the SCs, a special approach for tribal development and independent machinery to safeguard the rights of STs was considered necessary.

[17] The authorized share capital of the NSTFDC is ₹500 crore. DPL is Rs. 39,500 for rural and ₹54,500 per annum for urban areas (2018).

For getting financial assistance, the beneficiary as well as the Self-help Group (SHG) members should belong to the ST community, having annual family income up to double the poverty line. Similarly for Cooperative Society members, loan is extended to the eligible STs through society itself.

15.6.5 Tribal Cooperative Marketing Development Federation of India

The Tribal Cooperative Marketing Development Federation of India Limited (TRIFED) was set up in 1987 as a national-level apex body under the Multi-State Cooperative Societies Act, 1984 (now MSCS Act, 2002, with revised rules). TRIFED is now engaged in the marketing development of tribal products (natural and organic products, handicrafts, ratification, etc.) through its own shops (TRIBES India) and shops, selling its products on consignment basis.

15.6.6 Welfare Measures for the Tribal People

Some of the welfare measures taken for the tribal people are as follows:

1. *Special scheme for Adivasi mahila:* Adivasi Mahila Sashaktikaran Yojana (AMSY) is an exclusive scheme for the economic development of ST women. Under the scheme, NSTFDC provides term loan for scheme(s)/project(s) costing up to ₹50,000 per unit/profit centre. In addition, micro-credit scheme provides financial assistance for undertaking small self-employment ventures/activities by the eligible STs through existing profit-making SHGs.
2. *Recognition of forest rights of STs:* The Scheduled Tribes and Other Traditional Forest Dwellers (Recognition of Forest Rights) Act, 2006, seeks to recognize and vest the forest rights and occupation in forest land in forest dwelling STs and other traditional forest dwellers who have been residing in such forests for generations but chose rights on ancestral lands.[18]
3. *Vanbandhu Kalyan Yojana:* Major activities approved under Vanbandhu Kalyan Yojana (VKY) during 2017–18 are education, infrastructure, toilets in hostel and schools; health, sports, safe drinking water; self-employment, skill development, fruit farming, livelihood, dairy, fishery; irrigation; culture and tourism; monitoring cell, institution; and connectivity, market, electricity, solar energy.
4. *Umbrella scheme for education of ST children:* The ministry is re-engineering its educational schemes with the objective of providing adequate educational infrastructure for STs and incentive for education for ST children through scholarships. In the umbrella scheme, the following schemes have been merged:
   a. Establishing and strengthening of Ashram Schools
   b. Establishing and strengthening of hostels
   c. Vocational training in tribal areas
   d. Post-matric scholarship and
   e. Pre-Matric Scholarship

[18] The Act has been notified for operation with effect from 31 December 2007. Rules for implementing the provisions of the Act were notified in January 2008.

5. *National Overseas Scholarships (NOS) for ST students:* The Ministry of Tribal Affairs has approved revised scheme of NOS for ST students. The scheme is providing scholarship to students selected for pursuing higher studies abroad for postgraduation, PhD and post-doctoral research programmes. The ministry has revised some of its provisions to make it more beneficial for ST students.[19]

15.7 Welfare Measures for the Backward Classes

Backward classes (the term includes SCs, STs, denotified tribes and other backward classes/OBCs) constitute important segments of the society. A large number of people of backward classes continue to be socially and economically backward and are languishing at the bottom of the social pyramid.

15.7.1 Constitutional Provisions

Article 15(4) of the Constitution enjoins upon the states to create special provisions for the advancement of any socially and educationally backward classes or for the SCs and STs. Article 16(4) further enables the states to make provisions for the reservation of appointments or posts in favour of any backward class, which in the opinion of the state is not adequately represented.

The other provisions of the Constitution having a bearing on Article 16 are Articles 38 and 46. Clause (i) of Article 38 makes it obligatory for the state to 'strive to promote the welfare of the people by securing and protecting a social order'. Article 46 contains directive regarding the promotion of educational and economic interests of other weaker sections and protects them from social injustice and exploitation. Part XVI of the Constitution contains 'special provisions relating to certain classes', and, under Article 340, it envisages the appointment of a commission to investigate the conditions of backward classes.

15.7.2 Mandal Commission Report

The government considered the objectives of Articles 15 and 16 of the Constitution seriously, and the Second Backward Classes Commission (Mandal Commission) was appointed in 1979. The commission submitted its report on 31 December 1980.

As a consequence of office memorandum (OM) issued by GoI on 13 August 1990 providing 27% reservation for OBCs, there was widespread protest against this reservation and several writ petitions were filed in Supreme Court questioning the said reservation.

The Supreme Court, vide their majority judgement delivered on 6 November 1992, upheld the OM of 13 August 1990, providing for reservation for OBCs in government jobs subject to the exclusion of the socially advanced persons/sections (described by it as the 'creamy layer') from the notified OBCs.

[19] From the year 2016, out of total 20 awards, 3 awards have been earmarked for Particularly Vulnerable Tribal Groups (PVTGs) and 30% awards have been earmarked for girl candidates.

The Supreme Court in the Mandal Case judgement did not confine itself merely to the issue of providing reservation to OBCs but also proceeded to give its observations on various aspects of reservation policy. The view of the court was that these observations were made with a view 'to finally settle the legal position with regard to reservation'. The implications which have a bearing on the reservation policy for backward classes (ST/SC and OBC) are as follows:

1. Reservation for appointments or posts under Article 16(4) is confined to initial appointments only and cannot be extended to provide reservation in the matter of promotion.
2. The reservations contemplated in Article 16(4) shall not, as a rule, exceed 50%.
3. Certain services and posts, where, on account of the nature of duties, merit alone counts, should be excluded from the purview of reservation.
4. Reservation for economically backward classes of upper castes is constitutionally invalid.

The GoI in 1993 reserved 27% of vacancies in civil posts and services under the central government to be filled through direct recruitment in favour of the OBCs. With the amendment of Article 15 of the Constitution in January 2006 and the enactment of the Central Educational Institutions (Reservation in Admissions) Act in January 2007, listing of OBCs has become relevant for admission in central educational institutions as well. Under this Act, OBC students are entitled to 27% reservation in central educational institutions in a phased manner, over a period of three years, commencing from the academic session 2008–2009.

15.7.3 National Commission for Socially and Educationally Backward Classes (2017)

National Commission for Socially and Educationally Backward Classes (replacing NCBC set up on 14 August 1993, pursuant to the provisions of NCBC Act, 1993) would be set up to look into inclusion or exclusion of other backward castes for quotas, among other issues.[20] As per the NCBC, the number of backward castes in the central list of OBCs has increased to over 5,000 in 2016.[21]

15.7.4 National Backward Classes Finance and Development Corporation

The National Backward Classes Finance and Development Corporation was set up on 13 January 1992 as a not-for-profit organization under Section 25 of the Companies Act, 1956. The main objective of the corporation is to promote the economic development of the backward classes by granting financial assistance to them for viable self-employment ventures and upgrading their technical and entrepreneurial skills. The corporation also acts as an apex body for monitoring the work of all corporations and boards set up by the state governments for the welfare of OBCs.

---

[20] The bill of national commission for socially and educationally backward classes, which was passed by the Lok Sabha in April 2017, seeks to grant constitutional status to the NCBC.

[21] In October 2015, NCBC proposed that a person belonging to OBC with an annual family income up to ₹15 lakh should be considered as minimum ceiling for OBC.

15.7.5 Welfare Schemes for the OBCs

With a view to ensuring educational development among the students or members of the OBCs, a number of schemes have been launched which include pre-examination coaching, pre-matric scholarships, hostels for boys and girls, post-matric scholarships, and so on. In addition, financial assistance to voluntary organizations is given to establish centres and develop services which equip the OBCs to start income-generating activities.

15.8 Welfare Measures for the Minorities

The Constitution of India protects the interests of minorities, recognizes their rights to conserve their languages, scripts or culture, and establishes and administers educational institutions of their choice. Under the National Commission for Minorities (NCM) Act, 1992, six religious communities, that is, Muslims, Christians, Sikhs, Buddhists, Zoroastrians (Parsis) and Jains, have been notified as minorities. As per Census of 2011, the minority groups constitute nearly 18% of the total population of the country. The government has taken some measures for the welfare of minorities, which are discussed in the following sub-sections.

15.8.1 Ministry of Minority Affairs

The Ministry of Minority Affairs was created in January 2006 to ensure a focused approach to the issues relating to the minorities and to play a pivotal role in the overall policy planning, coordination, evaluation and review of the regulatory and development programme for the benefit of the minority communities. The ministry is also responsible for the administration and implementation of the (a) NCM Act, 1992, (b) Wakf Act, 1995 and (c) Dargah Khwaja Saheb Act, 1955.[22] In a short period of time, not only the ministry has been made fully functional but also concerted efforts have been made to streamline the ongoing programmes/schemes for the welfare of minority communities. With the 1995 amendment, the NCM composition was expanded to seven members, including a chairperson.

15.8.2 National and State Commissions for Minorities

The first statutory national commission (replacing the minorities commission set up in January 1978 by a resolution issued by the Ministry of Home Affairs) was set up on 17 May 1993 under the NCM Act, 1992.[23] The Act is primarily an instrument to protect and promote the minority communities.

In addition to the NCM, 13 state governments have set up statutory commissions for minorities.

---

[22] For purpose of advising the central government on matters relating to working of states, Wakf Boards were established. Similarly, for the proper administration of the Wakfs in the country, the Central Wakf Council was established as a statutory body under Wakf Act, 1995.

Under Dargah Khwaja Saheb Act, 1955, a central Act, the administration, control and management of the Dargah endowment has been vested in a representative committee known as the Dargah Committee, appointed by the central government.

[23] The provision under Section 3(2) of the Act stipulates that five members including the chairpersons shall be from among the minority communities.

15.8.3 Scholarship Schemes for Minority Students

The following three centrally sponsored scholarship schemes (with 30% scholarships earmarked for girl students) deserve attention, which are for students of minority communities.

1. *Merit-cum-Means Scholarship Scheme:* The scheme launched in 2007 is being implemented through state governments/UT administrations with entire expenditure borne by the central government.
2. *Post-Matric Scholarship Scheme:* The scheme launched in November 2007 is being implemented through the state government/UT administrations with 100% central funding.
3. *Pre-Matric Scholarship Scheme:* The scheme was approved in January 2008 and was launched as a centrally sponsored scheme. The scheme, with 100% central funding, is being implemented through the state governments/union territory administrations.

15.8.4 15-Point Programme for the Welfare of Minorities

The PM's New 15-Point Programme for the welfare of minorities was announced in June 2006. The objectives of the programme are (a) enhancing opportunities for education, (b) ensuring an equitable shares for minorities in economic activities and employment, through existing and new schemes, enhanced credit support for self-employment and recruitment to state and central government jobs, (c) improving the conditions of living of minorities by ensuring an appropriate share for them in infrastructure development schemes and (d) prevention and control of communal disharmony and violence. In order to ensure that the benefits of these schemes flow equitably to the minorities, the new programme envisages location of a certain proportion of development projects in minority concentration areas.

15.8.5 National Commission for Religious and Linguistic Minorities

For having a detailed examination to determine the criteria for identification of socially and economically backward sections among religious and linguistic minorities and to suggest measures for their welfare, the GoI constituted National Commission for Religious and Linguistic Minorities with the following terms of reference:

1. To suggest criteria for identification of socially and economically backward sections among religious and linguistic minorities
2. To recommend measures for their welfare including reservation in education and government employment
3. To suggest the necessary constitutional, legal and administrative modalities, as required for the implementation of their recommendations, and to present a report of their deliberations and recommendations

The office of the Commissioner for Linguistic Minorities (CLM) was created in July 1957, in pursuance of the provisions of Article 350B of the Constitution. The CLM takes up all the matters pertaining to the grievances arising out of the non-implementation of the constitutional and nationally agreed scheme of safeguards provided to linguistic minorities.

15.9 Welfare of Persons with Disabilities

In order to give focused attention to different policy issues and meaningful thrust to the activities aimed at the welfare and empowerment of the persons with disabilities, a separate Department of Empowerment of Persons with Disabilities was carved out of the Ministry of Social Justice and Empowerment in May 2012. The department acts as a nodal agency for matters pertaining to disability and persons with disabilities, including effecting closer coordination among different stakeholders—related central ministries, state/UT governments, NGOs, etc.—in matters pertaining to disability.

According to Census 2011, there are 2.68 crore persons with disabilities in the country (who constitute 2.21% of the total population). Out of the total population of persons with disabilities, about 1.50 crore are men and 1.18 crore are women. These include persons with visual, hearing, speech and locomotor disabilities, mental illness, mental retardation, multiple disabilities and other disabilities.

Sections 2(t) of the Persons with Disabilities (Equal opportunities, Protection of Rights and Full Participation) Act, 1995, defines a person with disability as someone suffering from not less than 40% of any disability as certified by a medical authority. The disability being (a) blindness, (b) low vision, (c) leprosy cured, (d) hearing impairment, (e) locomotor disability, (f) mental illness, (g) mental retardation, (h) autism, (i) cerebral palsy or (j) a combination of any two or more of (g), (h) and (i).[24] Mental illness has been recognized as one of the disabilities under the PwD Act, 1995. The treatment and care of the mentally ill persons are governed by the Mental Health Act, 1987. The Act is administered by the Ministry of Health and Family Welfare.

15.9.1 Department of Empowerment of Persons with Disabilities

The department deals with the following legislations governing different aspects of disability and welfare and empowerment of the persons with disabilities:

1. The Rehabilitation Council of India Act, 1992.
2. The PwD (Equal Opportunities, Protection of Rights and Full Participation) Act, 1995.
3. The National Trust for the Welfare of Persons with Autism, Cerebral Palsy Mental Retardation and Multiple Disabilities Act, 1999.

[24] Section 2(i) of the PwD Act 1995 read along with Section 2(j) of the National Trust for Welfare of Persons with Autism, Cerebral Palsy, Mental Retardation and Multiple Disabilities Act, 1999.

15.9.1.1 Persons with Disabilities Act

A comprehensive law, namely, the PwD (Equal Opportunities, Protection of Rights and Full Participation) Act, 1995, was enacted and enforced in February 1996. The law deals with both prevention and promotion aspects of the rehabilitation such as education, employment and vocational training, creation of barrier-free environment, provision of rehabilitation services for persons with disabilities, institutional services and supportive social security measures such as unemployment allowance and grievance redressal machinery both at the central and state level.

The National Trust, which is a statutory body under the National Trust for the Welfare of Persons with Autism, Cerebral Palsy, Mental Retardation and Multiple Disabilities Act, 1999, has the objective of enabling and empowering persons with these disabilities to live independently as fully as possible and supporting them requiring such protection.

The chief commissioner appointed under the PwD Act, 1995, is invested with powers of a civil court relating to summoning of witness, discovery, requisitioning and production of any document, etc. The functions and duties of the chief commissioner include coordinating the work of state commissioners for persons with disabilities, monitoring of utilization of funds disbursed by the central government, and taking steps to safeguard rights and facilities made available to persons with disabilities.

15.9.1.2 Rehabilitation Council

The Rehabilitation Council of India is a statutory body set up under the Rehabilitation Council of India Act, 1992. The council is responsible for regulating the training policies and programmes for various categories of professionals in the area of rehabilitation and special education. Its functions include the following:

1. Standardization and regulation of training courses at different levels in all the training institutions throughout the country
2. Recognition of institutions/universities running training courses in the area of rehabilitation of the disabled within and outside the country on a reciprocal basis
3. Promotion of research in rehabilitation and special education
4. Maintenance of a Central Rehabilitation Register for professionals possessing the recognized rehabilitation qualifications in the area of rehabilitation
5. Encouragement of continuing rehabilitation education programmes in collaboration with organizations working in the area of disability

15.9.2 National Institutes for Disabled Persons

In order to effectively deal with the multi-dimensional problem of the disabled population, the following national institutes/apex-level institutes have been set-up in each major area of disability:

1. National Institute for the Visually Handicapped, Dehradun
2. National Institute for Orthopedically Handicapped, Kolkata

3. Ali Yavar Jung National Institute for the Hearing Handicapped, Mumbai
4. National Institute for the Mentally Handicapped, Secunderabad
5. National Institute of Rehabilitation Training and Research, Cuttack
6. Institute for the Physically Handicapped, New Delhi
7. National Institute for Empowerment of Persons with Multiple Disabilities, Chennai

These institutes are mainly responsible for conducting innovative researches, organize training programmes for manpower development and deliver services in the country.

In addition to these, there is Artificial Limbs Manufacturing Corporation of India (ALIMCO), Kanpur, which is engaged in manufacturing of aids and appliance for persons with disabilities. Five Composite Regional Centres (CRCs) for the persons with disabilities are located at Srinagar, Lucknow, Bhopal, Sundernagar and Guwahati. These centres conduct training programmes to prepare professionals in the field of rehabilitation as well as provide rehabilitation services to the disabled.

15.9.3 National Handicapped Finance and Development Corporation (NHFDC)

NHFDC is an apex-level financial institution for extending credit facilities to persons with disabilities for their economic development. Funds assistance is disbursed through the channelizing agencies authorized by the state governments/UT administrations and NGOs. It also extends loans for pursuing education at graduate and higher levels. Besides, it assists in the upgradation of technical and entrepreneurial skills to enable beneficiaries to manage their production units efficiently.

15.10 Social Defence

In the area of social defence, the Ministry of Social Justice and Empowerment (GoI) is committed towards the welfare of older persons and rehabilitation of drug addicts. The programmes for the targeted groups are discussed in brief here.

15.10.1 National Policy for Older Persons

The National Policy for Older Persons (NPOP) was announced in January 1999 with the primary objective, namely, to encourage individuals to make provision for their own as well as their spouse's old age; to encourage families to take care of their older family members; to enable and support voluntary organizations and NGOs to supplement the care provided by the family; to provide care and protection to the vulnerable elderly people; to provide health care facility to the elderly; to promote research and training facilities to train geriatric care givers and organizers of services for the elderly; and to create awareness regarding elderly persons to develop them into fully independent citizens.

15.10.2 National Council for Older Persons

The government has reconstituted National Council for Older Persons (NCOP) to advise and aid the government on developing policies and programmes for older persons. It provides feedback to the government on the implementation of the NPOP and the specific initiatives for older persons. The NCOP is the highest body to advise and coordinate with the government in the formulation and implementation of policy and programmes for the welfare of the aged. Under Integrated programme for Older Persons, financial assistance up to 90% of the project cost is provided to NGOs for establishing and maintaining old age homes, day-care centres, mobile medicare units, and for providing non-institutional services to older persons.[25]

15.10.3 Prevention and Rehabilitation of Drug Addicts/Alcoholics

Under the scheme, grant-in-aid to the extent of 90% (95% in northeast states, Jammu and Kashmir, and Sikkim) of the expenditure is provided to voluntary organizations for rehabilitation of drug addicts and alcoholics. Assistance to voluntary organization for social defence services provides for undertaking programmes for the rehabilitation of various social segments at risk, not currently covered under the existing schemes of the ministry. In particular, the scheme provides for pilot projects in unchartered areas in which the ministry may like to formulate independent programmes in due course. A number of programmes are being supported for rehabilitation of children of sex workers. Initiatives have also been taken to support projects for rehabilitation of widows and for providing counselling and support to traumatized children and women, particularly those who have been victims of physical violence and sexual abuse.

Summary

Liberalization, globalization and privatization resulting from policies introduced since July 1991 have their impact on the welfare administration in India. Today, it seems that the state is withdrawing from the arena of welfare services. The industrialists and the rich in India lack commitment to the welfare state. Influence of Gandhism and religious values are not able to persuade them to pay their dues to the state. On the contrary, these people are largely responsible for commercializing education and health services in a big way. That has already adversely affected the social services in India.

The Fundamental Rights, Directive Principles of State Policy and Preamble stand testimony to the commitment of a welfare state. The institutions of the State have already played an important role in achieving welfare objectives. Specifically, the judiciary has played a pivotal role in forcing the state government to take effective steps for the implementation of welfare schemes for the poor

[25] In a landmark judgement, the Delhi High Court ruled, 'where the house is self-acquired by the parents, the son, whether married or unmarried, has no legal right to live there. He can stay at the parents' mercy up to time they allow it'. See *The Times of India*, 30 November 2016.

and weaker sections of the society. The social welfare administration needs proper administrative structures manned by the professional people with adequate budgetary support. There has to be a political support for the management of welfare programmes and services for the socially and economically weaker sections of the society. The governments operating both at the national and state levels have a moral obligation to secure to the people a welfare and healthy environment so that they feel that they are honourable subjects of the nation.

16 Reflections on Administrative Reforms

LEARNING OBJECTIVES

1. **To understand the meaning and significance of administrative reform**
2. **To discuss the changes and reforms in administration before India's independence**
3. **To comment on recent initiatives for administrative reforms**

Introduction

Administrative reforms are initiated by the government (Centre or state) on the presumption that there is a wide gap between well-intentioned planning and implementation, between policy statement and policy implementation. Undoubtedly, the country continues to be faced with formidable administrative problems, not the least of which are inefficiency, corruption, red tape and administrative discretion.

Although much of the present-day Indian administration reflects the imprints of the British India administration, the country's administration appears to have manifested impressive adaptability and resilience. Without departing from the essential concept of the civil service, it has changed its disposition and, to lesser degree, the character of its activity. The changes were made without serious impairment and with high degree of self-confidence. It was able to eliminate many of the objectionable qualities of an extreme exclusiveness incompatible with democratic ethos.[1] The major problems of administration were approached with frankness and reforms, involving the public, the legislature and the bureaucracy itself.

It is to be noted that gradual evolution of the structure of the British Raj was made possible by the relatively peaceful transition from colonial rule to India's independence (on 15 August 1947).[2] A strong apparatus of government was inherited intact. With respect to the state of administration,

[1] During British Raj, the ICS, holding key posts throughout the bureaucracy, determined the policy of administration and moulded the bureaucratic pattern. See B. Chakrabarty and P. Chand, *Indian Administration* (New Delhi: SAGE, 2016), 32–35.

[2] The transition of India from an empire of the British Crown to a dominion in the British Commonwealth of Nations was preceded by the enactment of the Indian Independence Act in July 1947 (repealed under Article 395) by the British Parliament, which provided for the abrogation of parliamentary authority over India's administration and the transfer of sovereignty to two dominions of India and Pakistan. Here, it may be mentioned that the solemnity of the transfer of power was, unfortunately, marred by violent mob disturbances in the partitioned province of the Punjab in the west and by the mass migration of refugees across the boundary lines demarcating the two dominions.

Appleby in 1953 observed that he had 'come gradually to a general judgement that now would rate the government of India among the dozen or so most advanced governments of the world'.[3] India is one of the few nations, indeed is the only country in Asia, which succeeded in bringing about administrative reforms and changes without massive financial or advisory help from foreign governmental sources.

Defining Administrative Reform and Its Objectives

Administrative reform means a planned or deliberate effort to induce desired fundamental changes in administrative system with a view to enhancing administrative capability for development. Gerald E. Caiden has defined administrative reform as 'the artificial inducement of administrative transformation against resistance'.[4] In his later article, Caiden comments that administrative reform is 'a risk, a gamble in which the odds are heavily against success … [and] it can take generations for administrative behaviour and values to change appreciably'.[5] He argues that administrative reform is "tossed around like a boat in a storm (since) from conception to finality is a long, arduous and difficult journey beset with numerous obstacles, unforeseen perils and unexpected surprises'.[6]

There is a consensus that administrative reform is intended to enhance and improve the administrative capacity of public administration to achieve national objectives or goals. Several United Nations documents define major administrative reform as specially designed efforts to induce fundamental changes in public administration systems through system-wide reforms or at least through measures for the improvement of one or more of its key elements, such as, administrative structures, personnel and processes.[7] All definitions accept that the objective of administrative reform is the improvement of the administrative system and enhancement of its capacity.

The need for administrative reform arises when the existing administrative machinery fails to meet the demands placed on it. In other words, reform is needed when 'a significant discrepancy exists between what it is doing and what it ought to be doing'. Thus, the inability of the administration to meet the present demands and anticipate future demands makes a space for administrative reforms.[8]

Caiden also makes a distinction between what constitutes 'reform' and what is 'change'. While the latter is a self-adjusting organizational response to changing conditions; reform is a device to remedy the malfunctioning of the administration. Reform, unlike change, is therefore a continuous effort directed towards transforming the 'structure', 'process' (procedure) and 'behaviour' of administration.

---

[3] Appleby, *Public Administration in India*, 8.

[4] Gerald E. Caiden, *Administration Reforms* (Chicago: Aldine, 1969), 8.

[5] Gerald E. Caiden, 'Administrative Reforms: Proceed with Caution', *International Journal of Public Administration* 22, no. 6 (1999): 815–32.

[6] Ibid., 827.

[7] United Nations, *Interregional Seminar on Major Administrative Reforms in Developing Countries, vol. I* (New York: United Nations Publications, 1971), 6–7.

[8] A. Downs, *Inside Bureaucracy* (Boston: Little, Brown, 1967), 191.

16.1 Trends in Administration Reform

Administrative reform is a continuous process. It entails a thorough reconstruction of the machinery of the government, including its administrative structure. The administrative reform in India is a legacy of the pre-British Raj period. This chapter discusses the changes and reforms in administration before and after India's independence.

16.1.1 Pre-British Raj Period

Administration in a dynamic society has to be dynamic; it has to be responsive. Appreciation of a need for administrative renewal is indeed a requisite of a dynamic administrative system. Even before pre-British period, the country already possessed of a degree of administrative sophistication, but handicapped by political discontinuities. Even in the ancient India, Hindu rulers, such Chandragupta Maurya and Asoka, initiated and introduced administrative reforms in government machinery. Treatises such as *Dharmashastra*, *Arthashastra* and Thiruvalluvar's *Kural* contain several norms for improving the administrative system.

During the Muslim rule (mainly from 1526 to 1803) in India, a series of administrative reforms were introduced in the administrative system. These were aimed mainly at securing centralization of authority, controlling administration and ensuring strong financial system.

In addition, the Mughal Empire witnessed significant reforms in areas of agriculture, land records, revenue administration and provincial management.

16.1.2 British Raj Period

The period following the British rule that ended in 1947 witnessed various administrative reforms that suited primarily the British. The British followed a time-honoured practice of setting up committees and commissions to study particular areas of administration and to make recommendations for improvement. Voluminous reports of commissions and committees, gazetters and statutes constituting a body of public record formed the bases of administrative reforms in the history of colonial rule in India. Such reports continue to be quoted and reproduced nearly two centuries after their first appearance. Of these reports—totalling some 50 published volumes appearing from 1887 to 1930—five emerged as *ad hoc* responses to the need for re-evaluation of the civil service (bureaucracy).

1. *Report of the Aitchison Commission (1886–87):* The report of the Public Service Commission determined the structure and the divisions of the services into imperial and provincial services.[9]
2. *Report of the Islington Commission (1915):* The report of the Royal Commission on public service abandoned exclusive reliance on the ICS provincial services distinction as a formula for equalizing opportunity between Indians and British in the services and formulated

[9] C. U. Aitchison and Public Service Commission, *Report of the Public Service Commission, 1886–87*, 8 vols. (Calcutta: Superintendent of Government Printing, 1888).

division of services by levels of work.[10] The historic Declaration of 20 August 1917 and the recommendations of the Islington Commission (1917) had thus envisaged acceleration of the process of Indianization of higher civil services.

3. *Report of the Montagu–Chelmsford Reforms (1918):* The report on Indian constitutional reforms was 'the most momentous utterance ever made in India's chequered history', which introduced the dyarchy that remained until 1937.[11]
4. *Report of the Lee Commission (1924):* The report of the Royal Commission on the superior civil services in India somewhat refined the bureaucratic pattern, adding public service commissions and revising the pay structure.[12]
5. *Report of the Simon Commission (1930):* The report of the Indian Statutory Commission was the massive effort to reassess conditions of British rule in India came in 1930 with the Simon Commission, whose report is the most comprehensive of the five.

These five analyses, three of which deal exclusively with the public bureaucracy, constitute the bedrock of the Indian administrative system. Even nearly two centuries after their first appearance, they created and sustained a public bureaucracy whose structure and power shifted with the times, but they are still seen in the pattern of contemporary Indian administration.

In addition to these five reports, there were seven other reports of significance to Indian administration. These are grouped together here because they are all concerned primarily with technical problems of administration rather than with broader aspects of bureaucratic structure and power.

1. *Report of the Macaulay Committee (1854):* In the history of civil services in India, the year 1854 is significant. Following the passage of the Charter Act, 1853, and submission of the Macaulay Report in 1854, the system of competitive examination was introduced from the year 1855 for entry into the ICS.[13] Thus, the ICS preceding the IAS owed its origin to the Macaulay Report.
2. *Report of the Hobhouse Commission (1909):* The crucial issue of spatial diffusion of power among districts, divisions, provinces and the Centre was the concern of the Hobhouse Commission, whose report is a comprehensive study of district administration and local government.[14]
3. *Report of the Llewellyn–Smith Committee (1919):* The Llewellyn–Smith Committee dealt with the problems of internal administrative procedure and efficiency.[15]
4. *Report of the Wheeler Committee (1937):* After the demise of dyarchy, the Wheeler Committee again dealt with the problem of secretariat reorganization.[16]

---

[10] Great Britain. Royal Commission, *Report of the Royal Commission on Public Service, 14 August 1915*, 20 vols. (London: Government Publication, 1917).

[11] *Report on Indian Constitutional Reforms* published in July 1918 is also known by the name of 'Montford Report' because it was the outcome of the joint venture of Edwin S. Montagu, the Secretary of State for India, and Lord Chelmsford, The Viceroy of India.

[12] Great Britain. Royal Commission, *Report of the Royal Commission on the Superior Civil Services in India* (London: Government Publication, 1924).

[13] The first successful Indian candidate for the covenanted service was Mr Satyendranath Tagore who gained his place in 1864.

[14] Great Britain. Royal Commission, *Report of the Royal Commission on Decentralization in India*, 10 vols. (London: Government Publication, 1909).

[15] H. Llewellyn-Smith, *Report of the Government of India Secretariat Procedure Committee* (New Delhi: GoI, 1919).

[16] Sir Henry Wheeler, *Report of the Government of India Secretariat Committee* (New Delhi: GoI, 1937).

5. *The Chapman Report (1938):* Probably the best empirical analysis of district administration in print is the Chapman Report, which avoids the usual nostalgia and sentimentality that characterize most of the writings on district administration.[17]
6. *Sir Archibald Rowland's Study (1945):* The Chapman Report is almost matched by Sir Archibald Rowland's study immediately before independence[18] and by the 447-page forerunner of India's Five-Year Plans prepared under the chairmanship of A. Ahmad (Post-war Reconstruction, Bengal Government's Plan).
7. *Sir Richard Tottenham's Study (1946):* Finally, Sir Richard Tottenham's study of the central government in which he urged the vigorous pursuit by government of welfare objectives and pressed for the 'section officer' scheme which, after independence, was adopted by GoI, completes the body of administrative analysis in the context of administrative reform.[19]

The administrative system that had evolved in India during British rule had the following features:

1. A system of bureaucratic organizations both at central and provincial levels
2. A system of elaborate rules and regulations designed for governance
3. A system of centralization as a means of maintaining control over decision-making power and administrative offices
4. A system of dominance of the general services—the ICS occupying the top position in the central and provincial hierarchies

Such an administrative system broadly preserved the structure of the Indian society. It did not concern itself with any radical socio-economic changes or administrative reforms. Thus, at the time of India's independence, the administrative system was not adequately prepared to handle the massive developmental, democratic and post-independence tasks.[20]

16.2 Administrative Reforms Since Independence

After the attainment of independence in August 1947, the independent government recognized that the capacity of public administration and finance systems in a developing welfare-oriented economy could be greatly enhanced by introducing administrative reforms on a wide scale. But, it also realized that there was a strong confrontation of ideas of administrative reforms within a bureaucratic tradition dominated by the ICS. Administration of the district was a major influence in shaping attitudes of the higher civil service. District work, however, was essentially autocratic, involving very little consultation among equals and equally little complex staff work.[21]

---

[17] L. A. Chapman, ICS, *Report Regarding the Establishment of Commissioners, Districts and Sub divisional Offices* (Alipore: GoI, 1938).

[18] Archibald Rowland, *Report of the Bengal Administration Enquiry Committee, 1944–45* (Alipore: GoI, 1945).

[19] R. Tottenham, *Report on the Reorganization of the Central Government, 1945–46* (New Delhi: GoI, 1946).

[20] E. N. M. Rai, *Patterns of Administrative Development in Independent India* (London: University of London, 1976), 30.

[21] Description of district administration can be found in the reports of Montagu–Chelmsford, the Simon and Hobhouse Commissions. See also the work of S. S. Khera, *District Administration in India* (New Delhi: National, 1960).

The transition from a colonial system of government to a parliamentary democracy with a federal structure of government, the adoption of planned economic growth and expansion of government activities have inevitably put a tremendous strain on the administrative system and steelframe bureaucracy. Simultaneously, the expansion or bureaucracies at both central and state levels have been accompanied by a proliferation of regulations, corrupt practices and misuse of powers. Thus, in India, as in many other developed and developing countries, administrative machinery necessitated administrative reforms and changes.

The Tottenham Committee's Report (1946) is quite significant in the history of administrative reforms in India.[22] The question of secretariat organization was further examined by the Secretariat Reorganisation Committee appointed by the GoI. The committee in its report submitted on 10 August 1947 suggested the reorganization of the methods of work in the secretariat.[23]

In 1948, an economy committee headed by Kasturbhai Lalbhai recommended several measures for effecting economy in central administration. A comprehensive review of the machinery of central government was done by the Ayyangar Committee (1949) which dealt with organizational changes and in the methods of transaction of governmental business (through the constitution of standing committees of the cabinet).[24] Earlier 1st PC (1946) submitted its report in 1947.

With the enactment and adoption of the Indian Constitution, backdrop of administrative reforms has been substantially changed. The provisions and schedules contained in the Constitution have in fact changed the pattern and complexion of the administrative system from steel-frame of administration to that of a dynamic administration. The years after the enactment of the Constitution witnessed a series of administrative changes and reforms. The Gorwala (an ICS officer) Committee Reports of 1951 and Appleby's (a Ford Foundation expert) two reports on Indian Administration in 1953 and 1956 made an appraisal of the Indian administrative system and called it 'archaic, feudalistic and unimaginative'.[25] Appleby's proposals served as basis for improving administrative machinery and methods both at central and state levels. It was on Appleby's first report, *Public Administration in India*, that the central government set up not only the Indian Institute of Public Administration at New Delhi but also created Organization and Methods units at different levels of administration. Appleby's second report, *Reorganization of India's Administrative System*, made several proposals for streamlining administration, recruitment and training and the relationship of administration with the Parliament. Besides, advocating greater coordination among the ministries, he underlined the need for the delegation of power. The reports of the Estimates Committee of the Lok Sabha on such issues as secretariat reorganization, public undertakings in general and government corporations reveal at least the beginnings of a system of parliamentary supervision over administration.

The year 1957 also witnessed the submission of the significant report to the NDC known as the *Balvantray Mehta Report* which became the base of decentralization and Panchayati Raj in Independent India.[26]

---

[22] Tottenham, *Report on the Reorganization*.

[23] G. S. Bajpai, *Report of the Secretariat Reorganization Committee* (New Delhi: GoI, 1949).

[24] N.G. Ayyangar, *Report on the Reorganization of the Machinery of the Government* (New Delhi: GoI, 1949).

[25] A. D. Gorwala, *Report on Public Administration* (New Delhi: Planning Commission, 1951); *Report on the Efficient Conduct of State Enterprises* (New Delhi: GoI, 1951); Appleby, *Public Administration in India*; *Re-examination of India's Administrative System with Special Reference to Administration of Government's Industrial and Commercial Enterprises* (New Delhi: GoI, 1956).

[26] India. Team for the Study of Community Projects and National Extension Service, *Report of the Team for the Study of Community Projects and National Extension Service* (New Delhi: GoI, 1957).

Earlier in 1955, the *Railway Corruption Enquiry Committee* under the chairmanship of J. B. Kriplani and the report of the Commission of Inquiry on Emoluments and Conditions of Service of Central Government Employees, 1957–59 (known as the Second Pay Commission, headed by Jagannath Das) had led to the changes in personnel administration. The Whitley Councils on the British pattern were set up on the recommendation of the Second Pay Commission. The *Report on Indian and State Administrative Services and Problems of District Administration* (1962), known as the Krishnamachari Report, also made recommendations pertaining to personnel administration in 1964. The *Report of the Committee on the Prevention of Corruption* under the chairmanship of K. Santhanam was presented, which recommended strengthening of vigilance organizations. Consequently, Central Vigilance Commission (CVC) was set up in 1964 and led to adoption of a code of conduct for civil servants.

Following recommendations of the Ayyangar Report in 1949 and later acceptance of Appleby's recommendation (1953), the Organization and Methods division was set up in March 1954 at the Centre. In 1964, the Organization and Methods division in the central government was merged and a new Department of Administrative Reforms in the Ministry of Home Affairs was constituted. The creation of the Department of Administrative Reforms was justified on the ground of 'the need for operating a vaster area than before and effecting improvement in administration on a larger scale and by the shift in emphasis from mere economy and routine office procedures to administrative reforms in its broader sense'.[27]

16.3 Administrative Reforms Commission (1966–70) Initiatives

The attempts at reforms in the pre-ARC period were considered to be too narrow in their scope to make any appreciable impact on the Indian administration. In August 1965, the PM Lal Bahadur Shastri announced in the Lok Sabha of the government decision to set up a high-powered commission.[28] Consequently, in January 1966, an ARC under the chairmanship of Morarji Desai (politician) was instituted with wide terms of reference embracing administration at the Centre as well as in the states. After functioning as the chairman for a little over a year, he was replaced by K. Hanumanthaiah.[29] Dozens of study teams and task forces were appointed to go into segments of the problem and a large secretariat was set up to support the commission as a whole. The commission, the work of which dragged on for four and a half years, made 20 reports (costing nearly $1.25 million). Although some reports were still to be formulated, the government mercifully terminated this experiment in macro reform. The catalogue of the reports of the ARC is as follows:

1. Problems of Redress of Citizens' Grievances (Interim) (1966)
2. Machinery of Planning (Interim) (1967)
3. Public Undertakings (1967)
4. Finance, Accounts and Audit (1968)
5. Economic Administration (1968)
6. Machinery of Government of India and its Procedures of Work (1968)
7. Life Insurance Corporation (1968)

[27] Department of Administrative Reforms, *Annual Report 1964–65* (New Delhi: GoI, Ministry of Home Affairs, 1965), 1.

[28] *Lok Sabha Debates*, vol. XLIV, no. 8 (New Delhi: Lok Sabha Secretariat, 1965).

[29] Morarji Desai left the Commission for the political posts of deputy PM and minister of finance.

8. Machinery for Planning (1968)
9. Central Direct Tax Administration (1969)
10. Administration of Union Territories and NEFA (1969)
11. Personnel Administration (1969)
12. Delegation of Financial and Administrative Powers (1969)
13. Centre–State Relations (1969)
14. State Administration (1969)
15. Small Scale Sector (1969)
16. Railways (1970)
17. Treasuries (1970)
18. Reserve Bank of India (1970)
19. Post and Telegraphs (1970)
20. Scientific Departments (1970)

Besides, the ARC brought out 33 reports of the study teams and working groups which together formed the basis of the main reports. These reports contained 581 recommendations. A few were important and useful and have been implemented, but many were trivial in nature. The commission made reports on such areas as machinery of GoI and its procedures of work, Centre–state relations, state administration, personnel administration, public undertakings and finance, accounts and audit. ARC's recommendations of bringing about unified civil services at top policymaking level and of ending the elite position of the IAS were not accepted by the central government.

On lines of Hoover Commission Report (1953–55) that believed that

> the government cannot be any better than 'the man and woman who make it function', the ARC also insisted that 'the road to the top must be open to every competent and qualified government servant' [and] to higher management in the Secretariat, talent must be drawn from every cadre and class of government servants.

Drawn on this philosophy, the ARC articulated its suggestions in the following four different ways:

1. A rational system needs to be devised for recruitment to policymaking positions with personnel possessing the required qualifications and competence.
2. Senior management personnel must be selected from all relevant sources—generalists and specialists.
3. A rational pay structure requires to be installed so as to truly reflect actual responsibilities, associated with each job.
4. In order to boost morale in the civil service, talented lower rank personnel should be given greater scope than what exists to move up the hierarchy on the basis of competence and performance.

In February 1970, on the recommendation of the ARC, the Department of Personnel was created and located it directly under the PM. In 1973, the Department of Administrative Reforms and Department of Personnel were merged to form the Department of Personnel and Administrative Reforms. This functioned under the PM until 1977 when it was shifted to the Ministry of Home Affairs. In January 1985, the department was converted into a ministry called the Ministry of

Personnel, Public Grievances and Pensions. This ministry comprises three separate departments, namely, Department of Personnel and Training, Department of Administrative Reforms and Public Grievances and Department of Pensions and Pensioners' Welfare. The Department of Administrative Reforms is the nodal agency of administrative reforms.

Perhaps the most important recommendation of the ARC (1966–70) has been the appointment of a Lokpal (at the Centre) and a Lokayukta (in the states), apart from the introduction of the concept and technique of performance budgeting. In addition, two most important areas touched upon by the ARC in its reports are the minister–civil servant relationship wherein the need for the depoliticization of the services is emphasized and the creation of a climate and culture of administration wherein the growth of person relationships between individual civil servants and the minister should be checked up and averted.

It was not surprising that the exercise ended in a good deal of disenchantment with the whole idea of bringing about reforms in administration. The regular bureaucracy had an important role to play in the strategy for implementation as devised by the government, although the ARC specifically asked the government not to involve the committee of secretaries in processing its recommendations. In a bid to enlist political support, the commission wanted a specifically constituted cabinet committee assisted by the cabinet secretary to be overall in-charge for implementation. But, arrangement devised by the government entrusted the work of commission's recommendations to the ministry directly concerned. Processing of resulting reports was made the responsibility of the Department of Administrative Reforms, wherein an implementing branch was created to see this work. The committee of secretaries was to comment upon the recommendations before these were placed before the union cabinet. In practice, the committee processed the recommendations in the light of its own wisdom. The Parliament was also kept out of the picture since no white paper on implementation was ever issued (as recommended by the ARC) nor any parliamentary committee set up. The central government simply placed before the Parliament the progress report showing the fate of each of the recommendations. There was little political will to implement the administrative reforms. Moreover, the bureaucracy commonly favoured the status quo and no change. However, the work of the ARC did help to highlight many issues which might otherwise not have received due attention.

16.4 Post-ARC Reforms Initiatives

Following the winding up of the ARC, the reform effort however did not cease. Reports in different facet of administration continued to be published. Major reforms on Indian administration are as follows:

1. *Third Central Pay Commission, 1973 (Chairman, Raghubar Dayal):* The report recommended the introduction of classification of posts contingent upon assumed equivalence of the work context of various occupational groups at different levels.
2. *Fourth Central Pay Commission, 1986 (Chairman, Justice P. N. Singhal):* The report dealt with various issues of personnel of central government including their pay structure and pensionary benefits.
3. *Fifth Central Pay Commission, 1997 (Chairman, Justice S. Ratnavel Pandian):* The report recommended the introduction of accountability, transparency and improving performance and integrity in administration.

4. *Sixth Central Pay Commission, 2008 (Chairman, B. N. Srikrishna):* The report sought to rationalize the governmental structure with a view to improve the delivery mechanisms for providing better services to the common man.
5. *Seventh Central Pay Commission, 2016 (Chairman, Justice A. K. Mathur):* The report was mainly concerned with pay, pension and allowances of the central government employees and pensioners, including those of the defence sector.
6. *Committee on Recruitment Policy and Selection Methods, 1976 (Chairman, D. S. Kothari):* The report recommended reforms in civil services examination, including preliminary and main examinations.
7. *Committee on Panchayati Raj Institutions, 1978 (Chairman, Asoka Mehta):* The report recommended the setting up of Mandal Panchayats.
8. *National Police Commission, 1977–80 (Chairman, Dharam Vira):* Eight reports contained several recommendations on the modernization of the law enforcement machinery.
9. *Economic Administration Reforms Commission, 1981–86 (Chairman, L. K. Jha):* Series of reports recommended the rationalization of the economic administrative system, including the ways of improving the functioning of public enterprises.
10. *Commission on Centre–State Relations, 1984 (Chairman, R. S. Sarkaria):* Its recommendations are still debated and some of them have been implemented, including the creation of ISC in 1990.
11. *Committee on the Recruitment Policy and Selection Methods for All India and Central Services, 1989 (Chairman, Satish Chandra):* The committee was set up by UPSC to recommend changes in the selection methods for the civil services examinations.
12. *Constitution (73rd and 74th Amendment) Acts, 1992:* 73rd and 74th Constitutional Amendments, relating to panchayats and municipalities to enable them to function as units of self-government, were passed in 1992 that came into effect in 1993.
13. *Expenditure Reforms Commission, 2001 (Chairman: K. P. Geetha Krishnan):* Ten reports contained meaningful recommendations on certain structural and procedural aspects of the functioning of the GoI.
14. *Civil Service Examination Review Committee, 2001 (Chairman, Y. K. Alagh):* The committee recommended introduction of an aptitude test (civil service aptitude test) which is in practice from year 2011–12.
15. *Report of Union Public Service Commission, 2004 (Chairman, P. C. Hota):* An important recommendation of this committee was the amendment of Article 311, empowering the president/governor to dismiss/remove public servants in the case of corrupt practices.
16. *National e-Governance Plan (NGEP):* It was approved by the GoI on 16 May 2006 to promote excellence in implementation of e-Governance initiatives at the central, state and local levels.
17. *Tax Reform:* The Constitutional Amendment (101st) Act, 2016, provides under Article 279A GSTC which is empowered to determine tax structure (presently four-tier tax rates of 5%, 12%, 18% and 28%) on goods and services. The main objectives of the GST rates are to protect the revenues of the Centre and the state governments and further to contain the inflationary pressures. The GST Act has been enforced from 1 July 2017 in the country.
18. *Curbing Black Money Initiative:* With view to curb financing of terrorism through the proceeds of Fake Indian Currency Notes (FICN) and use of such funds for subversive activities, and for eliminating black money, government decided and effected to cancel the

legal tender character of the high denomination bank notes of ₹500 and ₹1,000 from the midnight of 8 November 2016.[30]

19. Anti-Corruption Legislations.

To ensure effective vigilance against the menace of corrupt practices, the central government has worked out a set of following anti-corruption legislations:

1. The Prevention of Corruption Act, 1988
2. The Benami Transactions (Prohibition) Act, 1988
3. The Foreign Exchange Management Act, 1999
4. The Prevention of Money Laundering Act, 2002
5. The Central Vigilance Commission Act, 2003
6. The Whistleblowers Protection Act, 2011
7. The Companies Act, 2013
8. The Lokpal and Lokayuktas Act, 2013
9. The Black Money (Undisclosed Foreign Income and Assets) Act, 2015.

Besides these, there is of course the Indian Penal Code 1861 on the basics. The updated version of the Central Civil Services (Conduct) Rules, 1964, stipulates that every government servant shall at all times (a) maintain absolute integrity, devotion to duty, political neutrality and do nothing which is unbecoming of a government servant, (b) uphold the supremacy of the Constitution and (c) refrain from doing anything which is or may be contrary to any law, rules, regulations and established practices. In May 2011, India ratified UN Convention against Corruption of 2003—a defining document on anti-corruption. In August 2016, there was a major Amendment to the Benami Transactions (Prohibition) Act, 1988.

16.5 Second Administrative Reforms Commission (2005–2009)

The Second ARC was constituted on 31 May 2005, as a Commission of Inquiry, under the chairmanship of Shri Veerappa Moily for preparing a detailed blueprint for revamping the public administrative system. The commission was requested to suggest measures to achieve a proactive, responsive, accountable, sustainable and efficient administration for the country at all levels of government. It has presented following 15 reports to the government for consideration:

1. Right to Information: Master key to good governance (June 2006)
2. Unlocking Human Capital: Entitlement and Governance—A Case Study (July 2006)
3. Crisis Management: From Despair to Hope (September 2006)
4. Ethics in Governance(January 2007)
5. Public Order: Justice for Each … Peace for All (June 2007)
6. Local Governance(October 2007)
7. Capacity Building for Conflict Resolution: Friction to Fusion (February 2008)

[30] *The Tribune* (Chandigarh), 9 November 2016.

8. Combating Terrorism: Protecting by Righteousness (June 2008)
9. Social Capital: A Shared Destiny (August 2008)
10. Refurbishing of Personnel Administration: Scaling New Heights (November 2008)
11. Promoting e-Governance: The Smart Way Forward (December 2008)
12. Citizen Centric Administration: The Heart of Governance (February 2009)
13. Organisational Structure of Government of India (April 2009)
14. Strengthening Financial Management System (April 2009)
15. State and District Administration (April 2009)

The central government has considered 14 out of 15 reports and the decisions on the accepted recommendations of Second ARC are at various stages of implementation.

16.6 Recent Initiatives for Administrative Reforms

There is now growing recognition of the critical role of good governance as seen from the reports of the International Monetary Fund, World Bank (Development Report), UNDP or other international agencies. At the minimum, this role would consist of enforcing the rule of law and property rights, ensuring prevalence of transparent and corruption-free administration, providing basic infrastructure and healthy environment, and protecting vulnerable and disadvantaged sections of population.

16.6.1 Focus of Action Plan and Follow-up

The Conference of Chief Ministers convened by the PM in May 1997 endorsed the action plan with focus on the following:

1. Accountable and citizen-friendly administration
2. Transparency and right to information
3. Improving performance and integrity of civil services

Recent efforts for administrative reforms in India have largely been influenced by international experiences in the field of public administration. Much more is needed to initiate reforms in government structures in order to achieve the macro objectives of economic reforms and efficient policy formation and implementation. In the context of a large democracy with one-third of mass of people living below the poverty line and lacking access to health care and education infrastructure, the democratic governments at different levels need to perform tasks to provide an administration which is responsive, corruption-free and based on greater transparency and openness. The focus of attention has to be on follow-up action.

16.6.1.1 Transparency, Openness and Grievances Mechanism

The central and state governments are required to ensure greater transparency in government decisions and operations. The access to the government information (records in panchayats, employment exchanges, housing boards, etc.) would enable the people to exercise control over the government functioning.

The Right to Information Act, 2005, empowers the citizens, promotes transparency and accountability in the working of the government, combats corruption and makes the democracy work for people in real sense. The Act aims at creating an informed citizenry which would be better equipped to keep necessary vigil on the instruments of governance and make the government more accountable to the governed.

There are now improved efforts for strengthening the grievance redressal machinery at all levels—like computerised monitoring of replies and visits of collectors and district officials to the villages and blocks on pre-announced basis to deal with people's grievances on the spot. The institution of Lokayukta in most states—Odisha was probably the first state to have established the ombudsman institution—is required to enquire and investigate all complains made by citizens against abuse of discretionary powers, maladministration and take appropriate actions. The Parliament has also passed the Lokpal and Lokayuktas Act, 2013. Although, the Act came into force from 16 January 2014.

There is also, at the central level, the Directorate of Public Grievances (DPG) which was set up in 1988 to entertain grievances from the public after they fail to get satisfactory redress from the ministry/department concerned within a reasonable time. It is thus, an office of the last resort for the redressal of grievances relating to sectors in its purview. There is also a public grievance mechanism of PMO available on website[31] which is integrated with the central ministries, departments and state governments and monitored through online processes; it is known as the Centralized Public Grievance Redress and Monitoring System (PGRAMS).

16.6.1.2 Responsive Administration

The formulation and enforcement of Citizen's Charters by many central government departments and agencies with public interface, such as, Central Board of Excise and Customs (CBEC), Life Insurance Corporation, Directorate of Estates, Central Public Works Department, Passport Office and so on, manifest the commitment of the government to provide services to the people. Further, various consumer associations and welfare organizations are actively participating in the performance of government-funded agencies. They reflect a commitment of the administrative department to provide standards of service within a time schedule. At the central level, a department has been set up to monitor the progress of initiatives taken by ministries/departments with a substantial public interface.

16.6.1.3 Civil Service Reforms

While it is invariably recognized of the critical role of civil service in India, it is now increasingly accused of being corrupt, inefficient and unresponsive. The associations of civil servants, on the contrary, complain about the demoralization and lack of incentives, political interference and poor work environment. There is now the need for improving the efficiency, morale, integrity and responsiveness of the civil service through a series of measures which focus on the following:

[31] www.pmindia.gov.in

1. 'Agreement with the political leadership on institutionalised systems for stability of tenure and placement of officials;
2. Comprehensiveness assessment of various factors which have a bearing on motivation, incentives, productivity and working conditions of the civil services on the basis of recommendations of the commission; and
3. Steps to curb corrupt practices, prosecute offenders quickly, and to install a regime of self-regulation through code of ethics for Public Services'.

16.6.1.4 Changes in Regulatory Framework

Much more efforts are needed to be made to repeal obsolete regulations and rules and make them more citizen-friendly, simple and consistent with the requirements of liberalization and globalization. Such legal reforms will help to reduce delays and scope or corrupt practices and maladministration. Most of the central government departments have initiated efforts for the review of laws and regulations and some improvements have already been affected in the existing system.

A commission on review of administrative laws was set up on 8 May 1998 under the chairmanship of Shri P. C. Jain with a view to identify proposals for amendment/repeal of existing laws, regulations and procedures having inter-sectoral impact so as to make them objective, transparent and predictable. The commission submitted its report on 30 September 1998. Some of the important recommendation are as follows:

1. Repeal of almost 50% of the central laws (1,382 out of 2,500 laws)
2. Expeditious amendments to a list of 109 identified Acts
3. Documentation of administrative laws by all the ministries/departments
4. Harmonization or statutes and laws with reference to the perspective of domestic and foreign investors, trade and industry, consumers, exporters and importers
5. Development of a viable alternative disputes resolution machinery

Since 1834, some 6,612 central statutes have been enacted, of which 3,831 were repealed. Of the remaining 2,781, the Ramanujam Committee (set up in 2014) identified 1,741 Central Acts for repeal.[32] On 28 April 2016, the Parliament passed two Bills to repeal 1,053 outdated laws which had become redundant legislations.[33]

In a number of states, already new initiatives and reforms are being implemented, such as, the issue of the identity cards, permits under different laws, single-window systems for approvals, elimination of unnecessary procedures, self-assessment for the payment of taxes, use of citizen associations for management of services and so on. In addition, citizens groups are actively involved in operations of primary schools, health care, nutrition, women's welfare, etc.

16.6.1.5 New India @2022 Document

Government 'think tank', NITI Aayog, has envisaged a new India by 2022 that would be free from poverty, dirt, corrupt, terrorism, casteism and communalism. The document envisages that

[32] See *The Financial Express* (Chandigarh), 22 July 2015.

[33] See *The Tribune* (Chandigarh), 28 April 2016.

villages will have road connectivity by 2019. It says that India will have 20 world-class higher learning institutions by 2022.

16.7 Problems of Implementation of Reforms

Implementation of reforms is a serious problem. The impediments between what appear to be sound plans and effective implementation are surely among the principal problems of administrative reforms. All planned social changes at the implementing stage appear to be threatening to some of the people involved or potentially affected. Indian bureaucracy is so formidable that it is not easy to secure acceptance and implementation of measures of reform. K. Hanumanthaiah had once confessed it publicly, 'Our bureaucracy has capacity to virtually set at naught recommendations of any administrative reforms body, no matter how august it may be'.[34] A reform is apt to disturb the status quo and those who have developed vested interests in such a state of affairs. These vested interests are so deeply and solidly entrenched in the existing system that they conspire to frustrate most attempts at administrative reforms.

It may be that those seeking administrative reforms should have prepared an up-to-date contingency plan to be available for their time when their implementation becomes feasible. The ARC, therefore, gave good deal of attention to the question of acceptance and implementation of its recommendations. In this context, the commission outlined the following mechanism for consideration of its reports:

> In the first place, responsibility for piloting the reforms proposed by us should rest with a senior cabinet minister enjoying high political prestige and possessing wide administrative experience. We have already recommended that the Department of Administrative Reforms should be under the direct charge of the deputy PM. The commission feels that it should be his special responsibility to oversee the implementation of the proposed reforms. We have suggested … a cabinet committee on administration. The cabinet minister most concerned with a particular report of the commission or a set of separately identifiable recommendations may be co-opted as a member of this committee when considering that report or those recommendations. There seems to be some apprehension in the public mind that senior executives of the government are, by and large, averse to change and disposed to maintain the status quo. It is not, therefore, desirable to refer, as a matter of course, the recommendations of the commission to committees of secretaries. In view of the special nature of the commission's recommendations and the need for quick decisions by the government thereon, we would recommend that coordination of the processing of our reports should be handled by a special cell created in the cabinet secretariat for the purpose. This cell should function under the general supervision of the cabinet secretary. As a general coordinator of government policies, he is obviously the best person to ensure that the processing of ARC's reports is completed with speed and all the departments concerned have been duly consulted. Whenever necessary, he will consult the deputy PM, who, under our proposals will have the responsibility for implementation of our recommendations. The special cell, to be set up in the cabinet secretariat, should compile and collate the views of the different ministers concerned with a particular ARC report. The necessary papers for consideration by the cabinet committee on administration may thereafter be prepared in the cell under the supervision of the cabinet secretary. It is also imperative that speedy action is taken by government on the different reports of the commission. The recommendations in each report will fall into two types: (a) the basic ones and (b) the others. We feel that the government should

[34] Hanumanthaiah observed this at a seminar held in Hyderabad in November 1967. See *The Hindustan Times*, 21 November 1967.

> place before each house of parliament within three months of their receiving a report from the commission, a white paper indicating their decisions on the basic recommendations. It is also important to have an all-party parliamentary committee entrusted with the duty of watching the implementation of the accepted recommendations. The members of the committee may be nominated by the speaker and the chairman of the Rajya Sabha, having regard to their general knowledge, aptitude and/or administrative experience. The committee will see that the accepted recommendations are implemented expeditiously. The parliamentary committee should meet at least once in three months to review the progress of implementation.[35]

The First ARC was not in favour of assigning the task of implementation of reforms to the bureaucracy. It observed, 'The processing of the recommendations of the commission again by the secretaries is unnecessary'. Hanumanthaiah had even publicly pleaded for the formation of a special committee consisting of the PM, the deputy PM and the home minister to take decisions on the recommendations of the commission and implement those accepted by the government.

The commission's recommendations on this aspect was not given much attention. On the contrary, the government entrusted major responsibility of processing and implementation of the reports of the commission to the concerned ministers/departments. Elaborating this, the union minister replied in the Lok Sabha,

> After the reports are examined by the Committee of Secretaries, they are looked into by the minister concerned or by the Cabinet Minister, or a Committee that might be specially constituted or by the whole cabinet. That is the political level at which it is considered.[36]

Summary

Thus, it may be observed that implementation of reforms is not very easy. Among the impediments are the existing system of status, bureaucratic inertia, failure of communication between the planners and those who must implement the plans. Further, the main reasons for failures of administrative reforms lie with the reformers themselves—failure to appreciate the problems and motivations of those whose behaviour they would reform, to account for them in their plans and to communicate effectively the reasoning behind their proposals.

When a political decision is taken as to the implementation of the commission/committee recommendations, it is imperative on the part of the government to ensure that necessary staff, finance and infrastructure are made available to the organization entrusted with the tasks of implementing and monitoring the policy decisions.

---

[35] ARC, *Report on the Machinery of the Government*, 66–67.
[36] Lok Sabha Debates, vol. XXXV, no. 21, Col. 30, 31, 32.

17 Relationship Between Political Masters and Senior Civil Servants

LEARNING OBJECTIVES

1. **To understand the relationship theory between political masters and senior civil servants**
2. **To discuss the doctrine of accountability in relation to ministers and their civil servants**
3. **To highlight areas of potential conflict in the relationship between political executive and permanent civil service**

Introduction

Another important issue area on which depends the success of 'good governance' is the relationship between political executive (ministers) and administrative executive (civil servants). The Parliament in a democratic country such as ours has a legitimate interest in the quality of the governing process that provides it with its core business. It is, therefore, essential to get the key governing relationship between ministers and civil servants onto a clearer footing. The relations between ministers and higher or senior civil servants require a redefinition in the wake of welfarism and the rise of governance.

The Parliamentary system of government which India inherited from the British imperial rule brought forth the problem of the formation of appropriate relations between the political and permanent executives (ministers and civil servants). Before we discuss this in relation to India, we may briefly refer to the theory underlying this relationship.

17.1 Minister–Civil Servant Relationship Theory

With a view understanding the relationship between political masters (ministers) and administrators (civil servants) on a sound footing, we need to look at politics–administration approach. In his groundbreaking book *Politics and Administration*, Frank Goodnow contented that there were two functions of government. 'Politics', wrote Goodnow, 'has to do with policies or expression of the state will', while 'administration has to do with the execution of these policies'.[1]

[1] F. J. Goodnow, *Politics and Administration* (New York: Macmillan, 1900), 10–11.

This naturally leads on to explanation of relationship of the civil servant to political executive, but Sir William Harcourt's famous dictum, 'the minister exists to tell the civil servant what the public won't stand', is always to be born in mind.[2]

In a parliamentary system, civil service is an executive branch of the government. Civil servants or government officials are recruited in theory to render services to the ministers by carrying out their constitutional and policy decisions. The civil servants preserve, give advices and implement orders. They do not make policies, but help in the process. They are permanent servants of the government, whereas ministers are appointed from the elected MPs/MLAs. Legislators and ministers together constitute the chosen forces of progress and represent the will, the need and mood of the people. A minister is responsible to both the cabinet and the Parliament for the work of his department, and, if he loses their confidence or approval, he is expected to resign. Because of this constitutional responsibility, the minister has, subject to constitution, law and convention, the right to guide, direct and control the work of the civil servants of his department who are carrying out public policies and programmes approved either by him or the cabinet and legislature.

The theoretical basis of the minister–civil servant relationship and minister's responsibility to the Parliament in regard to the actions of civil servants in parliamentary democracies (including of India) is based upon the following lines or what may be called principles:

1. When the civil servant carries out the minister's explicit order, the minister must protect the civil servant concerned.
2. When the civil servant acts properly in accordance with the policy laid down by the minister, the minister must protect as well as defend him.
3. When the civil servant makes a mistake or causes delay but not on an important issue of policy and not when a claim of individual rights is seriously involved, the minister acknowledges the mistake and he accepts responsibility, although he is not personally involved. He states he will take corrective action in his department.
4. When action has been taken by a civil servant of which the minister disapproves and has no prior knowledge, and the conduct of the official is reprehensible, the minister is then under no obligation to endorse what he believes to be wrong or to defend what are clearly shown to be the errors of his officers. The minister is not bound to approve action of which he had no prior knowledge or of which he disapproves. But, of course, he remains constitutionally responsible to Parliament for the fact that something has gone wrong.

This minister–civil servant model in a parliamentary system emphasizes the non-partisan and neutral character of the higher civil service. The minister–civil servant relationship in any democratic country is aptly described by Peter Self thus, 'The style of ministerial-administrator partnership is pragmatic and flexible, stressing responsiveness to collective leadership and to general political ideas and policies while giving much less weight to specialized knowledge or experience'.[3] In this context, House of Commons (UK) says,

[2] Sir W. Harcourt, *The Civil Service in Britain and France* (London: Hogarth Press, 1892).

[3] P. Self, *Administrative Theories and Politics* (New Delhi: S. Chand, 1977), 152.

> An impartial civil service has a constitutional function. Civil service responsibilities are not simply to the government of the day; they should include responsibility to Parliament, and to the constitution. However, implementing the policies of the elected government is a core civil service role.[4]

The Second ARC (India) also made it very clear:

> A healthy working relationship between Ministers and civil servants is critical for good governance. While the principles governing the roles and responsibilities of Ministers and civil servants are well defined in political theory, in the actual working of this relationship this division of responsibility becomes blurred with both sides often encroaching upon the other's sphere of responsibility. In any democracy, Ministers are responsible to the people through Parliament and therefore the civil servants have to be accountable to the Minister. However, an impartial civil service is responsible not only to the government of the day but to the Constitution of the land to which they have taken an oath of loyalty. At the same time, implementing the policies of the duly elected government is a core function of civil servants. That is why the division of responsibility between the civil servants and ministers needs to be more clearly defined. A framework in which responsibility and accountability is well defined would be useful.[5]

17.2 Doctrine of Accountability

Running of a government department is the joint responsibility of political and administrative executives. It has long been clear that ministers cannot be expected to be responsible for everything which occurs within a department. Civil servants are charged to carry out the policy of the department which is laid down by the minister.

Thus, there exist two types of accountability—ministerial accountability and civil service accountability.

17.2.1 Ministerial Accountability

Ministerial accountability has come to mean that ministers have a duty 'to Parliament to account, and be held to account, for the policy decision and actions of their department'. Further, 'ministers who knowingly mislead Parliament will be expected to offer their resignation to the Prime Minister'. Similarly, ministers should require 'civil servants who give evidence before parliamentary committees on their behalf and under their directions to be as helpful as possible in providing accurate, truthful and full information in accordance with the duties and responsibilities of civil servants as set out in the Civil Service Code'.

However, 'it is not possible absolutely to distinguish an area in which a minister is personally responsible, and liable to take blame, from one in which he is constitutionally accountable. Ministerial responsibility is not composed of two elements which have a clear break between the two'.[6]

---

[4] UK, House of Commons, *Public Administration Select Committee, Politics and Administration: Ministers and Civil Servants* (London: Stationery Office Limited, 26 March 2007), 3.

[5] Second ARC, *10th Report (on) Refurbishing of Personnel Administration* (New Delhi: ARC, November 2008), 273, para. 15.1.3.

[6] UK, Public Service Committee, *Second Report of Session 1995–96, Ministerial Accountability and Responsibility, House of Commons*, para 21, pp. 313–14.

17.2.2 Civil Service Accountability

That civil servants were accountable to ministers has been asserted by Sir David Maxwell Fyfe:

> The position of the civil servant is that he is wholly and directly responsible to his minister. It is worth stating again that he holds his office 'at pleasure' and can be dismissed any time by the minister; and that power is nonetheless real because it is seldom used. The only exception relates to a small number of senior posts, like a permanent secretary, deputy secretary or principal finance officer, where since 1920, it has been necessary for the Minister to consult the Prime Minister, as he does on appointment.[7]

Thus, there is a clear democratic line of accountability which runs from the electorate through MPs to the government which commands the confidence of a majority of those MPs in the Parliament; and civil servants are accountable to ministers. A healthy working relationship between ministers and civil servants is of great importance for good governance.

But just as it is difficult to be definitive about the boundaries of ministerial accountability, so civil service accountability is far from clear. The Institute of Public Policy Research has suggested a radical extension of mechanisms to separate political and administrative responsibilities.[8]

It proposes that, while ministers would be responsible for setting policy, civil servants should be governed and managed by independent bodies and should be accountable internally to a civil service executive and externally to a new statutory governing body for the civil service, as is found in New Zealand (see Table 17.1).

17.3 Minister–Civil Servant Relationship Practice

The British view of the civil servant–master relationship has served as the model which the Indian constitutional and political scientists wish to be increasingly followed in India, at both the Centre and in the states. Let us now turn to the actual position in regard to this relationship in India.

The Rules of Business of Government (1961) do provide for the secretary to the government to advise his minister about the course of action proposed in a particular matter and to submit to him a note which tells him about the propriety or legality of his orders and suggests that either such orders not be given or that they be suitably modified. The relationship between the secretary and the minister is organic. The minister has the mandate of the people to govern, but the secretary has an equivalent constitutional mandate to advise the minister. Once his advice has been suitably considered, unless the minister passes an illegal order, the secretary is bound to implement it. The minister, on his part, is required to support the secretary who is implementing his order. Once a law is framed or rules and regulations are approved, they apply to everyone, whether a member of the political executive or of the permanent civil service. A civil servant is required to implement the orders of government without bias, with honesty and without fear or favour. A.K. Basu, former Jharkhand Chief Secretary, and H.C. Gupta, Ex-Coal Secretary, were sentenced to 3 years in jail in a coal scam in 2008.[9]

[7] UK, *House of Commons Debate*, 20 July 1954, vol. 530, p. 1285.

[8] G. Lodge and B. Rogers, 'Whitehall's Black Box: Accountability and Performance in the Senior Civil Service', *IPPR* (2006).

[9] See *The Tribune* (Chandigarh), 17 December 2017.

Table 17.1 Comparison Between Political and Administrative Executives

S. No.	Responsibility of a Minister	Responsibility of a Civil Servant
1.	Setting policies of the department	Providing honest advice to the minister enabling him to set policies
2.	Setting performance targets and holding officials accountable for delivery	Implementing policies set by the minister
3.	Accounting to Parliament and the public for policy delivery	Accounting to the minister for operational matters
	In doing so a minister is required to	***In doing so a civil servant is required to***
1.	Take and communicate clear and timely decisions	Take personal responsibility for delivery
2.	Ensure that decisions reflect resource constraints	Manage performance effectively and resolve issues quickly
3.	Focus on policy outcomes knowing resource constraints	Provide timely, honest and clear advice based on data
4.	Support the need for officials to make operational judgement	Support the minister in discharging his responsibility to Parliament
5.	Allow managers the freedom to deploy staff and resources to policy objectives	Ensure that the minister is informed properly about risks and operational issues that might affect the image of the department
6.	Review performance regularly and provide feedback	Ensure timely action in response to performance appraisal

Source: Adapted from House of Commons, *Politics and Administration. Ministers and Civil Servants* (March 2007).

Most of those who became ministers after India's independence had been in the midst of the political struggle for the emancipation of the country. Their background experiences consisted largely of agitational politics rather than politics which stressed the mature constitutional experience of the formulation and administration of public policies. Moreover, they and the civil servants had been on opposite sides of the country's political fence. While the politicians had struggled under the leadership of Mahatma Gandhi against the continuation of British control over India, the civil servants had served as the government's arm for maintaining law and order by attempting to suppress nationalist political agitations and movements. Thus, there were old unpleasant memories which could generate suspicion and misunderstanding between the two sides. In addition, the higher civil servants, by and large, were better educated, much better paid and maintained a social life of a more highly Westernized type than did the politicians. This created, then, somewhat different patterns of thinking between the two sides in regard to social and public affairs. Third, while the civil servants considered public interest as individual interest in terms of their consistency with laws, rules and administrative traditions, the ministers tended to attach more importance to measures which might bring quick relief to the people who had suffered from controls and the shortages of goods and services, dating from the days of World War II and the hardships caused by the partition, riots and disturbance of everyday life and commercial supplies at the time of Independence. They tended to be impatient with the slowness of administrative action caused by laws, regulations and rigid procedures, and the lack of requisite dynamism in bureaucracy. This impatience at times was aggravated when the ministers wanted individual cases brought to their attention by influential outsiders to be disposed of out of their turn or to be accorded few favourable treatments. At times, tempers were raised or snubs were administered to the bureaucracy or some punishment or withdrawal of an amenity was ordered by the ministers.

Sardar Patel had made the following observations in the constituent assembly to support the continuance of the pre-Independence civil service structures:

> It needs hardly to be emphasized that an efficient, discipline and contended civil service assured of its prospects as a result of diligent and honest work, is a *sine qua non* of sound administration under democratic regime even more than under an authoritarian rule. The service must be above party and we should ensure that political considerations either in its recruitment or in its discipline and control, are reduced to the minimum if not eliminated altogether.[10]

There were far-sighted politicians like Patel, Rajaji and Nehru and Pant, for example, who realized the futility and wastefulness of these tensions and attempted to provide a new lead in reorienting the minister–civil servant relationship. There were also administrators, Menon and Pillai, for example, who provided a lead to their fellow civil servants that ministerial directions must be obeyed, in letter and spirit, so long as the infringement of the Constitution and laws was not involved or the public interest was not jeopardized. It was not for the civil servants to disobey even in such cases but to resign from their posts.

Sardar Patel, the deputy PM in the Nehru government (1947–64) made following comment:

> Today, my Secretary can write a note opposed to my views. I have given that freedom to all my Secretaries. I have told them, 'If you do not give your honest opinion for fear that it will displease your Minister, please then you had better go. I will bring another Secretary!' I will never be displeased over a frank expression of opinion …

When the Planning Commission formulated the First Five Year Plan in 1951 for India's socio-economic development, the commission advised the political leaders and civil servants to work together in harmony as 'they have a common aim, the raising of standards of living through rapid economic and social development and better distribution of wealth and income; their functions are complementary, and neither can fulfil its part without the active help and trust of the other'.[11] Here, then a new dimension was added to the minister–civil servant relationship … the need for teamwork in the interest of promoting rapid development in the country. Although Jawaharlal Nehru repeatedly attacked the ICS as 'quintessentially colonial', he relied on bureaucracy as the central state agency for modernizing Independent India. He admitted shortly before his death that his 'greatest failure' consisted in not transforming the administrative machinery.[12] Senior administrators especially those in the Prime Minister's Secretariat created under the Lal Bahadur Shastri

---

[10] Constituent Assembly Debates, vol. no. 10, no. 3, 10 October 1946.

[11] Planning Commission, *First Five Year Plan, 1951–56* (New Delhi: GoI, 1951).

[12] See Jawaharlal Nehru, *An Autobiography* (London: Bodley Head, 1958), 445. As Nehru put it, 'that no new order can be built up in India so long as the spirit of the ICS pervades our administration and our public services'.

government became, at times, more influential than cabinet ministers. The assumption that bureaucracy stood in the way of development, it was argued that it needed to be transformed drastically. The ARC also exposed the strained relationship between the ministers and civil servants when it reported that 'There is disinclination among quite a number of ministers to welcome a frank and impartial advice from the Secretary'.[13]

The relationship between the two during late Mrs Indira Gandhi's regime underwent a radical change. She started using the bureaucracy as an instrument for achieving political goals (e.g., in the former Soviet Union and China where bureaucrats have to be faithful to the party). She called for a 'committed civil service' to carry out her political biddings and to provide her with policy advice. It progressively meant to serve interest of political party in power. This struck at the root of the form of administration that the British had left behind. The implication of commitment in civil service was broadly interpreted as loyalty to the party in power which had not been true before. Later, many of the senior bureaucrats welcomed Mrs Gandhi's Emergency rule (imposed on 25 June 1975). The Shah Commission in its reports after the Emergency found that 'even the cream of the talent of the country in the administrative field often collapsed at the slightest pressure'. Many collectors 'obediently carried out the instructions emanating from politicians and administrative heads issued on personal or political considerations'. These men said to the Shah Commission that they had no choice in the circumstances; they were 'helpless' for the fear of the consequences of not obeying.[14] There were many cases where officers curried favour with politicians by doing what they thought the people in authority desired, for 'many excesses did not originate at the political level'. In short, the Emergency represented, as one journalist remarked, 'the high water mark of the politicians' victory in the long drawn out struggle against the service'.[15]

When the Janata Party formed the government at the Centre and in some states in 1977, many of the senior administrators closely identified with the Gandhi's Emergency regime were marginalized or placed under suspension on charges of corruption. Again in January 1980, Mrs Gandhi came to power at the Centre, and, in May, the Congress was back in most of the states. Administrators formerly loyal to Congress were reinstated, whereas others who had done well under Janata were put into considerable demoralization.

Late PM Rajiv Gandhi (in power from 31 October 1984 to 1 December 1989) started with a negative perception of the higher bureaucracy. His tenure was marked by many controversies involving civil servants. Loyalty to the political boss tended to be the key ingredient of politician–civil servant relationship. Sarla Grewal and S. K. Bhatnagar were appointed, on their retirement, as governors of Madhya Pradesh and Sikkim, respectively. Gopi Arora was nominated for a coveted international job. On the other hand, some civil servants were axed due to their reluctance to fall in line with the PM. P.S. Appu, head of the Mussoorie Academy, had to resign. A. P. Venkateshwaran was removed from the post of foreign secretary for his brief during a visit to Pakistan. Bhure Lal, Director of Enforcement in the Ministry of Finance, was shunted out unceremoniously for his collaboration with the Finance Minister V. P. Singh in engaging the services of the Fairfax. Referring to the effects of the shabby treatment meted out to the senior civil servants by politicians, Arun Shourie quotes a civil servant approvingly, 'the civil service was reduced from the level of

[13] ARC, *Report of the Machinery of the Government*, 20–21.

[14] Shah Commission of Inquiry, *Third and Final Report* (New Delhi: GoI Press, 1978), 229.

[15] B. Vohra, 'Anatomy of Mal-administration', *Seminar* 230, (October 1978): 14.

guardians to that of courtiers with the more clever of them fulfilling the role of legitimizers and advisers'.[16]

Often, there is a pressure from a minister for instantaneous action, and any perceived delay by an officer is fraught with grave consequences. Suspension from service is perhaps the worst ignominy that can befall a government official. At the same time, some civil servants learnt the art of manoeuvring for favours in return for pliability in their decision-making.

In the 2G Spectrum case, the Secretary of Telecommunications Siddhartha Behura did indulge into corrupt practices by signing more than 100 letters in regard to the issue of licences within days of assuming charge as secretary. He was arrested by CBI along with the former minister, A. Raja, on 4 February 2011. If the secretary had put down his dissent on paper against the minister's decision, he would not have faced the peril of humiliation.

The drastic action by the CBI should shake the entire bureaucracy, especially the officers of IAS and IPS out of their complacency. It should make them introspect on how they should regulate their responses to ministerial demands for unequivocal compliance of directions.

Raghavan, a former director of the CBI, advised senior officers in the following words:

> Put down any dissent from ministerial directions in writing, and just abstain from any decision that even remotely suggests any irregularity or illegality. Do this even at the cost of being victimized through suspension or being ignored for a significant position that is legitimately your due.[17]

17.4 Areas of Conflict in Relationship

In its 10th report, Second ARC identified six areas of potential conflict in the relationship between the political executive and the permanent civil service:

1. The concept of neutrality
2. Advisory role of the civil servants in policymaking
3. Statutory role of the civil servants
4. Discharge of delegated functions
5. Appointment/recruitment of the civil services
6. Transfers and posting of civil servants[18]

There was also a tendency for some ministers at the Union and the state levels to focus more on routine administrative matters such as transfers in preference to policymaking. At the same time, some civil servants learnt the art of 'manoeuvring' for favours in return for pliability in their decision making. This trend was further accentuated by rising materialism and acquisitiveness in society as well as decline in values across the board. As a result, 'political neutrality' which was the hallmark of the civil service in the pre-Independence era as well as in the period right after Independence, was gradually eroded. These trends led to the phenomenon of 'politicization of the civil service' in India.

[16] Quoted in M. N. Buch, 'Restructuring of the Civil Services', *The Indian Express*, 6 January 1987.
[17] R. K. Raghavan, 'The Minister Versus the Civil Servant', *The Hindu*, 11 February 2011.
[18] Second ARC, *10th Report*, 274–75.

There are concerns that the recruitment process into the civil service is highly influenced by both the political and administrative leadership. The consequence is that it is not only the society that loses but also the political and administrative leaders of the service, who need the services of capable officers in order to achieve the mandate of their ministers.

Frequent transfer and postings of civil servants, including permanent secretaries, may also be a contributory factor to the impairment of relations between ministers and the administrative heads of ministries.

17.5 Politicization: Implications

Guy Peters and John Pierre define the term 'politicization' as 'the substitution of political criteria for merit-based criteria in the selection, retention, promotion, rewards, and disciplining of members of the public service'.[19] Normally, it can be taken to mean a system in which politicians are able to 'appoint directly to key posts, and in which those appointed retain their posts only as long as their political patrons retain power'. However, this concept of 'politicization' is different from that of civil service neutrality.

By contrast, David Blunkett (a former Home Secretary of British Government) asserted that civil service is willing and able to serve government of all persuasions. It is able to give both impartial advice and committed implementation and independence from the political process that presumes that the civil service has a life of its own. 'To fail to serve the government is to fail to carry out the inherent duty of the Civil Service'.[20] The corollary of this is that the elected ministers should have freedom to perform their functions as they see fit, within any framework set by the Parliament.

17.5.1 Beyond Impartiality: Political Appointments

In contrast to the proposals (as in the Institute for Public Policy Research [IPPR] report) for greater separation between politicians and the civil servants, Ed Straw argued for a Civil Service which was more political, and more open to direct ministerial influence. He believed that ministers should have the ability to appoint whom they wished. He argued that policies would be best implemented by those who believe in them. Ministerial appointments would be based on competence, not on political facilitation, and some appointments might well be acceptable to a different government.[21]

Straw argued that this change towards explicit politicization was necessary to strengthen electoral accountability and to increase the ability of those elected to get things done. Straw is right to point out that the British Civil Service is extreme in its insulation from political influence, compared with civil service in USA where it is commonplace for those elected to make senior

[19] B. G. Peters and J. Pierre, eds., *Politicisation of the Civil Service in Comparative Perspective* (London: Routledge Studies in Governance and Public Policy, 2004), 2.

[20] D. Blunkett, 'Evidence Before the House of Commons, Public Administration Select Committee', *Third Report of Session 2006–07* (London: SOL, 26 March 2007).

[21] Ed Straw, *The Dead Generalist: Reforming the Civil Service and Public Services* Demos, September 2004: 48.

appointments. In Britain, people have traditionally been suspicious of the 'spoils' system, but it is argued that politically appointed officials can be highly capable and well responsive. On a purely utilitarian basis, there remains a strong case for an impartial civil service.

In Northcote Trevelyan terms, even when appointment from outside becomes routine, able people are encouraged to apply to the public service because they know that appointment will be on merit, not by patronage. We do not believe wholesale introduction of appointments by politicians would necessarily solve problems of civil service performance in our country. Nor would it be consistent with our political culture. It is imperative to preservice political neutrality of the civil service.

17.6 Temptation to Collusive Practices

Before the National Democratic Party forming the government at the Centre (in May 2014), there had been arbitrary methods of appointments, promotions and transfers of civil servants by political masters which led to corrosion of the moral basis of independence. 'It has strengthened the temptation in services to collusive practices with politicians to avoid the inconvenience and to gain advantages by ingratiating themselves to political masters. They would do the politicians' biddings rather than adhere to rules'.[22]

With defections and mergers taking place almost continuously, it is difficult to keep count of parties. Naturally, the functioning of the political system has affected the bureaucracy as a whole, especially, the senior civil servants, who form an interface with the political executive. In the process, the concepts of neutrality and anonymity, which were the hallmark of the civil services in the past, have almost disappeared. Further, it is observed that, in the past two decades, more efficient civil servants, who have effectively carried out policies lawfully adopted by the political party in power, have suffered in their personal life as well as in their career. Every change of government becomes an occasion to harass senior civil servants. The new regime bears a suspicion that these civil servants were 'committed' to the political party previously in power. In the process, many individuals with exceptionally good record of service and reputation have suffered. This affects the morale of civil services.

Another contributory factor to sored relations is the lack of cooperation between democratic politicians and senior administrators on operationalization of policies. In this connection, an IAS officer writes,

> The problems between the civil servants and the political executive are not due to any basic ideological divide but due to tendency of the political executive to ignore the civil servants at the time of policy formulation and to unduly interfere in the process of policy implementation.[23]

It is now felt that senior administrators on the whole tend to bend more when coping with political pressure. No concerted and concrete policy is made, for the whole attention of the government is paid to keeping itself in the seat of power. The time of chief minister, which should mostly be devoted to making good policies and good governance of his state, is taken away in fighting off the intrigues of his dissidents and opponents. Today policies and laws are passed without serious

[22] National Commission to Review the Working of the Constitution, set up by the Atal Bihari Vajpayee government, (2000–2002).

[23] S. Arvind, *Indian Administration* (Bombay: Himalaya Publishing House, 1992), 169.

thought and almost without any discussion. When the PM or the chief minister of the day feels that a certain policy is desirable, it is drafted in a day or two by the administrator and is passed by the Parliament or state assembly on the next day. It seems that law does not matter to the MLAs or the ministers. Legislators who are supposed to frame policies have no interest in policies. Increasingly, the will of the minister or local MLA is reflected in the laws of the government. Furthermore, the ruling party legislators are encouraged or permitted to issue orders to the district administration. It seems that they are not interested in operationalization of initiatives of policies; on the other hand, they are interested in administrative matters such as appointment, transfer, promotion or dismissal of civil servants. The administrators taking advantage of the political void have started pressing the system for their own private gains. Moreover, the administrators refusing to toe the line of politicians in power are subjected to humiliation. For example, Chief Secretary of Delhi was roughed up by two to three MLAs of AAP at CM residence at mid-night on 20 February 2018 where he had gone for a meeting.

Unfortunately, however, such relationships are fostered with an eye on mutuality of benefit. Moreover, in recent years, political masters have actively promoted the formation of teams of officials, who are amenable to their wishes, in many cases, and become active partners in their irregular and sometimes illegal activities. In fact, if one were to closely analyse the scams and several activities highlighted in the CBI's investigations in the conduct of former ministers, including former PMs, the answer would be found in the nexus between the politicians and the civil servants.

Paradoxically, the increasing interference of politicians in the administrative process both at the local and state levels has not always been opposed by all the civil servants. Rather, they have learned to adjust to the compulsion of the politicians. The Vohra Committee Report (August 1995) has dutifully confirmed the 'nexus between criminals/mafia and anti-national elements on the one hand and bureaucrats, politicians and other sensitively located individuals on the other'.[24]

It seems the structure of political–bureaucratic relationships has been transformed in the direction of a patrimonial regime in which the political leadership selects officers who carry out their political biddings and who expect reciprocal preferment in return. In this context, Rajni Kothari observes, 'There has taken place a long process of erosion of democratic institutions, of the "rule of law," and of accountability of government and other institutions of the state'.[25]

In the recent past, there have been scandals and cases of corruption largely attributed to vicious circles in minister–civil servants relationships. Mention may be made of Airbus Scandal (April 1990); JMM Bribery case against the then PM P. V. Narasimha Rao (1992); Fodder Scam (1999–2000) against the former chief minister of Bihar, Lalu Prasad Yadav; Haryana Teachers' Recruitment Scam against ex-chief minister of Haryana (2008);[26] Bofors Scandal (1987); Sukh Ram Telecom Equipment Scandal (1996); Stamp Paper Scam (2002); HUDCO Scam (2003); Oil for Food Scam (Natwar Singh had to resign from the cabinet on 6 December, 2005); Taj Cooperative Group Housing Scheme Scam (2004) in which an IAS officer, Narayan Divakar, was convicted for two years; Delhi Jal Board Tanker Scam (2015) in which former Delhi Chief Minister Sheila Dikshit was accused of corruption charges; Gujarat Fisheries Scam (2015) involving two ministers; Chief Minister of Himachal Pradesh has been booked by CBI in Disproportionate Assets Case (2014);

[24] N. N. Vohra, *Report of the Vohra Committee* (New Delhi: GoI, 1993), para 6.2.

[25] R. Kothari, 'Interpreting Indian Politics: A Personal Statement', in *Crisis and Change in Contemporary India*, eds. Upendra Baxi and Bhikhu Parekh (New Delhi: SAGE, 1995), 159.

[26] Ex chief minister of Haryana, Om Prakash Chautala, and his son have been convicted for 10 years in teacher recruitment scam.

Case against Hari Kumar Jha (IFS) for disproportionate assets case (2014); Case against Mayank Jain (IPS) for disproportionate assets case (2014); and many more.[27]

Some of the unfortunate recent scams are a direct outcome in which the average IAS or IPS officer can hardly say 'no' to a ministerial fiat.

During the Congress-led governments at the Centre, bureaucrats and the politicians appeared to have built a protective shield around themselves against the rigours of the laws on corruption, malpractices and administrative collapse. The sorry state of the administrative machinery was greatly because of the working of the political system. For example, Prakash Chandra Parakh (1969 batch IAS officer of Andhra Pradesh cadre), who was appointed a union coal secretary in March 2004, dismissing the FIR by the CBI as 'baseless', said,

> If I have done anything wrong, then the Prime Minister (Manmohan Singh) who took the final call is also equally responsible. If the CBI has come to conclusion that allocation of Talabira Coal Blocks (in Odisha) to Hindalco was a conspiracy, then they should have made the Prime Minister also as an accused.[28]

Summary

Events over the past five decades have shown the need for wider review of understanding of ministerial and civil service responsibility. The relationship between ministers and civil servants is crucial to the efficient working of our democracy. This is good for the health of parliamentary democracy and for the preservation of directly and frequently to the legislatures' criticism. This should also encourage an administrative tempo better suited to developmental purposes. On the other hand, excessive ministerial direction and control in regard to bureaucracy can impair the initiative, sense of responsibility and active interest of the civil servants in public affairs. If this direction and control are not only excessive but aggressive and unscrupulous, they can impair even the integrity of the civil servants.

Although the theory of the correct relationship between ministers and civil servants is now widely understood, in practice, however, an administrative officer may have to work his way through a medley of pressures, 'keeping one eye on the law and merits of the case, and the other on the influence of the politicians, and particularly the weight he pulls, or can exert, with the ministers of the government', especially at the state level or the local level. Since the administrative decision or action tends to involve considerable delays, at present, these pressures begin to operate more strongly. The result is that the ministers, 'get more and more involved in routine administration, in particular problems, in particular individuals, and less and less in broad review and policy'. Not only this, but the existence of this type of minister's intervention and interference in routine administrative matters over a long period, and covering various subjects, 'provides opportunity for the ambitious or unscrupulous, be they ministers or civil servants or citizens, to cash in and to use it for further particular motives that may not represent public interest or policy'. Moreover, such conditions discourage the impartial civil servant and affords an opportunity for 'an ambitious, unscrupulous civil servant to play a game which borders on politics'. Moreover, these conditions create a general prejudice in the public mind that the administration is corrupt; although, in reality, this prejudice is disproportionately worse than the facts would indicate.

---

[27] List of scams and scandals involving cases of corruption and disproportionate assets against public servants (ministers and civil servants) since 1947 is very long.

[28] See *The Tribune* (Chandigarh), 14 October 2013.

What remedies are then being advocated to meet these administrative aberrations. One suggestion made is that a code of principles should be formulated by the GoI and informally approved by the ruling party, which should explicitly guide ministers and civil servants regarding their constitutional-cum-administrative relationships. A second suggestion is that there should be an ombudsman or a standing commission of inquiry to look into charges against both the ministers and civil servants of not only irregularities but also of administrative indiscretions and favouritism. While the first suggestion can be adopted more easily and its results watched, the adoption of the second suggestion can interfere not only with ministerial responsibility to the Parliament but also with the effectiveness of political direction of bureaucracy. The latter is needed in the interest of the developmental work of the administration and may not be provided by ministers who might fear the intervention or inquiry by an ombudsman or a standing commission reacting to varied complaints put forward by all sorts of people, scrupulous, unscrupulous and partisans. Moreover, unnecessary ministerial intervention or interference in routine administrative matters would tend to lessen the administrative delays and administrative inefficiency.

An impartial civil service has a constitutional function. Civil service responsibilities are not simply in the government of the day, they should include responsibility to the Constitution. However, implementing the policies and programmes of the elected government is a core civil service role and function.

The Constitution provides that the civil servants ought to be independent of the political executive and ought not to be swayed by the political biddings. However, the Constitution did not specifically prevent the minister from transferring, denying promotion or suspending a civil servant. These are the powers that have been used completely to demoralize the services. It is tragic that many civil servants including the IAS and IPS have not been able to uphold the traditions of impartiality, independence and efficiency.

After 70 years of independence, and after the bitter experience of the emergency, the nation should expect civil services to work only in the interest of the nation and to preserve the Constitution of India. Instead of asking for commitment to ideology of a political party, what should be expected is total commitment to the implementation of the programmes adopted by the government in power as long as the political executive is itself working within the parameters of constitutional propriety. This may also provide an answer to how to remedy the prevailing ethos in which the civil servants are aiding and abetting illegal or irregular decisions of their ministers and how the public could be saved from innumerable scams that have taken place in the recent years. Now there is the need to have a strong, independent and dedicated bureaucracy of administrative services imbued with public spirit which will not succumb to the pressure of political heads. What is required is that a developing democracy such as India should have a clear developmental programme for the future not in terms of only goals and policies in various spheres of socio-economic development but also in terms of politico-administrative system with such organization, personnel and procedure as would help it implement these goals and policies.

The Second ARC in its 10th Report recommended:

> There is a need to safeguard the political neutrality and impartiality of the civil services. The onus for this lies equally on the political executive and the civil services. This aspect should be included in the Code of Ethics for Ministers as well as the Code of Conduct for Public Servants.[29]

[29] Second ARC, *10th Report*, 280.

Further, the commission recommends that 'certain norms for recruitment in government to avoid complaints of favouritism, nepotism, corruption and abuse of power' be laid down.

What is more important is that appointments system for key posts, especially at the ministerial level, should recognize that ministers need to be able to work with those who are appointed, while ensuring that the civil service remains, as now, free from political patronage. In this way, a healthy working relationship between ministers (political executive) and civil servants (administrative executive), which is critical for good governance, can be promoted and strengthened.

18 Ethics in Governance

LEARNING OBJECTIVES

1. **To discuss the principles of ethics in public service**
2. **To suggest remedies to curb administrative corruption**
3. **To discuss concepts of ethics, morality and ethical governance**

Introduction

Although the study of ethics has been at the heart of intellectual thought since the earliest writings by the ancient Indians (e.g., Kautilya's *Arthashastra*), Greeks (e.g., Plato's *Republic* and *Laws* and Aristotle's *Politics*) and ancient Chinese (e.g., Confucius: *His Life and Thought*[1]), yet governance has been slow to recognize its own ethical practices. Governments in all nations lagged behind the public professions in recognizing ethical standards, but, by the mid-20th century, they were catching up. Today, more public sector organizations than either non-profit or private organizations (including businesses) have a code of ethics for their employees.[2]

The code of ethics is a commitment to ethical norms or professional conduct for governance practices in the public sectors. The legitimacy and stability of a political system get enhanced when appointed officials and public servants obey the constitutional rules, statutory laws and adhere to high professional standards and ethical precepts. Adherence to the rules also helps to prevent charges of corruption, misfeasance and embarrassing media exposure, thereby diminishing public cynicism and legal embarrassments to those in power and governing institutions.

[1] Kaizuka, Shigeki. Confucius: *His Life and Thought* (Dover Publications, 2002).

[2] For example, the US Congress first imposed a General Code of Ethics on federal administrators in 1958 (before this the first General Code of State Ethics was legislated in 1954 by the New York General Assembly) and with the passage of the Ethics in Government Act of 1978, expanded the code and founded the Office of Government Ethics. In India, there is the Central Civil Service (Conduct) Rules, 1954, for the central government employees. The Nolan Committee in the United Kingdom drew up the seven principles of public life which are included in Ministerial Code of conduct in 1995. Taking a cue from developed countries' road on ethics, the First ARC in its report on personnel administration (1966) recommended the enactment of a 'Code of Ethics' for civil servants in India. Similarly, the Second ARC set up by the GoI in 2005 in *Ethics in Governance* (fourth report) recommended the adoption of a code of ethics of ministers, members of the legislatures, judiciary, civil servants and regulators (all professions with statutory backing).

So long as behaviour and actions of the employees are within ethical framework and norms, well-being of the society remains unfettered. Deviations from external controls and acceptable limits may call for further constraints on their autonomy and functioning. A growing distrust of professions or individual professionals precipitates demands for more stringent actions. Professions in general, and specific professions or individual professions, do contribute to the development of internal controls on the conduct and behaviour of their members. They prescribe ethical norms or a code of ethics for their members to act with the highest standards of personal and professional integrity and honesty in their roles.

Ethics and Ethical Governance Defined

Ethics is a branch of philosophy that deals with the study of moral principles in human conduct. It is closely related to the concept of morality. The Second ARC defines the term 'ethics' as

> a set of standards that a society sets on itself and which helps guide behaviour, choices and actions. The crux of ethical behaviour does not lie in bold words and expressions enshrined as standards, but in their adoption in action, in sanctions against their violations, in putting in place competent disciplinary bodies to investigate allegations of violations and impose sanctions quickly and in promoting a culture of integrity. The commission is painfully aware that, standards do not, by themselves, ensure ethical behaviour; that requires a robust culture of integrity.[3]

Bottorff describes 'ethics' as 'a body of principles or standards of human conduct that govern the behaviour of individuals and groups'.[4]

According to Bowman, 'ethics' is being associated with rules and standards, morals, right and wrong, and values of honesty and integrity.[5] Further, he says that ethics has something to do with 'impartiality and fairness'. Likewise, Manoj Pandey states that moral values tell us what is the right, proper and acceptable way of behaving. Moral values are indispensable for good governance.[6]

While providing a good definition of administrative ethics, Thompson says that administrative ethics emphasizes:

> (a) the rights and duties that individuals should respect when they act in ways that seriously affect the well-being of other individuals and society; and (b) the conditions that collective practices and policies should satisfy when they similarly affect the well-being of individuals and society.[7]

In his discussion of *Integrity in the Public Service*, Thompson explains,

> Personal ethics originates in face to face relations among individuals, and it aims to make people morally better. Political ethics arises from the need to set standards for impersonal relations among people who may never meet, and it seeks only to make public policy better by making public officials more accountable.[8]

---

[3] Second ARC, *Ethics in Governance* (New Delhi: ARC, 2007).

[4] D. L. Bottorff, 'How Ethics Can Improve Business Success', *Quality Progress* 30, no. 2 (February 1997): 57–60.

[5] J. Bowman, 'Ethical Issues for the Public Managers', in *Handbook of Organization Management*, ed. William B. Eddy (New York: Marcel Dekker, 1983), 69.

[6] M. Pandey, 'Assessing Moral Values for Higher Civil Services Selection in India', *Indian Journal of Public Administration* 46, no. 2 (April–June 2000): 219.

[7] D. Thompson, 'The Possibility of Administrative Ethics', *Public Administration Review* 45, no. 5 (1985): 555–61.

[8] D. Thompson, 'Three Paradoxes in Government Ethics', *The Public Manager* (Summer 1992): 57–60.

In other words, administrative morality requires both good character and just behaviour. Administrative ethics is the opposite of administrative corruption, which is seen to be the abuse of one's government job to promote personal gain. Corrupt people go far beyond the norms of ethical standards. While adopting a practical approach to the ethics of public service, Denhardt defines administrative ethics as 'a process of independently critiquing decision standards, based on core social values that can be discovered, within reasonable organizational boundaries that can be defined, subject to personal and professional accountability'.[9] Her approach is about human nature. Cutting across these are issues of individual conduct and autonomy, all of which must be balanced with attention to administrative action.

John Rohr suggests that the moral problem is 'how to exercise his discretionary powers in a responsible manner even though he is not formally accountable to the electorate'.[10] Here, administrative morality requires 'integrity, personal responsibility and prudence'.[11] How does the moral administrator act in his role as 'principal agent'? In this context, Tinder explains, 'Moreover, the moral responsibilities of government should be carried out less through coercion than through example, through education, and through the respect, rather than fear, inspired by the laws'.[12]

Good Governance and Parameters

'Good governance' as a term is much larger than mere administration and management. It is a goal as well as a means. The idea of good governance has come into the fore in the academic discussions and administrative parlance during the 1980s as part of the neoliberal reform package. Actually, among all the institutions that advocated neoliberal reforms, the World Bank was the premier one that led the campaign with the spirit of a crusader to promote and popularize the new governance paradigm. The World Bank has identified three distinct aspects in the conceptualization of 'governance' such as, (a) the form of political regime, (b) the processes by which authority is exercised in the management of the country's economic and social resources and (c) the capacity of governments to design, formulate and implement policies and, in general, to discharge government functions. The features of good governance that could be gleaned from the World Bank publications included the following: An efficient public service, an independent judicial system and legal framework to enforce contract, an accountable administration of public funds, an independent public auditor responsible to a representative legislature, respect for law and human rights at all levels of government, a pluralistic institutional structure and a free press and so on and so forth.[13]

By promoting the idea of good governance, the objective of World Bank was to limit the power of the State and enhance the role of the civil society. As a concept, good governance is also characterized by elements of democracy, openness, transparency in administration, citizen participation in governance and application of ICTs in public administration. Thus, good governance represents a new set of structures or revamped version of old structures to manage political as well as economic relationships in a totally different way. Thus theoretically speaking, governance is wider than government and it refers to a regime of a minimal state. However,

[9] K. G. Denhardt, *The Ethics of Public Service* (New York: Greenwood Press, 1988), 26.

[10] J. Rohr, 'Bureaucratic Morality in the United States', *International Political Science Review* 9, no. 3 (1988): 170.

[11] P. Dobel, 'Integrity in the Public Service', *Public Administration Review* (May–June 1990): 354–66.

[12] G. Tinder, *Political Thinking: The Perennial Questions*, 5th ed. (New York: Harper Collins, 1991), 176.

[13] World Bank, *Governance and Development* (Washington, DC: WB, 1992).

neoliberal paradigm of governance associated with promotion of civil society as a non-violent instrument of democratic governance is subjected to a scatting criticism. 'But in actual practice the activities in the name of civil society paved the way for a kind of elitism with a depoliticizing effect on Third World societies'.[14]

As per the Annual Report (2005–2006), Union Ministry of Personnel, Public Grievances and Pensions, in a day-long conference of chief secretaries under the chairmanship of cabinet secretary focusing on good governance, administrative reforms and related issues had agreed to have a model code of governance which would enshrine the fundamental principles and benchmarks of good governance.

Accordingly, a model code of governance which is in the form of road map for the administration was finalized and sent to all chief secretaries of states/UTs in 2005. The main components of the model code cover action points under the following heads: (a) improving service delivery; (b) development of programmes for weaker sections and backward areas; (c) technology and system improvement; (d) financial management and budget sanctity; (e) accountability and transparency; (f) public service morale and anti-corruption measures; and (g) incentivizing reforms.[15]

18.1 Foundations of Ethics

In the Indian philosophical context, 'ethics' is equated with Dharma which literally means righteousness. In the Bhagavad Gita, there are references about *Sakam Karma* (performing actions with a motive) and *Nishkam Karma* (performing actions in a spirit of detachment from results). The Bhagavad Gita is a religious scripture which sets forth in precise and penetrating words the essential principles of ethical governance. Lord Krishna in the Bhagavad Gita (XVIII, 30) says:

> The understanding which knows action and non-action, what ought to be done and what ought not to done, what is to be feared and what is not to be feared, what binds and what frees the soul, O Partha (Arjuna) is of the nature of goodness.

The Ramayana teaches us that we should not drift from 'the path of truth', and also presents to us the picture of 'an ideal son', 'a model brother' and 'an ideal wife', besides expounding several other principles of moral conduct. Similarly, in the Mahabharata, we come across persons worthy of emulation, such as Yudhishthira, Arjuna, Vidura and Akroora, who are all embodiments of dharma. When the old Dhritrashtra and his wife Gandhari, the old Vidura and Kunti, mother of Pandavas, were going out of the capital of India for a quiet life in forest, Kunti asked Yudhishthira, the Emperor of India, to rule the State along with his brothers according to dharma, righteousness or justice (not any particular creed or religion).

Another ancient treatise, *Narada Smriti*, prescribed the guidelines for appointment of judges in the following words:

---

[14] M. B. Pillai, 'The Ethics of Neoliberal Governance Paradigm', *Indian Journal of Public Administration* 59, no. 4 (October–December 2013): 783.

[15] Ministry of Personnel, Public Grievances and Pensions, *Annual Report 2005–2006* (New Delhi: GoI, 2006).

Let the king appoint, as members of the Court of Justice, honourable men of tried integrity (*Sabhyas*) who are able to bear the burden of the administration of justice and who are well versed in the sacred laws, rules of prudence, who are noble and impartial towards friends or foes.

Equally important is the saying of Guru Nanak: 'Those who work hard for their livelihood and give something in charity to the deserving can alone recognize the path leading towards the Lord'. The individual has not only to perform duties for self but also for his family and society. The service of humanity leads us towards the lord. This is the social aspect of the spiritual culture (Guru Nanak Bani).

The father of the nation, Mahatma Gandhi, also prescribed certain ethical principles that can be formulated in terms of truth, ahimsa, *satyagraha* and *swaraj*. Only four days before his assassination, Mahatma Gandhi thus warned the country during his prayer meeting:

The subject of corruption referred to by the correspondent is not new. Only it has become much worse than before. Restraint from without has practically gone. Corruption will go when the large number of persons given to the unworthy practice, realise that the nation does not exist for them but they do for the nation. It requires a high code of morals, extreme vigilance on the part of those who are free from the corrupt practice and who have influence over corrupt servants.[16]

Dr Radhakrishnan, a philosopher, and a former President of India (1962–67) no doubt, but also a person involved in public affairs, had, while seconding the objective resolution in the constituent assembly, this to say, 'Much has been said that law… people, as well as kings, are subordinate to the *dharma*, righteousness which is the king of kings—Dharmaman Kshatrasaya Kshatram—it is sovereignty of this law which we have asserted'. Incidentally, even Kautilya, whose *Arthashastra* is regarded as the classic exposition of a moral statecraft, declared, 'in many matters where there is conflict between *Dharmashastra*, and any secular transaction, the king shall decide the matter by relying on *Dharma*'.[17]

18.2 Ethical Governance

Good government and not necessarily less government is the need of the hour. While the role of governments as facilitators is welcome, their basic function is ethical governance. 'Ethical values are indispensable for Good Governance, the core of which stands for decision-making and policy implementation characterized by accountability, transparency, responsiveness, effectiveness, equity participation and inclusiveness'.[18]

The Organisation for Economic Co-operation and Development (OECD) called for an ethical infrastructure referring to a range of tools and processes for regulating or checking undesirable behaviour and/or providing incentives to encourage good conduct of public officials.

It is instructive to note in this context the eight-point character evolved by the OECD. These are:

[16] M. K. Gandhi, *Delhi Diary*, 26 January 1948.

[17] Quoted by A. Goel, 'Ethical Governance and Society: Essential Parameters', *Indian Journal of Public Administration* 59, no. 3 (July–September 2013): 548–61.

[18] A. K. Mukhopadhyay, 'Ethics in Governance: Identifying the Crucial Issues', *Indian Journal of Public Administration* 59, no. 3 (July–September 2013): 477.

1. Political commitment for ethical governance
2. Evolving an efficient accountability mechanism
3. Creation of effective legal framework
4. Need for evolving workable codes of conduct
5. Professional socialization mechanisms (including training)
6. Creation of supportive public service conditions
7. Need for a central ethics coordinating body
8. Need for an energetic civil society able to act as a watchdog[19]

Good governance implies that affairs of the state are so managed that the material and social well-being of all the citizens are effectively looked after within a system of properly organized network of institutions. Values are important for this kind of society and herein comes the role of ethics. Collective good has to be promoted for harmonious social development. And this calls for ethics in governance.

The governance process in the Third World countries suffers from certain universally present features of the public service management namely apathy, evasion incompetence, obstructionism and unaccountability. In this connection, the observation of E. Sreedharan, who has formed an organization called Foundation of Restoration of National Values (FRNV), whose one of the declared objectives is to introduce 'ethical surveillance in public administration', is quite relevant. He explained that ethical surveillance means ensuring accountability and integrity at the top levels of public administration and thereby ensure an appropriate work culture of doing the day's work honestly. He insisted that in order to make this possible the general public should also imbibe 'the values of punctuality, integrity and professionalism'.[20]

The Second ARC in its fourth report in 2007 wondered why existing disciplinary procedures are not used to curb bribery, bad quality of public service and inefficiency. The report highlights the fundamentals of ethical governance starting with Mahatma Gandhi's famous words, 'You must be the change you wish to see in the world'.

Unfortunately, the Indian government sector cannot boast of high moral standards. Superior courts have made highly critical comments on the conduct of bureaucrats, and the media is full of reports of high-handedness, corruption and other forms of inappropriate conduct of the bureaucrats. Honest and upright civil servants themselves are concerned about the low morality of the bureaucracy and have been voicing concern at various fora.

India has marginally improved its ranking position in the anti-graft watchdog Transparency International's Corruption Perceptions Index (CPI) from 94 in 2012 to 81 in 2017.

Late K. R. Narayanan, President of India, while delivering his address on the eve of the Independence Day, on 14 August 2000, was critical of the nexus between politicians and criminals, who are in the process of polluting the environment of the country. The malpractices in every sphere have become mutually consensual and are engulfing the entire system.[21]

In studying the problem of the criminalization of politics and of the nexus among criminals, the Vohra (N. N.) Committee in its report (October 1993) said:

[19] OECD, *Ethics in Public Service* (Paris: OECD, 1996).
[20] *The Times of India* (New Delhi), 18 November 2008.
[21] *The Times of India* (New Delhi), 15 August 2000.

> The big smuggling Syndicates, having international linkages, have spread into and infected the various economic and financial activities, including *hawala* transactions, circulation of black money and operations of a vicious parallel economy causing serious damage to the economic fibre of the country. The Syndicates have acquired substantial financial and muscle power and social respectability and have successfully corrupted the Government machinery at all levels and wield enough influence to make the task of Investigating and Prosecuting agencies extremely difficult; even the members of the Judicial system have not escaped the embrace of the Mafia.

Justice V. R. Krishna Iyer has even blamed the elite clan for joining the criminals and making the nation stink by their frivolous activities. To quote Justice Iyer: 'Lawyers, Doctors, Company Secretaries, Chartered Accountants, Engineers and Scientists, not to speak of the talented bureaucrats, are all slowly selling their souls for a mess of pottage. Even the leaders in the professions have let us down'.

The modern world is marked by a widespread explosion of knowledge and tremendous achievements in science and technology, coupled with a general decline and reversal of human values as well as an alarming deterioration of moral and mental health both of individual and societies. The recent spate of crimes, violence, terrorism and drug abuse makes us aware of the significance of human values, without which human life loses all meaning.

There is not a day when you find newspapers, TV and other media without any news of unethical practices, or corruption, big or small, which has shattered the society and is more dangerous than any disaster. The paucity of ethical values is contagious and thus the society itself has become unethical. Mention may be made of India Coal Allocation Scam (2012) involving ₹186,000 crore; Wakf Board Land Scam (2008) involving 150,000 crore; 2G Spectrum Scam (2008) involving ₹176,000 crore; Commonwealth Games Scam (2010) involving ₹70,000 crore, Telgi Scam (2002) involving ₹20,000 crore; Satyam Scam (2009) involving ₹140,000 crore; Bofors Scam (1980s) involving ₹100 to 200 crore; Fodder Scam (1990s) involving ₹1,000 crore; Hawala Scandal (1990–91) involving ₹100 crore; and the list of scams under Congress–UPA government is too long and looks never-ending.

One wonders to find senior ministers of the government vehemently criticizing the CAG of India for pointing out gross irregularities in the allocations of important resources like '2G'. Another scam, which indicates the extent to which the virus of corruption has travelled, relates to the purchase of VVIP helicopters in which a retired Air Chief Marshal and other senior officers are involved. A young IAS officer Durga Shakti Nagpal was suspended on 27 July 2013 in Uttar Pradesh on frivolous grounds since she had taken on sand mafias.[22] Earlier, a young IPS officer had been killed by the 'sand mafia' in Morena (Madhya Pradesh).

It will be relevant to quote from the cover story in the 12 August 2013 issue of *India Today*:

> With no passion left for structural reforms, he (meaning Prime Minister) has spent most of his energy in defending the indefensible rather than running the country. Manmohan Singh the moderniser was once the wisest man from the East; he is today the meekest head of a moribund government that has already abdicated its responsibilities, economic as well as political. India was abandoned by its own government when the country needed most a redeemer.[23]

---

[22] *The Times of India* (Chandigarh), 28 July 2013.

[23] *India Today*, 12 August 2013.

Shekhar Gupta, Editor-in-Chief of the *Indian Express*, observed, 'But the UPA's most damaging contribution in its 10 years will be the undermining of the Office of the Prime Minister, and thereby the disturbing of the centre of gravity of India's governance'.[24]

It appears that the former PM had hardly any role to play in the selection of most of his ministers, allocation of their portfolios or take any action even when serious defaults came to his knowledge. Considering his reputation for integrity, it appeared improbable that he would have succumbed to the pressure of inducting colourful personalities like A. Raja in the cabinet, and then allocating the 'lucrative' portfolio of telecommunications again to him.

It is well known that some of the ministers at the Centre and the states have criminal background. Political corruption has been mounting rapidly due to entry of large numbers of criminal elements into the Parliament and state legislatures. It is pointed out that 1,581 lawmakers had criminal cases pending against them at the time of filing nominations in 2014. In an order aimed at decriminalizing politics, the Supreme Court on 14 December 2017 asked the Centre to set up 12 special courts by 1 March 2018 to exclusively hear cases against lawmakers facing criminal charges.[25]

18.3 Need for Administrative Ethics

Public employees in the course of taking or implementing decisions are often faced with the dilemma of choosing between obeying organizational policies and serving the needs of their clients. In a bureaucratic structure, an individual authority and responsibility is dictated by an individual's job description. The result is that he tends to follow blindly, regardless of any ethical dilemmas. This tendency clearly underscores the importance of adhering to administrative ethical values. Employees who work for public agencies with such incongruent policies are often placed in the uncomfortable position. They attempt to uphold organizational policies to the detriment of the very people the organization is serving. In choosing to meet the needs of their clients, employees violate organizational policies and put themselves at risk. Such policies need to be reviewed to eliminate this unnecessary ethical dilemma. Until then, choosing the client's interest over the organizational interest may be the most ethical action of all.[26] A potential cure for corrupt practice lies in organizational code of ethics. Strait contends that public employees 'must be able to remain within the framework of three goals: loyalty to the organization, responsiveness to the needs of the public and consideration for the employees' own objectives and desires. These goals provide an environment that is rich in ethical dilemmas'.[27]

But a reasonably effective, accountable, responsive, democratic administration will fail to deliver services to the satisfaction of the people at large, if it does not adhere to proper ethical standards. On the other hand, people themselves are bound to suffer economic and social deprivation and lose the benefits of good governance, if they themselves either patronize or practise corruption in their personal way of living.[28]

[24] *The Indian Express* (New Delhi), 10 August 2013.
[25] *The Times of India* (Chandigarh), 15 December 2017.
[26] P. B. Strait, 'Unethical Actions of Public Servants: A Voyeur's View', *Public Management* 80 (1998): 18.
[27] Ibid., 12.
[28] Mukhopadhyay, 'Ethics in Governance', 469–79.

18.3.1 Reasons for Unethical Behaviour

Unethical behaviour may result from individual and organizational factors. They may also occur despite clearly defined codes of ethics. In some cases, service terms and conditions, such as dissatisfaction with wages and benefits, may influence individuals to take what they feel is owed to them. Other factors may concern organizational culture, whereby a culture of 'getting the job done at any cost' prompt and promote disregard for ethical considerations in the interest of achieving results. Ferrell and Skinner argue that bureaucracy's centralized and hierarchical power base actually helps create opportunities for unethical behaviour.[29] As the discretion of rank-and-file and middle-level bureaucrats is severely limited, these bureaucrats tend to follow authority blindly, regardless of any administrative ethical standards. Nevertheless, codes of conduct are of tremendous importance towards enduring ethical conduct.

Public agencies, whether belonging to the public sector or cooperative sector, have an accountability towards the public since they contribute to the financial revenue of the government. The accountability of the public agencies is primarily concerned with preventing abuse of power and misuse of public resources. But it needs to be guided by values such as responsiveness, fair play and integrity. Public agencies must shun bias and arbitrariness in their actions and ensure a level-playing field to citizens.

Materialism, regarded as the most superior value, is the main cause of unethical deeds. 'Those who indulge in corrupt practices justify their actions as "being practical", else they would lose out in the race for power. No wonder everybody wants power, because we as a society, salute the powerful. We adore the richest people as our role models'.[30]

We know that we have to pay the price for the wrongs that we do to others. Erosion of ethical values results in corruption. Mervin Alexander has argued that corruption is harmful for three reasons. First, it is anti-national. The Hawala Scam showed how anti-national militants were getting money from abroad through hawala. Second, corruption is anti-poor since the resources meant for poverty alleviation schemes are siphoned off by corrupt politicians and bureaucrats. Third, it is anti-economic development as demonstrated by the collapse of the Southeast Asian economies.[31] It adversely affects administrative legitimacy by undermining the structures of administration and eroding the confidence of the people in administration.[32]

18.3.2 Charter of Ethics and Civil Service Code

Under the chairmanship of the cabinet secretary, a chief secretaries' conference was held in 1996 and finalized a charter of ethics and a civil service code based on values such as secularism, equality, impartiality, inclusive growth and social justice. This conference reiterated that the loyalty of the civil servants should only be to serve the public and the rule of law. But unfortunately, nothing

[29] O. C. Ferrell and S. J. Skinner, 'Ethical Behaviour and Bureaucratic Structure in Marketing Research Organizations', *Journal of Marketing Research* 25 (1988): 103–09.

[30] S. Rajneesh, 'Ethical Governance and Society: Social and Cultural Contexts', *Indian Journal of Public Administration* 59, no. 3 (July–September 2013): 515.

[31] M. Alexander, 'The Citizen's Guide to Fight to Corruption', *The Hindu*, 1 January 2002.

[32] P. K. Datta, 'Combating Corruption for Ethical Governance in India', *Indian Journal of Public Administration* 59, no. 3 (July–September 2013): 495–96.

concrete was heard about this recommendation in course of time. In 1997, first the judiciary and then a group of civil servants adopted resolutions for reinstating values such as integrity, professionalism, rule of law, probity, impartial leadership, transparency, efficiency and effectiveness in service delivery.

In Britain, the Committee on Standards in Public Life was sometimes referred to as Nolan Committee after its first Chairman Lord Nolan. It was set up in 1994 in the face of a series of scams and political scandals. The committee was constituted as a standing body with wide terms of reference to recommend on policy measures and organizational reforms for cleansing public offices and suggest the principles of a comprehensive code of conduct with a view to making the government offices, parliament, civil service and high-level financial institutions more transparent and accountable. In 1997 and in 2013, the committee's terms of reference were expanded. The first report, published in 1995, by the Nolan Committee, drew up the Seven Principles of Public Life as a restatement of the general principles of conduct underpinning public life, and stated that:

> All public bodies should draw up Codes of Conduct incorporating the Seven Principles: Internal systems for maintaining standards should be supported by independent scrutiny; more needed to be done to promote and reinforce standards of conduct in public bodies, in particular through guidance and training, including induction training.

These Seven Principles of Public Life, popularly known as the Nolan Principles, which are included in the ministerial code are as follows:

1. *Selflessness:* Holders of public office should act solely in terms of the public interest. They should not do so in order to gain financial or other benefits for themselves, their family or their friends.
2. *Integrity:* Holders of public office should not place themselves under any financial or other obligation to outside individuals or organizations that might seek to influence them in the performance of their official duties.
3. *Objectivity:* In carrying out public business, including making public appointments, awarding contracts or recommending individuals for rewards and benefits, holders of public office should make choices on objective criteria.
4. *Accountability:* Holders of public office are accountable for their decisions and actions to the public and must submit themselves to whatever scrutiny is appropriate to their office.
5. *Openness:* Holders of public office should be as open as possible about all the decisions and actions they take. They should give reasons for their decisions and restrict information only when the wider public interest clearly demands.
6. *Honesty:* Holders of public office have a duty to declare any, private interests relating to their public duties and to take steps to resolve any conflict arising in a way that protects the public interest.
7. *Leadership:* Holders of public office should promote and support these principles by leadership and example.

The GoI appointed the Second ARC on 31 August 2005 under the chairmanship of S. Veerappa Moily. The commission in its fourth report, *Ethics in Governance*, recommended 'greater transparency, accountability and ethical behaviour in politics, judiciary and administration. Corruption is an important manifestation of the failure of ethics'. Consequently, the commission also suggested measures for reducing or eliminating corruption.

The wide ranging recommendations of the ARC include partial state funding of elections, tightening of the anti-defection law and adoption of a code of ethics for ministers, legislatures, judiciary and civil servants. In order in check corruption, it has proposed that the provisions of the Prevention of Corruption Act, 1988 should be strengthened by making corrupt public servants liable for paying damages and confiscation of illegally acquired property. The commission has also proposed fast tracking of trials in corruption cases and establishment of strong institutions of Lokpal/ombudsman at national, state and local levels with powers to look into charges of corruption against high public functionaries, including chief ministers, ministers, MPs and MLAs. Recommending a code of ethics for civil servants, the Second ARC observes: 'Public Service Values towards which all public servants should aspire, should be defined and made applicable to all tiers of government and parastatal organisations. Any transgression of these values should be treated as misconduct, inviting punishment'.

The Second ARC recommended that, in addition to commitment to the Constitution, these values should include the following:

1. Adherence to the highest standards of probity, integrity and conduct
2. Impartiality and non-partisanship
3. Objectivity
4. Commitment to the citizens' concerns and public good
5. Empathy for the vulnerable and weaker sections of society

The commission also suggested the inclusion of the following principles in the *Code of Ethics for Civil Servants in India*:

1. *Integrity:* Civil servants should be guided solely by public interest in their official decision-making and not by financial or other considerations either in respect of themselves, their families or their friends.
2. *Impartiality:* Civil servants in carrying out their official work, including functions such as procurement, recruitment, delivery of services and so on should take decisions based on merit alone.
3. *Commitment to public service:* Civil servants should deliver services in a fair, effective, impartial and courteous manner.
4. *Open accountability:* Civil servants are accountable for their decisions and actions, and should be willing to subject themselves to appropriate scrutiny for this purpose.
5. *Devotion to duty:* Civil servants should maintain absolute and unstinting devotion towards their duties and responsibilities at all times.
6. *Exemplary behaviour:* Civil servants shall treat all members of the public with respect and courtesy and, at all times, should behave in a manner that upholds the rich traditions of the civil services.[33]

S. K. Chakraborty has suggested the concept of work ethics where everybody is motivated by the ethical and moral values and works with the doctrine of *Nishkam Karma*. The salient features of *Nishkam*

[33] Second ARC, *Ethics in Governance*.

Karma have been identified as under: (a) psychological energy conservation, (b) reactionless steady action, (c) perfection (as the aim), (d) inner autonomy, (e) freedom (*Swadheenta*), (f) socio-economically appropriate, (g) work commitment, (h) work as worship for excellence, (i) mind enrichment and (j) leads to yoga with the transcendent/higher self. *Nishkam Karma* will bring holistic transformation in work and will culminate in the following results: (a) stress-free mind at work, (b) a feeling for works as acts of consecration, (c) a pure, transparent mind, (d) an abiding instinct for ethical rectitude, (e) an inner sanctuary of fullness and (f) an all-embracing, other-related mind. All these factors can promote good governance, development and dynamism.[34]

Summary

James D. Wolfensohn, president of the World Bank, recognizing the praise and fears of globalization, says in the World Development Report (1999/2000):

> Globalization is praised for bringing new opportunities for expanded markets and the spread of technology and management expertise, which in turn hold out the promise of greater productivity and a higher standard of living. Conversely, globalization is feared and condemned because of the instability and undesired changes it can bring; to workers who fear losing their jobs to competition from imports; to banks and financial system and even entire economics that can be overwhelmed and driven into recession by flows of foreign capital, and, not least; to the global commons, which are threatened in many ways with irreversible change.

The necessity of good governance calls for observance of administrative ethics. Ethical governance cannot be sustained unless it is created by moral and social institutions. The government structures can only facilitate such a good governance. Building appropriate public morality and ethical conduct requires at all levels of the government functioning. 'It is an inexorable necessity like the oxygen cylinder to a suffocated patient as our contemporary society has come to be'.[35] As we find in this foregoing chapter, Indian administration has been, in comparison with other professions, slow to recognize its own ethical practices. Although, the government recognizes its importance, it lags behind the compliance programme of ethics code and regulations.

[34] S. K. Chakraborty, *Ethics in Management* (New Delhi: Oxford University Press, 1996). See also IJPA, 1997, 102.
[35] Mukhopadhyay, 'Ethics in Governance', 479.

19 Ombudsman: A Citizen's Defender

LEARNING OBJECTIVES

1. **To highlight origin, etymology and significance of ombudsman**
2. **To delineate efforts in the development of institution of ombudsman in India**
3. **To discuss the position and role of Lokayuktas at the state level**

Introduction

Most countries (around 150 nations) of the world have established a prototype of an ombudsman to investigate and address citizens' complaints against maladministration of public servants.[1] The term 'ombudsman' is traditionally viewed as a 'citizen's defender'[2] which is a rough translation of the Swedish word. In Swedish terminology, it refers 'to an officer appointed by the legislature to handle complaints against administrative and judicial action'.[3] 'Ombud', a Swedish word, stands for a spokesman of another person. In some countries, an 'inspector general', 'citizen advocate', 'parliamentary commissioner' (e.g., England), 'public complaints commissioner' (e.g., Nigeria), 'chancellor of justice' or any other official having duties similar to those of a national ombudsman may also be appointed by a legislature but with a significant degree of independence. Below the national (central) level, an ombudsman may be appointed by a state (e.g., Lokayukta in an Indian state), local or municipal government. More recent developments have included the creation of specialized children's ombudsman[4] and information commissioner agencies. In many countries, where the ombudsman's responsibility includes protecting human rights, the ombudsman is recognized as the national human rights institution. The post of ombudsman had by the end of the 20th century been instituted by most governments of the world.

[1] International Ombudsman Institute (IOI) was established in 1978 in Vienna (Austria) as an independent global organization to help more than 150 independent public sector, local, regional and national ombudsman institutions to cooperate. Typically, these organizations handle complaints from the public about the public administration in their country, protecting people against violations of their rights. http://www.theioi.org/the-i-o-i (retrieved 14 December 2016).

[2] Donald C. Rowat's work is quite significant in the ombudsman's field. His two books, *The Ombudsman: Citizen's Defender* (1965) and *The Ombudsman Plan* (1973), are outstanding.

[3] D. C. Rowat, 'The Spread of the Ombudsman Idea', in *American Government*, ed. Stanley V. Anderson (Englewood Cliffs, NJ: Prentice Hall, 1968), 7–36.

[4] Children's Commissioners exist in England, Northern Ireland, Wales and Scotland.

Origin and Etymology of 'Ombudsman'

A prototype of an ombudsman may have flourished in India during the days of the Mauryan Empire (321–185 BC) and in China during the reign of the Qin Dynasty (221 BC). The position of secret royal inspector was unique to the Josen Dynasty in Korea, where an undercover official directly appointed by the king was sent to local provinces to monitor governmental officials and look after the populace while travelling incognito.[5] The Roman Tribune had some similar roles with power to veto acts that infringed upon the plebeians. Other precursors to the ombudsman were Turkish Diwan-al-Mazalim and Qadial-Quadt. They were also attested in Siam, India, the Liao Dynasty (Khitan Empire), Japan and China.[6]

Use of the term in modern times began in Sweden, with the Swedish Parliament (Riksdag) establishing 'ombudsman' instituted by the instrument of government of 1809, to safeguard the rights of citizens by establishing a supervisory agency independent of the executive branch.[7] The predecessor of the Swedish Parliamentary Ombudsman (SPO) was the Office of Supreme Ombudsman which was established by the Swedish king Charles XII in 1713. The office commenced operation on 23 October 1714, and the role of the official was to ensure that judges and public officials acted in accordance with the laws, proficiently discharged their duties and, if not, he could initiate legal proceedings for dereliction of duty. This was the origin of the ombudsman institution in Sweden.[8]

Sweden was first in the field which developed this institution in 1809 and it remained in splendid isolation for some considerable period of time before it was copied in the other Nordic countries. It was created in Finland in 1919, Denmark in 1955 and in Norway in 1962. However, it was the adoption of the institution by New Zealand in 1964 and by Britain in 1967 which triggered the modern surge of fashionability. Of the great nations of the world, perhaps only the USA has remained persuaded of the need to adopt the institution. Even so there are local and, indeed, the occasional state ombudsmen in the USA. Of course, the due process clauses of the US Constitution have so permeated every level of executive activity in that country that the relative absence of ombudsmen has been less lamented than might otherwise have been the case.[9]

Much of the recent interest in this institution has been aroused because of the importance of such an institution 'as a bulwark of democratic government against the tyranny of officialdom'.[10]

The ombudsman institutions in India are normally cost-free at the point of use. They require a small registration fee and a sworn affidavit. Second, there is generally a provision for prosecution of someone who gives or makes false allegations. Third, the ombudsman conducts the investigation himself, though this is currently a bone of contention in some Indian states where the Lokayukta is

[5] S. Park, 'Korean Preaching, Han, and Narrative', *American University Studies*, Series VII, *Theology and Religion*, 2008.

[6] http://journal-of-conflictology.uoc.edu/joc/en/index.php/journal-of-conflictology/issue/view/vol2iss2.html (accessed on 24 May 2018), No. 2, Language, p. 57.

[7] The Parliamentary Ombudsman was established in 1809 by the Swedish Riksdag as a parallel institution to the still present Chancellor of Justice, reflecting the concept of separation of powers as developed by Montesquieu (Ombudsman, Riksdagens, *Historik*, retrieved 19 May 2017).

[8] In 1719, the Swedish Office of Supreme Ombudsman became the Chancellor of Justice. The Chancellor of Justice, in modern times, is a government official found in some northern European countries, broadly responsible for supervising the lawfulness of government actions.

[9] J. A. Barron and C. T. Dienes, *Constitution Law* (St. Paul: West Publishing, 1990), Chapter V.

[10] D. C. Rowat, *The Ombudsman Plan: Essays on the Worldwide Spread of an Idea* (Ottawa: McClelland and Stewart, 1973), 12.

not provided with adequate investigating staff. Fourth, the ombudsman can range much wider than courts of law. He can range widely across departmental files and materials to the extent of conducting what amounts to a system audit. Fifth, he can enquire into maladministration without being constrained by the need to identify illegality as such. Sixth, ombudsman investigations are conducted discreetly and informally, in contrast to courts which must sit in public. In the past, the courts protected the rights of the individuals. But the ordinary courts today are no longer an effective instrument of remedying the wrongs of administrative action, although the Supreme Court and High Courts often pull up the state and central governments for not protecting citizens' rights.

19.1 Features of Ombudsman in Sweden and the UK

The Swedish Ombudsman was intended to safeguard the rights and interests of the people in exercise of powers by public officials. Ombudsman is elected by the Swedish Parliament (Riksdag) to oversee the performance of public officials. Among the duties laid down for the parliamentary ombudsman, some sections of the relevant law are as follows:

> *Section 1:* The parliamentary ombudsmen shall … supervise the observance of laws and other statutes by those exercising public activity and that they in all respects properly fulfil their obligations.
>
> *Section 3:* It is the particular duty of the ombudsman to ensure that courts of law and administrative authorities observe the provisions of the instrument of government concerning objectivity and impartiality, and that the fundamental rights and freedom of citizens are not encroached upon in the process of public administration.
>
> *Section 6:* Should an ombudsman deem it necessary for the official to be dismissed or debarred from performing his duties on account of criminal act or repeated negligence of duty, he may make a report thereon to the person or body which has the authority to decide on such measures.

The Swedish Parliamentary Ombudsman (SPO) is elected by the Parliament (Riksdag) and is vested with wide powers of supervision over all public officials. Even the courts and judicial officers (i.e., the judiciary) are not excluded from his purview. He has also access to all official records. He is meant to ensure that administration is carried on in accordance with laws and statues; that public authorities do not exceed or abuse their powers; that justice is rendered fairly and impartially; and that the rights and freedom of the citizens are not violated. Further, the SPO has also been given the power to prosecute any erring public official or recommend departmental action for his removal or dismissal for any grave negligence in the performance of his duties. Even judges of the Supreme Court can be prosecuted by him. He is indeed a very powerful parliamentary official appointed to protect the citizens against injustice, abuse of power or any other act of misadministration.

Although the SPO cannot reverse or amend a decision already taken by any official, he can recommend or advise for modification or even for cancellation of any faulty order or decision to the competent higher authority of the official concerned. In this respect, he is neither a super-administrator nor a super-judge but a parliamentary supervisory official under the Constitution.

But when he comes across any fault, deficiency or shortcoming in the work or decisions of public officials, he may report to the appropriate higher authorities for corrective action and, where necessary, for initiating suitable penal or departmental action against an erring official.

The advice and recommendations of the ombudsmen are generally accepted by virtue of the power and prestige attached to the office. The ombudsman can initiate action either on the basis of an individual complaint or *suo moto*. He can also dismiss a complaint summarily if he finds it to be unfounded or trivial in content. Thus, the SPO is independent of the legislature, the judiciary and the executive.

Unlike MPs and Council of Ministers who come within the purview of the Lokpal in India, in Sweden, they are excluded from the purview of Swedish Ombudsman. On the other hand, members of judiciary are excluded from the purview of the Indian Lokpal, while in Sweden, they are included within the jurisdictions of Swedish Ombudsman. Further, since the level of corruption in Sweden (among the four least corrupt nations compared with India's 81st position in the 2017 crime figure results of 180 corrupt nations) is very low, the number of corruption cases prosecuted on the advice of the ombudsman constitute a very small fraction of the total number of all cases handled by him in a year.[11] The main activities of the ombudsman in Sweden are to deal with the complaints of citizens involving maladministration such as delay, negligence, improper or misapplication of laws and rules, and harsh or unjust decisions.

In the UK, the ombudsman, designated as 'Parliamentary Commissioner for Administration', is empowered to investigate complaints by any member of the public who claims to have sustained injustice in consequence of misadministration by any public authority which may relate to delay, negligence, arbitrariness, etc. The complaint of the aggrieved party has, however, to be routed through his MP. Similarly, action taken by the parliamentary commissioner on the complaint is intimated through the concerned MP. The people have thus no direct access to the UK Ombudsman. Parliamentary commissioner in UK is, therefore, described to be 'a muzzled watchdog' or a 'crusader without a sword'.

19.2 Development of Ombudsman Institution in India

As to the development of the institution of ombudsman in India, some efforts were made in early 1960s. In 1960, K. M. Munshi, a parliamentarian, demanded appointment of an institution similar to that of an 'Ombudsman' for controlling maladministration. M. C. Stelward, then Attorney General of India, in his speech at the All India Lawyers' Conference, held in 1962, suggested the idea of establishing ombudsman.[12] L. M. Singhvi also raised this issue in Parliament. The need for having an impartial machinery to provide redress to the citizens was emphasized again in 1964, and the minister of state for home affairs assured the House about examining the feasibility of evolving a suitable machinery for this purpose.[13] Later on 9 April 1965, a resolution on the subject was moved in Parliament and a Special Consultative Group of MPs on Administrative Reforms was constituted. One of its subcommittees was to look into the machinery for the redress of the

[11] In most of these countries (e.g., New Zealand, Denmark and the UK), the judiciary has been kept out of the ombudsman's purview, but ministers along with other public servants come within his jurisdiction.

[12] G. B. Sharma, *Implementation of Ombudsman Plan in India* (New Delhi: Ashish Publishing House, 1981), 24–25.

[13] Parliament of India, *Lok Sabha Debates*, vol. XXX, cc. 12356–416.

grievances. However, this committee suspended its work in 1966 when a high-powered commission on administrative reforms was appointed.[14]

The idea was extensively investigated by the ARC (1966–69). The commission observed, 'Our study of the institution of Ombudsman in Scandinavian countries and of the parliamentary commissioner in the UK and of the working of these functionaries convinces us that we can suitably adapt these institutions for our needs'.

The commission headed by Morarji Desai submitted an interim report 'Problems of Redressal of Citizen's Grievances' in 1966. In this report, the ARC recommended the creation of two special authorities designated as the 'Lokpal' and the 'Lokayukta' for the redressal of citizens' grievances: the former to deal with complaints against the ministers and secretaries to the government at the Centre as well as in the states, and the latter, that is, the Lokayukta, in each state and one at the Centre, to deal with complaints against other officials.

19.2.1 The Lokpal Institution

On the basis of the recommendations of the ARC, the government prepared the Lokpal and Lokayuktas Bill, 1968, and introduced it in Parliament in May 1968, which was referred to the Joint Select Committee (JSC) of both the Houses of Parliament. The JSC submitted its report in March 1969. In August 1969, the bill was passed by the Lok Sabha, but it lapsed due to dissolution of the House in July 1970. A bill with certain modifications was again introduced in August 1971 but this too lapsed. Another Lokpal Bill was introduced in the Lok Sahha by the Janata government in July 1977, which was referred to the JSC. However, this time the government itself withdrew the bill without advancing convincing reasons. The National Front government in 1989 once again introduced the Lokpal Bill, which also lapsed due to defeat of the government on the floor of the Lok Sabha.

The Lokpal Bill was introduced on 13 September 1996 'to provide for establishment of the institution of Lokpal to inquire into allegations of corruption against public functionaries' which was referred to the Parliamentary Standing Committee on Home Affairs by the speaker of the Lok Sabha.

The Lokpal Bill, 1998, was again introduced by the PM in the Lok Sabha on 3 August 1998, which was referred to the Department-Related Parliamentary Standing Committee on Home Affairs for examination and report. The standing committee presented its report to the Parliament on 25 February 1999 and made certain recommendations in regard to this bill. Before the government could take a view on the various recommendations made by the standing committee on this bill, the Lok Sabha was dissolved on 26 April 1999, and consequently the bill also lapsed. Similarly, the bill was introduced in 2001 with minor changes but it lapsed due to dissolution of the Lok Sabha.[15] The latest Lokpal and Lokayuktas Bill (9th in number) was introduced in the Lok Sabha on 22 December 2011 following massive public protests led by Anna Hazare (an anti-corruption crusader) and his associates. The bill was passed by the House on 27 December 2011

[14] Sharma, *Implementation of Ombudsman*, 81–82.

[15] The Lokpal Bills were introduced nine times in the Parliament: 1968, 1971, 1985, 1989, 1996, 1997, 2001 and in 2011, yet they were never passed.

as the Lokpal and Lokayuktas Bill, 2011.[16] The bill was passed in the Rajya Sabha on 17 December 2013 after making certain amendments to the earlier bill and in Lok Sabha on 18 December 2013. The bill received assent from the president on 1 January 2014 and came into force from 16 January 2014 and is officially called as the Lokpal and Lokayuktas Act, 2013.

19.2.2 The Lokpal and Lokayuktas Act: Salient Features

The historic Lokpal and Lokayuktas Act was enacted by the Parliament in 2013 paving the way for establishment of the institution of Lokpal at the central and Lokayuktas at the state levels. The purpose of this institution is to inquire into allegations of corruption against public functionaries and for matters connected therewith. The following are the major features of this Act.

Appointment and removal of chairman and members of the Lokpal: For appointment of chairperson and eight members of Lokpal (of which 50% shall be judicial members and another 50% of members shall be from SC/ST/OBCs, minorities and women), a selection committee is provided for consisting of PM, the speaker of the Lok Sabha, the leader of the opposition, the CJI or a sitting Supreme Court judge (nominated by the CJI) and one eminent jurist (to be nominated by the President of India on the basis of recommendation of the first four members of the selection committee.[17]

In order to ensure impartiality, it is provided that the chairman and the members shall not hold any office of profit and shall not be the members of legislature or any political party and after the expiry of their term shall be ineligible for any appointment under the State. Removal from office is only on the ground of proved misbehaviour and incapacity.[18] Salary and other service conditions of the chairman will be that of the CJI and of the members that of the judges of the Supreme Court. The expenditure on salary, allowances and pension shall be charged on the Consolidated Fund of India. The conditions of service of a member cannot be varied to his disadvantage after his appointment.

Jurisdiction: The Lokpal's jurisdiction will cover public servants, including the PM, Council of Ministers, current and former legislators and public sector employees (funded by the Centre). In addition, public servants and trustees and board members of NGO receiving government funds of more than ₹1 crore (under Foreign Contribution (Regulation) Act [FCRA]) or foreign funding of more than ₹10 lakh per year are under the jurisdiction of the Lokpal.[19]

---

[16] The term 'Lokpal' was coined in 1963 by Laxmi Mall Singhvi, an MP, during a parliamentary debate about grievance mechanism. The word was derived from the Sanskrit words 'Lok' (people) and 'Pala' (protector), meaning 'protector of people'.

[17] According to the Supreme Court (2 May 2017), the present legislation provides for Lokpal and members even in the absence of a recognized Leader of Opposition.

[18] The chairperson or any Member shall be removed from his office by order of the president on grounds of misbehaviour after the Supreme Court on a reference being made to it by the president on a petition signed by at least one hundred MPs in accordance with the prescribed procedure. He holds the office for 5 years or until he attains the age of 70 years.

[19] The Lokpal and Lokayuktas Act, 2013 (Amended in 2016) allows extension of the time given to public servants and trustees and board members of NGOs receiving government funds of more than ₹1 crore or foreign funding of more than ₹10 lakh to declare their assets and those of their spouses. The provisions of this Act would apply retrospectively, that is,

Power of Superintendence: The Lokpal will have power of superintendence and direction over any investigation agency including CBI for cases referred to them by the Lokpal. A high-powered committee chaired by the PM will recommend selection of the Director, CBI.

Enquiry and investigation: A complaint accompanied by an affidavit may be made to the Lokpal within a period of seven years from the date of commission of the alleged offence. The President of India may also require the Lokpal to enquire into an allegation in respect of a public functionary.

Alter the preliminary scrutiny, the Lokpal may enter into detailed scrutiny which will be in the nature of judicial proceedings to be held in-camera. Keeping in view the fundamentals of procedural fairness, the Lokpal may adopt a procedure appropriate in the circumstances. For the effective exercise of his functions, the Lokpal is authorized to secure the services of any officer, employee or investigating agency of the state or central government, with the concurrence of that state, any other person or agency.

The Act lays down clear time lines for preliminary enquiry (within 30 days) and investigation and trial towards this end, the Act provides for setting up of special courts. Anti-corruption inquiries should be completed within 60 days and the investigations completed within 6 months. The Lokpal shall order a probe only after hearing the public servant. An enquiry against the PM has to be held in-camera and will have to be approved by two-thirds of the full bench of the Lokpal.

For the purpose of any inquiry or investigation, the Lokpal shall have the powers of a civil court for the purpose of summoning witnesses and records, issuing orders for the seizure of documents.

Prosecution: The Act provides that the Directorate of Prosecution will be under the overall control of CBI Director. But the appointment of director of prosecution will be based on the recommendation of the central vigilance commissioner (CVC). The Lokpal can initiate prosecution through its prosecution wing before the special court, and the trial has to be completed within two years. The Act also incorporates provisions for attachment and confiscation of property acquired by corrupt means, even while the prosecution is pending.

Protection of whistleblowers: As in the case of some other countries, the Act provides adequate protection for honest and upright public servants.

Offences and penalty: In case of false and frivolous complaints, there is a provision of imprisonment of up to one year and a fine of up to ₹1 lakh. In case of public servants, the imprisonment is up to seven years. In case of criminal misconduct and habitually abetting corruption, the jail term is up to 10 years.

Bar to proceedings: The Lokpal institution lays down that no proceedings or decision of the Lokpal shall be liable to be challenged, reviewed, quashed or called in question in any court. This may bar the jurisdiction of the civil courts but will not oust the jurisdiction of the Supreme Court and the high courts under Articles 32 and 226 of the Constitution.

---

with effect from 16 January 2014. A provision was made in the amendment that relatives of (governmental) officers, including wife, children and others, will not have to submit details of their property every year. Anna Hazare alleged that this amendment provision has weakened the anti-corruption law. *The Tribune*, 16 December 2017.

Annual report: The Lokpal is required to make a consolidated report to the president annually who shall place it before Parliament within 90 days with an explanatory memorandum.

19.2.3 Criticism and Conclusion

The Lokpal and Lokayuktas Act, 2013, it appears, has diluted the purpose of the Lokpal (as mentioned in the Lokpal Bill of 1996 and 1998), that is, to deal with complaints of corruption against MPs, ministers and the PM by bringing all officers of the government and PSUs under the Lokpal jurisdiction. The number of such officials will run into several thousands and the Lokpal will be flooded with far too many complaints against them. As a result, the Lokpal may not be able to give sufficient attention to corruption allegations against MPs and ministers.

The CVC with his changed designation of Lokayukta could very well deal with other cases. The utility of the high-level Lokpal institution comprising of very high-level members would be far greater and more meaningful if its jurisdiction is restricted to ministers and MPs only for whom there is no vigilance machinery at present.

The Lokayukta institution at the Centre in the shape of the CVC may be taken to have been set up in 1964 as recommended by the Santhanam Committee in its report of 1963. The CVC deals with allegations of corruption against all categories of officials. That committee had stated that prevention of political corruption is the prerequisite for prevention of corruption among officials. According to the committee, 'ensuring absolute integrity on the part of ministers at the Centre and the states is an indispensable condition for the establishment of a tradition of purity in the public services'.

The 2013 Lokpal Act has, no doubt, some positive aspects, for example, the Lokpal having its own investigating and prosecution wings for purposes of investigation and prosecution. It will thus not be dependent on government agencies (like the CBI) whose neutrality, objectivity and fairness, rightly or wrongly, may be questioned.[20] It is also appropriate that the Lokpal under the Act is not to entertain complaints alleging abuse of power or other wrongdoings in cases which are more than seven years old. Such an upper limit for accepting and probing complaints is desirable so that public functionaries do not become victims of malafide complaints due to animosity or political vendetta long after retirement from the public services. Further, it is proper that Lokpal under the Act has been empowered to prosecute persons making false or frivolous complaints.[21]

Further, the 2013 Lokpal Act in Section 20(3) has accordingly provided that the Lokpal should afford a suspect public servant an opportunity of being heard before initiating inquiry against him. All these provisions and features would not only combat a substantial degree of corruption in the public domain but also would promote good governance.

The institution of Lokpal is quite important to ensure good system of administration. As this has been called the 'watchdog of the administration' or 'protector of the little man', it is important that it should be given the constitutional status. But the Lokpal institution is not the only remedial measure for all the ills in the politico-administrative system. For efficiency and effectiveness of the

[20] The Supreme Court is said to have used 'caged parrot' for the CBI.

[21] This would take care of the earlier apprehensions in not setting up the Lokpal body. Fear of false complaints and undue probe may tend persons in power to avoid as far as possible taking speedy or risky decisions which at times of urgency are necessary in framing and implementation of policies.

Lokpal institution, it is essential that adequate internal methods of redress in the form of complaint machinery need to be established. There is a strong and urgent need for paying proper attention to the total system for handling grievances within the Government of India.[22]

On the contrary, it is felt that a single ombudsman institution may not operate efficiently in India. According to J. Mukherjee, this institution which is 'accusatorial and inquisitorial' in nature shall not be suitable in India because such an institution would be unprecedented in a democracy with traditions of independent judiciary. So he concludes that it is an 'impracticable and disastrous experiment which will not fit into the Indian Constitution'.[23]

Lokpal and Lokayuktas and other related Law (Amendment) Bill, 2014, containing the proposed amendments in the law has been gathering dust from the date of its introduction in the Parliament on 18 December 2014. The law is yet to see the light of the day. This is despite the fact that India ratified the United Nations Convention against Corruption (UNCAC) way back in May 2011.[24]

19.3 Lokayukta in States

Section 63 of the Lokpal and Lokayuktas Act, 2013, provides for the establishment of a body, called 'Lokayukta for the state, if not so established, constituted or appointed, by a law made by the state legislature, to deal with complaints relating to corruption against certain public functionaries within a period of one year from the date of commencement of this Act'. The institution of ombudsman is getting popularity in many states of India. And already several states have enacted the Lokayukta Acts.[25] Orissa (Odisha) was perhaps the first state to have Lokpal and Lokayuktas Act, 1970, but the Act came into force on 2 October 1983. Maharashtra was the first state to appoint a Lokayukta by enacting the Maharashtra Lokayukta and Up-Lokayukta Act, 1971, in September 1971. Rajasthan enacted the Act in 1973. In Bihar, the office of Lokayukta was created through issuing an ordinance in 1973 and was replaced by regular legislation in 1974. Uttar Pradesh passed the Up-Lokayukta and Up-Lokayukta Act in 1975. The Act came into force only in October 1977. Other states which followed the enactment of Lokayukta Act are Kerala, Goa, Assam, Gujarat, Himachal Pradesh (1983), Haryana, Andhra Pradesh, Karnataka (1985), Madhya Pradesh (1981) and Punjab. Now, nearly all states have institutions of ombudsman with different titles.[26]

The establishment of Lokayukta institutions in the states proves that the principle of 'ministerial responsibility' as a means of providing continuous oversight over the administration is absolutely not correct. In a state, the Lokayukta is primarily 'concerned with corrective function, not punitive function'. His job is mainly to investigate into allegations made against a public servant.

Enough data is not available about the types of complaints received by the Lokayuktas in various states but whatever information is available clearly indicates that the main areas of

---

[22] India. Estimates Committee. 'System of Redressal of Grievances', First Report, 1991–92.

[23] Quoted by C. K. Thakker, *Administrative Law* (Allahabad: EBC, 1992), 474.

[24] *The Hindustan Times* (Delhi), 28 April 2017. Process for appointing Lokpal at Centre is on (June 2018).

[25] The ARC, headed by Morarji Desai, submitted a special interim report 'Problems of Redressal of Citizen's Grievances' in 1966. In this report, the ARC recommended the setting up of two special authorities designated as 'Lokpal' and 'Lokayukta' for the redressal of citizen's grievances.

[26] Presently, there are no Lokayuktas in the states of Jammu & Kashmir, Manipur, Meghalyas, Mizoram, Nagaland, Puducherry, Tamil Nadu, Telangana, Tripura, West Bengal and Arunachal Pradesh (2018).

grievance include police action or inertia, prison torture, malafide exercise of power and demand or acceptance of illegal gratification.

The ombudsman strategy as has been developed in various states has not been designed to cover the whole spectrum of administrative faults. In general, Lokayuktas have been given jurisdiction over ministers, public servants and officers.

19.3.1 Role of Lokayukta at State Level

Recently, the Supreme Court on 27 April 2017 found the Lokpal and Lokayuktas Act of 2013 an 'eminently workable' piece of legislation which has the purpose of combating corruption in the public administration. Lokayukta is a great check on corruption, brings about transparency in the system and makes administrative machinery citizen-friendly. His functions largely depend upon jurisdiction vested in him and facilities provided for taking cognizance of citizens' grievances promptly, dexterously and expeditiously through a simple, informal mechanism devoid of technicalities. Corruption is a social evil which is capable of endangering stability and security of society, threatening social, economic and political development and undermining the values of democracy and morality. Corruption is a cancerous disease, and if it is not timely detected, it will malign the polity of the country leading to disastrous consequences. In a case, the Supreme Court observed:

> Harassment of a common man by public authorities is socially abhorring and legally impermissible. It may harm him personally but the injury to society is far more grievous. Crime and corruption thrive and prosper in the society due to lack of public resistance. Nothing is more damaging than the feeling of helplessness. An ordinary citizen instead of complaining and fighting succumbs to the pressure of undesirable functioning in offices instead of standing against it.[27]

Corruption stalls the pace of prosperity and development of the country. It is, therefore, considered necessary to eradicate corruption with an iron hand, otherwise march towards progress and prosperity would be delayed considerably. In this context, Lokayukta at the state level has a contributory role. Lokayukta, being a legislative creation, can protect citizens' rights against maladministration, corruption and abuse of powers by the public agencies.

At the 11th All India Lokayuktas Conference, Delhi Lokayukta, Justice Sarin said, 'Corruption has entered the blood stream of our system and needs treatment including infusion of blood and new ideas'. As the judge has a constitutional responsibility to enforce the laws, so is the Lokayukta wielding legislative powers in reducing corruption, inefficiency and maladministration at the state level. Speaking at the inaugural function of the two-day 11th All India Lokayuktas Conference, 2012, Pranab Mukherjee said:

> Lokayuktas must at the same time remember that their duty is not just to indict public functionaries when they are guilty but also to protect them when nothing is found wrong with their conduct and to correct wrong perceptions about them with equal force and earnestness.

The former president also said, 'Institution of Lokayuktas is an ally to good governance, not an obstruction to development'.[28]

---

[27] *Lucknow Development Authority v. M. K. Gupta*, AIR 1994, SC 787.

[28] *The Times of India* (New Delhi), 3 November 2012.

Similar to the pattern followed in Scandinavian countries, where the ombudsman is appointed to bring about humanism in governance, can we have an anti-corruption body to strengthen existing institutions of accountability? In the states, where institutions of Lokayukta have been set up, they widely vary in respect of their jurisdictions, procedures and also powers. There is no uniformity in the functioning of Lokayuktas of different states, and their effectiveness differs from state to state. Owing to the fact that Lokayuktas only have recommendatory powers and no power to enforce their decisions, they are just toothless Lokayuktas in the states, who consider themselves as merely 'paperless tigers who can only name and shame'.

The Second ARC in its fourth report, *Ethics in Governance*, recommended uniformity in the general principles regarding the structure, power and functions of Lokayuktas in all states. Lokayuktas must be provided adequate financial and administrative autonomy. One of the main reasons for why the Lokayuktas have failed to make a mark across the states is the lack of uniformity about the selection and functioning.

In some states, chief ministers come under the ambit of the Lokayuktas, while in some others they do not. Since Lokayuktas are set up in states on the basis of a law defining their composition and role made by the respective state assemblies, the anti-corruption ombudsman in states has been reduced to a ceremonial post. Urging that the state executive needs a mind change, Justice Sarin said that Lokayukta should be given more powers so that all public officials who indulge in corruption should be dealt with by this institution.

In November 2012, after the conclusion of the 11th All India Lokayuktas Conference, as many as 16 Lokayuktas sent many recommendations to the GoI. The recommendations were as follows[29]:

1. Make Lokayukta the nodal agency for receiving all corruption complaints
2. Accord Lokayukta jurisdiction over state-level probe agencies
3. Bring bureaucrats under the ambit of the Lokayuktas
4. Accord Lokayukta powers of search and seizure and powers to initiate contempt proceedings
5. Provide Lokayukta administrative and financial autonomy
6. Bring NGOs funded by the government under Lokayukta's jurisdiction

Summary

In recent times, we have seen abolition of the office of the Lokayukta in some Indian states. This should not surprise us, for, if the ombudsman is to do the job for which he is appointed, he is bound to make enemies among the powerful elites. But he must do his job without fear or favour. What is more important is that this institution should work independently. The institutions of Lokpal and Lokayuktas in India must strive to retain their integrity, their moral authority and their utility to citizens in the country. Although in the context of globalization and privatization, this institution has gained wide popularity, it must be kept in view that 'Ombudsman cannot be a panacea. A number of people seem to regard "Ombudsman" as a kind of magic word that will cure all administrative ills'.[30] The ARC has also strongly emphasized in its *Interim Report on Problems of Redress of Citizen's Grievances* that

[29] Quoted from *Pioneer*, 9 November 2012, and *The Hindu* (Chennai), 9 November 2012.

[30] Rowat, *The Ombudsman Plan*, 54.

> The setting up of these authorities is not the complete answer to the problem of redress of citizens' grievances. They only provide the ultimate set-up for such redress as has not been available through the normal departmental or governmental machinery and do not absolve the department from fulfilling its obligations to the citizen for administering its affairs without generating, as far as possible, any legitimate sense of grievances.[31]

It is in this direction that the administration has to work, and the responsibility of the departments to deal adequately with public grievance must squarely be faced by them in the first instance.

On 27 April 2017, the Supreme Court directed the government to immediately implement the Lokpal and Lokayuktas Act and appoint a Lokpal.[32]

> As a policy of zero tolerance against corruption, the bill (the Lokpal and Lokayukta Bill 2011) seeks to establish in the country, a more effective mechanism to receive complaints relating to allegations of corruption against public servants, the Supreme Court said, underlying the necessity to have the watchdog.[33]

However, the first Lokpal is yet to be appointed (the process is on) and many states (11 in all) are dithering in appointing Lokayuktas.[34]

[31] ARC, *Interim Report on Problems of Redress of Citizens' Grievances* (New Delhi: Manager of Publications, 1966), 12–13.

[32] The statutory post of Lokpal has been vacant since 16 January 2014.

[33] *The Hindustan Times* (Delhi), 28 April 2017.

[34] see *The Tribune* (Chandigarh), 24 March 2018.

Index